Communicating for Results

Communicating for Results
ninth edition

A Guide for Business and the Professions

Cheryl Hamilton

Tarrant County College—NE Campus

WADSWORTH
CENGAGE Learning

Australia • Brazil • Canada • Mexico • Singapore • Spain • United Kingdom • United States

WADSWORTH
CENGAGE Learning™

Communicating for Results: A Guide for Business and the Professions, **Ninth Edition**
Cheryl Hamilton

Senior Publisher: Lyn Uhl

Executive Editor: Monica Eckman

Senior Development Editor: Greer Lleuad

Developmental Editor: Rebecca von Gillern

Assistant Editor: Rebekah Matthews

Editorial Assistant: Colin Solan

Media Editor: Jessica Badiner

Marketing Manager: Bryant Chrzan

Marketing Coordinator: Darlene Macanan

Marketing Communications Manager:
   Christine Dobberpuhl

Senior Content Project Manager: Rosemary
   Winfield

Art Director: Linda Helcher

Print Buyer: Justin Palmeiro

Text Permissions Manager:
   Margaret Chamberlain-Gaston

Production Service: Elm Street Publishing
   Services

Text Designer: Pronk Designs

Photo Manager: Amanda Groszko and Kevin
   McCane

Cover Designer: Pronk Designs

Cover Image: PhotoAlto Photography/© Veer;
   SSI Illustration/© Veer; Digital Vision
   Photography/© Veer; Comstock/© Getty
   Images; Aagamia/Iconica/© Getty Images;
   Ableimages/Riser/© Getty Images

Compositor: Integra Software Services Pvt.
   Ltd.

Library of Congress Control Number: 2009936169

For product information and technology assistance, contact us at
Cengage Learning Customer & Sales Support, 1-800-354-9706.

For permission to use material from this text or product,
submit all requests online at **cengage.com/permissions**.
Further permissions questions can be emailed to
permissionrequest@cengage.com.

ISBN-13: 978-1-4390-3643-3

ISBN-10: 1-4390-3643-8

Wadsworth
20 Channel Center St.
Boston, MA 02210
USA

Cengage Learning is a leading provider of customized learning solutions with office locations around the globe, including Singapore, the United Kingdom, Australia, Mexico, Brazil, and Japan. Locate your local office at **international. cengage.com/region**.

Cengage Learning products are represented in Canada by Nelson Education, Ltd.

For your course and learning solutions, visit **www.cengage.com**.

Purchase any of our products at your local college store or at our preferred online store **www.CengageBrain.com**.

Printed in the United States of America
1 2 3 4 5 6 7 14 13 12 11 10

Brief Contents

To my many classroom, online, and seminar students for reading the materials, trying out the activities, and making such excellent suggestions.

Contents

About the Author

CHERYL HAMILTON, an author well known for her writing style and award-winning teaching, understands the importance of oral and written communication as a lifelong skill. Also the author of two other texts—*The Essentials of Public Speaking* and *Communicating for Success*—she has conducted a number of research studies, including one published in the *Community College Journal of Research and Practice*. Dr. Hamilton has presented more than 40 papers at professional conventions, including those sponsored by the National Communication Association, Southwest Educational Research Association, Western Communication Association, and Texas Speech Communication Association. She has conducted seminars for groups such as the National Property Management Association, Bell Helicopter Textron, U.S. Postal Department, North Central Regional Police Academy, and LTV Aerospace. A native of Illinois, Dr. Hamilton received her bachelor's degree from Eastern Illinois University in Charleston, Illinois; her master's degree from Purdue University in West Lafayette, Indiana; and her doctoral degree from the University of North Texas in Denton, Texas. She is a professor of speech communication at Tarrant County College—NE Campus, which is an urban college district with over 47,000 students on five campuses in and around Fort Worth, Texas. She is active in college affairs where she has served as chair of the faculty senate and president of the faculty association. Although she has taught more than ten different communication courses at both two-year and four-year colleges, her favorite courses remain business communication, public speaking, and fundamentals. Her love of teaching is shown by the numerous teaching awards she has received including the Chancellor's Award for Exemplary Teaching.

Preface

Each year the National Association of Colleges and Employers (NACE) conducts research to determine how employers across the nation rank the skills and qualities of potential employees. Year after year, written and oral communication skills are chosen as number one in importance. At the same time, NACE research published in *Job Outlook 2009* notes that communication skills are also selected "as the number one skill that is most-lacking in new college graduate hires" (p. 24).

From this report, then, we can see the key importance that both oral and written communication skills will play in your career success. For example, even though interviewing is an oral process, if the letter of application and resume you send are poorly written, you may make such a negative impression that you will not be invited to an actual interview. Or your written skills may result in an interview, but if your oral skills during the interview are less than impressive, you may not get a job offer. Oral and written communications are intertwined even in everyday events. For example, you may be good at face-to-face communication but alienate people with your written e-mail messages.

As always, *Communicating for Results,* Ninth Edition, is directed at those who are interested in self-improvement. It is designed to introduce necessary communication skills to people with very little work experience, to improve the communication skills of entry-level managers and employees, and to serve as a reference book for experienced professionals who wish to refresh or update their oral and written communication skills. This text emphasizes important skills from three basic communication areas: interpersonal and organizational, interviewing and group, and public communication.

- *Interpersonal and organizational skills* include understanding organizational communication; improving communication and relationships with bosses, employees, and customers; handling conflict; improving listening; interpreting and using nonverbal communication; decreasing misunderstandings with others, both face-to-face and electronically; and overcoming obstacles to communication.

- *Interviewing and group skills* include preparing conventional, scannable, e-mail, and online resumes; conducting or participating in interviews of various types; knowing what questions are unlawful in preemployment interviews; conducting and participating in conferences; and making decisions in small groups.

- *Public communication skills* include giving individual or team presentations to employees, managers, and groups inside or outside the organization; using effective organization and delivery techniques for traditional and online presentations; preparing professional visual aids; and knowing how to manage presentation software.

Although the chapters in this book may be read in any order, they are organized so that each chapter builds on the skills taught in those preceding it. The skills are discussed practically and lend themselves to immediate application. In other words, what is read today can be applied at work tomorrow. Activities within the chapters (Awareness Checks) and at the end of chapters (Checkpoints and Collaborative Learning Activities) suggest ways for you to practice new skills and techniques. The *Communicating for Results* online resources and Instructor's Resource Manual feature additional application activities, test questions, and more.

In addition, a new feature in *Communicating for Results* is geared specifically toward improving written communication skills. This book has always included written communication pointers along with the oral aspects of interpersonal and team communication, interviewing, and oral presentations. However, in this new edition, I have added an appendix called "Written Communication" to showcase important business writing skills. See the next section, which outlines this book's new features.

Communicating for Results, Ninth Edition, not only features a skills orientation but also provides you with the theoretical basis for each skill discussed. It is my hope that you will find this book valuable and that you will add it to your personal library.

Features of the New Edition

The Ninth Edition of *Communicating for Results* showcases business writing skills with a new appendix, **Written Communication**. This new feature includes expanded and enhanced discussions of resume writing, e-mail messages, thank you letters, and written informative and persuasive speech outlines, providing more clarity and depth on these topics. New topics include the follow-up letter, the informative and persuasive written report, and general guidelines on powerful written communication. In addition to offering a more complete discussion of the importance of written communication skills, the appendix provides an easy-to-access place in the book to locate tips about and examples of written communication.

Also new to this edition are the end-of-chapter **Collaborative Learning Activities**. These group activities provide interesting and fun ways for students and seminar participants to apply the concepts in each chapter, thereby improving and cementing learning. Working together in teams improves communication and persuasive skills and prepares students for teamwork in the workplace. According to Tubbs (2009), team members are responsible for 80% of the success of an organization. Harvard Business School finds teams so important to student and business success that during orientation students are assigned to a study group that they will stay with during the first year of courses (www.hbs.edu/case/study-groups.html).

Newly revised features include the following:

- The **chapter-opening case studies,** which preview each chapter's content, have been updated with several new cases, highlighting communication issues related to Facebook, the University of Texas, AIG, and more. Updated **Revisiting the Case Study boxes** throughout each chapter ask students to consider the case study scenario in light of the concepts discussed in the chapter.

- New and updated **It Really Works boxes** in each chapter still highlight a real-world executive's use of the skills presented in the book, and the **Ethical Dilemma boxes** ask readers to think critically about how they might handle questionable situations in the working world.

- New and updated coverage of **communication technology and computer-mediated communication** are found throughout the text. For example, Chapter 1 features a new case study on Facebook and a new It Really Works box about eBay; Chapter 3 includes a new Ethical Dilemma box on bloggers getting fired for comments about work that they made on their personal blogs; and Chapter 6 features a new case study about how an unhappy customer placing a song on YouTube resulted in a positive response from United Airlines.

- Expanded coverage of **cross-cultural and gender communication**, both in the United States and internationally, includes a new case study on the University of Texas "hook 'em Horns" gesture and updated coverage about the importance of clothing and personal appearance (Chapter 5).

- Chapter 7 highlights a new type of interview, the **telephone interview**.

- New examples of a **letter of application and sample resumes** are included in Chapter 8 and in the new appendix on written communication.

- Chapter 11 and the Appendix include, respectively, **a new informative speech** and **a new persuasive speech**.

- All chapters have been streamlined and some have been reorganized for clarity and ease of reading.

Additional Student and Instructor Resources

Communicating for Results is accompanied by a full suite of integrated materials that will make teaching and learning more efficient and effective. **Note to faculty:** If you want your students to have access to the online resources for this book, please be sure to order them for your course. The content in these resources can be bundled with every new copy of the text or ordered separately. If you do not order them, your students will not have access to the online resources. *Contact your local Wadsworth Cengage Learning sales representative for more details.*

- The **Premium Website for** *Communicating for Results* provides students with one-stop access to all the integrated technology resources that accompany the book. These resources include an enhanced eBook, a student workbook, Audio Study Tools chapter downloads, Speech Builder Express™ 3.0, InfoTrac® College Edition, interactive video activities, interactive versions of the Awareness Check quizzes and Checkpoint activities, web links, and self-assessments. All resources are mapped to show both key discipline learning concepts and specific chapter learning lists.

- The *Communicating for Results* **interactive video activities** feature the Communication Situation communication scenario clips presented in the text so students can see and hear how the skills they are studying can be used in various workplace circumstances. Students can answer the critical thinking questions that accompany each video and then compare their answers to the author's. This online resource also features videos of the business informative and persuasive speeches referenced in the book. Each speech is accompanied by a transcript, a preparation outline and a speaking outline, note cards, the ability to time-stamp comments and e-mail them to instructors, and critical thinking questions. Also available in the interactive video activities, and new to this edition, are specially created **videos on organizational models (Chapter 2) and communication styles (Chapter 3)** that help bring challenging content to life.

- The **Speech Builder Express 3.0 organization and outlining program** is an interactive web-based tool that coaches students through the speech organization and outlining process. By completing interactive sessions, students can prepare and save their outlines—including a plan for visual aids and a works cited section—formatted according to the principles presented in the text. Text models reinforce students' interactive practice.

- The **InfoTrac College Edition with InfoMarks** is a virtual library that features more than 18 million reliable, full-length articles from 5,000 academic and popular periodicals. These articles can be retrieved almost instantly. This resource also provides access to InfoMarks—stable URLs that can be linked to articles, journals, and searches to save valuable time when doing research—and to the InfoWrite online resource center, where students can access grammar help, critical thinking guidelines, guides to writing research papers, and much more.

- The **Audio Study Tools** for *Communicating for Results* provide mobile content that offers students a fun and easy way to review chapter content whenever and wherever. For each chapter of the text, students will have access to a brief communication scenario or speech example and a 5- to 7-minute review consisting of a brief summary of the main points in the text and five to seven review questions. Students can purchase the Audio Study Tools through CengageBrain (see below) and download files to their computers, iPods, or other MP3 players.

- The **Cengage Learning Enhanced eBook** is a web-based version of *Communicating for Results* that offers ease of use and maximum flexibility for students who want to create their own learning experience. The enhanced eBook includes advanced book tools such as a hypertext index, bookmarking, easy highlighting, and faster searching, easy navigation, and a vibrant web-based format. Students get access to the enhanced eBook with the printed text, or they can just purchase access to the stand-alone enhanced eBook.

- The **Speech Studio™ Online Video Upload and Grading Program** improves the learning comprehension of public speaking students. This unique resource empowers instructors with a new assessment capability that is applicable for traditional, online, and hybrid courses. With Speech Studio, students can upload video files of practice speeches or final performances, comment on their peers' speeches, and review their grades and instructor feedback. Instructors create courses and assignments, comment on and grade student speeches with a library of comments and grading rubrics, and allow peer review. Grades flow into a light gradebook that allows instructors to easily manage their courses from within Speech Studio.

- The **CengageBrain.com** online store provides students with exactly what they've been asking for: choice, convenience, and savings. A 2005 research study by the National Association of College Stores indicates that as many as 60% of students do not purchase all required course materials; however, those who do are more likely to succeed. This research also tells us that students want the ability to purchase "à la carte" course material in the format that suits them best. Accordingly, CengageBrain.com is the only online store that offers eBooks at up to 50% off, eChapters for as low as $1.99 each, and new textbooks at up to 25% off, plus up to 25% off print and digital supplements that can help improve student performance.

- The **Online Student Companion** by L. M. Larry Edmonds, Arizona State University Polytechnic, offers chapter objectives and outlines, lists of important concepts that students can use to facilitate note-taking in class, skill-building activities, Internet activities and lists of helpful web pages, and self-tests. This workbook can be bundled with the text at a discount.

- The **Instructor's Resource Manual with Test Bank** by Lisa Benedetti, Tarrant County College Northeast, and Jolinda Ramsey, The Alamo Colleges – San Antonio College, features teaching tips, suggestions for online instruction, sample course outlines, lists of useful media resources, detailed chapter outlines, skill-building activities, forms and checklists, and an extensive test bank.

- The **PowerLecture CD-ROM** contains an electronic version of the Instructor's Resource Manual, ExamView® Computerized Testing, predesigned Microsoft PowerPoint presentations created by Ron Shope, Grace University, and JoinIn® classroom quizzing. The PowerPoint presentations contain text, images, and cued videos of student speeches and can be used as they are or customized to suit your course needs.

- **Special-Topic Instructor's Manuals** by Deanna Sellnow, University of Kentucky, are three brief manuals that provide instructor resources for teaching public speaking online, with a service-learning and problem-based learning approach that focuses on critical thinking and teamwork skills. Each manual includes course syllabi; icebreakers; information about learning cycles and learning styles; and public speaking basics such as coping with anxiety, outlining, and speaking ethically.

- **Videos for Speech Communication 2010: Public Speaking, Human Communication, and Interpersonal Communication.** This DVD provides footage of news stories from BBC and CBS that relate to current topics in communication, such as teamwork and how to interview for jobs, as well as news clips about speaking anxiety and speeches from contemporary public speakers such as Michelle Obama and Senator Hillary Clinton.

- The **ABC News DVD: Speeches by Barack Obama** includes nine famous speeches by President Barack Obama, from 2004 to the present day, including his speech at the 2004 Democratic National Convention; his 2008 speech on race, "A More Perfect Union"; and his 2009 inaugural address. Speeches are divided into short video segments for easy, time-efficient viewing. This instructor supplement also features critical thinking questions and answers for each speech, designed to spark class discussion.

- **TeamUP technology training and support** allows you to get trained, get connected, and get the support you need for seamless integration of technology resources into your course with Cengage Learning's TeamUP Program. This unparalleled service and training program provides robust online resources, peer-to-peer instruction, personalized training, and a customizable program you can count on. Visit http://academic.cengage.com/tlc to sign up for online seminars, first days of class services, technical support, or personalized face-to-face training. Our online or onsite training sessions are frequently led by one of our lead teachers, faculty members who are experts in using Wadsworth Cengage Learning technology and can provide the best practices and teaching tips.

- The **Flex-Text customization program** lets you create a text as unique as your course: quickly, simply, and affordably. As part of our Flex-Text program, you can add your personal touch to *Communicating for Results* with a course-specific cover and up to 32 pages of your own content, at no additional cost.

Acknowledgments

For their helpful comments and suggestions, I would like to thank the following reviewers of the Ninth Edition: Heather Allman, University of West Florida; Christa Brown, Minnesota State University, Mankato; Sue Cox, Wallace State Community College; Michele Foss-Snowden, California State University, Sacramento; Tracey Holley, Tarleton State University; Marianna Larsen, Utah State University; Martha Macdonald, York Technical College; Judith Norback, Georgia Institute of Technology; and John Parrish, Tarrant County College.

In addition, I would like to offer many thanks to reviewers of past editions: Ruth D. Anderson, North Carolina State University; Richard N. Armstrong, Wichita State University; Michael Laurie Bishow, Indiana-Purdue University; Cam Brammer, Marshall University; Pat Brett, Emory University; Linda Brown, El Paso Community College; Nicholas Burnett, California State University, Sacramento; Larry M. Caillouet, Western Kentucky University; Joan T. Cooling, University of Northern Iowa; Margie Culbertson, University of Texas, Austin; Ann Cunningham, Bergen Community College; Carolyn Delecour, Palo Alto College; Joe Downing, Western Kentucky University; Vella Neil Evans, University of Utah; Judyth Gonzalez, Delta College; G. Jon Hall, University of Northern Iowa; Martha Haun, University of Houston; Lawrence Hugenberg, Youngstown State University; Robin J. Jensen, St. Petersburg College; James A. Johnson, State University of New York at Geneseo; Pamela Johnson, California State University–Chico; J. Daniel Joyce, Houston Community College; Jim Katt, University of Central Florida; Frank L. Kelley, Drexel University; Sandra M. Ketrow, University of Rhode Island; Amos Kiewe, Syracuse University; Vivian Kindsfather, Texas Wesleyan University; Gary S. Luter, University of Tampa; Valerie Manno-Giroux, University of Miami; Steven R. Mark, University of Toledo; Katherine May-Updike, Mesa Community College; Donovan J. Ochs, University of Iowa; Steven Ralston, East Tennessee State University; Ken Rhymes, University of Texas at El Paso; Edwin N. Rowley, Indiana State University; Robert Sampson, University of Wisconsin–Eau Claire; Paul Scovell, Salisbury State College; Alan Shiller, St. Louis Community College–Meramec; Gary Shulman, Miami University; Gary F. Soldow, Baruch College/City University of New York; Del Stewart, Georgia State University; Robert A. Stewart, Texas Tech University; Bobbi Stringer, Tarrant County College Northwest; Susan Timm, Northern Illinois University; Tyler Tindall, Midland College; Rona Vrooman, Old Dominion University; Lionel Walsh, Virginia Commonwealth University; John L. Williams, California State University–Sacramento; and Thomas Wirkus, University of Wisconsin–La Crosse.

The staff and project team at Wadsworth Cengage Learning have also been extremely helpful, especially Rebecca von Gillern, the developmental editor for this edition. Additional thanks go to Monica Eckman, Greer Lleuad, Rebekah Matthews, Colin Solan, Jessica Badiner, Rosemary Winfield, Linda Helcher, Mandy Groszko, Chris Althof, Sarah D'Stair, Margaret Chamberlain-Gaston, Amanda Hellenthal, Bryant Chrzan, and Christine Dobberpuhl.

I would also like to thank my long-time colleague and coauthor, Dr. C. Cordell Parker (1940–2003), for his assistance with the first six editions; Charles Conrad for his help and advice on the organizational chapter in previous editions; Edward T. Hall for his suggestions on the three levels of culture; Dan O'Hair and Blaine Goss for writing the listening chapter for the second edition; Lisa Benedetti and Jolinda Ramsey for writing the Instructor's Resource Manual and test bank; L. M. Larry Edmonds for writing the Student Workbook; Debi Blankenship for the test bank in earlier editions and for finding Ted Goff and his wonderful cartoons; Ron Shope for producing the PowerPoint presentations for this edition; the many students who have allowed their speeches, outlines, and PowerPoint presentations to be used in this text and online; Erin Hamilton for writing many of the It Really Works features; Doris Redd and Erin Hamilton for their ready assistance in providing ideas and copyediting assistance; Howard Hamilton and Jon Thompson for the title; Doyle D. Smith for coauthoring the first edition; and the many communication and business students from my classes and seminars for their helpful advice.

Cheryl Hamilton
Ft. Worth, Texas

The Communication Process: An Introduction

Phil Boorman/ageFotostock

Case Study: Facebook Falters

As you read Chapter 1,

Define what is meant by *communication.*

Identify and **describe** each element of the basic communication model; pinpoint where in the basic communication model your main communication problems occur.

Identify how Americans view the honesty and ethical standards of several professions, including your own; summarize what can be done to encourage ethical communication.

What role does communication play in the many successes and failures of various organizations? Let's take a look at one organization that has had phenomenal success and some failures: Facebook. Mark Zuckerberg was a Harvard sophomore when he began operating Facebook for college and high school friends. Since then the site has gained close to 200 million active users and has doubled in size in less than 8 months and continues to grow at close to 1 million new users per day, which made Microsoft decide to invest $240 million for 1.6% ownership (Stone, 2009a, 2009b). According to Stone:

> Like other social networks, the site allows its users to create a profile page and forge online links with friends and acquaintances. It has distinguished itself from rivals, partly by imposing a Spartan design ethos and limiting how users can change the appearance of their profile pages. That has cut down on visual clutter and threats like spam, which plague rival social networks. In May 2007, Facebook revealed an initiative called Facebook Platform, inviting third-party software makers to create programs for the service and to make money on advertising alongside them. The announcement stimulated the creation of hundreds of new features or "social applications" on Facebook, from games to new music and photo sharing tools, which had the effect of further turbo-charging activity on the site.

It's not just people aged 18 to 24 years old who use Facebook either; they make up only one fourth of the new users and 70% of new users are from outside the

AP Photo/Paul Sakuma

As you read this chapter, see if you can (a) explain what caused so many people to react so quickly, (b) determine at which point in the communication model this misunderstanding occurred, and (c) theorize whether and how this misunderstanding could have been prevented.

United States (Hempel, 2009). Still, it is a social networking site and communicating relationships are all important. To meet the needs of so many people using the site for so many purposes, Facebook continues to experiment with new policies and features. Communicating these with all of the users has not been easy and keeping them happy hasn't been easy either.

In 2006, Zuckerberg introduced a feature that is now highly used and even taken for granted by new users: the *news feed* "which allows users to see their friends' most recent online activities" (The Editors, 2009). Customer backlash was considerable, but the new feature stayed and customers were allowed to opt-out if they wished. In 2007, users again became angry when a new feature called "Beacon" was implemented. According to Timothy Lee (The Editors, 2009), Beacon was "an ill-conceived advertising program that many users regarded as an invasion of privacy.... Facebook was forced to beat a hasty retreat in the face of widespread outrage." Apparently, users didn't like the idea of their friends seeing the sites they visited and the purchases they made. A new approach called "Connect" takes care of the previous complaints that information was being shared without their knowledge because users have to "opt-in" before any sharing occurs.

It's not just features that cause user outrage. Complaints numbered in the tens of thousands after May 2009 when Facebook "deleted a provision from its terms of service that said users could remove their content at any time, and added new language that said it would retain users' content after an account was terminated" (The Editors, 2009). This change seemed to say that Facebook would own materials users placed on their pages. As one blog noted, "never upload anything you don't feel comfortable giving away forever, because it's Facebook's now" (Stone & Stelter, 2009). Although Zuckerberg and other Facebook representatives did their best to assure users that there was a communication misunderstanding and that they had no intent of taking over ownership of their materials, it seemed that the only answer was to rescind the changes back to the previous terms of service, which Facebook did. In addition to this assurance, Facebook is asking for user contributions to a new Bill of Rights and Responsibilities to govern the site; how many people do you think will take them up on this offer? For the time being, users have quieted down while those in charge wonder how to communicate successfully in the future.

The chapter opener reminds us how important communication skills are to success in business and professional organizations. A 2009 survey of corporate recruiters from over 2,000 companies was conducted by the Graduate Management Admission Council (gmac.com). In the primary skills, knowledge, and experience category, 89% of these recruiters ranked communication skills (oral and written) as the number one hiring characteristic looked for in graduates with masters in business administration (Murray, 2009, p. 17). Communication skills are important in entry-level jobs as well. According to the *Job Outlook 2009* compiled by the National Association of Colleges and Employers (2008, p. 23), communication skills continue to receive top ranking as the most important quality or skill looked for by employers in new hires.

Despite evidence that communication skills are necessary for success in the workplace, individuals from new hires to managers continue to have problems in this area. According to *Job Outlook 2009*, "Once again, the largest group of respondents cited communication skills as the number one skill that is most-lacking in new college graduate hires" (2008, p. 24). It's not just new hires that have communication problems. A survey of 150 executives from 1,000 large companies found that "14 percent of each 40-hour workweek is wasted because of poor communication between staff and managers—amounting to a stunning seven weeks a year" (Thomas, 1999, p. 1). The best way to improve communication is to understand what communication is. This chapter introduces you to the communication process and the major causes of communication errors. Chapter 2 will deal more specifically with communication in the organizational setting.

Communication Defined

When business and professional people are asked to define *communication*, they often respond with something like this: "Communication is the process of transferring thoughts and ideas from one person to another." On the surface, this definition sounds good. It acknowledges that communication is a process (which means that it is ongoing), and it includes the idea of communicating our thoughts and ideas to others. However, the words *transferring* and *from one person to another* inaccurately imply that communication is like pouring liquid from a pitcher. The definition implies a simple, one-way action in which person A takes knowledge from his or her head and simply pours (transfers) it into the head of person B. Obviously, communication is not so simple. Person B may refuse to just accept person A's ideas without comment and may prefer to offer his or her own ideas (give feedback). Or person B may completely misinterpret person A's message. As communication scholar David Berlo (1960) once noted, "Communication does not consist of the transmission of meaning. Meanings are not transferable. Only messages are transmittable, and meanings are not in the message, they are in the message-user." (p. 175).

A more accurate definition of communication can be found by looking at its original meaning. *The Oxford English Dictionary* (1989) lists the Latin root of *communicate* as *communicare*, which means "to make common to many; share." According to this definition, when people communicate, they express their ideas and feelings in a way that is understandable (common) to each of them. Each person has a direct effect on the other person and on subsequent communication. Therefore, **communication** is the process of people sharing thoughts, ideas, and feelings with each other in commonly understandable ways.

ETHICAL DILEMMA

In 2002, the retail clothing chain Abercrombie & Fitch (A&F) launched a new line of underwear for preteen girls. Although A&F is known for its controversial, provocative ads, this new line sent an unprecedented number of parental e-mail complaints to the headquarters in New Albany, Ohio, resulting in the line being removed from A&F's Internet catalog. The thong underwear, marketed to girls aged 7 to 14, featured words like "eye candy" and "wink wink" printed on the front of them (Merskin, 2004). A statement released by Abercrombie said, "The underwear for young girls was created with the intent to be lighthearted and cute. Any misrepresentation of that is purely in the eye of the beholder" (AFA Online, 2002, para. 5). Supporters see nothing wrong with the line of underwear, but "critics think that the line is tasteless and that marketing it to young girls is contemptuous" (Lamb et al., 2006, p. 28).

QUESTIONS: What do you think? Based on your reading of the Communication and Ethics section in this chapter, was the action by A&F ethical?

The Basic Model of Communication

Whether you are communicating with one person, a small group, or many people, the same basic process occurs, and the same misunderstandings can arise. Successful business and professional communicators owe a large part of their success to their ability to minimize potential misunderstandings. Communication models allow us to pinpoint where in the process misunderstandings occur and to assess how to correct them. Communication models have evolved from Shannon and Weaver's one-way linear model (1949) to Schramm's interactive or circular model with feedback (1955) to today's dynamic transactional models in which communication from various directions may occur simultaneously. Successful communicators are aware of and can correctly use the basic elements of the communication process shown in the transactional model in Figure 1.1: person A/person B, stimulation and motivation, encoding and decoding, frames of reference, code, channel, feedback, environment, and noise. See which of these communication elements cause you the most difficulty.

Person A/Person B

Either person A or person B in the model could be the **sender** (the source of the message) or the **receiver** (the interpreter of the message). Actually, during most of their communication, they will both send and receive simultaneously. When conversations really get rolling, it can be difficult to determine at any one moment who is the sender and who is the receiver. However, to simplify our discussion of the model, we will continue to use the terms *sender* and *receiver*.

Stimulus and Motivation

Two things must happen before the sender even wants to send a message. First, the sender must be **stimulated**—an internal or external stimulus triggers a thought, which in turn triggers the desire to communicate. Here is an example: A publications supervisor, while briefing new personnel on basic procedures for lettering signs, suddenly remembers that he has not ordered the media equipment needed for the next day's briefing. He tells the new workers to take a 5-minute break, hurries to the office,

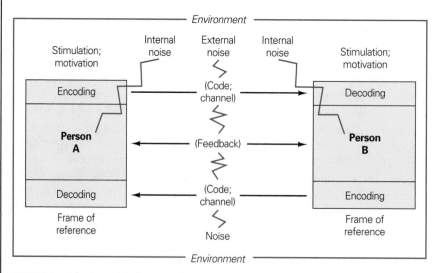

FIGURE 1.1 A basic model of communication.

and calls the media secretary. The supervisor's communication with the secretary was triggered by an *internal stimulus.*

An *external stimulus* can also trigger the desire to communicate. Meetings and professional gatherings that are filled with awkward silences are missing the external stimuli needed to start relaxed communication. For example, a sales representative who is promoting a new book at a convention is careful to arrange for appropriate external stimuli, such as drinks, appetizers, soft music, and the author of the book—all in a suite with a breathtaking view of the city. Carefully planned business meetings might include such external stimuli as coffee, a progress chart, or an outside consultant.

However, a stimulus alone is not enough to trigger communication. The second requirement for sending a message is sufficient **motivation**. Think of the times a manager or leader has asked a question and some of the people present were fairly sure they knew the answer (were stimulated) but did not respond. Why not? Probably because they were not sufficiently motivated—that is, they saw no personal benefit in answering. Or perhaps they saw greater benefit in not answering if they feared giving an incorrect answer. In contrast, if they suspected that their promotions could be influenced by the amount of their participation, they might be motivated to answer the question.

The importance of these two steps—stimulation and motivation—cannot be overlooked. Potential customers will rarely listen carefully to a sales presentation if the stimulus is absent, and they certainly won't buy unless they can see how they will benefit (motivation). The key to being a good salesperson lies in knowing how to stimulate and motivate the customer to buy. Good speakers are also aware of these two steps. In the introduction of an oral presentation, a good business speaker first gets the audience's attention (stimulation to listen) and then shows them how the presentation will be valuable to them personally (motivation to continue listening).

Encoding and Decoding

After being stimulated and motivated to communicate, the sender must decide how best to convey a message to the specific receiver. The process of putting a message into the form in which it will be communicated is **encoding**. For example, when a manager finds it necessary to reprimand an employee, he or she should think about how to encode the message: What type of words should be used—mild or firm? What volume should be used—loud or soft? Would a frown or a smile achieve the best result? What specific examples would help the employee understand? E-mail messages should receive the same careful encoding—for example, is my message clear and does it project the desired tone? Because senders encode messages before communicating them, the sender is often referred to as the *encoder.*

When the encoder's message is picked up, the receiver tries to make sense out of it—that is, to decode it. **Decoding** is the process the receiver goes through in trying to interpret the exact meaning of a message. When an employee is reprimanded by a supervisor, the employee may consider certain questions: How serious a mistake have I made? Is the boss serious or just joking? Am I going to lose my job or promotion? E-mail is even more difficult to decode, isn't it? Have you ever received an e-mail message that made you instantly angry? Because receivers decode messages, they are often referred to as *decoders.*

Frame of Reference

Inaccurate encoding and decoding can be responsible for some of our major communication breakdowns. These breakdowns occur because we use our own background and experience—our **frame of reference**—to encode and decode messages. Unless the backgrounds and experiences of both sender and receiver are identical, their messages may not be accurately encoded or decoded. Here are some examples:

- Nike withdrew its flame logo used on one of its basketball shoes when it received complaints from offended customers that the graphic resembled the Arabic script for *Allah*, the word for *God* (Ricks, 2006).

- Alka-Seltzer had problems with customers knowing how many tablets to take until the popular slogan, "Plop, plop, fizz, fizz, oh what a relief it is" clarified that point in an entertaining manner—sales doubled (Luntz, 2007).

- A popular toothpaste commercial that promised white teeth was considered unsuitable for parts of Southeast Asia, where black teeth, caused by the chewing of betel nuts, are a sign of higher social status (Lamb et al., 2004, p. 120).

- Doctors and psychologists have found that patients may not volunteer needed information because they are uncertain what is expected of them (Watts, 1983). For example, some patients think they should wait for their doctors to ask them questions, whereas many doctors would like their patients to volunteer information.

- After a voyage of 416 million miles, the $125 million Mars Climate Orbiter burned up in the Martian atmosphere because of a misunderstanding between Lockheed Martin, who built the spacecraft, and NASA, who designed it (Petit, 1999). When measuring the force of the small control thrusters, Lockheed Martin used pounds (an English measure), whereas NASA used newtons (a metric measure). A pound is approximately 4.45 newtons. Therefore, the thrusters sent the Orbiter 56 miles closer to Mars than NASA had intended.

- Lever Brothers mailed out samples of its new dishwashing liquid called Sunlight. The package had a large picture of a lemon and the phrase "with real lemon juice" on the label. Although the package clearly identified it as a household cleaning product, many people thought it was lemon juice (Lamb et al., 2006).

Each person's frame of reference includes educational background, race, cultural values, sex, life experiences, attitudes, and personality. Haney (1986) was the first to suggest that we should think of our frames of reference as an invisible window. Everything we see, touch, taste, smell, and hear takes place through our particular window. Some windows have a large frame that gives a broad view of what is going on outside them; others have a small frame that limits what can be observed. Some windows have clear glass, which allows for accurate viewing; others have thick or tinted glass that distorts images.

No Identical Frames of Reference   Based on what we have discussed so far, do you think it is it possible for any two people to have exactly the same frame of reference? Even identical twins have different personalities and react differently to the same experiences.

Managers and employees certainly have different frames of reference. In a now famous study (Bormann et al., 1969), managers and employees were asked to rank a list of morale factors according to their importance to employees. The managers rated appreciation of work done, a feeling of being "in on things," and sympathetic help on personal problems as eighth, ninth, and tenth in importance to employees. The employees, however, listed the same three factors as first, second, and third.

Differences in Cultural Values

Americans (U.S.)	Japanese	Arabs
1. Freedom	1. Belonging	1. Family security
2. Independence	2. Group harmony	2. Family harmony
3. Self-reliance	3. Collectiveness	3. Parental guidance
4. Equality	4. Age/Seniority	4. Age
5. Individualism	5. Group consensus	5. Authority
6. Competition	6. Cooperation	6. Compromise
7. Efficiency	7. Quality	7. Devotion
8. Time	8. Patience	8. Patience
9. Directness	9. Indirectness	9. Indirectness
10. Openness	10. Go-between	10. Hospitality

Source: Printed in Guffey, M. E. (2007). *Essentials of Business Communication* (7th ed.). Mason, OH: South-Western, p. 16. Based on Multicultural Management, 2000, by F. Elashmawi and R. Harris, p. 72

FIGURE 1.2 Cultural values of Americans, Japanese, and Arabs.

A more recent study (Schnake et al., 1990) that surveyed a large number of managers and employees also found major disagreements between what managers and subordinates thought managers communicated.

Frame of reference differences definitely play a role in international business. Consider the top 10 cultural values of Americans, Japanese, and Arabs (Figure 1.2). Compare these value differences with the individualistic/collectivistic cultures and the low context/high context cultures discussed in the Conflict section of Chapter 3.

If everyone's frame of reference is somewhat different, then we must assume that we will encounter difficulties in communicating. As you imagine the communication problems created by the value differences listed in Figure 1.2, consider the following examples that illustrate encoding or decoding breakdowns caused by differences in frames of reference. Remember that when you read these examples, you are doing so from your own frame of reference.

Example 1

A college professor was a member of a credit union. Needing a quick loan one day, she filled out all the necessary application forms and waited while the employee typed the request into the computer terminal. When the answer was received, the employee told the professor, "I'm very sorry, but we can't give you a loan."

"Why not?" asked the professor, who knew her credit was good.

"I don't know why, but the computer says we can't."

The words the computer had typed out were NO LOAN THIS MEMBER. Urged by the professor, the employee referred the matter to the manager and discovered that "No loan this member" meant that the professor did not have a loan. If she had already had a loan with the credit union, the computer would have responded with ONE LOAN THIS MEMBER.

Example 2

A new purchaser for overseas accounts received an urgent message on May 1 from a Dutch associate in Amsterdam requesting information needed "before closing time on 6/5." Feeling pleased with herself, the purchaser faxed the information three weeks early, on May 10. To her surprise, the Dutch office expressed anger and asked that she be taken off their account. The Dutch associate had really asked for information by May 6; Europeans usually write the day before the month (adapted from Ferraro, 1998, pp. 163, 172).

Example 3

On final approach, just short of touchdown, the pilot of a military plane determined that the runway was too short and that the landing must be aborted. He yelled to his engineer, "Takeoff power!" The engineer reached up and turned off the engines, and the plane crashed off the end of the runway. The pilot had wanted the engineer to give him extra power for takeoff!

These examples of communication breakdown might not have occurred if the senders had attempted to put their messages into the frames of reference of the receivers or if the receivers had attempted to decode the messages from the senders' frames of reference. Each communicator needs to remember that the message that counts is the one *received*. It does not matter what you really said, what you thought you said, or what you meant to say. As a sender, you need to be concerned with what your receiver thought you said. Therefore, the burden of communication lies with you as sender. It's a good idea to check the reception of your messages by asking receivers to **paraphrase** (summarize in their own words) what they think you meant.

A Communication Fallacy   After reading examples of communication breakdown, some people may think, "These examples don't apply to my business. We couldn't afford to make such ridiculous mistakes!" NASA probably thought so too until the loss of the Mars Climate Orbiter. The question we must ask is this: Is 100% communication—where the sent messages and the received messages are identical—possible in the business setting? Or is this a communication fallacy?

To answer this question, we must first decide whether 100% communication is *ever* possible. Let's move outside the business world for a moment to consider an example most of us have observed firsthand. Imagine that a couple who have been married for 50 years are at a social gathering. The husband and wife are on opposite sides of the room when one guest begins to tell the same joke he has told at every party for the past 10 years. The husband and wife look at each other from across the room and grimace. Obviously, both of them are showing disgust at the joke-telling guest, so general understanding has occurred between them. But is it 100%? No, because their intensity of feeling differs. The woman may find the joker so repulsive that she wishes to leave the party, whereas the man considers the joker annoying but tolerable. Also, the exact thoughts behind the husband's and wife's grimaces differ. The woman may be thinking, "How embarrassing for the hostess! How can she stand it when he makes a fool of himself at her party?" The man may be thinking, "The poor guy! How can he stand to make such a fool of himself?" In order for 100% communication to occur, husband and wife must have identical frames of reference. Obviously, they do not.

Now consider a business example:

A supervisor is sitting at her desk working on a prototype for a new production item. She has been working on it for several days and is angry about all the work required. She reaches for her jeweler's screwdriver but finds it missing. Wilson, a technician who works for her, walks by at that moment. "Wilson, bring me a set of jeweler's screwdrivers!" shouts the angry supervisor. Looking rather surprised, Wilson walks to the tool crib, picks up a set of jeweler's screwdrivers, and hands them to the supervisor.

Is this an example of 100% communication? The supervisor probably thinks so because she got what she requested. But she has forgotten that her tone of voice and facial expression also communicated something to Wilson. Although the supervisor may feel good about the communication, Wilson may be thinking, "What have I done wrong? She only picks on me when I've done something she doesn't like" or "I guess she doesn't like the way I handled the Smith job."

If no two individuals have the same frame of reference, how can we ever communicate 100% with anyone on any topic, even in the business setting? Perhaps we can reach 80 to 95% when communicating horizontally with other people in the same position or rank, but upward and downward communication gets progressively worse the greater the distance on the corporate ladder. One company researched 100 businesses and discovered that only 20% of a message communicated downward through five levels of management reaches the workers for whom it is intended (Killian, 1968); see Figure 1.3. Because of individual frames of reference, a message progressing up or down the chain of command may have the following characteristics:

- *Leveled*: Some details are lost.
- *Condensed*: The message becomes shorter and simpler.
- *Sharpened*: Some details are highlighted, thereby becoming more important.
- *Assimilated*: Ambiguities are "clarified" to conform to past messages and future expectations.
- *Embellished*: Details are added.

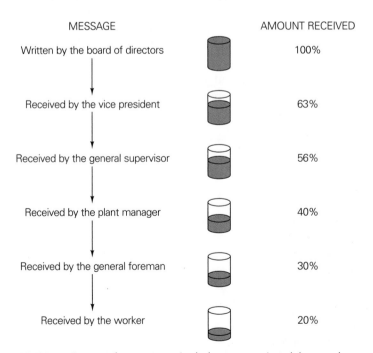

FIGURE 1.3 Amount of message received when communicated downward through five levels of management.

Business communicators who strive for communication excellence will probably have more success if they acknowledge that 100% communication is a communication fallacy and prepare for possible misunderstanding ahead of time. By anticipating different frames of reference, the effective communicator is able to prevent many errors.

Code

Another element of the basic communication model is the code. The **code** is the symbols that carry the message. There are three basic communication codes:

- *Language (verbal code)*: Spoken or written words used to communicate thoughts and emotions.
- *Paralanguage (vocal code)*: The vocal elements that go along with spoken language, including tone of voice, pitch, rate, volume, and emphasis. (Although paralanguage is often listed as a subcategory of nonverbal communication, it is separated here to emphasize the importance of each.)
- *Nonverbal cues (visual code)*: All intentional and unintentional means other than writing or speaking by which a person sends a message, including facial expressions, eye contact, gestures, appearance, posture, size and location of office, and arrival time at meetings.

Many business people think that the only important code is the language code. Researchers, however, have found that language is not as important to the meaning of a message as either the nonverbal or the paralanguage codes. R. L. Birdwhistell (1970) reports that "probably no more than 30 to 35 percent of the social meaning of a conversation or an interaction is carried by the words." This leaves 65 to 70% of meaning conveyed by the nonverbal and paralanguage codes. Analyzing the results from 23 studies, J. S. Philpott (1983) found that, indeed, the verbal code accounts for 31% of the variance in meanings between sender and receiver, whereas the vocal and visual codes account for the remaining variance (see Figure 1.4). Many other studies have found that when adults attempt to determine the meaning of a statement, they rely more heavily on nonverbal cues and paralanguage than they do on what is actually said (Archer & Akert, 1977; Burgoon & Hoobler, 2002; Thompson et al., 1998). This seems to be true for first impressions, attitudes, job interviews, and

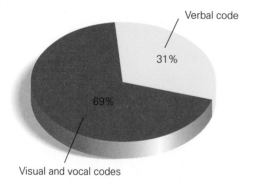

Verbal code

31%

69%

Visual and vocal codes

FIGURE 1.4 When interpreting a message, listeners rely more heavily on the visual and vocal codes (what they see and how you speak) than on the verbal code (what you say).

boss-employee conversations, to name a few (Burgoon, 1983; Burgoon et al., 1996). In other words, "the ability to encode and decode nonverbal messages is critically important to successful communication" (Burgoon & Hoobler, 2002, p. 247).

The difference among the codes can be illustrated in the following example. You arrive home after a hard day at work. You walk in, slam the door, plop down on your recliner, and let out a long sigh. When asked, "How was your day?" you reply, "Oh, it was fine!" In this instance, to which code would the questioner pay more attention: the slamming of the door (nonverbal), the loud sigh (paralanguage), or the actual words spoken (language)?

To communicate effectively, the sender must communicate the same message by all three codes. However, many people either deliberately or unknowingly send *conflicting* or *double messages*. Whenever there is a conflict among the messages received, people tend to believe more of what they see than what they hear. Grouping language and paralanguage together as verbal, Argyle (1973) found that "with initially equated signals the nonverbal messages outweighed the verbal ones at least 5 to 1, and where they were in conflict the verbal messages were virtually disregarded." (p. 78). For example, the flight attendants' reassuring words (language code) on a nearly disastrous Eastern Airlines flight were probably ignored by the passengers, who could see the fear on their faces (nonverbal code) and could hear the fear in the voice of the captain (paralanguage code). One passenger reported, "The worst part was when the captain told us that the ditching was imminent.... He had a real quivering voice, and it scared the hell out of everyone" (Lerner, 1983, p. 40).

To further illustrate the problem of conflicting messages, consider this example.

A supervisor was pleased at the way her employees had completed a very difficult and important project. She called a special meeting of the employees just to praise them. Five minutes before the meeting, however, she received a call from her boss telling her that she was wanted in the office of the vice president to discuss a problem relating to her department's budget. She was still concentrating on the phone call as she walked into the meeting. Her employees noticed her strained smile and abstracted manner and began to feel nervous. Maybe, they thought, they weren't going to be praised after all.

"I can't tell you how pleased I am with the way you handled last week's project," the supervisor began. "You worked together as a team, and I'm proud of all of you. Well, take a few minutes for coffee and donuts before getting to work." Then, instead of casually joining her employees for coffee as she usually did, the supervisor hurried from the room.

The employees were confused. Was she pleased with them or not? Her language said she was pleased. Yet her paralanguage (tone of voice and rushed delivery) and her nonverbal cues (strained smile, abstracted manner, and failure to stay for coffee) seemed to indicate displeasure.

Although most employees probably interpreted the conflicting messages to mean that the supervisor was unhappy, all she meant to communicate was "I'm pleased." She was completely unaware that she was sending conflicting, incongruent messages. Like many people, she incorrectly assumed that the only message she was sending was the verbal one.

Channel

The success of your message may depend not only on the consistency of your codes but also on the channel you select. A **channel** is the medium selected to carry the message. Examples of communication channels are face-to-face discussions,

TABLE 1.1

Shorthand for E-mail, Blogs, and Chat Room Messages			
Shorthand	**Meaning**	**Shorthand**	**Meaning**
BTW	By the way	SEC	Wait a sec
HTH	Hope that helps	TNX	Thanks
IDK	I don't know	TTFN	Ta-ta for now
IBTD	I beg to differ	(: & or >:-<	Angry or mad
IMHO	In my humble opinion	%-(or :/	Confused
IOW	In other words	:-I	Frowning
IWBNI	It would be nice if	:-) or :) or <g>	Happy, smile, or grin
LOL	Laughing out loud	{ }	No comment
OTOH	On the other hand	:(or :-(	Sad
PMFJI	Pardon me for jumping in	:-o or :-O or =O	Surprise or shock

telephone calls, memos, e-mails, instant messaging (IMs), blogs, newsletters, magazines, radio, and television.

Not all channels have the same capacity to carry information. The amount of information a channel can convey is referred to as **channel richness** (Daft & Lengel, 1986). The more codes a channel conveys, the higher its level of richness. For example, in a business meeting, when participants are using the face-to-face communication channel, all three codes—nonverbal, language, and paralanguage—carry messages. Television also carries all three codes. Radio and telephone communication, however, lack the visual clues of the nonverbal code. As a result, these channels carry a greater risk of communication breakdown. Memos, e-mail, and blogs are even more limited because they contain only the language code (although we attempt to add paralanguage by underlining, adding arrows, circling in red pen, or using emoticons, such as those shown in Table 1.1, or the animated emoticons now available on the Internet).

The extensive use of memos, e-mail, and the new use of blogs and video logs (vlogs) indicates the importance that business and professional people place on these channels of communication. The ethics dilemma in this chapter shows the persuasive power that e-mail and blogs had on Abercrombie & Fitch's decision to remove a controversial line of clothing from their Internet catalog. Keep in mind that memos and e-mail are most effective when used to follow up a face-to-face meeting, list the decisions reached during a meeting, or summarize the areas discussed. The receivers of these types of messages have less difficulty in decoding accurately because they were present at the meeting and their frames of reference are more closely attuned to the sender's. For specifics on how to write successful e-mail messages, see Appendix: Written Communication.

Channel Selection   In deciding which channel is most appropriate, there are other factors to consider in addition to channel richness (Timm, 1986):

- *The importance of the message.* Important messages usually require the face-to-face channel. If technology is used instead, Robert Heller's (1998) book *Communicate Clearly* offers three guidelines:

"Send only essential messages; keep messages short; and avoid delays in replying" (p. 31). Heller also recommends a few helpful rules of Internet etiquette, also known as netiquette: "Use meaningful subject titles; be as brief as possible; and distinguish business from non-business e-mail" (p. 30).

- *The needs and abilities of the receiver.* Some people are able to work from memos and phone conversations; others are better at interpreting face-to-face messages.

- *The amount and speed of the feedback required.* Complicated messages and messages needing immediate feedback are normally best with the face-to-face channel, where all codes are present. Keep in mind that although e-mail allows for fast feedback, it is easy to misinterpret. Charles Steinfield (1990), manager of Xerox, had the following to say:

  In the absence of immediate feedback and the tempering effects of nonverbal cues and the physical presence of receivers, electronic messages can sometimes be perceived as overly critical or blunt, or can simply be misinterpreted.... In situations in which a response is meant to be critical, the absence of context can lead to its being interpreted as stronger criticism than intended (p. 292).

- *The necessity of a permanent record.* Written instructions, memos, and e-mail can be used to verify a conversation and to serve as a permanent record of what was said.

- *The cost of the channel.* In the business world, time and energy equal cost. For example, it costs less to fax or send e-mail, more to speak on the phone long distance, and often much more to bring employees to a central place for a face-to-face meeting.

- *The formality or informality desired.* Although face-to-face communication can be quite formal, it is normally considered less formal than a newsletter or a memo but more formal than e-mail.

One supervisor found out the importance of the use of channels the hard way. During the lunch hour, he received a call from a person representing a key account who wanted to know if it was possible to get a special shipment of parts by 5:00 that afternoon. "No problem," assured the supervisor. "We can ship them to you by a special flight in plenty of time." "I'm counting on you," replied the caller. "If we don't get that shipment by 5:00, we will lose a big account!" The supervisor was scheduled to attend a very important meeting in 5 minutes, so he wrote a detailed memo and dropped it on the shipping foreman's desk on his way to the meeting. The supervisor was involved in this important meeting for most of the afternoon and soon forgot about the noon phone call. Two days later, he received a letter from the key account representative stating that they not only had failed to receive the parts by 5:00 but also had never received the parts at all. As a result, they were canceling all current orders and taking their business elsewhere!

What did the supervisor do wrong? First, he chose a poor channel for such an important message, and second, he failed to follow up the memo to make sure its meaning was clear to the foreman. When using a channel other than a face-to-face meeting, a sender must be sure to follow through by checking to see that the message has been received, understood, and carried out correctly.

Face-to-face communication is especially important in large organizations undergoing rapid change (Wagner & Hollenbeck, 2010). To help you decide which channel is most appropriate (face-to-face, written, or electronic), consider Table 1.2.

TABLE 1.2

Choosing the Best Channel: Should You Send Your Message Face-to-Face, in Writing, or Electronically?		
Use Face-to-Face	**Send Written Message**	**Send Electronic Message**
Immediate feedback needed	Immediate feedback not needed	Immediate feedback not needed, but speed important
Permanent record not needed	Permanent, verifiable record needed	Permanent record not needed, but wish to overcome time-zone barrier
Topic emotional, confusing, or complex; discussion required	Exact wording important; careful planning required	Message explicit, little inter-pretation needed, transferred quickly
Message important and new, or group cohesion needed	Follow-up to face-to-face meeting needed	Information used to support or expand face-to-face meeting
Confidence and trust need developing	Content more important than feelings	Speed, cost, or convenience crucial
Convenient and economical to assemble audience	Audience large and geographi-cally dispersed	Audience large and geographi-cally dispersed, but speedy back-and-forth messages important

Adapted from Bovee & Thill, 2004; Cliff, 1998; Hallowell, 1999; Rice & Gattiker, 2001; Sandberg, 2003.

The channel selected is also important when communicating with the public. When selling merchandise or ideas, the organization should select the channel that (a) is the least expensive but (b) reaches the target audience with (c) the appropriate codes needed to sell the item or idea. For example, suppose your company is planning to sell a new brand of laundry detergent. In deciding which channel to use for marketing, you would first want to identify the target audience—in this instance, probably homemak-ers or possibly college students. You would then decide which codes would be needed to sell the item. For example, do they need to see the item's size or packaging or would hearing about it be enough? Finally, you would decide which channel would be as inex-pensive as possible and still contain the necessary codes to reach the target audience. To reach the appropriate audience, ad campaigns often use more than one channel.

Word Choice   When memos or e-mail must be used to send important or new information, the sender should select language with extreme care. However, accord-ing to 80% of managers responding to a memo survey, the quality of written communication at work is only fair to poor (Buckley, 1999). Researchers have found that the tone of a written statement determines how the reader perceives the author of the message and even the organization for whom the author works. For example, one study (Kulhavy & Schwartz, 1980) found that when flexible-sounding words (e.g., asked, hesitate, agreeable, and offering) were used, readers judged the organization to be concerned with employees, fair to women and minorities, involved with commu-nity problems, generous in determining employee salaries, open in communication with the union, and liked by employees. However, when strict-sounding words (e.g., required, willing, forceful, and pushing) were used, the readers judged the organization to be exactly the opposite.

One company always substitutes the word *issue* for *problem*, feeling that people who don't wish to discuss problems will feel comfortable with issues. Here are some similar examples of corporate language selection: J. C. Penney, Physio-Control, and Quad/Graphics never refer to their people as "employees." At J. C. Penney, you're an associate; at Physio-Control, a team member; and at Quad/Graphics, a partner (Moskowitz, 1985). Automobile companies have found that they sell more used cars when the cars are referred to as "pre-owned" rather than "used." In the 1980s, oil companies outraged customers by charging a "credit surcharge" for credit card use (customers paying cash were not charged extra). Companies who offered a "discount for cash," however, were viewed as customer friendly. Both approaches charged customers more for credit card use and less for cash, but the language used to describe each approach affected customer perceptions (Wagner & Hollenbeck, 2010).

"Thank you for your opinion."

Feedback

When people observe their own behavior and resolve to do better next time, when people ask friends to give an opinion on how well they handled a certain situation, or when managers suggest ways in which employees can improve their performance, feedback is being employed. **Feedback** is the verbal and visual response to a message. Feedback can be a self-monitoring response that allows us to modify our behavior until it meets our expectations. Feedback is also the only way we can know whether messages we send are interpreted as we intended. Without feedback, all we can do is assume that the messages have been received correctly.

Advantages of Feedback Supervisors who encourage their employees to give feedback find that feedback improves the accuracy and productivity of both individuals and groups (Clampitt & Downs, 1983; Deal & Kennedy, 1999). Misunderstandings often occur because people honestly think they have understood the boss's or peer's instructions well enough that feedback is unnecessary. The few seconds that it would take to verify the assignment could save both time and money.

Another advantage is that feedback increases employee satisfaction with the job. People like to believe that their ideas and opinions are of value. When given the opportunity to ask questions or make suggestions, employees tend to feel more a part of the organization and are willing to take on responsibility for accurate communication. In a field study with nurses, Jackson (1983) found that bimonthly information-sharing meetings between nurses and supervisors resulted in less role conflict and ambiguity, as well as lower stress, absenteeism, and turnover.

Disadvantages of Feedback Despite the advantages of feedback, many managers and employees avoid its use for several reasons (Bormann et al., 1969, pp. 148–149). First of all, feedback can cause people to feel psychologically attacked. Even the most experienced manager or employee can become defensive when feedback seems negative. Sometimes, feedback indicates that the message was not communicated very well. However, people should worry when they don't receive any feedback; the receivers may be either so confused that they don't know what to ask or so confident of their understanding that they ignore the need for verification.

Another disadvantage is that feedback is time consuming. It takes time to make sure that everyone understands, but it takes more time (and money) to redo tasks that should have been accomplished correctly the first time. One consulting firm uses this slogan in its seminars: "If you don't have time to do the job correctly, when will you find time to do the job a second time?"

In addition, feedback can be difficult to elicit. Many people seek feedback by asking, "Are there any questions?" or "Are you sure you understand?" Then they can't understand why no one ever has any questions. Asking others if they understand pressures them to say, "No, I don't have any questions" or "Yes, I understand," even when the opposite may be true. When employees are afraid of appearing stupid in front of the manager, they will pretend to understand whether they do or not. Instead of asking employees *if* they understand, managers should ask them *what* they understand by asking them to paraphrase the instructions they have received. Paraphrasing allows managers to determine which part of the instructions, if any, are unclear.

Another reason people are reluctant to give feedback is past experience. They may have reacted negatively to feedback in the past, or others may have reacted badly to their feedback. It takes only a few negative verbal or nonverbal reactions to convince people that it is simply too risky to say what they think or to admit that they don't understand.

Effective Use of Feedback To improve your use of feedback, try adopting the following suggestions (based on Bormann et al., 1969, pp. 151–154).

When Receiving Feedback from Others
- *Tell people you want feedback.* When people feel that their opinions and observations may be used against them or that your feelings may be easily hurt, they withhold feedback. Therefore, let them know that you consider feedback (including personal opinions, questions, and disagreement) not only useful but also necessary. If you are hesitant to ask for feedback, try "360-degree feedback" (O'Reilly, 1994). In this process, you request anonymous feedback from a full circle of observers including peers, superiors, subordinates, customers, suppliers, and sales staff.

- *Identify the areas in which you want feedback.* If you want personal feedback, you might say, "I am trying to improve my delivery and am interested in how confident I appeared in today's meeting." If you want only feedback pertaining to the organization of your ideas, then specify that topic.

- If you are a manager, *set aside time for regularly scheduled feedback sessions.* Such sessions show employees that you value feedback and thus tend to make it easier for them to ask questions and express opinions.

- *Select the proper channel.* When feedback is routine, the channel can safely have low media richness. However, if the message is nonroutine, complicated, or negative, the channel needs to be high in media richness. Imagine how the 403 employees at Radio Shack felt when they received via e-mail the bad news that they had been fired (Augstums & Halkias, 2006).

- *Use silence to encourage feedback.* Too many people ask a question, wait only 2 or 3 seconds, and then begin talking again. It takes more time than that for most people to organize and verbalize their responses. If you remain silent for at least a full 10 seconds, you will probably get more responses.

- *Watch for nonverbal responses.* Because the nonverbal code carries a significant amount of the meaning of a message, it is an excellent source of feedback.

- *Ask questions.* Do not assume that you understand the meaning of the feedback you receive from others. When in doubt, ask for clarification.

- *Paraphrase.* Even when you feel sure you understand a person's feedback, it is a good idea to paraphrase. For example, if your boss says, "This rush job has top priority," you could paraphrase by saying, "Then you are telling me that this rush job has higher priority than any other job I'm working on now." As the need for message accuracy increases, the need for paraphrasing increases.

- *Use statements that encourage feedback.* People usually adjust their feedback by monitoring the listener's verbal and nonverbal reactions. If you want a person's honest opinion, you must encourage it by purposely saying such things as "Really?" "Interesting." "So, you feel that...."

- *Reward feedback.* If you are a manager, you can reward feedback by complimenting the person, preferably in front of colleagues. Some companies have a "Best Idea of the Month" contest and put the winners' names on a placard or give each of them a company pen with their name engraved on it. As an employee, you can sincerely thank people for their comments and perhaps write them a note of thanks.

- *Follow up.* Individual conversations and group meetings often require oral or written follow-up to ensure that successful communications occurred and to encourage implementation of any decisions reached.

When Giving Feedback to Others

- *Direct feedback toward behavior rather than toward the person.* A common mistake is to criticize the person rather than the behavior. Telling your assistant "You are a poor excuse for a secretary" is a personal attack rather than feedback on a particular behavior, and it only causes a defensive response. Your feedback is much more likely to be received positively if you identify the particular behavior and focus on what can be done to correct it in the future: "Janice, a mistake like this one costs way more than our weekly office budget. From now on, please check with me before finalizing any orders costing more than $100."

- *Use language that is descriptive instead of evaluative.* **Descriptive feedback** is tactfully honest and objective, whereas **evaluative feedback** is judgmental and accusatory. Evaluative feedback: "Where is your sales report? You know it is due on my desk no later than 9:00 each morning. You're obviously not reliable anymore." *Descriptive feedback:* "When you don't turn your sales reports in on time, I'm unable to complete the departmental report on time. This makes both me and the department look bad. You've been late twice this month. Is there something I can do to help you get those reports in on time?" Evaluative words cause defensiveness and hurt feelings; words that simply describe the situation are more likely to result in cooperation.

- *Recognize that feedback involves sharing ideas, not giving advice.* It is not always appropriate to give advice to other people. If your advice does not work, you will be blamed. One of the best ways to improve a relationship is by openly sharing opinions and ideas. Suppose a manager who is having trouble with some employees comes to you and asks, "What am I doing wrong?" Instead of giving advice, share a personal experience with the manager. For example, you might describe a similar problem you had and how you handled it. It is then up to the manager to decide what to do.

- *Include only as much information as the person can handle at one time.* Suppose during a performance appraisal, you give an employee a list of 20 items that need improvement. You may feel better now that you have fully expressed your feelings, but how can anyone improve on 20 things at the same time? Give only two or three suggestions—a number the person can reasonably handle.

- *Remember that effective feedback is immediate and well timed.* Immediate feedback is more valuable than delayed feedback because it allows the person to correct actions or behaviors while they are still fresh. For example, after a foul-up in shipping, discuss the problem with the responsible employee immediately, if possible, or at least within a day or two. Because feedback should also be well timed, sometimes it can't be immediate. For example, if you point out the employee's mistakes in front of a group of coworkers, it is likely to be resented. Or if it's after quitting time, your suggestions may not receive the attention they deserve. Sensitive feedback should be given in a private, relaxed atmosphere. Unfortunately, many people give feedback in anger without stopping to consider the consequences.

- *Allow face-saving when possible.* In an attempt to make themselves look good to others, a person will often continue to argue for a plan even when it is obviously not working or in the best interest of the organization (Brockner, 1992). People are more likely to accept negative feedback when allowed some degree of face-saving. For example, instead of saying, "Your idea was rejected," mention that the rejection was due in part to lack of funds or other factors, thereby allowing the person a face-saving out (Simonson & Staw, 1992).

IT REALLY WORKS!

Feedback

So you don't want to hold a garage sale but hesitate to throw away your old "stuff." Or maybe you are looking for something unusual to decorate your game room. Where could you go? How about eBay? People from all over the world can buy and sell items through eBay. In 1998, eBay had 2.1 million registered users and in 10 years that number had grown to 84 million (About eBay, 2009). eBay is an Internet commerce site that began with an annual revenue of $4 million and 138 employees when it went public in 1998 and has grown to $8 billion in revenue and 15,000 employees in 2008. Company success is indicated by its stock, which rose 5,600 percent during that 10-year period (Cohen, 2008).

Meg Whitman, company CEO from 1998 to 2008, credits eBay's phenomenal success to the feedback the company received from their many registered users through discussion boards, blogs, surveys, and personal contact. Whitman communicated directly with users about their experiences during the *eBay Live* conventions held in locations throughout the United States each year since 2002 (Lashinsky, 2003). Many of their ideas and innovations in the past have come from users. According to Whitman, "You are truly in partnership with the community of users. The key is connecting employees and customers in two-way communication. We call it 'The Power of All of Us.'" It remains to be seen whether recent changes will be approved by the eBay users and whether the new CEO John Donahoe will continue to listen to feedback.

What do you think?
- Have you used eBay, and does it seem to you that management is open to feedback from its registered users? Why or why not?
- Has eBay's dramatic increase in employees helped or hindered its ability to respond to users?

Environment

The effective communicator plans and controls the environment as much as possible. The **environment** includes the "time, place, physical and social surroundings" (Holm, 1981, p. 22) in which you find yourself. For example, the mood of your meeting, and consequently the success of your communication, can depend on the *time* of the meeting—8:00 a.m., 2:00 p.m., or 30 minutes before quitting time. The best time depends on the people involved, their expectations, and the purpose and expected length of your meeting. The *location* of a meeting also greatly affects communication. For this reason, your best business deals may take place outside the office, such as at a restaurant or on a golf course, where pressures are not felt so keenly. Communication is also affected by the *physical environment* of the location. Such conditions as the size of the room, the brightness of the lights, the room temperature, the comfort and arrangement of the chairs, the shape of the table, and the noise level can alter the type and success of communication. *Social environment*—the relationships of the people present—also affects your communication. For example, don't most of us feel and act differently when our supervisors are present at a gathering?

An organization's social and work environment is often referred to as its **climate**. An organization's climate is determined by the prevailing atmosphere and attitudes of its members. Climate can have such a powerful effect on communication that we will discuss it further in Chapters 2, 3, and 5.

Noise

Anything that interferes with communication by distorting or blocking the message is **noise**. *External noise* includes distractions in the environment, such as the speaker's poor grammar, papers being shuffled, phones ringing, people talking, cold air in the room, and lights that are too dim. *Internal noise* refers to conditions of the communicators such as a headache, daydreaming, lack of sleep, preoccupation with other problems, or lack of knowledge on the topic. Any of these noises can distort or block communication.

The effect of noise on communication is demonstrated by the following example. Suppose you are upset about not receiving the same raise as the other people in your office. You write a memo to your boss requesting a private interview. Two days after sending the memo and getting no response, you and your boss unexpectedly run into each other in a busy workroom. The boss, thinking that this time is as good as any other, motions you to sit down and says, "So what did you want to talk to me about?" How successful can this grievance interview be with phones ringing, machines running, and interested people walking in and out? These external noises are fairly obvious. Less obvious, but equally distracting, are the internal noises. We can only guess at the internal noise that the boss is experiencing—preoccupation with other problems or a perception of you as a satisfied employee, perhaps. However, your internal distractions seem fairly clear. You are unhappy and feeling mistreated. You will probably interpret your boss's interviewing you on the spur of the moment in such a noisy public place as further proof of disrespect and unfair treatment. The chance that the two of you will arrive at a mutually agreeable solution will be influenced by both external and internal noise.

As a communicator, you need to be aware of potential noise and its effect on messages. When possible, you should select an environment that is relatively noise free. If unexpected noise does occur, you should either postpone the message until the noise ends or eliminate the noise. If all else fails, simply acknowledge the problem and continue as best you can.

Revisiting the Case Study

Where in the communication model do Facebook's main problems occur?

AP Photo/Paul Sakuma

Communicator Quiz

How skilled a communicator are you? To check your communication effectiveness, take the following quiz. Compare your answers with those in the back of this book. You can also take this quiz online via the Premium Website for *Communicating for Results.*

Directions: For each of these statements about your communication, select one of the following answers: (*A*) usually, (*B*) sometimes, or (*C*) rarely.

_____ 1. Do you knowingly stimulate and motivate the receiver of the message?

_____ 2. Do you try to encode ideas so they will fit into the frame of reference of the receiver?

_____ 3. Do you try to decode messages using the sender's frame of reference?

_____ 4. Do you try to send each message by the nonverbal, paralanguage, and language codes?

_____ 5. Do you try to improve your communication success by controlling the environment?

_____ 6. Do you let the importance of the message and the ability of the receiver determine the channel you select?

_____ 7. Do you realize that 100% communication is unlikely and therefore plan for ways to avoid possible misunderstandings?

_____ 8. When you communicate, do you remember that the only message that counts is the one received?

_____ 9. Do you avoid becoming defensive or placing blame when communication breakdown occurs?

_____ 10. Do you view feedback as absolutely necessary for successful communication, and therefore both give and receive feedback on a regular basis?

Scoring:
Number of times you answered *A* (usually) _____
Number of times you answered *A* + *B* (usually and sometimes) _____
Number of times you answered *C* (rarely) _____

Results:
If you have seven or more *A* answers, you are an outstanding communicator.
If you have seven or more *A* + *B* answers, you are an average-to-good communicator.
If you have seven or more *C* answers, you need immediate improvement

Communication and Ethics

So far, we have discussed the basic elements involved in the communication process and identified some major causes of communication errors. Before finishing this chapter, we also need to take a careful look at the crucial role ethics plays in communication success. One author (Shockley-Zalabak, 2009) defines ethics this way:

> Ethics ... are the standards by which behaviors are evaluated for their morality: their rightness or wrongness. When applied to human communication, ethics are the moral principles that guide our judgments about the good and bad, right and wrong, of communication.... (p. 111)

According to Gallup poll surveys, the American public has lost faith in the honesty and ethics of most professional people, including business professionals (Saad, 2008). Since 1976 pollsters have asked, "How would you rate the honesty and ethical standards of people in these different fields—very high, high, average, low, or very low?" See Table 1.3 for the percentages of respondents from 2000 through 2005 who rated each profession as having "high" or "very high" ethical standards. Note that nurses continue to be the highest-ranked professionals, with 84%, followed by druggists and pharmacists with 70%. High school teachers and medical doctors scored in the 60% range; clergy and police officers scored in the 50% range. Dropping way down to the other end of the scale we find lawyers at 18%, congresspersons at 12%, whereas car salespeople and telemarketers ranked at the bottom with 7 and 5%, respectively.

TABLE 1.3

Percentages of Respondents Rating Each Profession as Having "High" or "Very High" Ethical Standards							
	Rating						
Profession	2002	2003	2004	2005	2006	2007	2008
Nurses	79%	83%	79%	82%	84%	79%	84%
Druggists, pharmacists	67	67	72	67	73	67	70
High school teachers	64	–	–	64	–	–	65
Medical doctors	63	68	67	65	69	63	64
Clergy	52	56	56	54	58	53	56
Police officers	59	59	60	61	54	53	56
Funeral directors	39	–	–	44	–	–	47
Accountants	35	–	–	39	–	–	38
Journalists	26	25	–	28	26	–	25
Bankers	36	35	36	41	37	35	23
Building contractors	20	–	–	20	–	–	22
Lawyers	18	16	18	18	18	15	18
Real estate agents	19	–	–	20	–	–	17
Labor union leaders	14	–	–	16	–	–	16
Business executives	17	18	20	16	18	14	12
Stockbrokers	12	15	–	16	17	–	12
Congresspersons	17	17	20	14	14	9	12
Advertising practitioners	9	12	10	11	11	6	10
Car salespeople	6	7	9	8	7	5	7
Telemarketers	5	–	–	7	–	–	5

Adapted from Lydia Saad, November 24, 2008, "Nurses Shine, Bankers Slump in Ethics Ratings," Gallup.com.

Apparently, the American public is skeptical about the honesty and ethics of its professionals. A May 2009 Gallup poll found that 71% of Americans think the moral values of the country are getting worse (Jones, 2009).

Pick up almost any newspaper to see reports of unethical practices in organizations, ranging from industrial sabotage, deceptive advertising, and failure to report negative drug reactions, to accounting fraud and discriminatory employment practices. In fact, Conrad and Poole (2005) report that "between 1975 and 1990 two-thirds of the Fortune 500 firms were *convicted* of serious crimes ranging from price fixing to illegal dumping of hazardous wastes" (p. 409). Although the conviction of former Enron executives Kenneth Lay and Jeffrey Skilling was thought to end the early 2000s era, where many top executives from Adelphia, Arthur Andersen, Enron, LLP, Tyco, WorldCom, and several other large corporations, including Martha Stewart, were indicted and convicted of various criminal activities including fraud (Barrionuevo, 2006), the conviction of Bernard (Bernie) Madoff in 2009 for stealing more than $65 billion from investors in a long-running Ponzi scheme makes the earlier fraud pail in comparison. And these only represent those that were caught. For example, when 2,300 employees of large corporations were surveyed recently, 75% reported observing a violation of company standards or a violation of the law during the previous year (Lamb et al., 2004).

To avoid unethical practices, G. R. Jones (2007b) recommends that managers and employees base their decisions on **four ethical rules** adapted from several ethics theories (Cavanagh et al., 1990):

- *The utilitarian rule.* Ethical decisions create "the greatest good for the greatest number of people."

- *The moral rights rule.* Ethical decisions protect people's "fundamental or inalienable rights." In other words, do unto others as you would have them do unto you.

- *The justice rule.* Ethical decisions provide fair and equal treatment for all individuals or groups involved.

- *The practical rule.* Ethical decisions are easy to "communicate to society because the typical person" would find them acceptable—thus, you feel good as well.

An example of a firm that could answer "yes" to these four ethics rules is Johnson & Johnson, which is well known for its code of ethics called "The Credo," which covers physicians, customers, employees, communities, and stockholders (Aguilar, 1994). The Credo begins with the following words: "We believe our first responsibility is to the doctors, nurses, and patients, to mothers and fathers and all others who use our products and services" (p. 66). Johnson & Johnson's top management credit this code of ethics with the action they took during the Tylenol scare of 1982 (Greenberg & Baron, 1995; Treviño & Nelson, 2004). When it was discovered that seven people in Chicago had died after taking Extra Strength Tylenol, the company pulled all Tylenol capsules off the shelves, urged people not to use any Tylenol they had at home, and offered a $100,000 reward for information leading to a resolution of the case (it was later found that the deaths

Louis Lanzano/AP Photo

Bernie Madoff was sentenced to serve 150 years in prison for stealing over $65 billion from investors.

were due to tampering). According to Greenberg and Baron, "Company officials credited the statement [the opening lines of The Credo] with helping them decide what to do at a time when there was no time to gather all the information and weigh all the options" (pp. 546–547). The decision was obviously a difficult one—management knew the costs would run high. Not only did the company experience a loss of revenue (31 million bottles of Tylenol were removed from store shelves), but many loyal customers switched brands. Fortunately, when Tylenol "reintroduced the product in tamper-proof packages," the company "very shortly thereafter regained 95 percent of the market share it had before the crisis" (Greenberg & Baron, 1995, p. 547). Texas Instruments is another company with a strong code of ethics. They have a hot line at 800-33-ETHIC, available from anywhere in the world, and they give their employees an ethics business card with the following information (which follows the four ethics rules discussed previously) on one side of the card:

TI Ethics Quick Test

- Is the action *legal*?
- Does it comply with our *values*?
- If you do it, will you feel *bad*?
- How will it look in the *newspaper*?
- If you know it's *wrong*, don't do it.
- If you're not sure, *ask*.
- Keep asking until you get an *answer*.

You can access the Texas Instruments Website via your Premium Website for *Communicating for Results*.

Companies like Texas Instruments with open communication and hotlines that encourage individual reporting can "cut their fraud losses … by 50 percent," according to a survey by the Association of Certified Fraud Examiners (Verschoor, 2003, p. 20). Why? The survey found that of all the fraud tips received by companies, "information from individuals resulted in the discovery of almost half the fraud schemes." (p. 20). Obviously, successful companies don't wait until a crisis to discuss ethics. Departments and employees should integrate "ethics into everyday conversations" (Coughlan, 2003, p. 33). Yet, a recent global survey of 1,800 respondents conducted by the International Association of Business Communicators (IABC) found that "less than half (46 percent) of companies encourage discussion of ethical issues at the workplace" (IABC News Centre, 2006, para. 3).

Although many companies have established ethics training programs (Treviño & Nelson, 2004; Weaver et al., 1999), many have not. For example, a sample of 1,000 U.S. employees found that only 28% had received any type of ethics training during the previous year ("Ethics training a low priority," 2004). A recent ethics training survey (PRNewswire.com, 2006) of 2,000 human resources, legal, and ethics professionals found the following:

- Over 70% of them were unaware of recent changes in the law (para. 3).
- Sixty percent were unaware that "all types of employers, whether public or private, and of whatever nature, including nonprofits and government units" must provide ethics and compliance training (para. 3).

- Forty-seven percent were not "tracking and archiving training completion records." If violations occur, companies that can prove they have effective ethics and compliance programs can greatly reduce any fines or punishments—sometimes by as much as 95% (para. 5)!

For companies that do have ethics programs, being aware of the company code of ethics isn't enough; employees need to know how to use it in their day-to-day decision making. To help with this problem, some companies have developed ethics games, including Lockheed Martin's "Ethics Challenge" game, BellSouth's "Ethics Scenarios" game, and Citigroup's "The Work Ethic" game (Williams, 2007, pp. 114–115). Even when ethics training is enjoyable, ethics specialists warn that unless leaders are perceived to live up to the high standards of ethical conduct they set, training programs and ethics codes will be meaningless (Daft, 2007; Greenberg & Baron, 2002; Weber, 1993). In *Managing Business Ethics*, Treviño and Nelson (2004) warn, "The most important thing for managers to remember about their job as role model is that what they do is infinitely more important than what they say. They can preach ethics all they want, but unless they live that message, their people won't" (p. 155). A commitment to ethical behavior must be made by all employees at all levels of the organization if it is to work. In the Employee/Employer Partnership section of Texas Instruments' online "Ethics at TI," Carl Skooglund (2003), former vice president and director of ethics, notes the following:

> We discovered some time ago that many new and entry-level employees believed they had little to do with TI's ethical reputation because they were not in a position to make significant decisions.... All employees, however, make decisions daily—such as how to charge time or how to use company assets—and can create ethical problems with poor decisions. For that reason, an effective ethics communications program must address the entire spectrum of employees in an intrusive, continuous manner, starting immediately after hiring. (para. 4)

As an employee, watch out for the following ethics traps that tempt business and professional communicators regularly (Bell, 1991, p. 68):

- *The trap of necessity.* "I really have no choice. If I suddenly stop charging as much, someone is sure to investigate."
- *The trap of relative filth.* "What I'm doing isn't half as bad as what others have done."
- *The trap of rationalization.* "It's all right if I call in sick. If I don't use my sick days before January, I lose them." It's estimated that "U.S. businesses lose about $40 billion annually from nonviolent, unethical behavior" (Wimbush & Shephard, 1994).
- *The trap of self-deception.* "So what if I claim my experience is more varied than it really is. No one will ever find out."
- *The trap of the end justifying the means.* "If I exaggerate the uses of this product just a bit, I will be able to increase my sales and get a promotion."

Being an ethical person is a responsibility we all share. In addition, there are some practical reasons for being ethical:

1. If people lose faith in you, or in your company, failure is inevitable. A 2005 survey by the American Management Association and the Human Resource Institute, finds that business ethics has a great impact on brands, reputations, customer trust, investor confidence, and public acceptance ("The Ethical Enterprise," 2006).

2. Not only do people enjoy dealing with honest people, but they also prefer working for ethical companies; being ethical is good business. A recent study found that employees are 6 times more likely to stay with a company they believe to be ethical (Smith, 2000).

3. Unethical behavior weighs heavily on your conscience; it's difficult to feel good about yourself.

Chapter 1 and this section on ethics end by asking you to think about your own personal ethics code. If you wait until an ethical problem arises to consider where you stand on ethical issues, you may not be prepared to handle the situation. Dennis Gioia (1992) was a young executive at Ford when ethical problems occurred involving the Pinto automobile. Gioia was part of the decision not to recall the Pinto (even though its gas tank could burst into flames in rear-end collisions at speeds as low as 25 miles per hour). In a special "Reflections on the Pinto Fires Case" written for Treviño and Nelson (2004), Gioia gives this advice:

> Develop your ethical base now! Too many people do not give serious attention to assessing and articulating their own values. People simply do not know what they stand for because they haven't thought about it seriously.... You need to know what your values are ... so that you can know how to make a good decision. Before you do that, you need to articulate and affirm your values now, before you enter the fray. I wasn't really ready. Are you? (pp. 131–132)

CHAPTER 1

R E V I E W

Key Terms

channel (11)

channel richness (12)

climate (19)

code (10)

communication (3)

decoding (5)

descriptive feedback (17)

encoding (5)

environment (19)

evaluative feedback (17)

feedback (15)

four ethical rules (22)

frame of reference (6)

motivation (5)

noise (19)

paraphrase (8)

receiver (4)

sender (4)

stimulated (4)

Summary

Now that you have read this chapter, has your frame of reference on communication changed? Effective communication involves more than just talking or listening; communication is hard work! Whether you are new to the business or professional world or have already launched your career, perfecting your communication skills will help ensure your success.

Organizations are looking for employees who can communicate. They are looking for employees who prepare carefully, execute effectively, and follow up their communications. For example, effective communicators check out the frame of reference of those with whom they communicate and try to encode their messages specifically for each person's understanding; they realize that 100% communication is unlikely to occur and plan ways to avoid misunderstanding. Effective communicators also realize the importance of stimulus and motivation, as well as, using all three codes (i.e., language, paralanguage, and nonverbal) when communicating. They attempt to select the best environment and channel for their communication and use feedback effectively. Even when communication seems successful, they follow up to make sure instead of assuming all is well. When communication misunderstanding occurs, they remember that the message to be concerned with is the one that is received and do not become defensive or assign blame for the problem. And of course, effective communicators ensure that their communication with colleagues, bosses, and customers is ethical at all times. Finally, effective communicators know that misunderstandings are going to occur; no one is perfect. However, when problems do occur, they will analyze them carefully so that the same problems won't happen again.

Communicating for Results Online

Before continuing to the next chapter, check your understanding of Chapter 1 at the Premium Website for *Communicating for Results*. Your Premium Website gives you quick and easy access to the electronic resources that accompany this text. These resources include:

- **Study tools** that will help you assess your learning and prepare for exams (e.g., student companion workbook, digital glossary, key term flash cards, and review quizzes).

- **Activities and assignments** that will help you hone your knowledge, analyze professional communication situations, build your public speaking skills throughout the course, and learn to work effectively in teams (e.g., Awareness Checks, Checkpoints, and Collaborative Learning Activities).

- **Media resources** that will help you explore communication concepts online (Web links), develop your speech outlines (Speech Builder Express 3.0), watch and critique videos of professional communication situations and sample speeches (Interactive Video Activities), upload your speech videos for peer reviewing and critique other students' speeches (Speech Studio online speech review tool), and download chapter review so you can study when and where you'd like (Audio Study Tools).

This chapter's key terms, Collaborative Learning Activities, and Checkpoint activities are also featured on the following pages, and you can find this chapter's Awareness Check activities in the body of the chapter. For more information or to access this book's online resources, visit www.cengage.com/login.

Collaborative Learning Activities

1. In small groups discuss which element of the communication model generally creates the most problems in understanding: environment/context, stimulation/motivation, encoding/decoding, frame of reference, code, channel, feedback, or noise. Why does your choice create more misunderstandings than other elements?

2. Divide into four groups representing ethics, gender, technology, and culture. Each group should:

   a. Discuss its topic and select two of the best examples of communication misunderstanding out of a list of several that are mentioned by members.

   b. Next, decide which of the four topic areas generally create the most misunderstanding in the workplace: yours, or one of the other three.

   c. Finally, share your examples and decision with the other groups.

3. As this chapter indicated, ethical decisions are not always clear cut. To think about some difficult ethical questions, complete the following activity.

   a. On your own paper, answer *yes* or *no* to the following list of questions, adapted from the *Wall Street Journal*'s Workplace Ethics Quiz (1999).

      1) Is it wrong to use company e-mail for personal reasons?

      2) Is it wrong to use office equipment to help your children or spouse do schoolwork?

      3) Is it wrong to play computer games on office equipment during the workday?

      4) Is it wrong to use office equipment to do Internet shopping?

      5) Is it unethical to blame an error you made on a technological glitch?

      6) Is it unethical to visit pornographic Websites using office equipment?

      7) Is a $50 gift to a boss unacceptable?

      8) Is a $50 gift from a boss unacceptable?

      9) Is it okay to take a $200 pair of football tickets from a supplier?

      10) Can you accept a $75 prize won at a raffle at a supplier's conference?

   b. In groups of four to seven compare individual answers. Discuss the reasons for your answers and work to come to an agreement on as many questions as possible.

   c. Compare answers with other groups. To see how business students and executives from the United States and college students from a Middle Eastern culture answered the questions, see the research study conducted by Lander et al. (2008) accessed in a database or at http://www.cluteinstitute-onlinejournals.com/PDFs/1040.pdf.

Checkpoints

Checkpoint 1.1 Is Your Feedback Descriptive or Evaluative?

To determine whether your feedback to others is evaluative (rather than descriptive), analyze others' responses to your questions. For example, when you and your date, spouse, or close friend are trying to decide where to eat, does the conversation sound something like this?

You: Where would you like to eat?

Other: Oh, anywhere is fine. I don't care.

You: Now come on. I decided last time. Tell me where you would like to eat.

Other: Really! Any place you like is fine with me!

And so on. The result may be that (a) you eat in a place neither of you particularly likes or (b) become angry and don't go out at all. If this type of conversation about what to eat or what movie to see occurs often, the chances are that you are *evaluative*. People send double messages (say one thing but mean another) when they fear that an honest opinion will be criticized. For example,

Other: O.K. Let's eat at Pizza Place.

You: Not again! I might have known you would pick Pizza Place! You know I don't like to eat there.

Checkpoint 1.2 Comparing Frames of Reference

Checkpoint 1.3 Ethical Dilemmas

Checkpoint 1.4 Communication Websites

2 Organizational Communication

Walter Hodges/Getty Images

Case Study: The Rise and Fall of Enron

What role do organizational structure and internal communication play in the rise and fall of a company?

Let's look at Enron, a company famous for its spectacular fall. Enron began with the merger of two fairly quiet energy companies, Texas's Houston Natural Gas and Omaha's Internorth, and grew to become a powerful and respected international organization. At one point Enron was the seventh largest corporation in the United States, and its stock reached $90 per share. For 6 years in a row, *Fortune* magazine named Enron "Most Innovative Company." Yet, when the company collapsed in 2001, 5,600 people lost their jobs, $2.1 billion was erased from pension plans, and stockholders around the world lost over $60 billion in market value. For their role in the collapse of Enron, company founder and chairman Kenneth Lay (now deceased) and CEO Jeffery Skilling were convicted of fraud and conspiracy. What caused such a disaster?

Enron thrived on its image of being a financially strong, innovative company so that it took on a life of its own (Conrad, 2003; Fusaro & Miller, 2002; McLean & Elkind, 2003). Because people wanted it to succeed, they ignored or misinterpreted the warning signs. Enron's complex and innovative business model, organizational practices, and employee reward system contributed to its fall as well. Soon after Enron was created, Skilling was brought on board to fashion a more successful business model that could help boost the company's image and balance sheets so it could get much-needed loans.

Conrad and Poole (2005) discuss two of Skilling's creative accounting changes, both of which were granted by government commissions because Enron successfully argued that their "regulatory structures needed to be adapted to the new global economy" (p. 436).

First, Enron lobbied the Securities and Exchange Commission (SEC) for permission to change from cost accounting (where stocks and commodities are recorded only when the company takes possession of them) to mark-to-market accounting (where such assets are recorded now, but the amount recorded is based on *reliable predictions* of future value rather than on their current worth). Second, Enron lobbied the Commodity Futures Trading Commission (CTFC) to exempt it from CFTC regulations. Regulating their own procedures would allow Enron to use "derivatives" in their accounting practices. Derivatives are financial contracts between companies that "are structured in ways that allow managers to keep them off of their companies' official books" (p. 435).

If these two practices seem complicated and difficult to understand, that was the point: Instead of clear communication, Enron's structure and accounting processes were supposed to confuse while creating an illusion of success (Fusaro & Miller, 2002). In fact, Conrad and Poole (2005) reported the following:

> Enron executives invested an incredible amount of time and energy, and spent literally millions of dollars on accountants and lawyers, in order to make their activities so complex they were not likely to be discovered, much less understood or successfully prosecuted against. (p. 429)

Not only were Enron's structure and accounting processes complex, but their employee reward system created a culture that was "absolutely cutthroat," in which "most employees were afraid to express their opinions or to question unethical and potentially illegal business practices" (Fusaro & Miller, 2002, pp. 51–52). Twice a year each employee was rated by peers and managers on sets of criteria. Then executive panels would "debate and rank each employee on a scale of 1 to 5" (McLean & Elkind, 2003, p. 63). Employees referred to this system as "rank and yank." Although criteria might include team and communication skills, what really counted was how much money each individual made for the company. To keep from being "yanked," most individuals had to show a "short-term paper profit" (Conrad, 2003, p. 436). People ranked "1" received huge bonuses, whereas those at the bottom were fired if they failed to improve. For example, in 1999 the top 200 employees (not including the top CEOs) made a total of $402 million, counting stocks, bonuses, and salaries (McLean & Elkind, 2003, p. 241).

As you read this chapter, see if you can (a) identify which type of formal and informal communication predominated at Enron and what changes, if any, could have been made to help the company survive; (b) explain which organizational model was used at Enron and what role it played in the company's collapse; and (c) discuss the role the company reward system played in the disaster. For more details on Enron, read one of the books referenced above or watch the 2005 documentary, *Enron: The Smartest Guys in the Room*, directed by Alex Gibney or the television movie, *GrookedE: The Unshredded Truth about Enron*, aired in January 2003 by CBS.

A s our opening discussion of Enron clearly shows, crisis and change in an organization not only affect the organization, but also have an impact on the lives of thousands of employees and their families, entire communities, states, and even other countries. With the rapid changes occurring in the job market because of technology, globalization, outsourcing, and even fraud, most people will go through many changes in their lives and will work for many different companies.

Therefore, to make effective job choices as an employee or a manager, one must understand (a) the types of internal communication found in organizations, (b) the methods used to coordinate people and groups to achieve success, and (c) the five major models used by organizations today and the effects of each model on communication.

Although it may seem to be nothing more than theory, in actuality this chapter has the potential to personally benefit your working career. Once you recognize that different organizations feature different models and cultures and figure out which ones you would enjoy working for and which you would dislike, you can better focus the goals of job hunts and manage your career success.

Communication Inside the Organization

In Chapter 1 we stated that the success of an organization depends on the communication skills of all its employees. We begin this chapter by looking inside the organization at two types of communication: formal and informal.

Formal Communication

Formal communication flows along the official paths prescribed by the organization's chain of command and is shown by its organizational chart (see Figure 2.1). Formal messages flow downward, upward, and horizontally.

Downward Communication

Formal messages that flow from managers and supervisors to subordinates are called **downward communication**. The importance of downward communication can be illustrated by this example:

> The computer operators in the data processing department of a large insurance firm were told to do an analysis of premium and claims payment at the end of each day. . . . Completing the run often held the operators past closing time.

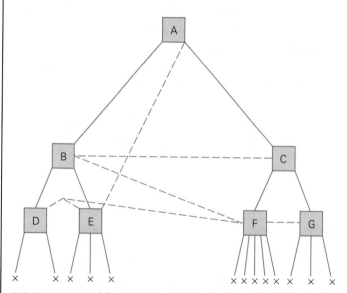

FIGURE 2.1 Pyramidal organization chart showing formal *(solid lines)* and informal *(dashed lines)* paths of communication.

Periodically, the operators would delay finishing the computer run until the next morning, which brought admonitions from management and excuses from the computer operators. During one of these failures the exasperated manager said, "Don't you realize how crucial this run is?" An operator replied, "Not really. You only told us that it was important and to do the job." The operators had never been told that the information not only reported the company's cash flow position but was used the next morning as the basis for short-term investments. Not having that information . . . had resulted in the company's losing millions of dollars of investment potential over the years. (Bradford & Cohen, 1984, p. 122)

Ideally, downward communication from managers should include such things as *job instructions, job rationale* (why a specific task is important and how it relates to other tasks in the organization), *policy and procedures, employee performance appraisals,* and *motivational appeals* (Katz & Kahn, 1966, p. 239).

Downward communication adds to employee satisfaction. Specifically, Goldhaber (1993) found the following:

Information about personal job-related matters (e.g., how to do my job, my pay and benefits, etc.) is needed to *prevent dissatisfaction,* but it will NOT create satisfaction. Information about organization-wide concerns (policies, plans, decision-making, failures, etc.) is needed to *create satisfaction* (p. 157).

Although downward communication can lead to information overload, one researcher found that employees with information overload were not necessarily dissatisfied with their jobs. However, all the employees who experienced information *under*load were dissatisfied (C. O'Reilly, 1980).

Another problem with downward communication is that it is often in written form. Although the redundancy of written English helps readers interpret messages, there are several problems with written messages:

- They are usually brief and may omit needed details; supervisors often assume that subordinates know more than they really do.

- Also, because of the need for brevity, memos normally do not include the job rationale.

- Frame of reference differences between sender and receiver make interpretation of messages difficult; we often wrongly assume that others see things as we do.

If memos and e-mails are accompanied by face-to-face communication (which is rich in information because all three codes—verbal, vocal, and visual—are operating), message interpretation is greatly improved (Conrad & Poole, 2005; Daft, 2007). In addition, employees at all levels often prefer oral communication (Turner, 2007) and managers prefer to hear it from people they know and like, even if they are less knowledgeable than others they could seek for information (Mackenzie, 2005).

Upward Communication

Formal messages that flow upward from subordinates to supervisors and managers are called **upward communication**. The following types of messages are valuable when upwardly communicated (Planty & Machaver, 1977, p. 167): reports of employee work, achievements, and progress; outlines of work problems that need to be solved; suggestions for improvements within the department or company; and how employees think and feel about their jobs, associates, and company. Bill Gates credits an employee's observation and concerned memo with changing Microsoft's

ETHICAL DILEMMA

Top executives have always received more compensation than the average worker. This is not surprising because CEOs (as well as COOs and CFOs) take more risks and have the special training and knowledge necessary to lead the company to financial success, and all company stakeholders from the suppliers and customers to the employees and stockholders benefit when the company succeeds. In 1982 the average pay difference between a CEO and a worker was 18%; however, by 2002 it had risen to 2,600% (Jones, 2007a)! This extravagant increase is due in part to tying executive compensation to stock options (Conrad & Poole, 2005). Take a look at the following compensation packages (Eisenberg, 2009; Jones, 2007b; Tse, 2009; Weber, 2006):

- Bob Nardelli, CEO of Home Depot since December 2000: $123.7 million, not including stock options. Nardelli received this package during a time when the company stock dropped 9%. During the same period, Lowe's stock increased 185%.

- Jack Welch, former CEO of General Electric: $500+ million in stock options. Welch generated hundreds of billions of dollars for the company.

- Michael Eisner, CEO at Disney for 19 years: $800+ million in stock options. Despite his considerable compensation, the company's performance lagged.

- Kenneth Lay, founder and former CEO of Enron: $252 million, including stock options in 1 year.

- The founder and CEO for Chesapeake Energy, Aubrey McClendon, received $112 million even though the company's stock declined 71% from the previous year.

- After receiving $45 billion in government bailout money, Bank of America planned to pay their CEO, Kenneth Lewis, a compensation package of over $16 million until the federal government stepped in.

QUESTIONS: Is it ethical for top executives to be paid so much more than average workers? List several pros and cons. How does extravagant pay for executives fare when considered in terms of the four ethical rules in Chapter 1?

placement of the Internet from a low priority to a top priority, resulting in the company becoming a leader in this new technology. The employee had visited Cornell University and noticed that the Internet was being used "for far more than just computer-science applications" (Krames, 2003, p. 163). Yet, in many companies there is no set procedure for sending messages upward ("Workers are Surveyed on Communication," 2004).

Effective decision making depends on timely, accurate, and sufficient information traveling upward from subordinates. On the other hand, if *all* information reached the top, information overload would hamper management decisions. For example, in his book *Inside Bureaucracy*, Downs (1967, p. 117; Conrad & Poole, 2005, p. 72) estimates that top decision makers would receive an unmanageable 4,096 messages per day in a seven-level hierarchy, with each supervisor having four subordinates and all employees producing one message per day to be sent to the top. Obviously, some messages need to be screened out or shortened, but in that seven-level hierarchy, if each person screened out only half of the upward-bound messages, 98.4% of the information would never reach the top of the hierarchy! Thus, the problem is how to get the information needed without information overload. E-mail only makes matters worse because computer information systems do not filter information (Rice & Gattiker, 2001).

For upward communication to be effective, it must be accurate. Unfortunately, many subordinates tend to conceal or distort upward communication to protect themselves and to make messages more acceptable to superiors. The desire to conceal bad news is referred to by researchers as the "MUM effect" (Lee, 1993). Upward messages are also more likely to be distorted or withheld when subordinates don't trust their superiors (Jablin, 1985) or when subordinates desire upward mobility or recognition (Sashkin & Morris, 1984).

In a high-tech environment, upward feedback must not only be accurate, but it must also be fast. For example, product sales data (received daily from salespeople using handheld computers) allowed Frito-Lay executives to observe a slump in sales in south Texas, to pinpoint a competitor's white corn tortilla chip as the cause, and, in 4 months, to produce a new white corn Tostitos chip, which rapidly regained the previous market share (Rothfeder et al., 1990).

Horizontal Communication

In **horizontal communication**, messages flow laterally between people of the same rank. Horizontal communication is important for coordinating tasks (with employees or departments), solving problems, sharing information, and resolving conflicts (Goldhaber, 1993, p. 163). Horizontal communication is especially valuable for unusually difficult or complex problems (Wilson, 1992). **Empowered teams**— teams with the power to make decisions—are especially adept in this situation and are the mainstays of the newest organization models: the multiunit and virtual organizations (see pages 54–56).

Organizations are paying much more attention to horizontal communication than they did in the past. In their bestseller *Re-inventing the Corporation*, Naisbitt and Aburdene (1985) state the following:

> The top-down authoritarian management style is yielding to a networking style of management, where people learn from one another horizontally, where everyone is a resource for everyone else, and where each person gets support and assistance from many different directions. (p. 62)

The Internet and company intranets have made it cheaper and easier for employees to communicate horizontally. The cost to send an average business letter in 1995 was $16.45 (Dartnell Corporation, 1995). Memos and e-mail obviously cost a lot less. However, information overload is still a real possibility. For example, Hewlett-Packard Company's 97,000 employees send 1.5 million e-mail messages per day (LaBarre, 1994).

Informal Communication

Not all messages flow along the official paths prescribed by the organization's chain of command. Many messages flow along an informal network commonly called **informal communication** or the grapevine (see Figure 2.1, page 30). Informal communication exists because of limitations of formal networks. Conrad and Poole (2005) state the following:

> Formal communication networks allow people to handle predictable, routine situations, but they are inefficient means of meeting unanticipated communication needs, for managing crises, for dealing with complex or detailed problems, for sharing personal information, or for exchanging information rapidly. (p. 123)

Although many people view the grapevine as unimportant, research indicates the opposite.

Consider the following:

- *The type of information the grapevine carries indicates the health of the organization.* If an organization's managers are fairly open with the employees and send all necessary information through formal channels, the grapevine usually carries only personal interest items, or gossip. Gossip is necessary to the maintenance of the grapevine. Without it the network would dry up (March & Sevon, 1982). However, when the formal communication channels fail to do the job, the grapevine begins to carry information about the organization, such as policy changes, impending layoffs, or workload revisions (Deetz, 1995). Daft reports that 55% of 22,000 shift workers across a wide variety of companies "said they get most of their information via the grapevine" (2008, p. 576).

- *Information carried by the grapevine is 75 to 95% accurate* (Caudron, 1998; Walton, 1961, pp. 45–49). Of course, some entirely false rumors are also spread through the grapevine, especially the electronic grapevine (Pitts, 1999). However, grapevine information can be confirmed, whereas rumors cannot. Grapevine messages are often more accurate than formal ones because status, power, and rank differences seem less important. In one study, middle managers reported that they often found informal communication to be a better source of organizational information than formal communication (Harcourt et al., 1991).

- *Information carried by the grapevine travels fast.* It is not uncommon for top management, who reached an important decision late at night, to arrive at work early the next morning only to find that the decision is common knowledge (Hymowitz, 1988; Simmons, 1985). According to *Inc.* magazine ("Reining in Office Rumors," 2004), Good news travels fast, bad news travels faster, and embarrassing news travels at warp speed" (p. 60). Use of e-mail and blogs have caused grapevine news to travel even faster, yet without the nonverbal and paralanguage codes—to be even more difficult to interpret correctly (Burke & Wise, 2003).

- *People who regularly use the grapevine are more satisfied with their jobs and more committed to the organization* (Caldwell & O'Reilly, 1982; Conrad & Poole, 2005, p. 119; Eisenberg et al., 1983).

- *Effective managers use the grapevine.* Managers who listen carefully to the informal communication network find it a useful source of information about employee concerns and problems. Some managers actually leak new ideas or proposals to the grapevine to test worker response. If an idea is greeted with hostility, they drop it or revise it. If the idea is received positively, they introduce it through official channels. Businesses have also been known to leak secret information in the hopes that a competitor would react and waste both time and money (Hitt et al., 1999, p. 76).

In his study of bureaucratic organizations, Peter Blau (1974) found two main advantages to using informal communication networks: (a) We can get advice and

Gossip is necessary to the maintenance of the organization's grapevine. Without it the network would dry up.

Yuri Arcurs/Shutterstock

information without formally having to admit we need it; and (b) we can "think out loud" about problems, thus increasing our self-confidence and problem-solving ability (p. 7). This "off-the-record" thinking stimulates innovative thinking as well (Albrecht & Hall, 1991).

As with horizontal communication, the Internet and company intranets have made the grapevine easier for employees to use, as well. Whereas the grapevine used to flourish around the water cooler or department coffee pot, now electronic forums and electronic bulletin boards allow employees to transfer information and inspire creative ideas (Sproull & Kiesler, 1992).

Although effective communication is important, organizations need more than communication if they are to achieve results.

Revisiting the Case Study

Which type of formal or informal communication caused the most problems for Enron?

Greg Smith

Coordination of People and Groups

Organizations must successfully coordinate people and groups to achieve maximum productivity. Knowing these coordination methods will help you better understand and appreciate the different organization models discussed in the next section.* According to Wagner and Hollenbeck (2010), organizations use three basic types of coordination: mutual adjustment, direct supervision, and standardization.

Mutual adjustment involves horizontal communication between peers who meet face to face (or by Internet) to make work-related decisions. They decide what job needs to be done, who will do it, and how it should be done. Because they can meet whenever they need to, this method is flexible and is implemented only when needed. Small mom-and-pop organizations may never need any other type of coordination. When an organization exceeds around 12 members, however, "process loss" occurs, which means that members "spend so much time communicating with one another that very little time is left for task completion" (p. 241). In these larger organizations, the next coordination method—direct supervision—is needed.

Under **direct supervision**, members do not make all their own decisions; instead, a supervisor has the authority to organize and direct their work. However, mutual adjustment is still used as a secondary means of coordination. Direct supervision is a more effective way to funnel information and coordinate the activities of midsize organizations—usually between 12 and 50 employees. Supervisors with more than 50 subordinates are likely to experience information overload trying to keep up with employee needs.

For organizations with over 50 employees, **standardization**—specific, written standards for tasks, output levels, skills, and workplace norms—is a more effective means of coordination. Global organizations may use videoconferencing (discussed in Chapter 6) to inform employees of standards and to train them as well. Standardization procedures are initially costly to set up, but once they are running, the need for coordination and communication is reduced, and the system basically runs itself. According to Wagner and Hollenbeck (2010), standardization of norms, behaviors, and tasks increases "the likelihood that people will behave appropriately and consistently over time" (p. 240). Direct supervision and mutual adjustment are used as secondary coordination methods when necessary.

---

* Much of the material in this section is based on Chapter 11, "Structuring the Organization," in John A. Wagner III and John R. Hollenbeck, Organizational Behavior: Securing Competitive Advantage (New York: Routledge, 2010).

Organizations that emphasize standardization are more bureaucratic in nature. One weakness of standardization is that it works only as long as conditions remain stable. In rapidly changing industries where procedures and standards quickly become obsolete—like the computer industry—standardization fails to work effectively and is usually replaced with the more expensive mutual adjustment method. Many large organizations that have traditionally relied on standardization for their coordination are finding that the flexibility offered by mutual adjustment teams is more effective in today's constantly changing market; the extra cost is considered necessary for survival. Therefore, the three coordination methods can be viewed as a continuum:

Mutual adjustment → direct supervision → standardization → mutual adjustment

(Wagner & Hollenbeck, 2010, p. 243). Although organizations may use more than one method, a single coordination method is primary.

Organization Models

Not until the beginning of the 20th century did anyone pay much attention to the internal workings of organizations. Since that time, theorists have searched for a "best way" for organizations to function. These theories ranged from decision trees and brainstorming in the 1960s, theory X/theory Y and management by objectives (MBO) in the 1970s, zero-based budgeting and quality circles in the 1980s, one-minute managing, total quality management (TQM), and six sigma in the 1990s, to current theories such as open book management, outsourcing, and 360-degree management. Some of these theories were passing fads; some are still to be proven; and others have had lasting effects on organizational structures and management. We can get a good feel for communication problems unique to organizations by looking at five main organization models in use today (Figure 2.2): the **traditional model**,

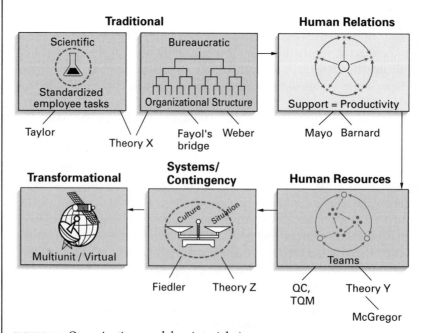

FIGURE 2.2 Organization models: pictorial view.

the human relations model, the human resources model, the systems/contingency model, and the transformational model.

To get a feel for the differences among the five organization models, let's listen as managers discuss their model's basic management techniques and assumptions. Which of these managers seems to be describing an organization with which you are familiar or in which you are especially interested?

Traditional Manager

Always remember to let employees know who is boss. If you are too friendly and get involved with their personal problems, they will take advantage of you and respect you less. To keep employee respect, you must take control. For example, tardiness should never be tolerated. When downsizing occurs, don't give employees a chance to sabotage their workstations or computer programs. Instead of giving notice of termination, have security escort them from the building.

To feel secure, employees need and want structure. Let them know where they fit in the company's organizational chart and clarify the expected chain of command. Tell them exactly how you want things done. Don't waste time asking for opinions. If you let them know that they are being watched and conduct time and motion studies to let them know how they stand, they'll appreciate it.

As we've seen, for productive employees, structure and control are essential. Employees are basically lazy, and they will goof off if you let them. If structure and control are not enough, money is a certain motivator. For a bonus, employees will do almost anything.

Human Relations Manager

I totally disagree with the traditional manager! Employees are more productive if they feel appreciated and content. You can't treat people like machines. Pushing a control, structure, or money button does not result in a more productive employee. Employees need and want tender loving care (TLC). If you are nice to people, they will respond by working extra hard for you when asked. For example, if downsizing becomes necessary, employees may be willing to take a pay cut so no one has to be laid off.

Social and psychological needs of employees should be an important management concern. We view our organization as "one happy family." Managers should call their employees by first names, be friendly, joke and laugh with them, and express sympathy with their personal problems. We show that we really care by celebrating birthdays and sponsoring company picnics and athletic events. Managers can gauge the happiness of employees by listening carefully to the grapevine. When conflicts do occur, we smooth over them, or even ignore them if possible, because conflict can damage our friendly atmosphere and hamper employee productivity.

Human Resources Manager

Both the previous managers have an inaccurate view of employees and of the employee-management relationship. First of all, employees aren't lazy, and they don't have to be bribed or manipulated with bonuses or with TLC. Employees want to work and will motivate themselves if they are allowed to participate in decision making.

Second, successful organizations use a team-oriented approach to employee-management relationships. Open communication and feedback flow freely up and down the organization. The organization's climate is supportive, flexible, and trusting. Therefore, the role of the manager is that of facilitator, allowing employees to take an active role in problem solving and in developing their potential. Employees must be allowed to make mistakes if you want them to be creative.

Long-term employee motivation comes from a feeling of self-worth, personal satisfaction, and achievement. When given a chance, employees exhibit self-control and self-direction compatible with the goals of the organization. In fact, downsizing reduces unnecessary jobs and controls and gives workers more challenges and opportunities for self-direction and productivity.

Systems/Contingency Manager

Regardless of what other managers may say, there is no single best way to manage. Any of the three organization models just described could be successful, depending on any number of internal and external factors. In deciding which management style would be the most effective in a particular situation, a manager should consider such internal factors as employee needs, expectations, and abilities; the complexity of employee jobs; the level of satisfaction available from each job; and the manager's own comfort with various communication approaches. A manager should also consider such external factors as customer expectations, local and national economy, and competition from other organizations.

In addition, managers and employees must be aware that every part of the organization is interdependent on every other part and that the actions of any one department or even one person can affect the entire organization. Therefore, communication and feedback within and between departments are extremely important. Now that global sales and constant change are the norm, effective communication is a must. Downsizing, which we plan and implement carefully, allows the company to improve communication even more, streamline work processes, and add flexibility while maintaining our "customer first" approach.

Transformational Manager

Actually, none of the previous management styles works in today's global market dominated by information technology. Constant change requires an absolute flexibility that's missing in the other styles. We're experimenting with new, decentralized structures, including multiunit and virtual structures. In a multiunit structure, each division is really an autonomous business under the same holding company. In a virtual structure (a temporary alliance among several companies with different areas of expertise), employees communicate through the Internet and videoconferences and may never meet face to face. Our employees have maximum personal autonomy and self-motivation. Most communication occurs via computer-connected teams that supervise themselves. Downsizing, like change, is a normal and positive part of organizational life (Cameron, 1994). Employees expect to change jobs fairly often.

Each manager approaches problems and relates to employees quite differently. We also can see that different kinds of communication are encouraged in the five organization models. Each model has its best way to do things, and each one has its strengths and weaknesses. Although each model is currently in use, not all fare equally well in today's diverse, global market. The influx of women and minorities into the workplace, the global competition for customers, and the rapid growth of the Internet have made constant change the norm. In 1993 Hammer and Champy noted in their book *Reengineering the Corporation* that "In today's environment, nothing is constant or predictable—not market growth, customer demand, product life cycles, the rate of technological change, or the nature of competition" (p. 17). Change has not slowed down. In fact, in *The World Is Flat* (2005), Thomas Friedman notes that changes in technology, lower hardware costs, and the explosion of software have flattened the international playing field so that "we are now connecting all the knowledge centers on the planet together into a single global network" (p. 8). For example, imagine hospitals sending computerized tomography (CT) scans at night to be read by doctors in India and Australia and having them ready for use the next morning; or major newspapers sending news stories to Bangalore, India to be typed into the proper electronic version ready for print or distribution online faster and cheaper than it could be done in the United States; or calling the help desk about your new computer and finding that the knowledgeable, friendly person on the other line lives in India. Organizations that succeed in today's changing marketplace may well be those that capitalize on diversity, are flexible, are fast at problem solving and operation start-up, encourage and reward innovation, and make use of new information-age technology (Ivancevich & Matteson, 2002).

As you read about the five models, consider which ones are more likely to succeed in today's changing environment. Understanding their differences should help you select your future working environment more effectively and communicate more successfully in it.

The Traditional (or Classical) Model

Early in the 20th century, large organizations were a new phenomenon with no role models except the military. A manager could not go to a bookstore and find self-help books on management. Concepts like the one-minute manager, 360-degree feedback, and open-book management were unknown. Therefore, companies were managed by hunch or intuition, and their attempts to motivate and control employees were inefficient and often inhumane. When managers' decisions (made with little planning and inadequate information) reaped less than desirable results, the managers blamed employees.

Two types of organization theorists (who we now call traditionalists) emerged (Figure 2.3): the scientific managers who wanted to improve organizations "from the bottom up" (meaning they were concerned with employee problems) and the bureaucratic theorists who felt improvements should occur "from the top down" (meaning they were concerned with management problems). Both types of theorists were interested in changing inefficient organizations into "systematically designed, objective, and fair systems of management and supervision" (Conrad & Poole, 2005, p. 68).

Traditional Model and Scientific Managers

Frederick Taylor (1911), a U.S. theorist, was responsible for the popularity of the scientific management approach. Taylor observed firsthand many of the organizational

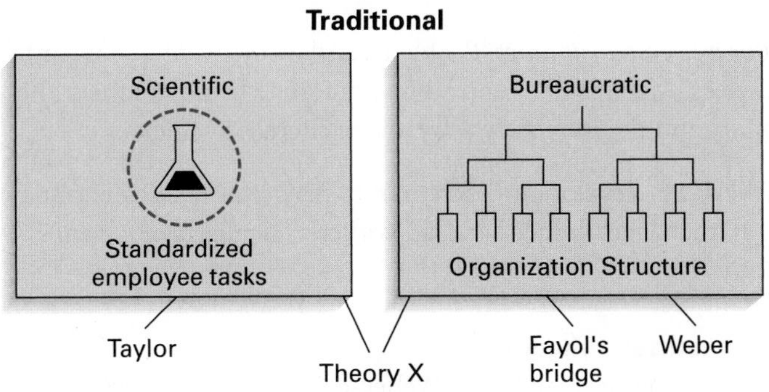

FIGURE 2.3 The traditional or classical model.

problems of the day. For example, workers' and managers' roles were not clearly defined; hostilities existed between them; decision making was based on too little information; and production was inefficient because of poorly motivated workers, poorly designed job procedures, minimal work standards, and inept employee placement (employees were often overqualified or underqualified).

Taylor's best way was to apply four scientific principles to the problems of production and management:

1. *Scientific design of each task.* With the help of subordinates, managers were to find the shortest and easiest way to perform tasks and then standardize them. For example, in the 1890s, Taylor conducted time-motion studies on coal shoveling at Bethlehem Steel Company (Rogers & Agarwala-Rogers, 1976). Because the workers provided their own shovels, there was a wide variety of sizes. From careful experimentation, Taylor found that maximum shoveling efficiency was obtained with a shovel load of 21 pounds. When workers were issued shovels with a 21-pound capacity, given instructions on the most productive and least fatiguing way to shovel, and offered a pay incentive for superior performance, the results were amazing:

   The average volume of material moved per day soared from 16 to 59 tons. Handling costs plummeted from 7.3 cents to 3.2 cents per ton (even after deducting the total cost of the experiment and incentive pay that boosted the average shovel pay from $1.15 to $1.88 per day). Bethlehem was able to reduce its yard crew from more than 400 to 140 employees. (Koehler et al., 1976, p. 12)

2. *Scientific selection of workers.* For each task, managers were to determine the necessary characteristics for an individual to perform that task successfully and then hire only workers with those characteristics (i.e., standardized hiring).

3. *Adequate training and rewards for productivity.* Once the managers had determined the most productive method to complete a task and had hired the appropriate workers, employees were trained to use this method and were carefully timed to see how much they could produce without exerting themselves. This level became a production standard on which their pay was based. Believing that workers could be motivated to higher efficiency if they were given the opportunity to make more money, Taylor advocated a piece-rate incentive or bonus for workers who produced above the standard rate. However, when workers earned too much, management reduced the piece-rate amount or raised the minimum needed to receive a bonus. Viewing this as punishment, workers began to produce no more than the minimum acceptable level, pressuring all workers to fall into line.

4. *Division of both labor and responsibilities.* Problems and errors were no longer to be blamed on employees. Management and labor were to be team members and share the responsibility and the monetary rewards for increased efficiency.

Although Taylor believed in developing "each man to his greatest efficiency and prosperity" (1911, p. 140), managers tended to treat workers "like parts of a giant industrial machine" (Conrad & Poole, 2005, p. 71).

Traditional Model and Bureaucratic Theorists

Henri Fayol, a French mining engineer, and Max Weber, a German sociologist, were Taylor's contemporaries. Whereas Taylor sought to improve organizational efficiency by standardizing employee tasks, these two bureaucratic theorists were interested in improving direct supervision through structure and control. The foundation of bureaucratic theory was **organizational structure**, the formal patterns of relationships and roles needed to get tasks accomplished (who works with whom and who reports to whom). Fayol and Weber believed that organizations must have a clear **division of labor**. The division of labor is the way an organization parcels out the work to be done (who does what). Division of labor works best when the organization has a clear chain of command. The **chain of command** is the communication structure of an organization and is shown by the pyramidal organization chart introduced by the bureaucratic theorists (Figure 2.3).

Although the bureaucratic theorists favored formal, downward communication, they were aware of the limitations of a pyramidal structure. Fayol's best way was the innovative suggestion that direct, horizontal communication between people in different departments be allowed, but only in legitimate crises. If person E needed information from person F before it could make its way through the formal chain of command, then person E could contact person F directly (Fayol, 1949). This method of bypassing the chain of command became known as Fayol's bridge (Figure 2.4).

The bureaucratic theorists also believed in a small **span of control**, referring to the number of employees that a manager can effectively supervise. They said that each employee should have only one manager, and each manager should oversee no more than five or six people. Span of control determines the shape of an organization. "If most managers throughout the organization have a small span, the overall shape of the organization will be tall. If the typical span is great, then the overall shape of the organization will be flat" (Goldhaber, 1993, p. 146). Figure 2.5 on page 42 illustrates tall and flat organization structures.

Despite the recommendation of bureaucratic theorists, the **flat organization** (with decentralized decision making and fewer levels of hierarchy) has several advantages over the tall organization: Complex problems are handled more efficiently; problems are handled faster; communication is less distorted because messages pass through fewer people; and employee morale and satisfaction are fairly high because employees make more of their own decisions. In contrast, the **tall organization** (with multiple levels and centralized decision making) is often used by large companies and has greater efficiency in handling uncomplicated tasks, slower communication, and lower employee morale and satisfaction (Carzo & Yanouzas, 1969; Conrad & Poole, 2005, p. 75).

Max Weber's (1947) best way was to formalize the bureaucracy, which he considered the best organization structure for the times. Some of his most enduring ideas, which typify the thinking of the bureaucratic theorists, are summarized here:

- The policies and rules of an organization should be specified in writing—high standardization.
- All decisions and actions should be put in writing, even those determined in oral conversations.
- Managers should keep all relationships with employees detached and impersonal so that no emotions will influence their decisions.
- Because authority in a bureaucratic organization is limited, the formal written rules should be the legal basis of authority and control over employees.

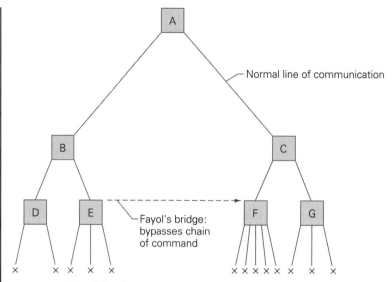

FIGURE 2.4 Fayol's bridge.

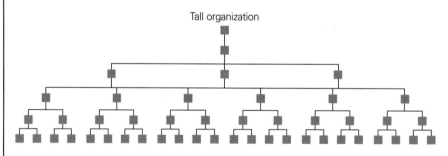

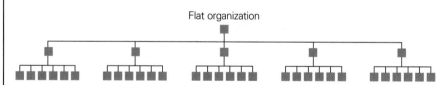

FIGURE 2.5 Tall and flat organizations.

The Traditional (or Classical) Model in Brief

Key Theorists and Landmark Books

Frederick Taylor, *Scientific Management* (1911)

Henri Fayol, *General and Industrial Management* (1949)

Max Weber, *The Theory of Social and Economic Organization* (1947)

Focus of Theory

Scientific: Concern with reducing production costs

Bureaucratic: Concern with administrative efficiency

View of Communication

Limited communication; restricted to downward use by managers

The Traditional Model in Today's World

Scientific and bureaucratic theorists have certainly left their mark on modern organizations. For example, automation, merit pay, time-motion studies, and reward systems introduced by Taylor are used to enhance productivity in many organizations today. Furthermore, practically every organization uses "some degree of bureaucratic control" (Daft, 2007, p. 339). For example, Weber's organization charts, division of labor, chain of command, and span of control are all now in common use. In fact, "The traditional strategy, with its tight hierarchy, focus on the structural dimension of communication, and written policies and procedures, is still the dominant strategy used in the United States for governmental agencies, educational institutions, and many private firms" (Conrad & Poole, 2005, p. 104). Many nonprofit organizations also prefer a bureaucratic structure (Daft, 2007).

If you have ever worked for the federal government, you know that Weber's bureaucracy still exists, especially when it comes to paperwork. In 1993, the Internal Revenue Service had 1,611 forms (Goldhaber, 1993). In 1988, the U.S. Department of Energy prepared an environmental impact study in conjunction with the site selection for the Superconducting Super Collider (a project that was canceled by Congress). Each copy of the report contained 8,000 pages and weighed 25 pounds!

The United Parcel Service (UPS) is an example of a large, successful bureaucracy. UPS employs over 425,000 people worldwide, delivers 15.5 million packages per day, and maintains an aircraft fleet of 262 planes and charters over 300 additional planes (Daft, 2008; Worldwide Facts, 2009).

> UPS is bound up in rules and regulations. It teaches drivers an astounding 340 steps for how to correctly deliver a package—such as how to load their trucks, how to fasten their seat belts, how to walk, and how to carry their keys. Specific safety rules apply to drivers, loaders, clerks, and managers. Strict dress codes are enforced—clean uniforms (called *browns*), every day, black or brown polished shoes with nonslip soles, no beards, no hair below the collar, and so on. Supervisors conduct three-minute physical inspections of drivers each day. The company also has rules specifying cleanliness standards for buildings, trucks, and other properties. No eating or drinking is permitted at employee desks. Each manager is given bound copies of policy books and is expected to use them. (p. 44)

The Human Relations Model

In addition to worker and labor union rejection of the traditional organization, by the time of the Great Depression many organizations had their own reasons to welcome the human relations movement (Figure 2.6). Engineering and business schools were turning out large numbers of educated, white-collar workers—workers so valuable that companies suddenly became concerned with the employee. At about the same time, one of the key ideas of scientific management—that employee productivity could be improved solely by economic motivation—was apparently disproved by a group of research studies conducted at Western Electric's Hawthorne plant in Cicero, Illinois.

One of these studies was designed to determine at what level of illumination the workers would be the most productive (Roethlisberger & Dickson, 1939). Surprisingly, productivity increased no matter what the researchers did. When lighting was increased from 24 to 46 foot-candles,

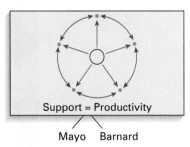

FIGURE 2.6 The human relations model.

then to 70, productivity increased both times; when lighting was decreased to 10, then to 3 foot-candles, productivity still increased. Productivity dropped only when the room became so dark that the workers could not see. Moreover, productivity even increased in the control group where the light level remained constant! These results were so unexpected that the Hawthorne executives contacted Harvard University.

Human Relations and Elton Mayo

The Hawthorne studies, conducted by Elton Mayo and his Harvard University colleagues between 1927 and 1932, substantiated the previous findings at the Hawthorne plant that changes in task conditions were not responsible for the increase in productivity. Although the original study varied the level of light, Mayo's studies varied such conditions as number of rest periods, time of lunch break, and the length of the work day. The Hawthorne studies reached two radical conclusions (Conrad, 1990, p. 202):

* Workers in relaxed and congenial work groups with supervisors who listen to them, are concerned about their needs, and are supportive are more productive than other workers, even when other working conditions are not favorable.

* Workers' satisfaction with the social and interpersonal relationships they have with their peers significantly influences their productivity, and workers feel substantial pressure from their peers to conform to the norms of their work group.

These conclusions served as the foundation of the human relations movement. In short, Mayo's best way was the concept that individual-centered tender loving care by supervisors and upper management would lead to greater work productivity. He replaced the "economic man" of the scientific managers with the "social man."

Human Relations and Chester Barnard

Chester Barnard, a contemporary of Mayo's and former president of the New Jersey Bell Telephone Company, was another important figure in the human relations school. Barnard's best way emphasized the importance of communication to organizational success. "The first executive function," he wrote, "is to develop and maintain

The Human Relations Model in Brief

Key Theorists and Landmark Books

Elton Mayo, *The Human Problems of an Industrial Civilization* (1933) and *The Social Problems of an Industrial Civilization* (1945)

Chester Barnard, *The Functions of the Executive* (1938)

Focus of Theory

Concern with social and psychological needs of employees

View of Communication

Downward supportive communication important; informal communication acknowledged a system of communication" (Barnard, 1938, p. 226). He also acknowledged the importance of informal communication, pointing out that informal groups within an organization establish norms and codes of conduct and provide cohesion, communication, and satisfaction to workers. Like Mayo, Barnard recognized that economic motives were not the only employee motivators.

Despite Barnard's opinion of the importance of communication, he still viewed it much as the scientific managers did—as a one-way tool to be used by managers for command functions. Indeed, he urged clearly established, formal communication channels and recommended that bypassing them not be allowed (Barnard, 1938, pp. 175–181).

The Human Relations Model in Today's World

An open, trusting climate—which is so necessary in the human relations organization—may be easier to implement in small, family-run organizations. A good example of the **human relations model** is provided by Southwest Airlines. According to Gary Kelly, CEO of Southwest Airlines, "Our People are our single greatest strength and our most enduring longterm competitive advantage" (southwest.com/careers, 2009).

Ideas, products, and procedures are relatively easy to come by; happy, productive employees are not. According to the founder and chairman of the board Herb Kelleher, "Our esprit de corps is the core of our success. That's most difficult for a competitor to imitate. . . ." (Krames, 2003, pp. 179–180). To maintain a fun-loving atmosphere, Southwest hires "attitudes," not just people and uses a targeted selection interview method to evaluate candidates on seven traits: "cheerfulness, optimism, decision-making ability, team spirit, communication, self-confidence, and self-starter skills" (p. 180). Southwest's fun-loving approach is represented by their blog called *Nuts About Southwest* (blogsouthwest.com); while you're there see the video of flight attendant David Holmes doing the GAAP Rap at the 2009 Shareholder's meeting in Dallas. In 2008 Southwest Airline was chosen as the "Friendliest Airline" by Time.com and in 2009 *Fortune* magazine selected Southwest as one of the 10 most admired companies in the world (Colvin, 2009). Some of the unexpected but "fun" things customers have experienced with Southwest include a gate agent singing happy birthday over the public address system; flight attendants singing safety regulations to the tune of the William Tell Overture (the *Lone Ranger* theme song); impromptu photos taken of passengers (copies sent by mail); boarding gates, as well as ramp agents decorated for Halloween; pilots pitching in to help at the boarding gate; and ticket agents loading luggage; CEO Kelly shaking hands with passengers as they board (Gittell, 2003; Krames, 2003; O'Brian, 1992; Williams, 2007; "Halloween," 2009). If a problem does occur, Southwest employees are empowered to solve it in the way they think best (Freiberg & Freiberg, 1996) fits their mission statement: The mission of Southwest Airlines is dedication to the highest quality of Customer Service delivered with a sense of warmth, friendliness, individual pride, and Company Spirit (Customer Service Commitment, 2009). Not only does this keep happy customers, but it makes for confident, satisfied employees.

Chief Executive Officer of Southwest Airlines, Gary Kelly, entertaining employees while wearing his bathrobe at a "put it to bed" ceremony for Southwest's last 737-200 aircraft. This is something you would not expect to see in a more traditional organization.

In addition to the fun-loving, family atmosphere, Southwest's human relations approach includes personal concern for its employees. Kelleher explains, "You have to recognize that people are still the most important. How you treat them determines how they treat people on the outside" (Lancaster, 1999). This personal treatment includes a strong dedication to job security. Even during the weeks following 9/11, Southwest continued its no-layoff policy—although they were reportedly losing "millions of dollars per day" (Trottman, 2001). The reason for this action was given by the director of Southwest's Office of Financial Analysis, who said, "It's part of our culture. We've always said we'll do whatever we can to take care of our people. So that's what we've tried to do" (Gittell, 2003, p. 242). As a result, employees are dedicated, devoted, and loyal to Southwest, although some labor problems do surface occasionally.

Southwest was one of the few airlines that continued to make an impressive profit after 9/11. In 2003, even though they ranked fourth in size among U.S. airlines, their profits were "greater than the combined revenues of the largest three airlines" (Cravens & Piercy, 2003, p. 3). Although "Southwest still enjoys some of the lowest costs, the best balance sheet, and the highest profit margins in the industry," they experienced a significant drop in earnings in 2006—possibly due to fuel costs and carry-on restrictions (Palmeri, 2006).

The Human Resources Model

The human resources model (Figure 2.7) grew out of the criticisms and problems of the human relations school, and by the late 1960s it had become a model in its own right.

IT REALLY WORKS!

Human Relations

Another company that puts employees first is Springfield ReManufacturing Corporation, part of SRC Holdings. In 1983 it began with an old plant, several million dollars of debt, and an "open-book management" desire to treat employees as partners. As Pfeffer and Veiga (1999) tell it:

> When General Motors canceled an order in 1986 that represented about 40 percent of Springfield's business for the coming year, the firm averted a layoff by providing its people with information on what had happened and letting them figure out how to grow the company and achieve the productivity improvements that would obviate layoffs. SRC has since enjoyed tremendous financial success. In 1983, its first year of operation, sales were about $13 million. By 1992, sales had increased to $70 million and the number of employees had grown from 119 to 700. (pp. 11–12)

CEO Jack Stack says, "The best, most efficient, most profitable way to operate a business is to give everybody a voice in how the company is run and a stake in the financial outcome, good or bad" (Daft, 2008; Daft & Marcic, 2006, p. 176). According to J. Case (1995), the "open-book management style" used by SRC involves four basic steps: a) getting job and company information out to employees, b) teaching business basics to employees, c) empowering employees to make decisions, and d) sharing company risks and successes with employees through targeted bonuses and stock ownership. SRC employees take an active role in keeping costs low: for 1.5 hours each week, small groups of employees meet to "study the company's weekly financial statements" and figure out ways to increase efficiency (C. Williams, 2003, p. 5).

What do you think?

- How does SRC's method of employee involvement fit the human relations model? Why does it seem to work so well?

- What do you suggest to SRC's management to keep problems from occurring as the company continues to grow?

There is no clear-cut line between the human relations and human resources models—only a gradual shift. Douglas McGregor (1960) and Rensis Likert (1961; 1967) started the transition by comparing traditional management with the human relations model and combining the best of both. Advocates of the human resources model liked it because it focused on both increased employee satisfaction and improved organizational decision making. At the same time, the human resources model emphasized both relational communication (i.e., open, supportive, friendly) and command communication.

Raymond Miles (1965) may have been the first to use the term *human resources*. In an article titled "Keeping Informed—Human Relations or Human Resources?" he compared the two models. Table 2.1 lists some of the basic differences. As the table indicates, the human resources model takes a more positive view of employee potential. Managers are encouraged to trust their employees and permit them to participate in important decisions and in their own development.

Let's take a look at some of the better-known human resource theorists and their best ways.

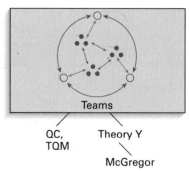

FIGURE 2.7 The human resources model.

Human Resources and McGregor's Theory Y

McGregor was critical of businesses following the traditional model. He felt that the traditional model significantly decreased employee performance. According to McGregor, when managers believe in the traditional model (which McGregor called Theory X), the following communication behaviors occur (Goldhaber, 1993, p. 78):

- Most messages flow downward from managers to subordinates. Information is often inadequate for employee needs.

- Upward communication is extremely limited (thus, the informal grapevine is very important to employees).

- Subordinates fear and distrust management.

TABLE 2.1

Comparison of Human Relations and Human Resources Models	
Human Relations	**Human Resources**
People wish to be liked and respected.	Most people desire a sense of accomplishment.
If their needs are met, employees will produce for the organization.	Most employees have untapped resources and are capable of more than most jobs allow.
Managers should convince workers that they are valuable team members.	Managers should tap and guide each employee's hidden talents and creativity to harmonize with organizational goals.
Managers should allow employee participation in routine decision making.	Managers should allow (and encourage) employee participation in routine and important decision-making situations.
Sharing information with employees will increase their satisfaction, which will improve morale and reduce resistance to authority, thus improving productivity.	Employee satisfaction is a by-product of improved performance.

Source: Adapted from Raymond Miles, 1965, "Keeping Informed—Human Relations or Human Resources?" *Harvard Business Review, 43*(4), pp. 148–163.

Although McGregor was critical of the traditional model of management, he wasn't completely satisfied with the human relations model either because he felt it did not do enough to encourage employee potential. Therefore, he developed a series of assumptions, which he called Theory Y. He felt they would produce the best managers and inspire employee trust and openness. The following communication behaviors are common when managers adopt Theory Y (or human resources) beliefs (Goldhaber, 1993, p. 79):

- Messages travel up, down, and across the organization.
- Decision making is spread throughout the organization. Even important decisions involve input from employees at all levels.
- Because feedback is encouraged in an upward direction—and management listens—no supplemental upward system is required.
- Frequent, honest interaction with employees takes place in an atmosphere of confidence and trust.
- The flow of messages downward is usually sufficient to satisfy the needs of employees.
- Decision making is based on messages from all levels of the organization, and thus the accuracy and quality of the decisions are improved.

McGregor based his theories on Abraham Maslow's hierarchy of needs (discussed in Chapter 14). Theory X deals only with the physiological and safety needs of the hierarchy; Theory Y covers all five levels of needs (i.e., physiological, safety, social, esteem, and self-actualization). See Table 2.2 for a comparison of McGregor's Theory X and Theory Y.

TABLE 2.2

Beliefs of Theory X and Theory Y Managers	
Theory X (Traditional)	**Theory Y (Human Resources)**
1 The average person has an inherent dislike of work and will avoid it if possible.	1 The use of physical and mental energy in work is as natural as play or rest.
2 Most people will not strive to achieve organizational objectives unless they are coerced, controlled, directed, and threatened with punishment.	2 External control and threats are not the only ways to motivate workers to meet organizational objectives. A person who is committed to the objectives will exercise self-direction and self-control.
3 The average person prefers to be directed, wishes to avoid responsibility, has relatively little ambition, and wants security above all else.	3 Commitment to objectives is both a motivator and a function of the rewards of achievement.
	4 Under proper conditions, workers learn not only to accept but also to seek responsibility.
	5 The capacity to exercise a relatively high degree of ingenuity and creativity is widely distributed in the population.
	6 The intellectual potentialities of most people are only partially utilized in modern organizations.

Norma Carr-Ruffino, 1985, *The Promotable Woman: Becoming a Successful Manager* (p. 230), Belmont, CA: Wadsworth. Reprinted by permission of the author.

Human Resources and Likert's Four Systems

Rensis Likert was another theorist who helped formulate the human resources model. He identified four management styles, which he called the Four Systems. System 1 (Exploitive/Authoritative) is similar to Theory X, and System 4 (Participative) resembles Theory Y. The other two systems (Benevolent/Authoritative and Consultative) fit between 1 and 4. Likert considered System 4 the ideal model for an organization. He and his colleagues from the University of Michigan found from their research that organizations high in System 4 characteristics also have high productivity. System 4 has three key elements: (a) supportive relationships based on trust, (b) group decision making and group supervision, and (c) high performance goals (Likert, 1961). In System 4 organizations, communication is both formal and informal, and upward, downward, and horizontal communication channels are used often and regularly.

The Human Resources Model in Today's World

The current application of the human resources model has a variety of names such as quality control circles (QCC) or quality circles (QCs), cross-functional teams, TQM, employee participation groups, high-performance teams, self-directed teams, or simply teams. Although the name and procedures may vary, essentially these are groups of employees who participate in generating ideas and decision making. Nonprofit organizations, businesses, educational groups, and governmental agencies all use participative employee involvement groups. Here are some examples:

- Quality-control decisions made by employee groups at the Honeywell facility in Phoenix resulted in the following decreases: 70% in defects, 46% in required inventory, and 75% in customer lead times (Daft & Marcic, 2006, p. 564).

- Federal Express has 4,000 Quality Action teams that are responsible for significant improvements in productivity, such as a 13% reduction in service errors in 1 year (Hackman & Johnson, 2000).

- Procter & Gamble's innovation panel was able to bring the Swiffer cleaning products to market in 10 months, half the normal P&G time (Cravens & Piercy, 2003, p. 241).

- A Hewlett-Packard cross-functional work team was able to reduce customer product delivery time from 26 to 8 days (Sherman, 1996).

- From 1999 to 2002, SSM Health Care improved patient survival well above national benchmark levels and lowered employee turnover rates from 21% to 13% by implementing 85 clinical collaborative teams ("SSM Health Care," 2003).

- Kodak "reduced its turnover rate to one-half of the industry's average and improved its handling of incoming customer calls by 100 percent after reorganizing into work teams" (Eisenberg et al., 2010, p. 213).

Although quality circles and employee teams have been very successful in some companies, other companies have experienced a high failure rate (the company represented in the cartoon may be one of them). The following characteristics are considered necessary for team success (Greenberg & Baron, 2007; Hitt et al., 1999; Preston, 2005; Smeltzer & Kedia, 1985):

1. Horizontal communication among departments and flexibility within departments.
2. Employees willing to work with each other and with other teams.

3. Managers willing to listen to employees.

4. Organizations open to change.

5. Rapid management response to suggestions.

6. Cooperation between management and the unions.

7. Support for team decisions and solutions.

Companies that have received the Malcolm Baldrige National Quality Award know the importance of training for their teams. For example, 1990 winner IBM Rochester yearly provides more than 45,000 days of training (5% of its payroll); 1999 winner Ritz-Carlton Hotel Company LLC provides 250–310 hours of training for first-year employees; 2000 winners Los Alamos National Bank and Clarke American Checks, Inc. trained 90% of employees, with associates receiving 76 hours of training ("1988–2002 Award," 2003). Medrad, Inc., a winner in 2003, spent more than $2,233 per employee on training in 2002, while Boeing Aereospace Support, also a 2003 winner, trained 98% of employees in 2002, up from 9% in 1999 ("President and Commerce Secretary," 2003). Even small businesses such as Park Place Lexus (PPL) a dealership in Plano and Grapevine, Texas (a 2005 winner) credit their gross profit increase in 2000–2004 of over 51% to training—the number of hours spent in training per member increased from 3 in 2001 to more than 32 in 2004 ("Park Place Lexus," 2005).

© 2003 Ted Goff

"After the merger, you may notice a few changes in our corporate culture."

The Human Resources Model in Brief

Key Theorists and Landmark Books & Articles

Douglas McGregor, *The Human Side of Enterprise* (1960)

Rensis Likert, *New Patterns of Management* (1961) and *The Human Organization* (1967)

Robert Blake and Jane Mouton, *The Managerial Grid* (1964; 1985)

Raymond Miles, "Keeping Informed: Human Relations or Human Resources," *Harvard Business Review* (1965) and *Theories of Management* (1975)

Focus of Theory

Equal emphasis on workers and management—a team-based orientation

View of Communication

Openness and trust in superior-subordinate communication very important; information and feedback flow freely up, down, and across the organization; informal communication encouraged

The Systems/Contingency Model

Although all the organizational theorists we have discussed so far have presented what they felt was the best way, each theory has fallen short in one or more areas. Current theories and the **systems/contingency model** (Figure 2.8) contend that there is no best way. Joan Woodward's seminal research (1965) supports this view. She decided to test important management principles to see whether successful companies applied these principles more often than less successful companies. Initially, she found no relationship between any one type of management principle and organizational effectiveness. However, upon reexamination of her data, she found that the effectiveness of certain management principles depended on the type of industry.

> In other words, there seemed to be a best method of organizing to fit each type of technology. Firms that stayed close to this best approach for their technical system were most effective. (Sashkin & Morris, 1984, p. 348)

Thus, it would seem that no organizational model will fit all organizations. A look at systems theory and contingency theory may help explain why this is true. Both theories, as they apply to organizations, grew out of general systems theory, which was introduced by a German biologist, Ludwig von Bertalanfy (1968). To summarize:

> General systems theory rests on the idea that the whole is more than the sum of its parts; each part must be considered as it interacts with, changes, and is changed by every other part within the system. The parts, or subsystems, of any given system are assumed to be interdependent, and it is primarily through communication that this interdependence is facilitated. (Andrews & Baird, 1999, p. 49)

To illustrate how one part of a system can affect the whole, imagine that you are traveling from Houston, Texas, to Santa Barbara, California, to help your colleague with a presentation at an important meeting. A surprise thunderstorm delays your plane's departure, and you arrive in Los Angeles 3 hours late. Then you sit on the plane for 45 minutes before a gate becomes available. Upon deplaning, you discover that the last commuter flight for Santa Barbara departed 30 minutes previously. By the time you stand in line to rent a car and drive the 91 miles to your meeting through heavy evening traffic, the presentation is over and your clients have gone. You missed the meeting for which you came. Not only do you feel stressed out and guilty, but your colleague is also furious that she had to give the presentation alone when she'd counted on your help. Uncontrollable external events affected you, who in turn affected the success of another part of the organization (the presentation).

Systems Theory

Applying the systems approach to organizations, Daniel Katz and Robert Kahn (1966) referred to organizations as open systems. An open system has flexible boundaries that allow communication to flow easily in and out of the organization. The people who "link the organization with outsiders," such as salespeople and purchasing agents, are boundary spanners. They gather useful outside information to help with decision making, they protect against external threats, they control the dissemination of information, and they present a good impression to outsiders (Conrad & Poole, 2005, p. 124). From new hires to company CEO, "the most successful companies involve everyone in boundary-spanning activities" (Daft, 2008, p. 83).

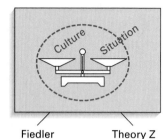

Systems/
Contingency

FIGURE 2.8 The systems/contingency model.

The strengths of systems theory are that (a) it recognizes the interdependence of all parts of an organization (what affects one part affects all parts), (b) it acknowledges both formal and informal communication as central to an organization's success, and (c) it integrates the biases of the traditional and the human relations models and gives them equal weight. According to systems theory, "Questions of job duty, chain of command, span of control, and decision making are equal in importance to questions of attitude, morale, behavior, role, and personality" (Goldhaber, 1993, p. 47).

Contingency Theory

Like systems theory, contingency theory evolved from general systems theory. Whereas systems theory is fairly mature, contingency theory is still being developed. There are several versions of contingency theory, but all have the same basic belief: "No one type of organizational structure or leadership style is most appropriate for all situations" (Rogers & Agarwala-Rogers, 1976, p. 45). Therefore, adaptability is required.

One of the best-known versions is Fred Fiedler's contingency theory. From his research with bomber crews, high school basketball teams, foundry workers, and management groups, Fiedler came to the conclusion that "which management style will be the most effective in a particular situation depends on the degree to which the group situation enables the manager to exert influence" (Carr-Ruffino, 1985, p. 277). Fiedler (1967) analyzes such contingent variables as leader-follower relations, position power, and task structure. For example, he found that a task or traditional orientation was most effective when (a) the manager was well liked, powerful, and the tasks were well defined or (b) when the manager was disliked, had little power, and the tasks were poorly defined. However, a human relations orientation was more effective when the manager was moderately liked, had some power, and the tasks were moderately defined. Research by Fiedler et al. (1976) shows that managers can be trained to identify and modify various situations to better fit their own communication and leadership styles.

Another version of contingency theory is Robert House's path-goal theory (1971). House's theory asserts that employees' overall job satisfaction and performance levels are contingent on (a) employee satisfaction with the job, (b) the uncertainty and difficulty of the job, and (c) the communication style of the supervisor (Conrad, 1994, p. 100).

Instead of employees adapting to fit management style, House suggests that managers adapt to fit a given situation (House, 1971; House & Mitchell, 1974). Direction and structure are needed when the task is uncertain, the procedure is ambiguous, or the employee is new or unfamiliar with the task. Supportive, considerate leadership is needed when the task is highly structured, dull, and unsatisfying or when employees are unfamiliar with the task but capable of doing it. Neither directive nor supportive leadership will be effective unless employees perceive the leader as helping them achieve desired goals. Successful leaders make the path to these goals clear and attainable.

The Contingency Model in Today's World

Theory Z, developed by William Ouchi (1981) as an alternative to Theories X and Y, is an application of contingency theory. According to Ouchi, successful organizations are those whose corporate culture reflects the values of their employees. In other words, instead of imposing its preferred management style on employees, a Theory Z company adapts its management style to the existing employee culture. **Culture** can be defined as the "patterns of beliefs and expectations shared by the organization's members, which produce norms that shape the behavior of individuals and groups

The Systems/Contingency Model in Brief

Key Theorists and Landmark Books & Articles

Joan Woodward, *Industrial Organization: Theory and Practice* (1965)

Daniel Katz and Robert Kahn, *The Social Psychology of Organizations* (1966)

Fred Fiedler, *A Theory of Leadership Effectiveness* (1967)

Robert House, "A Path-Goal Theory of Leader Behavior," *Administrative Science Quarterly* (1971).

Focus of Theory

Concern with the organization as a whole

View of Communication

All types of communication and feedback essential—even one person can affect the entire organization; used to build and maintain corporate culture

in the organization" (Schwartz & Davis, 1981, p. 30). Ouchi cites Hewlett-Packard, Dayton-Hudson Corporation, Rockwell International, Intel, and Eli Lilly as organizations with Theory Z cultures.

An organization's culture gives members a sense of identity, makes them feel a part of the whole and therefore more committed, and reinforces expected behaviors (Greenberg & Baron, 1997, p. 472). Culture is transmitted in part by stories, symbols and slogans, jargon, ceremonies, and principle statements (Oat, 1989). For example, evidence of a culture at Disney World is seen through "shared things (wearing the Walt Disney uniform), shared sayings (a good 'Mickey' is a compliment for doing a good job), shared behavior (smiling at customers and being polite), and shared feelings (taking pride in working at Disney)" (Ivancevich & Matteson, 1996, p. 83). Once a culture is established (such as the U.S. Marine Corps' "A few good men"; Ford's "Quality is job 1"; Disney World's "family feeling"), it tends to perpetuate itself. People who aren't interested in a particular culture won't want to work there, just as a student who wants to party won't apply to MIT. Because a culture is an attitude shared by employees, it is not always easy to identify.

In a speech titled "Employee Involvement," the senior vice president of operations for Miller Brewing Company verifies the importance of culture and contingency systems:

> We know that "Employee Involvement" is not a "corporate program" to be implemented "as is" at every Miller facility. We also know that how EI is implemented— the methods used and the timing—are going to vary with each different circumstance. Each of our plants is different. Each has its own culture, its own history, its own traditional way of doing things.
>
> What works in New York might not work at our Fort Worth can plant. The methods used at Albany, Georgia,

© 2002 Ted Goff

"Our task, then, is to decide how to decide how to decide."

might not be the same methods that will work out in Irwindale, California, or in Milwaukee. On the other hand, some might work with just a slight modification or alteration. And we encourage the sharing of ideas and projects in order to stimulate ideas that will work (Schumer, 1988, p. 564).

The Transformational Model

If you have looked at the business section in a bookstore recently, it may seem that the current organization model is "Management by Best Seller" (Kreitner, 2007, p. 51). *In Search of Excellence* (Peters & Waterman, 1982) sold over 5 million copies in 5 years; sales of *The One Minute Manager* (Blanchard & Johnson, 1982) reached 7 million copies by 2004 (Kreitner, 2007, p. 51). More recent management books that are selling well include, *First, Break All the Rules* (Buckingham & Coffman, 1999), *Jack: Straight from the Gut* (Welch, 2001), *The 360-Degree Leader* (Maxwell, 2006), and *The Speed of Trust* (Covey, 2006).

However, the newest organization models (see Figure 2.9) are the **transformational models**, which are the result of the problems that traditional models have experienced trying to survive in today's business environment. In fact, the very things that initially made traditional organizations so effective—direct supervision, standardization, and large size—have created many of these problems. According to *Busting Bureaucracy* (Johnson, 1992), many bureaucratic companies found that their formal, centralized, and complex structures made competition almost impossible in today's global market. Smaller, nonbureaucratic companies have proven better at innovation, flexibility, and customer service—requirements for productivity and growth. The *Wall Street Journal* reported that "all growth in the 1990s occurred in companies with fewer than 500 employees, and the vast majority of that occurred in firms with head counts of 20 or less" (Petzinger, 1999, p. R31). According to Wagner and Hollenbeck (2010), "Global competition, technological volatility, and trends toward the mass customization of products and services" require "the resources of a large organization, but the flexibility of a small one" (p. 279).

The new organizational models are known by several names. They are called *transformational* because they have transformed models from the past into the new multiunit and virtual structures discussed in the following paragraphs. They are called *postbureaucratic* because to compete in global markets, they must have more flexibility than bureaucratic models can provide. Finally, they are called *technological* (or networks) because they are made up of autonomous teams that "manage themselves" and "coordinate with one another by sharing information on computerized networks" (Wagner & Hollenbeck, 2010, p. 265; see also Conrad & Poole, 2005, p. 200). According to Poole et al. (1997), two new transformational structures seem to be emerging: the multiunit organization and the virtual organization.

The Multiunit Organization

A multiunit organization is made up of separate, autonomous businesses under the same holding company. This decentralized structure allows the large parent company to operate with the flexibility of the much smaller businesses. In addition, say Wagner and Hollenbeck (2010):

Transformational

Multiunit / Virtual

FIGURE 2.9 The transformational model.

The Transformational Model in Brief

Key Theorists and Landmark Article

Marshall Poole, Linda Putnam, & D. Seibold, "Organizational Communication in the 21st Century," *Management Communication Quarterly: McQ* (1997)

Focus of Theory

Concern with information technology and flexibility of decentralized structures

View of Communication

All types of communication important but horizontal communication among and between teams essential, as is knowledge of interpersonal relationships

> Compared with other types of bureaucratic structures, multiunit structures are extremely decentralized. Unit managers several levels below the holding unit's CEO have the authority to define their unit's purpose and formulate its mission. At the same time, routine activities within each business unit are coordinated as much as possible by standardization . . . to control the costs of process loss. (p. 255)

Multiunit organizations are often created when large bureaucracies downsize and restructure. For example, General Electric eliminated close to 170,000 positions, cut several levels of management, and organized its company into several independent businesses of 500 or fewer employees (Tichy & Sherman, 1994). In an attempt to improve earnings, McDonald's experimented with dividing the United States into five regions. The idea was to "create smaller companies within the larger McDonald's that will recapture its previous entrepreneurial zeal" (Cravens & Piercy, 2003, p. 296). In *Reengineering the Corporation*, Hammer and Champy (1993) suggest that successful organizations focus team efforts on business processes instead of tasks or jobs. For example, Cisco Systems, selected as number five of "The World's 50 Most Innovative Companies" (2009) by Fast Company, formed an Emerging Technologies Group, which produced eight products in three years "that are each expected to produce $1 billion in revenue" (p. 62).

The Virtual Organization

A virtual organization is generally a temporary venture among several companies, each with a special expertise or process specialty. For example, Motorola, IBM, and Apple created a virtual organization in 1994 to develop the PowerPC chip, a new computer memory chip. Once the task was completed successfully, they dissolved the temporary structure (Hof et al., 1994). In this case, the virtual model gave the three companies the combined resources and knowledge of a large conglomerate but the flexibility of a small company.

General Electric has created a virtual organization called Wipro GE Medical Systems with Wipro, a global IT services company in Bangalore to improve patient care by merging information technologies and healthcare services (Hamm, 2007). Of course, all members in a virtual alliance are dependent on one another. If one partner fails, the entire organization may fail (Chesbrough & Teece, 1996). Deere and

Company and Springfield Manufacturing Corporation joined together to produce a new company called ReGen Technologies LLC to remanufacture diesel engines for John Deere Agricultural Equipment and construction equipment in 1998—it is still going strong and will continue as long as its services are needed.

Virtual organizations use mutual adjustment as their primary means of coordination. Autonomous teams of employees communicate through the Internet and videoconferences and may never have any face-to-face meetings. For these teams to work effectively, they need trust and rapport and need to establish a type of "virtual water cooler" that allows for interpersonal connection (Conrad & Poole, 2005, p. 207; Kostner, 2001).

These new organizational models normally do not promise long-term employment. Instead, they use such terms as *conditional employment* and *employability*, which basically mean "Do not expect lengthy careers in this organization but expect to have your skills tested, polished, and acknowledged such that you will continue to be valued in the labor market" (Kunda & Van Maanen, 1999, p. 12; Waterman et al., 1994). Employees, who expect to change jobs fairly often, take an active role in managing their own careers. This model does not appear to be for the faint at heart.

The Transformational Model in Today's World

We have already discussed two thriving multiunit organizations—General Electric and Johnson & Johnson—and five large, traditional companies that successfully formed temporary virtual organizations —Motorola, IBM, Apple, General Motors, and General Electric. An additional example of a transformational model is the alliance made in 2000 between Toys "R" Us and Amazon.com to market toys through a "co-branded Web site" (Cravens & Piercy, 2003). Amazon.com has the Internet sales expertise whereas Toys "R" Us has the warehousing and purchasing knowledge.

The transformational model may be moving toward a blend of all models. In the multiunit and virtual alliances, all the following are important to organization and team success: structure, trust, strong relationships, team skills, flexibility, cultural values, environmental awareness, global awareness, and participative management. Stanley Deetz (1995; 2001) calls this approach the multiple stakeholder model. In this model, employees act like owners (see SRC Holdings discussed previously) and profitability occurs when "every stakeholder becomes responsible for decision making and is accountable for the outcomes of those decisions both to the business and to society" (Eisenberg et al., 2010, p. 210).

Communication Differences in the Organization Models

So far in this chapter, we have examined five organization models, as well as, basic types of communication and methods of coordinating people in organizations. Now let's look at the patterns of communication that typify each model.

Traditional Model

Communication in traditional organizations is rational, task oriented, formal, and usually written. It is mainly downward and used by supervisors and managers to clarify orders, rules, and tasks. The social side of communication is relatively unimportant. Traditional managers feel that employees are happier and more productive when they know what topics are appropriate to discuss, what behaviors are expected, and with whom they may communicate directly. Formally structured roles define what is expected of employees. In traditional models, employees are expected to fill predefined roles. Each position has its place in the chain of command and its set of expected behaviors. According to traditional managers, appropriate behavior and communication are

Revisiting the Case Study

Which organization model did Enron use, and how did it contribute to their ethical problems?

Greg Smith

determined by an employee's position. Decision making is the responsibility of management. Because communication is mainly downward and minimal, employees may feel the need to supplement it with information from the grapevine.

Human Relations Model

Although managers in human relations organizations provide a friendly, relaxed work environment, they still view communication as a command tool for use by management. Therefore, communication is basically downward, although it is also supportive. Human relations managers are concerned with the social and psychological needs of employees mainly because they believe that employees who are treated with TLC are more satisfied and therefore more productive. Managers seek feedback from employees and use the grapevine (informal network) to gauge employee satisfaction. Employees are allowed to make routine decisions; as we shall see in Chapter 10, employees who are involved in making a decision are much more likely to abide by it than are employees who are not involved in the decision. Communication skills are important in developing and maintaining relationships.

Human Resources Model

The human resources organization takes a team-oriented, or participative, approach to employee-management relationships. Employees are expected to take an active role in all decisions, big and small. To facilitate creative ideas and decisions, information and feedback flow freely up and down the organization; informal communication is encouraged; and the working environment is supportive, flexible, and trusting. For the information flow required in the human resources model, employees at all levels need to have the communication skills discussed in Chapter 1.

Systems/Contingency Model

The systems/contingency model asserts that there is no single best way to manage, and there is no single best way to communicate. Both management styles and communication processes are influenced by the particular situation and any number of internal and external factors—employees' needs and abilities, managers' personalities and communication skills, customers' expectations, and the economy. Communication flexibility is a must in the contingency organization and is valued even more than in the human resources organization. Therefore, communication skills are needed by employees at all levels.

Transformational Model

Horizontal communication among team members and between teams is essential for the transformational model, although upward, downward, and informal communications are readily used when needed. Therefore, team members in both the multiunit and virtual organizations must be skilled communicators who are aware of frame-of-reference differences—especially when working with members located across the United States and in different countries. In the virtual organization, much or all communication occurs electronically, and face-to-face communication may occur only by videoconferencing. Because the nonverbal code is missing, team members need to be especially skilled at communication and relationship building. According to Ishaya and Macaulay (1999), "The success of virtual teams depends largely on building and maintaining trust between the team members" (p. 140). How to develop interpersonal relationships and trust will be the topic of Chapter 3. For a discussion of technology used by virtual teams for communication, see the Technology section in Chapter 6.

AWARENESS CHECK

Organization Models

To check your knowledge of the five organization models, take the following quiz. Compare your answers with those at the back of this book. You can also take this quiz online via the Premium Website for *Communicating for Results*.

Directions: Identify which organization model the following manager statements describe: (A) Traditional, (B) Human Relations, (C) Human Resources, (D) Systems/Contingency, or (E) Transformational.

_____ 1. Employees are more productive when given tender loving care.

_____ 2. There is no single best way to manage. Both internal and external factors should be considered when selecting a successful organization style.

_____ 3. Today's global market requires immediate organization flexibility and change.

_____ 4. To keep employee respect, managers must take control and show who's boss.

_____ 5. Managers should allow employee participation only in routine decision making.

_____ 6. When employees—working face-to-face in teams—are allowed to make important decisions, they gain a feeling of self-worth and achievement.

_____ 7. Successful organizations have a culture that reflects the values of management and employees.

_____ 8. Employees are lazy and will usually goof off if not watched closely.

_____ 9. Because most contact occurs via computer-connected teams, good communication skills are essential for all employees.

_____ 10. The manager role is to serve mainly as a facilitator.

CHAPTER 2
REVIEW

Key Terms

chain of command (41)

culture (52)

direct supervision (35)

division of labor (41)

downward communication (30)

empowered teams (33)

flat organization (41)

formal communication (30)

horizontal communication (33)

human relations model (45)

informal communications (33)

mutual adjustment (35)

organizational structure (41)

span of control (41)

standardization (35)

systems/contingency model (51)

tall organization (41)

traditional model (36)

transformational model (54)

upward communication (31)

Summary

To be an effective communicator in an organization, you need to be aware of both formal and informal communication, realizing that sometimes the informal grapevine is more effective than formal (i.e., upward, downward, or horizontal) communication. It is also helpful to understand the three main ways organizations coordinate employees: mutual adjustment, direct supervision, and standardization.

Understanding communication and coordination methods will help you identify which model (i.e., traditional, human relations, human resources, systems/contingency, or transformational) a particular organization follows. Identifying its model will give you a feel for the organization's complexity and its typical communication problems. The traditional model is based on the work of two groups of theorists: the scientific managers, who urge the scientific design of each task and the scientific selection of workers; and the bureaucratic theorists, who want to improve the efficiency of managers by formalizing the chain of command, insisting that all decisions and actions be put in writing, and recommending a detached relationship with employees. The human relations model emphasizes employee-boss relationships and believes that giving employees TLC will result in greater productivity. The human resources model, represented by Theory Y, focuses on employee-manager teamwork, built on both employee satisfaction and management control. The systems/contingency model tries to select the management style that best meets the needs, expectations, and culture of the employees. And finally, the transformational model is a response to the constant change and the electronic media that characterize today's workplace. Both the multiunit organization and the virtual organization are changing the way businesses operate.

Communication in the traditional organization is mainly downward. In the human relations organization, communication is also primarily downward but supportive. In the human resources and contingency models, communication flows in all directions. The transformational model relies heavily on horizontal communication. Communication, feedback, and company expectations differ significantly from model to model. We hope you can now feel more comfortable identifying and selecting your work environment and communicating in any environment in which you find yourself.

Communicating for Results Online

Before continuing to the next chapter, check your understanding of Chapter 2 at the Premium Website for *Communicating for Results*. Your Premium Website gives you quick and easy access to the electronic resources that accompany this text. These resources include:

- **Study tools** that will help you assess your learning and prepare for exams (student companion workbook, digital glossary, key term flash cards, and review quizzes).

- **Activities and assignments** that will help you hone your knowledge, analyze professional communication situations, build your public speaking skills throughout the course, and learn to work effectively in teams (Awareness Checks, Checkpoints, and Collaborative Learning Activities).

- **Media resources** that will help you explore communication concepts online (Web links), develop your speech outlines (Speech Builder Express 3.0), watch and critique videos of professional communication situations and sample speeches (Interactive Video Activities), upload your speech videos for peer reviewing and critique other students' speeches (Speech Studio online speech review tool), and download chapter review so you can study when and where you'd like (Audio Study Tools).

This chapter's key terms, Collaborative Learning Activities, and Checkpoint activities are also featured on the following pages, and you can find this chapter's Awareness Check activities in the body of the chapter. For more information or to access this book's online resources, visit www.cengage.com/login.

Collaborative Learning Activities

1. In small groups of five to seven, show your understanding of the informal communication network—the grapevine—by answering these questions (If your group can't come to an agreement, do some additional research):

    a. What is the difference between gossip and rumours and what role does gossip play in maintaining the grapevine, if any?

    b. Who uses the grapevine the most—men or women?

    c. How fast and accurate are messages carried by the grapevine?

    d. How can you tell the health of your organization by listening to the company grapevine?

2. Assign each of the organization models to a small group of three to five members whose responsibility will be to gather and condense information about the model in preparation for a later interview. Follow these steps as a guide:

    a. Begin by getting two volunteers from your group.

    b. It will be the group's duty to coach your volunteers in exactly how a manager from your organization model would behave—allow 15 to 20 minutes.

    c. During this time, compile a basic list of characteristics including at least four things people who follow your model could be expected to do or say and four things they probably would not do or say.

    d. If time allows, consider what your volunteers would think about such things as structure and control, motivation of others, trust, productivity, employee feedback, personal problems, and technology.

    e. When time is up, a volunteer from at least three different models will move to the front of the room as though they are attending a press conference and being asked questions by employees. Each volunteer should have a place card stating his or her name and organization

model. Make sure to ask opinion questions and that all volunteers answer each question. Sample questions might be, "I hear through the grapevine that headquarters is planning on implementing a team approach when the new plant is completed. How do you think this will affect productively?" or "Do you really think that employees can be trusted enough to make important decisions that will affect the company?" The point of these questions is to see how managers from different organization models respond differently. In addition to asking questions, group members should make sure that their volunteers are answering questions true to their organization model.

    f. Change volunteers every 7 minutes until time is over or until all volunteers have participated.

Checkpoints

Checkpoint 2.1 Perception of Management
Think back to a job you have held in the last 5 years. Consider your perception of the management of the firm and answer the questions below using *Always*, *Sometimes*, or *Rarely*:

a. Management tried its best to treat employees fairly.

b. Management was concerned about the employees' personal problems.

c. Management did everything possible to make our customers happy.

Now assume that everyone else in the organization saw management in the same way. What would be the effects of these perceptions on the overall operation of the organization?

Checkpoint 2.2 Burden of Effective Communication

Checkpoint 2.3 Grapevine Information in Your Organization

Checkpoint 2.4 Downsizing

Checkpoint 2.5 Upward, Downward, or Horizontal Communication

Checkpoint 2.6 Volunteer Work and Organization Models

Checkpoint 2.7 Interviewing a Company Member about the Company's Organization Model

Checkpoint 2.8 Organization/Communication Websites

Improving Interpersonal Relationships

Inkastudio/iStockphoto

Case Study

American International Group Bailout Bonus Controversy

In the spring of 2008, a global economic crisis resulted in the U.S. government providing bailout monies to multiple companies in order to protect the stability of the economy. American International Group (AIG) received $200 billion of these funds. When the chief executive of AIG, Edward Liddy, used bailout funds to pay bonuses to 418 employees totaling $165 million, cries of outrage were heard from the White House, Congress, and the American people (Calmes & Story, 2009). When people realized that 73 of the employees received bonuses of $1 million each and that $33.6 million was paid to people no longer employed by AIG, the cries became even louder. The reality is that the bonuses were contractual agreements signed in 2007 before the bailout. According to Liddy the bonuses were paid to keep his best employees so they could help the company get back on its feet.

The AIG bonuses were the talk of the media and the American people for weeks as Congress held hearings and debated how to handle the situation. The *New York Times* received and published an interesting resignation letter from Jake DeSantis, an executive vice president of the AIG's financial products unit. Here is a portion of his letter:

> Dear Mr. Liddy,
>
> It is with deep regret that I submit my notice of resignation from A.I.G. Financial Products. I hope you take the time to read this entire letter. Before describing the details of my decision, I want to offer some context . . .

As you read Chapter 3,

Identify the role of interpersonal relationships in organizational success; **determine** your personal communication style by taking the Survey of Communication Styles, both long and short forms, discussed in the chapter.

Define the terms *clear expectations, reciprocal relationships, self-fulfilling prophecy,* and *trust cycles,* and **explain** what role each plays in developing and maintaining relationships.

List the four main communication styles typically used in the workplace and **summarize** when each is the most and least successful.

Identify several practical tips for relating with people of different styles and **plan** ways to become flexible in your personal use of these tips.

Identify types of conflict and strategies for managing conflict in business relationships; **explain** how each strategy works best especially when cultural differences exist.

As you read this chapter, see if you can (a) narrow down the main problem—was it the fact that bonuses were given, the size of the bonuses, or did something else cause the public outrage?, (b) determine which of the four communication styles best fits DeSantis based on his letter, and (c) assess the value of disclosing through the media and why you think DeSantis chose that method. For more details on AIG, go to **www.wsj. com** or **www.nytimes**.com and search on "AIG" or the names mentioned in this case study. If you'd like to read the remainder of DeSantis's letter, go to **www.nytimes.com** and search on "Jake DeSantis." You can access these Websites easily through your Premium Website for *Communicating for Results*.

After 12 months of hard work dismantling the company—during which A.I.G. reassured us many times we would be rewarded in March 2009—we in the financial products unit have been betrayed by A.I.G. and are being unfairly persecuted by elected officials. In response to this, I will now leave the company and donate my entire post-tax retention payment to those suffering from the global economic downturn. My intent is to keep none of the money myself.

I take this action after 11 years of dedicated, honorable service to A.I.G. I can no longer effectively perform my duties in this dysfunctional environment, nor am I being paid to do so. Like you, I was asked to work for an annual salary of $1, and I agreed out of a sense of duty to the company and to the public officials who have come to its aid. Having now been let down by both, I can no longer justify spending 10, 12, 14 hours a day away from my family for the benefit of those who have let me down.

You and I have never met or spoken to each other, so I'd like to tell you about myself. . . . I started at this company in 1998 as an equity trader, became the head of equity and commodity trading and, a couple of years before A.I.G.'s meltdown last September, was named the head of business development for commodities. Over this period the equity and commodity units were consistently profitable—in most years generating net profits of well over $100 million. . . .

But you also are aware that most of the employees of your financial products unit had nothing to do with the large losses. . . . I and many others in the unit feel betrayed that you failed to stand up for us in the face of untrue and unfair accusations from certain members of Congress last Wednesday and from the press over our retention payments, and that you didn't defend us against the baseless and reckless comments made by the attorneys general of New York and Connecticut. . . .

As most of us have done nothing wrong, guilt is not a motivation to surrender our earnings. We have worked 12 long months under these contracts and now deserve to be paid as promised. None of us should be cheated of our payments any more than a plumber should be cheated after he has fixed the pipes but a careless electrician causes a fire that burns down the house. . . .

Sincerely,

Jake DeSantis

Regardless of whether AIG should or should not have paid out the bonuses after receiving federal bailout money, the lack of communication from their CEO, Liddy, to his employees and the public is fairly obvious in this chapter's case study. Apparently, Liddy wasn't aware that good interpersonal relationships are essential to high productivity and quality customer service. Employees who develop and maintain strong interpersonal relationships with their bosses, coworkers, and customers have a different outlook on their jobs than do those who have poor relationships. Positive relationships produce confidence and trust and encourage free communication of opinions and feelings. Poor relationships inspire suspicion and lead to distorted communication.

The importance of customer service hasn't changed, but recent technology changes have allowed companies to approach customer service in a more personal and involved manner—to "tell their story" and allow "customers to join the conversation" (Pulizzi & Barrett, 2009, pp. 4–5). Social network sites like Facebook and Twitter, blogs, and YouTube have changed the way businesses approach potential customers. Take for example the success that company founder Tom Dickson has had demonstrating the strength of his Blendtec blender on YouTube in his video series called "Will It Blend?" Dickson blends items suggested by his audience including an iPhone, golf balls, a rake handle, an Olympus camera, as well as food items like avocados with the skin and seeds. The two-minute videos are fun, involve audience participation, and make the strength of his blender abundantly clear. According to Pulizzi and Barrett, this new approach which they call *content marketing* is really working for Blendtec—sales increased 500% after the video series began (p. 5).

Interpersonal Relationships and Organizational Success

Communication is more than just the exchange of information; it also involves the development and maintenance of **relationships**, which are mutual liking and interests between people. Regardless of your status in it, your organization's success is influenced by the quality of your relationships with your coworkers (Williams, 2005), supervisors, and customers. The quality of employee relationships affects (a) job satisfaction, (b) morale, (c) ability to meet others' communication needs, and (d) commitment to and knowledge of the organization (Conrad & Poole, 2005, p. 119). In addition, strong peer relationships appear to reduce turnover (Feely et al., 2008), enhance creativity (Yager, 1997), improve productivity (Ross, 1997), and even provide guidance and support with non-job-related problems (Sias & Cahill, 1998).

The quality of supervisors' relationships is equally important. Studies conclude that 40% of newly hired managers remain less than 18 months in their jobs mainly due to their "failure to build good relationships with peers and subordinates" (Fisher, 1998, p. 3). A survey by Lou Harris found that employees who were dissatisfied with their employee/boss relationships looked for other jobs four times as often as satisfied employees (Conrad & Poole, 2005). Managerial characteristics that are important to "high-quality" boss-subordinate relationships include praise, understanding, trust, friendliness, honesty, and openness to subordinates' disagreement (Goldhaber, 1993, p. 11). The need for strong interpersonal relationships is especially important in the new organization models—the multiunit and the virtual organizations—in which electronic commerce, globalization, cyberspace offices, and constant change can cause employees to feel both physically and emotionally isolated. In *Organizational Communication*, Eisenberg et al. (2010) note the following:

> It is highly likely that the development of virtual teams will increase exponentially with the development of more realistic telepresence and absorption of younger people into the workplace. ... From an employee perspective, members of the "millennial" generation are much more comfortable than their predecessors with multitasking and multiple, mediated forms of communication. (p. 218)

Keep in mind, however, that although technology-driven organizations often believe that the key to success is the number of messages sent, the key is actually using the media to build relationships and trust (Tapscott et al., 2000).

Not only does the quality of work relationships affect the organization, but the climate of the organization also determines the quality of relationships among its members. The father of organizational communication, W. Charles Redding (1964), said it best:

> A member of any organization is, in large measure, the kind of communicator that the organization compels him to be. In other words, the very fact of holding a position in an organization determines many of the ways in which a person speaks, listens, writes, and reads. (p. 29)

Even a trusting, sharing, hard-working person can become angry and uncaring in a company where most of the managers and employees are hostile and suspicious. *Everyone's* communication style is affected by the work environment. In fact, our lives at work may very well influence our lives at home as well (Kahn, 1984). Research analyzed up to 1991 concluded that job satisfaction spills over into life satisfaction (Rain et al., 1991). Thus, you need to be careful in selecting the organization for which you work because its atmosphere can directly affect your communication style, your relationships, and your communication behavior. Likewise, the organization must be careful about the type of person it hires because the way employees relate to others can affect the organization's communication success and even its atmosphere.

Building and Maintaining Relationships

The strong, lasting relationships that we develop with people at work (or anywhere, for that matter) fulfill a need for us. As long as the relationships are mutually satisfying, they will endure; if not, they will deteriorate. In developing and maintaining relationships, it is important to keep in mind several relationship keys, which include *expectations, the reciprocal nature of relationships,* and *trust.*

Make Expectations Clear

Every person in a relationship has certain **expectations** of other people and the job. In fact, the **climate** or social and work environment of an organization is often "a measure of whether or not people's expectations of what it should be like to work in an organization are being met" (Goldhaber, 1993, p. 69). For example, if we join an organization expecting a warm, social working environment but find a task-oriented, no talking environment, we are likely to react with frustration and anger and withdraw our trust. Unless the violated expectations are revised in some way or the situation changes, the quality of our working relationships will deteriorate or never develop and we may leave the job or even get fired. This is illustrated by a UPS distribution center in Buffalo, New York, that had an unexplained attrition rate of 50%. The fact that the job was difficult, the huge warehouse noisy, and the packages to be sorted nonstop didn't seem to be the problem. It took a new manager to realize that the Human Resources (HR) department was hiring anyone that could lift heavy packages without asking them their expectations. The job was part-time with almost no chance for full-time yet most of the new hires were really looking for full-time employment. When they realized that their expectations couldn't be met by the warehouse job, they quit—sometimes after only a few weeks. Once the job was offered to people who really wanted part-time work (like students and mothers), the attrition rate dropped to 6% (Daft, 2008).

If both employers and employees make their expectations clear from the start, job satisfaction and quality relationships have a better chance of developing (Chell & Tracey, 2005). However, most of our "expectations remain unspoken until they are violated" (Kreps, 1990, p. 150). We *assume* that others know what is expected of them without being told. For example, a supervisor assumes that all employees know they should take an active role in office decisions and becomes upset when a new employee expects others to make the decisions. Not only do most expectations remain unspoken until violated, but also our expectations "continually change, making the potential for the fulfillment of these expectations less likely" (Kreps, p. 150).

Making expectations clear is also important in virtual organizations, where virtual team members and telecommuters are physically isolated from others. E-mail, instant messaging (IM), blogs, teleconferencing, and other types of computer-mediated communication replace the normal face-to-face method of developing friendships (Ellison, 1999; Sias & Cahill, 1998). According to Sias et al. (2002), "In such cases, communication technologies enable 'virtual coworkers' to become 'virtual friends'" (p. 634). One woman who works on a virtual team said the following:

> "We've had more challenges than your typical office team. However, we've also had advantages over other teams, including improved relationships and the ability to avoid endless, pointless meetings." (Carter-Jackson, n.d.)

Utilize the Reciprocal Nature of Relationships

Interpersonal relationships are **reciprocal**, which means that a kindness from one person is usually returned in kind. For example, if a coworker helps you with a difficult task, you will most likely reciprocate and do something nice for the coworker (Wilson, 1993). No one actually said, "If you help me, I'll help you," but because of the reciprocal quality of relationships, "people communicate with others in accord with the way they perceive these others communicating with them" (Kreps, 1990, p. 153).

As long as we continue to reciprocate, the relationship will grow. On the other hand, if you do considerably more for me than I am able to do for you, the reciprocal quality of our relationship is out of balance, and the relationship will deteriorate or at least stagnate until the balance is restored. When our expectations of another person are reciprocated, a self-fulfilling prophecy is likely to occur. A **self-fulfilling prophecy** is where something that is expected actually occurs. For example, if a manager believes that a subordinate is dishonest or ineffective, the manager is likely to communicate these feelings to the subordinate through verbal and nonverbal behaviors, such as unwarranted questioning or criticism, dismissal of ideas, and unfriendly facial expressions. As a result, the subordinate now distrusts the manager and hesitates to present new ideas or disclose full and honest information. Because the subordinate fails to suggest new ideas and does not provide full and honest information to the manager, the manager's expectations about the subordinate are fulfilled (Fisher, 1998; Kreps, 1990).

Maintain Mutual Trust and Respect

Trust may be one of the most important determiners of manager-employee relationships (Hubbell & Chory-Assad, 2005; Lewicki et al., 1998). In their article, "Relationship Building in Small Firms," Chell and Tracey (2005) found **trust** and **mutual respect** to be "an intangible bond that secures the relationship in the present and prospectively into the future" (p. 606). High trust levels can be developed without a long acquaintance if the participants believe that the other is trustworthy based on such things as group membership, reputation, or information gained from a brief interaction about the other's intentions and motives (McKnight et al., 2006). This is fortunate because so many temporary and virtual teams must begin

---

IT REALLY WORKS!

Elder Relationships

A poll by *NewsHour* found that 43% of Americans considered living in a nursing home "totally unacceptable" for themselves, and 45% felt that elders are actually worse off after moving into a nursing home (Dentzer, 2002). According to William Thomas, physician, author (1999 and 2004), and creator of Eden Alternative—the typical nursing home is "utterly devoid of hope, love, humor, [and] meaning" (Salter, 2002, para. 2). He claims that America's institutionalized elders who live in nursing homes resemble convicted criminals who live in our prisons (Bell, 2002, para. 4).

What's the answer? "Relationships are the foundation of good health care," says Thomas (Bell, 2002). For relationships to flourish, elders need a sanctuary that feels like home—a place that is warm, uses smart technology, is connected with a green environment (Thomas, 2004, p. 221), and has a staff interested in relationships. Over 300 nursing homes and 15,000 care providers are now associated with Thomas's Garden of Eden approach, which includes well-treated, empowered staff who work in teams, elders who participate in personal and nursing-home operations when able, an environment that looks and smells like home (with personal furniture, home-baked bread, pets and children from the on-site center for staff children), and an inviting garden full of flower and vegetable beds at wheelchair height, benches, shade trees, and sometimes even a playground so residents can watch and interact with children (Bell, 2002; EdenAlt.org, 2006; Thomas, 2004;). Eden Alternative nursing homes provide an environment that encourages relationships.

Do they work? Residents bloom in the new homes (all the homes have long waiting lists), and research shows significant drops in the overall number of drug prescriptions, infection rates, pressure sores, behavioral incidents,

bedfast residents, and mortality rates (NCAOnline.org, 2006; Salter, 2002; Thomas, 2004). Employees, who traditionally have been encouraged not to develop relationships with residents, are also happy, as indicated by the staff motto at a home in South Bend, Indiana: "Our elders do not live in our facility. We work in their home" (EdenAlt.com, 2006). One staff member expressed the value of relationships this way:

> Today I had fried chicken and macaroni and cheese for lunch. It made me miss my friend Foby. She almost made it to her 99th birthday, missing it by only five days. . . . When I held her hand in the hospital bed that last day, I thought how lucky I was to have known her. Five years ago, I would have never thought that I would so dearly love this woman who stuck out her tongue when you walked by and would never let anyone sit with her. Oh, what I would have lost out on. And maybe, just maybe, I gave a little back to her. (CultureChangeNow.com, 2006, para. 9)

Not only are relationships the foundation of good health care, but they are also good for business. A registered Eden home in Michigan reported staff turnover and absenteeism drops of 75 and 60%, respectively, resulting in savings of approximately $100,000 (Steiner, 2004; Thomas, 2004). Not all is perfect; change is slow and a great deal of work remains, but Eden homes seem to be a good alternative.

What do you think?

- How do the new Eden Alternative nursing homes' successes relate to their quality of employee–elder relationships?
- Which communication style would be the most likely to inspire relationship development in a nursing home?

work immediately and have little time to spend developing trust. On the other hand, researchers have found that employees aren't necessarily feeling trust for their employers. For example, Kanter and Mirvis (1990) reported that 72% of employees felt their managers were taking advantage of them, and 66% believed their managers could not be trusted.

In *Managing for Excellence*, David Bradford and Allan Cohen (1984) suggest that instead of automatically attributing an employee's low productivity to a defect or negative personality trait, which could cause a negative self-fulfilling prophecy, the supervisor should check to see if something in the employee's work situation could be causing the problem. They suggest the supervisor take this view:

> Let me assume that this difficult subordinate is really a very competent, well-intentioned person. How then could such a nice, able person behave in such a negative way? What in the situation might be causing this behavior? (p. 149)

Such a view makes it easier "to move from an initial rejection position into a direct data-collection mode" (Bradford & Cohen, 1984, p. 149). Trust requires that we give everyone the benefit of the doubt. And it has a definite influence on the type of interpersonal relationships established and maintained in an organization. Trust is especially important to the success of groups and virtual teams (Meyerson et al., 1996).

Communication Styles and Business Relationships

Strong interpersonal relationships are not only the heart of a successful organization but also the foundation of our own business successes. To make relationships work, we need to be aware of more than expectations, the reciprocal nature of relationships, and trust. We also need to understand our **communication styles**. Our communication styles affect relationships with bosses, coworkers, teams, and customers. Each of us has a distinct communication style that we feel the most comfortable using. Many professions and businesses also seem to have preferred communication styles.

In the next few sections, we will look at four styles that managers, employees, and customers typically use when communicating: the closed, blind, hidden, and open styles. Few people are ever completely closed, completely blind, completely hidden, or completely open. Although a person may have some characteristics of all four styles, most people have one or sometimes two dominant styles they typically use when things are going well and another style (or styles) they use under stress. None of these styles is totally good or totally bad; each has its "best" and "worst" side.

To communicate more successfully and establish more meaningful working relationships, we need to (a) determine our personal communication styles, (b) understand the strength and weaknesses of each style, and (c) learn how to communicate effectively with people using styles different from our own (whether they are supervisors, coworkers, or customers).

Communication styles are determined by how often we use two important elements: feedback and disclosure (see Figure 3.1). **Feedback** (response from others in the form of information, opinions, and feelings) can vary on the feedback continuum from rarely seeking feedback to seeking it excessively. Either extreme can inhibit effective communication.

Similarly, **disclosure** (voluntarily sharing information, opinions, and feelings with others) can vary from rarely used to excessive. In his book *The Open Organization:*

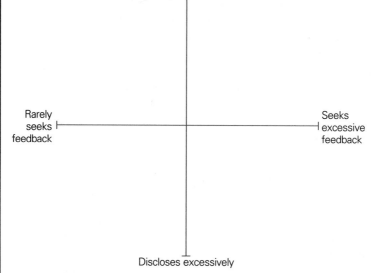

FIGURE 3.1 Feedback and disclosure continuums.

The Impact of Secrecy and Disclosure on People and Organizations, Fritz Steele (1975) offers the following:

> Disclosure can be of ideas, information from other sources, feelings, or any other topics we can pass on to another person. Individuals can disclose opinions, descriptions of past behaviors, future intentions, feelings, or anything else that can be conceptualized or acted out. Organizations can also disclose, that is, make information available, and in different degrees to different people. (pp. 7–8)

Too much or too little feedback can hurt communication, and too much or too little disclosure can hurt communication. For example, we've all met people who can't make a decision without input from others and people who rarely ask for suggestions or opinions from anyone. We know people who seldom volunteer ideas or opinions and other people who seem to volunteer everything that comes to mind!

Please realize that this classification system of four styles is not intended to serve as a method for stereotyping people but as a practical way of understanding your own and others' frames of reference. As you read the following sections, remember that the descriptions of these styles are not perfect or even complete; rather, they describe tendencies. As such, I hope you will find them helpful in your daily business and professional communication.*

When you complete the surveys please note that your largest total (or two totals if the totals are only one or two points apart) represents the style or styles that you typically use when things are running smoothly; the next largest total (or two if the totals are only one or two points apart) represents the style or styles you use under stress. For example, you might usually communicate in an open manner but under stress begin communicating in a hidden manner. As we have indicated, no one style

---

* The manager, employee, and customer styles presented in this section are a composite of Luft and Ingham's (Luft, 1969) "JoHari window" concept, J. A. Hall's (1975) "interpersonal styles and managerial impacts," Lefton's (Lefton et al., 1980) "management systems approach," and Bradford and Cohen's (1984) "manager-as-conductor" and "manager-as-developer" middle manager styles. The final result, although it does not contradict these authors' concepts, is my own product, and therefore, does not parallel any of the other five approaches exactly.

NOTE

Before reading further in this chapter, please complete the following two surveys:

1. *The Styles Survey— Short Form* on page 69 in this chapter

2. *The Survey of Communication Styles* (both the Manager and Employee sections) located online at your Premium Website for *Communicating for Results*. When you take the survey, it will be automatically scored and plotted for you and include the option to e-mail the results to your instructor.

AWARENESS CHECK

Styles Survey—Short Form

Take this styles survey and *compare* your results with the results you get when you take the Survey of Communication Styles—Long Form. You can take both surveys online at the Premium Website for *Communicating for Results*.

Directions: Answer each of the following questions by circling a number from 1 to 10 that represents how true or false each statement is to you: completely *false = 1*; completely *true = 10*. Write the number you circled on the line beside each question; this number represents your points for that question.

Points:

1. I feel more comfortable around things than people.   False 1 2 3 4 5 6 7 8 ⑨ 10 True
2. To keep the peace, I usually give in.   False 1 2 3 4 ⑤ 6 7 8 9 10 True
3. I find that I'm usually right on most issues.   False 1 2 3 4 5 6 7 8 ⑨ 10 True
4. I make sure that my opinions are known.   False 1 2 3 4 5 6 7 8 ⑨ 10 True
5. It's important to me that people like me; if they
   don't, I feel very uncomfortable.   False 1 2 3 4 5 6 7 8 ⑨ 10 True
6. I usually withhold my opinions until I know what
   other people think.   False 1 2 ③ 4 5 6 7 8 9 10 True
7. I like almost all of the people I meet.   False 1 2 3 4 ⑤ 6 7 8 9 10 True
8. Working on teams is fun and effective.   False 1 2 3 4 5 6 ⑦ 8 9 10 True

Scoring:

Add the points from questions 7 and 8: total = Open.   12
Add the points from questions 5 and 6: total = Hidden.   12
Add the points from questions 3 and 4: total = Blind.   19
Add the points from questions 1 and 2: total = Closed.   14

Your largest total represents the communication style you use when things are going smoothly. The next largest total (or two totals if the scores are very close) are the style or styles you jump back to under stress.

---

is perfect for every situation. Flexibility in use of styles is a desired communication skill. Which style is the most effective in a particular situation depends on (a) which styles you can use comfortably, (b) which styles could best handle the conflict or problem, and (c) which styles are preferred by your team, supervisor/employees, coworkers, or customers. Knowing the strengths and weaknesses of each style can help you adjust your own style and adapt to the styles of others.

The Closed Style

If you had the choice of a job in a room with five or six other people whom you would work with each day or a job in a room by yourself, working with a machine that only one person could operate at a time, which would you choose? If you selected to work alone, you probably have strong closed tendencies. **Closed style communicators** simply feel more comfortable working with things than with people—does this seem like you? For example, a closed employee might do well working at restocking items or finding glitches in a software program but be inefficient when handling customers at a complaint window or working in a group. A closed manager may enjoy inventory control, ordering supplies, and detail work but be less successful dealing with employees and employee problems.

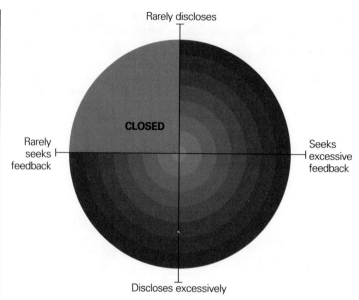

FIGURE 3.2 The closed communication style.

As Figure 3.2 indicates, communication with others is not high on the closed communicator's favorites list—they seek little feedback and disclose little information. In fact, people with a very large closed style not only feel uncomfortable around people, but they actually fear them.

Because closed people find it difficult to communicate their expectations to others, they are often disappointed by and disappointing to those around them. For example, the boss who expects closed employees to actively participate in group meetings and decision making will be disappointed. Asking their opinion in meetings does not make it easier for them to participate; instead, it increases their anxiety. Closed customers are often disappointed by salespeople (they really want to be led by the hand but are afraid to ask). If the product or service recommended by the salesperson turns out to be poor, rarely will closed customers openly complain. Instead, they may change stores without letting the store or the salesperson know why.

Closed people spend much of their energy in safety seeking to keep from looking like fools, being blamed for something, or even losing their jobs. One way closed people attempt to remain safe is to avoid making decisions. When decisions have to be made, they may use other safe procedures such as "going by the book," following tradition, and treating everyone alike. Actions taken by closed managers in an attempt to remain safe include treating all employees the same regardless of their performance, giving only brief, superficial employee appraisals (and then only when absolutely necessary), and never initiating upward communication.

REMEMBER

Closed Communicators . . .

At Their *Best* Are

- Productive as long as they can work in an environment free of interpersonal demands.
- Seen as reserved.
- Considered similar to the laissez-faire leader, who lets employees do whatever they want.

At Their *Worst* Are

- Likely to spend most of their energy looking for security; therefore, productivity is fairly low.
- Seen as difficult to get to know and unresponsive to needs of others.
- Thought to be aloof and noncommunicative.

Closed people can be quite productive as long as only minimal interaction with others is required. However, because of their communication anxiety, relationships with closed people are difficult—especially in the work environment. As a result, creative employees and employees who need guidance often become frustrated with the closed manager. On the other hand, other closed employees and highly trained and motivated employees who like to make their own decisions appreciate the closed manager.

To summarize, the closed style is most successful when little interpersonal interaction is required for the job, when going by the book is the preferred company stance, when subordinates are professionals who need little supervision, and when others in the department are closed or prefer things to people. The closed style is less successful when the job requires a high level of interpersonal interaction; when the organization is in a high-risk profession with creative, high-strung individuals; when subordinates need or want guidance; and when the profession or business is productivity-oriented.

The Blind Style

If you are looking for someone you can depend on to get the job done, someone to train a group of overconfident new hires, someone with the self-assurance to trouble-shoot a problem department, or someone who can command authority in a crisis, you couldn't do better than to hire a blind communicator. Whereas closed communicators would experience disabling anxiety in these situations, **blind style communicators** thrive in situations in which they can demonstrate their expertise and experience—does this sound like you?

As Figure 3.3 indicates, blind communicators tend to fall on the low-feedback and high-disclosure ends of the two continuums, which causes others to view them as authoritarian. As with closed people, blind communicators seldom ask for feedback, and yet they are the opposite of closed communicators in several ways. Instead of having a low self-image, blind communicators tend to be very confident (even overly confident) and are not afraid to express their views, expectations, or needs. People know where they stand with a blind communicator. Blind communicators don't ask

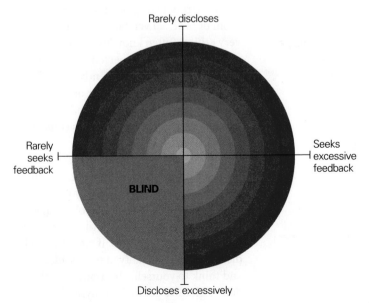

FIGURE 3.3 The blind communication style.

for feedback from others because they don't feel they need it; they already know what's best. Instead of avoiding others, blind communicators tend to overuse disclosure, telling others their opinions, how things should be done, and what others are doing wrong, even when their advice may not be wanted. For example, it's very difficult for blind managers to delegate responsibility. They want employees to *do* the work but do it the way they themselves would do it. Closed and blind communicators also differ in the way they handle conflict. Instead of ignoring conflict, blind communicators jump right in and solve the problem their way. Often, blind managers solve conflicts without asking for employee agreement or input.

Actually, blind communicators are often right when they say their ideas are better. They are usually experienced and very knowledgeable on the topic. But when people are not allowed to give feedback, to try things their way, or to make mistakes, they can't develop their potential. Therefore, even though blind managers are good trainers, they don't allow their employees the freedom to develop to the point where they can take over for the boss. When the manager is promoted or leaves, the organization usually discovers that there is no one within ready to fill the position.

Blind communicators are seen as very critical and demanding. For example, although blind managers mention employee strengths in appraisal sessions, they spend the majority of the time on weaknesses. Their comments probably don't include "face supportive" communication (Carson & Cupach, 2000)—comments and nonverbal gestures designed to show employee approval and give the employee some choices. In the same way, blind employees (feeling that their ideas are better than those of their bosses) are argumentative and have problems gracefully receiving criticism or orders. Even blind customers are very critical (often knowing more about a product than the salesperson) and are usually the first to tell their friends when they are unhappy with a particular organization. Such negative word-of-mouth advertising can reduce a company's business (Finkelman & Goland, 1990).

If you have blind tendencies, you have probably discovered that most people are not interested in the perfect way to do things. Most people want the job completed but are not impressed by all the hard work that "perfection" requires. If you often feel dismayed by the quality of others' ideas and think to yourself, "If I want something done right, I've got to do it myself," you are exhibiting blind tendencies.

© 2004 Ted Goff

"I don't have time to write performance reviews, so I'll just criticize you in public from time to time."

© 2004 Ted Goff. Reprinted by permission www.tedgoff.com

REMEMBER

Blind Communicators . . .

At Their *Best* Are

- Clear on what they want and where you stand with them—not afraid to exercise authority.
- Usually very loyal, organized, and dependable; others know the job will get done.
- Very helpful to those who want to learn as long as the help is appreciated.

At Their *Worst* Are

- Unable to delegate effectively.
- Very demanding and impatient; insist their way is best.
- Offer advice and criticism to others but unable to take it.
- Prefer to be in control at all times.
- Stifle growth and creativity of others by making most of the decisions.
- Expect others to mess things up ("To get things done right, do them yourself").
- Punish failure and mistakes.
- Often poor listeners.

Occasionally, a person who appears to be blind is really a very insecure, closed person who notices that blind communicators get more desired results (such as more job promotions) than closed ones and decides to try the blind style. Therefore, these people—we'll call them the **neurotic blind communicator**—hide their insecurity behind an authoritarian mask. Instead of the constructive criticism given by a blind manager, the neurotic blind manager's criticism is angry and includes unrealistic personal attacks. To hide the fact that they feel threatened by knowledgeable, hard-working employees, neurotic blind managers find a minor employee weakness and blow it out of proportion—often in front of other employees. Therefore, don't confuse the true blind communicator with the neurotic blind communicator. Blind communicators may be critical and demanding, but they appreciate quality work; neurotic blind communicators feel threatened by quality and are impossible to please.

To summarize, the blind style is most successful when untrained subordinates need the blind communicator's expertise, during a crisis or time of organizational change, or when an immediate decision is needed. The blind style is less successful when the organization has many personnel problems, when subordinates are professional people who expect to make their own decisions, or when creativity and risk taking are critical to the organization's success.

The Hidden Style

If you had to choose between an efficient, highly productive office in which people were friendly but not social, or a less efficient but social environment in which birthdays were celebrated, employees freely chatted while working, and everyone was treated as a family member, which would you pick? People with hidden tendencies prefer a social environment and want to be friendly with everyone. **Hidden style communicators** are interested in people, are good listeners, and are generally well liked. It's very important to them that everyone gets along and that conflicts are avoided. They are called "hidden" because they often hide their feelings and knowledge from others.

As Figure 3.4 indicates, hidden communicators fall on the low-disclosure, high-feedback ends of the two continuums. Although they like social

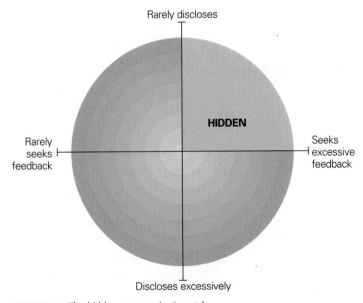

FIGURE 3.4 The hidden communication style.

environments, they find it difficult to disclose their opinions and expectations to others. For example, a hidden boss may cover only strengths in an employee appraisal and skip over weaknesses; a hidden employee may be unable to disagree with an unfair comment from the boss during an appraisal; and a hidden customer may agree with a salesperson's suggestions even if they don't reflect what the customer prefers.

Don't confuse the hidden communicator with the closed communicator. Hidden communicators are not afraid of people, and they don't hide from them. They do listen carefully to others and ask them how they feel, but tend to keep their own opinions and feelings private—does this sound like you?

Why do hidden-style people hide their opinions and feelings from others? They are motivated by *mistrust of people* or by the *desire for social acceptance*—or even both. Hidden people who tend to mistrust others feel more comfortable when they know what people are up to; they want to find out what is going on and to get feedback—someone is bound to let something slip. For example, a hidden customer who is motivated by mistrust will be suspicious that the salesperson is taking advantage in some way and will try to confirm these suspicions by asking questions.

Hidden people who are motivated by the desire for social acceptance want, above all, to please others. For example, hidden managers feel that keeping people happy is more important than productivity. After all, employee complaints can get you fired; moderate productivity usually doesn't. Hidden customers who are motivated by a desire for social acceptance would rather deal with friendly, sociable salespeople even if they have to pay more for the product.

Hidden people often *appear* to be sharing because they ask questions and stimulate others to share, thereby disguising their lack of disclosure. Hidden people disclose only on impersonal, safe topics and don't disagree with others. Hidden employees often appear overly friendly and eager to please ("yes" people). Hidden managers create the facade of being open in meetings when important decisions are to be made, but they usually speak up only after the majority opinion is clear or the top bosses' views are known. Hidden people fear conflict and disagreement and try to smooth over any discord.

As you can see, relationships with hidden people are basically one-way; hidden people do most of the listening, while others do most of the sharing. Often, when others realize this, they withdraw their trust or at least stop confiding as much to the hidden person.

To summarize, the hidden style is most successful when a social environment is expected; when the climate of the organization makes caution and political maneuvering necessary; when teamwork is a social occasion and rarely involves problem solving; and when adequate performance is all that is expected. The hidden style is less successful when the climate is more work oriented than social; when tasks require a high degree of trust among workers; when tasks are complex and involve team problem solving; and when excellent performance is expected.

REMEMBER

Hidden Communicators . . .

At Their *Best* Are

- Well liked, fun to be around, organizers of social events.
- Concerned with people and willing to listen.
- Busy smoothing over minor conflicts and keeping a happy office.

At Their *Worst* Are

- Suspicious of the motives of others.
- Not really interested in quality; adequate performance accepted.
- "Yes" people; pretend to agree to be liked.
- Unable to disclose opinions and ideas that might be rejected.
- Not always loyal and appear as two-faced.

The Open Style

Open style communicators tend to use both disclosure and feedback and are equally interested in people's needs and company productivity. Of the four styles, open communicators are the ones who most appreciate other people (closed communicators are nervous around people, blind communicators tend to view others as relatively unimportant, and hidden communicators don't always trust people). As Figure 3.5 indicates, open communicators fall on the high-disclosure, high-feedback ends of the two continuums. In fact, they may disclose too much too often and may ask for too much feedback. This type of forward communication makes many people uncomfortable—like the stranger sitting next to you on an airplane who tells you all about his or her family, latest surgery, and marital affair.

For most open people, the problem is not that they are too open but that they are too open too soon. In *The Open Organization*, Steele (1975) warns that the order in which we disclose different aspects of ourselves will determine how others react to us. For instance, new members of a group should first show their responsible, concerned side. When this stance results in their acceptance, then they can start to show their less perfect aspects and even make a critical observation. These same aspects or observations could get a nonmember rejected out of hand. For example, mentioning a problem you observed to your colleagues when you are a new hire of less than a week would likely get more of a negative response than if you had worked for the company 2 to 3 months. In new environments, open employees need to listen and observe others to determine the openness of the climate. Openness is most effective when it produces a gradual sharing with others.

Open people are generally sensitive to the needs of others and realize that conflict can be productive. Open managers are more likely to empower employees to take active roles in the affairs of the organization. These empowered employees usually develop quality relationships and increase productivity. Generally, "employees in open, supportive climates are satisfied employees" (Conrad & Poole, 2005, p. 144; see also Daft & Marcic, 2009, Chapter 12).

Revisiting the Case Study

What type of relationships and trust do you think existed at AIG prior to the bailout? Do you think it is realistic that the CEO of AIG has never met his own executive vice president whom he sent a bonus check for close to $1 million?

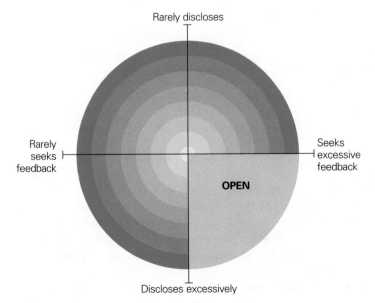

FIGURE 3.5 The open communication style.

Open Communicators . . .

At Their *Best* Are

- Flexible in meeting needs and using communication styles.
- Give and receive both praise and criticism.
- Genuinely like others and listen carefully.
- Seen as trusting, friendly, and dependable.
- Willing to share feelings, as well as knowledge.
- Productive.
- Empower others through team decisions and feedback.

At Their *Worst* Are

- Seen as ineffective managers especially by blind bosses.
- Frustrated by lack of creative opportunities under nonopen bosses.
- Impatient with time needed to implement organizational changes.
- So open that others feel uncomfortable around them.
- Open at inappropriate times.

Please do not assume from what has been said so far that the open style is advocated in all situations. *If* the organization's climate is open, *if* upper management favors the open style, *if* employees and managers are basically open, and *if* customers appreciate an open style, then the open style is appropriate. Within reason, the more open we are, the better communicators we are likely to be because we are better able to share our frames of reference and expectations with others. Many organizations, however, do not have an open climate. Upper management may not approve of open managers and may fail to promote them. Some employees may be uncomfortable around open managers and consider their requests for employee input as proof that they cannot make decisions. Some customers consider open salespeople as pushy or even nosy. In other words, what is too open for one group may be just right for another.

In general, a moderately open style is most successful when employee involvement in decision making is desired; when change is welcomed as a new opportunity; when tasks are complex and require teamwork; when quality work is expected; and when the organization is involved in global communication using one of the transformational

Communicator Styles

To check your knowledge of the four communicator styles, take the following quiz. Compare your answers to those at the back of this book. You can also take this quiz online and see the answers via your Premium Website for *Communicating for Results*.

Directions: Identify the communicator style each question describes: (A) closed, (B) blind, (C) hidden, or (D) open.

1. Which style employee prefers not to take any part in office discussions?
2. Which style employee has trouble accepting criticism and is usually argumentative?
3. Which style communicator may make others feel uncomfortable by using too much feedback and too much disclosure?
4. Which style customer prefers to deal with sociable salespeople even at the risk of paying more for the product?
5. Which style person more likely communicates expectations to others?
6. Which style communicator is motivated by mistrust of others?
7. Which style communicator uses too little feedback and too much disclosure?
8. Which style communicator is more likely to take responsibility for his or her mistakes?
9. Which style manager tends to concentrate more on an employee's strengths than weaknesses during an appraisal session?
10. Which style communicator prefers working with things to working with people?

models. The open style is less successful when upper managers or workers view the open style negatively; when tasks are extremely simple and require no teamwork; and when an immediate decision is needed. The key to good communication is *flexibility* of styles. There is a big difference between being closed, blind, hidden, or open because that is the style we generally use and deliberately choosing a certain style because it best suits the needs of the individual or group with whom we are dealing.

Practical Tips for Relating to People of Different Styles

The chances are that you have a boss, a coworker, or a customer with whom you have some difficulty communicating. If their communication style differs from yours, your expectations are probably different, which makes the relationship difficult to develop and maintain and negative self-fulfilling prophecies more likely. This section offers some advice on how to communicate with people of different styles. Remember, no one person exemplifies any one style perfectly; therefore, the advice should be taken as a guide to understanding, not as the complete answer to communication problems.

Closed Communication Style

- ***How to communicate with closed managers:***

  Carefully. Don't threaten them or increase their insecurity.

  Don't ask them questions. Ask other employees or make the decision yourself if you can do so quietly.

  Don't make waves, and downplay new procedures you develop.

  Don't expect any praise, guidance, criticism, or help from the boss. You may have to provide these for yourself.

- ***How to communicate with closed employees:***

  Put closed employees in environments that feel safe: ones with little interaction with others, little responsibility, and specific instructions about how, what, when, and where.

  Explain all policy changes face to face, before they hear rumors.

  Make the chain of command clear. To whom are they responsible?

  Limit criticism. They are overcritical of themselves already.

  Avoid interest in their personal concerns or family; it may threaten them.

  Don't expect their participation in meetings or appraisal interviews.

- ***How to communicate with closed customers:***

  Don't expect them to openly express what they really want (you must look for it).

  Help them make good choices; you could have a customer for life.

  Try to increase their sense of self-confidence by complimenting them on previous product choices.

  Avoid technical jargon; they may be overwhelmed by it.

  A flip chart presentation (see Chapter 13) may give them a sense of security.

  Avoid a team presentation; it may increase their insecurity.

  Treat them with respect; don't take advantage of them.

Blind Communication Style

- ***How to communicate with blind managers:***

  Take their criticism well and expect to learn from them. (Blind bosses often have extensive knowledge and training.)

  Meet the blind manager's expectations: Give proper respect.

  Be at work on time each day.

  Get projects in on time.

  Make projects neat, well supported, and accurate.

  Follow appropriate channels even if the boss does not; expect and give loyalty.

  Accept that your proposals will be changed by the boss.

  Review each stage of an assigned project face to face with the boss.

  Ask questions to see what information the boss has assumed you already know and to determine whether the boss already has a "correct" solution in mind.

  Appeal to the boss's self-confidence: "We need your help." "You've had a lot of experience in this, what do you think?" Let the blind manager feel in control. (Blind managers seldom care for quality circles, in which employees take on responsibilities.)

  Remember that if you get on the wrong side of a blind manager, it is very difficult to get off.

  Many blind managers tend to dislike any proposal (even those not in their area) that failed to get their backing before being made public. If any blind managers have power to hurt or help your idea, then get them behind it before you formally submit it.

  If the boss is a neurotic blind type (a closed boss pretending to be blind), expect personal attacks on your ego. The neurotic blind boss feels threatened by both logical appeals and well-researched, intelligent proposals. Therefore, your only survival mechanism may be to play dumb.

- ***How to communicate with blind employees:***

  Expect that blind employees are very self-assured.

  Often argumentative; take criticism poorly; blunt.

  Usually not team players but know the rules of the game and can play when it is to their advantage.

  Respectful of power and have little respect for those without it.

  Often, hard workers with little respect for those who do a less-than-competent job.

  Encourage blind employees to deal with others more flexibly because these employees could well become managers in the future; show them that you will reward team involvement.

  Let them see that you are in charge but that you appreciate the skills and knowledge of others.

  If possible, let them be in complete charge of a project. (You will still need to follow up and maintain some control.)

- ***How to communicate with blind customers:***

  Give a polished, well-supported sales presentation.

  Avoid reading a canned flip chart presentation; it will probably insult them.

A team approach, if professional, will probably impress them.

Be prepared for suggestions on how to improve your selling technique.

Blind customers like to feel in control; let them feel that they negotiated an exceptional deal (they probably did).

Don't keep them waiting.

Hidden Communication Style

- **How to communicate with hidden managers:**

  Expect the following: If you are too knowledgeable or have come from another department, you may be considered a spy.

  The boss will probably play politics and may not always be loyal.

  You will not always know where you stand.

  The boss is usually well liked, listens well, and is sympathetic.

  Don't expect the boss to disclose fully. Watch for nonverbal signs that the boss could say more.

  Lead into the topic yourself. ("I'm not sure about last week's presentation. Where do you think I need to improve?")

  Show how your work or ideas will bring recognition to the department and thus to the boss who wants social acceptance.

  Subtly bring your work to the attention of the boss's colleagues or superiors or get yourself appointed to an important committee. If other managers approve of your work, the boss who wants social acceptance will also approve (at least outwardly).

  Assure the mistrustful boss that you don't want his or her job.

  If appropriate, publicly applaud the boss for special accomplishments and occasions (such as a birthday).

  Don't be afraid to use tactful confrontation; the boss will often back down.

- **How to communicate with hidden employees motivated by desire for social acceptance:**

  Expect these employees to be "yes" people because they believe that pleasing you and others is the way to success.

  Motivate them by public praise (but criticism given in private), posting their names on a wall chart, asking them to give special talks, and other actions that will enhance their social acceptance.

  Show that you feel positive toward them.

- **How to communicate with hidden employees motivated by lack of trust:**

  Realize that hidden employees are hard to spot because they have learned how to play the game and appear open, are good listeners, and participate in group situations.

  It is difficult to get these employees to be team players because work experience or family training has taught them to express only the most acceptable ideas.

  Demonstrate (by promotions and performance appraisals) that honest team cooperation is the way to get ahead.

  Establish a climate in which differing opinions will not be penalized.

Expect your comments to be searched for a double meaning. Be specific; use examples; don't assume meanings are clear.

- ***How to communicate with hidden customers:***

   Spend time establishing a friendly feeling before giving your pitch.

   Share some bit of knowledge or a confidence to start the sharing, trusting cycle.

   Hidden customers will be more likely to buy if they feel the purchase will improve their social standing and acceptance.

   Use referral. They are more likely to buy if they feel that others they respect are sold on the idea, product, or service. Tell them that so-and-so recommended that you call them or that so-and-so is really happy with the item. (The customer may call to verify your statements.)

   Listen carefully and keep your opinions out of the picture (at least until the client's views are known) because hidden customers may say they agree even if they don't. For example, a real estate agent says to client, "I just love formal dining areas, don't you?" The client, despite not liking formal dining areas, agrees, but then rejects house after house for no apparent reason.

Open Communication Style

- ***How to communicate with open managers:***

   Be honest and open, but use tact.

   Look at all sides of a problem.

   Don't hesitate to share job feelings, doubts, or concerns.

   Share part of your personal life; follow the boss's lead.

   Accept shared responsibility and power.

- ***How to communicate with open employees:***

   Share confidences; open employees respond well. Examples of topics to share are your commitment to the company, hopes for recognition, aspirations within the organization, and probable length of stay in the department.

   Place them in an environment in which some friendships can develop.

   Give them constructive criticism; they usually want to improve and are the first to sign up for special courses offered by the company.

   Give them challenging tasks; they want to achieve.

   Praise them for work well done.

   Employees who are too open may talk too much, but don't assume that people can't talk and work at the same time. Some talkative employees are more productive than quiet ones.

- ***How to communicate with open customers:***

   Don't be pushy or manipulative.

   Listen carefully to their needs and wants; they are usually able to articulate them well. Build your persuasive appeals around these needs.

   Treat them as equals; don't talk down or defer to them.

   Canned flip chart presentations may be tolerated but are normally not impressive.

   Open customers are less impressed by flashiness and more impressed by facts. Brief demonstrations can work well.

ETHICAL DILEMMA

Blogging is one way that people develop relationships and share information about their lives with others. As indicated in the Zit's cartoon, bloggers share all kinds of information both good and bad in a kind of online diary. Eight percent of American Internet users kept a blog in 2006, which was around 12 million adults (Lenhart & Fox, 2006). As the number of people using blogs grows, so is the number of people getting fired for the information in their blogs—approximately 10% of companies surveyed have fired at least one employee for comments made on a blog (Singel, 2007). Take for example, Mark Jen, a new Google employee, who decided to chronicle his experiences posting both the good and the not so good. He even discussed Google's health benefits package which he said wasn't as good as Microsoft's—he was fired (Palan, 2008). Or Peter Whitney who worked as an administrative assistant for a brokerage owned by Wells Fargo and wrote about personal and work-related issues on his blog. One thing he remembers including is his unhappiness about being asked to contribute to a birthday card for a manager

he disliked—he was fired (Wallack, 2005). Ellen Simonetti, a Delta Airlines flight attendant was also fired after including on her blog "inappropriate pictures" of herself in uniform while onboard an airplane. She was just having fun she stated.

All these individuals were surprised that their blogs were discovered; they were just writing for family and friends, they thought. The Pew/Internet survey by Lenhart and Fox found that 49% of bloggers "believe that their blog readership is mostly made up of people they personally know" (p. 19). How to Blog Safely (2005) warns that the people that find your site "may be the people you'd least want or expect. These include potential or current employers, coworkers, and professional colleagues; your neighbors; your spouse or partner; your family; and anyone else curious enough to type your name, e-mail address or screen name into Google or Feedster and click a few links." Because only 55% of bloggers use a pseudonym (Lenhart & Fox, 2006, p. 10), more firings are sure to occur.

QUESTIONS: What about the decision to fire these employees? Was their desire to relate with others by sharing information by blog a breach of ethics? If so, did it warrant such drastic action? If not, what action would you recommend and why?

Becoming Flexible in Use of Styles

Is your communication style (or styles) and the way you typically manage conflict appropriate to your work environment? (If you have not yet done so, take the Survey of Communication Styles discussed on page 68.) As a result of your self-analysis, you may have found some discrepancies between your style and your work environment—in other words, some communication problems.

If you discovered some discrepancies, you may be down to two choices: either change your job (remember, we tend to become like the environment in which we spend our time) or adapt your style. The latter is a good choice even if a job change is in order; **flexibility** may well be your key to effective communication wherever you work. However, I don't recommend that you try a complete style change, at least not all at once. Before making any change, you should get enough feedback to be sure that a change is warranted and then start gradually. Adapt some of your responses to mirror those used by a person with a different style. When you feel comfortable with that new behavior, try another one. Communication behaviors can be changed, but not without hard work and patience. Few people find it easy to break an old habit. For example, a person with strong blind tendencies can learn to communicate in an open style and even solve conflict in a collaborative manner but will normally retain some blind behaviors, especially in times of stress.

Adapting or changing a style will require changes in your use of feedback, disclosure, or both:

- The person with *blind tendencies* needs to ask for more feedback from others to discover areas needing change.

- The person with *hidden tendencies* needs to disclose more and should slowly begin to share more information, opinions, and feelings with others.

- People with *closed or open styles* need to work equally on both feedback and disclosure; the closed person to use more of each, and the overly open person to use less of each.

Using Feedback Effectively

Guidelines for getting and using feedback are covered in Chapter 1. If you wish to improve your effectiveness in using feedback, a quick review of that section of the chapter should prove helpful. Remember when giving feedback to others, it should (a) be directed toward behavior rather than toward the person, (b) be descriptive rather than evaluative, (c) involve sharing ideas rather than giving advice, (d) include only as much information as the person can handle at one time, and (e) be well timed. Because an unusual interest in feedback may be viewed with suspicion by those who know you, move slowly, identify the specific type of feedback you want, and tell them why you want it. Remember also that you must accept any feedback in a positive manner. A negative or defensive response will convince others that being open with you is too dangerous.

Using Disclosure Effectively

For most people, disclosure is more difficult than feedback to use effectively. Many of us have grown up believing such statements as "It is better to keep silent and be thought a fool than open your mouth and remove all doubt" and "If you want to get ahead in business, keep your mouth shut." Many people who do disclose engage only in small talk or discussion of public information. They are still hidden when it comes to revealing and sharing personal information, feelings, and ideas.

Although both men and women appreciate the importance of disclosing in personal and work relationships, the way they accomplish it and the fears they have about it often differ (Floyd & Parks, 1995; Rosenfeld, 1979; Wright, 1982, 2006).

For example, men's primary concern about disclosure is loss of control; women are more concerned with personal harm and damaged relationships. Women are more likely to disclose feelings verbally and to appreciate verbal disclosure; men disclose feelings less by talking and more by doing. Therefore, women are more likely to disclose face-to-face whereas men are more likely to disclose side by side while completing an activity.

It is probably a good idea to be careful in using disclosure. In some climates, fears about the consequences of disclosure would probably be justified. In open climates, however, fear should be replaced by mild concern about when to disclose, how much to disclose, and with whom to disclose. Remember, "healthy relationships are built on self-disclosure" (Johnson, 2002, p. 233). In considering when and how to use disclosure:

Use Disclosure Only for the Purpose of Establishing and Developing Strong Interpersonal Relationships Although disclosure is a complex process (Dindia, 1994; Spencer, 1994), we are more likely to make disclosures to people we like, and we tend to like people who disclose with us more than those who do not (Worthy et al., 1969). Therefore, disclosure is necessary for a relationship to develop (Johnson, 2002). If a relationship is weak or dying, self-disclosure may not be considered worth the effort.

Disclosure Should Be Mutually Shared A healthy relationship cannot develop when only one person discloses. All people involved in the relationship must be willing to trust the others and to share openly with them. There is a reciprocal aspect to disclosure: People seem to view disclosure as rewarding and feel obligated to reciprocate (Worthy et al., 1969). If one person increases the amount of disclosure, so do the others (Cozby, 1973). The surest way to get others to disclose with you is to disclose with them. Disclosure normally results in trust and respect (Wheeless & Grotz, 1977), and people who trust each other are more likely to disclose (McAllister, 1980). However, the listener (using his or her own frame of reference) must perceive your comments to be disclosure to feel obligated to reciprocate (Montgomery, 1984).

Disclosure Naturally Involves a Certain Amount of Risk When you offer your opinions, ideas, and feelings to coworkers or your boss, you become more vulnerable to attack because they could use such knowledge against you. But if disclosure has been mutual, all members of the relationship are equally vulnerable. Although there is risk involved with disclosure, disclosure is necessary for quality relationships to develop.

Disclosure Should Be a Gradual Process In a new group, it is a good idea to avoid any discussion of task problems until the group has a chance to build cohesion (Steele, 1975). Similarly, to maintain a good image when you are the new member in a group, you should begin with more conservative disclosures. Relationships do not happen overnight. A truly open relationship may take months or years to develop fully. It would be a mistake to open up suddenly and dump your feelings on someone; the other person would probably wonder what game you were playing. Be cautious—lead up to disclosure slowly (Miell & Duck, 1986). If you are in the medical field, be aware that patients need to build up to an embarrassing disclosure and many of them don't get to it until the healthcare provider has a hand on the doorknob ready to leave (du Pre, 2000). Pay attention to others' nonverbal reactions. They will tell you if you are moving too fast or disclosing inappropriate information. Wait for your disclosures to be reciprocated before you disclose more. Someone must be willing to risk the first step. In organizations with an open climate, the managers generally should take the first step. When managers are open and supportive, employees tend to follow their lead.

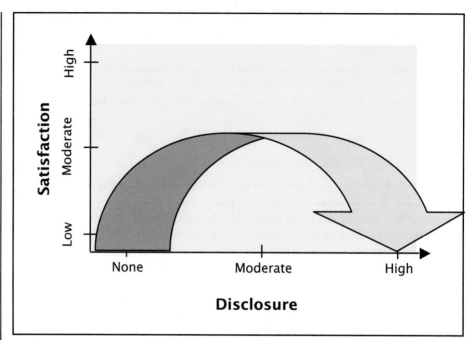

FIGURE 3.6 Curvilinear relationship between satisfaction and disclosure.

Communicate at a Moderate Level of Disclosure Although some researchers in the 1960s and early 1970s advocated full disclosure within relationships, today's researchers have found that high disclosure may be perceived by others as inappropriate and that moderate disclosure has more positive outcomes (Lombardo & Wood, 1979; Petronio, 1991). High levels of disclosure occur in relatively few communication transactions (Bochner, 1984) and even less in the business environment (Pearce & Sharp, 1973). According to Shirley Gilbert (1976), the relationship between disclosure and satisfaction is a **curvilinear relationship**, meaning that satisfaction is low when disclosure is both low and high; it is best when disclosure is at a moderate level (see Figure 3.6). Women typically find it easier to disclosure personal information than men (Punyanunt-Carter, 2006) and not all cultures view self-disclosure (even moderate disclosure) as a positive influence on relationships. For example, Chinese people tend to view disclosure as rude or in poor taste, whereas Japanese people often prefer to "put on a 'good face'" rather than risk displeasing another and may actually say yes when they really mean no (Caputo et al., 2000, p. 108).

Managing Conflicts in Business Relationships

By now, you know the importance of relationships in the workplace and should have a good idea of which communication styles you generally use in your daily business communication. Another way to verify your preferred communication style is to determine how you manage conflict. According to a survey conducted in 2000, "handling conflicts and managing workplace relationships were the issues that most seriously threatened productivity" (Murtha, 2005, p. 42).

Conflict is impossible to avoid. Whenever we deal with individuals or teams for any length of time, some kind of conflict is sure to occur. Fortunately, if managed effectively, conflict can result in improved team relationships, communication, and productivity (Chen et al., 2005; Frantz & Jin, 1995). The discussion of conflict will begin by looking at two types of conflict, then move on to five conflict strategies, look at when and how to use each strategy, and finally, compare U.S. responses to conflict with strategy preferences of other countries.

Conflict Types

Teams experience two basic types of conflict: A-type and C-type (Amason et al., 1995). **A-type conflict** is relationship conflict and sidetracks the team from the issues and creates defensiveness and anger; the *A* stands for affective or emotional. **C-type conflict** is task conflict and improves team productivity and relationships and creates a feeling of satisfaction; the *C* stands for cognitive. Although it seems obvious that teams should strive for C-type and avoid A-type, it's not as easy as it sounds. If team members have a strong relationship and trust each other, C-type conflict works well. During cognitive conflict, team members are open to serious debate and disagreement on the issues. They come prepared to support their ideas with facts, experiences, and solutions but don't take it personally when someone disagrees with them. A basic ground rule for successful C-type conflict is "ideas are separate from the person." Another ground rule is that feedback that is often in the form of a question should be *descriptive* (tactfully honest and objective), not *evaluative* (judgmental and accusatory); see Chapter 1 for more details. Comments might include "How will this design work for someone in a wheelchair?" or "This idea is a good start to our problem; can it be designed to stay in our limited budget? C-type groups can experience negative conflict occasionally; when this happens, one of the conflict strategies discussed in the next section can be used.

When team members do not have a strong relationship and trust is weak, A-type conflict will likely occur, especially when group members are emotional attached to the topic. In affective conflict, members may feel awkward giving and receiving feedback, and disagreements often become personal with people getting angry or avoiding comments entirely. When anger occurs, it distracts us from "relevant cognitive processing" (Zillmann, 1994). And, of course, making no comments at all is nonproductive. Feedback in A-type conflict tends to be evaluative, and comments might include "You apparently have no compassion for people in wheelchairs" or "You obviously haven't looked at our budget carefully enough—that design will be way too expensive!" or "No one likes my idea, as usual."

Teams with A-type conflict spend most of their energy dealing with emotions instead of solving complex problems and arriving at innovative ideas. Although the conflict strategies discussed next might help, the chance that A-type teams will be productive is slim unless definite steps are taken to provide change. Suggestions include bringing in a new leader from outside the team, replacing some of the members with people who work well with C-type conflict, or (this one probably has the best chance of working) providing relationship and trust-building training for the team. An excellent story of how this can be done is included in *The Five Dysfunctions of a Team* by Patrick Lencioni (2002).

Conflict Strategies

Each communication style (i.e., closed, blind, hidden, and open) tends to use a different **conflict strategy**, meaning they handle conflict differently. Take a moment and think how you typically handle conflict. When conflict occurs, are you more likely to (a) withdraw from it, (b) give in to others' wishes,

Revisiting the Case Study

What type of conflict strategy was DeSantis using when he took it upon himself to resign in such a public manner using a major newspaper's opinion page? Do you think he was expecting a win-win outcome?

(c) implement compromise, (d) convince others your way is best, or (e) search for a solution agreeable to all? Figure 3.7 illustrates these five strategies of avoidance, accommodation, compromise, competition, and collaboration (Kilmann & Thomas, 1975; Rahim & Magner, 1995; see also Thomas, 1992a, 1992b). Other researchers use slightly different terms. For example, in their well-known conflict grid, Robert Blake and Jane Mouton (1985) refer to the five strategies as withdrawal, smoothing, compromising, forcing, and problem solving. Compromise may be used by communicators of any style; the other four strategies correspond to specific communication styles.

As Figure 3.7 illustrates, the way you deal with conflict depends on the extent of your concern for self (low to high assertiveness) and for others (low to high cooperativeness). Which of the following methods of handling conflict best describes the way you typically resolve conflict? The way your manager, employees, or team resolve conflict?

Avoiding/Withdrawal

By employing the **avoiding strategy**, this person:

- Feels equally little concern for others and for self; places low value on both assertiveness and cooperation.

- Maintains neutrality at all costs; views conflict as a worthless and punishing experience.

- Removes self either physically or mentally from groups experiencing any type of conflict; stays away from any situation that might possibly produce conflict.

- Tends to communicate in the closed style.

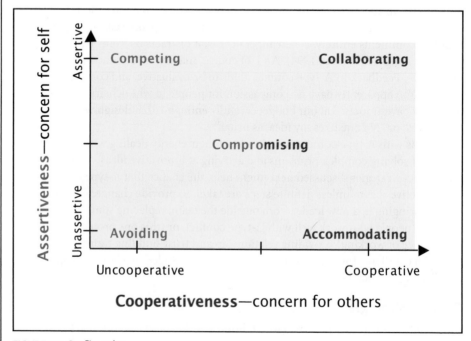

FIGURE 3.7 Conflict styles.
(Adapted from K. W. Thomas, 1992, "Conflict and Conflict Management: Reflections and Update," *Journal of Organizational Behavior, 13*, pp. 265–274.)

Accommodating/Smoothing

By employing the **accommodating strategy**, this person:

- Feels a higher concern for others than for self and, therefore, values cooperation over assertiveness.
- Views open conflict as destructive; gives in to the will of others when necessary.
- Believes that surface harmony is important to maintain good relationships and receive personal acceptance; tries to smooth over or ignore conflicts in an attempt to keep everyone happy.
- Tends to communicate in the hidden style.

Compromising

By employing the **compromising strategy**, this person:

- Takes a middle-of-the-road stance on assertiveness and cooperation and believes that a high-quality solution is not as important as a workable or agreeable solution.
- Views conflict as solvable but uses voting and other methods of compromise as a way to avoid direct confrontation.
- Tries to find a solution that everyone can live with, although all parties must sacrifice something important to reach a compromise.
- Usually views compromise as a second choice; may communicate in any style (i.e., closed, blind, hidden, or open).

Competing/Forcing

By employing the **competing strategy**, this person:

- Views personal goals as much more important than the goals of others; therefore, values assertiveness (even force when necessary) over cooperation.
- Views conflict as a win-lose situation or as a contest of power: One person must fail so the other can succeed; compromise is not acceptable.
- Has great respect for power and will submit to arbitration only because the arbitrator's power is greater.
- Tends to communicate in the blind style.

Collaborating/Problem-Solving

By employing the **collaborating strategy**, this person:

- Gives equal consideration to others and self; values high cooperation and assertiveness.
- Views conflict as beneficial if handled openly; lays all cards on the table.
- Guides groups through the basic problem-solving procedure (see Chapter 9).
- Attempts to reach a consensus; willing to spend a great deal of time and effort to achieve consensus.
- Tends to communicate in the open style.

Although individuals (regardless of their cultural background) may use any of the preceding methods to resolve conflict, it is interesting to note that Western cultures (like the United States and Canada) often select different strategies than Eastern cultures (like Japan, China, and Taiwan) when solving conflict (Ting-Toomey et al., 1991). Ting-Toomey (1988) found that competition was preferred by Americans, accommodation by the Chinese, and avoidance by the Taiwanese.

Choosing the Best Conflict Strategies

When selecting a conflict strategy for a specific situation, consider (a) the strategy you feel the most comfortable using, (b) the strategy your organization or team prefers, and (c) the advantages and disadvantages of each strategy. Each conflict strategy is productive in some cases and best avoided in others (Amason, 1996; Conrad & Poole, 2005; Thomas, 1992a, 1992b). In the words of Johnston and Gao (2009), "No one seems to benefit if they stick to one style" (p. 106).

Avoiding

Avoiding (withdrawal) may be the best response to conflict when:

- The issue is trivial.
- Power relationships make successful resistance impossible.
- Parties lack the communication skills necessary to prevent destructive escalations.
- Potential losses from an open conflict outweigh potential gains.
- There is insufficient time to gather needed information or to work through the issue adequately (Conrad & Poole, 2005, p. 325).

The drawback to handling conflict by avoidance is that the confrontation is usually only delayed or transferred to another issue.

Accommodating

Accommodating (smoothing) may be the best response to conflict when:

- The issue is minor.
- The damage to the relationship would harm both parties.

Creasource/Corbis

If managed effectively, conflict can result in improved group communication and productivity.

- A temporary reduction in conflict is needed to give time for additional research or information.

- Tempers are too hot for productive discussion.

The drawback to handling conflict by accommodation is that it only temporarily solves the problem; it's like putting a bandage on a cut that requires stitches.

Competing

Competing (forcing) may be the best response to conflict when:

- A decision or action must be immediate.

- The parties in the conflict expect and appreciate the force and power necessary in a win-lose situation.

- The combatants recognize the power relationship between themselves.

The drawbacks to handling conflict by force are (a) the real cause of the conflict is usually not resolved, and (b) the solution may be only temporary; when the losers gain more power, they may reinstate the conflict.

Compromising

Compromising may be the best response to conflict when:

- Both parties stand to gain.

- An "ideal" or "quality" solution is not required.

- Time is short.

- A temporary solution is needed for a complex problem (with a problem-solving discussion held later to determine the best solution).

- The parties in the conflict are equals.

The drawbacks to handling conflict by compromise are that everyone loses something, and the best solution is probably not reached.

Collaborating

Collaborating (problem solving) may be the best response to conflict when:

- Members are trained in problem solving.

- The parties have common goals that require everyone's cooperation.

- The conflict has arisen from misunderstandings or communication breakdown and parties are willing to reframe their conflict in a new manner.

- The conflict occurs during a crisis.

One drawback to collaboration is that it may not be successful when the parties have different values or goals. For example, a person who feels that conflict should be resolved in a competitive manner has goals and values completely opposed to the "everyone wins" view of the collaborator. Another drawback to the collaboration is that it usually takes longer to achieve than other strategies.

One final thought about choosing the best conflict strategy comes from Raymond Friedmanand his colleagues (Friedman, et al., 2000) whose research combined A-type (task) and C-type (affective or relationship) conflict with conflict strategies. They found:

- Collaborating reduces both C-type conflict and A-type conflict. However, because C-type conflict usually creates A-type, it must be handled carefully.

Simons and Peterson (2000) suggest that high levels of trust can keep A-type conflict from developing when group members are emotionally involved in the task outcome.

- Avoiding and competing increase C-type conflict, which almost always results in an increase in A-type conflict as well.

- Accommodating decreases A-type conflict and the stress that goes with it; however, because people who use this strategy do not assert their own needs, C-type conflict remains.

Reaching Consensus in Conflict Management

The five conflict strategies previously discussed can be divided among three categories according to type of outcome (Weaver, 1984):

- **Win-lose**. Only one party achieves objective. Competition and voting are examples of the win-lose category.

- **Lose-lose**. Neither party achieves objective, or both get only a small part of what they wanted. Compromise, arbitration, accommodation, and avoidance are examples of the lose-lose category.

- **Win-win**. All parties receive acceptable gains. Collaboration and consensus are examples of the win-win category.

Although all of these strategies can be used to handle conflict, the most productive and satisfying over the long run is usually collaboration (Friedman et al., 2000; Thomas, 1992b). The collaborating problem solver (who values both assertiveness and cooperation) helps the group reach a **consensus**, that is, all members agree to accept a specific decision even though some members originally preferred a different choice. They agree to this final decision either because they have come to like it better than their original choice or because they feel their original choice, although not selected, was given a fair hearing.

Of course, sometimes it is impossible to reach a consensus. But keep in mind that settling for just any solution could be worse than no solution. If the group seems to have reached a stalemate—that is, if collaboration appears impossible—try the following procedure before yielding to compromise or force:

1. *Clarify the situation.* Include such comments as "We seem to have reached an impasse. Further discussion along the same lines would be a waste of time. Let's try a new approach."

2. *Urge the person or group to set the two conflicting solutions aside temporarily and to pretend they do not exist.*

3. *Guide the person or group to seek new solutions through brainstorming or the two-step nominal group technique.* (The rules for these procedures are covered in Chapter 9.) Once a new list has been created, work with the person or group to evaluate these solutions and select the best one.

4. Finally, *join the person or group in comparing the original two solutions with the new solution to see which of the three is now the best.* Often, the new solution is more creative and effective than either of the original conflicting solutions and is selected as the new best solution.

This four-step procedure is not a compromise because no concessions are required to reach a consensus agreement. The discussants believe that the new solution is better than the original solutions and usually wonder why they didn't think of it sooner. If a consensus is still not possible, the conflict will have to be resolved by another method—perhaps compromise, mediation, or even force.

Cultural Differences in Conflict Management

Michael Keaton's character in the movie *Gung Ho*, is an excellent example of communication problems that can occur when organizations attempt to conduct business with people from other cultures and countries. In an effort to save a failing automobile-assembly factory in Pennsylvania, Keaton flies to Japan to try to persuade a Japanese company to invest in a joint venture. However, he knows nothing about the Japanese culture; he shows up alone, is late, is dressed informally, speaks informally, and makes jokes. He is met with silence and stony faces. He has no idea what he has done wrong. Do you?

Global teams don't always view conflict in the same way as Western teams. Even so, C-type conflict is possible.

Not all cultures view conflict and conflict strategies discussed above in the same way. In fact, it's probably safe to say that no two cultures (even those within our own country) are identical in how they view conflict and conflict resolution. Yet, understanding these differences, as well as, similarities is crucial to business and team success. It would be impossible to discuss every culture's differences, but we can identify several similarities and differences by looking at two dimensions: individualistic—collectivistic cultures and low context—high context cultures.

Western cultures like the United States tend to be **individualistic cultures** because the individual and individual rights are valued more highly than group identity or group rights. Asian cultures like Japan tend to be **collectivistic cultures** because they put more value on group membership, group obligations, and group goals than on the individual. Individualistic cultures are problem oriented; collectivistic cultures are more relationship oriented. Individualistic cultures value autonomy, assertiveness, and democracy and prefer competing strategies (Triandis, 1995), although they also use collaborating and compromising to solve problems. Collectivistic cultures value empathy and listening and prefer avoiding and accommodating strategies to preserve friendships and save face for themselves and others (Choi, 1991; Morris et al., 2004). Notice in Table 3.1 (which includes a list of countries and an individualistic score for each on a 100-point scale) that the United States, Australia, Great Britain, and Canada rank the highest on individualism while Venezuela, Colombia, Pakistan, and Peru rank the lowest and are, therefore, more collectivistic.

The second dimension which enriches our understanding of cultural differences deals with high and low context (Hall, 1976; Hall & Hall, 1990). **Context** does not refer to the words in a message; it is defined as "the information that surrounds an

TABLE 3.1

Individualistic Scores of Various Countries*			
Country	**Score**	**Country**	**Score**
United States	91	India	48
Australia	90	Argentina	46
Great Britain	89	Japan	46
Canada	80	Iran	41
Netherlands	80	Brazil	38
New Zealand	79	Greece	35
Italy	76	Philippines	32
Denmark	74	Mexico	30
Sweden	71	Portugal	27
France	71	Hong Kong	25
Switzerland	68	Chile	23
Germany	67	Thailand	20
South Africa	65	Taiwan	17
Finland	63	Peru	16
Austria	55	Pakistan	14
Israel	54	Colombia	13
Spain	51	Venezuela	12

*Higher scores are more individualistic; lower scores are more collectivistic

From Hofstede, G., & Hofstede, G. J. (2005), *Cultures and Organizations: Software of the Mind* (2nd ed.), pp. 78–79. New York: McGraw-Hill.

event" (Hall & Hall, 1990, p. 6). Ting-Toomey (2000) notes that people who communicate with low context messages tend to come from individualistic cultures; people whose messages are high context tend to come from collectivistic cultures. In **low-context cultures**, messages are clearly spelled out—that is, they are direct and explicit. It is the speaker's responsibility to make sure the meaning is provided by the words and to be well organized and structured. The person's gestures, facial expressions, status, and so on may add subtle meaning but are not considered to be of major importance. On the other hand, **high-context cultures** rely only minimally on spoken words that tend to be brief, indirect, and implicit. Words have the power to hurt, so they are used very carefully (Cohen, 1991). This is the reason high-context nations like Japan find it hard to say and receive a direct "no." It seems like the rejection is given to the person, not the idea (Stefani et al., 1997). Instead, it is the receiver's responsibility to determine the meaning—usually from the setting, the speaker's face and nonverbal gestures, the speaker's friends, family background, age, status, silence, and so on. High-context cultures are homogeneous, tightly bound by experiences, family, and tradition; messages and responses are basically consistent (Hofstede, 2001; Samovar & Porter, 2004).

So, what do these two dimensions tell us about how different cultures handle conflict? The preceding information is summarized in Table 3.2 by Ting-Toomey (2000) and includes important cultural assumptions about conflict.

Remember that the information in this section should be used as a starting point only; behaviors vary greatly within each country. As more and more companies expand into other nations, we are likely to experience intercultural conflict. Individualistic, low-context team members need to be aware that solving intercultural conflicts requires some careful reframing such as, "It is not a conflict that is resolved but a relationship that is mended" (Cohen, 1991, p. 51). Collectivistic, high-context team members also need careful reframing, such as "It is not just a relationship that was mended but a conflict that was resolved." A recent article by Chen, Liu, and Tjosvold (2005) indicates that Chinese management teams, rather than avoiding conflict as many collectivistic countries do, have learned to approach conflict in a cooperative manner. Regardless of the culture, team members could improve communication by using the following tips from Bradford J. Hall (2002):

- Realize that there is more than one reasonable position in a conflict.

- Look for the "trigger" to the conflict (triggers are "small acts or comments that push already difficult situations into open conflict," p. 255).

- Use storytelling as a way to talk about conflict when a direct approach is undesirable.

- Use a neutral third party to mediate really serious conflicts.

TABLE 3.2

Cultural Assumptions about Conflict	
Individualistic–Low Context Cultures	**Collectivistic–High Context Cultures**
• Conflict viewed from "problem-solving" model.	• Conflict viewed from "face maintenance" model.
• Conflict can be functional or dysfunctional.	• Conflict is mainly dysfunctional.
• Conflict is dysfunctional when not confronted openly.	• Conflict shows lack of self-discipline and emotional immaturity—is cause for embarrassment and distress.
• Conflict is functional and exciting when it provides open opportunity to solve problems.	• Conflict, when forced upon one, provides testing ground for skillful facework
• Contextual and relational issues should be handled separately.	• Contextual and relational face issues are intertwined.
• Conflict should be handled openly and directly.	• Conflict should be handled discreetly and subtly.

Source: S. Ting-Toomey, *Managing Intercultural Conflicts Effectively*. In L. A. Samovar & R. E. Porter (Eds.), *Intercultural Communication: A Reader* (9th ed.), Wadsworth, 2000, 388–400; L. A. Stefani, L. A. Samovar, & S. A. Hellweg, *Culture and Its Impact on Negotiation*. In L. A. Samovar & R. E. Porter (Eds.), *Intercultural Communication: A Reader* (8th ed.), Wadsworth, 1997, 307–317.

CHAPTER 3
REVIEW

Inkastudio/iStockphoto

Key Terms

accommodating strategy (87)

A-type conflict (85)

avoiding strategy (86)

blind style communicator (71)

climate (64)

closed style communicator (69)

collaborating strategy (87)

collectivistic cultures (41)

communication styles (67)

competing strategy (87)

compromising strategy (87)

conflict strategies (85)

consensus (90)

context (91)

C-type conflict (85)

curvilinear relationship (84)

disclosure (67)

expectations (64)

feedback (67)

flexibility (82)

hidden style communicator (73)

high context cultures (91)

individualistic cultures (91)

lose-lose (90)

low context cultures (92)

mutual respect (66)

neurotic blind communicator (72)

open style communicator (75)

reciprocal (65)

relationships (63)

self-fulfilling prophecy (65)

trust (66)

win-lose (90)

win-win (90)

Summary

The quality of your interpersonal relationships with other members of any business or professional organization will directly affect your ability to communicate, as well as, the success of your organization. In building and maintaining quality relationships with managers, employees, customers, and colleagues, we need to make our expectations of each other clear and to use the reciprocal nature of relationships to help build interpersonal cooperation and trust.

It is easier to communicate successfully with our bosses, employees, customers, and colleagues if we understand their frames of reference. One way to do this is to determine their style of communication. Do they tend to be more closed, blind, hidden,

or open? And which is our preferred communication style? Are the styles compatible? Each style varies in the amount of feedback obtained from others and disclosure volunteered to others. Each style also varies in the strategies used to solve conflicts (i.e., avoidance, accommodation, compromise, competition, or collaboration). Intercultural conflicts can be explained by the two dimensions of individualism–collectivism and low or high context.

We need to realize that there is no perfect style. Each style has its own strengths and weaknesses; each style is effective in some situations and less so in other situations. If you are interested in changing your style or becoming more flexible in style use, carefully monitor your feedback and disclosure and plan to make minor changes in how you use them as needed for specific situations. It is not recommended that you make a drastic change in your communication style; it's better to know your style's best and worst sides and then build on your strengths and minimize your weaknesses.

Communicating for Results Online

Before continuing to the next chapter, check your understanding of Chapter 3 at the Premium Website for *Communicating for Results*. Your Premium Website gives you quick and easy access to the electronic resources that accompany this text. These resources include:

- **Study tools** that will help you assess your learning and prepare for exams (student companion workbook, digital glossary, key term flash cards, and review quizzes).

- **Activities and assignments** that will help you hone your knowledge, analyze professional communication situations, build your public speaking skills throughout the course, and learn to work effectively in teams (Awareness Checks, Checkpoints, and Collaborative Learning Activities).

- **Media resources** that will help you explore communication concepts online (Web links), develop your speech outlines (Speech Builder Express 3.0), watch and critique videos of professional communication situations and sample speeches (Interactive Video Activities), upload your speech videos for peer reviewing and critique other students' speeches (Speech Studio online speech review tool), and download chapter review so you can study when and where you'd like (Audio Study Tools).

This chapter's key terms, Collaborative Learning Activities, and Checkpoint activities are also featured on the following pages, and you can find this chapter's Awareness Check activities in the body of the chapter. For more information or to access this book's online resources, visit www.cengage.com/login.

Collaborative Learning Activities

1. Go to the Communication Situation, "Hasty Resignation," at the end of Chapter 6. Read the situation or watch a video of it at your Premium Website for *Communicating for Results*. Then in small groups, discuss the situation looking for the communication style (i.e., open, blind, hidden, or closed) that seems to most closely describe the police chief, James Ferguson and the style that best describes the police sergeant, Cal Richards. Make a list of all the specific events that convince you that your style choice is correct. As a group, be prepared to share your ideas with other groups.

2. In groups of three to five discuss and select a character from a current or well-known movie that clearly illustrates each communication style. Some movies to consider include *No Reservations* (2008), *The Devil Wears Prada* (2006), *Ambulance Girl* (2005), *50 First Dates* (2004), *Lost in Translation* (2003), *My Big Fat Greek Wedding* (2002), *Jerry Maguire* (1996), and *Groundhog Day* (1993). To watch the movie trailers, search for them on YouTube.com.

3. In small groups, share the way conflict was handled when you were growing up—was it considered beneficial or something to be ignored? Was conflict usually Type-A or Type-B? What is your main conflict strategy today: avoiding, accommodating, compromising, competing, or collaboration, and how has it changed since you were a child? Now that you know the various conflict styles you have in this small group, how effective would this group be as a problem-solving team? Give specific reasons to support your position.

4. In small groups, compare the four communication styles used by individuals with the five organization models discussed in Chapter 2. Which styles would likely feel the most and least comfortable working in or with each organization model (e.g., would the closed employee/manager/customer feel more comfortable in the traditional or the human resources models?) Give reasons for your answers.

Checkpoints

Checkpoint 3.1 Assessing Your Method of Conflict Resolution

 Think about two or three situations that occurred over the last few months involving conflict. For each situation, answer the following questions using this scale: 1=not at all; 2=sometimes; 3=often

1. *I tried to resolve this conflict by avoidance (withdrawing from it).*

2. *I tried to resolve this conflict by accommodation (giving in).*

3. *I tried to resolve this conflict by competition (trying to win).*

4. *I tried to resolve this conflict by compromise (finding the middle ground).*

5. *I tried to resolve this conflict by collaboration (working with others to find a solution agreeable to all).*

Look at your answers to see if there were any similarities in the way you handled conflict in the various situations. How did your success in solving the conflicts relate to the method(s) used? Does your communication style seem to agree with your conflict resolution choices? Give an example to explain your answer.

Checkpoint 3.2 Survey of Communication Styles

Checkpoint 3.3 Communication Styles

Checkpoint 3.4 Analyzing the Climate and Attitudes of an Organization

Checkpoint 3.5 Becoming More Flexible in Use of Communication Styles

Checkpoint 3.6 Communication Styles and Conflict Resolution

Checkpoint 3.7 Friendship and Disclosure

Checkpoint 3.8 Interpersonal Websites

Monkey Business Images/Shutterstock

Effective Listening

As you read Chapter 4,

List at least two practical tips for improving your listening skills with each of the following groups: customers, employees, supervisors, and coworkers.

Identify and briefly **describe** the signs of poor listening.

Distinguish among the main barriers to poor listening and **determine** which of these barriers cause you the most problems.

Discuss several guidelines for improving your listening and the payoffs for using them correctly.

Case Study: An Engineer's Experience With Listening

Problems are often discovered and solved through listening. A fascinating problem with the 59-story Citigroup Center tower in New York City (formerly the Citicorp Center) came to light when a nationally known structural engineer, William J. LeMessurier, listened to a student's concerns about the strength of the columns that support the building. Although the student's concerns proved to be unfounded, as a result of the call, LeMessurier discovered a much more serious problem with the structural integrity of the building. The following story was adapted from "The Fifty-Nine-Story Crisis" by Joe Morgenstern (1995).

The beautiful Citigroup tower was designed by architect Hugh Stubbins Jr., but it was engineered by LeMessurier and his firm. There were several design "firsts" in this project. One innovation was the wind braces hidden inside the structural skin—instead of one piece, two pieces coming from opposing sides if soldered together in the center would be as strong as a single brace. The second was the "tuned mass damper" (TMD)—a 400-pound block of concrete located near the top of the building that was designed to greatly reduce the natural sway of such a tall building. The third innovation of LeMessurier's was the placement of the four columns on which the building rested. These massive, nine-story stilt-like columns were located at the center of each side of the building instead of at the corners. This made the building appear to "float" over the church, shops, and plaza underneath it. The student's questions were about these columns.

LeMessurier was very proud of this building, which had won much engineering praise. He patiently explained to the student, who was writing a paper on the building, that the placement of the columns was exactly correct to "resist what sailors call quartering winds—those which come from a diagonal and, by flowing across two sides of a

William Perry/iStockphoto

As you read this chapter, see if you can, (a) evaluate LeMessurier's listening skills on a scale of 1 (poor) to 5 (excellent), (b) determine whether he was guilty of any signs of poor listening and why, and (c) decide whether it was ethical for LeMessurier and others involved in the crisis to withhold this information from the public for 20 years (until Morgenstern's 1995 article).

For more details on this story, go to the website of the Online Ethics Center for Engineering and Science at www.onlineethics.org and search on "LeMessurier." You can access this site through your Premium Website for Communicating for Results.

building at once, increase the forces on both" (p. 6). Because LeMessurier was teaching a structural engineering class at Harvard, the student's call reminded him that his own students would benefit from this information on quartering winds, as well as, the new wind braces he had had installed in the columns to resist strong winds. Although New York building code required that such braces pass only perpendicular wind tests, as background for his lecture, he calculated the strength of the braces when hit by quartering winds. To his surprise, he found that these winds would increase the strain on several of the braces by 40% and would increase the strain on the joints of the columns by 160%. Even this increase would be no problem for soldered joints (but a few weeks before, LeMessurier had discovered that the steel company who built Citicorp tower had decided to use bolted joints—which in most cases would cost less yet be just as safe).

LeMessurier still was not overly worried because "a margin of safety is built into the standard formulas for calculating how strong a joint must be" in structural columns. However, when he discovered that the building team had defined the braces as "trusses" and not as "columns," he became very worried! Because trusses are exempt from the extra safety margin, LeMessurier knew that there would be too few bolts in these joints for safety under the force of quartering winds even with the TMD designed to reduce building sway.

LeMessurier decided to ask the labs of Canada's Boundary Layer Wind Tunnel Laboratory to run some wind tunnel tests. The results were not encouraging. After working through each floor and each joint, LeMessurier determined that the thirtieth floor had the weakest joint: "If that one gave way, catastrophic failure of the whole structure would follow" (p. 22). The likelihood of a storm serious enough to create this disaster was calculated to be once every 16 years; with the TMD calculated in, it dropped to once in every 55 years. However, the TMD required electricity, which would likely fail in this type of storm! By now it was the end of July, and hurricane season was rapidly approaching. His worry now escalated to panic.

There was a way to correct the problem: A heavy steel plate could be welded around each of the 200 bolted joints like a "giant Band-Aid." The joints were readily accessible by simply removing the carpet and sheetrock that covered them. This fix would raise the safety of the building to a once-in-every-700-years storm. However, as Morgenstern noted, "To avert disaster, LeMessurier would have to blow the whistle quickly on himself. That meant facing the pain of possible protracted litigation, probable bankruptcy, and professional disgrace" (p. 24). This would be in addition to the cost of repairs (which would be at least $1 million), the problem of evacuating thousands of people, and the panic all of this would create. Although the student had been wrong about the exact problem, his concern had uncovered a serious structural weakness.

To see how LeMessurier handled the crisis, read the summary for this chapter.

Are you a good listener? Most of us assume we are. We take for granted that **listening** just comes naturally, when in fact effective listening requires as much skill as the other forms of communication: reading, writing, and speaking. But unlike writing, reading, and especially speaking, few overt motor skills are necessary to engage in listening. The effort involved in listening is primarily mental, and this may account for deceiving ourselves that listening is easy.

One reason effective listening is so important is that we do so much listening each day. According to research, we are listening during 80% of our waking hours (Powell, 1983). That makes it our most frequently used communication skill. The business world is certainly aware of the importance of listening. For example, one study estimated that 60% of worker errors is due to poor listening (Cooper, 1997). In another study, 80% of the executives ranked listening as the most important workplace skill. At the same time, 28% of them also ranked listening as the skill most lacking in the workplace (Salopek, 1999). In addition, studies confirm that good listeners make good managers (Penley et al., 1991; Ramsey & Sohi, 1997; Weitz et al., 2008) and that good listening is essential for business success (Goby & Lewis, 2000). In a survey of industrial salespeople, failure to listen was cited as one of the main reasons salespeople are unsuccessful (Ingram et al., 1992). In a survey of customers, listening was rated as the most important skill a salesperson can possess (Boyle, 1999; Moore et al., 1986).

Indeed, most working professionals recognize that listening is a skill that can and should be improved. Only through knowledge and application can we become more effective listeners. The information in this chapter will provide you with the knowledge to become a better listener on and off the job, but it will take effort on your part to apply it. To get an idea of how much effort will be needed, complete the Awareness Check on pages 110–111.

Effective Listening in Organizations

Most of us consider listening important when we know that the information we are receiving can benefit us in some way. At other times, we may feel that careful listening is a waste of time. But there is no guarantee that what we ignore is unimportant. How will we know unless we listen? An attitude of "I already know what they're going to say" can make us miss important information. In the working world, four sources of information demand effective listening: customers, employees, supervisors, and coworkers (Horton, 1983).

Listening to Customers

Several popular business-related books, such as *The 7 Habits of Highly Effective People* and *The 8th Habit: From Effectiveness to Greatness* (Covey, 1990, 2005), *Customers for Life* (Sewell & Brown, 1998), *The Lost Art of Listening* (Nichols, 1996), and *What the Best CEOs Know* (Krames, 2003), contend that the best-run companies in the United States actively listen to what their customers are saying. By listening to customers, the organization can learn objective information about its products or services. For example, customers can suggest product improvements that the research and development department may have overlooked.

Listening to customers can tell us a great deal about the competition. Most companies like to compare themselves with other companies' people, information, goods, and services. It is simply good business practice to do so. Customers will communicate their opinion of your company and its competition if they

ETHICAL DILEMMA

How would you feel knowing that your surgeons were using a product on you that the developing company had paid them to use? Is this just one way that companies get their products known to physicians who then use the products and report valuable feedback on the products to the company, or is this an ethics breach?

One company that uses this method to promote its products is Medtronic, Inc. Medtronic refers to the physicians it pays to use products, give presentations, write articles, and train other surgeons as "consultants." Whistleblowers in a recent lawsuit claimed that in 2006 Medtronic paid over $8 million to consultants to use a product called Infuse Bone Graft ("New suit against Medtronic," 2009). According to Medtronic, "consulting arrangements with surgeons are critical to the development of new products" (Armstrong & Burton, 2009). Infuse Bone Graft is a product that helps bones heal more rapidly and replaces the often painful process of harvesting or surgically removing bone from an area in a person's body for use in a later surgical procedure (Medtronic.com, 2008). Infuse Bone Graft was cleared for use by the Food and Drug Administration (FDA) for Degenerative Disk Disease, fractures of the tibia, and two dental procedures requiring bone grafting ("Did Medtronic promote dangerous off-label use?", 2008). Surgeons can use the product as they see fit, but it is unlawful for Medtronic to encourage other uses. The lawsuit mentioned accuses Medtronic of paying surgeons to use Infuse in non-approved or "off-label" surgeries.

The latest accusation involving Infuse was reported by the *Wall Street Journal* (Armstrong & Burton, 2009). Timothy Kuldo, a consulting surgeon paid almost $800,000 by Medtronic, was accused of falsifying data that "reported advantages in healing the legs of injured soldiers when Infuse was used" (B1). According to the article, the Army has claimed the study to be fraudulent. The names of 22 other consultants who worked on "Infuse-related matters" were provided to Congress by Medtronic.

QUESTIONS: Although it appears that medical companies and doctors need to listen to each other to develop quality products for patients and it appears that as patients, we would want our surgeons to be trained by and listen to more experienced surgeons, ethical questions remain. For example, is it ethical for doctors who use their products and doctors who train other physicians how to use the products to accept payment from medical companies? How would you recommend that both Medtronic and the doctors who use their products maintain a winning yet ethical relationship?

are encouraged. One way to listen to and communicate with customers is through a public or company blog. General Motors has had great success with its blog called GM FastLane (see the "It Really Works" story in Chapter 6). According to the Blog Herald.com (Duncan, 2006), there are approximately 200 million blogs in existence today, but the readership exceeds 500 million! See Chapter 6 for more on blogs.

Listening to customers can also increase sales and customer satisfaction. Starbucks +66Coffee Company considers listening as "a vital component of customer service" and "expects their employees to listen to customers" (Hitt et al., 1999, p. 143). When customers perceive that a salesperson is listening to them, they are more likely to trust, are more satisfied with, and more likely to do future business with that salesperson (Aggarwal et al., 2005; Bergeron & Laroche, 2009). This is also true of medical patients: They want their doctors and nurses to listen to them; as a result they feel much more satisfied (Frankel, 1995; Perry, 1994).

Listening to Employees

In *The Change Masters*, Rosabeth Moss Kanter (1983) tells of a textile company that had a high frequency of yarn breakage for years. Management considered the breakage an unavoidable business expense until a new manager, who listened to the employees, discovered a worker with an idea about how to modify the machines to greatly reduce the breakage. The new manager "was shocked to learn that the man had wondered about the machine modification for *32 years*. 'Why didn't you say something before?' the manager asked. The reply: 'My supervisor wasn't interested, and I had no one else to tell it to'" (p. 70).

Management can't afford *not* to listen to employees. Michael Nichols, in *The Lost Art of Listening* (1996), warns that people who aren't listened to feel unappreciated and assume that neither they nor their ideas matter. Listening to employees is a way of showing support, which makes for a more open climate, and an open climate increases employee satisfaction and productivity (Conrad & Poole, 2005, p. 135). To show that they are listening, managers' responses must communicate acceptance

TABLE 4.1

Responses That Can Communicate Nonacceptance	
Listener's Response	**Implied Message**
Ordering, demanding: "You must try . . .", "You have to stop . . ."	Don't feel, act, or think that way; do it my way.
Criticizing, blaming, disagreeing: "You aren't thinking about this properly . . ."	You are wrong if you have that feeling, act, or think that way.
Advising, giving answers: "Why don't you . . .", "Let me suggest . . ."	Here's a solution so you won't have that feeling, act, or think that way.
Praising, agreeing: "But you've done such a good job . . .", "I approve of . . ."	Your feelings, actions, and opinions are subject to my approval.
Reassuring, sympathizing: "Don't worry . . .", "You'll feel better . . ."	You don't need to have that feeling, act, or think that way.
Interpreting, diagnosing: "What you need is . . .", "Your problem is . . ."	Here's the reason you have for feeling, acting, or thinking that way.
Diverting, avoiding: "We can discuss it later . . .", "That reminds me of . . ."	Your feelings, actions, and opinions aren't worthy of discussion.
Kidding, using sarcasm: "That will be the day!" "Bring out the violins . . ."	You're silly if you persist in having that feeling, acting, or thinking that way.

From Norma Carr-Ruffino, 1985, *The Promotable Woman: Becoming a Successful Manager* (p. 230), Belmont, CA: Wadsworth. Reprinted by permission of the author.

of the person. If you are a supervisor, check your usual responses against the list of **nonacceptance responses** in Table 4.1. If you are not a supervisor, see if you recognize your boss's typical responses. Do they make you feel like no one supports or listens to you?

Employees in organizations that have recently been downsized, merged, or reengineered are especially likely to be insecure and feel that their ideas don't matter. It is important for employees to know that management will be honest and open with them about both the good and the bad news. (See Appendix: Written Communication for how to send bad news by e-mail). Listening is the key to communicating with and understanding employees. For example, managers and supervisors can ask hard-hitting opinion questions of groups or teams of employees and then answer and discuss the employee responses in an open and direct manner. Questions that ask employees if they have the tools, feedback, and respect needed to excel at their jobs can be real eye-openers for management. The Gallup Organization has developed 12 questions that relate to employee morale and engagement that they call Q12. The questions are answered on a 1- to 5-point scale, with 5 being most positive and compiled into a total score that predicts employee performance. Gallup results show that companies in the top quartile based on employee scores have "engaged" employees that feel an emotional attachment with the company. Top quartile companies experience from 12 to 18% higher customer loyalty, higher productivity, and higher profitability; companies in the lower quartile "have 51% more shrinkage, 31% to 51% more employee turnover, and 62% more accidents than business units in the top quartile" (Robinson, 2009, p. 2).

One company that successfully listened to employees is Procter & Gamble who in 2000 had half of its "top 15 brands . . . losing market share," as well as demoralized, unhappy employees (Stengel et al., 2003, p. 107). The feedback they received from listening to employees through surveys, focus groups, e-mail, and interviews allowed them to make dramatic redesign changes resulting in growth in 19 of the top 20 brands and an employee confidence increase from 26 to 56% in less than 2 years (p. 116). Listening and participating in company blogs is another effective way to see what employees are thinking and saying. Monster.com is an excellent example of a company that uses its employees as its blogging voice (Wright, 2006, p. 60). So does Starbucks, who is discussed in the "It Really Works" box later in this chapter.

Listening to Supervisors

Although it is obvious that employees should listen to their bosses, many employees are unaware of how important it is to *show* that they are listening. Of course, giving the appearance of listening without actually listening is unwise, but effective listening requires not only good listening skills but also an indication that listening is taking place. Listeners can show that they are sensing what the speaker is saying by maintaining good eye contact (Yrle & Galle, 1993) and can show interest by other nonverbal behaviors: maintaining a relaxed posture, shaking the head, and making responsive sounds like "really" or "uh huh" (Stewart & Logan, 1999).

Too often, when managers give instructions, they must guess whether the employee is processing the information. Managers who don't see an appropriate listening response are likely to suspect that the information was not received correctly and repeat themselves, ask for feedback, or become frustrated. All of these alternatives are time consuming and could hurt the career of the employee who appears not to be listening.

Effective listening can help you improve your relationship with your boss by helping you understand the boss's expectations and frame of reference. Allan Glatthorn and Herbert Adams (1983, pp. 71–74) offer the following suggestions for listening and responding to your supervisors:

- *Listen to know your supervisors.* When do they prefer meetings? What nonverbal behaviors do they use, and what do the behaviors mean? When are they the most receptive to bad news? In Episode 2, Season 1 of *The Apprentice*, Donald Trump advised his contestants to "deal directly with the boss" because it establishes a working relationship and you avoid the "go-between who may not have your passion or knowledge" (Kinnick & Parton, 2005).

- *Use that knowledge to guide your general interactions with your supervisors.* Frame bad news in the manner that they find most acceptable. If they prefer certain jargon terms, such as "team player," use these terms in your comments when appropriate.

- *Develop the expertise your supervisors value.* Without competing with them, build your knowledge and expertise in needed areas (preferably in areas in which a supervisor is weak). Make yourself valuable.

- *Be wary of giving advice.* If you are right, the supervisor may resent it; if you are wrong, you may be blamed. Instead, serve as a sounding board for your supervisors. Ask questions and paraphrase in an attempt to help them think through the problem.

Effective listening involves more than actual listening; the listener must also appear to be listening.

- *Build off your supervisors' ideas.* Don't make counter-suggestions; instead, piggyback your ideas off the supervisor's. For example,

  Your supervisor says, "We could increase sales if we changed our advertising agency." You think the packaging is the problem. So you say, "That sounds good. That would give us a shot in the arm, and if we did that, we could have them take a look at the way we package the product. There are probably some other ways they could help us as well. What do you think?" (Glatthorn & Adams, 1983, pp. 72–73)

- *Know how to praise appropriately.* "Your praise is one of the few rewards you have for your boss" (Glatthorn & Adams, 1983, p. 73). Avoid extravagant or insincere praise. Use tact; be subtle.

- *Don't criticize your superiors.* Behind-the-back criticism has a way of traveling through the grapevine back to them. Direct criticism, even when sought, may not be appreciated. Be gentle and use tact.

Listening to Coworkers

Businesses depend on strong interpersonal relationships among coworkers, as discussed in Chapter 3. Relationship development depends on careful listening to coworkers. According to Purdy (2003), "Listening creates community" (p. 1). Brownell (2006, p. 276) suggests that effective listening with peers is improved when we are aware of which listening method is needed: *comprehension* (questions asked to clarify areas of confusion), *therapeutic* (supportive responses given), or *critical* (objective assessment of facts and ideas needed).

If your company is a global one, you may find yourself a part of a cross-functional or virtual team where "listening" to coworkers is made more difficult and stressful by technology, cultural differences, or lack of personal knowledge about team members. On the other hand, technology, especially e-mail and instant messaging (IM), can improve communication. As Brownell (2003) emphasizes, "The *only* way that we can develop meaningful relationships within our families, communities, and across continents is through effective listening" (p. 10). If you are part of a global organization, you may find the following global listening tips helpful (Boland & Hoffman, 1983; Brownell, 2006; Ferraro, 1998; Hall, 2002; Reisner, 1993; Varner & Beamer, 1995):

- *Use humor as a morale booster* as long as members' cultural differences are respected.

- *Learn to tolerate ambiguity*—be open to many differing viewpoints. Listen not only to accomplish the task, but also to appreciate another culture's view of the world.

- *Explain your ideas completely and explicitly when members have few shared experiences.* In this situation, member communication will be **low context**—the situation or context provides only minimal information so the majority of meaning must come from explicit content cues. This approach may need team discussion because cultures that are **high context**, such as Japan and Saudi Arabia, believe it is the listener's responsibility to understand and may feel insulted if too much information is given. Low-context cultures such as the United States and Canada feel that listener understanding is the responsibility of the speaker and feel frustrated if messages are too brief or vague.

- *Show you are "listening"* by answering e-mail as soon as possible, showing interest in the ideas of others, making occasional personal inquiries, and including some personal comments and data.

- *Concentrate more on information gathering and sharing rather than persuasion.* Avoid using words that may be considered arrogant or pushy such as *should*, *must*, *ought*, or *have to*, and use *we* instead of *I* when possible to show team membership.

Signs of Poor Listening

Regardless of how you previously perceived yourself, after reading this far you may be wondering, "How good a listener am I?" Fortunately, there are certain signs that can alert you to poor listening skills on the job (Horton, 1983). Because most people will not tell you that you are a poor listener, you have to monitor your own habits. By watching for these signs, you may be able to detect whether poor listening is affecting your performance on the job.

Breaking the Chain of Command

As a manager, one of the surest signs of poor listening is that employees go around you or over your head to talk to others. This breaking of the chain of command—frustrating for both the manager and the employee—results when the manager's poor listening leaves the employee with no alternative. To carry out their responsibilities effectively, employees must have someone in authority who will listen to them. The following example illustrates this sign of poor listening:

Jim was the shift supervisor and Bob's boss at a chemical plant. Jim and Bob had worked together for over a year when Jim began to notice that Bob had quit discussing safety problems with him. Jim was glad because he really felt that

Bob was somewhat paranoid and cried wolf much too often. Recently, however, the operations vice president called Jim and demanded to know why Jim was unaware of or unconcerned with the safety problems in the plant. Obviously, Bob had been discussing safety problems with the vice president. When confronted by Jim about his discussions, Bob replied, "Safety is too important not to have someone listen to the problems in this plant!"

If you find that others are going around you or over your head to talk about issues that are really your business, it may indicate (as it did to Jim) that you have demonstrated poor listening skills.

Learning About Events Too Late

Another sign of a manager's poor listening is learning about important events too late. In many organizations, oral messages are not always followed up by written memos or letters. Managers are expected to act on information without having it repeated. When important events occur without your knowledge or participation, poor listening may be the culprit. A manager in the corporate office of a restaurant chain related the following story:

> I arrived at work one day and was surprised to find that all of my colleagues were missing. I asked one of the secretaries where everyone was and was shocked by her reply: "All of the corporate managers are in a special meeting with our public relations firm. Aren't you supposed to be there?" When the special meeting was over, I asked one of my colleagues when the meeting was called, and he replied that it was announced in our weekly meeting with the president. I was at that meeting, but never heard (listened to) the announcement.

If you find that you must rely on others or on memos to ensure that you are on top of important events, or if these events pass you by, you can take this as a sign of poor listening.

Always Putting Out Fires

If a manager is always putting out fires or having to handle problems after they have reached crisis proportions, this too could be a sign of poor listening. Most warnings that a problem is imminent are direct, but sometimes they are not, such as "I'm not sure I can handle this alone" or "We may want to consider replacing it soon." It is important to pick up on these indirect warnings to head off problems before they get out of control. Listening for these indirect comments takes special effort, but one of the fundamentals of good management practice is spotting problems before they reach the crisis stage.

Information Must Be Repeated

As an employee, if you find that your supervisor or coworker has to repeat information to you constantly, it is probably a sign of poor listening. Repetition is costly for the manager, for you, and for the organization. Every time information must be repeated, time is wasted. Just as important is the harm that repetition does to perceptions of your abilities and your chances for promotion. A supervisor may say, "I cannot recommend Tom for promotion because he doesn't seem to catch on very fast. I always have to repeat instructions for him!" In most cases, the truth is not that people don't catch on very fast, but that they do not use listening skills to their advantage (Tannen, 1994, p. 26).

"Did you just say that anyone who asks another question will be fired?"

Tasks Given to Others

Tasks once entrusted to you and now being given to others may be another sign of poor listening. Supervisors may be communicating that they do not trust your listening skills when they avoid delegating complicated responsibilities to you. Clearly, your career advancement is threatened: Promotions and raises often are based on one's ability to take on complex tasks.

Increase in Written Communication

Another sign of poor listening is receiving an unusual amount of written communication (i.e., memos, letters, e-mail, or faxes) when oral communication (i.e., face to face, telephone) would be a more appropriate channel. Oral communication is often the better method (assuming the receiver's listening skills are good) because it is more rapid and allows for instant feedback. When the message is lengthy or complicated, however, senders may feel that in writing you will not misunderstand it. Those who choose to write memos or letters to you may be aware that your listening skills are not what they should be.

Increase in Poor Listening Habits

Ralph Nichols, one of the first researchers to concentrate on listening, has identified several bad habits that people develop (Wolff et al., 1983). Using three or more of these habits is a sign of poor listening. Fortunately, these habits can be corrected with effort. Poor listening habits include:

- *Calling the topic boring.* Many poor listeners justify their inattention by declaring the speaker's topic uninteresting. Good listeners try to find some fact or idea that they can use in the future even if the presentation isn't as interesting as they had hoped.

- *Criticizing the speaker's delivery.* Poor listeners make a game of criticizing speakers including their walk, clothes, mannerisms, voice, grammar, and dialect instead of listening to the message. In contrast, good listeners may notice the speaker's faults but concentrate on the message anyway.

- *Orally or mentally interrupting to disagree.* Poor listeners are easily provoked to disagree. Instead of listening, they are planning a rebuttal. Good listeners pay attention to the entire idea before deciding whether they agree or disagree with the speaker.

- *Listening only for facts.* The best way to remember facts is to relate them to a theme, principle, or concept. Facts are more meaningful when the feelings behind them are clear. Good listeners, make sure they understand not only the speaker's facts and feelings, but also any principles to which they relate.

- *Takes detailed notes of everything.* Poor listeners become so involved in taking notes that they are not really listening. The best notes are brief key words and phrases that will later refresh the listener's mind. They do not have to be in outline form; many speakers don't even follow an outline.

- *Pretending to listen.* Poor listeners pretend to listen (by staring at the speaker and appropriately nodding from time to time) while really thinking about something else. Good listeners look like they are listening because they really are listening.

- *Tolerating or creating distractions.* People conversing while a speaker is talking is very distracting to those sitting near the conversationalists and can be distracting to the speaker and a sure sign of poor listening. Allowing these distractions to continue is just as bad as creating them. Good listeners will either ask the conversationalists to be quiet or ask the speaker to talk louder.

- *Avoiding difficult material.* When the topic is complicated or includes technical terms, many poor listeners immediately tune out. Periodically, we all should attend professional training sessions or watch challenging TV programs to practice our listening skills.

- *Reacting emotionally and tuning out the speaker.* Sometimes a speaker will use a word that is emotionally charged for some listeners. Good listeners may not care for certain words, but they do not let their reactions block what the speaker is saying.

- *Daydreaming during longer presentations.* Poor listeners become so engrossed in their own thoughts that they forget to tune in the speaker. Good listeners use "spare" time to ponder the speaker's ideas, to evaluate the quality of evidence, and to commit important ideas to memory.

In addition to being aware of poor listening signs, it is important to know the main barriers to poor listening. Understanding them will allow you to plan ways to minimize potential problems.

Barriers to Poor Listening

People are not born with the ability to listen effectively; the signs to poor listening we just discussed must be learned. In addition to these bad signs and habits, which we have some power to change, four other barriers to effective listening should be recognized: physical, personal, gender, and semantic barriers (Callarman & McCartney, 1995).

Physical Barriers

Most **physical barriers** to effective listening are not directly under our control. For example, a hearing disability, noisy office equipment, or a loud conversation could prevent us from hearing an important message. According to the American Hearing Research Foundation (2006), any noise over 85 decibels can cause hearing loss (e.g., a normal conversation and keyboard clicks produce 60 decibels). Visual distractions also pose barriers to effective listening. For instance, during a conversation with your boss, you see someone make an obvious filing mistake; while a subordinate is delivering a report, you are watching birds land on the ledge outside your window; or while listening to a technician's report, you can't help but be distracted by his inappropriate three-piece suit. (See the section on clothing and personal appearance in Chapter 5.)

Because we cannot control or eliminate many physical barriers, we have to control ourselves when these distractions are present. It may be difficult to devote our entire mental effort to the message we are supposed to be receiving, but it is necessary for effective listening.

Personal Barriers

We might assume that it is easier to control the **personal barriers** to effective listening because we create them ourselves. This is not always true, especially if they are subconscious aspects of our personalities. The first step is learning to recognize them.

Obviously, our *physical well-being* affects the listening process. Illness, fatigue, and discomfort make us unable to concentrate. Our main concern is relief of our aches and pains. When we go to work ill, we jeopardize the opportunity to listen well.

Psychological distractions are another type of personal barrier. Psychological distractions can arise from almost any source. Personal problems such as finances, buying a house, or the behavior of a spouse or children could all be psychologically distracting. Distractions can also originate in events or conditions at work. We may be worried, for example, that our idea will not be received favorably.

Attitudinal biases against the speaker are still another personal barrier to listening. We tend to attribute or explain people's behavior after looking at only a "thin slice" (brief samples) of their behavior (Ambady et al., 1999). Often we are fairly accurate, but just as often our judgments are biased and overgeneralized. In any case, our listening is affected by these attributions. For example, honestly answer the following questions (Glatthorn & Adams, 1983, p. 9):

- Do you have trouble listening to a colleague of the opposite gender?
- Do you have trouble listening to coworkers from different ethnic groups?
- Do you have trouble listening to someone much older, or much younger, than you?
- Do you have trouble listening to coworkers with whom you feel competitive?
- Do you have trouble listening to someone whose manner or personal appearance displeases you?
- Do you have trouble listening to coworkers whom you judge to be less competent than you?

You probably answered yes to at least one of these questions. Everyone has some biases. As the workforce becomes more socially and culturally diverse (Simon, 1991, it will be even more important for communicators to acknowledge attitudinal biases and try to minimize their effect. For example, "I know I have a problem listening to that young know-it-all engineer—I'll watch it in tomorrow's meeting." Personal barriers are a natural human tendency, but it is critical to put aside physical, psychological, and attitudinal distractions and concentrate on listening effectively.

Gender Barriers

If we are not careful, gender differences can cause **gender barriers** to listening. *Gender* refers to the traditional masculine and feminine characteristics and behaviors that are influenced by culture and society. The influx of women into occupations and positions traditionally held by men—the number of female managers continues to rise from 29.3% in 1990 to 39.5% in 2008 (U.S. Department of Labor, 2009); executive positions from 2.9% in 1986 to 4.8% in 1992 (Fisher, 1992)—and the movement of some men into traditionally female occupations, such as nursing and office jobs, have increased the likelihood of gender-related barriers.

Complete the following Awareness Check to see if your perception of gender listening differences agrees with research findings.

Gender Barriers

How accurate are you in determining gender differences? To find out, take the following quiz and check your answers against those in the back of this book. You can also take this quiz and view the answers online at your Premium Website for *Communicating for Results*.

Directions: For each question, write "**M**" if you think the answer is men; write "**W**" if you think it is women; write "**S**" if you think it is the same for both men and women. Then compare your responses with the answers and explanations drawn from the latest research (questions adapted from Rozema and Gray, 1989, and updated from current research).

_____ 1. In office discussions, who usually talks more often?

_____ 2. Who is better at interpreting nonverbal cues while listening?

_____ 3. When speaking to others, who tends to attach more tag questions (such as "Don't you agree?" and "Right?") to statements?

_____ 4. Who is more likely to view a conversation in a competitive rather than cooperative manner?

_____ 5. In office discussions, who usually works harder to keep the conversation going?

_____ 6. During a conversation, who tends to interrupt more often?

_____ 7. While listening, who is less likely to ask questions, especially if asking will reveal a lack of knowledge?

_____ 8. Who do colleagues consider the better listener?

To summarize the Awareness Check answers (available at the end of the text), women typically are better at decoding nonverbal cues in messages, view communication as a cooperative tool, and work harder to maintain discussions by initiating topics and by making supportive responses. Men, on the other hand, talk more often and longer, view communication as a competitive tool, and tend to interrupt more often. At the same time, they give minimal response cues during conversations and are less likely to ask questions. Both men and women (especially in power positions) tend to use tag questions (such as "Isn't it?") at the end of comments. However, women tend to be more tentative when the topic is masculine; men are more tentative when the topic is feminine; little difference appears when topics are gender neutral.

Are differences in the way men and women listen due to real, biological differences between the sexes, or are they learned behaviors that correspond to social stereotypes? In general, men are seen as more *task oriented*, whereas women are seen as more *supportive*. However, reviewing the statistical procedures used in gender research, Thorne, Kramarae, and Henley (1983) concluded that "very few expected sex differences have been firmly substantiated by empirical studies of isolated variables" (p. 13), and Wilkins and Andersen (1991) found that sex differences between male and female managers accounted for only 0.5% of the variance and was basically insignificant.

Perhaps the business communicator of the future will be more androgynous. The term *androgynous* comes from the Greek words for "male" and "female," and denotes the integration of both masculine and feminine characteristics (Quackenbush, 1987; Wood, 2009). Already, Geddes (1992) reports that union members judged the androgynous manager (whether male or female) as the most effective and satisfying manager, and Heath (1991) found that androgynous people are generally more successful at work and at home.

More research on listening and gender differences needs to be conducted before we can confidently answer whether gender differences are due to biological traits or to social role expectations. Both probably play a part, but many of the gender-related differences will likely disappear as more women move up in their organizations and women managers become commonplace. Conrad and Poole (2005, p. 270) explain that:

> "in Western societies men often do not learn to listen at the emotional and relational levels. . . [which can lead to] misunderstandings, frustrations, and communication breakdowns. In contrast, Western women often learn to focus on the relational level of meaning and to respond by expressing understanding, sympathy, and emotional support. . . [which also can lead to] misunderstanding and frustration."

In the meantime, the most effective listeners of both sexes will be those who understand the communication principles discussed throughout this text and who apply them in a considerate and flexible manner.

Semantic Barriers

The word *semantic* refers to the meaning of words. How often have you disagreed with someone over the meaning of a message simply because the two of you had different frames of reference and interpreted the words differently? Many ideas, objects, and actions can be referred to by more than one word. Additionally, many words have several different meanings (referents). Consider the following example:

> A woman called the help desk at her company completely upset. "It's just not here," she complained. "I've spent over an hour looking, and it's just not here! Can you help me?" "What's not there?" asked the technician, thinking this might finally be a problem worth his time. The woman said, "The program says to press any key and there simply is no Any Key on my keyboard!"

Even the sounds of words can be the same but have entirely different meanings (*red, read*). **Semantic barriers** can be frustrating because the problem stems from oddities of language, not from the listeners' lack of effort.

Listening Skills

How are your listening skills? To check your listening effectiveness, take the following quiz. Compare your answers with those in the back of this book. You can also take this quiz and view the answers online at your Premium Website for *Communicating for Results*.

Directions: For each of these statements about your listening skills, select one of the following: **A** = yes, **B** = sometimes, or **C** = no.

_____ 1. I feel uncomfortable when listening to or responding to my supervisor.

_____ 2. When I disagree with a person, I pretend to listen to what they are saying.

_____ 3. I usually focus on facts when people are speaking.

(continued on next page)

Continued

_____   4. I have difficulty concentrating on the instructions that others give me.

_____   5. When speakers say something that makes me mad, I usually tune them out.

_____   6. I seldom seek out the opportunity to listen to new ideas.

_____   7. I find myself daydreaming when others seem to ramble on.

_____   8. I often argue mentally or aloud with what someone is saying even before he or she finishes.

_____   9. I find that others are always repeating things to me.

_____   10. When listening to speakers, I often concentrate on what they are wearing or on their mannerisms.

Number of times you answered **A** _____
Number of times you answered **B** _____
Number of times you answered **C** _____

Listening to Blogging Customers

One company that is changing the way they listen to customers is Starbucks Coffee Company, in business since 1971. On March 19, 2008, Starbucks introduced a new blog site called *My Starbucks Idea* where customers share ideas, view other people's suggestions, post comments, and finally, vote on and even vote down ideas. One year later to the day, customers had posted over 70,000 ideas; 94 of those ideas were "put into action," and 25 ideas were actually "launched" according to an employee whose blog title is ssbx_bean.

One customer suggested a mini Starbucks card and that idea was launched on June 30, 2009. Four days before its launch, the following blog was posted by Chuck Davidson under the Heading, *You Asked for It: Introducing the Mini Starbucks Card!!*

> Hi there, I'm Chuck Davidson and I work on innovation with the Starbucks Card team. We are VERY excited about the new Mini Starbucks Card—something you have been asking for and we are pleased to launch it on June 30. The Mini Starbucks Card is a convenient way to always have your Starbucks Experience at your finger tips—just clip it to whatever you like (keys, gym bag, etc.) and continue to enjoy your on-the-go lifestyle. I clipped mine to my racing bike, so I am never

> without a doppio espresso when I need it—I just cycle to a Starbucks store and swipe my Mini Starbucks Card—no wallet required!….

Chuck Davidson. (2009, July 4). "Asked for it: Introducing the Mini Starbucks Card!!" [Blog Post]. Retrieved from http://mystarbucksidea. force.com.

Starbucks certainly isn't the first company to launch a customer blog; Dell and Chrysler are just two others that have experienced success by listening online to customer suggestions and complaints (Hachmann, 2008). However, many companies shy away from such a commitment perhaps because they fear what they might hear. According to Jeff Jarvis (2008), "Starbucks, of all companies, with its loyal and opinionated customers, should have been doing this years ago. Every company should be doing it now. . . . What an incredible wealth of information, ideas—and caring—from customers. All you have to do is listen." And Starbucks is listening.

What do you think?
- Do you think Starbucks will benefit from *My Starbucks Idea* blog?
- What is making this site a success?
- What problems might result that they should be prepared to handle?

Listening Skill: Improvements Lead to Payoffs

In the previous section, we made several suggestions for correcting bad listening habits and overcoming listening barriers. This section explores strategies for strengthening listening skills.

Understanding the Stages of Listening

One way to improve your listening skills is to understand the listening process. The basic stages of listening (as shown in Figure 4.1) are sensing, interpreting, evaluating, responding, and, if those steps are completed correctly, storing in our memory what we hear (Steil et al., 1983).

Sensing Stage In the **sensing stage**, listeners select or ignore one or more stimuli from the multitude of stimuli that bombard us continually. It's impossible to notice every sound, every sight, and every smell, or to acknowledge every feeling that occurs around us. We have learned to become highly selective. We pay attention to things that are important to us or of interest to us; the other things we essentially tune out. Arthur K. Robertson (1994), in his book *Listen for Success*, illustrates the sensing stage with this example:

> A zoologist [is] walking down a busy city street with a friend amid honking horns and screeching tires. He says to his friend, "Listen to that cricket!" The friend looks at him with astonishment. "You hear a cricket in the middle of all this noise?" The zoologist takes out a coin and flips it into the air. As it clinks to the sidewalk a dozen heads turn in response. The zoologist says quietly, "We hear what we listen for." (p. 45)

In addition to needs and interests, listeners' sensing abilities are also affected by gender, age, cultural background, bias, emotion, and environmental distractions. For communication to really be effective, of course, you must not only look like you are listening, but you must be genuinely concerned with what is being communicated (Comer & Drollinger, 1999).

Interpreting Stage In the **interpreting stage**, listeners assign meaning to the messages that they have seen, heard, and felt in the sensing stage. In other words, they attempt to decode what the speaker really means. The difficulty is that we often have different meanings for the same word. As a result, some of the most serious listening problems occur in the interpreting stage. Many of these problems are explained by **attribution theory**, which describes how the average person processes information and uses it to explain the behavior of others and self (Littlejohn & Foss, 2008). Sometimes these problems occur because of semantic barriers (recall the woman we mentioned previously who tried to find the key called *Any Key* on her keyboard).

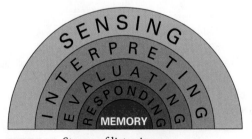

FIGURE 4.1 Stages of listening.

Sometimes they occur because listeners assume that they understand and don't bother with questions or paraphrasing (summarizing the speaker's ideas in their own words). Sometimes listening problems result from jumping to conclusions or from fatigue or information overload. And many interpreting problems arise because both speakers and listeners believe in the communication fallacy discussed in Chapter 1—that is, that 100% understanding is possible as long as the speaker is clear and the listener is paying attention. Brody (1994) found that customers felt positively toward salespeople during this stage of listening if the salesperson listened without interrupting, tried hard to understand by paraphrasing the customers' questions, and asked for more details when needed.

Evaluating Stage   In the **evaluating stage**, listeners "think about the message, make more extensive inferences, evaluate and judge the speaker and the message" (Goss, 1982, p. 306). In assigning a value judgment to what they have sensed and understood, listeners must decide whether the speaker is qualified, the information and evidence are accurate, and the comments are relevant and worth the time.

Listeners' evaluations are often affected by their attitude toward the speaker. Imagine yourself speaking before business colleagues who think you are too young, doubt you because of your gender or ethnicity, or mistrust the department you represent. Listeners' evaluations are also affected by previous experiences, expectations, and even their beliefs and emotions. As a result, listeners sometimes make evaluations based on assumptions without having all the facts. A rescue squad member related this incident about a call for help the squad received from a patrolman:

> A 38-year-old man had pulled off the road and hit an obstruction. [After calling the rescue squad, the] patrolman had called back: "Cancel the call. The man is not really injured. He's just complaining of chest pains and probably bumped into the steering wheel." The squad went out anyway. When they arrived they could see immediately that the man was having a heart attack. "What happened," he told them between gasps, "was that I had this chest pain and went off the road." And with that he passed out. We got to work on him right away and got him to a hospital, but it was too late. Now he had told the patrolman the same thing he had told us—"I had this chest pain and went off the road." The patrolman heard him, perhaps understood him, but despite his knowledge and experience did not evaluate what he heard and in this case not evaluating correctly was fatal. I never forgot that. (Steil et al., 1984, pp. 27–28)

Revisiting the Case Study

What role did attribution theory play in the Citicorp tower crisis, if any?

Attribution Theory

Original Theorist: Fritz Heider, *The Psychology of Interpersonal Relations,* 1958.

Definition: The process of drawing inferences or how people process information and use it to explain the behavior of others and self.

Involves a Three-Step Process: (a) Perceive an action, (b) judge intent of action, and (c) attribute reason for action.

Fundamental Attribution Error (Ross, 1977): Our tendency to overestimate the role of the person's character and underestimate the role that the situation has on behavior (i.e., we usually assume that the things that happen to people are a result of something they did).

Digital Vision/Getty Images

What value judgment do you think the listeners in this picture are making?

When speaking to others, remember that they are evaluating your message based not only on the words you use (language code), but also on the quality of your speaking voice (paralanguage code) and your appearance, gestures, and visual aids (nonverbal code)—as we saw in Chapter 1.

Responding Stage When listeners have sensed, interpreted, and evaluated you and your ideas, they are ready for the **responding stage**. This stage is very important because, without feedback, speakers can only assume that they have communicated. Listeners won't always agree, but their responses show whether they were listening and whether they understood. Listener response can take many forms. Ideally, listeners will verbally indicate their understanding (i.e., agreement, disagreement, or confusion). If not, watch for nonverbal facial expressions (such as frowning or head nodding). Although accurately interpreting nonverbal responses can be difficult, Chapter 5 will discuss specific nonverbal cues that may be helpful. Also, don't forget that listeners sometimes fake attention. Attentive posture and constant eye contact do not necessarily equal listening. People who are listening attentively may shift in their seats, doodle on their papers, cough, glance at the clock, and look at the floor. It's usually the people who sit perfectly still who are mentally somewhere else.

Memory Stage The **memory stage** is the final stage of effective listening. Listeners (assuming that they completed the sensing, interpreting, evaluating, and responding stages) decide what parts, if any, of your message to retain and then attempt to store them in memory. Unfortunately, no matter how brilliant the speaker's ideas, or how intently people listen, most of us will remember only about 10 to 25% of a presentation the next day, week, or month (Wolff et al., 1983).

Much of this problem occurs because listeners fail to transfer what they have just heard from their short-term memory into their long-term memory (Schab &

Crowder, 1989). In addition, Miller (1994) warns that our short-term memory holds only about seven "bits" of information, plus or minus two bits (in other words, five to nine bits). Cowan's more recent research (2001) suggests that many of us can retain no more than four bits of information in our short-term memories. A sound, letter, word, sentence, or even an idea is considered to be a bit of information. More than four to nine bits and we start to forget, unless we take notes or rehearse in some way in 30 seconds or less (Kosslyn & Rosenberg, 2006). Actually, some of us can forget even one bit of information if we don't rehearse. For example, have you ever left your office for the workroom to pick up some items, but forgot what you needed by the time you got there? Frustrating isn't it?

Speakers should know that listeners are more likely to remember information that is organized, effectively delivered, repeated, related to their backgrounds and interests, and accompanied by professional-looking visual aids. The power of visual aids cannot be overstated. Audience retention and comprehension are definitely increased when visual and verbal communication channels are properly teamed. (Chapter 13 discusses the benefits and power of using visual aids.) The Improving Your Listening—Key Points section that follows gives specifics on transferring information from short-term memory into long-term memory. As listeners, pay particular attention to these three points: (a) listen for key words, (b) write down the key words, and (c) constantly summarize/rehearse the key points in your mind.

Listening More Each Day   As you recall from the beginning of the chapter, we spend a great deal of time listening each day. Nevertheless, we probably could listen even more than we do. A very successful businessman once said that the more listening he did, the less speaking he did, and the more successful he became. He discovered that by listening more, not only did he learn more about his job, his colleagues, and the product they were making, but he also said the wrong thing less often, he appeared more industrious, and people talked to him more about pertinent issues. All of these factors contributed to his successful career.

As an experiment, figure out how much time you spend listening and speaking on a typical day. Don't include time spent reading, writing, reflecting (thinking), or watching TV. Just log the time you spend interacting with other people—for a log sheet to use, see Collaborative Learning Activity 1 at the end of this chapter. Once you get a reasonably accurate idea of your average listening and speaking time, deliberately attempt to adjust those percentages, spending more time listening and less speaking each day. The mere act of consciously attempting to listen more will alert you to the process of listening and help you practice being a good listener.

REMEMBER

In the Five Stages of Listening, Listeners . . .

1. Sense	Hear what is important to them
2. Interpret	Assign meaning to what is seen, heard, and felt
3. Evaluate	Determine speaker credibility and message importance
4. Respond	React to speech usually through nonverbal cues
5. Remember	Retain parts of message in memory

Improving Your Listening—Key Points

Instead of daydreaming or allowing yourself to get distracted, improve your listening by following these simple guidelines:

- *Identify the speaker's main points with a* **key word** *or phrase.* Key words and short phrases are easier to remember than complete sentences. Recalling a key word will trigger your mind to recall related facts as well.

- *Take* **brief notes** while you listen. Writing down phrases or key words will help reinforce your memory. Then review your notes. Studies show that people who take notes while listening but never review their notes retain no more than people who listen without taking notes (Kiewra et al., 1991). It's best to review while listening and not wait until later (Stettner, 1998).

- Therefore, *constantly summarize the speaker's previous points by repeating the key words in your mind.* Refer to your notes any time you are uncertain. With practice, you should be able to summarize a list of 10 items and still not miss anything the speaker says. This type of **constant summary** can increase the length of time ideas are held in short-term memory and may actually transfer them into long-term memory (Kiewra, 1985). **Note:** These first three guidelines—key word, brief notes, and constant summary—work together as key points in improving memory. Practice them when listening to speakers.

- *Listen for the facts, as well as, the feelings behind the facts.* If there is an emotional tone to the message, listening for facts alone will result in an incomplete message.

- *Relate information to current policies and procedures.* When listening to information about the organization, good listeners associate what is said with current policies and procedures. Associated information is easier to understand and remember.

- *Avoid prejudice.* We all have prejudices, and we need to remember that they affect the information we process. Good listeners listen to information objectively first and then evaluate it according to their beliefs. Allowing prejudice to intrude during the listening process distorts the meaning of the message.

Payoffs of Effective Listening

When we listen more effectively, we gain several advantages. The following list is not exhaustive, but it does suggest payoffs most people can obtain through more effective listening (Robinett, 1982). Your own personal payoffs will be even more numerous!

- *Effective listeners discover the values, needs, expectations, and goals of those with whom they work.* When listening is effective, we get a better understanding of what motivates our superiors, colleagues, and subordinates. We recognize that their values and expectations are either similar to or different from our own, and this information facilitates our own and the organization's goals. The following comments from two business managers illustrate this payoff of effective listening:

    It wasn't until management and the labor union at my plant really started listening to one another that we realized that both parties in the labor dispute were trying to attain the same goal: job security for the workers.

For several years I became quite angry with several of my subordinates when they would gripe, "We are not appreciated around here." Their discontent was not reduced by several pay raises, which were quite generous. It was not until I really listened to their complaints that I found money was not the appreciation they desired. Verbal recognition was the answer. I now praise my employees each time they do a good job. They seem much happier and more motivated, and I am saving the company money, which would have been spent on excessive salaries.

- *Better management-employee relations develop.* When employees feel that their managers are really listening and responding appropriately to their messages, good relationships will develop (as we saw in Chapter 3 on interpersonal relationships). Even when a manager is not able to grant employees' requests or suggestions, employees are much more likely to accept the decision and respect the manager if they know that they have been heard, and if the manager explains the reasons for the decision. In making decisions, good managers take employee concerns into consideration by listening to them and understanding them.

- *Better decisions are made in emergency situations.* For example, many people ignore safety briefings given by airline attendants because they feel they've heard it all before. Yet studies show that people who listen to these briefings are more likely to get through an emergency on an airline safely than those who don't listen. In an effort to encourage passengers to listen more to the safety instructions, Northwest Airlines uses video safety briefings instead of live briefings. Results show that while only 45% of passengers watch live safety presentations, 70% watch video briefings ("Listen Up," 2001).

- *We learn from others' experience.* Managers and employees who listen effectively realize that other members of the organization experience many of the same problems that they do. By listening carefully, we can learn from others' successes and avoid their mistakes.

All of these advantages of effective listening make us more valuable employees.

CHAPTER 4

REVIEW

Monkey Business Images/Shutterstock

Key Terms

attribution theory (112)

brief notes (116)

constant summary (116)

evaluating stage (113)

gender barriers (108)

high context (104)

interpreting stage (112)

key word (116)

listening (99)

Summary

Effective listening is not passive. It takes a great deal of effort and motivation to become an effective listener. Good listening is a prerequisite for success in business and the professions. Although effective listening is certainly not the answer to all business problems, it is one of the first steps leading to solutions. Organizational effectiveness is hampered by employees and managers who do not listen well. Individual career advancement also can be hindered by poor listening. Unfortunately, poor listening is often more apparent to others than it is to the poor listener.

The suggestions in this chapter about breaking bad listening habits and improving listening skills should be used as a guide. Some suggestions may be more beneficial than others. It is up to you to try them and monitor how they are working. Becoming an effective listener takes a great deal of work, but the payoffs are worth the effort. Few people are effective listeners. Once you attain this skill, you will be in an elite group indeed.

To conclude this chapter, let's take a look at how our case study crisis ended: Once LeMessurier realized how serious the danger could be from a rare quartering wind, he took immediate action and notified the lawyers, the architect, and the top brass at Citicorp. After discussions, the following steps were taken: Emergency generators for the TMD were set up; contracting engineers inspected an exposed joint on an unused floor and agreed that LeMessurier's steel Band-Aid idea was feasible; a number of constantly monitored strain gauges were attached to the building; an advisory group of weather experts were gathered to provide wind alerts; an evacuation plan for the building and surrounding area was planned by Citicorp and the American Red Cross's director of disaster services; the building commissioner and nine city officials were briefed about the danger and proposed actions; and a short, fairly vague press release was sent out. Anticipation was high. To minimize concern, welding occurred only at night and was cleaned up before office workers arrived each morning. By the time Hurricane Ella headed for New York, repairs to the most serious joints had been completed, and with the TMD operating, the building could withstand a 200-year storm (fortunately, the hurricane veered out to sea). Another fortunate thing was that the city newspapers were on strike during the repairs, so no citizen awareness or panic occurred. Although Citicorp filed a claim against LeMessurier and the architect, they agreed to accept the insurance company's payment of $2 million and dropped the suit. Robertson, the structural expert brought into the case by Citicorp, had this to say: "I have a lot of admiration for Bill, because he was very forthcoming. While we say that all engineers would behave as he did, I carry in my mind some skepticism about that" (Morgenstern, 2005, p. 69).

Communicating for Results Online

Before continuing to the next chapter, check your understanding of Chapter 4 at the Premium Website for *Communicating for Results*. Your Premium Website gives you quick and easy access to the electronic resources that accompany this text. These resources include:

- **Study tools** that will help you assess your learning and prepare for exams (student companion workbook, digital glossary, key term flash cards, and review quizzes).
- **Activities and assignments** that will help you hone your knowledge, analyze professional communication situations, build your public speaking skills throughout the course, and learn to work effectively in teams (Awareness Checks, Checkpoints, and Collaborative Learning Activities).
- **Media resources** that will help you explore communication concepts online (web links), develop your speech outlines (Speech Builder Express 3.0),

watch and critique videos of professional communication situations and sample speeches (Interactive Video Activities), upload your speech videos for peer reviewing and critique other students' speeches (Speech Studio online speech review tool), and download chapter review so you can study when and where you'd like (Audio Study Tools).

This chapter's key terms, Collaborative Learning Activities, and Checkpoint activities are also featured on the following pages, and you can find this chapter's Awareness Check activities in the body of the chapter. For more information or to access this book's online resources, visit www.cengage.com/login.

Collaborative Learning Activities

1. After team members each take the following listening survey on an appointed day, combine results for a team total. Are the results as expected? Why or why not?

Listening Survey

a. Please estimate the total amount of time you spend in school or doing school work on your assigned day:

b. Now estimate the amount of time you spend in school or doing school work on your assigned day in each of these communication methods. *Note*: Your total should add up to the estimated total you wrote.

Writing: |--------|--------|--------|--------|--------|--------|--------|--------|--------|--------|
[Hours]   0   1   2   3   4   5   6   7   8   9+

Reading: |--------|--------|--------|--------|--------|--------|--------|--------|--------|--------|
[Hours]   0   1   2   3   4   5   6   7   8   9+

Speaking: |--------|--------|--------|--------|--------|--------|--------|--------|--------|--------|
[Hours]   0   1   2   3   4   5   6   7   8   9+

Listening |--------|--------|--------|--------|--------|--------|--------|--------|--------|--------|
[Hours]   0   1   2   3   4   5   6   7   8   9+

Phone: |--------|--------|--------|--------|--------|--------|--------|--------|--------|--------|
[Hours]   0   1   2   3   4   5   6   7   8   9+

E-mail |--------|--------|--------|--------|--------|--------|--------|--------|--------|--------|
[Hours]   0   1   2   3   4   5   6   7   8   9+

Internet: |--------|--------|--------|--------|--------|--------|--------|--------|--------|--------|
[Hours]   0   1   2   3   4   5   6   7   8   9+

2. Complete the questions about gender barriers in the Awareness Check on p. 109. Check your answers against the correct answers located in the back of the text. In small groups of five to seven, compare answers and discuss any that were missed by group members. If your group disagrees with the answer key, be prepared to explain your group's preferred answer to other groups or the entire class if asked. Be prepared with an example to support your answer.

3. In small groups, discuss the "It Really Works" essay about Starbucks and the way they listen to customers on a new website called My Starbucks Idea, and answer the "What do You Think?" questions listed at the end. Be prepared to share your answers with other groups.

4. Summarize the main points in the Citigroup case study at the beginning of the chapter—see the conclusion of the situation in the chapter summary. In small groups of three to seven come to an agreement on what the chapter has to say about the following questions: (a) evaluate LeMessurier's listening skills on a scale of 1 (poor) to 5 (excellent) and explain why you gave him the score that you did; (b) determine whether he was guilty of any signs of poor listening and why, and (c) decide whether it was ethical for LeMessurier and others involved in the crisis to withhold this information from the public for 20 years.

Checkpoints

Checkpoint 4.1 Listening Test
Go to Randall's ESL Cyber Listening Lab at www.esl-lab.com and take one of the tests in the General Listening Quizzes columns to test your listening skills. After taking one of the tests, write a short essay explaining what you now know about your listening habits that you did not know before. Are you a better listener than you thought? Do you need to improve your listening skills?

Checkpoint 4.2 Practicing Your Listening Skills

Checkpoint 4.3 Listening Websites

Nonverbal Communication in the Organization

Dreamstime.com

Case Study

As you read Chapter 5,

Define the term *nonverbal communication*, and **explain** how it differs in each of the three cultural levels: technical, formal, and informal.

List the seven major types of nonverbal communication in the workplace, and **summarize** at least three practical tips for effective use of each type.

Describe the role that nonverbal symbols and culture shock play in international business transactions and what can be done to minimize any negative effects.

Identify how to improve your nonverbal skills through immediacy behaviors and effective habits.

Hook 'em Horns Gesture Causes Problems at 2005 Inauguration

Communication misunderstandings caused by nonverbal messages and gestures can be especially serious when multiple countries and cultures are involved. In January 2005 at his second inauguration, George W. Bush along with his wife and daughters flashed several hook 'em horns hand gestures as the University of Texas Longhorn Band marched by them during the inaugural parade. This certainly wasn't the first time President Bush had used this gesture, nor was it the first time that a student from the University of Texas had received negative press overseas for using the hook 'em horns gesture (Douglas, 2005). However, the heavy media coverage of the inauguration, which was shown around the world, led to more people and countries taking notice and many of them expressing shock and anger.

The hook 'em horns hand gesture began at the University of Texas in 1955 to represent their mascot, the Texas longhorn, which is a breed of cattle known for its unusually long horns (Douglas, 2005). The hand sign representing the longhorn is made with the two middle fingers pressed against the palm of the hand and the other two fingers pointing upward like cattle horns. The hook 'em horns sign looks similar to the American Sign Language sign for "I love you," which you may have seen on an American postage stamp except that the thumb is extended in the "I love you" sign but crosses the middle fingers in the hook 'em gesture. The palm and fingers generally face away from the body in both signs.

The hook 'em horns gesture is used by the University of Texas alumni, students, faculty, and cheerleaders as a greeting and as a sign of respect during sporting events. For example, during football games use of the sign begins when the

Ronald Martinez/Getty Images

As you read this chapter, see if you can determine (a) who was the most responsible for the misunderstanding—Bush, his advisors, or the people from other countries and why, (b) which of the four types of gestures would best describe the hook 'em horns sign, (c) and how important a role do you think a misunderstanding over a gesture such as this one would play in international affairs.

Longhorn Band runs onto the field at home games "in its burnt orange uniforms, hands raised with 'hook 'em' signs. Fans leap to their feet, and soon 'hook 'em' signs fill the stadium to its farthest reaches" ("Showband of the Southwest," 2002). Because Bush had been governor of Texas and his wife and daughters have degrees from the University of Texas, the entire family feels a close connection to the university and its mascot.

The problem with the hook 'em horns hand gesture, as well as other gestures used around the world is that they don't mean the same thing to all people in all countries. According to David Thomas (2008) in his book *Cross-Cultural Management*, "trying to learn all the hand gestures that exist across cultures would be virtually impossible" (p. 135). However, in President Bush's case, the gesture he and his family used has different meanings in other countries that are serious enough that he probably should have saved the gesture for a more private time. For example, in Nordic countries, the sign is viewed as a salute to Satan or devil worship. Italians use the sign to mean that a wife is cheating on her spouse. Some Africans interpret the sign to mean that a curse is being placed on the one to whom the gesture is made, and some Mediterranean countries consider the sign to be an insult similar to the single middle finger sign used in the United States (Axtell, 2007). Although there are many other meanings for the hook 'em horn sign that do not have a negative meaning—such as in baseball where the sign is used to mean "you have two outs," you can see why some international viewers felt both shock and confusion seeing the president of the United States portraying such a sign, smiling all the while.

Managers, employees, and team members constantly send messages to those around them. Some of these messages are sent intentionally, but many are sent unconsciously. Managers at all levels send messages with their clothes; the size and location of their offices; the arrangement of their office furniture; where they sit during meetings; their facial expressions, gestures, and posture; their distance from others; and many silent messages with their eye contact; their posture; their facial expressions, gestures, and clothing; their distance from others; the time it takes them to complete their work; the way they handle conflict; and even the way they decorate their desks. The success of communication in an organization often depends on how well managers, employees, and teams can read these silent messages—especially in today's global economy where organizations represent a variety of cultures that have different views of individualism and context (see Chapter 3 for a review).

Recall from our discussion in Chapter 1 that nonverbal code (including paralanguage) is responsible for more than half of the meaning of a sender's total message and that when the language, paralanguage, and nonverbal codes send conflicting messages, people tend to pay even more attention to the nonverbal code (Burgoon & Hoobler, 2002). Therefore, we shouldn't be surprised that successful use of nonverbal communication helps in establishing and maintaining necessary interpersonal relationships (Burgoon et al., 1996). According to Barnlund (1989), there is a reciprocal quality to nonverbal communication: "The habits of posture, gesture, and touch of one person tend to prompt similar acts from the other" (p. 127), thereby improving rapport and decreasing awkwardness. Effective use of nonverbal communication also improves the likelihood that others will comply with our requests (Gladwell, 2002; Segrin, 1993). The impact of nonverbal communication on your success in business *cannot* be overemphasized. For example, research indicates that 60 to 70% of the interpersonal communication involved in effective sales is nonverbal (Dimmick, 1995; Fill, 1995). This chapter, therefore, concentrates on improving your skill in understanding, detecting, and sending nonverbal messages.

Nonverbal Communication: Definition and Principles

Although the term can be defined in several different ways, this text defines **nonverbal communication** as all intentional and unintentional messages that are not written, spoken, or sounded. Although many texts include paralanguage (vocal sounds) as part of nonverbal communication, this definition omits it because the three codes (language, paralanguage, and nonverbal) are easier to understand when each is considered separately. (See Chapter 1 for a discussion of paralanguage and Chapter 12 for a discussion of language, paralanguage and cultural differences.)

To accurately determine the meaning of a nonverbal (silent) message in a business or professional setting, you must know the sender's personal frame of reference and cultural background, as well as the specific situation. Although facial expressions for such emotions as happiness, surprise, sadness, disgust, anger, and fear are fairly universal (Ekman, 1994, 2003; Ekman et al., 1987), the meaning of most nonverbal messages depends on the culture in which they occur. For example, in the United States nodding your head usually means agreement; in Japan nodding the head means only that the message was received (James, 1989); and in Bulgaria nodding the head shows disagreement (Axtell, 2007). Another example of cultural differences is illustrated by the gesture made by forming a circle with the thumb and forefinger: In the United States this gesture means "A-OK"; in Japan it refers to money; in France it means zero or worthless; in Australia, Brazil, Germany, and Tunisia it is considered an obscene gesture (Hansson, 1999; Munter, 1993; Samovar et al., 2010).

One way to enrich our understanding of culture and nonverbal behaviors is to view it through several dimensions. We will examine three of them here and another one later in the chapter. The first two important dimensions were

If this boxer were visiting Australia or Germany, people would view his "A-OK" gesture as obscene.

AP/Wide World Photos

discussed in Chapter 3: *individualistic–collectivistic* cultures and *low-context–high-context* cultures. If you recall, collectivistic cultures prefer empathy, listening, and nonverbal communication, whereas individualistic cultures prefer individual rights, assertion, and telling it like it is. Low-context cultures are direct and explicit and consider clear communication to be the responsibility of the sender who provides meaning primarily through words; high-context cultures prefer a more indirect route and consider clear communication to be the responsibility of the receiver who gets the meaning from context and nonverbal messages. See Chapter 3 for a more detailed discussion.

A third way to understand the relationship between culture and nonverbal messages is through the dimension of the *technical–formal–informal* levels of culture (Hall, 1973).

Technical Level

At the **technical level**, the rules for cultural and nonverbal behaviors are openly known and easily stated by most citizens of a particular culture. These rules, as well as, the reasons for the rules, are deliberately taught, such as in a new-employee orientation session where various procedures, techniques (correct use of a machine or computer program), regulations, and behaviors (greeting a customer) are taught. When a technical rule or behavior is broken unintentionally, very little emotion is involved; the mistake is pointed out and a correction is made. Of course, people who deliberately choose to ignore a company's technical rules will likely find themselves out of a job.

Formal Level

At the **formal level**, the rules for behavior are clearly stated, but the reasons for the rules are not. They are simply accepted without question by most people. Some generally accepted workplace examples of the formal level include typical office hours in the United States (9 to 5 with lunch from 12 to 1), arrive on time or early, and the boss sits at the head of the table. Formal rules that include rituals, traditions, and etiquette are considered extremely important and if violated, cause a strong emotional response. People who question these rules are not viewed as team players and are told, "That's just the way things are!" Compared with many other countries, the United States has few formal rules. Furthermore, many of these formal rules allow for a fairly wide range of variation before the rule is considered to be violated. Formal rules based on tradition change slowly, but they do change—for example, "Male managers should wear ties and white shirts."

Informal Level

At the **informal level** of culture, neither the rules for behavior nor the reason for the rules are taught; they are unconsciously learned by imitation (modeling ourselves after others). The informal level includes rules for nonverbal behaviors, such as gestures, eye contact, status, office size, appointment arrival time, and the proper physical distance for conversations. Once the behaviors of the informal level are learned, they usually become automatic and are taken for granted. We are often unaware that these behaviors are dictated by rules. However, when someone breaks one of these unstated rules (e.g., staring at us longer than we feel is polite or standing too close in an elevator), we may become uncomfortable and even withdraw from the situation.

There are many different cultures and subcultures in the United States, so it is dangerous to make assumptions about nonverbal meanings—especially because what is a formal rule in one culture may be a technical or informal rule in another. Nevertheless, the *majority* of our business-related nonverbal behaviors are governed by informal-level rules. Because we are generally not consciously aware of these rules, it is no wonder that so many people overlook the importance of nonverbal messages to successful communication.

Types of Nonverbal Communication and Their Effects on Business Communication

The types of nonverbal communication are almost limitless. However, in this chapter, we cover only those types that are most applicable to business communications: facial expressions and eye contact, other body movements and gestures, clothing and personal appearance, distance and personal space, physical environment, and time.

Facial Expressions and Eye Contact

The face is responsible for most of the meaning in nonverbal messages. Although basic facial expressions (such as happiness, surprise, fear, and anger) are fairly universal, the subtle and spontaneous expressions we encounter at work each day are more difficult to interpret (Ekman, 1994; Motley, 1993) and differ across cultures. For example, although facial expressions are fairly open in the United States, Asian countries are more likely to suppress facial expressions (Andersen & Wang, 2009). Nevertheless, expressions like raised or lowered eyebrows, nervous tics, clenched teeth, or tensed, pursed lips give clues to a person's feelings, thus enabling us to improve communication.

The eyes are the most expressive part of the face and have considerable effect on communication. In U.S. culture, eye contact performs several functions.

Eye Contact Shows Interest and Attentiveness In U.S. culture, people in business or the professions expect those to whom they are speaking to look at them. A listener's lack of eye contact is interpreted as disinterest or even disrespect. At the same time, a speaker's lack of eye contact may cause the listener to interpret the message less favorably (Exline & Eldridge, 1967).

Petro Feketa/Shutterstock   Ximagination/Shutterstock   Donald Macalister/iStockphoto

The face is responsible for most of the meanings in nonverbal messages. Can you identify which face is expressing elation? dread? fear?

The informal rules do not call for constant or prolonged eye contact (except in cases of extreme anger or intimacy). In the United States, people tend to look at others more while listening than while speaking. Speakers tend to look away at the beginning of an utterance (perhaps to plan what to say), look back occasionally to check the listener's response, and look again at the end to signal that feedback is expected (Malandro et al., 1989; Wiemann & Knapp, 1975).

Generally, two people conversing will maintain mutual eye contact only 31% of the time; the average length of a mutual gaze is only 1.18 seconds (Harper et al., 1978; Knapp & Hall, 1997). When the gaze is not mutual (e.g., when the listener looks at the speaker, who has glanced away), it lasts an average of only 2.95 seconds (Argyle & Ingham, 1972). When people maintain eye contact for longer than the expected lengths—as Arabs, Latins, Indians, and Pakistanis do—North Americans become uncomfortable, whereas some Africans and East Asians view it "as conveying anger or insubordination" (Thomas, 2008, p. 137).

Eye Contact Signals a Wish to Participate People who want to interact usually make eye contact and smile (Burgoon & Hoobler, 2002). The following example illustrates how eye contact can be read as an indication of the desire to participate.

> Tonya, a young nurse at a large hospital, complained that in the 6 months she had been working at the hospital, she had been appointed to four committees even though she hadn't volunteered for any of them. Each time one of the head nurses asked for volunteers, Tonya sat quietly and said nothing. What the young nurse did not realize was that whenever the head nurse said, "We need one more volunteer," Tonya looked directly at the head nurse, nonverbally signaling "I volunteer," and thus prompting the request, "Tonya, how about you?" Her nonverbal volunteering was just as loud as the verbal assents given by other nurses. Nurses who did not wish to volunteer most likely looked down and refused to meet the searching eyes of the head nurse.

You have probably had a similar experience when your boss asked the group a question. The moment you made eye contact with the person, you knew that you were going to be called on—and you were, weren't you? The opposite is also true: Avoiding eye contact can signal a desire to be left alone.

Eye Contact Controls and Persuades Others In U.S. culture, eye contact signals others that it is okay to talk. Consider, for example, the project director who, after explaining the project, asked for individual responses from the group but looked directly at Joe. Even though Joe was looking down and missed the signal, no one else spoke; they had not received permission yet. Only when the director glanced across the group with slightly raised eyebrows did someone else speak. Because response to eye contact is at the informal level, quite possibly neither the director nor the members were consciously aware of what had happened. Other people use it deliberately, such as withholding eye contact from a person they are unhappy with while making direct eye contact with everyone else. If a supervisor does this, it sends a strong message: "I'm displeased" (Reardon, 2000, p. 87).

Lack of eye contact can also control the flow of communication by signaling that it is time for a conversation to end. Suppose, for example, that you are busy on an important task when a colleague stops by and asks if you have a minute to discuss a problem. You reply that you are busy but can spare 5 minutes or so. At the end of 5 (or maybe even 10) minutes, when the visitor shows no signs of leaving, you can either tell the person that you must get back to work or terminate the conversation nonverbally by breaking eye contact and glancing down at the papers on your desk. If you choose the latter course, in most cases the person will automatically end the conversation, thank you for your help, and leave without being consciously aware of the role that eye contact played.

Eye contact is such a powerful control that a seminar speaker who stands facing the left side of the audience with his or her back slightly toward the right side of the group will usually get comments only from those on the left. If, halfway through the seminar, the speaker turns and faces those on the right side of the room, those who have eye contact with the speaker will begin to respond, and the other side will become silent.

"See? That means, 'What do you clowns want?"

In the food service industry, eye contact is a valuable way to move customers rapidly while still giving them the feeling that they are receiving personal service. In line at a cafeteria one day, we observed a food server who would say, "May I help you with a meat dish?" but would look at the food while speaking. When no one replied, he would repeat the question several times and finally look up in exasperation. At that point, the person he made eye contact with would say, "Oh, I'll have the. . . ." That server must have been exhausted by the end of the day! The salad server had much more success simply by making direct eye contact with each customer and raising her eyebrows slightly.

Eye contact and facial expressions also play a role in persuasion. A study conducted by Brian Mullen and colleagues (1986) and discussed in Gladwell (2002) took place during the presidential campaign between Walter Mondale and Ronald Reagan. All ABC, NBC, and CBS nightly newscasts were videotaped for 8 days prior to the election. All references to the candidates were organized into 37 segments, each approximately 2.5 seconds long with no sound. Subjects were asked to watch each segment by each newscaster (Peter Jennings at ABC, Tom Brokaw at NBC, and Dan Rather at CBS) and score the facial expressions on a 21-point scale from 1, "extremely negative," to 21, "extremely positive." The results indicated that Brokaw and Rather used practically the same expressions for both candidates (scores averaged in the 10s for Rather and 11s for Brokaw), but Jennings had a 13.38 when talking about Mondale and a 17.44 when discussing Reagan. When regular watchers of each program were called and asked whom they voted for, those who watched ABC voted for Reagan significantly more often than those who watched the other two stations, even though additional research showed that ABC was the "most hostile to Reagan" (Gladwell, 2002, p. 76). The study was repeated in the Michael Dukakis–George H. W. Bush campaign with the same results. The researchers concluded that it was a subtle pro-Republican bias showing in Jennings's face that influenced the viewers.

Eye Contact and Other Cultures Because nonverbal expressions have different meanings in various cultures, be careful about assigning your culture's meanings for eye behavior to all people. For example, in some parts of the country Brazilians tend to avoid eye contact with people of different status or ages with the younger person generally looking down (Axtell, 2007); yet Americans working overseas report that the eye contact used by Brazilians is so intense that it appears to be rude even to Americans who generally appreciate direct eye contact (Wood, 2010, p. 127). In the United States, the informal rules governing eye contact for blacks and Hispanics differ somewhat from those for whites. The following example illustrates this point:

> A New York department store manager fired a young Hispanic clerk suspected of pilfering. "She wouldn't meet my eyes when I questioned her," he told a union representative. "I knew she was lying."
>
> The union representative, himself Hispanic, explained, "What you don't understand is that a well-bred Hispanic girl will not make eye contact with a man who is not a relative. It's just considered too bold. . . . She'll look away or drop her eyes." (Fast, 1991, p. 29)

One researcher feels that different eye expectations may contribute to perceptions of racism, especially between whites and blacks. According to F. Erickson (1979), many white listeners use a combination of three behaviors to show attentiveness: fairly direct eye contact, vocal noises (like "uh huh"), and head nodding. However, many blacks show attentiveness with only one of these (usually head nods). Therefore, although whites may view a single nonverbal behavior as insufficient to show attentiveness, blacks may consider use of all three nonverbal behaviors as unnecessary and as a sign of hostility or superiority. This research was published in 1979. Is Erickson's observation still true today?

What other cultural differences dealing with facial expressions and eye contact have you observed in your part of the country? As we learned in Chapter 1, assuming that you and another person have identical frames of reference usually leads to misunderstanding.

Other Body Movements and Gestures

Movements and gestures of other parts of the body are even more closely tied to culture than are facial expressions and eye contact. Therefore, it is extremely misleading to isolate a single body movement (such as crossing the legs) and give it a universal meaning, as do many popular body language books. Keep in mind, however, that others may attribute specific meanings to your body movements and gestures regardless of your intentions. For example, poor posture during an interview may be interpreted as disrespect, lack of enthusiasm, or indicative of poor work habits. Audiences may consider speakers' poor posture and nervous movements as proof that they are insincere or even inept. In one-to-one or small-group situations, posture can indicate like or dislike: Leaning forward signals a positive feeling toward others; leaning backward, a negative feeling (Mehrabian, 1969). The way a person stands may indicate self-confidence, status, friendliness, or mood. Even weak or overly strong handshakes will be given some significance by many people (Figure 5.1). Overall, a firm handshake (known as the continental grab) makes the best impression in the United States (Chaplin et al., 2000) for both men and women. Ninety percent of the personnel managers from 30 companies considered a firm handshake by the applicant in an interview to be important (Harris, 1993). Most Americans react negatively to the flaccid, or "dead-fish," handshake

The early grab

The over-confident

The continental grab

FIGURE 5.1 Typical handshakes—which do you prefer? dislike?

(Nierenberg & Calero, 1973). Not all countries greet with a handshake; "Arab men often greet by kissing on both checks. In Japan, men greet by bowing, and in Mexico they often embrace" (Samovar & Porter, 2004).

Gestures and body movements can be divided into four categories: emblems, illustrators, regulators, and adaptors (Ekman, 1992, 2003; Ekman & Friesen, 1969).

- **Emblems** are intentional body movements and gestures that carry an exact verbal meaning (Ekman, 1992). For example, even if no words accompanied an obscene gesture, the chances are good that you would understand its meaning. Different cultures might interpret emblems differently. For a discussion of emblems used around the world, see Axtell (2007) and Kendon (1994).

- **Illustrators** are intentional movements or gestures that add to or clarify verbal meaning—for example, pointing in the correct direction while explaining how to get to the mall or turning your hands palm up as you say, "Now this is my point."

The gestures used by police officers to direct traffic replace the need for most words.

- **Regulators** control the flow of a conversation. For example, the interviewer who breaks off eye contact with the interviewee may be signaling that it's time to wrap up the discussion; the listener who nods her head several times while saying, "Yeah, yeah, right" is probably signaling that it's time to switch speakers.

- **Adaptors** are habitual gestures and movements we use in times of discomfort. Flipping your hair behind your ear, scratching your nose or cheek, or rubbing the back of your neck while giving a presentation are examples of adaptors (Cooper, 1987). Adaptors often contradict the message we wish to send. Suppose you are a customer trying to negotiate a price reduction. Any nonverbal adaptors the salesperson displays indicate to you that he or she is weakening, and you renew your efforts to reduce the price. According to Navarro and Karlins (2008), adaptors are clues that a person is experiencing or has experienced an uncomfortable situation. People use these adaptors, what Navarro and Karlins call **pacifying behaviors**, as a way to calm themselves by stimulating nerve endings. In addition to the examples given, playing with a necklace or tie stimulates the neck below the Adam's apple,

ETHICAL DILEMMA

If you glance through the news archives from 2002, it's hard to miss the cover-up scandal involving accounting firm Arthur Andersen and its most famous client, Enron. Even with an ethics policy in place and an 89-year-old stellar reputation, the top managers somehow conveyed the threat of unemployment to those working beneath them. When the middle managers were ordered to shred documents related to the company's dealings with Enron (Jones, 2007b), the nonverbal "do as I do" message received from their bosses was more powerful than the "think straight, talk straight," motto that the original Arthur Andersen had brought to his company back in 1913 (McLean & Elkind, 2003, p. 143). As a result of all the shredded documents and cover-ups done for Enron, Arthur Andersen was found guilty of obstruction of justice. However in May 2005, the Supreme Court overturned the conviction because of faulty instructions given to the jury and returned the case back to the lower courts (Mears et al., 2005). Even though revenue from Enron was "less than 1 percent of Andersen's $9.3 billion annual revenues" (Fusaro & Miller, 2002, p. 128), having a felony conviction kept other companies from using them, and Andersen was forced to declare bankruptcy. In the end, all those middle managers who had been afraid to lose their jobs lost them anyway (Jones, 2007b).

QUESTIONS: What ethical procedures need to be implemented to help employees reject unethical orders received from supervisors and managers? Is there a way to protect employees from the consequences of ethical behavior when ordered to do otherwise?

rubbing the head or neck with your fingers or the inside of the mouth with the tongue stimulates nerves, and so does rubbing the tops of your legs with the palms of your hands.

As a business or professional person, you can improve your communication techniques by monitoring your conscious and unconscious body movements and gestures. Ask colleagues and family for feedback, and review a videotape of yourself (taped during a meeting, interview, or oral presentation).

Clothing and Personal Appearance

Clothing and personal appearance also communicate nonverbal messages. In fact, people use your clothing and appearance to determine your status, credibility, and persuasiveness (Benson et al., 1975; Knapp & Hall, 2002; Michelsen, 1993). Businesses and professions have learned from experience that the public's perception of their organization depends in part on the appearance and dress of their personnel. For this reason many companies require uniforms and most others have a dress code. UPS, Bank One, and Sears are just a few of the companies that specify the career apparel employees can wear (Jones, 2003; Merx, 2003). Even the Mayo Clinic requires business attire in place of casual dress or white coats for its more than 2,800 staff physicians except when they are in surgical scrubs (Berry & Bendapudi, 2003). Even the White House under President Barack Obama's leadership is moving from traditional business dress to a more casual approach (Stolberg, 2009).

Your company may be like IBM and many others that have relaxed their strict business dress codes and now allow employees to dress in a **business casual** manner. But you may be as confused as others about what business casual really means. Image consultant Sherry Maysonave (1999) calls this confusion **casual confusion syndrome (CCS)** and says that it leads to people wearing inappropriate casual attire. "The business-casual trend has created entire companies of people who are unsure of what to put on in the morning," says Christina Binkley in an article for the *Wall Street Journal* (2008, D1). She notes that in most cases, business casual is more formal than "casual" and does not include jeans, shorts, t-shirts, or halter-tops. Maysonave (1999, p. 79) offers these business casual basics: dark colors (for contrast mix with a white or light-hue blouse or shirt); simple, classic lines; long sleeves and quality fabrics; high-quality shoes in immaculate condition—all-leather tie shoes for men and classic closed-toes with moderate heels for women; clean, shiny hair, professionally cut; and simple, high-quality jewelry kept to a minimum. According to New York psychologist Jon-Scott Turco, you may be judged more when wearing business casual than when wearing traditional business attire because people "assume they're seeing the real person" (Binkley, 2008, p. D1).

If you are uncertain about what clothing is appropriate, take your lead from what managers are wearing and keep these pointers in mind:

- The most basic business colors are navy, gray, and neutrals such as tan or beige; business casual also includes green, gold, and black (Damhorst & Fiore, 2000).

- Color shows status in business offices just as clearly as uniforms show rank in the military (Greenleaf, 1998). The darker the color, the higher the rank and the more authority it communicates. Researchers have consistently found that interviewers tend to rate applicants dressed in darker colors as more competent than applicants dressed in lighter colors (Damhorst & Reed, 1986; Forsythe, 1990). This holds true even in sports organizations. Researchers found that football and hockey players who wear black uniforms are perceived by fans as being rougher and more aggressive and even receive more penalties from referees (Frank & Gilovich, 1988).

- Sport coats or jackets for men and women and a tie for men continue to be important in the business wardrobe—keep these handy to put on when needed. Keltner and Holsey (1982) suggest that wearing a jacket is important to the female manager because it allows her to look part of the team. Jackets are also a great equalizer between men and women. For men, although a tie is normally not a requirement for

Jacob Wackerhausen/iStockphoto

Business casual generally does not mean casual and does not include jeans.

business casual, nothing says authority more than a tie especially when no jacket is worn.

- Color and style are equally important for job interviews because the first impressions created by clothing and personal appearance impact hiring decisions (Rowe, 1989). Patrick Dailey, director of business HR for Nokia Corporation says the dress code for men "remains a dark suit, a light or white shirt and a bright-colored but sophisticated tie" ("Business Casual Can Be Confusing," 2006). Although attractive pantsuits work for women, when asked to select the best from 100 photos of women's business attire, both men and women preferred skirted suits that had visual symmetry, skirts below the knee, conservative colors, and light-colored shirts with round necks (Damhorst & Fiore, 2000).

- On the job and in interviews, don't overlook the importance of professional demeanor, which includes direct eye contact and pleasant social interaction. It may be as important as or even more important than what you wear. Researchers report that physical appearance (especially grooming and neatness) has "some effect" on hiring decisions but that professional demeanor has "a marked influence" on them (Boor et al., 1983; Mack & Rainey, 1990). (See Chapter 8 for a more thorough discussion of successful nonverbal behaviors in interviews.)

IT REALLY WORKS!

Nonverbal Imagery

Take a look at the word *Sapworth*. What sorts of nonverbal images do you take from a word like that? It's not very hearty or strong, is it? Admiral Elmo "Bud" Zumwalt Jr. certainly knew the power an image can create in the minds of team members—even early in his career.

Zumwalt was born in 1920, served in the U.S. Navy from 1939 to 1974, and was promoted on a fairly consistent basis until—as the youngest man ever to do so—he reached the rank of Chief of Naval Operations in 1970 (Zumwalt, 2006). So powerful and positive was his influence—in part due to his excellent communication skills—that the Navy has named a ship after him (*The Waterline*, 2006).

Earlier in his career, upon taking command of the *Arnold J. Isbell*, Zumwalt learned that the crew's morale was considerably lower than that of other ships. In addition to various other communication issues, he discovered that the voice call sign, a sort of nickname for naval ships, was Sapworth. In his own words, "When in company with such stalwarts as 'FIREBALL,' 'VIPER,' and others, it is somewhat embarrassing and completely out of keeping with the quality of the sailormen aboard to be identified by the relatively ignominious title 'SAPWORTH'" (Zumwalt, 1976, p. 187). So, realizing that Sapworth did not make for an exciting T-shirt and recogniz-

ing the nonverbal effects on his crew, Zumwalt decided to make a change. No longer would the *Isbell* be subject to the scorn—real or imagined—associated with Sapworth, for the ship would now be called Hellcat.

Though a small word change, Zumwalt's use of the Hellcat image proved successful. "*Arnold J. Isbell*'s officers and men proudly wore sleeve patches and baseball cap patches showing a black cat with a forked tail stepping out of the flames of hell and breaking a submarine with its paws. The impact on morale was remarkable" (Zumwalt, 1976, p. 189). Nonverbal communication expressed by his crew gave him exactly the results he wanted, and all because of a simple switch in image.

What do you think?

- A company's image is so important that image consultants are often hired. How does this compare with the action taken by Zumwalt to change *Isbell*'s call sign?

- Research discussed in this chapter found that football and hockey players who wear black uniforms receive more penalties from referees. Discuss why the *Isbell*'s sailors with the new call name might be perceived by others and even themselves as more aggressive and dangerous.

Distance and Personal Space

The informal distance rules for conversing in various situations differ from culture to culture, family to family, and person to person. When you violate an individual's personal space requirements, that person becomes uncomfortable and will move away to correct the distance. Many people are completely unaware of their personal distance requirements because, as mentioned previously, such requirements usually are at the informal level of culture.

Careful observation of business and professional people in the United States led one well-known anthropologist (Hall, 1973) to divide personal reactions to distance into four categories (see Figure 5.2). Except for comforting gestures (such as an arm around the shoulder) or greetings between close friends or loved ones, most Americans reserve the **intimate distance** (from touching to 18 inches) for private use. **Personal distance** (from 18 inches to 4 feet) is used by close friends or colleagues as they eat lunch together or stand around the coffeepot during a break. How closely they sit or stand within the personal distance range depends on their own personal space requirements, the environment, and how much they like one another. Most business transactions are conducted within the **social distance** (from 4 to 12 feet). People attending a social function after work, or people who normally work together or meet to solve problems, converse approximately 4 to 7 feet apart. Distances of 7 to 12 feet

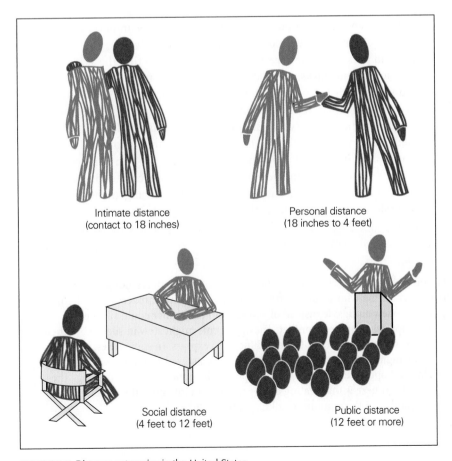

Intimate distance
(contact to 18 inches)

Personal distance
(18 inches to 4 feet)

Social distance
(4 feet to 12 feet)

Public distance
(12 feet or more)

FIGURE 5.2 Distance categories in the United States.

are reserved for formal business transactions with strangers. Finally, **public distance** (from 12 to 15 feet or farther) is maintained between a speaker and a large group of listeners.

Knowledge of these distances is important to your business or professional success. Although there may be times when you wish to deliberately ignore the unwritten rules of appropriate distances (e.g., to demonstrate power or status), generally you will want to improve communication by ensuring that everyone feels comfortable (Burgoon & Hoobler, 2002; Burgoon & LePoire, 1993). Be aware of any nonverbal reactions that signal discomfort. The following example demonstrates the problem:

> A dispatcher at a trucking company had a habit that routinely annoyed all the truckers. Several truckers would be standing at a personal distance, drinking coffee and relaxing after making their deliveries. The minute the dispatcher received a delivery request from headquarters, he would, according to instructions, present the request to the appropriate trucker. The problem was that instead of calling to the trucker, or joining the group by also adopting a personal distance, he would walk between two truckers to present the message, thus violating the intimate space of both people.
>
> When the truckers complained to the supervisor, they could not verbalize exactly what the dispatcher did that irritated them. All they could say was that he seemed rude and unfriendly. Although he had never noticed the dispatcher behaving rudely, the supervisor was forced to replace him after several truckers threatened to quit.

If the supervisor or any of the employees had been aware of the importance of personal distance requirements, the problem might have been solved.

Distance and personal space are also important in selecting the seating arrangements for various tasks. Some of the most helpful research findings are diagrammed in Figure 5.3 (Cook, 1970; Hall, 1983; Mehrabian, 1980; Sommer, 1967). Why are these research findings on seating arrangements important to you? Regardless of who you are or what job you hold, an individual will usually be more comfortable talking with you if you are not separated completely by a desk. However, if the individual is positioned at any angle to you narrower than 45 degrees, he or she may become nervous. Also, if you are conducting a meeting, you can control the amount of discussion by the seating arrangement you select. To keep discussion to a minimum, arrange the chairs in straight rows; to encourage discussion, try circular seating. You may want to designate individual seats (e.g., by place cards) to control interaction. Koneya and Barbour (1976) suggest the following:

> Groups could conceivably change the patterns of interaction among their members by changing who sat across from whom. Putting two holders of conflicting points-of-view alongside instead of across from each other could silence the verbal expression of their conflict. The opponents might stew in silence but their verbal disagreements would be very difficult to express. In some cases, however, a group might welcome opposing viewpoints as a stimulus to discussion and might want opposites in opinions to be physically opposite in the meeting. The powerful fact here is that seating arrangements can influence the direction of talking and even the amount of talking. (pp. 69–40)

People (whether in a doctor's office, in the boss's office, or at home) are more comfortable conducting *conversation* when they are at right angles (90° or 45°) and no more than 4 feet apart.

When working closely together, *cooperating* on a task, people prefer corner seating or side-by-side seating.

When people are working on different tasks, *co-acting*, but need to be in close proximity to each other, they prefer more distant seating, facing opposite each other.

Competing people also prefer to sit opposite each other, with more distance between them.

People sitting side by side (on a sofa, for example) rarely converse with each other, preferring to converse with those across or at right angles to them.

Individuals in a group are more likely to participate if the group is seated in a circular pattern rather than in a rectangular pattern or in straight rows.

When a group sits in a circle, individuals are more likely to ask questions of or make comments to the persons directly across from them. Again, they are less likely to communicate with those sitting closest to them.

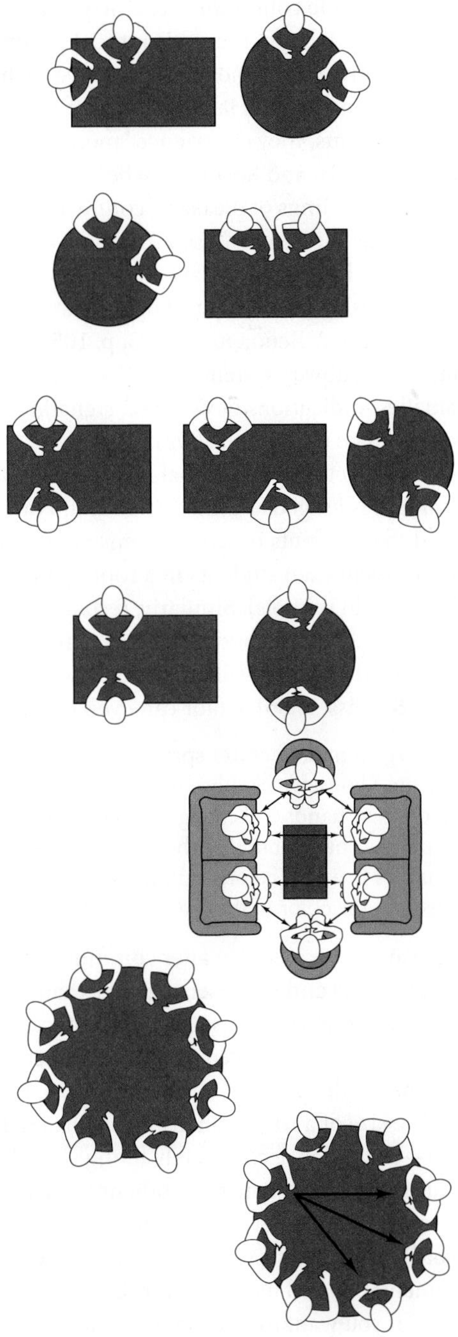

FIGURE 5.3 Seating arrangements.

Physical Environment

Have you ever noticed how some rooms and offices seem friendly and inviting, whereas other rooms (or buildings) seem cold and unfriendly and seem to create a feeling of stress? Do you feel uncomfortable talking to your boss (or instructor) in his or her office? Your reaction may be caused by the room itself.

Physical environments reveal characteristics of the owner of the territory; they also affect how people communicate. One prominent psychologist (Mehrabian, 1980) noted that for each person, the environment produces an emotional response, with "approach" (positive) or "avoidance" (negative) behaviors. Various research studies, summarized by Knapp and Hall (2002), have found that when participants perform tasks in "ugly" rooms, they experience "monotony, fatigue, headache, discontent, sleepiness, irritability, and hostility"; when performing tasks in "attractive" rooms, they experience "feelings of pleasure, comfort, enjoyment, importance, energy, and desire to continue the activity" (p. 123). In an attempt to decrease stress, convey caring, and promote healing, the Mayo Clinic has designed its buildings "to create open, welcoming spaces with soft, natural light" that include gardens, fountains, and even piano music (Berry & Bendapudi, 2003, p. 105). New York City cut the crime and vandalism in the subway system by getting rid of all graffiti, broken windows, trash, and the smallest indications of violence, signaling to everyone that this was a safe, pleasant place to be (Gladwell, 2002).

Color also affects our emotional response and is a determining factor in whether an environment is judged as attractive or not. For example, one researcher (Ketcham, 1968) found that students in schoolrooms painted yellow, rose, blue, or green showed more improvement than students in a room painted buff or white (the more common colors used in schools). Similarly, restaurant proprietors who want customers to eat and leave quickly may choose red and orange for their restaurant decor. Hospitals use colors instead of white walls so patients will relax more (Fishback & Krewson, 1981; Karlin & Zeiss, 2006). Color can even impact the public's buying habits:

> One detergent manufacturer sprinkled red granules throughout his white soap powder, and housewives subsequently complained that the detergent was too rough on their hands. He changed the color to yellow, and women said it was easier on their hands but that the clothes were not as clean. Finally, he changed the granules to a blue color, and the women said it was just right. Nothing had changed but the color of the granules. (Malandro et al., 1989, p. 157)

Lighting and *room size* also alter communication. Soft lighting causes people to speak more softly and sit closer together than in brightly lit rooms (Meer, 1985). A lighting design expert tells us that "most offices are generally overlit with often twice as much light as they need. . . . The result can be inefficiency, fatigue and perhaps a sense of dislocation" (Kowinski, 1975, p. 46). Room size works much the same way. The size of a room can also affect listener attitudes toward the event or the speaker—an audience completely filling a small room gives the appearance of a well-attended event; the same size audience in a much larger room gives the appearance of a poorly attended event. Management consultant Ken Cooper (1987) says, "I always avoid a small classroom in my training sessions because the audience is much more argumentative and hard to control. The same holds true for a business meeting. . . . However, if you want to hold an efficient, spirited meeting, keep the space tight" (pp. 19–20).

Odor, too, communicates nonverbally, especially in a dental or medical office where chemicals and disinfectants stir up unpleasant memories and increase already existing anxiety. Noise level, heat, ventilation, lack of windows, and furniture arrangements (which will be discussed in detail in this chapter) are other environmental factors that can nonverbally affect communication.

Closely related to physical environment is *ergonomics*, the science of mating machines to human requirements. Poor ergonomics can result in eyestrain, backache, headache, and fatigue. For people who spend a large portion of their day at the same workstation using a computer terminal, ergonomics can be extremely important to physical well-being and, therefore, to communication according to the Occupational Safety and Health Administration ([OSHA], 2008). When we feel better, we communicate better. Perhaps your communication could be improved by ergonomic changes in your working environment.

Time

Time is another nonverbal communication factor in the business world. One way to understand the relationship between time and culture is to look at the dimension called *monochromic–polychromic*. **Monochromic (m-time)** cultures, such as the United States, Switzerland, and Germany, view time as a "scarce resource which must be rationed and controlled through the use of schedules and appointments" (Smith & Bond, 1994, p. 149), "Saving" time is good; "wasting" time is not. On the other hand, **polychromic (p-time)** cultures, such as Africans, Arabic, Asian, and Latin American countries, see "the maintenance of harmonious relationships as the important thing, so that the use of time needs to be flexible in order that we do right by the various people to whom we have obligations" (Smith & Bond, 1994, p. 149). "Saving" time is not as important in these cultures. M-time relates closely to low-context, individualistic cultures, whereas p-time corresponds to high-context, collectivistic cultures.

Although American reactions to time occur at all three levels of culture, business life is generally regulated on the informal level. For example, the consequences of arriving late for an appointment often depend on whether you are meeting someone of equal rank, someone more important, or someone less important (Richmond & McCroskey, 2003). Also, anyone who is consistently late for appointments or in completing work assignments may be deemed inconsiderate or undependable. These informal aspects of time in business are manifest in the use of *as soon as possible (ASAP), in a while,* and other similarly vague terms. The amount of time an important person spends with us also has informal significance. For example, an employment interview that lasts longer than 30 minutes may mean that the interviewee's chances of getting the job are good (Hall, 1973). And the amount of time that a physician spends with a patient may tell the patient how much the physician cares (Gladwell, 2005; Roter et al., 1997).

Reactions to these types of time behaviors may vary depending on where we were raised and our cultural background. For example, a woman born and reared in the North moved to the South and found it frustrating to adjust to what she called the "Southern concept" of appointments: The cable TV representative refused to give her an exact appointment time other than "sometime during the morning," and the plumber who promised to show up at 1:00 finally arrived at 6:00, just as she was leaving for the evening. In contrast, when a Southern family moved to the North, they were just as frustrated by what they considered the hectic pace set by Northerners. Expecting a repairman to arrive late, they went shopping only to return and find they had missed him and he would be unable to return for at least a week!

Although cultural and regional differences do add some confusion to the nonverbal aspect of time, when we deal with people from other nations, we all become American in our view of time. As a Japanese businessman told us, "If you keep Americans waiting long enough, they will agree to anything."

Revisiting the Case Study

What specific types of nonverbal communication could have helped President Bush and government officials defuse the misunderstanding over Bush's use of the hook 'em horns gesture?

Ronald Martinez/Getty Images

Status Symbols

Clothes are a nonverbal status symbol. As we've already seen in the discussion of clothing, darker colors signal higher status. In addition, Molloy (1988) tells us that "the tie is probably the single most important denominator of social status for a man in the United States today. Show me a man's ties and I will tell you who he is or who he is trying to be" (p. 93). Researchers also have found that people are more likely to take orders from and follow the lead of people, even strangers, who are dressed in high-status clothing (Levine et al., 1998; Segrin, 1993). William Thourlby, author of *You Are What You Wear* (1990), also notes the following:

> Although they don't say it, most managers when pressed agree that "You never get promoted to a position you don't look like you belong in." Understanding this can help you realize you dress for the position you want, not the one you're in. (p. 36)

Although dressing for the job you want is important, overdressing can lead to failure. For example, a three-piece suit is normally worn only by those in authority. Golden (1986) warns, "If you wear high-authority symbols on a low-authority job, managers may consider you foolish and your coworkers may feel threatened. You may lose the trust you've worked hard to gain" (p. 41).

Other important nonverbal status symbols are the location and size of a person's office (Remland, 1981). The following observations on office status are adapted from Michael Korda's (1991, pp. 75, 79–80) popular book on power:

- Because corner offices are usually larger and have more windows, corner offices carry more status; therefore, "offices in the middle of a row are less powerful than the ones at either end of it."

- Offices that are out of the traffic mainstream confer more power than do others. However, a secretary gains power by having a view of as many directions as possible.

- In most cases, power diminishes with distance. Put someone's assistant next to his superior's office, and he benefits from being close to the source of power. Promote the assistant to a larger office that is farther away, and his power is likely to decrease. Only if he is given a title and a job that allows him to create his own power base can he benefit from moving.

Along with size and location, the interior arrangement of an office conveys the authority of its owner (Monk, 1994). Which office arrangement shown in Figure 5.4 conveys the most authority?

Office *a* nonverbally assigns the most authority to its owner mainly because visitors are allotted only a small amount of space and because the desk separates visitors from the owner. Visitors would probably feel more comfortable and would communicate more freely in office *c* because they could sit at a right angle to the owner. However, of the three, office *b* gives the owner the most flexibility; he or she can speak to the visitor from behind the desk when authority is necessary or come from behind the desk to sit either in the chair or on the sofa for relaxed conversation with the visitor.

Other office amenities that lend a person status are solid-wood furniture, green plants, and quality artwork. And, of course, it doesn't hurt to have a personal secretary!

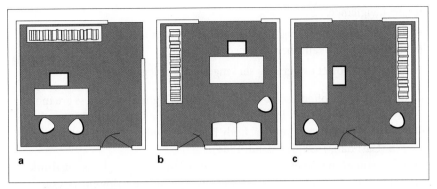

FIGURE 5.4 Possible office arrangements.

Time—that is, how it is handled—is another nonverbal indicator of status. For example, your boss may call a meeting at a specific time. The boss is allowed to arrive late, but you are not. A job interview that lasts 45 minutes or longer usually conveys the prospective employer's interest, whereas a 10-minute interview may indicate disinterest. If you wish to talk with your supervisor, you are expected to make an appointment; however, your supervisor may stop by your office without giving you any prior notice.

A male executive can nonverbally indicate that he is more powerful than female executives or even other male executives by putting a comforting arm around them or always opening the door for them (Korda, 1991). Of course, these gestures may have other meanings, but the recipients of such gestures need to be aware of their possible status implications. One way to counteract them as status symbols is simply to use similar gestures yourself.

There are many other nonverbal ways to convey status (Andersen, 1999, ch. 12; Burgoon et al., 1996; Edinger & Patterson, 1983; Remland, 2000). For instance, a person with high status is more likely to have a preferred parking space, to demand (nonverbally or verbally) direct eye contact from others, to violate subordinates' personal space by touching or closeness, arrive late to appointments, fail to acknowledge others with a greeting, and to be allowed more space by lower-status people.

Others' perceptions play a large role in a person's success. The reason more women don't hold management positions is because the people who promote and hire do not perceive women as being as capable as men in power positions.

Norma Carr-Ruffino (1997, p. 251) lists the following strong and weak nonverbal behaviors for both men and women in the United States (see Figure 5.5):

Signs of Power

- Expansive, confident movements.
- Tall, upright standing posture; arms at sides; feet placed slightly apart.
- Relaxed, affable, familiar behavior.
- Ability to turn one's back on another to get an object.
- Comfortable, relaxed, seated positions: legs crossed, arms asymmetrically placed, body leaning sideways and reclining slightly.

Signs of Weakness

- Small, controlled movements.
- Any form of bowing or bowed posture; using hand to cover face.

- Tenseness, vigilance.
- Hesitantly standing or sitting forward attentively with feet together on the floor, with arms in lap or in another balanced position.
- Playing with an object or nervous shaking of foot or leg.

Signs of power are more often used by bosses, whereas signs of weakness are more often displayed by subordinates. Even if we don't know the two people involved in a face-to-face discussion, their nonverbal body behaviors will usually clearly signal the status of each (Cashdan, 1998; Remland, 1981).

If you feel you aren't taken seriously by your coworkers or boss, or think that others see you as having low status or power, practice using more powerful behaviors such as the following (adapted from Carr-Ruffino, 1997, pp. 250–255):

- Be pleasant, but smile less often.
- Lower the pitch of your voice, and speak with firmness.
- Use steady, relaxed, frequent eye contact.
- Keep head straight and still (avoid tilting to side).
- Maintain a relaxed yet strong stance (not stooped); walk in unhurried fashion using smooth movements.
- Occasionally, turn your back on others when reaching for an item; move casually around the room while speaking.
- Use strong, definite movements (avoid nervous movements such as shaking leg, tapping foot, or clasping hands).
- Try using the *steepling* gesture (with hands pointing upward, place fingertips together).
- Initiate firm handshakes (continental grab).
- Videotape yourself using these power behaviors, or practice using a full-length mirror.
- Create a mental picture of yourself as a powerful, relaxed person.

Some of you, especially those just beginning in a business or profession, may be thinking, "This is all ridiculous. I don't want to play these games. I can work well in extremely casual clothes, and where my desk or office is located makes no difference to my performance." And you may very well be right. Many companies have tried to downplay status differences. However, recall the first principle of communication: The message that counts is the one *received*. People are receiving nonverbal messages about you regardless of whether you intend to send them or not. Although you are capable of handling a particular job, you will not be assigned that job unless other people (especially your boss) think you are capable. Their perceptions of you are probably colored by their opinions of your clothing, office, and other nonverbal messages. Even if no one has a private office, the people closest to the boss are perceived as having higher status; if personnel are required to wear the same uniforms, status will be determined by some other indicator such as an expensive watch, fountain pen, or leather clipboard (Janus et al., 2000, p. 267). Look around you. What are the most successful managers wearing? How are their offices arranged? Imitate people in the positions you desire to achieve.

(a) Powerful and (b) weak nonverbal behaviors described on pages 139 and 140.

Nonverbal Messages and International Business Transactions

The nonverbal symbols and gestures discussed in this chapter are understood by most people in the United States. However, people of other countries and cultures have different nonverbal symbols and meanings for each level culture, especially the informal level. For example, people from different cultures use touch quite differently. In a study of how often adult couples in coffee shops touch, Sidney M. Jourard (1968) found that couples in San Juan, Puerto Rico, touched 180 times per hour; couples in Paris, France, touched 110 times per hour; couples in Gainesville, Florida, touched only 2 times per hour; and in London, England, couples touched 1 time per hour. It is just as difficult for the American businessperson, even one prepared for differences, to interpret accurately the nonverbal communication used in other countries as it is for businesspeople from other countries to interpret ours. An informal rule in the United States may even be a formal or technical rule in another nation.

Mistakes and Culture Shock

When a company sends representatives abroad to conduct business or to manage or work in a plant whose employees are primarily from the host country, two mistakes are often made. The first mistake is the company's. American companies, for example, seldom give their representatives (expatriates) much training in the language and customs of the country they will visit. Hogan and Goodson (1990) report two seemingly related facts: (a) 65% of companies fail to provide cultural training for employees going abroad, and (b) 40% of managers return home from overseas assignments before completing them. Apparently, companies assume that employees will cope. But without training, how would you know that the Japanese nod to acknowledge hearing rather than agreement? What if, while visiting Taiwan, you and several Taiwanese colleagues go to a restaurant and you take the "wrong" seat? Without training, how would you know that the host, the person who is paying the bill, always sits facing the door? If you were supposed to pay the bill but chose the wrong seat, or if you were not the host but sat facing the door, the group would likely become upset. Business relations would be strained.

The second mistake is made by the visiting employees, who assume the people in the foreign country will behave basically the same as Americans. When the natives do not react as expected, the expatriates experience **culture shock**, or confusion because they cannot understand or be understood by the people of their host country. The visitors may negatively stereotype the people of the host country and withdraw from personal contacts. Marx (2001) found that the average length of time managers experience culture shock in overseas assignments is 7 weeks.

To become culturally sensitive, Americans need to be aware of the effects of culture shock in the workplace and realize how people from other countries view us. Here are some comments made by foreigners while visiting the United States (Adler & Gundersen, 2008, p. 83). Do you think these observations are accurate? If so, how would you explain them?

> **India:** "Americans seem to be in a perpetual hurry. Just watch the way they walk down the street. They never allow themselves the leisure to enjoy life; there are too many things to do."

> **Vietnam:** "Americans are handy people. They do almost everything in the house by themselves, from painting walls and doors to putting glass in their windows . . ."

> **Turkey:** "Once we were out in a rural area in the middle of nowhere and saw an American come to a stop sign. Though he could see in both directions for miles and no traffic was coming, he still stopped!"

> **Japan:** "Americans seem to feel that they have to say something instead of having silence—even when what they say is so well known that it sounds stupid . . ."

> **Columbia:** "I was surprised to see so many young people who were not living with their parents, although they were not married. Also, I was surprised to see so many single people of all ages living alone, eating alone, and walking the streets alone. The United States must be the loneliest country in the world."

> **Iran:** "The first time . . . my [American] professor told me, 'I don't know the answer; I will have to look it up,' I was shocked. I asked myself, 'Why is he teaching me?' In my country a professor would give the wrong answer rather than admit ignorance."

Complete the Awareness Check on page 143 to see if you would experience culture shock in a couple of hypothetical situations. Compare your responses with those of a colleague from a different culture.

To minimize culture shock, the following guidelines are suggested (Gonzalez, 2006; Marx, 2001; Overman, 2004): Learn the language as much as possible; ask for cross-cultural training or take a continuing education course from a local college; keep a sense of humor; get plenty of rest; listen with an open mind; ask for a family sponsor or company mentor to serve as a "cultural translator" or make a friend in the host country to help you; keep a positive attitude and view the visit as a "great adventure;" and realize that just because things are done differently, doesn't mean they are wrong.

Expectancy Violations Theory

We all have expectations about others' nonverbal behaviors, but these behaviors are not always met, as our discussion of culture shock shows. When our expectations

Nonverbal Symbols Across Cultures

How aware are you of the nonverbal symbols and meanings used by people from other countries in their everyday lives? Check your knowledge by selecting the best response to each of the following hypothetical situations.* Then check your answers against those in the back of this book. You can also take this quiz online, test yourself with additional hypothetical situations, and view the answers through the Premium Website for *Communicating for Results.*

Situation 1: You volunteer for assignment at your company's plant in a West African country. You are aware of how difficult it is to step into a manager's position where the majority of the managers are not of your nationality. To get to know the other managers better, you host several informal cocktail parties in your home. None of your guests reciprocates by inviting you to a party at their homes, and several of them failed to attend your last party. What could be the reason for this behavior?

_____ a. Informal parties in West Africa are only for family; business parties are expected to be formal affairs.

_____ b. Many of your African associates can only afford to entertain on a much smaller scale, and they are not sure you would be interested in their parties.

_____ c. Your guests think you are cheap and probably feel insulted because you served no food at your parties.

_____ d. Africans generally are not a social, party-loving people. No insult is intended.

Situation 2: You are excited that you have been selected to travel to England to help solve a technical problem at your company's English manufacturing plant. You have always wanted to visit London. The visit is very pleasant until you actually begin discussions with the English management. The managers continually stare at you and blink their eyes as though bored. This behavior on their part is very distracting. What nonverbal meaning, if any, can be drawn from their behavior?

_____ a. The managers resent the fact that an U.S. outsider, especially a mere technician, was sent to handle such a major problem. They are nonverbally communicating to you their unhappiness.

_____ b. The English smog is so bad that most British have eye irritations. Just ignore the behavior.

_____ c. In England, eye blinking is a sign that people are listening. No disrespect is meant.

_____ d. In England, eye blinking indicates confusion. Somehow, you are not getting through to them.

* These situations are based on the authors' personal experience or adapted from R. W. Axtell. (1998 & 2007). *Gestures: The do's and taboos of body language around the world* (1st & 3rd ed.). New York: Wiley; E. T. Hall. (1969). *The hidden dimension*. Garden City, NY: Anchor; Hall, E. T. (1973). *The silent language.* Garden City, NY: Anchor; E. T. Hall, & W. F. Whyte. (1960, Spring). Intercultural communication: A guide to men in action. *Human Organization, 19,* 5–12.

are met, we judge the person favorably; if they are not met or violated, we judge the person unfavorably. **Expectancy violations theory**, developed by Judee Burgoon (1983, 1993), deals with how people respond when their nonverbal expectations are not met. Nonverbal expectations can involve any of the nonverbal behaviors

Ronald Martinez/Getty Images

mentioned in this chapter, such as eye contact, distance, gestures, personal appearance, and even immediacy behaviors covered in the next section of this chapter. It's easier to have our expectations violated when the person or persons involved come from another culture and our expectations are based on incomplete information or stereotypes.

Improving Nonverbal Skills

In the Secret Handshake, Reardon (2000), is quite blunt about the importance of nonverbal communication when she says, "People who can't read these subtle and not-so-subtle messages don't last long at companies. They keep making the same mistakes" (p. 87). If you are serious about improving your skills in sending and interpreting nonverbal messages, you can use immediacy behaviour and adopt more effective nonverbal behaviors.

Immediacy Behaviors   With specific nonverbal, vocal, and verbal behaviors, you can promote a sense of closeness with business colleagues and customers; this interaction is referred to as **immediacy behaviors**. Research has found that students learn significantly more and have an improved attitude toward the classroom experience when instructors use immediacy behaviors (Mottet et al., 2007). Although research on immediacy behavior has focused on teachers and students, the findings can apply to work situations as well. The greater the group size, the more distant people feel unless the person in charge uses immediacy behaviors (Gorham, 1988). For example, because of his use of verbal and vocal immediacy behaviors during his radio "fireside chats," President Franklin D. Roosevelt made Americans feel like he was speaking to them personally, as individuals (Ryfe, 1999). Immediacy behaviors include the following:

- *Verbal behaviors* (language). Using humor sensitively; citing personal experiences during conversations; using *we* and *our* when speaking with colleagues or employees about company projects; praising others for their work, actions, or comments; referring to people by name; asking for opinions and questions; and conversing with others before and after meetings.

- *Vocal behaviors* (paralanguage). Being vocally expressive when speaking—that is, using good volume, pitch, emphasis, and rate (see the section on delivery and voice in Chapter 12).

- *Visual behaviors* (nonverbal). Making eye contact, smiling appropriately at individuals, as well as, the whole group, keeping a relaxed posture, gesturing naturally, and moving around rather than staying behind a barrier such as a desk.

Effective Habits   In addition to learning to use immediacy behaviors, you can improve your nonverbal communication by adopting more effective habits. A good place to begin is with these steps:

1.   Develop awareness of nonverbal differences.
2.   Do not judge others according to your own nonverbal meanings.
3.   Do not assign nonverbal meanings out of context.
4.   Observe your nonverbal behavior on videotape or ask others for feedback.

The first step in using nonverbal communication effectively is to be aware that differences in nonverbal symbols and meanings exist on the technical, formal, and informal levels. You have to be extremely observant to perceive even a few of these differences. Unobtrusively observe the nonverbal behaviors of your family, friends, coworkers, and even strangers. And, of course, be aware of your own nonverbal reactions in various situations and what those reactions are saying about you to others.

Second, when you observe nonverbal behaviors, do not immediately assume that you know what a particular behavior means. Judging others according to your own nonverbal system is a natural reaction, but it leads to errors. You will make fewer errors in interpretation if, instead of analyzing only one nonverbal response at a time, you evaluate several responses as a whole. For example, suppose you are interviewing an employee about some missing machinery. If the employee fails to look you in the eye while responding, it might indicate that he or she is guilty. But it might also indicate embarrassment that you are questioning his or her integrity, or it might be a gesture of respect for your authority. Suppose, however, that the employee squirms in the chair, begins to perspire, gives evasive answers to your questions, and makes nervous hand gestures in addition to avoiding eye contact. Now you have much stronger support for your assumption that the employee is guilty. But guilty of what? You are still making an *assumption*! Perhaps the employee appears guilty because he or she knows who took the machinery but does not want to betray anyone. Be careful about jumping to conclusions.

Third, do not assign meanings to nonverbal behaviors out of context. Consider the specific situation, environment, cultural background, and personal frame of reference. No nonverbal behavior has the same exact meaning in all situations. To understand the meaning of a nonverbal behavior, you must know its context.

A fourth suggestion for improving your nonverbal skills is to watch yourself on videotape and observe your nonverbal behaviors. Participate in a small-group discussion of job-related problems and record the session on videotape. Analysis of the videotape should indicate both positive and negative nonverbal behaviors. If videotaping is not possible, ask for specific feedback on your use of nonverbal communication from the other group members.

A final way to observe your nonverbal skills is to role-play using hypothetical situations. For example, you might play the role of an employer who is interviewing an unfriendly or shy job applicant, played by a colleague. Again, videotapes of these sessions can be quite revealing. Simulated pressure situations like this give participants insight into the effects of their own and others' nonverbal (and verbal) behavior. One businessman comments on the success of role-playing:

> The observers will often be surprised at how quickly they can tell if one of the role-players is falling under attack or is trying to mislead the others. Even though a role-player thinks he is hiding his discomfort or impatience, observers read the hidden messages quite clearly. (McCaskey, 1979, p. 148)

CHAPTER 5
R E V I E W

Dreamstime.com

Key Terms

adaptors (129)

business casual (130)

casual confusion syndrome (CCS) (130)

culture shock (142)

emblems (129)

expectancy violation theory (143)

formal level (124)

illustrators (129)

immediacy behaviors (144)

informal level (124)

intimate distance (133)

monochromic time (m-time) (137)

nonverbal communication (123)

pacifying behaviors (129)

personal distance (133)

polychromic time (p-time) (137)

public distance (134)

regulators (129)

social distance (134)

technical level (124)

Summary

The relationship between culture and nonverbal communication can be understood by examining the three levels of culture: technical, formal, and informal. In the United States, most nonverbal behaviors are governed by the informal level, where the rules for behavior are unstated and most people use them unconsciously. When an informal rule is violated, people may become extremely uncomfortable and even angry without knowing why.

To make you more aware of these unconscious rules, we covered the types of nonverbal communication most applicable to business life: (a) facial expression and eye contact, (b) other body movements and gestures, (c) clothing and personal appearance, (d) distance and personal space, (e) physical environment,

and (f) time. Nonverbal status symbols in business, such as clothing, office size, and the manipulation of time, strongly influence how others perceive us and thus are key factors in career advancement. For success in international business dealings, we must be aware of differences between our nonverbal messages and those of other countries.

Although knowledge of nonverbal communication can be a powerful tool for the business and professional communicator, a little bit of knowledge can be dangerous. Use caution when interpreting others' nonverbal behaviors. Don't jump to conclusions, and don't read nonexistent meanings into simple gestures. Overreacting to nonverbal messages will cause just as many misunderstandings as ignoring them.

Communicating for Results Online

Before continuing to the next chapter, check your understanding of Chapter 5 at the Premium Website for *Communicating for Results*. Your Premium Web-

site gives you quick and easy access to the electronic resources that accompany this text. These resources include:

- **Study tools** that will help you assess your learning and prepare for exams (student companion workbook, digital glossary, key term flash cards, and review quizzes).

- **Activities and assignments** that will help you hone your knowledge, analyze professional communication situations, build your public speaking skills throughout the course, and learn to work effectively in teams (Awareness Checks, Checkpoints, and Collaborative Learning Activities).

- **Media resources** that will help you explore communication concepts online (web links), develop your speech outlines (Speech Builder Express 3.0), watch and critique videos of professional communication situations and sample speeches (Interactive Video Activities), upload your speech videos for peer reviewing and critique other students' speeches (Speech Studio online speech review tool), and download chapter review so you can study when and where you'd like (Audio Study Tools).

This chapter's key terms, Collaborative Learning Activities, and Checkpoint activities are also featured on the following pages, and you can find this chapter's Awareness Check activities in the body of the chapter. For more information or to access this book's online resources, visit www.cengage.com/login.

Collaborative Learning Activities

1. In small groups of three to seven make a list of the major gestures used as emblems in the United States. Then using Google, research databases available through college and city libraries, or books such as *Gestures: The Do's and Taboos of Body Language Around the World* by Roger Axtell (2007) or *What Every BODY is Saying* by Navarro and Karlins (2008), determine as many different meanings for each gesture both in the United States and abroad as possible. Which 10 gestures would your team select as the most likely to cause international incidents and the most important to be avoided by the current and future U.S. presidents? Specify reasons for your choices.

2. In groups of two to five, do some extra research on business casual dress in the workplace. Find at least three articles from a Google search and a search of library and college databases such as EBSCOhost and see what specific clothing suggestions you can find. Also, interview several businesses in your area to see how they interpret business casual and what specific clothing dos and don'ts they suggest. Compare what you find with the information in this chapter and be prepare to share it with other individuals or groups.

3. In pairs or small groups consider the answers to the following questions: (a) What nonverbal behaviors do you consider to be the most valuable in the college classroom or in workplace training sessions? (b) Which nonverbal behaviors do you think would be inappropriate in the college classroom or in workplace training sessions? Explain your reasons.

Checkpoints

Checkpoint 5.1 Nonverbal Characteristics of Various Office Arrangements
Walk the corridors of the place where you work, paying particular attention to various office arrangements. What nonverbal characteristics do you feel create a favorable impression? What nonverbal characteristics account for any unfavorable impression? What symbols communicate power? Based on nonverbal characteristics, can you determine the hierarchy within the workplace?

Checkpoint 5.2 Evaluating Personal Use of Nonverbal Communication

Checkpoint 5.3 Checking Your Awareness of Cultural Differences—Additional Situations

Checkpoint 5.4 First Impressions

Checkpoint 5.5 People-Watching

Checkpoint 5.6 The Artifact Arsenal

Checkpoint 5.7 Nonverbal Communication Websites

6

Overcoming Obstacles to Communication in Organizations

As you read Chapter 6,

Define the terms *situational anxiety* and *trait anxiety*, and **list** several specific tips for managing each type of anxiety.

Briefly **describe** each of the following obstacles to communication, and **list** at least two practical tips to correct each obstacle: inadequate preparation, vague instructions, jumping to conclusions, and bypassing.

Define the term sexual harassment, and **specify** how the courts use the reasonable person rule in deciding sexual harassment cases.

Identify three tips for successfully communicating using each of the following types of technology: e-mail, podcasts, blogs, and electronic meetings.

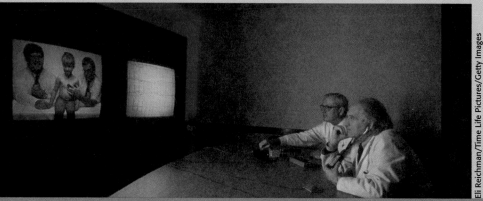

Eli Reichman/Time Life Pictures/Getty Images

Case Study: Technology, a Songwriter, and United Airlines

Technology has given customers powerful ways to retaliate if they are ignored or mistreated. Take for example, Canadian musician and songwriter Dave Carroll whose guitar was broken by United Airlines luggage handlers on his way to a performance in March of 2008. After 9 months of getting the run-around by officials at United, Carroll took matters into his own hands by writing and recording an entertaining musical video called "United Breaks Guitars," which he posted on YouTube on July 6, 2009 (Mutzabaugh, 2009). In the video, Carroll (accompanied by his band Sons of Maxwell) sings of how his guitar was smashed and of his frustrations in dealing with United Airline employees.

The facts of the story according to Carroll (2009) include the following: Prior to deplaning in Chicago for the last leg of a trip to Omaha from Halifax, a passenger sitting behind Carroll noticed that the baggage handlers were throwing guitars, which just happened to belong to Carroll and his band. He tried to complain to three different United flight attendants before leaving Chicago with no success, and when they arrived in Omaha at 12:30 a.m., there were no employees available at all. Early the next morning after being picked up by the tour manager, he discovered his $3,500 Taylor guitar was broken into two pieces. As frustrating as this was, it didn't compare with the frustration of trying to file a claim and contact the "correct" person to discuss reimbursement for his guitar; at various times he was told to talk to all the following: the ground crew in Omaha, the airport where the trip began (Halifax), the airport where the damage occurred (Chicago), United's 1-800 number in India, and Central Baggage in New York. Carroll notes that "The system is designed to frustrate affected customers into giving up their claims and United is very good at it." The last person he spoke with, Ms. Irlweg, told him nothing could be done even after he offered to settle for payment of $1200 in flight vouchers to reimburse having the guitar repaired. He gave up after telling her that he would write three songs about his experiences with United in video form, offer them as a free download online, and ask viewers to vote on their favorite song. His goal, he told her, was "to get one million hits in one year"—a modest goal as it turned out.

"United Breaks Guitars" was posted on Monday, July 6, and by Thursday, July 9, it had 400,000 hits and, according to Benet Wilson in her blog post titled "United Airlines Sees Power of Viral PR Up Close and Personal" (2009), Carroll's video already had over 100 news stories and 2000 blogs written about it, including multiple television network reports. Even United Airlines was on Twitter explaining its actions and making apologies. On July 10th, United posted on Twitter that following Dave's request, they had donated $3,000 to the Thelonius Monk Institute of Jazz. A spokeswoman for United told the *Chicago Sun Times* that they were interested in using the video "for training purposes to ensure that all customers receive better service from us" (Jackson, 2009). By evening on Sunday, just 6 days after the video was posted, more than 2.4 million viewers had listened to it. In addition to making a point, and getting the attention of United, Carroll and his band were a hit! The song was clever, the video funny, and the music really enjoyable. Carroll (2009) ended his background on the incident with this statement:

> I should thank United. They've given me a creative outlet that has brought people together from around the world. We had a pile of laughs making the recording and the video while the images are spinning on how to make "United: Song 2" even better than the first. So, thanks, United! If my guitar had to be smashed due to extreme negligence, I'm glad it was you that did it. Now sit back and enjoy the show.

Courtesy of Dave Carroll

As you read this chapter, see if you can (a) decide whether the action taken by United Airlines to repair the damage done by Carroll's video was adequate, (b) discuss the actions that United should take to prevent future customer service incidents, and (c) determine whether technology is more of an advantage or more of a obstacle to effective communication in today's society. For the complete story, go to **www.davecarrollmusic .com**, and click on "News" and then "United Breaks Guitars."

Regardless of your business or professional position, you have probably acquired a few poor habits that create obstacles to communication. These obstacles can be avoided with patience and practice, but first they must be identified. To help you identify your own communication obstacles, this chapter describes those that are most common in organizations. Anyone, employee or employer, can create such obstacles. As you read this chapter, determine how skilled you are at recognizing and avoiding each obstacle.

Communicator Anxiety

Whether you are expressing your ideas to a colleague, giving instructions or information to your employees, participating in a group discussion, interviewing or being interviewed, or giving a presentation, communicator anxiety can definitely

NOTE

To help you determine which type of anxiety you have, take the PRCA-24 (Richmond & McCroskey, 1998), accessible through your Premium Website for *Communicating for Results*. A total score of 80 or above or 24 or above on any subscore indicates some *trait anxiety*. A total score of 65 or above or 18 or above on any subscore indicates some *situational anxiety*.

be an obstacle to effective communication in the work environment. According to research, the higher a supervisor's anxiety, the less potentially important information employees receive (Bartoo & Sias, 2004). Research also indicates that people who experience a high level of communication anxiety are at a disadvantage when compared with more talkative, outgoing employees. For example, people with high anxiety are perceived as less competent, are less likely to be offered an interview, make a poorer impression during interviews, typically hold lower-status and lower-paying positions, experience less job satisfaction, and are less likely to be promoted to supervisory positions (Richmond & McCroskey, 1998). In fact, Richmond and McCroskey reported that approximately 95% of those surveyed in the United States have some degree of communication anxiety. Hearing-impaired people experience communication anxiety as well (Booth-Butterfield & Booth-Butterfield, 1994). Not all cultures express the same levels of communicator anxiety, possibly due in part to the low-context collectivistic nature of their culture, as discussed in Chapter 3. For example, researchers found that the Chinese (Zhang et al., 1996) and Chinese in Taiwan (Hsu, 2004) are more apprehensive about communication than Americans, but Puerto Ricans are much less apprehensive than Americans unless they are asked to communicate in English (McCroskey et al., 1985).

Before you can manage your anxiety, you need to know what kind of anxiety you have. There are two types of communication anxiety: situational and trait. **Situational anxiety**—often referred to as *state anxiety* (Booth-Butterfield & Booth-Butterfield, 1992; Motley, 1995)—is anxiety caused by factors in a specific situation, such as speaking for the first time before an audience, speaking in front of the boss, and being critiqued while speaking. **Trait anxiety** (Beatty et al., 1989; Daly & Friedrich, 1981) is the internal anxiety an individual brings to the speaking situation, such as feelings of inadequacy or fear of looking like a fool in front of others. In other words, situational anxiety is caused by a new or different situation, and trait anxiety is caused by the speaker's internal apprehensions and feelings regardless of the situation. Your own anxiety may be situational, trait, or a combination of both.

Situational Anxiety

Feeling nervous prior to a new communication situation is perfectly normal. Firing a troublesome employee, being interviewed for a job, presenting a controversial idea to your team leader or supervisor, selling a product to a new client, and approaching a banker for a loan are all situations that could cause a nervous, butterflies-in-the-stomach feeling in just about anyone. Anytime we become anxious, afraid, or excited, our body's nervous system prepares us for action with a big shot of adrenaline, which accelerates the heart rate; sends extra oxygen to the central nervous system, heart, and muscles; dilates the eyes; raises the blood sugar level; and causes perspiration.

Actually, we should be grateful for this boost from our nervous system. Can you imagine a runner at an Olympic competition with absolutely no anxiety? The runner's performance would no doubt fall far short of real potential. People who view increased heart rate, dry mouth, and sweaty palms as normal excitement necessary for a dynamic job of communicating find that their anxiety becomes manageable and often disappears completely once they begin speaking. Poor communicators, who tend to view physical reactions to situational anxiety with fear and as further proof that they are poor speakers, often find that their anxiety becomes worse as the presentation proceeds.

Even very experienced speakers—like Katie Couric of the *CBS Evening News*—experience speaker anxiety. Accept the fact that almost every speaking situation will produce that sinking feeling in the pit of your stomach. According to Edward R. Murrow, a great journalist of the past, "The only difference between the pros and the novices is that the pros have trained their butterflies to fly in formation" (Bostrom, 1988, p. 57). The following advice will help you stay in control during situational anxiety.

Prepare and Practice! Nothing will make you more nervous than knowing you are not adequately prepared. After all, isn't your nervousness really fear that you will make mistakes or be humiliated in front of your colleagues, boss, or customers (Bippus & Daly, 1999)? Lack of preparation makes a poor presentation much more likely. Sometimes—perhaps because they feel overwhelmed—anxious people prepare less instead of practicing more thoroughly (Daly et al., 1995). However, Lilly Walters (1993), a speech consultant and author of *Secrets of Successful Speakers*, estimates that careful preparation can reduce anxiety by as much as 75%! Preparation is essential—tackle one small step at a time. Helpful guidelines on preparing your presentation (i.e., analyzing the audience, selecting and researching the topic, organizing, choosing interesting supports, and preparing visual aids) are covered in Chapters 11 to 14 in this book.

Once you have prepared your presentation, make easy-to-follow notes and practice your presentation three or more times from beginning to end, speaking aloud. Mentally thinking through your speech is not the same as practicing aloud. The environment you practice in should be as close as possible to the actual speaking environment. If you will be standing during your presentation, stand while practicing; if you will be using visual aids, practice presenting them as well. Once you begin to feel comfortable with the flow of the presentation, it is time to get some feedback on any needed changes either by taping yourself, speaking in front of a mirror, speaking before an audience of friends and family, or all three. Researchers have found that both taping yourself and speaking in front of a mirror provide valuable feedback, but that practicing in front of an audience is even better (Smith & Frymier, 2006). In fact, these same researchers found that students who practiced in front of an audience made better grades than students who practiced alone. Even one audience member was better than none, but four or more was best. Time yourself to see if you need to shorten or lengthen the presentation. Finally, anticipate possible audience questions, and prepare to answer them. Knowing that you are well prepared will help ease much of your anxiety (Behnke & Sawyer, 1999).

Warm Up Prior to giving your presentation, stretch your neck and arm muscles and warm up your voice. Sing up and down the musical scale, as singers do before a concert; read aloud a memo or page from a book, varying your volume, pitch, emphasis, and rate; do several stretching exercises such as touching your toes and rolling your head from side to side; practice various gestures such as pointing, pounding your fist, or shrugging your shoulders. Speakers are no different from singers who warm up their voices or athletes who warm up their muscles before a performance. Warm-up helps you relax and ensures that you are ready to perform at your best (Richmond & McCroskey, 1998).

Use Deep Breathing One quick way to calm your butterflies is to use **deep breathing**—take a deep breath (through your nose), hold it while you count to five, and then slowly exhale (through your mouth). As you exhale, feel your stress and tension slowly draining down your arms and out your fingertips, down your body and legs and out your toes. Do the same thing a second or third time if needed. You can do this quietly so that no one even notices. Deep breathing slows the heartbeat and lowers the tension, making us feel more in control (Pletcher, 2000). One researcher (Hamilton, 2000) found that using deep breathing can lower our feeling of anxiety by up to 15%. A good time to use deep breathing is right before you go to the front of the audience to begin your presentation.

Use an Introduction That Will Relax You Most speakers find that once they get a favorable audience reaction, they relax. This is one reason why so many speakers start with humor; it relaxes them, as well as their listeners. If a humorous introduction is inappropriate or you are not comfortable with humor, perhaps relating a personal experience, some interesting statistics, or using a dynamic quotation would relax you and get the attention of the audience. Whatever your preference, make your introduction work to put *you* at ease.

Concentrate on Communicating Your Meaning Instead of worrying about how you look or how you sound, center your energy on getting your *meaning* across to your listeners. Don't think of your speech as a performance; instead think of your speech as a way to provide valuable information to others. Pay close attention to their nonverbal reactions. If they look confused, explain the idea again or add another example. A speaker who is really concentrating on the listeners soon forgets about being nervous.

Use Visual Aids Some speakers do not know what to do with their hands. Using visual aids, such as transparencies or flip charts, not only adds eye-catching movement to your presentation but also keeps you so busy there is no time to worry about hand gestures. Visuals also make it almost impossible to forget a point or idea; if you forget, simply move to the next visual. Chapter 13 gives specific advice on preparing and using visual aids.

Trait Anxiety

Whereas nearly everyone experiences situational anxiety, fewer people experience trait anxiety known as *communication apprehension*—a personal, internal feeling that you may experience regardless of the situation. For example, if you feel like you are a poor speaker, it won't matter whether you are speaking to a large or small audience; if you feel you are unskilled at interviewing, it won't matter whether the interviewer is someone you know or a stranger. The situation isn't the main cause of the anxiety—you brought it with you to the situation.

Researchers now feel that trait anxiety is both learned and inborn. In this chapter we are especially interested in speaking situations. If your anxiety about speaking is learned, you may experience two or more of these characteristics: (a) feel that you are different from and less effective than most other speakers, (b) have a history of negative speaking experiences, and (c) consider yourself inferior to others (Beatty, 1988; McCroskey & Beatty, 1998). In other words there is a good chance that you have learned trait anxiety if you feel you are more nervous than anyone else in your group, if you have had several negative speaking experiences in the past, and if you are worried that your audience will know more about your topic than you do.

Trait anxiety may be an inborn trait for some people as well. Researchers who believe that communication anxiety is primarily an inborn or genetically caused behavior use the term *communibiology* (Beatty et al., 1998; McCroskey & Beatty, 2000). Other researches like Conditt (2000) disagree and feel that biology is only one of several factors causing anxiety and that anxious individuals can learn to control their anxiety with effort. In fact, biopsychologists, view behavior as the *interaction* of three factors: (a) our genetic endowment, (b) our experiences, and (c) how we see our current situation (Kimble, 1989; Pinel, 2006, p. 23). Each of these factors influences and is influenced by the others.

Regardless of the cause, there are many techniques used to manage trait anxiety (Booth-Butterfield & Booth-Butterfield, 1992), although most of them require professional assistance. One successful technique that you can do by yourself is positive imagery. Research has found positive imagery to help with both situational and trait anxiety, have a long-term effect, and to be easy to use (Ayres, et al, 1997; Bourhis & Allen, 1992; Zagacki, et al., 1992). Using **positive imagery** (also called **visualization**) requires using your imagination in a positive way. Instead of thinking of all the things you will do wrong and how nervous you will feel when you speak, create a detailed, positive, and vivid mental image of yourself confidently preparing for and giving a successful presentation. In other words, instead of imagining failure—as most speakers with trait anxiety do—imagine success.

Psychologists tell us that we act as the person we "see" ourselves to be (Maltz, 1960). If we say to others and ourselves such things as "I don't see myself ever becoming a professional speaker," then we won't. No amount of encouragement or practice will make us a confident professional speaker as long as we believe ourselves to be an ineffective speaker. Therefore, to change negative pictures you have of your speaking ability into positive ones, try positive imagery (Porter, 2003; Porter & Foster, 1986; Tice, 1980). First, look 2 or 3 months into your future and picture yourself as the speaker you would like to be. Write down the specific characteristics you want to develop. Now, close your eyes and mentally picture this "ideal you" on the day of your speech, feeling confident and giving a great presentation. Make this mental picture as detailed and vivid as possible (Ayres et al., 1994; Marks, 1999). For example, see yourself walking confidently up to the front of a group; see how professionally you are dressed; see yourself giving a clear, well-organized, and entertaining talk; feel yourself enjoying the talk; feel relaxed and warm; notice the direct eye contact you use and the way you retain your composure when a latecomer slams the door; hear yourself giving a great finish to the presentation and the audience applauding as you walk proudly back to your seat. Say to yourself, "I am a good speaker," and say it with conviction. As you picture yourself being successful, don't forget to feel successful. Words + vivid mental pictures + feelings = confidence. You need to say it, see it, and feel it if you want to change a negative mental picture into a positive one (Zagacki et al., 1992). Each time you vividly imagine yourself giving a successful presentation, your confidence will grow just as it would if you had actually given a successful presentation.

Positive imagery has been used in athletic programs for years. Sports psychologist Jim Loehr (1989) says that 80 to 85% of the top athletes use positive imagery in their training. For example, basketball great Michael Jordan; golfer Tiger Woods; swimmer Michael Phelps, and gymnast Nastia Liukin regularly use mental imagery. Says Nastia when asked about her Olympic secrets that led to winning a Gold medal in all-around gymnastics, "I visualize all of my routines before I compete on each event" ("Graceful Competitor," 2008).

Athletes such as swimmer Michael Phelps—winner of 8 gold metals at the 2008 Beijing Olympics—commonly use positive imagery to enhance performance.

Houston (1997) reports that "numerous studies have confirmed the fact that vividly experienced imagery, imagery that is both seen and felt, can substantially affect brain waves, blood flow, heart rate, skin temperature, gastric secretions, and immune response" (p. 11). In other words, just imagining yourself being attacked while walking to your car creates many of the same physiological responses as actually being attacked. In fact, neuroscientists using brain imaging technology on athletes have found that athletes who imagine a movement activate the same areas in the brain as athletes who actually perform the movement (Kosslyn et al., 1999; Stephan et al., 1995). Imagining yourself speaking also creates responses similar to actually speaking. Researchers (Wise et al., 1991) have found that imagined and spoken words both activate the prefrontal and premotor areas of the brain. Although top performers obviously use both their muscles and their minds when practicing, these findings do show the value of using positive imagery.

The Awareness Check on page 155 is a positive imagery exercise written by a seminar participant in an attempt to overcome her speaking anxiety. You may want to write and practice your own imagery exercise and include the specific speaker qualities of interest to you. As you complete this exercise, imagine that you are the person being described.

How did you do? Could you see yourself? If not, don't be concerned. Visualizing is easier for some people than for others (Isaac & Marks, 1994). If you are used to picturing your speaking abilities negatively, trying to see yourself in a positive light may feel not only phony but almost impossible. But if we can't even imagine ourselves giving a confident presentation, how can we expect to actually give one? As Gail Dusa, past president of the National Council for Self-Esteem, says the following:

> Visualization, in many ways, is nothing more complicated than involving your imagination in goal-setting. It's not hocus-pocus or magic. When you use your imagination to enhance goal-setting, you get fired up, excited. This enthusiasm equips you with more mental energy to put into the task. (McGarvey, 1990, p. 35)

To become confident speakers, we must think of ourselves as confident. Studies support that speakers who use a visualization script only once have less communication anxiety than speakers who do not use it or who use some other anxiety reduction technique (Ayres & Hopf, 1995). You may need to practice positive imagery for up to 4 weeks before you begin to feel comfortable with the new you.

Don't forget that positive imagery can be used to manage more than just speaker anxiety: It can help us control our anxiety in employment interviews, problem-solving discussions, meetings with angry customers, or any situation where our confidence needs a boost.

Once you have mastered positive imagery, you may wish to try other anxiety reduction techniques. In addition to visualization, colleges often offer courses or workshops

AWARENESS CHECK

Positive Imagery

Directions: For the best effect, have someone read the following visualization to you, or tape it and then listen to it. You can also view this visualization online through the Premium Website for *Communicating for Results*.

It is important to get in the mood to visualize. Close your eyes and get as comfortable as you can. Remember to keep an open body posture with your feet flat on the floor and your arms resting comfortably but not touching. Now, slowly take a deep breath . . . hold it . . . and exhale slowly. As you exhale, feel the tension draining away. Take another deep breath . . . hold it . . . and slowly exhale through your mouth. Now one more time, breathe deeply . . . hold it . . . slowly exhale and begin normal breathing. Imagine yourself as the "I" in the following visualization:

> I am leaning toward the mirror in my bathroom so I can get a good look at my face. Suddenly, the mirror clouds over. When it clears, I am looking at myself sitting in my speech seminar on the day of my first speech. It is my turn to speak.
>
> As I rise from my seat, I direct the butterflies of excitement in my stomach into positive energy. I can do this because I have practiced carefully and know I am well prepared. As I turn to face my colleagues, I draw in a deep breath, stand up straight, and begin to speak. An aura of confidence radiates from within as I speak. My body is relaxed and calm. My breathing is paced. My motions are fluid, and my gestures are graceful. My shoulders stay relaxed and down. My voice remains strong and steady. It is pitched low and is well modulated and easy for everyone to hear. My eyes scan from person to person, drawing their complete attention. My mind is rested and calm, allowing my words to flow evenly and to be clear and concise.
>
> As I speak, I easily remember each point of my speech. I can see the outline of my speech clearly in my mind and refer to my notes only briefly. I make use of dramatic pauses to stress important points within the speech. It is obvious that the audience understands what I am saying and that they are enjoying my speech. My words continue to flow smoothly and my transitions are especially good. Each idea is spoken clearly and confidently. There are no mistakes.
>
> As the speech winds down, my words are chosen carefully and powerfully. The audience is paying complete attention. I end with a bang! I know from the enthusiastic applause and positive comments that my speech has been a total success! I feel proud as I gather my visuals and walk to my seat. The mirror clouds over again, and I am back in my bathroom. I feel confident and happy. I am looking forward to giving my speech. I begin to dress for the day.

Now take a deep breath . . . hold it . . . and slowly let it out. Do this several more times and slowly return your awareness to the room.

in one or a combination of these other techniques: systematic desensitization, cognitive restructuring, and skills training. According to researchers, "the widest possible combination of methods" is often the most effective in reducing communication apprehension (Allen et al., 1989, p. 63; see also Dwyer, 2000; Kelly & Keaten, 2000). Taking a course in communication such as this one is a form of skills training that researchers claim is often as successful as other forms of treatment (Duff et al., 2007). Also keep in mind that if you have high communication apprehension (total scores higher than 80

Other Anxiety Reduction Methods

- **Systematic desensitization** involves (a) learning to relax using deep muscle relaxation and breathing, and (b) learning to remain relaxed while visualizing a series of communication situations progressing from low anxiety to high anxiety (McCroskey, 1972; Richmond & McCroskey, 1998).
- **Cognitive restructuring** involves (a) identifying irrational self-talk that produces speaker anxiety, (b) developing alternative coping statements, and (c) practicing the coping statements in stressful situations (Ellis, 2004; Fremouw & Scott, 1979).
- **Skills training** involves (a) identifying reasonable speaking goals, (b) determining behaviors or skills needed to achieve each goal, and (c) developing procedures for judging the success of each goal (Duff et al., 2007; Kelley, 1989; Phillips, 1991). Taking this course is a form of skills training.

ETHICAL DILEMMA

Napster and Music File Sharing

Before 2000, free peer-to-peer (P2P) music sharing was relatively ignored. In 1999, Shawn Fanning, an 18-year-old college student at Northeastern University in Boston, changed all that when he began a company called Napster. Fanning wrote the software using P2P that allowed people to easily share MP3 music files with each other by making their directories available online. What began with 150 users grew to 15,000 then soared to 60 million worldwide (Evangelista, 2009). Although Napster was a free service making no money for Fanning, it was allowing people to download music without paying the artists a royalty. Eventually, the band Metallica started the wave of lawsuits against Napster when it came to light that one of their unreleased songs was now in the hands of millions and on radio stations across the United States without a single cent paid to the artists.

In February 2001, lawsuits filed by the Recording Industry Association of America (RIAA) resulted in decisions by the U.S. District Court and a federal appellate court that Napster was violating copyright laws. In the RIAA's own words, "We want Napster to play by the same rules as everyone else, including the copyright laws honored by businesses offline and legitimate sites online that are licensed to download music" (RIAA.com, 2006). Eventually, a nearly destroyed Napster was sold to the company Roxio in 2002 and then to Best Buy in 2008 who retained the Napster name and became a legal music downloading service. According to Benny Evangelista (2009), although paid music downloads reached $3.8 billion in 2008, P2P file sharing has not gone away. In fact, many new companies exist that facilitate shared downloading of music, television shows, and even movies. He also notes that in addition to the United States, countries that are most guilty of copyright infringement include England, Italy, France, and Spain.

QUESTIONS: What do you think? Is file sharing unethical or just illegal? Refer back to the Chapter 1 discussion of ethics as you formulate your answer.

on the PRCA), and because a part of this apprehension is likely influenced by genetics, learning to handle your anxiety won't happen overnight. Awareness or perception of your anxiety and its effect on you and others around you is a definite beginning.

Anxious people do not have to take a back seat to more confident people. Taking control of nervousness and anxiety is much easier once we identify it and take steps to manage it. Positive imagery is one step, thorough preparation is a second, and giving yourself time to change is another.

Inadequate Preparation

Inadequate preparation can make communicator anxiety even worse. Unfortunately, many of us believe that, outside of public speaking, most communication requires little special preparation. The following story, adapted from Howell and Bormann (1971, pp. 152–153), illustrates potential problems that can result from such false confidence:

Cass Carlyle, the manager of a television station, found out the hard way the results of poor preparation. Several newscasters had complained about errors in a special newscast prepared by Al Mendez, the man Carlyle was grooming for the position of top newscaster. Although Carlyle thought Mendez's newscast was exceptionally good, he promised to speak to Mendez about the matter. He was discussing a problem sponsor with his secretary when Al walked by. Acting without thinking, Carlyle called Mendez into his office. Al noticed the uneasiness in Carlyle's voice and wondered what was wrong.

"I've, uh, wanted to talk to you about your news special," Carlyle began. "We don't . . . we aren't always as careful of the basic information . . . the foundation of—facts as it were . . . not as careful as we should be."

"What do you mean?" Al asked, standing and putting his hands flat on Carlyle's desk.

"Well, it's just that some of the others feel you plunged ahead a little too fast without checking on certain basic background information."

"Are they questioning my competence as a news analyst?"

"No, no, it's nothing like that. . . . They just note, for example, that your treatment of the Middle East crisis was not historically accurate."

Mendez leaned over the desk and raised his voice, "They're saying I did a bad job of research, is that it?"

"Well, no, I wouldn't say that precisely." Carlyle wasn't sure what he wanted to say. Things weren't going as he had expected.

From this point on, with both men emotionally upset, the simple, friendly conference that Carlyle had intended turned into a shouting match and ended with Al's resignation. It had never occurred to Carlyle that the final result of the conference would be so disastrous. He had lost an extremely valuable employee, one he might not be able to replace.

If Carlyle had planned what he wanted to say and had anticipated its possible effect on Mendez, and if he had selected a time when his own mind was free from other problems, the conversation might have ended very differently.

Good communicators are aware the communication is irreversible (once a particular idea has been expressed, its effect cannot be completely erased). As a result, they know that they must prepare their messages carefully.

Vague Instructions

Giving and receiving instructions are weaknesses in many organizations. Take, for example, medical professions where the instructions given by the nurse or doctor are misunderstood; the results can result in minor to serious physical harm and possibly even death (Green-Hernandez et al., 2004). To get an idea of how difficult it is to give instructions, complete the Awareness Check on page 158 before reading further in the chapter.

Many of us give vague, easily misunderstood instructions due to lack of preparation. But in some cases, we give confusing instructions even when we prepare the instructions ahead of time. The Awareness Check activity will give you an idea of the obstacles that can arise when communicating instructions to others. Chances are that your listeners or patients will interpret your instructions differently from what you intend. Don't rush to blame them if they don't follow your instructions correctly; *your* instructions may be the problem.

Were you successful? If not, compare your instructions with the following eight rules for giving clear instructions (Stewart, 1973):

1.   Begin with an overall picture.

AWARENESS CHECK: GIVING INSTRUCTIONS

Situation: Project F

You are an engineer in an aerospace corporation and are working on a control panel for a top-secret missile.* A demonstration is planned for the Air Force this afternoon. The unit was sent to the demonstration site by Federal Express. To make sure no one tampered with the panel, you designed a secret access device, composed of parts that must be properly assembled into an F shape (F for fail-safe) and then scanned by a computer.

Five minutes before the demonstration is to begin, you receive an urgent message from a technician asking for the secret instructions for assembling the access device; the two engineers who know the instructions and were to conduct the demonstration have not arrived. The Air Force insists that the demonstration must go on at the scheduled time. Knowing there is no time for questions, how would you instruct the technician to assemble the pieces? Try the following experiment:

Solution

Directions: Using a copy machine, enlarge and then cut out the pieces of the fail-safe device at the bottom of this paragraph. Carefully plan the easiest way to explain Project F, and then, giving each person a set of the cutout parts (but not the solution), instruct various people (e.g., colleagues, employees, friends) on how to assemble the device. Stand far enough from them so that you cannot see what they are doing. Have them sit so that they can't see each other's work. Don't let them ask any questions. Remember, they must finish in 5 minutes.

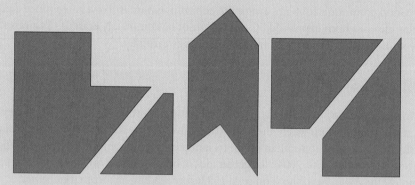

You can go to your Premium Website for *Communicating for Results* to access this Awareness Check online and download the image of the fail-safe device.

*The instructions were developed by Cheryl Hamilton and Cordell Parker. The puzzle pieces are from "How to Assemble a Framus," in M. Sashkin & W. C. Morris, *Organizational Behavior: Concepts and Experiences,* pp. 127, 137 (Englewood Cliffs, NJ: Prentice-Hall). Copyright 1984. Reprinted by permission of Pearson Education, Inc., Upper Saddle River, New Jersey.

2. Use a minimum number of words.

3. Use simple, easily understood words.

4. Be specific.

5. Use simple comparisons.

6. Use repetition.

7. Number or "signpost" objects or steps.

8. Use good delivery techniques.

Let's take a careful look at each rule. Although you probably don't instruct people at work on how to draw geometric shapes (such as those shown in Figure 6.1), we are using such tasks to clarify certain rules. The principles for giving instructions are the same whether you are explaining how to boot a new computer, how to assemble a piece of machinery, or what work must be completed by your employees before noon.

Rule 1: Begin with an overall picture. The first step in giving instructions of any kind is to give a brief, but vivid, mental picture of the task. In other words, give a frame of reference from which the person can interpret your instructions. For example, the overall picture for geometric shape *a* in Figure 6.1 might include the following information:

> Before we begin with specifics, let me give you a brief overview. This drawing includes three squares that are 1 inch on each side. They resemble a child's stack of building blocks that is beginning to topple to the left. Because each square on your graph paper is 1/4-inch wide, each building block you draw will be four graph squares high and four graph squares wide. Only one corner of each square touches the one below it; they do not overlap. I will begin my instructions with the top square and work downward. Okay . . . now draw a 1-inch square in the top left portion of your paper. . . .

This overall picture will give the listeners a mental image of the drawing, which should make it easier for them to follow your subsequent instructions accurately.

To make accurate decisions, employees must also be aware of all relevant information. Therefore, an *overview* could include such information as the importance of the assignment, management's ideas about the task, the importance of completing

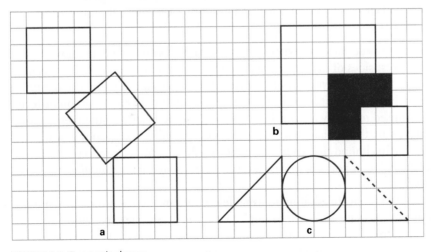

FIGURE 6.1 Geometric shapes.

the task by a certain time, and reasons why past attempts at completing the task failed.

Rule 2: Use a minimum number of words. The more words you use, the more likely you are to cause confusion. If you are prepared and know what you want to say, you should be able to convey your message in as few words as possible. For example, compare "Draw a 1-inch square in the center of your paper" with the following wordy instructions:

> About half an inch above the center of your paper draw a 1-inch line that is parallel with the top of the paper. Now go to the right end of that line and draw a 1-inch line downward that is parallel to the right side of the paper. Next, go to the left end of the original line and draw another 1-inch line downward. You should have three sides of a square. Complete the square by connecting the bottom points of the two vertical lines.

Although these instructions are fairly clear, such a detailed explanation of how to draw a square is unnecessary and a waste of time.

Rule 3: Use simple, easily understood words. In giving instructions, you should not be trying to impress people with your vocabulary. Do not assume that everyone knows jargon or technical terms. Here's an example of the difference between jargon and simple words.

> A plumber wrote to the U.S. Bureau of Standards about using hydrochloric acid to clean drainpipes; several days later he received this reply: "The efficacy of hydrochloric acid is indisputable, but the corrosive residue is incompatible with metallic permanence." Confused, he wrote again and asked if the acid is "okay to use or not." A second letter advised him, "We cannot assume responsibility for the production of toxic and noxious residue and suggest that you use an alternative procedure." Still baffled, he wrote, "Do you mean it's okay to use hydrochloric acid?" A final letter resolved the question. "Don't use hydrochloric acid. It eats the hell out of pipes." (Dunworth, 1980, p. 190)

The skilled communicator uses terms that fit into everyone's frame of reference. For example, suppose you were explaining how to draw the second square in geometric shape *a* in Figure 6.1. You might give the following instructions:

> Go to the bottom right corner of your first square and draw a half-inch line at a 45-degree angle toward the northeast corner of your paper. Then go back to the same point and extend that line half an inch downward toward the southwest corner of your paper.

Most adults should know what a 45-degree angle is and where the north, east, south, and west sides of the paper are located. They should also know the meanings of such words as *perpendicular, tangent, parallel, horizontal, vertical, diameter,* and *circumference.* Unfortunately, however, many do not. Even for jargon or technical terms used regularly in your business, you should briefly define their meaning to make sure that all have the same frame of reference. Using simple words increases the likelihood that your instructions will be accurately followed. It also reduces the risk that you will misuse a term (such as saying *horizontal* when you mean *vertical*).

Rule 4: Be specific. In addition to using few words and simple words, you must also be as specific as possible. For example, a specific yet simple explanation of how to position the second square in geometric shape *a* (Figure 6.1) is shown in Figure 6.2. For the right-hand triangle in geometric shape *c*, you might use instructions like those in Figure 6.3.

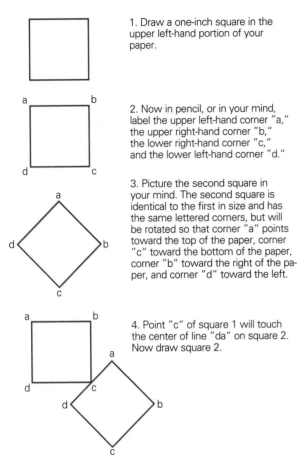

1. Draw a one-inch square in the upper left-hand portion of your paper.

2. Now in pencil, or in your mind, label the upper left-hand corner "a," the upper right-hand corner "b," the lower right-hand corner "c," and the lower left-hand corner "d."

3. Picture the second square in your mind. The second square is identical to the first in size and has the same lettered corners, but will be rotated so that corner "a" points toward the top of the paper, corner "c" toward the bottom of the paper, corner "b" toward the right of the paper, and corner "d" toward the left.

4. Point "c" of square 1 will touch the center of line "da" on square 2. Now draw square 2.

FIGURE 6.2 Instructions for second square of shape *a* in Figure 6.1.

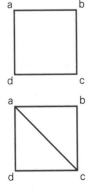

1. Draw a one-inch square on the right side of your paper. Label the corners.

2. Inside the square from point "a" to point "c," draw a dashed or broken line.

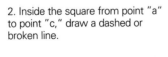

3. Erase line "ab" and line "bc." You should now have a triangle "acd" with two solid lines and one dashed or broken line.

FIGURE 6.3 Instructions for right-hand triangle shape *c* in Figure 6.1.

Rule 5: Use simple comparisons. People learn more easily when they can compare or contrast a new task with an old one. Mentioning that today's task is identical to yesterday's except for one additional step makes today's task much easier. To make sure that your comparisons fit into the frames of reference of those who are to follow your instructions, keep all comparisons simple. For example, look at the shapes in Figure 6.1. You might say that geometric shape *a* resembles a stack of three building blocks toppling to the left or that shape *c* looks like a large ball wedged between two triangular bookends. What does shape *b* look like to you—what comparison could you make to clarify its shape?

Rule 6: Use repetition. Most people need information repeated before they completely understand it. When giving instructions, repeat each set of instructions or steps. If the instructions are especially long or complicated, give a brief summary after explaining several steps. Finally, after you've given all instructions, review the entire procedure. Some managers eliminate the final summary because they are rushed, but the final summary often clarifies a confusing item or points out an area of possible misunderstanding. The final summary also gives you a chance to ensure that all necessary instructions were given correctly.

Rule 7: Number or "signpost" objects or steps. Instead of saying "And the next step . . . ," say "The third step. . . ." Instead of saying "When you finish that, I want you to . . . ," say "The third thing I want you to do before noon is. . . ." This makes it easier for everyone to keep track of the instructions. Also, when possible use mnemonic devices (i.e., memory formulas such as acronyms, rhymes, and acrostics) to simplify encoding of your instructions (Bellezza, 1982; Mastropieri & Scruggs, 1998). Some common mnemonic devices are the rhyme "Thirty days hath September . . . ," used to remember the number of days in each month; the acronym HOMES, to remember the names of the five Great Lakes; and the acrostic "Every good boy does fine," to remember that the lines on the treble clef are for the notes EGBDF. Make it as easy as possible for your listeners to remember your key ideas.

Rule 8: Use good delivery techniques. Glance at each of your listeners while you are speaking, and watch for nonverbal indicators of confusion (such as a frown or raised eyebrows). Look and sound confident. If you don't appear to have confidence in your instructions, why should others? And of course, make sure you speak loudly enough to be heard easily.

If you follow these eight rules, your instructions will be understood. Don't assume, however, that you have communicated what you meant. Listeners often think they understand completely when they do not. Therefore, when possible, ask them to rephrase your instructions in their own words, encourage them to ask for clarification of any confusing points, and supply a written copy of your instructions for further clarification.

Jumping to Conclusions

When we fail to distinguish between what we observed firsthand and what we only inferred or assumed, **inference-observation confusion** (better known as jumping to conclusions) has occurred. The following story is about an employee who made an inference and then acted on the inference as though it were fact:

> Arlene Johnson, 36, had worked for the Farwell Sheet and Tube Company as an inside salesperson for 10 years. Her duties consisted of handling telephone

orders from customers, processing orders placed by outside Farwell salespeople, and responding to letters of inquiry about company products.

Outside sales positions paid substantially more and held more prestige than inside jobs. Johnson had requested a transfer to outside selling at the time of her annual performance review in December. Henry Browning, sales manager, had promised her the first opening in a sales territory. The most likely possibility was George Madison's territory because Madison was to retire on his 65th birthday in March. It became general office knowledge that Johnson was to have Madison's post.

In mid-January, Browning began interviewing applicants for sales positions in the firm. Johnson heard via the grapevine that the company was looking for a salesperson from the outside to take over Madison's territory. Johnson decided to check with Browning and was again assured that the next vacant territory would be hers.

Facts Versus Inferences

Directions: How skilled are you at distinguishing facts from inferences? To check your effectiveness, carefully read the following story* and answer the statements by writing T (definitely true), F (definitely false), or ? (not stated in the story) in the blanks. Check your answers against those in the back of this book. You can also take this quiz online and view the answers at your Premium Website for *Communicating for Results.*

John Phillips, the research director of a Midwestern food products firm, ordered a crash program of development on a new process. He gave three of his executives authority to spend up to $50,000 each without consulting him. He sent one of his best men, Harris, to the firm's West Coast plant with orders to work on the new process independently. Within 1 week Harris produced a highly promising new approach to the problem.

Statements

_____ 1. Phillips sent one of his best men to the West Coast plant.

_____ 2. Phillips overestimated Harris's competence.

_____ 3. Harris failed to produce anything new.

_____ 4. Harris lacked authority to spend money without consulting Phillips.

_____ 5. Only three of Phillips's executives had authority to spend money without consulting him.

_____ 6. The research director sent one of his best men to the firm's West Coast plant.

_____ 7. Three men were given authority to spend up to $50,000 each without consulting Phillips.

_____ 8. Phillips had a high opinion of Harris.

_____ 9. Only four people are referred to in the story.

_____ 10. Phillips was research director of a food production firm.

_____ 11. Although Phillips gave authority to three of his best men to spend up to $50,000 each, the story does not make clear whether Harris was one of these men.

*From W. V. Haney, 1962, "Test Your Judgment," *Nation's Business,* January, pp. 66–69, 81. Reprinted with permission of *Nation's Business.*

Two weeks later, Johnson, whose desk faced Browning's inner office, saw a tall, well-groomed young man enter the sales manager's office at 9:30 Monday morning. Around 10:00, Browning, Madison, and the young man emerged. Johnson heard Browning tell Madison, "Although Mr. Calvin will not graduate officially until next week, he's finished his exams and is ready to start at once. I suggest you take him along with you, George, for the rest of the day and tomorrow as well, so he can get the feel of your territory."

Henry Browning shook hands with Calvin and said, "Good luck, Sam. We're glad to have you with us. I knew your father well."

At lunch, three other members of the office staff told Arlene the word around the office was that a new man was being hired to take over Madison's territory. Johnson blurted out, "Well, that's about all I can take!" She returned to her desk, collected her personal effects, and stomped out of the office.

The next morning, two events occurred that, to Browning, seemed unrelated. He received a bitter letter of resignation from Johnson, and he placed Sam Calvin on the payroll—as a trainee for the *inside* sales force. (Bergen & Haney, 1966, pp. 107–108)

As you will no doubt notice when you take the Awareness Check on page 164, we all make assumptions. It is quite possible that your job requires you to make a certain number of inferences or assumptions, and sometimes you may also need to act on those inferences. However, in such cases, you are *aware* that you are making an inference and you also know that there is a certain amount of risk involved. In other words, you are taking a calculated risk. Problems are more likely to arise when people are *unaware* that they have made any inferences and think, instead, that their inferences are facts as Arlene did in the example. When these inferences include other workers, management, job assignments, and interests of clients or customers, communication breakdown is likely to occur. If Arlene had checked her sources more carefully (in this case the grapevine did not have accurate information), asked questions to get facts instead of assuming, and listened carefully to the answers to her questions, the outside sales position would likely have been hers. How often do you jump to conclusions in your communication with others?

Bypassing

Another kind of assumption that causes communication obstacles is **bypassing**, which happens when we assume that a word has the same meaning for other people that it does for us.

Managers and employees often have different meanings for the same words. When a boss tells an employee that a raise is "likely"—which to the boss means a 51% chance but to the employee means an 85 to 95% chance—misunderstanding and disappointment are sure to arise.

To further your understanding of bypassing, select three people with whom you regularly communicate and ask them each to take the test in the following Awareness Check without looking at the others' answers. See how closely all of you agree on meanings. Do you see any terms that could cause misunderstandings among you?

Vague phrases such as *good job*, *as soon as possible*, and *in a couple of minutes* are sure to have different meanings for different people and will cause misunderstandings if we are not careful.

AWARENESS CHECK

Meanings of Terms

Directions: Decide what percentage of certainty (from 0 to 100%) is implied when you use each of the following terms*—for example, if you tell someone that your attendance at the staff party is *likely*, do you mean there is an 85% chance of being there, a 30% chance, or what? Write the percentage that expresses your usual meaning next to each term. Ask three other people to do the same thing, and compare answers. You can take this quiz online and view the answers at your Premium Website for *Communicating for Results*.

Terms Commonly Used in Business

_____ 1. absolute

_____ 2. certain

_____ 3. a cinch

_____ 4. indefinite

_____ 5. open to question

_____ 6. possible

_____ 7. probable

_____ 8. risky

_____ 9. settled

_____ 10. a sure thing

_____ 11. a toss-up

*Adapted from Schneider, Donaghy, & Newman, 1975, *Organizational Communication*, (pp. 22–23), New York: McGraw-Hill.

Cultural differences also cause bypassing problems. Here is one example:

Mr. Sato, manager for Kumitomo America, told Jane Brady to ship any lots of more than 25 units to the parent corporation in Japan immediately. Jane assured him that she would "get right on it." Six weeks later she was summoned by an unhappy boss wanting to know why she had not shipped the lots as requested.

"Sir," replied Jane, "I shipped every lot more than 25. Those were my orders, and I carried them out."

Mr. Sato shouted, "I checked this morning. We have 40 lots of more than 25 units each."

"That's not so. We don't."

"We do!"

"No, we don't!"

Finally they agreed to go and look. When they counted the first lot, it contained 25 units. Each looked at the other triumphantly. To Mr. Sato, "more than 25" always included 25. To Miss Brady, "more than 25" began with 26. (Adapted from Sullivan & Kameda, 1991, pp. 1–2)

Now that so many companies have plants around the globe, cultural bypassing is sure to cause many costly misunderstandings.

Another way bypassing happens is when people have different words for the same meaning. For example, an American motorist made the following observations about the meaning of British road signs:

If we saw a sign ROADUP, we came to learn that it meant "Road Taken Up" or "Road Repairs Ahead." Near Chepstow we were asked to detour (the

British call it DIVERSION) because, said the man who directed us, there had been a BUMP down the road. We could see two cars locked together in a collision. Near London, you may find a warning DUAL CARRIAGE WAY, meaning "Divided Highway." Instead of "No Passing" the sign reads NO OVERTAKING.

When the danger zone is passed, you come to END OF PROHIBITION! You are told not to "Stop" but HALT at highway intersections. If you try to park in a no parking area, you find a sign NO WAITING. (Haney, 1973, pp. 259–260)

To prevent bypassing, both managers and employees should ask for feedback from one another to determine what each really means. Assuming that the listener's frame of reference is the same as yours can only lead to misunderstanding. Refer to Chapter 1 for additional examples of frame of reference differences that can cause bypassing. Frame of reference also plays a role in our next obstacle, sexual harassment.

Sexual Harassment

One of the surest obstacles to communication in the workplace is sexual harassment. We would like to think that sexual harassment occurs rarely, but in 2008, over 13,800 sexual harassment charges were filed with the Equal Employment Opportunity Commission (EEOC); 11,731 cases were resolved resulting in $47.4 million in benefits paid (U.S. EEOC, 2009). According to the U.S. EEOC (2009),

> Unwelcome sexual advances, requests for sexual favors, and other verbal or physical conduct of a sexual nature constitute **sexual harassment** when this conduct explicitly or implicitly affects an individual's employment, unreasonably interferes with an individual's work performance, or creates an intimidating, hostile, or offensive work environment.

The definition of sexual harassment includes two basic concepts:

1. *Quid pro quo* ("something for something")—Includes the promise of rewards for sexual favors (such as job promotion or perks) or the threat of punishment for rejection of sexual overtures (such as loss of promotion or job).

2. Hostile work environment—Occurs when conditions are sexually "intimidating, hostile, or offensive" and interfere with performance on the job. A one-time vulgar remark does not constitute sexual harassment; however, repeated verbal or nonverbal behaviors, which affect work performance and morale would be considered sexual harassment.

Since the Civil Rights Act of 1964, it has been unlawful in the United States to discriminate in hiring on the basis of sex. In 1980, sexual harassment became a violation of Title VII of the Civil Rights Act; in 1991, an amendment to Title VII entitled employees to monetary damages; in 1998, the U.S. Supreme Court ruled that same-sex harassment is also governed by Title VI; and in 2000, educational institutions became liable for sexual harassment of students (Conrad & Poole, 2002).

Sexual harassment can occur in many circumstances including the following:

• The victim, as well as the harasser may be a woman or a man. The victim does not have to be of the opposite sex.

- The harasser can be the victim's supervisor, an agent of the employer, a supervisor in another area, a coworker, or a non-employee.

- The victim does not have to be the person harassed but could be anyone affected by the offensive conduct.

- Unlawful sexual harassment may occur without economic injury to or discharge of the victim.

- The harasser's conduct must be unwelcome (U.S. EEOC, 2009).

Harassment is judged by its effects on the recipient, not by the intentions of the harasser. Because some people may regard a particular behavior as offensive and others not, the courts use what is called the **reasonable person rule** to determine whether a "reasonable person" would find the behavior in question offensive. There has been a gender problem in applying this rule to sexual harassment because "a reasonable woman and a reasonable man are likely to differ in their judgments of what is offensive" (Riger, 1991; Sandler, 1996; Solomon & Williams, 1997). Although both women and men consider blatant behaviors, such as sexual bribery or sexual assault, to be harassment, they disagree in other areas. For example, women are more likely to consider gestures, stares, and teasing as harassment (Deutschman, 1991; Kirk, 1988); men do not typically consider these behaviors harassment (Konrad & Gutek, 1986; Powell, 1986). Women tend to view sexual overtures from men at work to be insulting, whereas men often view similar overtures to be flattering (Diehl, 1996; Gutek, 1985).

Our ever-changing, high-tech society has brought about a new form of sexual harassment: sexual harassment through e-mail (Volokh, 2000). E-mail harassment can include distributing photographs, cartoons, or jokes, and in some cases, surfing the Internet and viewing offensive websites in the presence of coworkers. For example, the following litigation was reported by the EEOC (2003):

> In this Title VII lawsuit, the Los Angeles District Office alleged that defendant subjected four current and two former female employees at its manufacturing plant in Henderson, Nevada to a sexually hostile working environment and retaliated against some of the women for complaining about the harassment. The harassment included groping and sexual advances by male supervisors and coworkers and the circulation of pornographic pictures, dirty jokes, and e-mails. The case was resolved through a settlement agreement which provides for a total payment of $217,500.

Organizations need to prepare themselves for potential problems by developing strong policies and procedures regarding use of e-mail and the Internet, as well as dealing with sexual harassment (Ingram et al., 2004). It is the responsibility of the employer to provide a safe workplace, free of sexual harassment, to all employees. Fortunately, most companies have thorough policies that cover these issues and clearly state how offenses will be handled. But having procedures in place isn't always enough, as Wal-Mart discovered when it settled two sexual harassment suits for $315,000 because although Wal-Mart did have a written harassment policy in place, the staff in charge "failed to take appropriate corrective action" (U.S. EEOC, 2006). Wal-Mart also agreed to provide yearly sexual harassment training for its managers and to be monitored by the EEOC for 3 years.

Effective company sexual harassment policies ensure confidentiality, freedom from retaliation, prompt investigation, and punishment for offenders. If you become aware of sexual harassment within your organization, or you believe that you are a victim of sexual harassment, you should do the following (Tamaki, 1991; Carr-Ruffino, 1997):

- Review the organization's policies on harassment.
- Project a friendly but professional image of a person who won't put up with harassment.
- Confront your harasser in an assertive manner, giving the person a chance to stop the behavior.
- Document the incidents of harassment.
- Report the incident to an immediate supervisor or the human resources department.
- Weigh the consequences of further action; hopefully the company will handle the complaint.

When individuals and organizations become more sensitive to individual rights and differences, we will all benefit.

IT REALLY WORKS

Blogging

In the beginning, **blogs**—short for web logs—were used mostly by students to express opinions on everything from politics to what kind of wine goes best with a meal. Today, however, there are an estimated 200 million blogs in existence, both personal and corporate, and used regularly in hundreds of countries including South Korea, Iraq, and Croatia (Duncan, 2006).

One company that realizes the value of blogging is General Motors—both before and after their bankruptcy. When General Motors—now referred to as the New GM—began their company blog, GM FastLane.com, vice chairman Bob Lutz used the blog to allow "customers to engage with him directly about products, services, and the future of the company" (Wright, 2006, p. 73). Blog comments ranged from the cheerleading to useful critiques to vocal criticism. After declaring bankruptcy on June 1, 2009, GM used their company blog to communicate with employees and consumers about their financial situation, and downsizing of plant facilities, car brands, dealerships, and employees. For example, on July 13, Lutz hosted a live webchat to answer questions about his new role as GM Vice-Chairman "responsible for all creative elements of products and customer relationships." One blogger asked: "Bob, will we see improvements in GM commercials now that you are in charge of them? The new Buick commercial is very embarrassing . . ." Lutz gave this reply: "Let me put it this way: That Buick commercial tested very well, which is not the same as saying that it's an effective ad. I think you will very quickly see a drastic change in the tone and content of our advertising. And if you don't, it will mean that I have failed" (Lutz, 2009).

From their experience with blogs, General Motors suggests the following (Wright, 2006, pp. 76–77):

> *Be honest* (negative comments don't go away by ignoring them, but tackling them can create reader trust); *use blogrolls* (links to other quality blogs); *ask people for their thoughts; be passionate; be fair to your competition;* and *have a genuine voice* (speak like a real person so people can relate to you).

What do you think?
- What do you think about the advice from General Motors' vice chairman, Bob Lutz, for effective use and maintenance of a blog?
- What advantages and disadvantages do blogs offer when communicating with customers and coworkers?

Communication Technology

The final communication obstacle we'll discuss is that caused by communication technology. The newest communication technologies use the Internet. According to ComScore.com, on February 2009, 164.3 million U.S. citizens were online (Radwanick, 2009). The United States is the number one Internet user in the world followed in order by China, Japan, Germany, Great Britain, and South Korea (McPhail, 2006). Blogs (web logs) are gaining in business use—as we saw in the "It Really Works" example. In 2007, Technorati reported approximately 70 million active blogs with 120,000 new blogs being added each day (Sifry, 2007). Sifry also reported that the blog messages are posted in many different languages and that English bloggers do not top the list; instead, Japanese is the number one blog language followed by English, Chinese, Italian, and Spanish (see Figure 6.4). Of all the Internet activities, e-mail is used more often—91% of U. S. adults online send or read e-mail ("Internet Activities," 2009). A relatively new web attraction is Twitter.com with 17 million U.S. citizens visiting the site in April 2009 (Lipsman, 2009). Instant messaging has also gained multiple users—and not just with teenagers and college students although 75% of young adults use instant messaging (Nadler, 2008). In 2003, 84% of North American companies surveyed made regular use of instant messaging (Nasaw, 2003). And of course, there is the ever popular cell phone used by everyone. Employees and managers who know how to effectively harness the power of the technology of the information superhighway without letting it become an obstacle, have an edge on the competition. Let's look at several of these types of technologies in more detail along with their advantages and disadvantages.

E-mail, Instant Messages, and Blogs

There are some definite advantages to using **e-mail** and **instant messages** (IMs) in an organization—increased access to and faster retrieval of information, to name

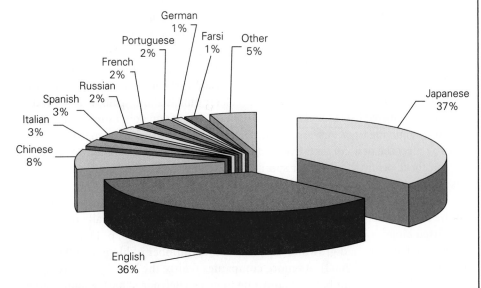

FIGURE 6.4 Blog posts by language.
Source: From State of the Live Web, April 2007. David Sifry, Technorati.com. Accessed at http://www.sifry.com/alerts/archives/000493.html.

Courtesy of Dave Carroll

just two. For example, Manistique Papers, Inc., was having a problem in their recycling plant; when ink was removed from old magazines, the paper wasn't white enough. They contacted Buckman Labs, which "immediately posted a message on their Internet discussion board." Within less than 48 hours the answer came from employees in Finland and Belgium: A rare bacterium was breaking down the peroxide; fortunately, an antidote was available (Cravens & Piercy, 2003, p. 164). The U.S. Army uses IM technology "to transmit communications about weather conditions and the latest intelligence," and the Navy uses IM "to communicate within ships, across Navy divisions, and back to the Pentagon in Washington, D.C." (Daft & Marcic, 2006, p. 502).

Another advantage to e-mail may actually be the social uses, such as hobbies and recreational activities. A study conducted by Xerox Corporation supported their belief that their employees' social use of e-mail outweighed the costs. They found that social use of e-mail had the following advantages (Steinfield, 1990):

- Employees learned to use the system more rapidly.
- Social contacts often became valuable in later work tasks.
- Quality of work life improved for some employees.
- Creativity was enhanced.

On the other hand, there are a number of disadvantages to using e-mail. For one thing, e-mail messages are not private and may live as long as "five years in someone's backup file or memory bank" (Haddock, 1996, pp. 148–149). For example, as part of the settlement with Enron, "company e-mail used as evidence was published on the web. Also published were thousands of e-mail messages unrelated to the case, both business-related and personal, sent by Enron employees during the period under investigation" (Young, 2006, p. 123). This probably occurred because according to the Electronic Communications Privacy Act (Fraser, 1999), it is legal to view or disclose personal electronic communication if it is "readily accessible" to the public—which most e-mail is. It is also legal for employers to inspect employee e-mail on the company intranet, so it's never a good idea to send any e-mail that you wouldn't want on the front page of the local paper. Another disadvantage is that, because e-mail messages are usually brief and informal, senders often do not give them the same care they would give to a letter or memo; this is especially true for IMs. Always read your message at least twice before sending to check for punctuation, spelling, tone, and clarity; use bulleted lists to make your ideas stand out. If you aren't sure, don't send it. If you are replying to or forwarding an e-mail message, be sure to change the subject line to reflect the new content. Even IMs, when business related, should be given a careful check before sending. For specifics on writing successful e-mail, see Appendix: Written Communication.

Although the use of personal blogs is growing rapidly, in 2006 only 5.8% of the Fortune 500 companies and 1.5% of the Forbes 200 best small companies used blogs as part of their regular business (Belcher, 2006, p. 1). By 2008, corporate bloggers had grown to 12% of the total number of bloggers ("State of the Blogosphere," 2008). As more companies realize the benefits to having a company blog, this number will continue to grow (Belcher, 2006). E-commerce which is one of these benefits is growing by 33% each year (Ingram et al., 2008). You don't have to be a company to sell products online—individuals worldwide have found that the Internet and blogging have leveled the playing ground for communication and sales. Blogs are better than one-way communication says Jeremy Wright in *Blog Marketing* (2006), because with blogs, "you're engaging with your customers, as every reader is reading your blog by choice, every reader is choosing to interact with your business, and every reader wants to hear more from you" (p. 56). Whether you are a large or small company or an individual, the suggestions for using blogs offered by General Motors in the "It Really Works" section in this chapter are good. At the same time, be aware of the power of technology. As United Airlines found out in our chapter opener, technology like YouTube and the comments people make on blogs can be quite persuasive. Also, look ahead to the Chapter 8 opener where RadioShack's past CEO, Dave Edmondson, resigned due in part to blogger comments about him and the company. When inaccuracies in Edmondson's resume were made know but company response was slow, trust was lost and bloggers created what Hewitt (2005) calls a "blog swarm," which is "an early indicator of an opinion storm brewing, which, when it breaks, will fundamentally alter the general public's understanding of a person, place, product, or phenomenon" (p. 2). RadioShack didn't have a company blog at that time, but that didn't keep them from being hit by a blog swarm as they discovered; so having a blog and managing the blog may be the way to go. Additionally, blogs allow a low-cost way to present new products and brands (Hewitt, 2005).

A word of warning to employees who have their own blogs: Don't think that your blog goes no further than family and friends. There have been many reported cases of employee firings because of blog content, such as Michael Hanscom, who was fired by Microsoft in 2003, and Mark Jen, who was fired by Google in 2005 (Bishop, 2003; Perez, 2005). Management may have found these job-related comments by using Technorati.com, a search engine for blogs. According to Technorati, they make "it possible for you to find out what people on the Internet are saying about you, your company, your products, your competitors, your politics, or other areas of interest—all in real-time" (About Technorati.com, 2006). A survey of 308 U.S. companies found that 9% of them had fired an employee for comments made on a blog or message board (Singel, 2007). Also, companies and interviewers are beginning to search blogs such as Facebook, MySpace, Xanga, and Friendster for additional information on job candidates (Hechinger, 2008). If you have considered these sites safe places to blow off steam, you may want to revisit your posts.

Electronic Meetings

In today's era of global involvement, telecommuting, and virtual offices, electronic meetings (such as teleconferences and videoconferences) are important communication avenues. Davenport and Pearlson (1998) found that "despite e-mail, fax machines, cell phones, and pagers, workers do not communicate as well with one another in virtual environments as they do in the traditional office" (p. 58). A study of **telecommuters** (workers who complete tasks offsite) found

© 2005 Ted Goff

"If you ever forget your cellphone, this model will hop up and run after you."

that many "felt a profound sense of loss akin to grief at job loss" (Hylmö & Buzzanell, 2002, p. 349). Not only do these workers need information, but they also need involvement to feel more a part of the company. Although research indicates that "video dampens feelings of social contact" (Fulk & Collins-Jarvis, 2001, p 629), when face-to-face meetings are not an option, electronic meetings would seem a good alternative.

Videoconferencing is used by multiple-location companies to communicate with their employees—for training, business updates, to introduce new products or procedural changes, or just to keep employees from feeling isolated ("Videoconferencing," 1995). As the chapter opening photo shows, videoconferencing is also used regularly by medical personnel as a consulting tool. Recently, 20 doctors from three Mayo Clinic locations spent 1.5 hours discussing a risky skin cancer case. They arrived at "a course of treatment, including specific recommendations on how aggressively to sample the patient's lymph nodes and how best to construct the surgical wound" (Berry & Bendapudi, 2003, p. 104). Design consultants help businesses (such as Computer Sciences Corporation) design conferencing quarters with suggestions such as make the ceilings 13 feet high to "wash the boundary walls with light" and "provide full-frequency absorption"; keep the doors "out of the line of the camera" so late-comers won't be on film; and minimize camera movement because "it can cause a slower frame rate" (Lawlor, 1998; Sommerhoff, 1998, p. 52).

A summary of research includes the following characteristics of videoconferencing when compared with face-to-face meetings (Fulk & Collins-Jarvis, 2001):

- Discussants show less emotion and experience less conflict during meetings.
- Participation is more organized and orderly, which may account for shorter meetings.
- Decision-making quality is generally equal to face-to-face groups except when bargaining or negotiation is required.

An executive briefing room like this one often features a large multipurpose screen used for video presentations, videoteleconferences, and viewing of the Internet and intranet.

- Participation is more equal (status differences are less noticeable and less threatening).
- Discussants find videoconferencing less satisfying than face-to-face meetings.

Electronic meetings can also benefit from conferencing tools on company intranets, videoconferencing software (such as NetMeeting by Microsoft), and desktop videoconferencing systems (DVCS), discussed in Chapter 10.

Videoconferencing is not for everyone. How and when to use videoconferences depends on the communication needs and capabilities of the participants and planners. In Chapter 1 we said that memos are best used to follow up a face-to-face meeting; in some cases, this may be true of videoconferences as well. Technological innovations can become obstacles to communication unless we consider them as just another resource to improve communication.

Hasty Resignation

COMMUNICATION SITUATION

Directions: The following conversation between Chief Ferguson and Sergeant Richards results in Richards's resignation. Both men contributed to the problem. Referring to the first six chapters in this text, what specific things did each do wrong? You can use your Premium Website for *Communicating for Results* to watch a video clip of this Communication Situation and answer this question and, if requested, e-mail your responses to your instructor. You can also further critique the interaction between Chief Ferguson and his employee and access Checkpoint 6.4 to see a similar communication situation and sample answers to analysis questions.

Cengage Learning/Jason Harris

Situation

James Ferguson was a dedicated and able police chief who had worked hard since taking over as police chief 6 months previously. Long before Ferguson was hired, a new manufacturing plant had moved into the area, causing the city to double its population in 5 years. The city council had not been prepared for such rapid growth, and when Ferguson was hired, the police force was quite understaffed. The city council claimed that there wasn't enough money to hire more police officers. It had taken Ferguson hours of time spent with community members and the city council before the police force was increased. The pay was still below the state level, however, and many officers were grumbling about the low pay and the extra long shifts they were required to work. Silently, Chief Ferguson agreed with the officers.

Even with all the problems, the department had greatly improved in the last 6 months and the chief was pleased. He was especially pleased about the young police sergeant he had recently hired. Cal Richards had graduated from the state academy with highest honors, and Ferguson hoped to groom him to take over direction of the local police academy when its current director, William Newsom, retired next year. Newsom was very conservative in his concept of what should be taught in the academy, and the chief was looking forward to the new techniques and approaches sure to be instigated by Sergeant Richards. He was even letting him make some minor changes now.

Things were moving along very well until the city newspaper broke a story with the front page headline "Local Police Instructed to Shoot to Kill Regardless of the Offense!" The story was written by a reporter who had been invited by Sergeant Richards to sit in on a class at the academy as a public relations gesture. When Chief Ferguson came to work the next morning, an angry group of senior officers led by William Newsom was waiting in his office. According to Newsom, the new sergeant had invited the reporter without letting anyone else know he was coming—and this was after Newsom had voiced his doubt to Richards about the possibility of such an event. The reporter had arrived unannounced during the middle of a class discussion, and no one had seen him enter. Newsom took Richards's actions as a direct attempt to undermine his efforts. The chance of the city council appropriating additional money for new uniforms now seemed certainly doomed. The chief was visibly disappointed in Richards's behavior and promised the men he would speak to him that day.

Later that morning, the chief was in his outer office discussing with his secretary an irritating problem relating to the cancellation of an order for some much needed supplies, when Richards stepped into the doorway with a cheerful greeting. The chief looked up with a frown. Seeing Richards, he was forcibly reminded of the unpleasant task that lay before him, and in characteristic fashion decided to handle it immediately. "Hello, Cal," he said. "Could you step in a minute?"

Richards caught something of the chief's discomfort from his voice and noticed the frown on his face. He felt a moment of panic. Something serious had happened. "Sure, Chief," he said. "I've got a minute."

The two men went into the office and the chief closed the door. Richards noticed the move, which was somewhat unusual, and again thought that something was up for sure. He searched his mind for a problem or crisis that might have upset the chief, but he could think of nothing.

Ferguson took a deep breath and cast about for some way to begin. To Ferguson the pause seemed short, whereas to Richards it seemed very long. "As you know, Sergeant," the chief began, "I have had great hopes for you in this department and have given you basically a free hand to try new things."

Richards felt a wave of relief and relaxed. "Yes, thank you very much, Chief." He felt good about his performance in the department. His colleagues seemed to respect him and several council members had even complimented him on his concern for the community. Probably the chief was going to complement him on getting the press and the academy together. And heaven knew how difficult that had been! He had been unable to attend the final meeting due to an accident at the plant but had left Newsom a message on his desk earlier the same morning warning him to call the reporter if his visit was inconvenient.

"Introducing new ideas can be very difficult, of course," the chief said, drumming his fingers on a newspaper.

"That's true," Richards said, somewhat puzzled because the chief was still noncommittal. He noticed the newspaper on the chief's desk. Perhaps the article had already been published.

Ferguson was proceeding slowly, trying to find precisely the right words. Suddenly Richards realized that something was going wrong. He was not going to get a compliment.

The chief was upset about something.

"Of course," said the chief, "newspapers do tend to sensationalize. . . . Hell, I thought you could handle the position!"

"What do you mean?" an angry Richards asked, standing up and putting his hands flat on the chief's desk.

The chief felt uncomfortable looking up at the sergeant, yet he did not want to stand. The temperature of the meeting was rising too fast for him. "Newsom and some of the older men feel that you mishandled the reporter situation."

"Are they questioning my competence to handle the position?"

"No, no, it's nothing like that, but. . . ." Ferguson wasn't sure what he wanted to say.

Things weren't going as he would have liked.

"What would you say, then? Dammit, Chief, I like to have all the cards on the table!"

"All right." The chief stood up. "You disappointed me in how you handled Newsom and the reporter situation. I guess you're still a little too impetuous to take over as director of the academy. You're going to have to learn. . . ."

"If you think I'm incompetent, why don't you fire me?"

"Now, wait a minute," said Ferguson. "Don't take that tone with me."

"Either I'm incompetent and you ought to fire me or I'm not and you have no right to take potshots at my attempt to get good P.R. for the department."

"Just a minute. . . ."

"Do you think it was correct or not?" Richards asked.

The chief lost his temper. "No, I think it was poorly handled!"

"All right, you can have my resignation as of right now!"

"Good. I accept it."

Richards threw open the door and left the room. The chief had some sober second thoughts. It had never occurred to him that the end result of the conference would be Richards's resignation. Richards was also sorry about his hasty decision, but both were proud men and neither would back down, so Richards was terminated.

The chief had lost an extremely valuable man, one that he might be unable to replace adequately. Richards had lost an excellent position with a place of distinction in his profession. What had gone wrong?

Note: Some of the dialogue adapted from Howell and Bormann, 1971, *Presentational speaking for business and professions* (pp. 152–153), New York: Harper & Row.

CHAPTER 6

REVIEW

Eli Reichman/Time Life Pictures/Getty Images

Key Terms

blogs (168)

bypassing (164)

cognitive restructuring (156)

communibiology (153)

deep breathing (153)

e-mail (170)

inference-observation confusion (163)

instant messages (170)

positive imagery (153)

reasonable person rule (167)

sexual harassment (166)

situational anxiety (150)

skills training (156)

systematic desensitization (156)

telecommuters (172)

trait anxiety (150)

videoconferencing (172)

visualization (153)

Summary

Communication obstacles can create problems for managers and employees. Communicator anxiety (both situational and trait) is an obstacle to communication success in one-to-one, group, interview, and public speaking situations. Positive imagery is one method of managing such anxiety. Inadequate preparation is another obstacle; preparation is necessary not only for public speaking but also for many business interactions. The experiment with Project F demonstrated how to overcome the third obstacle: vague instructions. The fourth obstacle, jumping to conclusions, occurs when we fail to distinguish between what we observed firsthand and what we inferred. Bypassing, the fifth obstacle, is caused by the multiple meanings of words—either we have different meanings for the same word or we use different words for the same meaning; asking for feedback can prevent bypassing. The sixth obstacle, sexual harassment, causes loss of human dignity and decreased productivity in the workplace. And finally, even technological advances in communication can create obstacles to understanding if not used with care.

Successful communication is a result of constant effort. If you are willing to work at avoiding communication obstacles, your communication and your business success should improve.

Communicating for Results Online

Before continuing to the next chapter, check your understanding of Chapter 6 at the Premium Website for *Communicating for Results*. Your Premium Website gives you quick and easy access to the electronic resources that accompany this text. These resources include:

- **Study tools** that will help you assess your learning and prepare for exams (student companion workbook, digital glossary, key term flash cards, and review quizzes).

- **Activities and assignments** that will help you hone your knowledge, analyze professional communication situations, build your public speaking skills throughout the course, and learn to work effectively in teams (Awareness Checks, Checkpoints, and Collaborative Learning Activities).

- **Media resources** that will help you explore communication concepts online (web links), develop your speech outlines (Speech Builder Express 3.0), watch and critique videos of professional communication situations and sample speeches (Interactive Video Activities), upload your speech videos for peer reviewing and critique other students' speeches (Speech Studio online speech review tool), and download chapter review so you can study when and where you'd like (Audio Study Tools).

This chapter's key terms, Collaborative Learning Activities, and Checkpoint activities are also featured on the following pages, and you can find this chapter's Awareness Check activities in the body of the chapter. For more information or to access this book's online resources, visit www.cengage.com/login.

Collaborative Learning Activities

1. In groups of five to seven people make a list of all the technology (such as social networks, YouTube, and e-mail) that people in your group use to communicate with (a) friends and family, (b) in class and training situations, and (c) in the workplace. As a group, rank the communication effectiveness of each technology on your list using a scale from 1 (extremely ineffective) to 7 (extremely effective). Select the most successful and least successful technology in each of the three situations and share specific problems and successes using them. Was there an overlap of most and least effective technologies across the three areas? Why or why not? Select one of the ineffective technologies and discuss ways that communication could be improved using it. Be prepared to share your conclusions with other groups.

2. Watch the video for the Communication Situation: Hasty Resignation and read the text of the situation on pages 173–176. In groups, discuss answers to the following questions:

   a. What specific things did Chief Ferguson do that contributed to the communication breakdown?

   b. What specific things did Sergeant Richards do that contributed to the communication breakdown?

   In deciding on your answers, refer to the information in Chapters 1–6 of your textbook. Be specific and use terminology. Discuss any areas of disagreement. Conclude your evaluation by summarizing what each should have done in the first place. When you have finished, compare your answers with other groups.

3. In groups of three or four follow the instructions in the Awareness Check on page 158 relating to Project F. Your task is to use the rules for giving effective instructions presented in this chapter to explain how to assemble the pieces of the fail-safe device in 5 minutes or less. Practice on each other until you think you have the clearest, fastest instructions.

Each group member should then present the directions at a later time to at least three people one at a time. Remember that participants can't ask you questions once the instructions begin; you may watch their faces, but should not see what they are actually doing; begin with an overall picture and end with a complete summary. When the 5 minutes are over (or sooner, if the participant is finished), show the correct answer and ask for suggestion on how to make your instructions even better. Revise your instructions and try them on the next person.

Return to class and share your successes and failures. As a group, answer these two questions: (a) what did you learn about the way you give instructions? And (b) what did you learn about the way others follow instructions? If asked, be prepared to share your experiences with other groups.

Checkpoints

Checkpoint 6.1 Overcoming Speaker Anxiety

 Select a situation in which anxiety seems to bother you (e.g., conversations, interviews, group discussions, or public speeches).

Determine which type of anxiety bothers you the most, situational or trait—one way is to take the PRCA-24 or the PRPSA surveys located on your Premium Website for Communicating for Results. Write a positive imagery exercise where you visualize yourself giving a positive, confident presentation, and read it out loud at least once prior to each oral presentation.

Checkpoint 6.2 Obstacles to Organizational Communication

Checkpoint 6.3 Communication Situation: Input Systems, Inc.

Checkpoint 6.4 Research on Communication Anxiety

Checkpoint 6.5 Bypassing the Meaning

Checkpoint 6.6 Overcoming Communication Obstacles Links

Basic Information for All Types of Interviews

matzaball/iStockphoto

Case Study: A True Tale of a Case Interview Gone Bad

A job-seeker's true story. . . . The following is the sad-but-true story of what can go wrong in a case interview. The narrator was a liberal arts graduate in political science who worked for a short and unhappy time after graduation as a financial consultant and aspired to a position in management consulting. He interviewed at McKinsey and Company. The names in the story have been changed:

> I scrambled in the mist from my parking lot to the third tallest building in Atlanta, and headed for the top floor. As I was greeted by the recruiter, I had condensation or perspiration—I'm not sure which—trickling down my temple. She led me back to an area with two sofas already accommodating three other interviewees. That caught me off guard slightly. For some reason I figured I'd be alone since it was the end of recruiting season. Seating myself, I realized I hadn't really had a chance to contemplate what to expect. I waited there in the morgue.
>
> Finally, I was greeted by a young woman in her late 20s and pregnant. I'll call her Mandy for the sake of this anecdote. She was welcoming, and we chatted as she led me to a narrow little station where we could talk. I found Mandy to be warm, personable, and helpful. She put me at ease in what I realized was a completely unknown environment. She asked me several "interview-type" questions, but her tone was always helpful and inquisitive.

I think I made three mistakes during this interview: (1) I felt as though I was always trying to give some nebulous right answer and falling short. I had difficulty being concise because my nerves were so shot, and I think my stammering didn't help. (2) When she asked a question about where I saw myself in ten years, I gave a very honest and unusual answer about how people create stress for themselves trying to plan and not being able to be flexible. I instead gave goals but probably wasn't as concrete as I should have been. I wondered if my honesty was appreciated less than a strong goal-oriented statement. (3) Although I was vaguely familiar with case questions, I wasn't well versed or practiced. . . . Had I been more practiced, I could have been more systematic in my approach and then stuck to my answer instead of feeling the need to add something I may have left out.

When my final inquisitor—I'll call him Ken—finally arrived, I heard the hammer hit the nail. . . . Nothing Ken did or said put me at ease or made me feel like the interview was anything other than adversarial. I also knew that the moment I became confrontational, I would lose. He started out with a series of questions that were harmless enough, but sent me scrounging.

"What was your most rewarding leadership experience?" I told him about how I started at the age of 15 playing hockey, without knowing which way to hold my stick or how to skate backwards, and the next year was chosen captain, and the next again when I led our team to the playoffs. Ken's enthusiastic response, "That's nice, but how about something you did?"

Maybe I chose the wrong thing by giving a heartfelt answer as opposed to an ideal answer, or perhaps I just wasn't clear in my point of leadership by example. Either way, I felt his response to be colder than the February air.

He then asked me a case question: "How much does a Boeing 757 weigh?"

Again, I knew he was less concerned about the number I came up with as opposed to my process, but he was no help. I asked him all sorts of questions, and he just shrugged his shoulders and sat tight-lipped until after the fifth attempt he finally said, "To answer your one question, you can assume that the seats are empty and the tank is full."

He corrected me a few times, too. "Now I heard recently that the Concorde that they mounted atop a building near Times Square weighs 25,000 tons. . . ."

"Tons or pounds?" asks Ken.

"I thought tons . . . right???" I asked as I felt the last bead of self-esteem trickle down the small of my back.

"I don't know," helped Ken smugly.

Well I figure the Concorde seats about 300 people, so the 757 probably somewhere around 350-375.

"Actually, it's more like 500," helped Ken again, "and you have two more minutes."

I could barely stand up after our time was up; my legs were weak. Ken started down some stairs, and I mentioned, "I need to pick up my umbrella and briefcase from the waiting area," and he said, "OK, meet me at the door afterwards."

I didn't know what to make of it all, but I was scared. I could hardly keep the tears back as I headed for the job I so desperately wanted out of. I had a bad feeling in my stomach.

If I am to glean some powerful lessons from this experience, they are:

- Although it sounds like I did not prepare for this interview, I did. I, however, did not prepare the right way or understand really what I was getting myself into. Those approaching interviews need to know what is expected in interviews of various types of companies and positions, I obviously was clueless. I was especially clueless about the rigidity and formality of these interviews.
- Another valuable lesson I've learned from this experience is to practice those case studies and all your answers to those questions that I thought were too trite to be asked (like "what's your greatest accomplishment?").
- And most importantly, leave nothing to chance. Prepare every unthinkable scenario. There is no replacement for hard work, especially when you get only one shot.

Copyright by Quintessential Careers. The original article can be found at http:// www.quintcareers.com/bad_case_interview.html. Reprinted with permission.

Rubberball/Jupiterimages

As you read this chapter, see if you can (a) identify which type of questions Mandy and Ken asked in the interviews described in this case study, (b) assess the quality of the job candidate's answers compared with the advice given in the last section of this chapter, "Be Prepared to Answer Questions," and (c) think about the interviews you've experienced in light of the advice given by the candidate—were his observations correct? You can find even more information about job interviews by searching on "interview" at quintcareer. com. You can find easy access to this link at your Premium Website for *Communicating for Results*.

Whether you are a production worker, supervisor, teacher, police officer, executive, or self-employed, you will spend much of your business time involved in various types of interviews. By the term *interview*, we are referring to all types of planned, face-to-face encounters in which at least one of the participants has a specific objective in mind. According to this definition, interviewing includes gathering information, appraising employee performance, settling grievances, and many other interactions. In this chapter, we'll discuss 10 of the most common types of interviews, the basic organization of an interview, and effective questions and answers. Because interviewing is a form of communication, all the communication theories, skills, and obstacles discussed in previous chapters are important for interviewing success. Also remember that interviewing is a reciprocal process: Interviewees, as well as, interviewers should actively question, paraphrase, and add information.

Types of Interviews

Although there are dozens of types of interviews, an understanding of the 10 most common types can easily be transferred to other interview situations that you may encounter (Allen, 2009; Stewart & Cash, 2008; Still, 2006). For ease of reference, we will list the types in alphabetical order.

Counseling Interview

The intent of the **counseling interview** is to help the interviewee uncover and solve "career-related personal or interpersonal problems" (Bell, 1989, p. 169). Counseling interviews may deal with job-related problems such as stress, a job change, and relationships with a boss or coworker, or they may deal with personal problems such as alcoholism, smoking, drug abuse, or family discord. Although counseling interviews are not used by all organizations, the "best" companies try to meet all the needs of their employees.

Because the interviewee may be emotional or defensive, communication skills such as empathetic listening, nonevaluative feedback, careful paraphrasing, and sympathetic nonverbal responses are important to establish the needed climate of trust. In some cases, a directive approach in which the interviewer takes complete control works best; in other situations, a nondirective approach in which the interviewer is merely a facilitator is needed, and occasionally, a combined approach may be best (Arkowitz et al., 2008; Shea, 1998; Stewart & Cash, 2008).

Employment Interview

The **employment interview** is one of the most important types because in it some of the most critical organizational and personal decisions are made (Stewart & Cash, 2008; Still, 2006). The ultimate productivity of an organization depends on the ability of its management to recruit and select the best personnel. However, over 30 years of research points to the fact that the business interview does not predict employee success with any accuracy (Cascio, 1998). It can, however, discover information not available from other sources, such as "employee 'fit,' communication skills, job motivation, and work-related values" (Kirkwood & Ralston, 1999, p. 55).

Typically, the employment interview involves one prospective employee and one prospective employer. However, some companies use various group approaches, which will be discussed in this chapter. Although the prospective employer usually takes the lead during the interview, the person seeking employment should also ask questions of the employer. Chapter 8 offers information and advice to both interviewers and interviewees who wish to improve the employment interview.

© 2003 Ted Goff

© 2003 Ted Goff. Reprinted by permission. www.tedgoff.com

"I'm in the middle of a job interview. What are you doing?"

Exit Interview

Whether an employee was laid off, fired, or simply quit, it can be to the organization's benefit to discover the perceptions of this employee who has "nothing to lose." Company problems can be identified and corrected while they are still small (Bruce, 1988). **Exit interviews** require careful listening and reading between the lines because many people will only hint at their real reason for leaving—never saying, for example, that the boss was impossible to work with. The exit interview is also a good way to create goodwill for the organization. For example, many companies include outplacement counseling to help employees find and qualify for new jobs (Skyes, 2007).

Grievance or Confrontation Interview

The **grievance** (or **confrontation**) **interview** is any type of one-to-one encounter involving conflict and its resolution. Situations leading to this type of interview include employer-employee disputes over working hours or wages, customer-salesperson conflicts, and teacher-student conflicts. Although emotions may run high, it is very important that participants express their feelings honestly and remain cooperative (Greenberg & Baron, 2007). The interviewer in a grievance interview must be both a good listener and a problem solver. The basic problem-solving procedure discussed in Chapter 9 is an effective way to organize the interview.

Group Interview

Although interviews with one interviewer and one interviewee are the most common, **group interviews** (such as panel and board interviews) are gaining in popularity (Drake, 1998; Edmunds, 2000). When there are more interviewees than interviewers, the interview is called a **panel interview**. Product researchers use panel interviews, often called *focus groups*, as a quick, inexpensive way to sample customers' opinions about a product. Psychologists and health care professionals use the panel interview as a counseling and diagnostic tool. For example, in an attempt to help a child who has been stealing items from school, a family counselor might interview the entire family together to observe family interaction styles and relationships. Employment personnel in both profit and nonprofit organizations use panel interviews as a way to save time and to observe leadership and communication skills. For example, American Airlines uses panel interviews extensively for reservation clerks and flight attendants.

When there are more interviewers than interviewees, the interview is called a **board interview**. Board interviews are used by nonprofit, public, educational, and business organizations. The WorldCom hearing conducted by the U.S. Senate was a board interview. Other examples include parole board hearings, graduate student oral examinations, and selection, or hiring, interviews (such as those used by educational institutions, government agencies, and even museums). Board interviews allow interviewers to share responsibility and expertise and to check interviewee answers under stress.

Because group interviews can catch you off guard, here are a few suggestions to keep in mind if you are the interviewee (Drake, 1998; Edmunds, 2000):

General Suggestions for Group Interviewees
- *Be prepared for confusion and noise.* Don't let them make you rush your answers or feel pressured.
- *If possible, learn who the panelists are ahead of time.* Find out their names, who is in charge, and who has the most clout.

- *If possible, determine why a group interview is being used.* Is it merely convenience, to create stress, or to save the interviewer time and money? This information may indicate how to focus your answers.
- *Appear confident and in control.* Keep a relaxed posture, including open body with chin down, direct eye contact, appropriate dress, and natural gestures to convey a positive attitude.
- *Make your answers direct, brief, honest, and sincere.*

Specific Suggestions for Panel Interviewees

- *Speak to everyone, not just the interviewer.* The interviewer is probably interested in how you interact with a group, so think of the other applicants as your friends. If the interviewer asks all interviewees to direct their answers to the group, consider the interviewer as part of the group and speak to everyone.
- *Take an active role but don't always speak first.* If the group is asked to solve a problem, listen carefully, draw in nontalkers, help structure the process, and use other good leadership skills discussed in Chapter 10.

Specific Suggestions for Board Interviewees

- *Try not to be one of the first applicants interviewed.* It may take several interviews before board members become organized and feel comfortable with one another.
- *If possible, sit where you won't have to constantly move your head back and forth to see all the interviewers.*
- *Make eye contact with all interviewers and not just the person who asks a question.* Be sure to speak to those both on your right and on your left.
- *Stick by your answers.* If challenged, "defend your view or just acknowledge that there are several ways to look at it and you subscribe to one particular view" (Bamford, 1986, p. 191).

A board interview occurs when there are more interviewers than interviewees, as is the case in this Chicago city council meeting where a local alderman is being interviewed about a local "living wage" issue.

Informational Interview

Informational interviews give or seek information. In an **information-giving** interview, the interviewer wants to impart important information. Examples include a dental hygienist advising a client on how to brush teeth, an automobile salesperson demonstrating for a customer the correct operation of the cruise control, or a supervisor informing an employee about a new company policy.

In an **information-seeking interview**, the interviewer wants information from the interviewee. Examples include a lawyer interviewing crime victims or witnesses, a physician interviewing a patient about his medical history, or a journalist conducting a public opinion poll.

Information-seeking interviews are especially useful for people who are planning a career, anticipating a career change, or planning for future promotion. For example, most job hunting guides recommend that readers conduct several information-seeking interviews before going on a job interview (Bolles, 2009; Petras & Petras, 1995). These interviews, which should take no longer than 15 minutes, can provide a wealth of information. These are some of the questions you might ask:

- Exactly what does your job entail?
- What are the educational requirements for this position?
- What experience is required or recommended?
- What do you like most about the position? Like least?
- If you could start over, would you choose the same career? Why or why not?
- What problems could I expect to encounter in a position of this type?
- What future changes do you see in this field (or position)?
- Describe the ideal person for this career (or position).
- What is the average salary for a person just starting out in this career?
- What questions could I expect if I were interviewing for a job of this type?
- What professional organizations (journals, newsletters) do you recommend?
- Could you give me the name of another person whom I might interview?

Find people to interview through friends, coworkers, professors, and even parents and bosses. You may also want to call the human relations (personnel) department of a relevant company and ask for the name of a person to interview. When conducting an information-seeking interview, be sure to follow the basic organization of opening, question-response, and closing phases discussed in the next section of this chapter. Take only minimal notes, use verbal and nonverbal probes, ask follow-up questions, and listen carefully. Follow up with a thank-you note. Later, if an interview suggested to you by the previous interviewee uncovers a helpful bit of information, why not call and share it. This way you are not only developing friendships, but also future references.

Interrogation Interview

In **interrogation interviews**, there is usually some type of offense involved. For example, a firm representative may interrogate a customer in a case of shoplifting, an employer may interrogate an employee in a case of missing company funds, or a police officer may interrogate a suspect. The interviewer should begin the interview by discussing a topic of interest to the interviewee to assess his or her nonverbal behaviors when relatively relaxed. The interviewer should

ETHICAL DILEMMA

In his book *A Million Little Pieces*, James Frey describes overcoming his addictions to alcohol and drugs. Oprah picked up the book, and in October 2005 she added it to her book list, saying how deeply it had touched her. Oprah interviewed Frey on her October 26, 2005, show and in front of millions of viewers he discussed the book and what Oprah called his "gut-wrenching memoir of detox, pain, blood, vomit . . . and hope" ("A Powerful Story," 2005, para. 2).

However, an investigation by The Smoking Gun—a website devoted to posting documents relating to various controversies and scandals—revealed that large portions of Frey's facts were "wholly fabricated or wildly embellished" ("A Million Little Lies," 2006).

In 2006, Frey again appeared on Oprah's show, titled "*The Million Little Pieces* Controversy," along with several journalists, to answer questions about his actions. When asked if he felt he had conned everyone, Frey replied, "No . . . because I still think the book is about drug addiction and alcoholism and nobody's disputing that I was a drug addict and an alcoholic" ("Did He Con His Readers?," 2006, para. 6). Richard Cohen, a columnist for the *Washington Post* responded that Frey's approach "was a betrayal of his readers" and that the publishing industry needs to take more responsibility for checking facts. "A fact checker would have found out in a half an hour that some of this book didn't work." ("Journalists Speak Out," 2006, para. 2). Audience comments were varied but are represented by this Oprah message board post ("Bigger Liars Out There," 2006):

> Although I don't agree with Frey's choice to lie [and] embellish his book, I'm happy that the book was written. Many people have been positively affected by it; maybe lives were saved by it. My point is, does this story really warrant so much news coverage?

QUESTIONS: What do you think? In his book (which has sold close to 3 million copies) and in a media interview, Frey misrepresented the facts. Were his actions ethical?

also gather information by using many open-ended questions (Gordon & Fleisher, 2001; Lee, 1996), such as those illustrated later in this chapter.

Performance Review

One of the keys to the successful operation of any organization is the accurate and consistent evaluation of the performance of employees, regardless of their level. When planned and executed under the proper conditions, these are some excellent ways to use a **performance review**:

- Recognize and reward employee contributions.

- Give employees feedback on their standing in the eyes of the company.

- Discover and help solve communication problems between employees or between employer and employee.

- Motivate employees by setting future performance objectives.

The content of the performance review should be relevant to the job, include only "observable" aspects of the job, and avoid vague factors such as "desire to succeed" (Muchinsky, 1999). The performance review is covered by equal employment opportunity guidelines and civil rights legislation (covered in Chapter 8) and therefore must be standardized in form, method, and application, and should avoid assessment of traits that can't be judged objectively (Stewart & Cash, 2008). The performance review will be more productive if the employee is actively involved in assessing his or her performance. Usually an assessment form is filled out by both the employee and supervisor prior to the meeting and then compared and discussed during the meeting. The review should include a written, as well as an oral appraisal; the written form is normally kept in the employee's file. This written appraisal protects the employee from unfair dismissal, gives the company concrete support for dismissing a person with a consistently poor job record (Cleveland et al., 1989), and provides concrete support for promotion or salary raises.

You can read a sample performance review at the end of this chapter and assess whether Alan O'Connor, a manager, followed these guidelines successfully. What could Alan have done to improve his interaction with his employees?

Persuasive Interview

Many employee-customer, employee-boss, or employee-employee interview situations are really persuasive in nature. For example, selling a customer a new product, convincing your boss you deserve a raise, or persuading your colleagues to go along with your suggested office rearrangement are all examples of **persuasive interviews**.

Although it influences the choices a customer makes, persuasion is not coercion or trickery. According to Stewart and Cash (2008, p. 297), persuasive interviews are more likely to succeed if you can convince the interviewee that your proposal will satisfy one or more unmet needs; is consistent with beliefs, attitudes, and values; is practical and affordable; has benefits that outweigh any objections; and is the best course of action available.

Telephone Interview

As the cost of transportation increases, companies are using the **telephone interview** more often as a way to collect survey information, as follow-up with customers to determine their satisfaction with a purchase or a procedure such as a car repair, and to screen job applicants. When collecting information or determining customer satisfaction, the introduction or opening phase is very important because one-third of the respondents hang up or refuse the interview in the first seconds of the call (Stewart & Cash, 2008). Also the interviewer's voice (i.e., faster rate, louder volume, standard American pronunciation, and a competent and confident sound) seems to be as or more important in getting the respondent to agree to an interview than the words spoken (Groves et al., 2001).

The best phone interviews occur when you are dressed and using the same facial expression and gestures you would use in a face-to-face interview.

Companies that conduct job interviews by telephone are screening applicants "to evaluate whether the candidate is qualified to do the job and to address any areas of concern in the resume" ("Telephone Interview Techniques," 2009). The following are a few suggestions to keep in mind if you are interviewed by telephone (Ceniza-Levine, 2009; Hentz, 2009; Needleman, 2009a, 2009b):

- Prepare the same way you would for a face-to-face interview.

- Keep a file of your personal information as well as a list of the companies you have contacted and information about each company close by the phone.

- Make sure the message on your answering machine is brief and professional and that family members or roommates know that you are expecting an important call.

- Plan for a detailed interview that may last as long as an hour.

- Show complete attention to the interviewer.

- Prepare to sound sincere, enthusiastic, friendly, yet professional.

- Listen to questions carefully before answering.

- Thank the interviewer and ask for their e-mail address so you can send a more detailed thank you—then send it before the day is over.

Basic Interview Organization

All interviews are organized in pretty much the same way. They consist of three phases: the opening phase, the question-response phase, and the closing phase.

Opening Phase

The opening phase of an interview is just as essential for understanding as the introduction of an oral presentation. We know one manager who completed an entire interview before he discovered that the woman he was talking to was not the person he was scheduled to see. Interviews for the position she wanted were being held in another department two doors down the hall. Because the manager had omitted the opening phase, neither person was aware of the error.

The **opening phase** of an interview includes three steps: rapport, orientation, and motivation. Normally, these steps are followed in the order listed. However, feel free to order the steps in the way that best fits your preference, the type of interview, and the occasion.

Rapport Rapport is a comfortable, I-respect-you-as-an-individual feeling that makes both participants receptive to the interview. The initial 1 to 4 minutes of the interview may be the most important of the entire interview; their impact on its outcome cannot be overstated (Zunin & Zunin, 1994). First impressions are difficult to erase. In an employment interview, the applicant who makes a good first impression has a better chance of being hired (see Chapter 8 for more on the relationship between first impressions and hiring). In a grievance interview, rapport is likely to make the conflict easier to resolve. In a performance review, rapport typically makes the employee more likely to accept the review. In a persuasive interview, rapport between the salesperson and the customer usually makes it easier to sell the product. And in an informational interview, rapport makes the information easier to obtain.

There is no magic formula for establishing rapport or making a good first impression. However, the interviewee can begin to create a good first impression by being on time, dressing appropriately, being well prepared, and appearing confident and relaxed. The interviewee can also help establish rapport by referring to a mutual acquaintance or some topic of mutual interest. The interviewer can aid the process by supplying a relaxed but businesslike environment, selecting a spot relatively free from distractions, and coming from behind the desk to sit near the interviewee. (An exception might be an interrogation interview in which the interviewer wishes to maintain a psychological distance.) When the interviewee arrives, the interviewer should stand up, shake hands, and make the person feel welcome. To start a relaxed conversation, the interviewer might refer to a mutual acquaintance or interest, a local or national event, or even the weather. In some types of interviews, such as the grievance interview, the interviewer might create rapport by sharing some personal feelings or opinions to give the interviewee a feeling that someone understands and cares. Some interviewees can be put at ease by moving immediately to the orientation step with a reference to the subject of the interview. Once interviewees start talking, they are likely to forget to be nervous.

Orientation In addition to establishing rapport in the opening of an interview, the interviewer should give the interviewee a clear orientation, or overall view, of the interview. The orientation should include at least the following information:

- Verification of the interviewee's name (if not included previously).

- The interviewer's name and why he or she is the person conducting the interview. Why this particular manager or supervisor is conducting the interview (instead of someone else the interviewee was expecting) is especially important in the exit, grievance, and performance interviews.

- The purpose or desired outcome of the interview. In some interviews, such as a grievance interview, the interviewer may not know the desired outcome. But even when the purpose is fairly obvious, as in an employment interview, it should be stated—never assumed!

- What information is needed and how it will be used. In general, interviewees are more willing to talk openly, and their answers are more precise once they realize what information is needed and how their comments will be used. When possible, the interviewer may wish to assure the interviewee of the confidentiality of his or her responses.

- Approximate length of the interview. It is common courtesy to give the interviewee a general idea of how much time will be needed to complete the interview.

Motivation   The interviewer's third step in the opening phase of an interview is to motivate the interviewee to give straightforward, complete answers. The type of motivation depends on the person and the circumstances. Here are sample motivational approaches for three types of interviews: employment, exit, and information.

Employment Interview

> This interview is an important part of the application process with our company, Mr. Riley—not just a formality. I feel sure that you are as interested as we are in finding you a position in which you will be most successful. To place you appropriately, we need accurate, detailed information from you, okay?

Exit Interview

> Management is interested in your perceptions of our company. Anything you tell me will be kept in strict confidence. After your comments are added— anonymously, of course—to our exit interview suggestion pool, this form will be destroyed. No mention of this interview will be added to your permanent file.

Information Interview

> Ms. Smith, so far you are the only witness to the robbery. Our ability to apprehend the thieves depends on you and how much information you can give us about them. Thieves tend to come back to the same neighborhood, so I'm sure you want them apprehended just as much as we do.

Question-Response Phase

The **question-response phase** is the heart of the interview, for in this phase both interviewer and interviewee have the opportunity to ask and respond to questions. The primary objective of an interview is explored during the question-response phase.

Regardless of the type of interview, both participants should carefully prepare for the question-response phase. Few interviewers can compose effective questions on the spur of the moment, and even fewer interviewees can give good answers to questions that take them by surprise. So, for example, giving employees the list of questions that will be discussed during their performance review allows them to give more complete and honest answers (Lefton et al., 1980).

To plan for the question-response phase of an interview, the interviewer should decide what information needs to be sought and then plan the necessary questions.

Revisiting the Case Study

Although the story provides limited information, how well do you think Mandy and Ken handled the opening phase of their interviews?

Rubberball/Jupiterimages

The interviewer should also anticipate possible responses and be prepared to change the type and the organization of the questions if necessary. The advantages and disadvantages of various types of questions and how best to organize questions are discussed in the next section of this chapter.

Likewise, the interviewee should outline the information he or she wishes to communicate to the interviewer. For example, for a grievance interview, the interviewee should prepare a clear picture of the grievance with documentation if available. For a performance review, the interviewee should prepare a list of strengths, weaknesses, and accomplishments for the year, as well as future performance objectives, all with documentation if possible. For an employment interview, the applicant should prepare a list of strengths, areas of knowledge, and accomplishments (usually in resume form). And the interviewee in an informational interview should make sure that the necessary information to answer the interviewer's questions is readily available.

In preparing for the question-response phase, the interviewee should also anticipate possible questions and think through honest answers to each one. When appropriate, the interviewee should ask the interviewer for a list of possible questions or talk to someone who has been through a similar interview. Suggestions for answering various types of questions are covered in the final section of this chapter.

Closing Phase

The **closing phase** of any type of interview should begin with a summary of the major points covered in the interview and of any conclusions reached. Summaries allow both parties to make sure that all important topics have been discussed and that no information has been misunderstood. The interviewee should also have a chance to ask questions. Finally, the interview should always end with the participants thanking the other for their time and cooperation.

When appropriate, the closing phase should also include agreement on what the follow-up will be and a date for another meeting if one is needed. For example, a person applying for a job needs to know if there is a chance of being hired, when a decision will be made, and how candidates will be notified. Interviewees in grievance interviews or performance reviews want to know what steps will be taken in the future and how these steps may affect their standing in the organization. Likewise, witnesses to crimes want to know if they will be interviewed again and if they may have to appear in court.

Using Questions Effectively in the Interview

To use questions effectively in an interview—whether you are the interviewer or the interviewee—you must understand the different types of questions that can be used. Additionally, interviewers should organize their questions appropriately, and interviewees should be prepared with answers.

Determine the Types of Questions to Ask

Different types of questions elicit different types of responses and maintain different amounts of control. An effective interviewer knows what types of questions to ask to get particular responses. Consider the interviewer who could not understand why an employee in a grievance interview would not talk much. After all, the employee was the one with the grievance! The interviewer did not realize that she was asking only direct and **closed questions**, which are designed to get short, brief answers. To encourage the employee to talk, she should have asked open-ended or **hypothetical open questions**.

Effective interviewers also know what types of questions give them the most control and what questions give more control to the person being interviewed. As you read the following types of questions, notice where each type fits on the control continuum in Figure 7.1: A and B questions give the interviewer the most control, F and G questions give the interviewee the most control, and C, D, and E questions fit in the middle because control could go either way depending on the specific situation.

Open-Ended Questions These are broad questions that allow the interviewee maximum freedom in deciding how much and what type of information to give. The following are examples of **open-ended questions**:

"In your own words, evaluate your accomplishments this year."

"Tell me about your complaint."

"We hope to hire someone who will stay for at least three years. We know plans can change, but could you describe the sort of opportunity or circumstances that would tempt you to leave sooner than this?" (Kirkwood & Ralston, 1999, p. 73)

"Why are you leaving our company?"

"Describe a time during your current job when your work was criticized. Tell me how you responded and the outcome of the complaint."

Open-ended questions can be effective because they tend to relax most interviewees who find the questions easy to answer and nonthreatening. Also these questions reveal what the interviewee thinks is important and may uncover information or attitudes that may need further probing. It is difficult to hide information when answering open-ended questions. Because of these advantages, most interviews should begin with open-ended questions.

Open-ended questions do have some drawbacks. The responses may be time consuming, cover information of little interest to the interviewer, and even cause the interviewer to lose control of the interview. Also, the ambiguity of open-ended questions may make extremely nervous interviewees even more nervous because they do not know where to begin their answers. Even so, the advantages of using open-ended questions far outweigh the disadvantages.

Hypothetical Open Questions These questions allow the respondent maximum freedom in deciding how to respond to an invented, but possible, situation. The following are examples of hypothetical open questions:

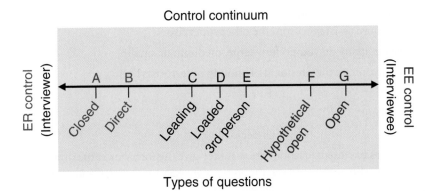

FIGURE 7.1 Control continuum for types of interview questions.

"On your first day of work, you arrive an hour late. How would you explain this and to whom?"

"Suppose you were on regular patrol duty and observed an elderly woman run a red light. You signal her to stop, and she pulls into a busy parking lot. What would you do if she refused to roll down the window and accept the traffic citation?"

"Suppose you were supervisor of this department and someone came to you with a complaint similar to yours. How would you handle it?"

Hypothetical open questions have the same advantages and disadvantages as open-ended questions. In addition, they allow the interviewer great flexibility in designing a question to fit any situation, and the response gives the interviewer an idea of how the interviewee would react in a specific circumstance.

Direct (or Specific) Questions These are short questions requiring a short answer or a simple "Yes" or "No." Here are some examples:

"Is the accusation against you accurate?"

"Did you accomplish your top priority this year?"

"Who recommended you to us?"

"What word-processing software can you use?"

"How long have you been in this field of work?"

"Do you think you should receive a promotion?"

The advantages of **direct questions** are that they limit responses, save time, and may be more relaxing for some interviewees than open-ended questions. However, researcher E. Duff Wrobbel (1991) has found that many interviewees will expand on a short answer or a yes or no answer with an explanation of their response. Therefore, an interviewer who wants only short answers without explanations should make this clear during the orientation step of the opening phase. Another disadvantage of direct questions is that they usually reveal only limited information, especially if the interviewer does not know which direct questions to ask. In most types of interviews, direct questions that can be answered with a yes or no should be kept to a minimum.

Closed Questions These questions limit the interviewee's choice of answers to one of the answers supplied in the question. The following are examples of closed questions:

"Do you prefer to work with Doris, Carol, or Bob on this assignment?"

"Which would best help you meet your performance objectives—more guidance from me or more assistance from the other supervisors?"

"What size company do you prefer—large, medium, or small?"

"How would you rate the president's handling of terrorists?"

a. Superior   d. Fair

b. Excellent   e. Poor

c. Good   f. Undecided

The advantages of closed questions are that they give the interviewer maximum control over the questions and answers, the answers are easy to interpret, and more questions can be asked in less time. However, closed questions do not allow for detailed explanations. Also, unless the answers include an "other" option, there is no certainty that the interviewee's answer was his or her "real" preference. If you wish to encourage an emotional or frustrated interviewee to talk freely, it is best to avoid closed questions.

Loaded Questions **Loaded questions** are those questions that have no correct answers but are designed to get an emotional response. Here are some examples:

> "Have you stopped drinking yet?"
>
> "Are you still difficult to get along with?"

Loaded questions are seldom used, even by expert interviewers; unless care is taken, they can backfire. But they can be valuable in determining how well a person handles pressure or in stimulating a reticent or hostile respondent. Once a loaded question is answered, be sure to mention why the question was asked and discuss any emotion in the answer—for example, the following:

> "I asked you that question to see how well you handle stressful situations. You became quite upset, didn't you? Working in our complaint window is a very stressful job. It doesn't appear that you would be at your best with angry customers. What do you think?"

Leading Questions A **leading question** implies the correct answer. The following are examples of leading questions:

> "You want the kind of car that gets good gas mileage, don't you?"
>
> "We are looking for creative people here. What do you have to offer?"
>
> "I don't think you have been working up to your potential. What do you think?'"

Leading questions can be helpful in determining whether the respondent is giving honest answers or merely being a "yes person." For example, suppose in the early part of an interview you said, "I just love working in teams, don't you?" and the respondent answered "Yes." Then later you reversed the question (indicating your dislike for teams), and the respondent agreed again. These responses could indicate a lack of honesty or a high desire to please. To clarify the situation, point out the discrepancy and ask the respondent which answer is accurate.

A disadvantage to using leading questions is that interviewers often confuse them with direct questions. For example, "Do you plan on furthering your education?" is a direct question, but "Education is important to this company. Do you plan on furthering your education?" is a leading question. As a general rule, unless you have a specific purpose in mind, avoid leading questions.

Third-Person Questions Embarrassing or personal questions may be phrased in a less threatening way by involving a third person. The following pairs of examples show how a question can be rephrased as a **third-person question**:

a) "What do *you* think about the latest merger proposal?"

b) "What does *your group* think about the latest merger proposal?"

a) "Do *you* think the new raise is fair?"

b) "Do *the employees in your department* think the new raise is fair?"

The answer to a third-person question is usually the personal opinion of the respondent, which is generally what the interviewer really wants to know. Well-known interviewers like Barbara Walters and Oprah Winfrey use third-person questions to get guests to speak openly about subjects they had planned to avoid.

Verbal and Nonverbal Probes **Probes** are used to urge the respondent to add more information to a previous response. Verbal probes are usually single words or phrases requesting more information or a judgment. The following are examples of verbal probes:

"Tell me more."

"I see."

"Really?"

"Uh-huh."

"That's interesting."

"How do you mean?"

"Why?"

"Why do you feel that way?"

"Anything else?"

"What happened next?"

"In probing for information," suggests one author (Zima, 1983), "useful questions begin with the words *what, when, where,* and *who.* When seeking judgments, ask questions that begin with the words *why* and *how*" (p. 70). Repeating in your own words the response just given is also an excellent probe.

A nonverbal probe often can produce the same result as a verbal probe. Silence, raising the eyebrows, frowning, and nodding are examples of nonverbal probes.

Knowing the different types of interview questions, their strengths and weaknesses, and the control each gives to the interviewer and interviewee leads to better interviews. Complete the Awareness Check on page 195 to see how many types of questions you can identify.

If you had any problems in identifying the various types of questions, go back and reread those sections. Effective interviewers should not ask questions that they cannot identify, and interviewees will do a better job answering questions if they know what to expect.

Decide How to Best Organize Questions

Using questions effectively in an interview involves not only knowing what type questions to ask but also organizing them carefully into general areas. In an employment interview, all questions relating to past work experience might be asked first; then, questions about leadership abilities; and finally, questions about educational background. In a performance review, questions might be organized into four areas: general performance over the past year, ability to get along with other employees, specific achievements, and possible areas needing improvement. Interviewers who jump back and forth between general areas find it difficult to remember what was discussed and what answers were given.

When you are conducting an interview, think of yourself as a detective. You are trying to gather enough facts to make a decision of some sort. For example, if you are asking a candidate about her educational background, at the conclusion of your questions you want to be able to say, no, she doesn't meet our educational requirements, or, yes, she does. Some interviewers assign a rating of 1 to 5 for each general area covered.

The questions asked within any general area are usually organized in either the funnel sequence or the inverted funnel sequence.

AWARENESS CHECK

Types of Questions

To check your knowledge of the various types of questions, take the following quiz and check your answers against those in the back of this book. You can also take this quiz online and view the answers at your Premium Website for *Communicating for Results*.

Directions: Identify each question below. Is it (A) open-ended, (B) hypothetical open, (C) direct/specific, (D) closed, (E) loaded, (F) leading, (G) third-person, or (H) a verbal probe?

_____ 1. If you were a supervisor in this department, what changes would you implement to make employees feel more a part of the organization?

_____ 2. Do you still arrive late to most meetings?

_____ 3. About how long does it take you to drive to work?

     Less than 15 minutes

     16–20 minutes

     21–30 minutes

     31–40 minutes

     Over 40 minutes

     Don't know

     Refused/NA

_____ 4. Tell me about one or two aspects of your last job that you hope will never occur again.

_____ 5. Oh?

_____ 6. The communication teams in manufacturing are very excited about this procedural change. What do you think about it?

_____ 7. Could you give me an example?

_____ 8. Suppose you had an employee who was consistently late to work. Every time you talked to him about his lateness, he apologized and promised to do better, but he never improved for more than one day. How would you handle the problem?

_____ 9. If I could lower the price another $300, would you buy this item today?

_____ 10. Where did you work immediately after you graduated from college?

_____ 11. How did the majority of officers in A Company view the chief?

_____ 12. Which do you enjoy the most—working on your own or working under close supervision?

Funnel Sequence Questions following the funnel sequence move from the general (open-ended or hypothetical open questions) to the specific (closed or direct questions). The following series of questions illustrates the **funnel sequence**:

1. "Tell me what overall problems you see occurring in the Harrison project." (open-ended)

2. "Why do you feel Shelton is an ineffective communicator?" (open-ended)

3. "Are you willing to accept Shelton and Jackson as coworkers?" (direct)

4. "What makes you say that?" (verbal probe)

5.   "Whom do you recommend for director of the Harrison project—Jackson, Shelton, or yourself?" (closed)

The funnel sequence is probably the most common method of organizing questions. Beginning with open-ended questions usually relaxes the interviewee and often eliminates the need to ask many of the planned questions because the interviewee volunteers the information. Moreover, in many interviews, the interviewer does not know enough about the interviewee to begin with direct, **specific questions**. The funnel sequence gives the interviewer a chance to listen and learn more about the interviewee.

Inverted Funnel Sequence   Questions following the **inverted funnel sequence** move from specific to general. The following series of questions illustrates the inverted funnel sequence:

1.   "Who do you recommend as director of the Harrison project—Jackson, Shelton, or yourself?" (closed)

2.   "What makes you say that?" (verbal probe)

3.   "Are you willing to accept Shelton and Jackson as coworkers?" (direct)

4.   "Why do you feel Shelton is an ineffective communicator?" (open-ended)

5.   "Tell me what overall problems you see occurring in the Harrison project." (open-ended)

The inverted funnel sequence is typically used with reluctant, shy, or unmotivated respondents. Short, closed, or direct questions may prompt these people to talk, while open-ended questions might cause only frustrated silence.

Remember that the effective interviewer is flexible and can switch from funnel to inverted funnel as needed. Some topics seem more appropriately organized in one sequence than the other. Don't be afraid to use variety. As the interviewer, maintain control of the interview to cover as much as possible in as short a time as possible. Rambling interviews are frustrating to both participants. To keep the answers on track, interrupt when necessary with comments such as the following:

"I understand what you're saying, but let me ask you this. . . ."

"Let's go back to . . . for a minute."

"I am more interested in. . . . Could you expand on that particular topic for me?"

Although the funnel and inverted funnel are the most common sequences for questions, you may occasionally want to use their variations: the hourglass and the diamond sequences. These two sequences are used as follow-up when answers are unexpected or unclear.

Hourglass Sequence   When the interviewee's answer to the last (specific or closed) question in a funnel sequence isn't at all what you expected, you will want to reopen the questioning to clarify the missing information. Each question would then become more and more general until you end with a final summary (open-ended) question. A diagram of your questions would resemble an hourglass, hence the **hourglass sequence**. For example, refer to the first five questions below. Suppose the respondent's answers to questions 1 to 4 had clearly indicated both knowledge of the project and a dislike for Shelton as leader, but the respondent answered "Shelton" to question 5. Obviously, some piece of information is missing, and additional questions are needed.

1. "Tell me what overall problems you see occurring in the Harrison project." (open-ended)

2. "Why do you feel Shelton is an ineffective communicator?" (open-ended)

3. "Are you willing to accept Shelton and Jackson as coworkers?" (direct)

4. "What makes you say that?" (verbal probe)

5. "Who do you recommend for director of the Harrison project—Jackson, Shelton, or yourself?" (closed)

6. "Let me clarify a few items. Did you previously indicate leadership as a possible problem with the Harrison project?" (direct)

7. "Did you not express serious reservations about Shelton as project leader?" (direct)

8. "Then, could you please explain why you selected Shelton and not yourself, Jackson, or even someone else as director of the Harrison project?" (open-ended)

Diamond Sequence The **diamond sequence** is used when the answer to your final (open or hypothetical open) question in an inverted funnel sequence is unexpected or unclear. To clarify the answer, you will want to reopen the questioning, starting with a general question and then moving to more and more specific ones until you end with a closed (or direct) question. A diagram of your questions would resemble a diamond shape.

IT REALLY WORKS!

Interviewing

There are many types of interviews and many uses for interviewing. The National Education for Assistance Dog Services (NEADS) is a nonprofit organization established in 1976 and now located in Princeton, Massachusetts, which trains dogs specifically to help out blind, hearing impaired, or physically disabled people (Daft & Marcic, 2006). The newest program with NEADS is the Canines for Combat Veterans program that places service dogs with disabled veterans ("Canines for combat veterans," 2009).

Through an extensive interview and application process, potential owners are matched up with the right kind of dog for their personality, lifestyle, and disability. The interview process is necessary to ensure a good match between dog and owner. According to the NEAD website, "We match the personality and skill of the dog to the personality and need of his human partner, so we cannot provide a dog immediately. It generally takes a year (and sometimes up to two) to find and train the right dog for an applicant" ("FAQ's," 2009).

After an application process, an interviewer conducts an in-person interview to determine such things as the potential client's disability (i.e., how it occurred, how serious it is, and its prognosis), specific physical and emotional needs, lifestyle, expectations and preferences (i.e., size, breed, and energy level) for a dog (Daft & Marcic, 2006). The interviewer is not only interested in finding out about the client, but also about "the care and safety of the dogs they place. Being able to continue the dog's socialization and training, along with providing a healthy environment for the life of the dog, are both crucial factors for placement" (Killion, 2004). All types of dogs are trained, but most service dogs are Labradors or golden retrievers. Once the interview is completed and it is clear that the needs of the applicant can be met, the process to find and train the perfect dog begins. Because of their rigorous interview process, over 1,300 assistance dogs placed by NEADS have brought "security, freedom, independence and relief from social isolation to their human partners" ("About NEADS," 2009).

What do you think?
- Which type interview do you think is being used by NEADS, and which method of organizing questions do you think would produce the most useful information: the funnel sequence or the inverted funnel sequence? For more information on the program, go to www.NEADS.org. You can find easy access to this link at your Premium Website for *Communicating for Results*.

Be Prepared to Answer Questions Effectively

Just as effective interviewers know what type of questions to ask to get particular responses, effective interviewees come prepared to answer those questions. The following suggestions can help interviewees in any type of interview:

- *Try to relax and be yourself.* A psychologist's suggestion to a friend who was testifying in court for the first time is good advice for all interviewees: Imagine how you feel when you are sitting in your own living room in a favorite chair, entertaining a guest (the interviewer). You are comfortable, relaxed, warm, and friendly.

- *If a question catches you off guard, don't rush unprepared into an answer.* Think about your answer first. If you feel you are taking too much time, say something like, "I'd like to make sure I completely understand your question. You're asking . . ." (then paraphrase the question as you understand it). Repeating the question aloud often helps stimulate thinking.

- *If you don't know or can't remember certain information, say so.* Never lie. On the other hand, there are things you probably should avoid mentioning. There is a fine line between disclosing too much and saying too little. Without falsifying facts, you should present as positive a picture of yourself as possible.

- *Don't be pressured into saying more than you want to say* by such interviewer techniques as silence, leading questions, or nonverbal probes.

- *Use open-ended questions to present the information you want the interviewer to know.* Open-ended questions give you the floor. "Tell me about yourself " is one prompt that all interviewees should be prepared to answer. In an employment interview, you can tell your age, marital status, spouse's occupation, and number of children (all unlawful for the interviewer to ask about), but it's better to speak of past career achievements, past employment, and why you feel especially qualified for this job.

- *Listen carefully to hypothetical open questions* to make sure you understand the situation. Interviewers may use hypothetical open questions to check the consistency of your answers or your commitment to an ideal, to check your knowledge, or to determine whether you rush to make decisions.

- *Be attentive to the interviewer's intentions when direct (or specific) questions are asked.* Because these questions require only brief answers or yes or no answers, most interviewers use them to verify known information. For these interviewers, keep your answers short. On the other hand, interviewers who are not very skilled at asking questions may really want you to give detailed answers. If they seem frustrated by your brief answers, try to answer their specific questions in an open manner. For example:

  Q: How long have you been in this field of work?

  A: Two years. (Experienced interviewers expect this.)

  A: I've been a certified financial planner for 2 years. After my training and apprenticeship with the Smith Company, I began working for Black's Financial Planners in. . . . (Untrained interviewers might expect this.)

- *Don't let closed questions limit you to an incorrect answer.* Closed questions, normally used in surveys, give the interviewer the most control of any type of question.

- Always answer the question as given, but if your preferred answer is not one of the choices in the question, make sure to express it also. For example:

> **Q:** Which of the following college courses best prepared you for this position: psychology, technical writing, Pascal, or management theory?
>
> **A:** Of those four choices, I would select management theory. However, if I could pick any course, I would say my business communication course best prepared me to handle people as individuals.

- *Avoid answering yes or no to a loaded question.* Loaded questions are designed to put you under stress for some reason known to the interviewer. For example:

> **Q:** Are you still difficult to get along with?
>
> **A:** I don't think I am ever difficult to get along with. As a matter of fact, three months ago I was voted employee of the month by my colleagues.

- *Beware of leading questions.* They are normally trick questions designed to determine how much of a "yes person" you are or to get you to agree to purchase a product.

- *Don't let the interviewer put words in your mouth.* Listen to the question carefully. If it is confusing, ask for an explanation. For example:

> **Q:** This product does meet the majority of your needs, doesn't it?
>
> **A:** Yes, but I still want to comparison shop.

- *Be aware that third-person questions are often aimed at getting you to say more than you planned to say.* Third-person questions are face savers that allow us to give our opinion without having to say that it is our opinion. As such, they are good, but be careful not to say more than you intended.

Performance Review

COMMUNICATION SITUATION

Alan O'Connor, manager in the following excerpt from a performance review, is trying to follow the guidelines we've discussed in this chapter. He tries to be honest with his employees about what they need to improve, but often they seem to resent it. What is he doing wrong? You can go to your Premium Website for *Communicating for Results* to watch a video clip of this Communication Situation, critique the

Cengage Learning

interaction between Alan O'Connor and his employee, and if requested, e-mail your responses to your instructor.

O'Connor: How do you feel about your work over the last 6 months since we last reviewed it?

Andrews: I guess I've done okay. Uh, I'm not sure what you're after here.

O'Connor: I'd just like to know your own appraisal before we talk about my perceptions of your work.

Andrews: Like I said, I guess I've done pretty good work.

O'Connor: You've missed a lot of days. And you're often late getting in.

Andrews: Well, there have been some family issues. My son developed a serious medical condition, and we had to go through testing with several doctors and then some treatments. It took a lot of time.

O'Connor: [obviously feeling uncomfortable] I don't want to get involved in your family issues. Let's focus on the work. I'd like to know if you think you'll be on time and not absent much from now on.

Andrews: Not if my son needs help. [Andrews is getting angry.] I mean, he comes first. I'm sure you can understand that. But when I'm here, I do my best and sometimes I stay late if I've had to come in late.

CHAPTER 7

R E V I E W

matzaball/iStockphoto

Key Terms

board interview (183)

closed questions (192)

closing phase (190)

confrontation interview (183)

counseling interview (182)

diamond sequence (197)

direct questions (192)

employment interview (182)

exit interview (183)

funnel sequence (195)

grievance interview (183)

group interview (183)

hourglass sequence (196)

hypothetical open questions (191)

informational interviews (185)

information-giving interview (185)

information-seeking interview (185)

interrogation interview (185)

interview (181)

inverted funnel sequence (196)

leading questions (193)

loaded questions (193)

open-ended questions (191)

opening phase (188)

panel interview (183)

performance review (186)

persuasive interview (187)

probes (194)

question-response phase (189)

rapport (188)

specific questions (192)

telephone interview (187)

third-person questions (193)

Summary

Although there are many types of interviews, the same basic approach can be used in all of them. Therefore, you will find that you can apply the information in this chapter to almost any situation, from counseling and grievance interviews to informational interviews to employment, telephone, and performance reviews. All effective interviews are organized into the same three phases: opening phase (including rapport, orientation, and motivation), question-response phase (the body of the interview), and closing phase.

Interviews also include a variety of types of questions. The most common are open ended, hypothetical open, direct, closed, loaded, leading, and third-person questions, as well as, verbal and nonverbal probes. They all have advantages and disadvantages, and the interviewer should use them with a specific purpose in mind. By grouping questions in general subject areas, the interviewer can evaluate information in coherent chunks as the interview progresses. The funnel sequence and the inverted funnel sequence are the two most common methods of organizing questions within general subject areas. The diamond and hourglass sequences are used as follow-up when answers are unexpected or vague.

Interviewees, too, should be aware of the purposes of various types of questions and the types of responses expected. Effective interviewees know that open-ended questions give them the floor but that direct and closed questions indicate that a brief response is desired. They also know to answer leading and loaded questions with extreme care.

As with all skills, effective interviewing involves both knowledge and practice. The next chapter will look in greater detail at the employment interview.

Communicating for Results Online

Before continuing to the next chapter, check your understanding of Chapter 7 at the Premium Website for *Communicating for Results*. Your Premium Website gives you quick and easy access to the electronic resources that accompany this text. These resources include:

- **Study tools** that will help you assess your learning and prepare for exams (student companion workbook, digital glossary, key term flash cards, and review quizzes).

- **Activities and assignments** that will help you hone your knowledge, analyze professional communication situations, build your public speaking skills throughout the course, and learn to work effectively in teams (Awareness Checks, Checkpoints, and Collaborative Learning Activities).

- **Media resources** that will help you explore communication concepts online (web links), develop your speech outlines (Speech Builder Express 3.0), watch and critique videos of professional communication situations and sample speeches (Interactive Video Activities), upload your speech videos for peer reviewing and critique other students' speeches (Speech Studio online speech review tool), and download chapter review so you can study when and where you'd like (Audio Study Tools).

This chapter's key terms, Collaborative Learning Activities, and Checkpoint activities are also featured on the following pages, and you can find this chapter's Awareness Check activities in the body of the chapter. For more information or to access this book's online resources, visit www.cengage.com/login.

Collaborative Learning Activities

1. In groups of four to seven, develop a list of five or more quality interview questions that could be asked in an information-seeking interview. Select a specific job (such as sales associate or waiter) and a category into which the questions would fit (e.g., education and work experience required or job duties and responsibilities). Identify each question as to its type and list them in either the funnel or inverted funnel sequence making sure that the sequence used is obvious. Be prepared to present your questions to others and justify why you decided to use the sequence you selected.

2. In groups of four to six people (use an even number if possible), prepare two quality questions for each type listed on pages 191–194—one question for each type may come from the text; the other questions should be created by the group. Keep in mind that most questions asked by interviewers regardless of the type are poorly worded. Make sure your questions are clear, quality questions. Once the questions are ready, break into pairs and conduct mini interviews. Take turns asking and answering the questions. Work on sounding confident and maintaining good eye contact while answering questions. When finished, discuss how you each felt and which questions were the most difficult to answer and why. Which type questions would normally not be included in an employment interview?

3. In small groups share personal experiences or stories of people you know who have asked for raises. In addition, find at least one article on asking a supervisor or manager for a raise. Decide on the best answers to the following questions: (a) What questions and techniques work best in a persuasive interview when asking for a raise? (b) What questions do you think the boss will ask of you? (c) What are the best answers to these questions that will show you are an effective communicator and increase your chances of getting the raise?

(d) What questions should you avoid asking the boss? Why?

Checkpoints

Checkpoint 7.1 Conducting an Information-Seeking Interview

Conduct a 15-minute information-seeking interview with someone who currently holds approximately the same job and title that you would like to have sometime in the future. You act as interviewer, and have the person be the interviewee. Ask him or her questions that will either help you decide whether you want this particular job or help you prepare effectively for it. For suggested questions see the informational interview in this chapter. Keep in mind that it is better to conduct at least three or more information-seeking interviews so you can compare your results and feel confident in the advice you've obtained.

Checkpoint 7.2 Effective Questions for Performance Reviews

Checkpoint 7.3 First Impressions

Checkpoint 7.4 Funnel and Inverted Funnel Questioning Sequence

Checkpoint 7.5 Telephone Interviews

Checkpoint 7.6 Preparing for a Performance Review

Checkpoint 7.7 Information on Interviews: Websites

The Employment Interview

As you read Chapter 8,

Identify the basic methods for successful job hunting including locating specific jobs; preparing a conventional, scannable, e-mail, and web resume; and writing a powerful letter of application.

Summarize suggestions for interviewees when preparing for an interview including creating the right impression, handling different types of interviews, answering tough standard and behavioral questions, and asking the interviewer appropriate questions.

Identify the phases of a successful interview, and **discuss** what an interviewer should include in each phase.

Summarize important suggestions for interviewers when conducting an interview especially how to know which interview questions are lawful and which are not.

Adam Gregor/iStockphoto

Case Study: False Information on Resume Brings Down CEO

The days when you can falsify information on your resume and expect to get away with it are over. Just ask past-CEO of RadioShack, Dave Edmondson. As this story shows, if the newspaper reporters don't catch you, then a blogger using one of the 200 million blogs currently online likely will (Duncan, 2006).

Edmondson was hired as vice president of marketing for the Retail Division of RadioShack in 1994, and by May 2005 he had become president and CEO of the nearly 7,000-store company. Nine months later, the local newspaper broke a story titled "RadioShack CEO's Resume in Question," reporting that an investigation had "uncovered discrepancies in the academic credentials of RadioShack Chief Executive Dave Edmondson, including inaccuracies on his resume and corporate biography" (Landy, 2006, para. 1). Edmondson denied any wrongdoing, and the board gave him a prompt vote of confidence.

By the next day, the story was different: Edmondson was backpedaling, and the board was refusing to discuss the matter, calling the investigation "out of place" (Landy, 2006). According to Edmondson's biography and resume, he had earned degrees in theology and psychology from Pacific Coast Baptist College in San Dimas, California. (The college had changed its name to Heartland Baptist Bible College and moved to Oklahoma City in 1998.) However, a call to the registrar determined that Edmondson had attended only two semesters and that the college had never offered a degree in psychology.

Confronted with this information, Edmondson said he was unaware of this error on his corporate paperwork but that his degree was a 3-year degree in theology called

Chris Gardner/Associated Press

As you read this chapter, see if you can (a) decide what policies RadioShack could implement to make sure no resume inaccuracies occur in the future, (b) list two advantages and disadvantages for RadioShack if they decide to develop their own company blog (refer back to Chapter 6), and (c) discuss why you think Edmondson falsified information on his resume. For more information on RadioShack, go to their home site at **www. radioshackcorporation.com** and browse for information. You can find easy access to this link through your Premium Website for *Communicating for Results.*

a "Thg" degree, completed by correspondence courses, and that he had only minored in psychology. A second call to the registrar revealed that the college had no record that Edmondson had ever graduated.

When asked to produce his diploma, Edmondson replied that he could not because it had been destroyed in a fire at his home (the fire was verified), but he suggested that Jack Baskin, the executive vice president of Pacific Coast Baptist when he was a student at the college, might be able to verify that he had graduated. In a phone conversation, Baskin said he had spoken with Edmondson the previous week and since then had consulted with other former employees and that it was "pretty well a consensus that he did graduate in 1980" (Landy, 2006, para. 32). In addition, the registrar faxed the following statement to Edmondson:

> In the life of a small school, where increased workload and student workers in the offices is the norm, the possibility exists that papers, file inserts, and various documents could get lost, misfiled, or misplaced—and moving from California to Oklahoma could have compounded the problem. (Landy, 2006, para. 22)

With these last two "verifications" of graduation, the incident might have been over except for two things: time and the blogosphere. From the time the story broke on Tuesday until Edmondson resigned on Monday, "RadioShack made searing headlines at home and across the nation, in print and in broadcast" (Schnurman, 2006). For shareholders, potential shareholders, and customers, RadioShack's image took a beating. Even worse were the comments on message boards, various blog sites, and newspaper blogs. The comments on the local newspaper blog (which included comments from many employees) went from mild but insightful to anger at Edmondson's behavior to anger at the board's actions to discussion of a cover-up and a demand that the entire board resign. The board members were following these comments, and the chairman admitted to the newspaper that he "sensed the rage, the pain of a hurt company" (Schnurman, 2006, para. 7).

In the end, the board of RadioShack announced they were to begin their own investigation into possible discrepancies, and Edmondson offered this apology: "The contents of my resume and the company's website were clearly incorrect. I clearly misstated my academic record, and the responsibility for these misstatements is mine alone" (CBC News, 2006). On Monday, after meeting with the board over the weekend, he resigned.

I f you follow the current norm, you will be searching for a job several times during your lifetime. Arranging for employment interviews through telephone contacts, letters of application, computer searches, and a good resume (conventional or electronic), and then communicating effectively in the actual interview are important skills you need to practice. And on the job, you may be interviewing others seeking employment. Knowing how to conduct an effective interview that accurately assesses the qualifications of applicants without restricting their individual rights (as specified by law) also requires up-to-date skills and information.

Chapter 7 covered the basic organization used by almost all interviews (the opening, question–response, and closing phases), the types of questions normally asked along with their advantages and disadvantages, and how to effectively organize the questions during the interview. This chapter will apply this basic information to the employment interview; add specific, current information; and organize these tips into the responsibilities expected of the interviewee and those of the interviewer.

Interviewee: Preparing for the Job Hunt

As the interviewee, you cannot take a passive role in the employment interview process. The following sections discuss some of the things you can do to increase the likelihood that you will find a job that specifically fits your abilities and interests.

Investigating the Employment Market

Various job-hunting methods show the following rates of success according to Richard Bolles (2009) in *What Color Is Your Parachute 2009?* and Peter Weddle in *Weddle's Newsletter: March 27, 2008*:

- Networking (through informational interviews)—86%.
- Cold-calling potential employers—47%.
- Asking friends/acquaintances for job leads—33%.
- Asking relatives for job leads—27%.
- Answering newspaper ads—4 to 24%.
- Using college placement office—21%.
- Using job agencies—5 to 28%.
- Answering an ad posted on an Internet job board—13%.
- Posting a resume on the Internet—4 to 6% (maybe as much as 10 to 20% if seeking a job in finance, health care, engineering, or information technology; or even 45% if seeking a computer-related job).
- Using a social networking site (like MySpace)—3.9%.

Although some methods have a higher success rate than others, aggressive job hunters use multiple methods. You will certainly want to use networking, based on the information-seeking interview discussed in Chapter 7. A **network** is a web of contacts and relationships designed to benefit the participants by providing leads and referrals. However, as *Weddle's Newsletter* (2006a) pointed out: "People who don't know you are unlikely to take the risk of referring you to friends or colleagues who may have an opening that is just right for you" (para. 2). Therefore, you have to "work" at getting people to know you. Or as Ellen Reeves notes in her book *Can I Wear My Nose Ring to the Interview?* (2009), you should be looking for people, not jobs because "The right person will lead you to the right job" (p. 1). A recent survey found that the number one recruitment strategy of companies in the United States is employee referrals ("Corporate Recruiters Survey," 2009). The importance of employee referrals is mentioned over and over from Fortune's

100 Best Companies to Work For (Yang, 2009). For example, Judy Merkel, senior director of recruiting for Booz Allen Hamilton, made this comment: "Our best source of new hires is our employee referral program, which is where we get about 50% of our new hires" (Yang, 2009, para. 3).

Based on the value of networking, before going on any job interviews, begin networking by conducting from 10 to 40 **information-seeking interviews**. Interview successful people who do what you would like to do, people who have access to information you need, and people who have access to other people you may want to contact (Bolles, 2009; Damp, 2005; Weddle, 2006b). One new way to find contacts and to research a company is through blogs (web logs). For example, go to Google and type in "business blogs," and you will be amazed at the results (Maher, 2004).

It's not as difficult as you might think to find qualified people to interview. For leads, ask your friends, schoolmates, family members, family friends, acquaintances from organizations and clubs (including religious and volunteer organizations), business colleagues, and professors. In fact, one researcher (Rosaluk, 1983) claims each of us knows approximately 40,000 people we could ask. Rosaluk suggests that you start with 200 people you know—friends to casual acquaintances. Don't overlook acquaintances—they are more likely than your friends to know people that you do not (Gladwell, 2002). Each of those 200 people also knows 200 people. Out of these 40,000 people, you should come up with at least 40 people to interview. If you are a member of LinkedIn.com, which claims to have over 45 million professional members worldwide, coming up with 40 people could be a breeze.

A survey conducted by Goodrich & Sherwood Company, a human resources management consulting firm, found that serious networking reduces the length of a job search (Weinstein, 1993). For example, if you see 2 people a week, you may expect the search to last up to a year; if you meet 10 people a week, your search will usually be cut about 6 months. But if you see 20 people a week, you're likely to land a new job in 90 days or less. Reeves (2009) suggests the Rule of Three—three informational interviews or three actual interviews, three e-mail, and three letters each workday which equals close to 200 contacts a month. Information-seeking interviews should provide you with the following information:

- *Specific information* about the career, job, or company in which you are interested (including jargon, keywords, trends, potential problems, expected salary range, organizations to join, and leading journals and magazines to read).

- *Feedback* on your career goals, resume, interviewing skills, and appearance.

- *Names* of other people (referrals) you can contact for further information.

Informational interviews are best when conducted in person, but phone interviews will do if a personal interview is impossible. Once you have all the information you need about a specific job area, you are ready to prepare one or more types of resumes: a conventional paper resume, a scannable paper resume, an e-mail or

Martin Purmensky/iStockphoto

Before applying for a job or making a career change, conduct between 10 and 40 information-seeking interviews.

plain text resume, or a web (HTML) resume. These resumes are summarized below; for specific details see the appendix: "Written Communication."

Locate Specific Jobs of Interest

A large number of employers post openings on free sites (such as Indeed.com, Simplyhired.com, or Jobster.com), their own websites, or on employment websites like Monster.com or Careerbuilder.com. Employers search for resumes and applicants on employment websites, Google, and Zoominfo.com, (Reeves, 2009; Weddle, 2006b, 2009; Yate, 2008b). Job sites can be used for more than just posting your resume or looking for job openings. They are also an excellent source of information, such as interviewing advice, facts about specific companies or jobs, an up-to-date list of average salaries, cost of living across the country, and names of people you may want to call for additional information (Bolles, 2009). You can even get ideas by looking at other people's resumes.

Most employers now have their own websites where they post job openings. To see if a company you are interested in has a website, do a Google search, or go to Monster.com, Weddles.com, or JobHuntersBible.com for a listing of company sites. (You can find links to these sites through your Premium Website for *Communicating for Results*.) Some companies include an Internet address in their newspaper ads and instruct applicants to e-mail their resumes. Virtual job fairs allow you to check who's hiring in your area and to post your resume for jobs that are of interest.

Prepare a Resume

The resume is a way of communicating with a prospective employer. If properly done, it can give you an advantage over others applying for the same position. The information you gathered during your information-seeking interviews will help you decide the type and length of resumes to plan. There are four basic types of resumes—you will probably want to prepare more than one:

- The **conventional paper resume** is formatted to look attractive and designed to be mailed or handed to the reviewer (see Figure 8.1) but cannot effectively be scanned by computers or stored electronically. They vary in length, style, and content, depending on the type of job, the work experience of the applicant, and the preference of the particular company or firm. Most conventional resumes are organized in one of three basic ways: the **chronological resume** that emphasizes the applicant's work experience in chronological order beginning with the most recent; the **functional resume** that emphasizes skills rather than work experiences and downplays dates; and the **combination resume** or **hybrid resume** that begins by highlighting specific skills and abilities and follows with a chronological list of jobs and a brief look at education. The chronological resume is generally preferred by interviewers; in most cases, they also prefer a brief resume of one or two pages. The best conventional resumes begin by placing the most important information about the applicant first—for example, if education is not your strong suit, begin with work experience or a summary of your skills. When you list your job duties, be sure to include how effectively you handled each one when possible. Also, omit any personal information that does not relate to the job. For specific details in how to write a conventional resume and a look at several sample resumes, see Appendix: Written Communication.

LYNDA C. MORGAN
1777 Manual Street ♦ Baltimore, Maryland 21201
lmorgan@verizon.net ♦ 410.837.5555 (Home) ♦ 410-837.5554 (Cell)

QUALIFICATIONS SUMMARY

Honest, hardworking leader and team player with keen judgment and dependability, poised to leverage education and experience toward launching a successful career in Sports Psychology.

♦ **Teaching Knowledge:** MS in Kinesiology, coupled with experience providing group instruction in Weight Training/Body Conditioning while Department/Teaching Assistant.
♦ **Athletic Training:** Two-year Letter Winner for Athletic Training of athletes in various intramural sports, including Basketball, Softball, Volleyball, and Gymnastics.
♦ **Communication:** Exceptional interpersonal skills in handling sensitive matters. In-depth experience educating for individual needs. Proficient in MS Office Suite and Windows OS.
♦ **Key Strengths:** Finely tuned analytical and research skills. Able to maintain an exceptional rate of productivity, accuracy and efficiency while providing exceptional staff support.

EDUCATION

Master of Science in Kinesiology, 2009. Maryland Christian University, Baltimore, Maryland. Specialization: Sport & Exercise Psychology with G.P.A. 3.6.
Bachelor of Science in Human Biology, 2004. Maryland Christian University. Specialization: Kinesiology; G.P.A. 3.7; Two-year Letter Winner.

EXPERIENCE HIGHLIGHTS

GRADUATE STUDENT AND DEPARTMENT ASSISTANT, MARYLAND CHRISTIAN UNIVERSITY   2007 to 2009
- Completed Master of Science program in Kinesiology and Sports Psychology; Specialized in Research Methods, Physiology of Exercise, and Psychology of Youth Sports; Graduate thesis dealt with Eating Behaviors among Middle School Adolescents.
- Served as department assistant responsible for coordinating assigned department projects, research, and reporting; maintaining department project calendar to ensure timely completion of all projects; assisting the campus community for the Director; and teaching college courses in weight training and body conditioning.
- Selected as Teacher's Assistant for coursework instruction in Elementary Methods, Secondary Methods, Team & Group Sports, and Foundations of Kinesiolog & Sports Psychology.

ANDROLOGY TECHNICIAN, CENTER FOR ASSISTED REPRODUCTION, Baltimore, Maryland   2004 to 2007
- Responsible for providing customer service to patients receiving andrology and IVF services and coordinating biopsy and testing services with outside laboratories.
- Participated in the external audit process of laboratory credentialing and licensure to ensure compliance with state and federal requirements.

MEDICAL RECEPTIONIST, GASTROENTEROLOGISTS OF MARYLAND, Baltimore, Maryland   2001 to 2004
- Responsible for answering telephones, scheduling patient appointments, explaining policy to patients, scheduling hospital admissions, and filing medical reports and insurance forms.
- Gained broad based experience in all aspects of medical office administration.

PROFESSIONAL AFFILIATIONS

Association for the Advancement of Applied Sports Psychology; Golden Key National Honor Society

Conventional Resume

```
RONALD STRINGER
408 Emmett Avenue
Bowling Green, KY 42101
502-796-2784/ASRS815@gmail.com

------------------------------------------------
Sales Representative / Marketing
------------------------------------------------

Commission and retail sales. Customer service.
Management assistant. Inventory control. Team player.
Interpersonal, oral, and written communication.
Presentation skills. Television commercial. Advertising
campaign. Windows operating system. Microsoft Office 2007.
AA in Communication. BA in Business communication-2007.

------------------------------------------------

Experience
------------------------------------------------

SEARS -Bowling Green, KY
Commission salesperson, 6/09 to present.
* Profiting company by selling product lines & services.
* Demonstrating benefits of merchandise requests &
  problems.
TRUTH BOOKSTORE -Bowling Green, KY
Management assistant - Internship, 2/08 to 8/08
Created letters to increase sales and profits. Assisted
In inventory control. Updated customer records on
Microsoft Office 2007.
* Developed & implemented an advertising campaign.
* Wrote, directed & voiced company television
  commercial.
CASUAL MALE BIG AND TALL - Bowling Green, KY
Sales associate, 10/06 to 1/08
Greeted and assisted customers. Demonstrated merchandise
& advised customers on fitting fashion and style selections.
* Maintained highest average item per customer (IPC).
* Led all employees with the highest sale for the year.

------------------------------------------------

Education
------------------------------------------------

WESTERN KENTUCKY UNIVERSITY - Bowling Green
BA in corporate & Organizational Communication, December 2007
FLORDIA COLLEGE -Temple Terrace, FL
AA in Communication, May 2005

------------------------------------------------

Professional Affiliations & Awards
------------------------------------------------

Graduated Cum Laude, Florida College
Athletic Director for Arête Society at Florida College
```

E-mail Resume

LYNDA C. MORGAN
1777 Manual Street Baltimore, Maryland 21201
lmorgan@verizon.net 410.837.5555 (Home) 410-837.5554 (Cell)

KEY WORD SUMMARY

Honest, confident and hardworking leader. Team oriented. Keen judgment and dependability. Specialist in sport and exercise psychology. Weight training. Body conditioning. Intramural athletic events. Interpersonal skills in handling sensitive matters. MS Office and Windows operating systems. Analytical and research skills. Productive staff supports services. College teaching experience. MS in Kinesiology.

EDUCATION

Maryland Christian University	**Baltimore, Maryland**
Masters of Science in Kinesiology	May 2009
Maryland Christian University	**Baltimore, Maryland**
Bachelor of Science in Human Biology	May, 2004

EXPERIENCE

Maryland Christian University   **Baltimore, Maryland**
Graduate Student and Department Assistant   2007 - 2009
- Completed Master of Science program in Kinesiology and Sports Psychology; Specialized in Research Methods, Physiology of Exercise, and Psychology of Youth Sports; Graduate thesis dealt with Eating Behaviors among Middle School Adolescence.
- Served as department assistant responsible for coordinating assigned department projects, research, and reporting; maintaining department project calendar to ensure timely completion of all projects; assisting the campus community for the Director; and teaching college courses in weight training and body conditioning.
- Selected as Teacher's Assistant for undergraduate coursework instruction in Elementary Methods, Secondary Methods, Team & Group Sports, and Foundations of Kinesiology and Sports Psychology.

Center for Assisted Reproduction   **Baltimore, Maryland**
Andrology Technician   2004 - 2007
- Responsible for providing customer service to patients receiving andrology and IVF services and coordinating biopsy and testing services with outside laboratories.
- Participated in the external audit process of laboratory credentialing and licensure to ensure compliance with state and federal requirements.

Gastroenterologists of Maryland   **Baltimore, Maryland**
Medical Receptionist   2001 - 2004
- Responsible for answering telephones, scheduling patient appointments, explaining policy to patients, scheduling hospital admissions, and filing medical reports and insurance forms.
- Gained broad based experience in all aspects of medical office administration.

PROFESSIONAL AFFILIATIONS

Association for the Advancement of Applied Sports Psychology
Golden Key National Honor Society

Scannable Resume

Lynda C. Morgan

E-Mail: lmorgan@verizon.net

E-Mail Resume

Download a text version of my resume. Use the "Save" command in your browser to save to a disk.

Complete Resume

View or print a fully formatted copy of my resume.

Feedback

lmorgan@verison.net

Objective

Career in sports psychology and kinesiology.

Additional information to support my qualifications:

▶ Qualifications Summary
▶ Experience Highlights
▶ Education
▶ Affiliations & Awards
▶ Computer skills
▶ Brief Video Clip

Last Updated 3/21/10

WEB Resume

FIGURE 8.1 Sample resumes.*

*Resumes in Figure 8.1 were adapted from a resume provided courtesey of Deanne Arnath, President of Career Wizards, Inc. For additional resumes see careerwizardsinc.com and the Appendix: Written Communication in this text.

- The **scannable resume** is a conventional resume that is altered to be computer friendly and is used for companies or online job sites that electronically scan, search, and store resumes they receive (see Figure 8.1). If you aren't sure whether your resume needs to be scannable, call the company and ask. Scannable resumes differ from conventional resumes in two main ways. First, because they will be read by optical character recognition (OCR) scanners, they must be plainer and thus easier to scan. For example, avoid using colored or patterned paper; type sizes smaller than 12 point (scanners have problems reading small print); fancy fonts or fonts with letters that touch; graphics and formatting such as underlining, italics, boxes, and shading (although boldface type works well). Also, dates scan more accurately if you write them as May 2010 or 5/10 and place them on the left side of the page rather than the middle or right side as many conventional resumes do. Second, because electronic scanners are looking for a set of terms specified by the job searcher, it is important to add a either a keyword summary or a qualifications summary with keywords either after or in place of the objective. A **keyword summary** is a brief summary of your skills and qualifications in a running list with each word or phrase separated by a period. A **qualifications summary** usually begins with a clear and powerful career goal and is followed with a bulleted list of three to five values and qualifications in keyword-packed phrases beginning with action verbs (Nishimura, 2009). Make sure that your keywords are up to date and incorporate any terms that relate to you gathered from the written job description. Don't overlook your communication and interpersonal skills. The number one skill that corporate recruiters look for is communication skills (oral and written)—as selected by 89% of recruiters surveyed (Corporate Recruiters Survey, 2009). For a list of several requested interpersonal keywords used in job searches, see Figure 8.2. In addition to the keyword summary, scannable resumes include headings for experience, education, and professional affiliations/awards. For detailed specifics on how to write an effective scannable resume and a look at an additional sample resume, see Appendix: Written Communication.

- The **e-mail resume**—also called an e-resume or ASCII resume—is a plain-text "bare bones" resume designed to be pasted into an e-mail message and read by any computer using any e-mail or word processing software (see Figure 8.1). To avoid the possibility of a virus, more and more companies are refusing to accept attachments and request that you send your resume by e-mail. Although many

Interpersonal and Communication Keywords		
Adaptable	Follow-up	Persuasive
Assertive	Industrious	Public speaker
Communicator	Innovative	Self-starter
Creative	Open minded	Supportive
Customer oriented	Organizationl skills	Takes initiative
Ethical	Problem solver	Team player

FIGURE 8.2 Interpersonal and communication keywords.

companies use e-mail that reads html and allows for standard word processing formatting such as underlining and boldface, don't assume that all do. Therefore, the e-mail resume is designed for ASCII (American standard code for information interchange) and uses only keyboard characters. This means that no boldface, underlining, italics, bullets, boxes, pictures, graphics, or special characters or symbols can be used in an e-mail resume. The safest fonts to use are Courier and Courier New. To add some interest, you can highlight titles by using all caps or placing dashed lines above and below each title; the plus sign (+) or asterisk (*) can also be used in place of bullets. To keep your resume from having ragged lines or added blank lines when sent through e-mail, keep each line to no more than 60 characters and end each line with a space and a hard return instead of letting the lines wrap automatically. Although the e-mail resume is plainer than the scannable resume, it typically includes the same headings: keyword summary, experience, education, and professional affiliations/awards. The e-mail resume does not take the place of a paper resume. You will want to take a hard copy with you to interviews. It does, however, eliminate the possibility of sending a virus along with an attached resume and speeds the job search. For detailed specifics on how to write an ASCII e-mail resume and a look at two sample resumes using different styles, see Appendix: Written Communication.

- The **web resume**—also called an electronic or **e-portfolio** (Lehman & Dufrene, 2008)—includes an e-mail resume, a link to a conventional resume, and links to additional information showcasing your qualifications and abilities all posted to your personal website (see Figure 8.1). Information could include career goals; problem-solving examples; honors and awards; research completed; languages spoken; military service; education and training including degrees, certificates and licenses; and perhaps a brief video of projects you have completed like a movie clip you produced, an oral presentation or you teaching a class; using PowerPoint, or answering interview questions. However, include only the information that is directly related to the job—if you include too much, the chances are good that it won't be seen. Web resumes aren't advised for all applicants, but are especially effective for those interested in technology, advertising, marketing, theatre, film, art, or design (Kennedy, 2007). When invited in for an interview, always take a conventional resume and a list of your references; also, you may want to take a couple DVDs of your web resume just in case it seems appropriate to leave a copy with the interviewer. For detailed specifics on how to write one or more sections for the web resume, see Appendix: Written Communication.

Check Resume Content for Accuracy and Honesty

As our chapter opening case clearly indicated, you can't be too careful about the accuracy and honesty of your resume. Although companies

"I want my résumé to be the one you remember. It's also available as a music video, interpretive dance, and a haiku."

expect you to present yourself in a positive light, as Guffey (2010) warns, "Distorting facts on a resume is unethical; lying is illegal. Either practice can destroy a career" (p. 395). Although some resumes have total lies in them, many people stick to exaggerations and distortions, perhaps because these forms of lying seem less serious to them. **Exaggeration** is overstating or presenting facts as more important than they are; **distortion** is misrepresenting or twisting facts, or stating that they are true when they are only partially true. After conducting 2.6 million background checks in a single year, ADP Screening and Selection Services reported the following: "44% of applicants lied about their work histories, 23% fabricated licenses or credentials, and 41% falsified their educational background" (Kidwell, 2004, p. 177). According to Guffey (2010, p. 396), before you send your resume to potential employers, carefully check it for the following: *inflated* education, grades, or honors; *enhanced* job titles; *puffed-up* accomplishments; and *altered* dates of employment (such as saying you worked several months longer than you actually did to cover an employment gap).

Once you have investigated the employment market, located several potential jobs, and prepared one or more resumes, you are ready to prepare a letter of application also called a cover letter.

Prepare a Letter of Application

The purpose of the **letter of application** is to give enough information about you and your capabilities so that the employer will be interested in talking with you personally (Krannich & Krannich, 2006; Lurie & Welz, 2006; Yate, 2008a, 2008c). If you write it correctly, your letter presents a good first impression making you sound like a fun, interesting, and confident person. In addition to previewing what is in your resume, it showcases your communication skills and writing style (Reeves, 2009). Each letter should relate specifically to the company and person to whom you are writing (see Figure 8.3). Ideally, you will have already conducted an informational interview with someone at the company. If not, try to talk with someone who has been working with the firm; ask for literature, such as the annual report, that explains the firm and its policies; check the company's website or blog (look on Google or Twitter for both); or read about the organization at the following sites: CareerBuilder.com, CareerJournal.com, FastCompany.com, Monster.com, QuintCareers.com, Wetfeet.com, or Jobster.com. (You can access links to these sites through your Premium Website for *Communicating for Results*.)

You can also check your college or city libraries for the following databases:

- Business and Company Resource Center by the Gale Group (type in company name or browse; also includes links to articles about the company).

- Associations Unlimited by the Gale Group (contains information on nonprofit organizations).

- EBSCOHost (click on Company Profiles, then type company name or browse; includes complete company reports in PDF format).

If the company doesn't have a website and is too small to appear in any of the preceding sources, call the company receptionist or the sales, marketing, public relations, or human resources departments for information. Once you have discovered as much about the company as possible, you are ready to complete your letter of application. The key to writing a good letter is to place the focus on the needs or problems of the company and what you can do for them—not on you or how the job fits your interests. For guidelines on how to write an outstanding letter—one

LYNDA C. MORGAN
1777 Manual Street ♦ Baltimore, Maryland 21201
lmorgan@verizon.net ♦ 410.837.5555 (Home) ♦ 410.837.5554 (Cell)

[Month, Day, Year]

[Mr./Ms. First Name, Last Name]
[Company Name]
[Company Address]
[City, ST Zip]

Dear [Mr./Ms. Last Name]:

Your need for a [position title] caught my attention as my qualifications appear to be well aligned with your needs. Please accept the enclosed résumé for your consideration.

As you will see, in addition to a Master of Science in Kinesiology, my background encompasses four years of progressively responsible experience in teaching and training at the university level, from Athletic Trainer for Baltimore Woman's University to my most recent position as Department Assistant for Maryland Christian University. In this capacity, I taught college level courses in Kinesiology and Sports Psychology as well as Weight Training and Body Conditioning to classes consisting of 25 to 30 undergraduate students.

Currently, I am poised to excel in a position with an organization that offers continued professional development and the opportunity for advancement in the field of [job/industry]. I am very eager to learn more about the responsibilities of the position and how I can begin to make a contribution to your overall success. Please contact me by phone or email to arrange a mutually convenient time for an initial conversation.

I look forward to hearing from you; thank you for your time and consideration.

Sincerely,

[Signature]

Lynda C. Morgan
Enclosure

FIGURE 8.3 Sample letter of application.*

*Letter of Application provided courtesey of Deanne Arnath, President of Career Wizards, Inc. For additional letters see careerwizardsinc.com and the Appendix: Written Communication in this text.

that is sure to improve your chances for a telephone or face-to-face interview—see Appendix: Written Communication.

Interviewee: Preparing for the Interview

Once your resumes and letters of application have landed one or more interviews, it is time to carefully prepare for the interview process. Although the advice in this section may seem like common sense, it can make a real difference in how interviewers view you and your abilities.

Have a Positive Attitude

Once you have a date for an interview, the next step is to prepare for it by adjusting your mental attitude as necessary. Regardless of the type of interview, attitude is immensely important. Know that you are a person of worth and integrity with a genuine right to be considered for the job. Be confident in your ability to respond openly and honestly with favorable effect. Approach the interview with a positive attitude no matter what has happened in the past. No one wants to hire a bitter, depressed person. Use the confidence-building techniques discussed in Chapter 6. Think success!

On the other hand, adjusting your attitude does not mean that you should try to alter your personality or style just for the interview: Be yourself. You will make a better impression if you avoid role-playing and pretense. Remember, the interview also helps you decide whether this position is right for you.

Communicate and Dress for the Occasion—Impression Management

Impression management refers to the efforts people make to improve how others see them (Rao et al., 1995; Rosenfeld, 1997). An early study found that when a negative impression was created during the first 5 minutes of the interview, applicants were not hired 90% of the time; however, when a positive impression was created in the first 5 minutes, applicants were hired 75% of the time (Blakeman et al., 1971, p. 57). More recent studies (Burgoon & LePoire, 1993; Zunin & Zunin, 1994) confirm the power of first impressions. Furthermore, Burgoon and Hoobler (2002) point out that "first impressions based on nonverbal cues tend to be highly persistent, even in the face of subsequent contradictory cues" (pp. 263–264). In other words, once the initial impression of the interviewee is formed, the interviewer tends to view the remainder of the interview as supporting this original view, even when some information may indicate otherwise. In job interviews, all three codes contribute to first impressions: *verbal* (what we say), *vocal* (how we say it), and *visual* (our dress, appearance, and nonverbal behaviors).

Candidates' verbal comments affect the kind of impression they make on interviewers. Stevens and Kristof (1995) found that successful applicants most often used the following five types of comments, or impression-management techniques: (a) describing self in a positive manner, (b) describing past events with positive personal stories, (c) expressing opinions that agree with the interviewer, (d) claiming personal responsibility for successful past events, and (e) making statements that compliment the company or interviewer. These five comments can be divided into two basic impression-management styles: the **controlling style** (where comments are focused on self-promotion) and the **submissive style** (where comments are focused on the interviewer). As long as the comments are not phony, manipulative, or false, research indicates that the controlling style of impression management results in more job offers and higher ratings of the candidate for motivation, enthusiasm, and technical skills (Kacmar et al., 1992; Stevens & Kristof, 1995).

The vocal sounds that candidates make during interviews also help form the impressions of

© 2003 Ted Goff

"We're in awe of your ability to fit in here, Ms. Stoughton."

interviewers. Researchers (Buller & Aune, 1988; Burgoon et al., 1990; Burgoon & Hoobler, 2002; Ray, 1986) have found the following:

- Variety in pitch and tempo and a moderately loud volume add to the impression of power and credibility. A heavy accent does the opposite.

- A pleasant-sounding voice adds to the image of attractiveness and likeability.

- Speaking fairly rapidly and forcefully with few nonfluencies ("uh" and "um") adds to the impression of competence and authority. On the other hand, speaking slowly or moderately can increase the impression of honesty.

Interviewers' decisions are more heavily influenced by unfavorable first impressions and behaviors than they are by favorable ones (Rowe, 1989; Watson & Smeltzer, 1982). This is especially true of visual impressions. For example, if you are poorly groomed, there is a good chance that the prospective employer will view you as a person with a low self-concept—a person unable to function effectively in the position being discussed. (See Chapter 5 for suggestions on how to dress for acceptance in the business world.) Table 8.1 summarizes five common grooming and appearance mistakes that men and women applicants make that lead to negative first impressions.

Nonverbal behaviors also affect interviewers' evaluations of applicants (Burnett & Motowidlo, 1998; Ralston & Kirkwood, 1999). For example, 26 people interviewed candidates with good nonverbal behaviors and candidates with poor nonverbal behaviors. Good nonverbal behaviors included direct eye contact, high energy level, smiles, and smooth delivery; poor nonverbal behaviors included little eye contact, low energy level, nonfluent delivery, and few smiles. When asked if they would invite the candidates back for another interview, none of the 26 would invite the candidates with poor nonverbal behaviors, but 23 of the interviewers would invite back the candidates with good nonverbal behaviors (McGovern & Ideus, 1978). Another study (Einhorn, 1981) found that successful interviewees were more likely to do the following:

- Speak rapidly and forcefully.

- Gesture and smile often.

- Look directly at the interviewer.

TABLE 8.1

Common Mistakes Men and Women Make in Dress and Appearance	
Men	**Women**
1. Clothes that don't fit properly or are wrinkled or dirty	1. Clothes that are ill fitting or wrinkled
2. Shirts that fit too snugly at the collar or around the waist	2. Clothing that is inappropriate especially when too short or too revealing
3. Hands, hair, or nails that are dirty	3. Too much perfume; too much or too little makeup
4. Scuffed or the wrong color shoes; white socks	4. Scuffed or inappropriate shoes
5. Cheap-looking tie or tie that is too short	5. Inappropriate or too much jewelry

Source: R. J. Ilkka, 1995, "Applicant Appearance and Selection Decision Making: Revitalizing Employment Interview Education," *Business Communication Quarterly,* 58(3), pp. 11–18; Martin Yate, 2008b, *"Knock 'em Dead: The Ultimate Job Search Guide 2009,"* pp. 123–136.

- Nod their head in a positive manner.
- Lean forward while maintaining natural, comfortable postures.

And finally, Watson and Smeltzer (1982) report that there are three things that interviewers remember most after the interviewee is gone: *eye contact*, *appearance*, and *facial expressions*.

You might find it helpful to think of impression management as another skill that can help you communicate effectively. However, be sure to avoid dysfunctional impression management relating to your dress, expressions, or resume (Kidwell, 2004). You still want to be the *real* you—just a polished you. Dressing professionally or sending a thank-you note (which are examples of positive impression management) play an important role at work. Consider carefully the following impression management tips (de Janasz et al., 2002): "Be punctual, dress appropriately, flatter legitimately, have a good sense of humor, be friendly and approachable, and make friends" (p. 204).

Be Prepared for Any Type of Interview

You cannot always predict which type of interview you will have. In the course of job hunting, you may experience one or all of the following types.

The Nonstructured Interview   In the **nonstructured interview** you are usually expected to take most of the initiative during the interview. Expect to be asked open-ended questions (such as "Tell me about yourself" or "Why do you feel we should hire you over other candidates who have applied for this position?") and behavioral questions (such as "What was the most difficult problem you had to overcome in your last job, and how did you solve it?"). This interviewer wants detailed, fairly long responses. To respond effectively, you must anticipate possible questions and carefully think through your responses in advance. Veruki (1999, pp. 14–17) advises applicants to develop key messages or themes to present during an interview, such as passion for the business, skills and experience, professionalism, creativity, compatibility with the job, cultural compatibility, interpersonal skills, problem-solving ability, and accomplishments. Think of what you want to say; jot down the major points if you wish, and practice aloud "until the words come easily in an organized yet comfortable, conversational way" (p. 14).This type of interview gives you a chance to demonstrate your intelligence, creativity, and ability to adapt to a difficult situation.

The Structured Interview   In the **structured interview** everything is planned in advance and you have much less opportunity to be creative in your responses. The structured interviewer follows the standard interview format discussed in Chapter 7 and asks the same basic structured questions of all applicants. This interviewer asks many direct and closed questions and wants specific, to-the-point answers. As a result, this interviewer succeeds in learning a great deal of information in a short time.

The best way to respond to the structured interviewer is to provide the most direct, forthright answers you can.

Regardless of the type of interview, remain confident yet relaxed and relate all your answers directly to the job.

Phillip Jones/iStockphoto

Keep explanations brief while still including all necessary information. However, if the interviewer suddenly becomes silent to test how you handle the unexpected, use this silence as an opportunity to expand on your key themes.

The Hostile or Stress Interview   On rare occasions, you may find an interviewer who seems to delight in constantly evaluating the interviewee, often with belittling and embarrassing comments or questions and subtle nonverbal signals. If so, you are in a **hostile or stress interview**. This interviewer either has low self-esteem and feels threatened by the interviewee or is a well organized, experienced interviewer trying to see how the interviewee handles stress to find the "real" person underneath (Yate, 2008b, pp. 214–215). Take your time, lean back in your seat, and smile. To give yourself more time to think, answer with a question such as "Why do you ask?" or "That surprises me. Why do you say that?" When possible, reply with one of your key themes. Keep your answers positive and give personal examples that present you in a positive light. As Yate advises, "Stay calm, give as good as you get, and take it all in stride. Remember that no one can intimidate you without your permission" (p. 239).

The Group Interview   As you will see in this chapter's "It Really Works" section about the Container Store, the **group interview**—including a panel or board interview—is becoming more common in both for-profit and nonprofit organizations and at all levels (Lehman & Dufrene, 2008; Edmunds, 2000). As discussed in Chapter 7, panel interviews usually have one interviewer and several interviewees; board interviews have two or more interviewers and usually only one interviewee. American Airlines uses the panel interview as a screening tool for many positions (such as reservation clerks and flight attendants) and board interviews for follow-up management interviews. Many businesses today—especially those that follow the human resources or transformational model—use team involvement in their hiring processes. These board interviews may include five or more team members who plan the questions, determine selection criteria, interview and evaluate candidates, and make "call-back" and hiring decisions (Lehman & Dufrene, 2008, p. 516). As noted in Chapter 7, some companies even use group interviews that include several interviewers and several interviewees. Unless you know for sure that your interview will not be a group interview, be prepared just in case.

The Video or Virtual Interview   For global companies, face-to-face interviews can be expensive. Therefore, "many companies, ranging from IBM, Microsoft, Nike, and Hallmark Cards, are now screening candidates through a **video or virtual interview** from remote locations and saving money and time in the process" (Lehman & DuFrene, 2008, pp. 601–602). Videoconferencing provides more information than a telephone interview and can be used for board or panel interviews with applicants around the world. In addition, a tape of the interview is available for later viewing. Vicers (1997) reports that video interviews can save as much as 15 to 20% of usual recruiting costs. The new Flip Cameras have made the interview video even easier (read one of many comments about these cameras on the Cisco Blog at http://blogs.cisco.com/tag/video).

Lehman and DuFrene (2008) suggest that you arrive early at the interview site and familiarize yourself with the equipment and camera. Of course, you will want to pay special attention to your visual image (review the previous section on impression management in Chapter 8). We suggest that you lower the camera so it is at eye

IT REALLY WORKS!

Employment Interviewing

The Container Store specializes in organization and storage. Since 1978 they've adhered to "a fundamental set of business values entered around deliberate merchandising, superior customer service and constant employee input" ("There's No Containing Our Growth," 2009). They also maintain the business model that "1 great person = 3 good people." It is this business model that most greatly affects their hiring of new employees (Jones, 2007b, p. 237).

Once an applicant begins the hiring process, he or she will first go through a group interview. "The group setting offers managers a glimpse of how candidates function as part of a team (Powers, 2004)," and once they determine which of the original applicants made the cut, they can proceed to one-on-one interviews that may take as long as 3 hours. By instituting such a rigorous interview process, the Container Store management ensures that they will be "hiring people who are self-motivated and team-oriented with a passion for customer service" ("Our Stores: The Best Service," 2009).

By using combined group and individual interviews to find those people who best fit their needs, the Container Store has managed to hire high-quality employees, provide a high level of customer service and satisfaction, and maintain a turnover rate that is 75% lower than the national average (Jones, 2007b). The Container Store has been on *Fortune* magazine's "100 Best Companies to Work For" over 10 years in a row.

What do you think?
- Based on what you've learned about the Container Store, which type of questions do you think their interviewers would prefer using—standard or behavioral questions—and why?
- Which keywords would likely make the best impression on Container Store management who are reading an applicant resume?
- Describe the nonverbal communication that Container Store interviewers would likely look for in applicants during the group interview.

level when you are sitting. When the camera is pointed downward, you are more likely to appear unfriendly and even dishonest. Lehman and DuFrene (2008, p. 517) recommend that you (a) speak clearly, (b) sit straight and make sure you are centered in the picture frame, (c) concentrate on looking up and into the camera, and (d) use gestures but avoid excessive movement that could look blurred on the videotape.

In addition to being prepared for any type of interview, you must be prepared for all probable questions.

Carefully Plan Answers to Probable Questions

One researcher (Einhorn, 1981) suggests that when answering questions, job applicants should do the following:

- Use technical jargon that is common in their field.
- Use active, positive, and concrete language.
- Support answers with specific examples, comparisons, illustrations, and statistics taken from personal experience, coworkers, supervisors, and company publications. (See Chapter 12 for an explanation of supporting materials.)
- Use humor when appropriate. If the interviewer uses humor, you can; if not, don't.
- Describe job weaknesses or physical disabilities in a positive manner.

Detailed lists of typically asked questions, as well as good and bad answers are included in many excellent books, such as *101 Great Answers to the Toughest Interview Questions* (Fry, 2006), *Knock 'em Dead: The Ultimate Job Search Guide* (Yate, 2008b), and *What Color Is Your Parachute 2009?* (Bolles, 2009).

Many questions interviewers ask are **standard questions** that are designed to determine basic skills and abilities. Anticipate these questions, plan your answers (include research specific examples and statistics in your answers), and practice your answers aloud until you feel confident about them. Here are a few typical "tough" standard questions (Bolles, 2009; Fry, 2006; Yate, 2008b):

What do you know about our company?

Why do you want to leave your current job?

What do you think of your present job?

What salary are you expecting?

Where do you want to be 5 years from now?

Describe yourself in three adjectives.

What is the best idea you've had in the last 3 years?

How would your coworkers describe you? Your supervisor describe you?

Why should we hire you over others applying for this position?

Another kind of question you may be asked is the **behavioral question**. This type of question requires you to give examples of your skills or behaviors. One method for framing your answers to behavioral questions is called SAR: *situation* or problem/task, *action*, and *result* or outcome (Hansen, 2006). Interviewers often ask behavioral questions to avoid the memorized answers that candidates sometimes give to standard questions. The Mayo Clinic is an example of a large company that uses behavioral interviews (Berry & Bendapudi, 2003). They try to avoid questions or situations that have a "right" answer; instead, their behavioral questions "probe for specific details that reflect true experiences and perspectives" (p. 102). Here are a few "tough" behavioral questions (adapted from Berry & Bendapudi, 2003; Fernandez-Araoz et al., 2009; Fry, 2006; Yate, 2008b):

If you had to give a presentation to a group of clients with only 2 hours notice, how and what would you prepare?

Suppose you were given a project that required you to interact with employees at all levels of the organization. Select three levels and explain specifically how you would communicate with each level.

Tell me about a situation in which you benefited from a personal mistake.

Explain how you saw a new project through to completion.

I'm going to describe a conflict between two employees. I want you to describe each employee's position and present a solution to the problem that might be acceptable to both.

Suppose you had an important decision to make, but the information to base it on was conflicting. How would you handle the situation?

Listening is an important employee skill. I'm going to present a brief opinion on working overtime, and I want you to demonstrate your listening ability by paraphrasing my opinion.

It is impossible to predict exactly what is going to happen during an interview, but if you take time to consider probable questions and think through your answers, your confidence and chances of success will be greatly improved. Don't think of the interview as an interrogation; instead, imagine the interview as a conversation with a fellow employee on your first day at work (Breen, 2000). Of course, your answers should always be truthful, should come from you, and should never sound memorized. Practice your interviewing by conducting several informational interviews, as discussed in Chapter 7.

Be Prepared with Questions to Ask the Interviewer

Most interviewers will invite you to ask questions. You should be prepared to ask a few—first, because you want to get enough information to decide if you really want this particular job, and second, because your questions show that you are interested. If the interviewer does not give you the opportunity to ask questions, simply say, "Excuse me, but I have a few questions I would like to ask about. . . ." Here are some questions you might want to ask (adapted from Bolles, 2009; Stewart & Cash, 2008; Yate, 2009b):

> How creative am I allowed to be on this job?
>
> Your company recently experienced a downsizing of 10% of the workforce. What has been the impact on efficiency and customer service?
>
> I know there is some turnover in every job. Approximately how many people that you hired in the last 3 to 5 years are still with the company?
>
> Would the company support me if I went back to school?
>
> What is the typical career path of an individual entering the organization at this level?
>
> Why is this job open and how many people have held this job in the last 5 years?
>
> What would be the three main results expected of me during the first year in this position?
>
> What could I do or read while you are considering my application that might help me on the job if I'm hired?
>
> How will my performance be measured by you and by higher-ups?
>
> It's been a pleasure meeting with you. Now that we've talked, I really want this job. Can you tell me what the next step will be? (Or "Can you offer me this job?" which most interviewees fail to ask, but should ask according to Richard Bolles (2009, p. 101). Although it is a bold step, it often works. If not, you can drop back to asking what the next step in the process will be).

Remember, your questions reflect your training and education, your ambitions, and your level of commitment.

Be Prepared to Follow up the Interview

Most interviews end with some plan for future action on the part of one or both of the participants. When the decision will be reached and how it will be communicated are usually specified by the interviewer. Make certain that you carry out whatever responsibility you have been assigned during the interview. If you do not hear from the company within a reasonable amount of time (usually 1 to 2 weeks), e-mail, write, or call reconfirming your interest in the position and again thank the interviewer for his or her time.

Send a Thank-You Card

Always send a **thank-you card** immediately after the interview; it could be a factor in whether you are called back for a second interview. Bring a thank-you card with you to the interview—some candidates have them already written, sealed, and stamped before the interview—and mail it on your way home. For specifics on how to write a thank-you note, see Appendix: Written Communication.

Interviewer: Planning the Interview

If you are the interviewer, you usually have more responsibility for the manner in which the employment interview is conducted than does the interviewee. Keep in mind that interviewees prefer interviewers who do the following (Jablin et al., 1987, p. 691):

1. Show high levels of nonverbal immediacy behaviors (discussed in Chapter 5), such as eye contact and an open body posture.
2. Listen to interviewee answers and limit the number of interruptions.
3. Ask open questions and allow sufficient time to answer them.

Also keep in mind that successful interviewing is difficult and requires careful preparation. In fact, poor interviewers are likely to select a candidate to hire that is less qualified than a person selected completely at random (Fernandez-Araoz et al., 2009, p. 81). However, if you follow the suggestions in this section and check references carefully, you are likely to make a wise hiring decision.

Get to Know the Interviewee Ahead of Time

Read the resume and application forms carefully (along with the background check if you have one) looking for any problem areas, and for areas needing follow-up during the interview. Review your structured interview format, making sure you have an evaluation form, which meets equal employment opportunity requirements, ready to use. You may want to search on Google or Yahoo! for the interviewee to see what other information is available, if any. Some companies also search on blog sites such as MySpace, Facebook, Xanga, or Friendster for additional information (Finder, 2006). The key is to know the applicant before he or she arrives. Regardless of whether you hire this person or not, their impression of your company and what they tell their friends about your company depends on you.

Plan the Environment

The nature of the interview usually determines the type of environment you will want to establish. In almost all instances, privacy is essential. Select an area that will be free from phone calls and distractions. The seating should be planned so that participants feel comfortable. You may want to come from behind the desk, and sit across from the interviewee, free from psychological and physical barriers. However, a recent high school or college graduate with minimal work experience may actually feel more comfortable if you remain behind your desk.

Organize the Interview Carefully

Interviewers who conduct poorly planned, unorganized employment interviews learn little useful information about the candidate. Consequently, their decisions will be based solely on gut reactions, often resulting in ineffective hiring. Such mistakes cost the company money. One researcher estimates that replacing an employee can cost as much as 1.5 times 1 year's salary (Lamb et al, 2004). As an interviewer, you cannot afford to make wrong decisions. Therefore, plan and organize each phase of the interview carefully. Some suggestions for organizing each phase are summarized here (see Chapter 7 for more detailed explanations).

Plan the Opening Phase   Establishing rapport is the first responsibility of an interviewer during the **opening phase** of an interview. The best way to establish rapport depends on the interviewee; each person should be handled individually. Your prior look at the applicant's resume and letter of application should have provided some clues as to what subject would be of most interest to the person. If you plan to establish rapport by discussing general interest topics, be careful not to overdo it—usually a minute or two of rapport-building is plenty. Your candidate may become suspicious and nervous if idle talk continues for too long. Instead of discussing general subjects, you may want to ask the applicant to verify information listed on the resume or application form or to discuss his or her reasons for wanting the particular position.

Regardless of the topic discussed, remember that your purpose is to get the applicant talking, relaxed, and ready for the interview. Also, try not to be overly dependent on your first impressions of the applicant; they could be inaccurate.

As you establish rapport, give the interviewee a brief orientation to the interview. Don't assume! Verify the interviewee's name and the position sought. State your name and the reason you are the one conducting the interview. Give a clear overview of the job and any responsibilities connected with it. Once the specific job has been clarified, the interviewee may no longer be interested; if so, you have saved yourself valuable time. If the applicant is still interested, clarify the type of information you are specifically interested in and the type of responses you prefer—detailed or brief answers. Give the applicant a general idea of the length of the interview and ask whether that is agreeable.

Don't conclude the opening phase of the interview before motivating the applicant to give you candid, carefully thought-out answers. Most applicants are already motivated simply because they want the job. However, they may feel a need to impress you by pretending to have qualities or characteristics they don't have. Tell applicants that you are sure they are as interested as you are in finding a position in which they will be most successful and that to help you place them accurately, you want them to answer all questions honestly and to put aside false modesty.

Plan the Question-Response Phase   Asking whatever question comes to mind is an extremely ineffective way to learn and remember information about the applicant. The skilled interviewer decides what general areas (such as past work experience, leadership abilities, and personality characteristics) should be covered in the **question-response phase** of the interview and then plans specific questions for each area. For example, if the personality characteristics of your company's ideal employee include sociability, stability, leadership, maturity, and industriousness, you would need to plan a series of questions designed to help you rate the applicants on each category. To determine the industriousness of a sales candidate you might ask these standard questions:

Tell me about your first job.

How many jobs have you held since you left school and which one did you enjoy the most?

How many clients did you service in your last position?

How often did you see these clients?

What were your sales for the past year? Preceding year?

The real heart of a quality interview includes behavioral questions which ask candidates "to describe specific experiences they've had that are similar to situations they'll be facing in your organization" (Fernandez-Araoz et al., 2009, p. 81). For example, a behavioral question to determine the industriousness of a sales candidate might include this question: "Describe a time when sales were down and what steps you took to generate new or repeat sales."

To remember data and to comply with Equal Employment Opportunity Commission (EEOC) regulations, interviewers must keep an accurate record of each interviewee. For example, a rating of 1–5 or "well above average" to "well below average" could be given for each characteristic or topic area such as maturity or industriousness. Another example of rating scales comes from a sample form prepared by HRdirect.com: When evaluating education and training, the answers could include:

☐ Has no education or training relevant to this position.

☐ Has limited education or training relevant to this position.

☐ Education and training are relevant and adequate for this position.

☐ More education and training than the average applicant for this position.

☐ Education and training are outstanding and directly related to this position ("Applicant Interview," 1998).

To locate additional interviewee evaluation forms, go to Google.com and type in "job applicant rating form" and search until you find one that is a close fit for your position. Adapt it or combine several forms making sure that all evaluation areas are lawful. Software such as Microsoft Inpath 2007 allows for creation of a template for rating job applicants that could include various skills to be assessed for such general headings as job experience, applicant preparation for interview, and academics.

Most employment interviewers organize their questions for each general area into the funnel sequence (described in Chapter 7), which begins with open-ended questions and ends with direct or closed questions. Open-ended questions at the beginning of the interview usually relax the applicant, uncover a great deal of information (which means the interviewer will not have to ask so many questions), and reveal areas that need to be investigated in more detail. Organized questions will allow you, the interviewer, to make a more valid assessment of the applicant. Notes of important job-related information taken discreetly during the interview and written in the appropriate spot on the applicant rating form will further help you in your assessment.

Plan the Closing Phase   The **closing phase** of the interview is as important as the opening, for you will want to make sure the interviewee leaves with a positive feeling and an accurate understanding of what will happen next. Let the applicant know that the interview is ending by summarizing its content and outlining the times and nature of any future contact. Give the interviewee a chance to ask questions, and thank the interviewee for his or her time and cooperation.

Interviewer: Conducting the Interview

Although careful planning for each interview goes a long way in assuring interview success, it is crucial that interviewers conduct the interview carefully as well. For example, asking only lawful questions, listening carefully to the answers interviewers give, and asking appropriate follow-up questions are three important areas discussed in this section.

Ask Only Lawful Questions

In accordance with federal and state laws (see note page 230),* interviewers cannot ask certain questions of applicants during preemployment interviews. These laws are based on the belief that all persons—regardless of race, sex, national origin, religion, age, or marital status—should be able to compete for jobs and advance in the job market based on what the law terms their "bona fide occupational qualifications": experience, education, and specific skills. An employer does not have to hire anyone who is not qualified, but race, sex, national origin, religion, age (in most cases), disabilities, or marital status cannot be used to determine whether a person is qualified (except in rare instances in which an employer can prove that one of these traits is job-related). Thus, skills, experience, and education are the only factors that should be used to determine whether a person is qualified for a particular job.

There are two basic **EEOC guidelines** to follow in deciding the legality of an interview question (whether it's asked during the interview or included on the application form):

1. *All questions must be job related.* The interviewer must be prepared to prove that the questions are related to the specific job.

2. *The same basic questions must be asked of all applicants for the position.* In other words, an interviewer cannot have one set of questions for minorities, another for women, and still another for white males.

Using these two guidelines, answer the questions in the Awareness Check on page 224. (These questions are often asked in interviews and found on application forms.) Determine whether these questions would be considered lawful if used by the average organization. Then compare your answers with those in the back of this book. Be sure to read the discussion provided with each answer; additional questions are covered there as well.

You may have discovered while checking your answers that what seemed fair or reasonable to you may not be considered fair or reasonable in the eyes of the law. As an interviewer, you must depend on court rulings and not on personal opinions. Court rulings are constantly changing the interpretations of various laws, so stay up to date. Check with the *Federal Register* or an Equal Employment Opportunity website regularly. Some of the answers we have given here may have already changed. Ask your placement director or personnel supervisor about possible changes.

Keep in mind that it is illegal in the United States to unfairly discriminate "in any aspect of employment" (not just in hiring practices) when race, color, religion, sex, national origin, disability, or age are involved. The areas covered include "hiring and firing; compensation, assignment, or classification of employees; transfer, promotion, layoff, or recall; job advertisements; recruitment; testing; use of company facilities; training and apprenticeship programs; fringe benefits; pay, retirement plans, and disability leave; or other terms and conditions of employment" (EEOC, 2004), If you find job applicants are answering any of your questions in the ways listed, you need to review your questions for possible discriminatory content (Bolles, 2009; Jablin & Tengler, 1982; Stewart & Cash, 2008; Wilson, 1991):

Less Effective Answers to Unlawful Questions

- Silence.
- "That's illegal; you can't ask me that."
- "I prefer not to answer that question at this time."

AWARENESS CHECK

Lawful and Unlawful Questions

Discover your knowledge of unlawful questions by taking the following quiz.* Compare your answers to those at the back of this book. You can also take this quiz online through your Premium Website for *Communicating for Results*.

Directions: For each of the questions and statements below, select *L* for those you feel are lawful, *U* for those that seem unlawful, and *Q* for those that seem questionable (could be either lawful or unlawful depending on the situation).

_____ 1. What is your wife's maiden name?

_____ 2. Are you a citizen of the United States?

_____ 3. Have you ever been arrested?

_____ 4. Do you play golf?

_____ 5. How old are you?

_____ 6. Would you be willing to submit a copy of your birth certificate or baptismal record to prove your date of birth?

_____ 7. How many words per minute do you type on the keyboard?

_____ 8. Do you have any physical disabilities?

_____ 9. Have you ever been fired from a previous job?

_____ 10. What work experiences have you had that adequately prepared you for this job?

_____ 11. Tell me about your educational background and your grade point average.

_____ 12. Are you married, divorced, or single?

_____ 13. Do you have any children? Are you planning on having any children?

_____ 14. What foreign language(s) do you speak, read, or write fluently?

_____ 15. What personal qualities do you have that you think would be helpful in working with the people within our organization?

_____ 16. What type of discharge did you get from the service?

_____ 17. What are the names and addresses of your parents, grandparents, or other relatives?

_____ 18. Please include a photograph with your application form.

_____ 19. What religious holidays do you observe?

_____ 20. What office machines can you operate?

_____ 21. What club or organization memberships do you hold?

_____ 22. Do you own your own home?

_____ 23. What is your weight, height, and color of eyes, hair, and complexion?

_____ 24. You sound Oriental. Are you from Taiwan?

_____ 25. Can you get along with people of different races?

*Adapted and updated from M. Bordwin, 1998, The courts get you coming and going. *Management Review,* 87(10), 51–53; J. Boyd, 1999, Wrong questions can turn job interview into lawsuit. *Business Journal, 14*(11), 29–30; J. G. Frierson, 1987, National origin discrimination: The next wave of lawsuits. *Personnel Journal, 66,* 97–108; "How to Conduct a Lawful Employment Interview," 1987, Des Moines: Batten, Batten, Hudson and Swab; V. A. Hoevemeyer, 2005, *High-Impact Interview Questions: 701 Behavior-based questions to find the right person for every job.* New York: AMACOM; F. M. Jablin & C. D. Tengler, 1982, Facing discrimination in on-campus interviews. *Journal of College Placement,* 57–61; R. L. Minter, 1972, Human rights laws and pre-employment inquiries. *Personnel Journal,* 431–433; N. L. Perkins, 1991, What you need to know about the Americans with Disabilities Act. *Supervisory Management,* 4–5; N. L. Perkins,1992, *Americans with Disabilities Act.* New York: Wiley; G. L. Wilson, 1991, Preparing students for responding to illegal selection interview questions. *The Bulletin of the Association for Business Communication,* 47–48; and M. Yate, 2008b, *Knock 'em dead: The ultimate job search guide 2009.* Avon, MA: Adams Media.

- Ignoring the legality of the question and giving a candid answer. (Although employers may prefer this answer, why should applicants give information that may be used against them? Also, if applicants continue to answer unlawful questions, interviewers will continue to ask them.)

More Effective Answers to Unlawful Questions

- "I'm not clear on how that relates to my ability to handle this job. Could you clarify it for me?"

- With sincerity, the applicant asks the same question of the interviewer. For example, if the interviewer asks if the applicant has children: "Yes, I have two lovely children. They are such a joy, aren't they? Do you have children?"

- Laughter, and then, "Is having children a requirement for this job?"

Answering the fear behind the question, not the question itself. For example:

Q: Do you have plans for a family?

A: If what you are concerned with is my ability to manage or my commitment to my job, I can assure you that I am quite aware of the job's responsibilities and take them seriously.

A: If you are concerned about my regular attendance, let me assure you that I have only missed 1 day of work in the last 3 years, and on that day I had the flu.

Q: Do you have any physical disabilities?

A: Any disabilities I may possess would not interfere with my ability to perform all aspects of this position.

As well as being careful to ask only lawful questions, you must be careful to listen to the person you are interviewing.

Listen Carefully to the Interviewee

It is fairly easy for an employment interviewer to become so preoccupied with the tasks of the interview that he or she forgets to listen carefully to what the applicant is saying. As an interviewer, you need to be aware of the mistakes that poor listeners tend to make. Some of the more common ones are listed here.

- Being distracted by something in the environment (e.g., a stack of letters that must be read before quitting time).

ETHICAL DILEMMA

Bloggers were partly responsible for the action taken by the board of directors when it was reported that the CEO of RadioShack had falsified information on his resume (see the opening case study). Most people see this as a good thing. However, the *Wall Street Journal* reports that some bloggers are now posting embarrassing and sensitive information about their place of employment on the Internet (Mattioli, 2009). In the case of the law firm Schwabe, Williamson & Wyatt, information about lay off plans appeared online less than 41 minutes after the first employees were notified but before all those being laid off had been notified. In the case of Yahoo Inc., their plans to cut costs and lay off employees, as well as the actual e-mail sent to managers on how to handle the lay offs were published on the blog Valleyway.com. Neither the law firm nor Yahoo was able to locate the persons responsible for the leak. Mattioli reports that a recent survey of 586 U. S. employees found that 14% admitted to sending "potentially embarrassing company emails to outsiders" (2009, p. B4).

The question is what can companies do to stop these leaks? Mattioli (2009) reports the following actions taken so far:

- Install software such as *Optenet* that blocks e-mail sent to certain addresses and scans e-mail attachments.

- Block employees from using personal e-mail accounts.

- Actively locate and fire those who leak sensitive information.

- Hope that once the economy recovers from the 2009 recession that leaks will greatly diminish.

- Change communication practices—send internal messages to employees at the same time (rather than before) the information is released to the media.

Questions: What do you think? Is leaking sensitive information unethical? Refer to the Four Ethical Rules and the Practical Reasons for Being Ethical" section in Chapter 1 in making your decision. What are the advantages and disadvantages of the above steps taken to block information leaks? Should a new interview question be: Have you ever posted embarrassing or sensitive information about your company or management to a blog or social networking site?

- Listening only for the factual parts of the applicant's responses (ignoring the applicant's feelings toward these facts and the reasons behind the facts).

- Becoming so overstimulated by something the applicant says (such as a belief that all students should work while attending college) that you miss his or her following comments.

- Getting upset when the applicant uses emotional words.

- Making snap judgments about the applicant's worth based on only one or two comments.

- Failing to follow up on important information.

Additional listening errors were covered in Chapter 4. We suggest that you reread that chapter carefully in preparation for an interview.

Remember, you can't listen while you're talking! Allow the interviewee to do most of the talking—while *you* listen. Researchers have discovered that interviewers generally talk more than interviewees in many interview situations.

Clarify and Verify Responses; Avoid False Inferences

Even interviewers who listen carefully can make mistakes when they assume they understand exactly what the interviewee means. In Chapter 1, we stated that everyone receives messages through their own frame of reference. Because the interviewee and the interviewer have different frames of reference, each may misinterpret the other's meanings.

When a statement is unclear, the interviewer should *clarify* the interviewee's response by asking questions. Ask a question when you don't understand exactly what the applicant is talking about. For example, you might say, "I'm not sure I understand. Would you explain . . . ?" Sometimes you may understand what the applicant is saying but fail to understand the reason behind it. In this case, you might say, "I understand what you are saying, but I don't think I quite understand why you feel this is important. Why *do* you feel it's so important?" Even when the applicant's statement seems clear, the interviewer should *verify* the response by paraphrasing— repeating the statement in your own words to see if you understood correctly. You might say, "Then what you are saying is. . . . Is that correct?" or "Are you saying . . . ?"

It is easy for interviewers to confuse inference with facts (see "Jumping to Conclusions" in Chapter 6) and reach a costly hiring error due to **false inference**. To avoid making hiring errors as a result of false inferences, be careful to base your decisions on real facts and not on inferred or assumed information. Ask for clarification and verification of interviewee comments.

Employment Interview

Elliott Miller, job applicant in the following excerpt from a job interview, is trying to follow the guidelines we've discussed in this chapter. He dresses appropriately, arrives on time, and does a good job answering some tough interview questions. What techniques does he use to answer his questions that impress his interviewer, Karen Bourne?

You can go to your Premium Website for *Communicating for Results* to answer this question online and, if requested, e-mail your responses to your instructor. You can also watch a video clip of this Communication Situation and further critique the interaction between Elliott Miller and Karen Bourne.

Cengage Learning

Bourne: Mr. Miller, I see you're right on time. That's a good start. [They shake hands.]

Miller: Thank you for inviting me to interview today.

Bourne: Sit down. [He sits in the chair in front of her desk; she sits behind the desk.] So you're about to finish college, are you? I remember that time in my own life—exciting and scary!

Miller: It's definitely both for me. I'm particularly excited about the job here at Community Savings and Loan.

Bourne: [smiles] Then there's a mutual interest. We had a lot of applications, but we're interviewing only eight of them. What I'd like to do is get a sense of your interests and tell you about our managerial trainee program here, so that we can see if the fit between us is as good as it looks on paper. Sound good to you?

Miller: Great.

Bourne: Let me start by telling you about a rather common problem we've had with our past managerial trainees. Many of them run into a problem—something they have trouble learning or doing right. That's normal enough—we expect that. But a lot of trainees seem to get derailed when that happens. Instead of finding another way to approach the problem, they get discouraged and give up. So I'm very interested in hearing what you've done when you've encountered problems or roadblocks in your life.

Miller: Well, I can remember one time when I hit a real roadblock. I was taking an advanced chemistry course, and I just couldn't seem to understand the material. I failed the first exam, even though I'd studied hard.

Bourne: Good example of a problem. What did you do?

Miller: I started going to all the tutorial sessions that grad assistants offered. That helped a little, but I still wasn't getting the material the way I should. So I organized a study team and offered to pay for pizzas so that students who were on top of the class would have a reason to come.

Bourne: [nodding with admiration] That shows a lot of initiative and creativity. Did the study team work?

Miller: [smiling] It sure did. I wound up getting a B in the course, and so did several other members of the study team who had been in the same boat I was in early in the semester.

Bourne: So you don't mind asking for help if you need it?

Miller: I'd rather do that than flounder, but I'm usually pretty able to operate independently.

Bourne: So you prefer working on your own to working with others?

Miller: That depends on the situation or project. If I have all that I need to do something on my own, I'm comfortable working solo. But there are other cases in which I don't have everything I need to do something well—maybe I don't have experience in some aspect of the job or I don't have a particular skill or I don't understand some perspectives on the issues. In cases like that, I think teams are more effective than individuals.

Bourne: Good. Banking management requires the ability to be self-initiating and also the ability to work with others. Let me ask another question. As I was looking over your transcript and resume, I noticed that you changed your major several times. Does that indicate you have difficulty making a commitment and sticking with it?

Miller: I guess you could think that, but it really shows that I was willing to explore a lot of alternatives before making a firm commitment.

Bourne: But don't you think that you wasted a lot of time and courses getting to that commitment?

Miller: I don't think so. I learned something in all of the courses I took. For instance, when I was a philosophy major, I learned about logical thinking and careful reasoning. That's going to be useful to me in management. When I was majoring in English, I learned how to write well and how to read others' writing critically. That's going to serve me well in management, too.

Bourne: So what led you to your final decision to double major in business and communication? That's kind of an unusual combination.

Miller: It seems a very natural one to me. I wanted to learn about business because I want to be a manager in an organization. I need to know how organizations work, and I need to understand different management philosophies and styles. At the same time, managers work with people, and that means I have to have strong communication skills.

CHAPTER 8
REVIEW

Adam Gregor/iStockphoto

Key Terms

behavioral questions (218)

chronological resume (207)

closing phase (222)

combination resume (207)

controlling style (213)

conventional paper resume (207)

distortion (211)

EEOC guidelines (223)

e-mail resume (209)

e-portfolio (210)

exaggeration (211)

false inference (226)

functional resume (207)

group interview (216)

hostile or stress interview (216)

hybrid resume (207)

information-seeking interview (206)

keyword summary (209)

letter of application (211)

impression management (213)

network (205)

nonstructured interview (215)

opening phase (221)

qualifications summary (209)   standard questions (218)   thank-you card (219)

question-response phase (221)   structured interview (215)   video or virtual interview (216)

scannable resume (209)   submissive style (213)   web resume (210)

Summary

Both the job-seeking interviewee and the employment interviewer have specific responsibilities if meaningful communication is to occur. Interviewees are responsible for preparing job-hunting tools and preparing for the interview. Preparing job-hunting tools includes: investigating the employment market, preparing one or more resumes including conventional, scannable, ASCII, and web resumes, preparing letters of application, and checking resume content for accuracy and honesty. Preparing for the interview includes having a positive attitude, dressing for the best effect, anticipating various types of interviews, planning answers to possible questions, as well as, questions to ask the interviewer, and following up the interview and sending a thank-you card.

Interviewers are responsible for carefully planning and organizing the interview ahead of time, asking necessary (but lawful) questions, listening carefully to the interviewee, clarifying and verifying responses, and avoiding false inferences. The interviewer perhaps has the greatest responsibility for the success of the interview. Interviews that are poorly planned, poorly organized, and poorly executed result in neither participant learning anything valuable about the other. Often the wrong person is hired for the job—a costly mistake for everyone involved.

The practical advice offered in this chapter should help you make your next interviews more productive.

Communicating for Results Online

Before continuing to the next chapter, check your understanding of Chapter 8 at the Premium Website for *Communicating for Results*. Your Premium Website gives you quick and easy access to the electronic resources that accompany this text. These resources include:

- **Study tools** that will help you assess your learning and prepare for exams (student companion workbook, digital glossary, key term flash cards, and review quizzes).

- **Activities and assignments** that will help you hone your knowledge, analyze professional communication situations, build your public speaking skills throughout the course, and learn to work effectively in teams (Awareness Checks, Checkpoints, and Collaborative Learning Activities).

- **Media resources** that will help you explore communication concepts online (web links), develop your speech outlines (Speech Builder Express 3.0), watch and critique videos of professional

communication situations and sample speeches (Interactive Video Activities), upload your speech videos for peer reviewing and critique other students' speeches (Speech Studio online speech review tool), and download chapter review so you can study when and where you'd like (Audio Study Tools).

This chapter's key terms, Collaborative Learning Activities, and Checkpoint activities are also featured on the following pages, and you can find this chapter's Awareness Check activities in the body of the chapter. For more information or to access this book's online resources, visit www.cengage.com/login.

Collaborative Learning Activities

1. Form into groups of four or six then further divide into teams of two. Each person should prepare a resume or list of education, work experiences, and desired job or career. Exchange lists/resumes and plan three standard and three behavioral questions that relate to the personal

information received. Either face-to-face, by telephone, or in front of a larger group, each group member will interview the other. (If a speaker phone is available, have each team member separated by a wall of some sort conducting interviews by phone with the conversation available on speaker phone for an audience.) If possible, video tape the interviews for later viewing possibly using a Flip Camera. If there is an audience, share a strength and weakness of each person as interviewer and interviewee. If not, each team should comment on the strengths and weaknesses they saw in each other and in themselves.

2. In small groups, select five interview questions (three included in this chapter and two that you create) and write both good and bad answers to each question. Be prepared to explain what makes each answer either a good or bad one.

3. In small groups and without looking at the answers ahead of time, complete the Awareness Check on page 224. Try to come to a group agreement on each question. When finished, check your answers with those provided at the end of the text. As a group, discuss those questions that you missed. Refer to the two rules used by the EEOC in determining the legality of questions. Share any problems with other groups.

Checkpoints

Checkpoint 8.1 Analyzing Application Forms
Write or phone for application forms from prominent firms in your community. Take a careful look at the form used in your current organization. Analyze each form carefully and evaluate the appropriateness and effectiveness of each. Are any unlawful questions included?

Checkpoint 8.2 Applying for a Position

Checkpoint 8.3 Conventional, Scannable, and E-mail (ASCII) Resumes

Checkpoint 8.4 Preparing and Practicing Answers to Interview Questions

Checkpoint 8.5 Employment Interview Links

Note from page 223:
*Federal legislation and guidelines include Title VII of the Civil Rights Act of 1964, amended 1972; the Age Discrimination in Employment Act of 1967 (ADEA), amended 1978; the Equal Pay Act of 1963, amended 1972; the Equal Employment Opportunity Act of 1972; OFCC (Office of Federal Compliance Commission) Affirmative Action Guidelines of 1972; the Rehabilitation Act of 1973; the Vietnam Era Veterans Readjustment Act of 1974 (VEVRAA), amended 1980, and in 1999 to include veterans of World War II, Korea, the Persian Gulf War, Somalia, and Bosnia; the Immigration Reform and Control Act of 1986 (IRCA); the EEOC 1987 policy statement regarding national origin, discrimination and IRCA; the Americans with Disabilities Act of 1990 (ADA), amended in 2009 to include a broader coverage of individuals; and the Civil Rights Act of 1991, which provides monetary damages to employees in cases of intentional discrimination. Many states have employment laws stricter than the federal laws. Check the *Federal Register* for current federal rulings.

Small-Group Communication and Problem Solving

Walter Hodges/Getty Images

Case Study: Groupthink and the *Columbia* Space Shuttle Disaster

9

As you read Chapter 9,

Define the term *small group*, and **list** the uses and values of teams in the effective organization.

Briefly **describe** the seven characteristics of successful problem-solving teams, and **determine** which ones are normally the most important and why.

List the steps of the basic problem-solving procedure, including how to use criteria correctly in step 5, and **determine** which steps are the most crucial to successful problem solving.

Briefly **describe** these group formats: round-table, panel, symposium, and forum.

Most teams who produce faulty solutions have a chance to correct their errors and try again. That wasn't the case for the NASA personnel responsible for the safe return of the space shuttle *Columbia*. In 2003, the shuttle's seven astronauts were killed when it disintegrated upon reentry, disabled by a crack in its left wing heat shield that allowed superheated air of 5,000° F to penetrate and melt the aluminium wing spar (*Columbia* Accident Investigation Board [CAIB], 2003, p. 12). This problem began during liftoff, "when a suitcase-sized piece of foam weighing 1.67 pounds peeled off the massive external tank" and hit the wing (Borenstein, 2006). However, the extensive damage to the wing couldn't be seen clearly from the liftoff photos. In addition, a complete inspection of the damage and discussion of options for the safe return of the crew were hampered by multiple communication problems, including several symptoms of *groupthink*, which is an uncritical way of thinking that is characteristic of some groups.

On the day of the launch, NASA's Intercenter Photo Working Group began normal viewing of launch photos from the many tracking cameras. The next day, they observed possible debris striking the wing, and fearing serious damage, contacted the Shuttle Program to request closer imagery of the wing. Engineers and program managers began exchanging e-mails to assess the damage and discuss possible action plans. However, program managers sent out various memos stating that "the strike posed no safety issues" and that "there was no need for a review to be conducted over the weekend," because Monday was a holiday (CAIB, 2003, p. 142).

Why would the program managers conclude there was no real danger before any official report was issued? According to the *Columbia* Accident Investigation Board

AP Photo/NASA

As you read this chapter, see if you can (a) identify which symptoms of groupthink contributed to this disaster; (b) determine what role e-mail played in the engineers' attempts to communicate; and (c) explain why the CAIB report summary stated, "We are convinced that the management practices overseeing the Space Shuttle Program were as much a cause of the accident as the foam that struck the left wing" (CAIB, 2003, p. 11).

(CAIB) report, among other reasons, the Shuttle Program labeled the foam loss as an "action" rather than an "in-flight anomaly," giving the impression that the loss of foam, a normal occurrence during flights, was "not a safety-of-flight" issue (p. 137) and NASA's safety culture was unjustifiably optimistic, as well as complacent and overly risk oriented (pp. 180–181).

Nevertheless, on that Monday, 30 NASA engineers and contractors of the newly formed Debris Assessment Team met, looked at the available evidence, and agreed that they needed additional images to clarify the severity of the damage. The team sent an e-mail to the shuttle engineering manager, requesting that the astronauts try to visually locate the strike. When they'd received no reply, they sent a second, more urgent, message: "Can we petition (beg) for outside agency assistance?" (Glanz & Schwartz, 2003, para. 27). It took two days for the shuttle engineering manager to reply that management had decided against seeking additional images. Astonished, the team asked why, and the engineering manager told them, "I'm not going to be Chicken Little about this" (paras. 30–31). The team wrote an angry reply but decided not to send it, remembering that "engineers were often told not to send messages much higher than their own rung in the ladder" (para. 36).

The engineering manager wasn't the only one to fail to take the team's requests seriously. For example, one NASA manager noted, "As engineers, they're always going to want more information" (Glanz & Schwartz, 2003, paras. 4 & 26). In another instance, in a meeting where Boeing engineers had concluded that "the shuttle probably took the hit without experiencing fatal damage," a NASA engineer who wanted to discuss remaining areas of uncertainty, was cut off by the chair of the shuttle mission management team and no further mention of the wing area was made in the meeting (para. 45).

In another attempt, some of the team members contacted a United Space Alliance manager with their concerns. In response, he phoned the Department of Defense (DOD) Manned Space Flight Support Office to request additional imagery of *Columbia* while it was in orbit. Later e-mail obtained by the CAIB "shows that the Defense Department had begun to implement [this] request" (CAIB, p. 150). However, a later discussion between the DOD, the chair of the shuttle mission management team, and other program managers resulted in the cancellation of the request. The following day, the team tried again by contacting mission operations about obtaining more images of the wing damage via spy satellites. Mission operations, impressed by the team's concerns, presented them to a *Columbia* flight director, who said he'd see what he could do. However, after speaking with the mission management team, he determined there was no reason for additional images, saying, "I consider it to be a dead issue" (Glanz & Schwartz, 2003, para. 7).

The shuttle tragedy resulted in major restructuring and policy changes at NASA. Following CAIB's recommendations, NASA "has reached agreements with outside agencies to take images during every flight. And 11 of the 15 top shuttle managers have been reassigned . . . or have retired" (Glanz & Schwartz, 2003, para. 66).

To download the CAIB report, go to nasa.gov and type in "Columbia accident investigation board report" in the search window. For easy access to the NASA website link, go to your Premium Website for *Communicating for Results*.

Have you ever been a member or leader of a committee or other small group and found it an unsatisfying experience? Have you thought to yourself, "No one cares about my opinion," as the engineers in our opening case did? If so, you may be one of many people who seldom use groups because they feel that, although teams sound good in theory, in reality they fail to work effectively.

Of course, there are times when an individual is more effective than a group. For example, an individual can make decisions more quickly, which can be crucial when time is short. And many individuals in managerial positions certainly have enough expertise and experience to make the right decision for others. It would be ridiculous to appoint a committee to make the minor, daily decisions necessary to run an office.

On the other hand, there are many times when teams can be more effective than individuals. Consider some of these advantages of group decision making (Beebe & Masterson, 2006; Bowen, 1981; Newstrom & Davis, 1996):

- Resistance to change is reduced, and decisions that are arrived at jointly are usually better received because members are committed to the solution and therefore are more willing to support it.

- Group decisions may be superior to, and more accurate than, individual decisions because people with different viewpoints give input making the amount of information greater.

- Because decisions are better, they may be more readily accepted by those outside the group.

- Personal satisfaction and job morale are greater.

- Hostility and aggression are significantly reduced.

- Productivity is increased.

- Responsibility for the decision is diffused, so there is less risk for any individual. This is especially important when the solution is unpopular or unpleasant.

The problem with group decision making, both in the business world and in society in general, is that often neither the leader of the team nor the participants know how to work effectively as a group. To prepare you for managing and participating in teams in business and professional environments, this chapter emphasizes problem-solving techniques; Chapter 10 will discuss how to be an effective group leader and participant.

Definition of a Small Group

Three characteristics define a small group or team: size, type of interaction, and action. **Small-group communication** involves a small number of people, usually engaged in face-to-face interaction, actively working together toward a common goal.

1. *A small number of people* (the optimum size is five). A group of fewer than three people usually has difficulty supplying enough information for efficient decisions. A group of more than eight makes it difficult for everyone to participate freely. Five is considered the most productive size for a small group because it is large enough to supply needed information and to share the workload, yet small enough to give each member a chance for maximum participation. (In business, however, groups of 15 or 20 are common—perhaps explaining why groups often seem to function slowly and poorly.) Having an uneven number of people in a group is also a good idea because it can prevent votes from ending in ties.

2. *Face-to-face interaction.* This is simply a meeting that occurs in the presence of all the group members. The importance of this characteristic should not be overlooked. A successful virtual team meeting conducted by e-mail, teleconference, or videoconference would be much more difficult because of the lack of instant feedback and the absence of nonverbal cues to meaning. In fact experts on virtual teams recommend that teams will be more successful if they have met at least once face-to-face and multiple times throughout a project is preferred (Davis & Scaffidi, 2007).

3. *Actively working together toward a common goal.* Just having the same goal is not enough. To be classified as a group or team, members must be working together to achieve the common goal.

According to this definition, four people discussing politics while waiting for a bus to take them downtown would not constitute a small group. They may be engaged in face-to-face interaction and have the same goal (to catch the bus), but they are not working together toward that goal. However, if the bus failed to arrive, and the people discussed how they were all going to get downtown—walk or share their money for a taxi—they then would be considered a small group.

Use and Value of Teams in the Effective Organization

A brief look at business surveys indicates that the small-group team (e.g., the committee, task force, quality circle, or performance team) may be one of the most often used communication methods within organizations:

- It is estimated that by 2010 over 75% of the U.S. workforce will work in teams of some sort (Shockley-Zalabak, 2009, p. 194).

- A global, cross-functional team successfully designed the website for GE Global eX-change Services "so it would have the same simple, intuitive-looking feel in English, French, Spanish, German, and Italian (Williams, 2007, p. 317). Today the website (gxs.com) is used successfully in 58 countries.

- Team suggestions at a Cleveland Maytag plant caused production to double, yearly production costs to drop by $7 million, and required on-hand inventory to drop by $10 million (Williams, 2003, p. 578).

- Rubbermaid created 20 cross-functional teams of five to seven people to develop new products. In 1 year the teams developed over 365 new products. The problem now is not finding innovative product ideas, but deciding which new product ideas to select (Jones, 2007b, p. 225).

- At Honeywell's Industrial Automation and Control plant in Phoenix, quality control decisions by employee teams lowered defect rates by 70% (Daft & Marcic, 2006).

- The new Windows 7 operating system by Microsoft has many outstanding "Wow!" features created by an "eclectic team of architects, industrial designers, and writers" (Rockwood, 2009, p. 56). The task bar with its "sheet-of-glass effect" and icons that glow when you hover over them and trail along with you when you move is one of these features.

Because group communication is one of the most often used methods of communication within the organization, let's take a look at the three categories of groups generally used:

1. **Learning groups** are involved in seeking or sharing information—for example, a department conference of the supervisor and the department employees, a management-training seminar, or an orientation group for new employees.

2. **Self-maintenance groups** seek to inspire desirable attitudes, understanding, and communication patterns rather than merely to inform. Companies that project a corporate culture use self-maintenance groups to train employees to interact, feel, and communicate as team members.

3. **Problem-solving groups** make a series of decisions in an attempt to solve a particular problem:

   Decision making refers to the act of choosing among options that already exist. Problem solving is a more comprehensive, multi-step procedure through which a group develops a plan to move from an unsatisfactory state to a desired goal. Problem solving usually requires a group to make numerous decisions, but it also involves creating or discovering alternatives, not just choosing among them. (Galanes & Adams, 2010, p. 232)

   Some examples of problem-solving teams are a group of purchasing representatives discussing how to expedite critically needed materials from a subcontracting firm behind in deliveries; a quality circle suggesting ways to improve the general work environment; or a group of supervisors trying to figure out how to increase production in their departments without sacrificing quality. Problem-solving groups can have tremendous influence on others, as the passengers on United Airlines Flight 93 from Newark did on September 11, 2001. After four hijackers took over the plane, and the passengers realized from cell phone calls that these hijackers were likely on another suicide mission similar to the previous crashes into the Pentagon and the World Trade Center, Todd Beamer and others decided to take action. They discussed what to do and even voted on various courses of action. Over an open cell phone, Todd Beamer was heard to say, "Are you ready? Okay, let's roll." A few minutes later the phone went dead as the plane crashed into the ground near Shanksville, Pennsylvania (Beamer & Abraham, 2002). The plane had been headed toward Washington, D.C.—possibly for the White House.

   Because problem solving is the most complicated yet most often used type of team process, this chapter concentrates on various problem-solving procedures.

Characteristics of Effective Problem-Solving Teams

Successful problem-solving teams have seven basic characteristics in common. They (a) are well organized, (b) receive periodic training, (c) examine assumptions and opinions, (d) evaluate possible solutions, (d) avoid groupthink, (e) manage cultural diversity, and (f) operate virtually. Let's look at each of these characteristics in more detail.

Effective Teams Are Well Organized

Researchers generally agree that groups following an organized procedure are more productive (Hirokawa & Rost, 1992). In fact, organized teams are more likely to avoid sloppy thinking, have fewer problems and negative behaviors, handle conflicts better, build on the strengths of members, and feel more empowered (Jarboe, 1996; Poole, 1991).

This does not mean that all groups follow exactly the same procedure, nor that they always move smoothly from step to step. Researchers have found that although effective groups tend to move toward a solution in a "linear" fashion, the actual process appears to be accomplished in a "cyclical" manner (Poole & Roth, 1989; Segal, 1982). In other words, "forward movement toward a solution is sometimes accompanied by backward steps to anchor ideas in prior discussion, and lateral moves to consolidate the thinking of all members" (Brilhart, 1978, pp. 120–121; see also Galanes & Adams, 2010, Chapter 9). Effective teams follow an organized procedure, but they aren't overly rigid; some overlapping and backtracking can be expected.

Effective Teams Receive Periodic Training

One way to ensure the failure of a problem-solving team is to not train the leader and participants in problem solving. Research shows that group productivity can be improved when group training is improved (Pfeffer & Veiga, 1999). John Deere, based in Moline, Illinois, certainly thinks so. One of the things John Deere implemented to turn around their high losses in the 1990s and to create a "work smarter" environment was employee training. Now, not only are John Deere's employees some of the most skilled and productive in the industry, but their self-managed work teams have also cut manufacturing costs by 10% and reduced customer complaints as well (Jones, 2007b, pp. 222–223).

In discussing needed resources for self-managing teams, two professors of organizational behavior said the following:

> Team members need to be trained in basic problem-solving and group-dynamic skills. Over time, the employees' skill base should be broadened to include statistical quality control, conflict resolution and other useful problem-solving tools. Training in the philosophy of participation, responsibility, and management-worker cooperation is also essential. . . . Keep in mind that it is necessary to continue providing training as new workers and managers enter the system; to periodically "retrain"; and, especially, to reinforce the training over time. (Sims & Dean, 1985, p. 31)

Periodic training is especially important for virtual teams (Robey et al., 2000; Wardell, 1998). In addition to the training needed by all teams—basic problem solving, conflict resolution, trust building, and intercultural, nonverbal, and group-dynamic skills—virtual teams also need training in information and communication technologies, including the potential problems of each medium (e.g., Internet, e-mail, desktop videoconferencing systems, collaborative software programs, and electronic brainstorming). In addition, new members should be given a complete record (i.e., print, audio, and even video) of the team's past history, especially discussions leading to crucial decisions.

Training can dispel a variety of prejudices people have about teams. People who have had poor experiences with teams, fear teams for some reason or view teams as a waste of time expect all new team experiences to be negative. They have an attitude referred to as *grouphate* (Keyton et al., 1996). One researcher developed a scale to measure how much or how little people enjoy working in teams and found that those with a higher level of grouphate had *no training* in group communication skills (Sorenson, 1981).

Effective Teams Examine Assumptions and Opinions

Researchers have found that ineffective groups tend to accept opinions and assumptions without adequately evaluating them and may even view such inferences as though they were facts. On the other hand, effective teams question the opinions and assumptions expressed by group members (Hirokawa & Pace, 1983). Here is an example of how an ineffective group failed to question assumptions in deciding how to punish a student caught plagiarizing:

A: Well, let's see, we could recommend anything from letting him off to kicking him out of school. . . .

B: Kicking him out is unreasonable, don't you think?

C: Yeah, no way that would be justified. . . . This is his first offense . . . right?

B: Uh. . . .

C: Has to be, I mean, he's a journalism student, right? They must write a lot of papers, and since the student has never been caught plagiarizing before, this had to be the first time he did it. . . .

A: Okay. . . So kicking him out of school is out. . . . Also, failing him in the course would be out, too? Huh?

B: Has to be . . . if it's his first offense and all. . . . (Hirokawa & Pace, 1983, p. 370)

Effective Teams Evaluate Possible Solutions

The best way to evaluate a possible solution is to compare it to predetermined criteria—guidelines or rules that the group previously agreed to use to reach a

Many problem-solving meetings are ineffective because they fail to follow an organized procedure.

solution (how to establish criteria will be discussed in this chapter). For example, in selecting the employee of the month, a team of employees might agree on the following criteria:

- Employee's supervisor should have received at least one letter of recommendation from a satisfied customer.

- Employee should have at least an increase of 20% in sales over the previous month.

- Employee should be liked by fellow workers.

Although researchers have found that both effective and ineffective groups weigh possible alternatives against determined criteria, effective teams are more thorough in considering the consequences of each alternative. In one study, ineffective groups

> appeared to test each alternative against the four pre-established criteria in almost a perfunctory manner—that is to say, they appeared to "go through the motions." . . . In most instances, members of the "ineffective" groups would simply ask each other whether the recommendations met each of the four criteria and would simply respond to each question with a simple "yes" or "no" response. (Hirokawa & Pace, 1983, pp. 370–372)

The ineffective teams rarely brought up facts to support their "yes" or "no" responses and ignored the consequences of the possible solutions.

Effective Teams Avoid Groupthink

Groupthink, a term developed by Irving Janis, is an uncritical way of thinking, often characteristic of groups in which the desire to avoid conflict and reach agreement is more important than careful consideration of alternatives (Janis, 1989; Turner & Pratkanis, 1998). Teams are often guilty of the following symptoms of groupthink (Janis, 1971, 1982, 1989):

- *The illusion of invulnerability*. Like the military advisors who decided to concentrate on training and supplies rather than defense because they felt Pearl Harbor was impregnable, teams may make risky decisions, feeling that their decisions cannot possibly be wrong.

- *Shared stereotypes*. Ideas that conflict with the majority opinion are often presented stereotypically—for example, "Well, you know how those guys in engineering are! Always ready to push the panic button." Such stereotypes make it easier for a team to discount the "other" as unimportant.

- *Rationalization*. Justifying or making excuses for a particular course of action hampers a team's critical thinking.

- *Illusion of group morality*. The unquestioned belief that the team's decisions will be moral and good keeps group members from considering the possible negative consequences of their decisions.

- *Self-censorship*. When members believe that they are the only ones with doubts or are afraid any expression of doubt or disagreement will destroy the team's harmony, they remain silent.

- *Illusion of unanimity*. Self-censorship leads to the mistaken assumption that everyone is in agreement when actually some members have doubts.

- *Direct pressure*. If a member does voice a doubt and is persistent in that objection, direct pressure is applied by the leader or other members to reestablish a feeling of harmony. Usually a simple comment such as "Let's stay in agreement on this! I'm sure John didn't mean to upset anyone on the team" is enough to silence the doubters. If not, members may withdraw eye contact, reposition their chairs, and even refuse to listen by talking as though the deviant were not speaking.

- *Mind guarding.* Members protect each other from mental harm (i.e., information that might cause the team to question its decisions or opinions) just as a bodyguard protects a person from physical harm.

Groupthink is more likely in teams with hidden-style leaders or members. As you recall from Chapter 3, hidden communicators have a strong desire for social acceptance. As a result, they are unlikely to express openly any disagreements or even to introduce any ideas that might cause conflict. They smooth over any conflicts in an effort to reach a consensus and preserve the harmony of the group. In contrast, effective teams view conflict as a healthy way to ensure that all ideas are considered (Frantz & Jin, 1995)—conflicts are resolved, not smoothed over.

To avoid groupthink, Janis (1971, 1989) suggests the following techniques:

- Bring in outside experts with opinions that differ from those expressed by the team.
- Ask all members to be "critical evaluators" who look at all sides of the problem regardless of personal opinions.

To keep from unduly influencing the team, the leader should:

- Keep personal opinions to self until others have expressed their opinions.
- Occasionally miss a meeting and allow someone else to lead.
- Impress on the group the importance of looking at many options.
- Once a tentative solution has been reached, give members a "second chance" to rethink their choice and to openly express any doubts before agreeing to the final solution.

Effective Teams Manage Cultural Diversity

Increasingly, we will be participating in decision making with people from other parts of the world. Not all cultures view or solve problems in the same way (Adler & Gundersen, 2008; Ivancevich & Matteson, 2002; Triandis & Albert, 1987). For example, managers in the United States expect problems to occur and are quick to identify them when they do. Managers in Asian countries, such as Thailand, Malaysia, and Indonesia, are more likely to accept situations for what they are and take longer to identify problems. Also, in the United States a single individual (usually a manager) assumes the final responsibility for decisions—hence our saying "The buck stops here." In Sweden, the responsibility for decisions also rests with an individual, but that individual may be a low-level employee. On the other hand, in Japan it is the team that makes and assumes responsibility for decisions.

Americans put great value on speed and decisiveness. In other countries, such as Egypt, a fast decision means that little importance was attached to the problem or business deal. In Japan and China, people tend to want to discuss all alternatives before making any decisions, whereas Canadians and Americans prefer to make decisions as the discussion proceeds. Italians tend to base decisions on tradition and past experience, whereas Australians and Americans prefer unique and innovative solutions.

Even though countries view problem solving differently, research discussed by Nancy Adler (Adler & Gundersen, 2008) shows that multicultural groups have

Revisiting the Case Study

Which of Janis's techniques do you think could have helped NASA management avoid groupthink?

AP Photo/NASA

definite advantages: Because of their different backgrounds, the members are less susceptible to groupthink and more likely to produce a creative range of alternatives. These advantages are especially important when problems are complex. Adler points out that successful teams do not ignore their diversity; they manage it. To manage diversity, Adler recommends that multicultural groups do the following:

- *Recognize differences.* Begin by describing the range of cultures present.
- *Elect members for their task-related abilities.* Members should be "homogeneous in ability levels and heterogeneous in attitudes."
- *Find a purpose, vision, or superordinate goal* "that transcends individual differences."
- *Avoid cultural dominance.* Encourage equal participation.
- *Develop mutual respect for each other.*
- *Seek a high level of feedback* from each other and the leader. (pp. 126–147)

Effective Teams Operate Virtually

When face-to-face (FTF) meetings are difficult, or even impossible, technology makes virtual teams or **computer-mediated communication** (CMC) teams a reality. These technologies include e-mail, desktop videoconferencing systems (DVCS), and electronic brainstorming systems (Drucker, 2000; Freed, 2000; Townsend et al., 1998; Vaas, 1999).

DVCS allow team members to speak to and see one another without ever leaving their own offices. All it takes is a small camera and microphone mounted on or near

---

IT REALLY WORKS

Managing Global Diversity

Formed in 1969 in the living room of one of the cofounders, Advanced Micro Devices (AMD) is now one of the largest producers of microchips in the world (AMD.com, 2009). This U.S.-based company has enjoyed success, but it did not come without difficulties.

In 1995, when AMD decided to build a factory overseas, the company was faced with a big challenge: cross-cultural teams. Their factory-building project brought together the United States, East Germany, and West Germany (Klyukanov, 2005). Several problems soon became apparent, and as tensions rose among the Americans, East Germans, and West Germans, AMD had to find a solution. The team members from the United States thought the Germans' system was too rational and bound up with too many regulations; the West Germans thought the Americans did not spend enough time thinking about ideas; the East Germans felt the West Germans were arrogant and too commercialistic; and the West Germans viewed the East Germans as behind the times.

How was this problem solved? "The AMD start-up team first considered alternating German-style formal meetings

and American free-form brainstorming sessions" (Klyukanov, 2005, p. 235). However, they realized that in a situation like this, neither side would be reaching their full potential in meetings, so eventually a new format was settled upon in which meetings would start with brainstorming and end with a formal reflective process and wrap-up. Also, it was decided that both the English and German languages would be spoken at meetings so everyone could express ideas in either language. This use of "cultural symbiosis" allowed both groups to learn and grow from the positive aspects of the other and make the new factory in Dresden, Germany, their most successful start-up yet (p. 236).

What do you think?
- Compare the way AMD solved its diversity problem with the suggestions given previously in this chapter. What similarities and differences do you see?
- Read about the various brainstorming methods discussed in this chapter and decide which one you think would have worked the best for this AMD team. Explain your reasons.

Teams with multicultural members are more likely to produce creative alternatives.

the computer monitor of each team member, software such as Microsoft's NetMeeting, and an Internet/intranet hookup. DVCS allow approximately 15 members online at one time, with the faces of all members displayed on the screen. (Fewer participants, however, yields a clearer video.) NetMeeting supports "chat, application sharing, whiteboard, file-transfer and Internet telephone functions" (Freed, 2000, p. 165). Although there is no video, Centra 7, a voice-enabled web service, offers a virtual conference room for up to 20 members—the first 5 members are free for a 15-day trial. The meeting planner can broadcast any application running on his or her desktop (including PowerPoint slides). All members can see and hear, make suggestions (only one person can speak at a time), and even send information during the meeting. Once received by the planner, the new information can be broadcast to everyone.

In deciding whether to use an audio only or a video system, keep in mind some of the interesting research that compared teams using FTF communication and teams using CMC communication. Basically, researchers have concluded three important differences: (a) CMC teams communicate less and share less information than FTF teams; (b) when completing intellective tasks (tasks where a "correct" answer exists), CMC teams underperform FTF teams—but only slightly; and (c) CMC teams are better able to predict the success of their decisions than FTF teams, thereby allowing them to determine when additional information is needed (Baltes et al., 2002—a meta-analysis of 27 studies; Hollingshead & McGrath, 1995; Roch & Ayman, 2005). The Elaboration Likelihood Model (Petty & Cacioppo, 1986a, 1986b) may explain these differences (Figure 9.1).

The **elaboration likelihood model** (ELM) describes how people evaluate arguments: they use either (a) a *central route* and take the time to thoroughly consider the argument or (b) the *peripheral route* and are distracted by secondary cues, like what the speaker is wearing, and make rapid decisions with little critical thinking. Applying the ELM model, Roch and Ayman (2005) observe that even though CMC teams exchange less information and fewer messages—which is a definite drawback in problem solving—they make up for it by carefully and critically evaluating the written message (using the central route). There is no message giver to

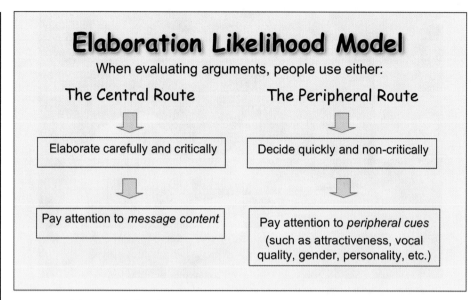

FIGURE 9.1 Elaboration Likelihood Model Used to Explain Differences between Face-to-Face (FTF) Communication and Computer-Mediated Communication (CMC).

Basic Problem-Solving Procedure

1. Define the problem.

2. Research and analyze the problem.

3. Establish a checklist of criteria.

4. List possible alternatives.

5. Evaluate each alternative.

6. Select the best alternative(s) and discuss how to implement it.

serve as a distraction. On the other hand, FTF teams have both the message and the message giver to observe while listening, so they are more likely to allow secondary cues from the presenter to distract them from a careful consideration of the arguments presented. If you are in a virtual or CMC team, encourage team members to be careful not to suppress their ideas; the chance that members will communicate too much shouldn't be a worry. Also, if the team feels that their solution isn't a good one, believe them, and help the situation by finding additional information or bringing in one or two new members to serve as consultants.

The Basic Problem-Solving Procedure

To ensure productive meetings, both the leader and the team members should be trained in using the basic problem-solving procedure. If training is impossible—for example, if a new team is formed to handle an emergency—then at least the leader should be trained in problem solving. Before jumping into the problem-solving procedure, even if the team members already know each other, it is a good idea to highlight their talents and skills so that they can "develop a deep appreciation for their colleagues" (Preston, 2005).

The **basic problem-solving procedure** includes six steps adapted from Dewey's classic reflective thinking process (Dewey, 1910): (a) define the problem, (b) research and analyze it, (c) establish a checklist of criteria, (d) list possible alternatives, (e) evaluate each alternative, and (f) select the best alternative. Many groups skip steps 1 through 3 and go immediately to step 4, listing possible alternatives. However, each of these steps must be addressed for the basic problem-solving procedure to be successful.

Step 1: Define the Problem

Step 1 is often omitted because the team members assume that everyone already knows exactly what the problem is. This is especially true when the team's task has been decided by management or someone outside the group. Eliminating step 1, however, can waste valuable time. Teams often are unaware that everyone's basic understanding of the problem is different until they are unable to agree upon a solution.

Discuss the Problem's Symptoms, Seriousness, and Impact Defining the problem may be the only purpose of some meetings. If the problem is vague, or too broad, or even unknown, then a discussion of its *observed symptoms* and *perceived seriousness* may help the team define the problem. For example, a supervisor who has noticed that production has dropped and that morale seems quite low knows the symptoms but not the problem.

Identifying the exact problem may also help to determine its *impact*. One consultant found that average managers focus their evaluation on the problem itself, whereas "super executives," who solve problems with apparent ease, view "the problem as merely a stepping stone to the *problem impact*—the effect of the problem" (Ford, 1982, p. 6). Whereas the average person is considering the cause of the problem, the super executive is determining the cause of the problem's impact and what to do about it. This is important because

> the initial focal (or takeoff) point generally determines the train of thought that follows . . . starting with the problem instead of the problem impact invariably results in a narrower evaluation of the total situation and final decisions are less prone to be fully responsive to overall needs. (Ford, 1982, pp. 10–11)

Write the Problem in Question Form When the problem finally seems clear to everyone, test that understanding by writing the problem in *question form*. Discuss the wording of the written question until all members are satisfied. Even when the problem to be solved seems obvious, the team should summarize it by stating it precisely in question form. If the team cannot agree on the specific wording, then the problem has not been defined clearly enough.

Step 1: Defining the Problem

A. Discuss the symptoms.

B. Discuss the size (seriousness) and the impact (effect) of the problem.

C. State the problem in question form.

D. Define any confusing terms in the question.

Keep the following characteristics in mind when wording your question (Wood et al., 2000):

- *Written in a manner that allows for the widest range of answers.* "Yes" or "no" answers should be avoided. For example, the question "Should Tooling Incorporated increase online sales?" asks for only a yes or no answer. If the question is rewritten as "What position should Tooling Incorporated take toward increasing online sales?" the team would have a range of possible responses.

- *Specific rather than general.* For example, in the question "Should we encourage employees to give to the United Way?" the words *we* and *encourage* are vague. Who are we and what is meant by encourage? The question might be reworded as "What position should the management of Park's Furniture take toward employees giving to the United Way?"

- *Specific about who should act.* In the question "What can be done to clean up the debris around Johnson Lake?" the person or group who is to act has not been named. Should the question be directed toward the police, the Boy Scouts, the City Council, or the business community? A better question might read as follows: "What suggestions for cleaning up the debris around Johnson Lake should the local Parents League make to the City Council at the council meeting on Friday?"

- *Written in an unbiased manner.* Sometimes, questions are worded in such a way that the group's biases are obvious. "What can management do about the ridiculous hiring practices required by the Equal Employment Opportunity Commission?" is not an objectively worded question. How can a group be objective in its answers when the question is biased?

Thus, an effectively worded problem avoids yes or no answers, is specific, states who is to act, and avoids biased phrasing. Can you see what is wrong with the following question: "Should the speed limit be raised to a decent speed?" This question violates all four rules! It can be answered yes or no. It is too general. (What speed limit—national? state? or on company property? What is meant by "decent speed"?) It fails to state who is to act (perhaps the U.S. Congress or the state legislature or the company policy board). And it includes biased phrasing ("decent speed" implies that the present speed is not decent).

You may find it helpful to think of problem-solving questions as questions of fact, value, or policy. In **questions of fact**, the team tries to determine whether something is true or to what degree something is true. In **questions of value**, the team tries to assess the desirability of some object, idea, or person. In **questions of policy**, the team tries to arrive at a specific course of action, usually a change from the present system. Questions of fact base the solution on detailed research; questions of value base the solution on value judgments (opinions); and questions of policy consider both researched facts and value judgments in reaching a solution.

Define Any Confusing Terms The last part of step 1 is to define any unusual or ambiguous terms in the problem question. Defining terms further clarifies meaning and prevents misunderstandings. Of course, if your question has been carefully worded, few terms will need clarification, and the team will be ready for step 2.

Step 2: Research and Analyze the Problem

Teams that omit step 2 usually arrive at unsound solutions because they do not know enough about the situation to make an effective decision. Even teams that do

Step 2: Researching and Analyzing the Problem

A. List topics needing research/discussion.

B. Gather information.

C. Discuss information/opinions in organized fashion.

    1. Identify a topic.

    2. Allow all members to give research/opinions on that topic.

    3. Ask if anyone wishes to add additional thoughts.

    4. Summarize the group's findings.

    5. Identify the next topic and repeat until finished.

analyze the problem often reach ineffective solutions because their discussions are disorganized. To prevent these difficulties, follow the three simple guidelines outlined in points A, B, and C in the Step 2 summary box.

List All the Topics That Must Be Researched and Discussed This will inform team members of the information needed for them to reach an intelligent solution. To answer the question "What position should our county take toward the federal government's proposal to build a nuclear power plant in Glen Rose?" you would need to research current laws, public opinion, accident records of present nuclear power plants, and safety features. Most problem-solving discussions should also include research on causes of the problem and past efforts to solve the problem: What are the real causes of this problem? Has the problem come up before? How was it handled then? Was the solution successful? If so, why does the problem exist today? What are some possible negative consequences to various solutions? Based on a meta-analysis of problem-solving groups, Orlitzky and Hirokawa (2001) concluded that *groups that consider the negative consequences of proposed solutions are 86% more likely to reach effective solutions* than groups who do not consider them. If your group is unwilling to risk group reactions, assign one or two people at each meeting to play the role of "devil's advocate."

When the cause of a problem is unclear or unknown (such as when a piece of machinery suddenly begins to turn out inferior products), your group may find it helpful to answer the following four pairs of questions (Kepner & Tregoe, 1981). Write the answers on a chalkboard or flip chart so everyone can see them.

1. What is involved? What is not involved?

2. Where is it found? Where is it not found?

3. When does it occur? When does it not occur?

4. To what extent (how much/how often) does it occur? To what extent does it not occur?

For each pair of answers, ask two additional questions: (a) What is the main difference, if any, between the answer to the first question and the answer to the second, and (b) what change, if any, caused the difference? When as many

© 2002 Ted Goff. Reprinted by permission. www.tedgoff.com

"Our mission will be to turn this plan into a reality."

answers as possible have been found, summarize your information by stating the most likely cause. If this possible cause does not account for the facts obtained by answering the four pairs of questions, reject it and look for some other cause. Look carefully for differences and changes that might have been overlooked earlier.

Gather Needed Information   At this point, the leader should postpone further discussion until members have gathered necessary information. Possible sources of information include company records and data, personal opinion surveys conducted by the team, and company or community library. The Internet, company intranets, and even blogs have greatly improved the ease and speed of information searches. (See Chapter 12 for advice on researching using the Internet.) There may be times when decisions must be made on incomplete information. Lisa Simpson, president of Sony's Online Entertainment unit admits, "We can't afford to wait for perfect or even near-perfect information to execute our business." (Hymowitz, 2000) Most teams find, however, that the more information, the better their decisions. Even when no outside research is needed, the discussion will take less time if members are given a chance to organize their thoughts and do some careful thinking before sharing the information they know with their team members.

Discuss the Information and Opinions for Each Topic in an Organized Manner
A classic study found that most groups changed topics or themes on an average of every 58 seconds; although topics were usually mentioned more than once, few of them were completely discussed (Berg, 1967). Obviously, jumping from topic to topic is unproductive. To organize your team's discussion, try using the following pattern:

1. State the topic to be discussed.
2. Give all members a chance to cite their research and opinions on the topic.
3. Ask if anyone has anything further to say on the topic.
4. Summarize the group's findings on the topic.
5. State the next topic to be discussed and repeat the preceding steps until all topics have been discussed.

Gathering, analyzing, and discussing information relevant to the problem are necessary components of the team's problem-resolution process.

Step 3: Establish a Checklist of Criteria

Establishing criteria is one of the most important steps of all. Without criteria, the procedure we have been discussing would not be "the basic problem-solving procedure." To clarify the importance of criteria, we will examine them from four angles: *what* are criteria, the *types* of criteria, *when* in the procedure to establish criteria, and *how* to use criteria in reaching quality solutions.

What Are Criteria? **Criteria** are the guidelines that a group agrees to follow to reach a solution. For example, your group might agree that any solution selected should receive unanimous support from all group members; fall within current state and national laws; treat all persons equally; not result in any increase in taxes; and receive the backing of both the union leaders and management.

You can also view criteria as a checklist of requirements that a possible solution must meet in order to be selected by your group. For example, a checklist of criteria for the selection of a chief executive officer of a corporation might be as follows:

*   Should meet all requirements listed in the bylaws.
*   Should have at least 10 years' experience in policy-making positions.
*   Should be a good public speaker and present self well on camera.
*   Should have prestige with major companies in the United States and abroad.

Step 3: Establishing a Checklist of Criteria

A. Brainstorm for possible criteria.

B. Discuss each criterion in order to:

1. Reduce list (combine and eliminate).
2. Divide into groups of "musts" or "wants."
3. Assign each want a rank or numerical weight.

Types of Criteria First, criteria can be either task or operational. **Task criteria** relate to the actual problem or task being discussed. **Operational criteria** relate to group procedural matters. Examples of *task criteria* for choosing Employee of the Year might include the following: should be an employee of the company for at least 5 years; should have received merit pay at least once in the last 5 years; should be a current member of a work team; and should have presented a suggestion to the company that saved $5,000 or more. Examples of *operational criteria* might include the following: selection of employee of the year must be completed in 2 weeks; selection should be unanimously supported by group members; selection should be agreeable to the division manager; and selection costs (duplication of papers, and so on) should not exceed $50.

Second, criteria can be divided into "musts" and "wants" (Kepner & Tregoe, 1981). **Must criteria** are required items, and **want criteria** are desired items. Must and want criteria can be either task or operational items. If an alternative fails to meet even one of the must criteria, it will be rejected by the group. Therefore, *there is no need to rank must criteria.* On the other hand, *want criteria must be ranked to be effective.* For example, imagine that two solutions meet all of your group's must criteria, and solution A meets want criteria 2, 3, and 4, but solution B meets want criteria 1, 2, and 3. In this case, solution B is the best solution because it meets the most important want criteria.

Once the want criteria have been ordered from most desirable to least desirable, your group might wish to assign a numerical weight to each criterion (see Figure 9.2). For example, if there are five want criteria, the group might assign the most important criterion a numerical weight of 5, the next most important a weight of 4, and so on. Another method is to assign each want criterion a weight of 1, 2, or 3 regardless of the number of items being considered:

1 = important

2 = very important

3 = extremely important (almost a must)

For example, in deciding what computer to buy, your department might arrive at the following criteria:

Musts

- Must not cost more than $1,500 (top allotment for office purchases).
- Must include a 14-inch flat-screen monitor.
- Must have a 300GB hard drive.
- Must include a CD/DVD burner.

Wants	Assigned Weight
Includes a printer	3
Cost of computer low enough to allow for large flat-screen	3
Keyboard comfortable to use	1
Business software included in cost of computer	2
Hard drive larger than 300GB	2
Speakers produce music-quality sound	1

FIGURE 9.2 Want criteria given an assigned weight.

When to Establish Criteria Deciding *when* to establish the criteria to be used in evaluating possible solutions is almost as important as deciding *what* your criteria will be. Other than requirements specified by management and given to the group at its first meeting, *criteria should not be established before step 2* (researching and analyzing the problem) because the group will not know enough about the problem. For example, in the hypothetical list of criteria for selecting a CEO, how did the group know that experience in policy making was an important quality in a CEO?

It was because in step 2, one of the group members researched the experience of past corporate CEOs. In discussion of this topic, the group discovered that CEOs who were judged effective by their corporate structures had at least 10 years' prior experience in policy-making positions. If the group had found that experience seemed to make little difference in the performance of past CEOs, then experience would not be listed as a criterion.

Whether criteria should be established before or after listing alternatives (step 4) is more difficult to say. Research has produced conflicting answers. On the one hand, once solutions are listed, it is difficult for group members to remain objective. It is only natural that they will favor criteria that support their preferred alternative. For example, suppose CEO candidate A has only 6 years of policy-making experience and candidate B has 12 years of experience. You prefer candidate A. If your group discusses criteria after narrowing the field to these two candidates, you might insist that experience should not be used as a criterion.

On the other hand, establishing criteria before listing alternatives makes it more difficult to think of novel alternatives. Once criteria are set, tunnel vision occurs. Therefore, if your group's main purpose is to produce a great number of solutions for group consideration, perhaps you should reverse steps 3 and 4 (Galanes & Adams, 2010). Nevertheless, it's advisable to establish criteria *before* listing alternatives in the following situations:

- If the task is complex.
- If the topic is emotional or involves value judgments.
- If team members have little or no problem-solving experience and are likely to allow preferred solutions to dictate the criteria.

How to Use Criteria Effectively Once a team has decided when to establish criteria, they must focus on producing quality criteria. Criteria are easy to confuse with solutions. Criteria are guidelines for reaching solutions, but are not solutions. For example, in discussing whether city police officers should be allowed to strike, "The strike should not last longer than 48 hours" is a solution, whereas "Citizen safety should be considered" is a criterion. To keep your group from confusing criteria with possible solutions, precede each criterion with this phrase: "Any decision we reach should (or should not). . . ." For example, "Any decision we reach should be agreeable to all sides" or "Any decision we reach should not result in any increase in taxes."

The following procedure is an effective way to organize your group's discussion of criteria:

1. List all possible criteria (make sure everyone gets a chance to respond).
2. Evaluate each criterion to determine its importance or unimportance, thereby

   a. Reducing the list of criteria to a workable length by combining or eliminating.

   b. Dividing the remaining criteria into musts and numerically ranked wants.

Establishing criteria is the key to the basic problem-solving procedure. Once a group agrees on the criteria to be used in evaluating the solutions, the most difficult part of the process is over.

Step 4: List Possible Alternatives

List as many alternative solutions as are feasible within your team's time and budget limits. Most teams have trouble listing possible alternatives without evaluating

AWARENESS CHECK

Use of Criteria

To check your knowledge of the various types of criteria and how to use them, take the following quiz. You can also take this quiz online and view the answers via your Premium Website for *Communicating for Results*.

Directions: Which types of criteria are represented by the following statements or questions: **(A)** *must* criteria, **(B)** *want* criteria, **(C)** *task* criteria, or **(D)** *operational* criteria. More than one answer may be used.

1. Which type of criteria (must or want) does not need to be rank ordered?
2. Any criteria we select cannot cost more than $150.
3. If possible, our decision should be a unanimous one.
4. Any supervisor we select should be a current member of a work team.
5. Any child care facility we select must be independently owned.
6. Selection of a child care facility must be completed in one month.

Step 4: Listing Possible Alternatives

A. List as many ideas as time and resources allow.

B. Use brainstorming or nominal group technique (NGT), or a combination.

them at the same time. But to use step 4 effectively, all evaluations must be postponed until step 5. Evaluating alternatives as soon as they are mentioned tends to hamper creative thinking. Remember to *list first* and *then evaluate*. Brainstorming, electronic brainstorming, and nominal group technique are only three methods for producing innovative lists of ideas such as Glass Chalk (chalk that can write on glass) invented by Pennzoil–Quaker State and Spirit Foam (a nondripping decorative spray in a variety of colors) invented by Valvoline (Lamb et al., 2006). Both of these nonautomotive products were invented by automotive scientists using effective brainstorming for alternative products.

Brainstorming One way to obtain creative, detailed lists of ideas such as the alternative products mentioned previously is **brainstorming**, which is the spontaneous contribution of ideas by all members of the team. Neither a debate nor an evaluation session, brainstorming's sole purpose is to generate lists of items. For effective brainstorming, follow these basic guidelines (Osborn, 1993):

- *Avoid negative feedback* (both verbal and nonverbal). The only comments allowed should be words of praise and encouragement or requests for clarification of an idea. Negative comments usually put an end to creative thinking.

- *Strive for the longest list possible* rather than for a high-quality list. Discussions of the quality of the ideas should be postponed until step 5. The leader or a recorder should make a list of all ideas. The more ideas, the better your chances of finding a really good one. For example, one good idea out of 5,000 is common in the pharmaceutical business (Lamb et al., 2004, p. 321).

- *Strive for creative, unusual ideas.* It is often the crazy-sounding idea that proves to be the best when combined with other ideas. Even if it would not be acceptable to the group, a bizarre or extraordinary suggestion often stimulates someone to think of a valuable idea that may have been overlooked otherwise.

- *Try to build from previously mentioned ideas.* If your team is really thinking, there should be no long pauses. Effective brainstorming moves quite rapidly as one idea stimulates another.

Brainstorming can also be used in step 1 to define the problem, in step 2 to generate the list of topics needing research, and in step 3 to generate the list of possible criteria. Many companies use consumer focus groups to brainstorm for new products. The Dustbuster vacuum, Stick-up room deodorizers, and Wendy's salad bar were all the results of group brainstorming (Lamb et al., 2004, p. 320). For additional brainstorming ideas, see Van Gundy (1994).

Brainstorming works best when team members are outgoing and enjoy being creative and building on one another's ideas (Bachman, 2000; Kramer et al., 1997). It is less effective when one or two members monopolize the time and don't give others a chance to participate or when some group members are afraid to talk because of real or perceived group pressures. They may withhold an excellent idea simply because they are afraid someone will criticize it. In these cases, electronic brainstorming or nominal group technique is recommended.

Electronic Brainstorming Instead of rapidly throwing out ideas around a table with other group members, in **electronic brainstorming systems (EBS)**, ideas are generated individually (and often anonymously) by typing them and sending them electronically. The ideas are recorded by the software program and combined for later group viewing. EBS thus allows team members to interact with their individual identities revealed or concealed (Dennis et al., 1999; Roy & Gauvin, 1996). Compared to traditional brainstorming and nominal group technique, EBS generally produces more ideas (Pinsonneault & Barki, 1999; Valacich et al., 1994), sometimes better-quality ideas (Gallupe et al., 1994), and it tends to work better with large groups (Dennis & Valacich, 1993; Gallupe et al., 1992).

Royal Dutch/Shell Oil uses the Internet for brainstorming. Each week, teams of six employees meet around the globe to brainstorm ideas. For example, in 1999 teams produced "more than 300 new-product and process-improvement ideas . . . including four of the company's five most crucial initiatives" (Stepanek, 1999, p. 57).

Nominal Group Technique Another method of listing alternatives is a procedure known as the **nominal group technique** (Delbecq et al., 1986). Because nominal group technique (NGT) gives all team members an equal chance to participate, it has some advantages over brainstorming. It encourages shy members to participate freely and prohibits overly talkative or negative members from dominating. NGT can be used both for generating lists of ideas and as a method of decision making.

When NGT is used as a method for generating ideas, these two steps are followed:

1. *Ideas are silently generated by each individual.* Each person writes down ideas or solutions privately. There is no discussion at this point.

2. *Ideas are recorded on a chalkboard, markerboard, or flip chart.* All ideas are recorded in a round-robin procedure: The leader accepts one idea at a time

from each person until all ideas are listed, including any additional ideas that members have thought of while others were speaking. There is no discussion of ideas in this step. (We suggest the use of flip charts because they can be rolled up and taken with you; chalk and markerboards often get erased.)

When NGT is used as a method of decision making, four steps are followed:

1. *Ideas are silently generated by each individual.*

2. *Ideas are recorded on a chalkboard or flip chart.*

3. *Each idea is discussed for clarification only.* Debate, criticism, or persuasive appeals are not allowed; suggestions for combining or rewording ideas and for clarifying meaning are allowed.

4. *Each member privately selects the top five (or more) preferred items* and ranks them according to importance, assigning the most important a rank of 5, the next most important a 4, and so on. When all votes are recorded, one page of a flip chart for the problem "How can our department become more productive?" might look like Figure 9.3.

When using NGT as a problem-solving procedure, the third and fourth steps may have to be repeated until a definite solution is clearly present—that is, until one idea clearly wins the highest score.

The advantage of NGT—privacy—can also be its weakness. Researchers have found that the quality of both individual and group decisions is improved by open exchanges of information, ideas, and criticism. NGT allows an exchange of information, but no criticism. Critical evaluation appears to be necessary for superior decisions.

Combination Methods A combination of brainstorming (oral) and NGT (written) methods may also be effective. One popular combination method begins with the two-step NGT and concludes with a brief brainstorming session. The new ideas derived from the brainstorming session are added to the flip chart. Another combination method calls for each member to suggest an idea. All ideas are recorded (even if they are the same or similar to previous ideas). Each mem-

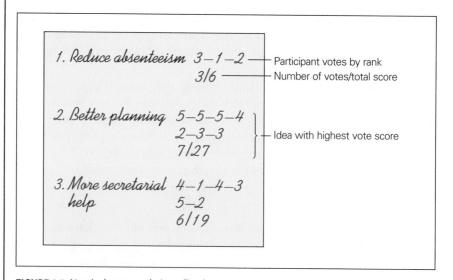

FIGURE 9.3 Nominal group technique flip chart.

ber is asked explicitly to contribute (Sashkin & Morris, 1984). This method follows the brainstorming procedure but takes the pressure of speed off the participants. Another combination method called *brainwriting* was developed at the Battelle Institute in Frankfurt (Van Gundy, 1987). Brainwriting instructions are as follows (Van Gundy, 1984):

- Write down four ideas on a sheet of paper, place the sheet in the center of the table, and exchange it for another person's sheet. No discussion is permitted.

- Use the ideas of the other team members for stimulation and list as many additional ideas as possible. These new ideas may be combinations and improvements of the listed ideas or entirely new ideas. Keep exchanging sheets and adding your ideas until time is called.

- There will be a 30-minute time limit. At the end of this time, all papers will be collected so that the ideas can be evaluated.

Combining brainstorming, EBS, and NGT may provide more effective ways to generate lists of ideas than the traditional brainstorming method alone (Holt, 1996). Try all three to see which works the best for you and your organization.

Step 5: Evaluate Each Alternative

If the team has done a good job of determining criteria, step 5 in the basic problem-solving procedure should be amazingly simple. The following guidelines will enable your group to evaluate the possible alternative solutions:

1. Read through the list of alternatives, eliminating those that the team feels do not meet the criteria agreed on in step 3.

2. Further reduce the list to a workable number by combining any similar alternatives.

3. Discuss each remaining alternative's strengths and weaknesses (referring to research presented in step 2 when necessary). If no one feels comfortable playing the role of devil's advocate, assign one or two members to criticize and question each solution. According to Williams (2007), *there is a 58% chance that groups who assign critical evaluators will end up with better decisions*. He also suggests that assigning someone to play the role of devil's advocate is a good way to encourage the group to use C-type or cognitive conflict that was discussed in Chapter 3.

4. Determine how well each alternative meets the criteria; consider the number and the importance of criteria met.

5. Continue reducing the list until the best alternative (or alternatives) is reached.

> ## Step 5: Evaluating Each Alternative
>
> A. Eliminate unacceptable alternatives.
>
> B. Combine similar alternatives.
>
> C. Eliminate any alternatives that do not meet all must criteria.
>
> D. Compare remaining alternatives to want criteria and assign numerical values. Calculate totals.

Want Criteria	Assigned Weight		Computer A*		Computer B*		Computer C*	
—Includes printer	3	×	5	= 15	1	= 3	5	= 15
—Cost allows for flat-screen monitor upgrade	3	×	1	= 3	3	= 9	4	= 12
—Keyboard comfort	1	×	5	= 5	3	= 3	5	= 5
—Bundled software	2	×	4	= 8	1	= 2	4	= 8
—Hard drive larger than 308GB	2	×	5	= 10	5	= 10	5	= 10
—Music-quality speakers	1	×	3	= 3	1	= 1	5	= 1
				total = 44		total = 28		total = 51

* Each computer ranking (on a scale of 1–5) for how well it meets each criterion.

FIGURE 9.4 Using criteria to narrow down possible solutions.

One drawback to group problem solving is that so much time is required. *Teams that use criteria correctly can substantially cut the time needed to reach a solution* because criteria limit the solutions that must be considered. In the example in step 3 about deciding what computer to buy for the department, four must criteria were listed. Suppose that only three of the computers currently on the market meet our must criteria. At this point, we may wish to do additional research or personally test each of the three computers. Next, we determine how well each of the top computers meet the want criteria in Figure 9.4.

Step 6: Select the Best Alternative

The best solution is simply the solution (or solutions) that best fulfills the group's criteria. Sometimes, however, even after using criteria to eliminate poor solutions, the team is left with several alternatives—a decision must still be made.

A decision can be reached by one of several methods: consensus, compromise, or vote (Wood, 1984). *The best decision is the consensus.* In a **consensus** decision, all members agree to accept a particular solution even though it may not have been their original choice. Commitment to the solution is greater in teams that can reach consensus, but the team needs to beware of groupthink, discussed previously in this chapter.

If a consensus cannot be reached, the next best decision is a **compromise**. Of course, no one completely wins in a compromise; all parties must forfeit some of their requirements, but at least no one completely loses, either.

If a consensus or a compromise is not possible, the group may have to **vote** for the best solution, which would be the alternative that receives more than 50% of the

Step 6: Selecting the Best Alternative(s)

A. Best solutions—those with highest totals.

B. In case of tie, select more than one solution; or create additional criteria; or use consensus, compromise, or vote.

vote. Voting should be used only as a last resort because it often causes resentment by creating winners and losers.

Discuss How to Implement the Best Alternative Once the best solution to the problem has been selected, the team must discuss how to implement it. In other words, the team must decide what should be done to ensure that the solution becomes a reality. During this discussion, the team may decide that although the solution sounds great in theory, it is too costly or management would never agree to it. In this case, go back to step 5, select the second-best alternative, and discuss implementing it.

The team has then completed the decision-making process and is ready to report all recommendations to the appropriate person(s) or, if the group has the power, to initiate the implementation. (See Chapters 13 and 14 for suggestions on making individual and team presentations.) If the team is to remain a group even after the solution has been reached, it is important to *follow up* on the implementation and to keep a record of both successes and failures for future use.

Although the basic problem-solving procedure can be modified to fit specific needs, it tends to work best when both the leader and members are trained in the process, the group is relatively small, and the members have had ample time to prepare. According to one group of researchers, a procedure that works should guide "a group to analyze a problem thoroughly, to establish criteria for a good solution, and to evaluate the positive and negative qualities of alternative choices" (Hirokawa et al., 1996, p. 277).

Selecting the Group Format

We conclude this chapter on small-group communication and decision making by taking a brief look at various group discussion formats.

- The most often used format, generally referred to as the **roundtable**, is a small group discussion conducted in private using the basic problem-solving procedure.
- The **panel** discussion is a small group of well-informed individuals discussing a problem or topic of interest in front of a larger group. All panel members contribute freely

ETHICAL DILEMMA

Baseball players in the Major Leagues have to be in peak physical condition in order to compete in the game still known as America's Pastime. In general, training in baseball comes down to explosive power and protection against injuries (Burtt, 2006). But because steroids can take all that power and magnify it, many players—Jose Canseco, an American League MVP, and Ken Caminiti, a National League MVP, to name two—decided to use steroids to improve their game. Caminiti, one of the first players to admit using steroids, says that so many players are users that those who don't are at a real disadvantage (Daft & Marcic, 2006, p. 123). In his book, *Juiced* (2005), Canseco says that "intelligent, informed use of steroids, combined with human growth hormone, will one day be so accepted that everybody will be doing it" (p. 2). Boston Red Sox pitcher Curt Schilling calls Canseco's book "a disgrace," noting that it sends entirely the wrong message to youths ("McGwire Mum on Steroids," 2005).

Besides giving users an unfair advantage over other players, using steroids is dangerous, causing strokes, seizures, heart attacks, and violent behavior in adults, plus reduced height and injury to bones, ligaments, and cartridge in children (Hamilton, 2005). In an open letter to fans, Baseball Commissioner Bud Selig said, "We ban and test for amphetamines. And human-growth hormone is banned as well. We have cracked down and will continue to crack down on steroid users, but the use of HGH represents a threat to all sports everywhere [currently there is no reliable test for HGH]. . . . These players who use performing-enhancing substances offend all of us who care for the game and I will not tolerate their actions" (Rogers, 2006).

Fans may agree with the commissioner. A *Chicago Tribune* commentary noted that when the Giants' slugger Barry Bonds (who has denied using steroids but was named by Canseco as a user) plays away from his home field, he is met with a "vociferous medley of boos" (*Chicago Tribune*, 2006).

Questions: What do you think? Is it ethical for baseball players to use steroids and HGH? What should be done about the records of those players who previously used steroids? What impact on team morale do teammates using performance-enhancing drugs create?

and equally and are usually guided through the basic problem-solving procedure by a leader or chairperson.

- The **symposium** is composed of a small group of experts, also in front of a larger group. Instead of the free exchange of ideas found in panel discussions, each member of a symposium gives a formal, 5- to 10-minute presentation on an aspect of the problem relating to the member's expertise. The chairperson introduces each presentation. When all presentations are finished, the speakers may choose to discuss the ideas presented by the other speakers or to use the basic problem-solving process. However, if the symposium is intended to educate or stimulate the audience, the leader may invite everyone to enter the discussion.

- When audience members are allowed to participate following a panel or symposium, the discussion is called a **forum**. Thus, both a panel-forum and a symposium-forum are possible. A forum may involve a simple question-and-answer period, a general discussion, or organized groups.

Most problem-solving groups select the roundtable format and conduct their discussions privately. However, if your group is asked to discuss a problem in front of a larger group, you will need to select either the panel or symposium format for your discussion. The basic problem-solving procedure can be used with either format with only minor modification.

Now that we have covered the basic procedures of group discussion, the next chapter will discuss how individuals can become more proficient in small-group participation and leadership.

COMMUNICATION SITUATION

Group Discussion

As members of the Student Government Financial Committee, Davinia, Joyce, Thomas, and Pat make decisions on how much funding, if any, to give to various student groups that request support from the funds collected from student fees. They are meeting for the first time in a campus cafeteria. What role does each participant play in this group? You can use your Premium Website for *Communicating for Results* to answer this question online after you've watched a video clip of this Communication Situation, further critique the interaction among Davinia, Joyce, Thomas, and Pat, and, if requested, e-mail your responses to your instructor.

Thomas: Well, we've got 23 applications for funding and a total of $19,000 that we can distribute.

Davinia: Maybe we should start by listing how much each of the 23 groups wants.

Joyce: It might be better to start by determining the criteria we will use to decide if groups get any funding from student fees.

Davinia: Yeah, right. We should set up our criteria before we look at applications.

Thomas: Sounds good to me. Pat, what do you think?

Pat: I'm on board. Let's set up criteria first and then review the applications against those.

Joyce: Okay, we might start by looking at the criteria used last year by the Financial Committee. Does anyone have a copy of those?

Cengage Learning

Thomas: I do. *[He passes out copies to the other three people.]* They had three criteria: service to a significant number of students, compliance with the college's nondiscrimination policies, and educational benefit.

Davinia: What counts as "educational benefit"? Did last year's committee specify that?

Joyce: Good question. Thomas, you were on the committee last year. Do you remember what they counted as an educational benefit?

Thomas: The main thing I remember is that it was distinguished from an artistic benefit—like a concert or art exhibit or something like that.

Pat: But can't art be educational?

Davinia: Yeah, I think so. Thomas, Joyce, do you?

Thomas: I guess, but it's like art's primary purpose isn't to educate.

Joyce: I agree. It's kind of hard to put into words, but I think educational benefit has more to do with information and the mind, and art has more to do with the soul. Does that sound too hokey?

[Laughter.]

Pat: Okay, so we want to say that we don't distribute funds to any hokey groups, right?

[More laughter.]

Davinia: It's not like we're against art or anything. It's just the funding we can distribute is for educational benefit, right?

[Everyone nods.]

Joyce: Okay, let's move onto another criterion. What is the significant number of students?

Thomas: Last year we said that the proposals for using money had to be of potential interest to at least 20% of students to get funding. How does that sound to you?

Pat: Sounds okay as long as we remember that something can be of potential interest to students who aren't members of specific groups. Like, for instance, I might want to attend a program on American Indian customs even though I'm not an American Indian. See what I mean?

Davinia: Good point—we don't want to define student interest as student identity or anything like that.

[Nods of agreement.]

Thomas: Okay, so are we agreed that 20% is about right with the understanding that the 20% can include students who aren't in a group applying for funding? *[Nods.]* Okay, then do we need to discuss the criterion of compliance with the college's policies on nondiscrimination?

CHAPTER 9

REVIEW

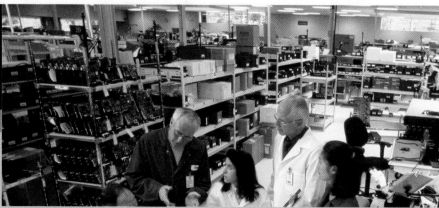

Walter Hodges/Getty Images

Key Terms

basic problem-solving procedure (243)

brainstorming (250)

compromise (254)

computer-mediated communication (CMC) (240)

consensus (254)

criteria (247)

elaboration likelihood model (ELM) (241)

electronic brainstorming (EBS) (251)

forum (256)

groupthink (238)

learning group (235)

must criteria (248)

nominal group technique (251)

operational criteria (247)

panel (255)

problem-solving groups (235)

questions of fact (244)

questions of policy (244)

questions of value (244)

roundtable (255)

self-maintenance groups (235)

small-group communication (233)

symposium (256)

task criteria (247)

vote (254)

want criteria (248)

Summary

Team decision making is not the answer to all business or professional problems, but, when used correctly, it can be quite effective. Now that you have read this chapter, you should feel more confident about participating in and even leading committees or other small groups. Most typically, you will be asked to work in small groups to solve problems. Unfortunately, problem solving can be one of the most difficult group tasks. Teams can be effective problem solvers if they are well organized, receive training in problem solving, carefully examine members' assumptions and opinions, evaluate all possible solutions, avoid groupthink, manage cultural diversity, and operate virtually when needed. If the group follows the basic problem-solving procedure outlined in this chapter,

decision making can be less frustrating and more productive. The six steps of basic problem solving are to (a) define the problem, (b) research and analyze the problem, (c) establish a checklist of criteria, (d) list possible alternatives, (e) evaluate each alternative, and (f) select the best alternative. This six-step procedure can be altered to fit most group or individual problems. For example, to practice the procedure, why not use it to solve family problems at home? Because your family group will not be familiar with the process, you will not have to use the terminology discussed here. A skilled leader, regardless of the setting, can guide a group through the six steps without the group even being aware of the process.

Communicating for Results Online

Before continuing to the next chapter, check your understanding of Chapter 9 at the Premium Website for *Communicating for Results*. Your Premium Website gives you quick and easy access to the electronic resources that accompany this text. These resources include:

- **Study tools** that will help you assess your learning and prepare for exams (student companion workbook, digital glossary, key term flash cards, and review quizzes).

- **Activities and assignments** that will help you hone your knowledge, analyze professional communication situations, build your public speaking skills throughout the course, and learn to work effectively in teams (Awareness Checks, Checkpoints, and Collaborative Learning Activities).

- **Media resources** that will help you explore communication concepts online (web links), develop your speech outlines (Speech Builder Express 3.0), watch and critique videos of professional communication situations and sample speeches (Interactive Video Activities), upload your speech videos for peer reviewing and critique other

students' speeches (Speech Studio online speech review tool), and download chapter review so you can study when and where you'd like (Audio Study Tools).

This chapter's key terms, Collaborative Learning Activities, and Checkpoint activities are also featured on the following pages, and you can find this chapter's Awareness Check activities in the body of the chapter. For more information or to access this book's online resources, visit www.cengage.com/login.

Collaborative Learning Activities

1. In small groups, practice writing good discussion questions by first evaluating what is wrong in each of the following discussion questions; and then rewriting each question to conform to the guidelines in this chapter.

   a. Should General Motors produce electric cars?

   b. Should something be done to alter the ridiculous prices charged by phone companies for long-distance calls?

   c. What can be done to help eliminate waste in the federal government?

2. In small groups, practice brainstorming by listing the qualities you look for in a teacher—stop at the end of 2 minutes. Count your list and compare its length with other group lists. Discuss which of the rules for effective brainstorming gave your group the most trouble and why. Take your list of qualities and discuss how to divide them into wants and musts. Keep your must list relatively short—if you have too many musts, you will never be able to find a teacher that meets them all. When finished, rank the wants from most important to least important striving to get a group consensus. Compare your list with other groups.

Checkpoints

Checkpoint 9.1 Establishing Criteria
Assume that someone in your organization must be transferred to a branch store and that the decision as to who will be transferred has been left to the employees. The branch store is 18 miles from your current store, and all jobs in this organization are considered functionally equivalent. Establish criteria to determine who should be transferred. Show your list to a fellow worker or friend and get some feedback.

Checkpoint 9.2 Evaluating a Decision-Making Meeting

Checkpoint 9.3 Groupthink and Hurricane Katrina

Checkpoint 9.4 Groupthink in Business and World Situations

Checkpoint 9.5 Global Cultural Norms

Checkpoint 9.6 Positive Characteristics

Checkpoint 9.7 Suggestion Box

Checkpoint 9.8 Small Group Communication and Problem Solving Websites

Participation and Leadership in Teams

As you read Chapter 10,

Summarize the communication skills needed by effective team members and why these skills are so important.

Define *task*, *maintenance*, and *dysfunctional roles* as used by effective team participants, and briefly **list** and **explain** the group behaviors that fall under each category.

Describe each of the *different types* of leadership described in this chapter and **explain** what contribution each makes to the person learning to be an effective leader.
Identify the leader's responsibilities during a team meeting.

Andersen Ross/Digital Vision/Getty Images

Case Study: FEMA Leadership in Hurricane Katrina Problematic

When Hurricane Katrina struck Louisiana in August 2005, the Federal Emergency Management Agency (FEMA) responded with mixed leadership. Although FEMA leadership in Baton Rouge was excellent, the leadership shown in New Orleans by FEMA director Michael Brown was completely ineffective (Brinkley, 2006; Heerden & Bryan, 2006; Horne, 2006).

Hurricane Katrina made landfall slightly east of the downtown area on a Monday morning, and as late as Tuesday federal officials thought that the city had "dodged the bullet." In actual fact, the storm surge had created breaches in the flood walls around New Orleans, and millions of gallons of water a minute were pouring into the city eventually flooding 148-square-miles of urban land, killing at least 1,300 people, and trapping thousands on rooftops and in hotels (Horne, 2006; Hudson, 2006). FEMA director Brown had been apprised of the dire conditions in New Orleans on Monday evening, but failed to take any action. He even prevented others from dealing with the problems, which resulted in the absence of needed personnel, supplies, buses, planes, and rescue boats.

When the *only* FEMA employee in New Orleans on Monday morning, Marty Bahamonde, realized the seriousness of the situation, he informed FEMA immediately, which in turn promised food, water trucks, and medical teams (Horne, 2006, p. 52). That evening, when very little of these resources had arrived, he spoke directly with Brown, informing him that the levees had been breached; the city was under water; thousands were trapped on rooftops across town; 20,000 hungry people were camped out in the Superdome; 30,000 tourists were trapped in hotels with no power; and hospitals were not responding to his calls (pp. 58–59).

Lee Celano/Corbis

As you read this chapter, see if you can determine (a) what specific factors made the handling of evacuees so difficult; (b) what leadership style was used by Brown—was it the best for handling a disaster of such magnitude; and (c) which organization model from Chapter 2 best describes FEMA and what role did this model play in this disaster?

At that point, Brown sent a memo to Michael Chertoff, secretary of Homeland Security, requesting that 1,000 employees from the Department of Homeland Security be made available in 2 days and that 2,000 more report in 7 days (Brinkley, 2006, p. 272). The next morning, Brown flew to New Orleans with the Louisiana governor and senators to meet with Mayor Ray Nagin—but he brought no supplies or staff. Before Brown left, Bahamonde twice reiterated how dire the situation was and stressed the hungry and dehydrated people in the dome and the need for oxygen and toilet paper. He told Brown, "Sir, the situation is past critical." Brown responded, "Thanks for the update. Anything specific I need to do or tweak?" (Horne, 2006, p. 64). Brown's response expressed perfectly his seeming apathy and ineffective leadership. The following information is just a sample of additional mind-boggling facts now known (Brinkley, 2006; Heerden & Bryan, 2006; Horne, 2006):

- The USS *Bataan* hospital ship was ready off the coast with 600 hospital beds, six operating rooms, and the capability to make 100,000 gallons-of-water per day—it was not used by FEMA.

- The state Department of Wildlife and Fisheries "had appealed to FEMA's headquarters in Denton, Texas for 300 rubber rafts"—later upped to 1000. They were denied because of possible "debris" in the water (Horne, 2006, p. 89).

- The Department of the Interior (a federal organization) "with hundreds of boats available for rescue work" never got a return call from FEMA so no boats were deployed (Horne, p. 89).

- On Monday, Brown sent out a press release stating, "It is critical that fire and emergency departments across the country remain in their jurisdictions until such time as the affected states request assistance" (FEMA, 2005). For those who came anyway, many were sent home by the National Guard, which had been instructed by FEMA to "keep emergency responders out" so local, state, and federal officials could become "well-coordinated" (Brinkley, 2006, p. 254). FEMA employees "were mortified" (p. 251).

All this happened even after a week-long Hurricane Pam exercise conducted by FEMA in 2004 was designed to clarify "who would be doing what during an actual hurricane emergency" in New Orleans—especially in case of catastrophic flooding (Heerden & Bryan, 2006, p. 149); and after senior FEMA professionals in 2004 expressed to Brown their grave concerns over "unprepared teams and zero funding for training, exercises and team equipment" (Kagan, et al., 2006).

For more information on Hurricane Katrina, go to the Louisiana State University website at Katrina.LSU.edu and browse for information. You can find easy access to this site via your Premium Website for *Communicating for Results*.

The basic problem-solving procedure presented in the previous chapter is a useful way for teams to organize their decision-making processes. As we saw in the opening story about FEMA, poor organization can cause team failure. However, for a small group or team to operate effectively, it must be more than well organized and well trained (as covered in Chapter 9). It also must have team members who know how to participate effectively and leaders who know how to lead. For example, have you ever been in a team where members often wait for the leader to initiate each step, but then become angry when the leader does so? As a result, they feel that they play no real part in the decision-making process. On the other hand, leaders are often confused about their role as well. They want to let team members make decisions but believe that leaders should hold firm control if the team is to accomplish anything.

To help you avoid such problems in your teams, this chapter discusses effective team participation and effective team leadership.

Effective Team Participants Have Good Communication Skills

For successful communication to occur, team members must successfully use the communication skills of commitment and preparation, active listening, open-mindedness, and flexibility in dealing with people of different personality types.

Commitment and Preparation

Effective team members come to their meetings committed and prepared. A committed member is one who is willing to devote time and energy to the team by faithful attendance and is committed to supporting the final decision of the team. When the facts and figures presented during a discussion point to a solution that is agreeable to all but a few members, the majority opinion must stand until new evidence is presented. In the business world, members who are not willing to support their team's final decisions are not committed members. This does not mean that the members should avoid disagreement or productive conflict during the discussion, but once a solution is reached, it should be supported by everyone in the team.

Effective team members also prepare carefully for each meeting. Obviously, meetings run more smoothly when members are prepared. Probably the best way to prepare for a problem-solving discussion is to work through the six basic problem-solving steps before the meeting as discussed in Chapter 9. Come prepared with facts, possible criteria, and possible solutions. Be prepared to research and discuss all pertinent viewpoints and alternatives, thereby avoiding groupthink.

Active Listening   Many times when we are discussing a problem in a group, we listen to gather ammunition for our rebuttals and to determine when to insert our viewpoints. **Active listening**, however, requires us to listen from the speaker's viewpoint. The active listener:

1. *Receives* the speaker's total message—verbal, visual, and nonverbal.
2. *Interprets* the speaker's meaning as closely as possible.
3. *Checks* the interpreted meaning for accuracy by rephrasing it for the speaker.
4. *Repeats* steps 1 through 3 until the speaker is satisfied with the interpretation.

Only after you are sure you understand the speaker's argument should you present your views. This type of active listening is necessary for effective group participation (Larson & LaFasto, 1989).

Jetta Productions/Corbis

For effective group participation to occur, team members must be active listeners, open-minded participants, and able to communicate with teammates of different personality types.

Open-mindedness While preparing for a group discussion, team members sometimes become convinced that a certain solution is best. They come to the discussion prepared to convince the other members to agree with their choice. If all participants were equally closed-minded, the discussion would become a debate. Productivity would decrease, and the meeting would drag on.

Productive team discussion requires that members listen with an open mind and respect others' views (Larson & LaFasto, 1989). But **open-mindedness** does not mean that there will be no disagreement. Conflict over opinions can stimulate the team's thinking. If no one disagreed, the group could fall into a groupthink pattern and arrive at a risky or unsuccessful decision.

Open-minded participants try to reach a decision that benefits the group or company as a whole. They work together as a team, not as unyielding advocates of a particular position.

Effective Personality Types Productive team discussion also requires that members respect and work with the differing personality types of their teammates. Depending on their personality, people interact with others, gather data, make decisions, and orient their lives differently especially during times of crisis. Five personality characteristics often referred to as the "**Big Five" personality factors** are considered important in successful teams (Daft & Marcic, 2009, p. 382):

1. *Extroversion*—how "outgoing, talkative, assertive, and comfortable with inter-personal relationships" the team member may be.

2. *Agreeableness*—how well the team member gets "along with others by being good-natured, likable, forgiving, understandable, and trusting."

3. *Conscientiousness*—how well the team member focuses on team goals in a "responsible, dependable, persistent, and achievement oriented" manner.

4. *Emotional stability*—how "calm, enthusiastic, and self-confident, rather than tense, depressed, moody, or insecure" the team member is.

AWARENESS CHECK

The Big Five Personality Factors Questionnaire

Directions: The following phrases describe various traits and behaviors. Rate how accurately each statement describes you, based on a scale of 1 (low) to 5 (high) accuracy. You can also fill out this questionnaire online using your Premium Website for *Communicating for Results*.

Extroversion

I am usually the life of the party.   1 2 3 4 5

I feel comfortable around people.   1 2 3 4 5

I am talkative.   1 2 3 4 5

Agreeableness

I am kind and sympathetic.   1 2 3 4 5

I have a good word for everyone.   1 2 3 4 5

I never insult people.   1 2 3 4 5

Conscientiousness

I am systematic and efficient.   1 2 3 4 5

I pay attention to details.   1 2 3 4 5

I am always prepared for meetings.   1 2 3 4 5

Emotional Stability

I usually feel proud and pleased with myself.   1 2 3 4 5

I am happy for other people when they receive special recognition.   1 2 3 4 5

I am a relaxed and cheerful person.   1 2 3 4 5

Openness to New Experiences

I am imaginative.   1 2 3 4 5

I am open to new ideas and like to try new things.   1 2 3 4 5

I find it easy to discover creative solutions to problems.   1 2 3 4 5

Interpretation: Determine which traits are your most prominent. If you have a moderate to high degree of each personality factor, you are likely to be an effective team member. If you have a low degree in any factor, be especially aware of how you communicate in future discussions.

Based on Daft, R. L., & Marcic, D. (2009). *Understanding management* (6th ed.). Mason, OH: Thomson South-Western, p. 383.

5. *Openness to experience*—the degree to which the team member "has a broad range of interests and is imaginative, creative, artistically sensitive, and willing to consider new ideas."

Effective Team Participants Perform Needed Task and Maintenance Roles

Team members are responsible for 80% of the success of an organization (Tubbs, 2009), but this success only occurs when members display good communication skills and are able to perform needed task and maintenance roles and be willing to handle any *nonfunctional behaviors* that may appear in the team.

Task and Maintenance Roles

Just as we perform numerous roles in our lives—as a spouse, a student, a member of the church board, a manager, and a friend—so we may perform many task and maintenance roles in the life of a group (Benne & Sheats, 1948; Mudrack & Farrell, 1995). **Task roles** are functions that must be performed if the group is to accomplish its task or solve its problem. **Maintenace roles** are functions that must be performed to maintain the interpersonal relationships and harmony of the group. The number of task and maintenance roles that need to be performed in a particular group depends on the personalities of the group members, the goal of the group, and even the leadership style of the leader (see situational leadership). Task roles are stressed more by the traditional/classical manager, whereas maintenance roles are stressed more by the human relations manager (see Chapter 2). The following lists give examples of various task and maintenance roles (Benne & Sheats, 1948; Keyton, 1999, pp. 65–66).

Group Task Roles
- *Initiate.* Propose new ideas, procedures, goals, and solutions to get the discussion started.
- *Give information.* Supply evidence and experiences relevant to the task.
- *Seek information.* Request and clarify information from other members.
- *Give opinions.* State beliefs, attitudes, and judgments.
- *Seek opinions.* Solicit and clarify opinions and feelings of others.
- *Elaborate.* Clarify and expand the ideas of others through examples, illustrations, and explanations.
- *Energize.* Stimulate the group to be energetic and active.
- *Review.* Summarize the discussion throughout.
- *Record.* Record group suggestions and decisions.

Group Maintenance Roles
- *Encourage.* Provide a warm, supportive interpersonal climate by praising and agreeing with others (especially important during conflict).
- *Harmonize.* While recognizing the value of conflict to a group, members reconcile differences in a productive manner. Compromise and mediation may be used when necessary.
- *Relieve tension.* When necessary, relax the atmosphere through informality or humor.
- *Gatekeep.* Control the flow of communication: Draw the nontalkers into the discussion, and tactfully cut off the monopolizers and other dysfunctional members in an attempt to give all members an equal chance to communicate.

The positive behaviors of task and maintenance functions are necessary in groups. Gatekeepers are needed to minimize nonfunctional behaviors.

Dysfunctional Behaviors Some behaviors are dysfunctional because they serve individual needs while inhibiting group needs. Although these behaviors often cause problems, some of them can also stimulate healthy conflict and jar a group out of its groupthink pattern. Some of the common **dysfunctional behaviors** of group members are listed here (Benne & Sheets, 1948; Keyton, 1999, pp. 66–67).

Dysfunctional Behavior

- *Blocking.* Constantly putting down the ideas and suggestions of others.
- *Aggression.* Insulting and criticizing other members, perhaps out of jealousy or dislike.
- *Storytelling.* Luring the group off track with irrelevant stories, often very interesting.
- *Recognition seeking.* Calling attention to personal achievements and successes.
- *Dominating.* Monopolizing group interaction; often, domination is the result of excellent preparation and involvement in the discussion.
- *Confessing.* Using the group as a sounding board for personal problems and feelings.
- *Special-interest pleading.* Representing the interest of another group, regardless of whether it fits the topic being discussed.
- *Distracting.* Distracting the group with antics, jokes, and comments at inappropriate moments.
- *Withdrawing.* Participating very little or not at all, possibly from lack of preparation, nervousness, or the climate of the group.

Handling Dysfunctional Behaviors   When it is obvious that these behaviors are causing unproductive conflict, handle them with care and tact. The key to handling these behaviors lies in the reason for them. Careful observation of both the verbal and the nonverbal behaviors of these team members should give the gatekeeper or leader valuable clues to their motives. Although the appointed leader often takes responsibility for handling dysfunctional behaviors, committed team members should be willing to help as well. Here are some helpful hints for minimizing the effect of dysfunctional behaviors:

- *Plan your opening remarks carefully.* When you are the leader, open the meeting with a reference to the short time allotted for the meeting and request that all remarks be brief and specific. Mention that you will be interrupting conversations when necessary to keep the discussion on track. Listing expected topics or the criteria for performance is surprisingly effective in directing group behavior. Most members are willing to conform to necessary limitations as long as they know what they are and the reasons for them.
- If you know ahead of time that a person with potentially dysfunctional behavior will be present, *seat the person immediately next to the leader.* It is easier to bypass a person in this position. If the leader is sitting on one side of a rectangular table, make sure the person with dysfunctional behavior is not at one of the ends of the table (the traditional power seats) or across from the leader, where direct eye contact is impossible to avoid.
- *Avoid direct eye contact* with anyone performing dysfunctional behaviors. Eye contact in American society is a nonverbal signal that encourages talking. Therefore, when asking a question of the group, look only at those to whom you wish to speak.
- *Assign dysfunctional members specific tasks* to keep them occupied. For example, ask them to help you relieve tension during the sure-to-come tense moments or

Revisiting the Case Study

Were FEMA's problems mainly due to poor leadership, ineffective team participation, or poor training? What solutions would you recommend?

Lee Celano/Corbis

to be the recorder. By having to concentrate on their tasks, these nonfunctional people will likely become productive team members.

- *Ask members to speak in a specific order* to make sure that everyone gets a chance to participate. Such regimentation will make the group more formal, however, and should be used only when necessary.

- When a person who is displaying a nonfunctional behavior stops to take a breath, *break in!* Briefly summarize the previous comments, or quickly ask someone else for an opinion. Don't ask, "Is that correct?" He or she will simply begin speaking again.

- *Place an extremely talkative member between two extremely quiet members.* Such seating seems to stimulate the quiet members and restrain the talkative member.

- *Encourage withdrawers* by giving only positive feedback to their comments or by asking them specific questions.

- *Give praise and encouragement* when possible to those who seem to need it, including the distracters, the blockers, and the withdrawn.

Effective Team Leadership

In addition to an organized procedure and committed participants with good communication skills, an effective team must have good leadership. Without it, situations like Brown's handling of Hurricane Katrina (covered in the chapter case study) can occur. With good leadership, even complicated and stressful situations like Katrina can be handled effectively. Contrast, for example, the disaster in New Orleans with the Baton Rouge success that involved FEMA crisis communications officer, Robert Alvey (Alvey, 2005):

> Two days before Hurricane Katrina touched down, the Louisiana Department of Health and Hospitals (LDHH) prepared a field hospital on the LSU campus in Baton Rouge and began to stockpile supplies. They also requested a crisis communications officer from FEMA, Robert Alvey, to serve as media manager for the hospital and lead LSU's inexperienced crisis communication team in handling the large number of media expected to descend on the hospital.
>
> The crisis communication team had to work within the field hospital's nonnegotiable rules: "No disruption of medical care, no talking to patients or medical staff, no identifying images of patients, no more than five or six media per tour, and all media needed to be escorted by armed security" (p. 12). Alvey had his own unbreakable rules for the team: limit comments to the field hospital's activities or conditions; talk about the news, don't make it; and be proactive with the media by establishing the team as "the source" for information. Under Alvey's guidance, the team conducted more than 125 media tours and facilitated almost 300 interviews in one week. They also "produced stock photos and video footage for the media" (p. 12), established their own disaster website, held press conferences, and worked to unite children with missing families. Avery and his team played a large role in the Baton Rouge success story because they handled evacuee, staff, and media needs rapidly and effectively, allowing the medical teams the time and quiet they needed to concentrate on evacuees.

There are many theories of leadership (see Table 10.1). Research does not completely validate any of these theories, and they are not all equally helpful to those who want advice on how to become a good leader. Therefore, we summarize here those theories that are the most important if you wish to assess your leadership skills.

TABLE 10.1

Leadership Theories	
Behavior Theories	
Trait	Leaders are born with certain leader characteristics.
Two-dimension	Leaders have either task orientation or people orientation (Stogdill, 1948).
Function	Leadership is determined by a set of functions—task functions and maintenance functions. Anyone can perform functions, thereby sharing leadership responsibility (Benne & Sheats, 1948).
Three-dimension	Leader behavior is thought of in terms of three basic styles: autocratic, democratic, or laissez-faire (White & Lippitt, 1968).
Situational Theories	
Situational contingency	Leader style determined by (a) leader-member relations, (b) how clearly task is structured, (c) leader's power position (strong or weak). Different leader styles successful in different sets of circumstances. Leaders normally don't change styles (Fiedler, 1967, 1996).
Situational leadership	Leaders can change styles to fit the situation. Which of four styles to use—delegating, participating, selling, or telling—depends on the ability and willingness of subordinates to carry out the task (Hersey & Blanchard, 1996; Hersey, Blanchard, & Johnson, 2007).
Path-goal	Leader effectiveness depends on leader's abilities and group's needs. Leader is responsible for assisting followers in attaining their goals while providing needed direction—making the path to those goals clear (House, 1971; House & Aditya, 1997).
Recent Theories	
Normative decision	Provides a step-by-step guide for selecting one of five basic decision-making strategies (Vroom & Yetton, 1973; revised by Vroom & Jago, 1988).
Transformational	A charismatic leadership style that inspires employees to exceptional performance, enthusiasm, and loyalty (Bass, 1985, 1995; Burns, 1978).

Trait Theory of Leadership

Do you believe that some people are "born leaders"? Such a belief is based on the **trait theory** of leadership, which claims that a person must have certain traits to become a leader. Although it may be helpful and even desirable for a leader to have such traits as self-confidence or flexibility, research on leadership does not completely support the trait theory. Keith Davis (1972) reports the following:

> Research has produced such a variegated list of traits presumably to describe leadership that for all practical purposes it describes nothing. Fifty years of study have failed to produce one personality trait or set of qualities that can be used to discriminate between leaders and nonleaders. (p. 3)

In a search for leader traits, Stogdill (1948) reviewed more than 25,000 books and research articles on leadership and management and failed to find any "magic" traits that fit all leaders in all situations (see also Bass, 1995). In more recent reviews of trait research (Kellett et al., 2006; Kirkpatrick & Locke, 1991; Kouzes & Posner, 2002), researchers report that successful leaders do seem to be different from less successful leaders: Successful leaders are more likely to be ambitious, fair-minded, inspiring, empathetic, trustworthy, motivated to lead, self-confident, able to integrate and interpret large amounts of information, knowledgeable of their industry and of technical matters, creative, and able to adapt to people and situations.

Even so, most experts believe that *good leaders are not born, they are trained.* Practically anyone willing to spend the time for training can become a team leader. People who seem to be natural leaders have usually observed leaders (perhaps a parent or mentor) and had leadership experience (various clubs and organizations). Determine your leadership traits in the following Awareness Check.

AWARENESS CHECK

Leadership Trait Questionnaire

The main benefit of trait theory is that you can use it to indicate leadership characteristics that are strengths and those needing some long-term improvement. To determine your leadership traits, complete the following questionnaire. You can also fill out this questionnaire online using your Premium Website for *Communicating for Results.*

Directions: *You and two other individuals* should complete the following questionnaire about *you* as a leader. Indicate the degree that each adjective describes you (as leader) and *see how closely their perceptions match yours.*

5 = Strongly Agree   4 = Agree   3 = Neutral   2 = Disagree   1 = Strongly Disagree

	Rater One	Rater Two	Your Rating
1. **Articulate** (communicates effectively with others)	1 2 3 4 5	1 2 3 4 5	1 2 3 4 5
2. **Perceptive** (discerning and insightful)	1 2 3 4 5	1 2 3 4 5	1 2 3 4 5
3. **Self-confident** (believes in oneself and one's ability)	1 2 3 4 5	1 2 3 4 5	1 2 3 4 5
4. **Self-assured** (secure with self, free of doubts)	1 2 3 4 5	1 2 3 4 5	1 2 3 4 5
5. **Persistent** (stays fixed on goals, despite interference)	1 2 3 4 5	1 2 3 4 5	1 2 3 4 5
6. **Determined** (takes a firm stand, acts with certainty)	1 2 3 4 5	1 2 3 4 5	1 2 3 4 5
7. **Trustworthy** (acts believably, inspires confidence)	1 2 3 4 5	1 2 3 4 5	1 2 3 4 5
8. **Dependable** (is consistent and reliable)	1 2 3 4 5	1 2 3 4 5	1 2 3 4 5
9. **Friendly** (shows kindness and warmth)	1 2 3 4 5	1 2 3 4 5	1 2 3 4 5
10. **Outgoing** (talks freely, gets along well with others)	1 2 3 4 5	1 2 3 4 5	1 2 3 4 5

Interpretation:
Use the ratings from your two friends to compare with your personal ratings to more accurately determine *your strengths and weaknesses* as a leader. When all three of you agree, those adjectives are the most accurate.

Adapted from Northouse, P. G. (1997). *Leadership: Theory and practice.* Thousand Oaks, CA: Sage., pp. 28–29.

Function Theory of Leadership

Suppose that you have just been promoted to supervisor and the first day with your new employees will be in 1 week. Or suppose that your boss has asked you to lead a problem-solving team that will meet in 2 weeks. Is it possible to train yourself to be a leader in 1 or 2 weeks? Not if you believe in the trait theory! You could have a nervous breakdown trying to acquire Kirkpatrick and Locke's (1991) list of "successful leadership characteristics": ambitious, trustworthy, motivated, self-confident, intelligent, knowledgeable, creative, and flexible. How long would it take to train yourself to be ambitious, self-confident, and creative? Thinking of leadership as a list of personality traits is counterproductive.

Instead, think of leadership as an activity composed of various functions or roles (Benne & Sheats, 1948; Keyton, 1999, pp. 65–67; Sayles, 1993). The **function theory** claims that there are certain functions or roles that must be performed if a group is to be successful. Any time you perform one of these roles, you are the leader for that period of time.

As mentioned previously, **leadership** may be defined as the use of power to promote the goal accomplishment and maintenance of the group (Johnson & Johnson, 2002). In other words, the leader is the person (or persons) who performs the task and maintenance roles discussed previously in this chapter. In many groups, the appointed leader performs most of the task and maintenance roles. However, in democratic groups in which the members are committed and involved, the leadership functions or roles are shared. Because it is difficult for one person, the designated leader, to guide a group through the basic problem-solving procedure and, at the same time, to be aware of all the roles that need to be performed, another member can handle some leadership roles. For example, you may be sitting next to someone who has been trying to participate in the conversation for several minutes, but the leader and the other members are so involved in what's being said that they haven't noticed. When you say, "Carol has a point she wishes to make," you are performing gatekeeping, an important leadership role. Furthermore, in some groups the appointed leader is inept, and the only way the group will succeed is for one or more members to emerge as the real leaders. If you wish to develop leadership skills, begin by simply learning to perform the task and maintenance roles discussed previously. The Awareness Check on page 272 will help you assess your task and maintenance skills.

Leadership Styles or Three-Dimension Theory of Leadership

To become a skilled leader, you should be aware of your **leadership style** (the way you handle yourself and others in a group). The leadership styles or **three-dimension theory** of leadership describes three different leadership styles: authoritarian, democratic, and laissez-faire. J. Kevin Barge (1994, pp. 203–204) summarizes the three main leadership styles as follows:

- *Authoritarian leadership style.* Leaders are central authority figures who retain a high degree of control and power over their followers. Leaders make the decisions, whereas followers' participation in decision making is minimal. Leaders use one-way communication.

- *Democratic leadership style.* Leaders and followers make decisions together and jointly determine courses of action. They are viewed more as equals because two-way communication exists between leaders and followers.

Leadership Function Questionnaire

Directions: After you have participated in at least one group discussion, complete the following questionnaire *indicating how often you performed each task and maintenance function.* You can also fill out this questionnaire online using your Premium Website for *Communicating for Results.*

5 = Several times	4 = A few times	3 = Twice	2 = Once	1 = Never

1. **Initiator** (proposed new ideas, procedures, goals, etc., to get the discussion started)   1 2 3 4 5

2. **Information giver/seeker** (supplied evidence and experiences/requested information and ideas from others)   1 2 3 4 5

3. **Opinion giver/seeker** (stated beliefs and judgments/ asked others for opinions and feelings)   1 2 3 4 5

4. **Elaborator** (clarified and expanded ideas of others through examples and illustrations)   1 2 3 4 5

5. **Energizer** (stimulated group to be energetic and active)   1 2 3 4 5

6. **Reviewer/recorder** (summarized group's opinion and/or kept official record of discussion)   1 2 3 4 5

7. **Encourager** (helped provide a supportive climate by praising and supporting the ideas of others)   1 2 3 4 5

8. **Harmonizer** (helped group members settle differences in productive manner)   1 2 3 4 5

9. **Tension reliever** (helped relieve tense situations by poking fun or using humor)   1 2 3 4 5

10. **Gatekeeper** (encouraged nontalkers/tactfully cut off monopolizers and nonfunctional members)   1 2 3 4 5

Interpretation: Roles that received a 4 or 5 show leadership skill. Roles that received a 1 or 2 need additional improvement for effective leadership performance.
Adapted from Benne, K. D., & Sheats, P. (1948). Functional roles and group members. *Journal of Social Issues, 4,* 41–49. (The Leadership Function questionnaire used by permission.)

- *Laissez-faire leadership style.* This style of leadership is best characterized by leaders who are not involved with the team's decision making. . . . Team members make work assignments and evaluate task completion among themselves.

Authoritarian Leader The **authoritarian leadership style** is similar to the traditional organization model and the blind communication style discussed in Chapters 2 and 3.

- Advantages: the team reaches a solution quickly, often makes few errors, and gets more work accomplished than groups that get bogged down in detailed discussion. Also, large groups often need an authoritarian leader to maintain control.

- Disadvantages: members may develop a dependence on the leader rather than a trust in their own abilities and initiative and they tend to display more discontent and even hostility with their low level of participation. Manz and Sims (2001) found group hostility to be 30 times greater in autocratic teams than democratic teams.

- Level of use is declining. Wagner and Hollenbeck (2010) note, "In today's project-oriented, team-driven business environment, autocratic leadership is becoming more and more rare" (p. 225).

Democratic Leader The **democratic leadership style** is similar to both the human resources model and the open communication style discussed in Chapters 2 and 3.

© 2002 Ted Goff. Reprinted by permission. www.tedgoff.com

"I'd like to take this opportunity to acknowledge my wonderful coaching, which resulted in your accomplishments."

- Advantages: motivation, initiative, and creativity are higher than in autocratic groups. Also, under democratic leadership, team members experience a high level of personal satisfaction and are more committed to the team and its final decision.

- Disadvantages: tasks take longer to accomplish under a democratic leader because so many employees have ideas to share.

- Level of use is increasing.

In the business world, team commitment to decisions can be important—especially because people tend to resist change. One way to reduce resistance to change is to allow employees to share their ideas in small teams and to take part in deciding how the change is to take place. People who have been involved in a decision are much more likely to abide by it (even if they aren't completely happy with it) than people who have not. Therefore, the democratic style of leadership is a good choice when member satisfaction and personal commitment are crucial. In fact, Manz and Sims (2001) call democratic leadership that involves and empowers team members *SuperLeadership*; Tubbs (2009) calls this type leadership "the trend in leadership development of the future" (p. 237). Keep in mind, however, that democratic leadership can be difficult and time consuming. It takes much skill and patience to become a good democratic leader.

Laissez-Faire Leader Most groups seem to need more guidance than the **laissez-faire leader** gives. As a result, this style of leadership tends to result in a low level of group productivity and poor member satisfaction. Only one type of group usually excels with this "nonleader": a group of highly trained, highly motivated experts (such as a group of vice presidents) who perform leadership roles themselves.

Situational Contingency Theory of Leadership

Another approach to leadership is to adapt to the situation and the contingencies involved. Before choosing a leadership style, you would weigh the style you are most comfortable with, the needs and expectations of the group, the situation, and the goals of the group. For example, if group members expect a good leader

Revisiting the Case Study

Do you think Brown's leadership was more autocratic, democratic, or laissez-faire? How do you know?

Lee Celano/Corbis

to be autocratic, they may not perceive you as a good leader if you use the democratic style.

Because of the normal pressures of the business world, the *situation* may be the primary factor that dictates the most effective leadership style. Fred Fiedler remains the best-known exponent of **situational contingency theory** (see Chapter 2, p. 52 for a more detailed explanation). In summary, Fiedler (1967, 1978, 1993, 1996) found that leadership in any given situation depends on the *power* of the leader, the nature of the *task*, and the *relationship* between the leader and the team members.

AWARENESS CHECK

Least Preferred Coworker (LPC) Measure

Directions: Use Fiedler's LPC Scale to rate a difficult coworker. Do not describe yourself as you answer this questionnaire, instead, *describe a person you have major problems working with.* Circle the number between each pair of adjectives that best describes this person and record it in the Scores column. When finished, total the Scores column for your LPC score. You can also fill out this questionnaire online using your Premium Website for *Communicating for Results.*

Scores

Pleasant	8 7 6 5 4 3 2 1	Unpleasant	_____
Friendly	8 7 6 5 4 3 2 1	Unfriendly	_____
Rejecting	1 2 3 4 5 6 7 8	Accepting	_____
Tense	1 2 3 4 5 6 7 8	Relaxed	_____
Distant	1 2 3 4 5 6 7 8	Close	_____
Cold	1 2 3 4 5 6 7 8	Warm	_____
Supportive	8 7 6 5 4 3 2 1	Hostile	_____
Boring	1 2 3 4 5 6 7 8	Interesting	_____
Quarrelsome	1 2 3 4 5 6 7 8	Harmonious	_____
Gloomy	1 2 3 4 5 6 7 8	Cheerful	_____
Open	8 7 6 5 4 3 2 1	Closed	_____
Backbiting	1 2 3 4 5 6 7 8	Loyal	_____
Untrustworthy	1 2 3 4 5 6 7 8	Trustworthy	_____
Considerate	8 7 6 5 4 3 2 1	Inconsiderate	_____
Nasty	1 2 3 4 5 6 7 8	Nice	_____
Agreeable	8 7 6 5 4 3 2 1	Disagreeable	_____
Insincere	1 2 3 4 5 6 7 8	Sincere	_____
Kind	8 7 6 5 4 3 2 1	Unkind	_____
Total:	_____		

Interpretation of total score: 57 or below indicates that you are more *task* motivated; 64 or above indicates that you are more *relationship* motivated.

Adapted from Fiedler, F. E., & Chemers, M. M. (1974). *Leadership and effective management.* Glenview, IL: Scott, Foresman.

He determined task and relationship preferences by how each leader reacted to a "least preferred coworker" (LPC). If you tend to react fairly negatively to coworkers you least like, Fiedler would say you are a *low LPC leader* (authoritarian) who is more task oriented than relationship oriented. If you react fairly positively to coworkers you least like, he would say you are a *high LPC leader* (democratic) who is more interested in relationships than tasks.

Researching both leader types, Fiedler found that authoritarian (or low LPC) leadership is more effective at two extremes: When the leader is powerful, the task is well defined, and relations are good; or when the leader has little power, the task is poorly structured, and the leader is disliked by the group. Democratic (or high LPC) leadership is more effective when the three conditions are somewhere between the two extremes—when the leader has some power, is moderately liked, and the task is somewhat vague.

To determine whether you are more *task oriented* or more *relationship oriented*, complete the Awareness Check on page 274.

Another situational variable is *time*. In selecting an appropriate leadership style, you need to consider the time needed to (a) reach a decision, (b) get group commitment, and (c) implement the decision. The chart in Figure 10.1 compares the total time for the three leadership styles. Although the autocratic approach is usually assumed to be the fastest, the chart shows that it is actually the slowest when the

IT REALLY WORKS!

Innovative Leadership

The late Bill Gore was the founder of W. L. Gore & Associates, a private company that makes over 1,000 innovative products including Gore-Tex fabric, which is used by soldiers, astronauts, and clothing designers. This fabric has a transparent plastic coating that makes it windproof and waterproof but also breathable (Deutschman, 2004).

Gore's innovative leadership style was based on an epiphany he had one day that "the best communication happened in the carpool because that was the one place where there was no hierarchy," and that people in a crisis solve problems faster and more creatively when they throw out the rules (Daft & Marcic, 2006, p. 299). Because he didn't want to wait for a crisis, "Bill Gore threw out the rules. He created a place with hardly any hierarchy and few ranks and titles. He insisted on direct, one-on-one communication; anyone in the company could speak to anyone else" (Deutschman, 2004, para. 7). Gore put salespeople, research and development, and production workers all in the same location so they could work readily together as needed for various projects. Although new employees in his corporation have a "sponsor" and are told to spend at least 10% of their time working on innovative ideas, they usually have a hard time grasping that there really isn't a boss to keep track of what they do (para. 15). All employees are called associates, and all employees are free to be leaders. If

they have an idea, passion for the idea, and the ability to sell their idea to others, that is all that is needed for leadership. The current CEO, Terri Kelly, continues with the goal "to provide overall direction and guidance, not to micromanage and tell people how to do their jobs" (Daft, 2008, p. 492).

Gore's leadership innovation didn't stop there. He helped ensure successful teamwork by organizing his employees into buildings that housed no more than 150 people (Deutschman, 2004). In the *Tipping Point*, Gladwell (2002) calls this "the Rule of 150": Groups made up of smaller teams work well together as long as the number of group members remains below 150. As Gore discovered, however, "things get clumsy" with larger groups (p. 184). This principle is illustrated by the corporation's expansion policy: When an associate was asked how management knew it was time to build a new plant, the reply was simple: "When people start parking on the grass" (p. 185).

What Do You Think?

- Which leadership theory or style do you think Gore was using?

- What are some advantages and some disadvantages of this style?

- Why do you think groups that include more than 150 people have problems communicating?

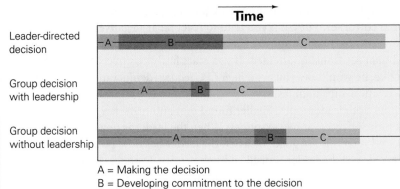

A = Making the decision
B = Developing commitment to the decision
C = Implementing the decision

FIGURE 10.1 The decision time line.

Source: Marshall Sashkin and William C. Morris, 1984, *Organizational Behavior: Concepts and Experiences,* Reston, VA: Reston Publishing, p. 190. Printed by permission of Prentice-Hall, Inc., Englewood cliffs, NJ.

time required to implement a decision is included. The autocratic style is quick at reaching a solution but slow at implementation, possibly because group members are not fully committed. The democratic style takes longer to reach a decision but is faster to implement, probably because the group is actively involved in the decision.

Generally, the *autocratic leadership style* works best in the following conditions:

- Group agreement is not required for implementation.
- The group is very large.
- Time for a decision is short.
- Tasks are fairly simple.

Democratic leadership is suggested when the following are true:

- Greater employee satisfaction is needed.
- Group commitment is needed for implementation.
- Tasks are complicated and require lengthy discussion.
- Increased productivity is needed (Galbraith, 1967).
- Reduced resistance to change is sought.

Selecting the wrong leadership style can result in wasted time, unacceptable solutions, unhappy or hostile employees, and resistance instead of commitment to an idea.

Situational Leadership Theory

Believing that a good leader is flexible and can change styles when needed, Hersey and Blanchard (1996, pp. 516–517; Hersey et al., 2007) describe the following four leadership styles—style selection depends on the ability and willingness of subordinates to carry out a particular task:

- *Delegating style.* Employees make and implement decisions on their own. This style works best when employees are both willing and able to do the job.
- *Participating style.* Employees and leader share in decision making. This style works best when employees have the ability but require encouragement.
- *Telling style.* Employees receive detailed instructions with close supervision. This style works best when employees are able but lack the knowledge needed to do the job.

- *Selling or coaching style.* Employees receive structured but supportive instructions. This style is needed when employees have neither the ability nor the willingness to do the job.

Although research has yet to prove the validity of this **situational leadership theory**, companies such as Xerox, Caterpillar, and Mobil Oil have found it a successful tool in their leadership training (Greenberg & Baron, 1997, p. 510).

To determine which situational leadership style you tend to prefer, complete the following Awareness Check.

AWARENESS CHECK

Situational Leadership Questionnaire

Directions: Read each of the following questions and decide which action you would most likely take: A, B, C, or D.

A = Let the group members decide what to do.

B = Ask members for input, but make the final decision yourself.

C = Make the decision yourself, but explain your reasons.

D = Make the decision yourself, but tell the group exactly what to do.

You can also fill out this questionnaire online using your Premium Website for *Communicating for Results*.

_____ 1. In the face of financial pressures, you are forced to make budget cuts for your unit. Where do you cut?

_____ 2. To meet an impending deadline, someone in your secretarial pool will have to work late one evening to finish typing an important report. Who will it be?

_____ 3. As coach of a company softball team, you are required to trim your squad to 25 players from 30 currently on the roster. Who goes?

_____ 4. Employees in your department have to schedule their summer vacations so as to keep the office appropriately staffed. How is the decision made?

_____ 5. As chair of the social committee, you are responsible for determining the theme for the company ball. How do you do so?

_____ 6. You have an opportunity to buy or rent an important piece of equipment for your company. After gathering all the facts, how do you make the choice?

_____ 7. The office is being redecorated. How do you decide on the color scheme?

_____ 8. Along with your associates, you are taking a visiting dignitary to dinner. How do you decide what restaurant to go to?

Interpretation:
Delegating score is the number of times you chose A _____.
Participating score is the number of times you chose B _____.
Selling score is the number of times you chose C _____.
Telling score is the number of times you chose D _____.
From Marshall Sashkin and William C. Morris, 1984, *Organizational Behavior: Concepts and Experiences* (Reston, VA: Reston Publishing) p. 190. Reprinted by permission of Pearson Education, Inc.

Transformational Leadership

Franklin D. Roosevelt, Martin Luther King Jr., Mary Kay Ash (of Mary Kay Cosmetics), Lee Iacocca, and Rudolph W. Giuliani are examples of **transformational leaders**, that is, **charismatic leaders** who inspired followers to exceptional performance, enthusiasm, and loyalty. Iacocca was the executive who took over Chrysler Corporation when it was several billion dollars in the red, convinced Congress to approve a $1.5 billion loan guarantee, and motivated workers to pull together and the public to buy. As a result, Chrysler was able to pay back the federal loan 7 years before it was due (Iacocca & Novak, 1986). Giuliani was the mayor of New York City who in 7 years was able to decrease felony crimes by 57% and murders by 68%, raise property values, redevelop Manhattan, encourage growth in tourism, and lead the city through the worst terrorist attack ever on U.S. soil. Working 20-hour days, Giuliani encouraged rescue workers, consoled survivors, spoke with compassion and optimism, and within days convinced the world that "New York City was getting back to normalcy" (Bass & Riggio, 2006, p. 57; Robbins, 2003, pp. 334–335). Reuben Mark, chairman of the board and CEO of Colgate for over 20 years, is another example of a transformational leader (Ellison, 2004). He helped raise company profits to over $10 billion with sales in 222 countries. Mark "meets regularly with Colgate employees and is the corporate cheerleader, discussing Colgate's core values: caring, continuous improvements and teamwork" (p. B1). It was under his guidance that the Bright Smiles, Bright Future program began, whose goal is to teach oral hygiene to over 100 million children in the United States and around the world (UnityFirst.com, 2003). Transformational leadership as shown by Iacocca, Giuliani, and Mark includes the following components:

> [Transformational] leadership is charismatic, and followers seek to identify with the leader and emulate him or her. The leadership inspires followers with challenge and persuasion, providing both meaning and understanding. The leadership is intellectually stimulating, expanding the followers' use of their abilities. Finally, the leadership is individually considerate, providing the follower with support, mentoring, and coaching. (Bass & Riggio, 2006, p. 5)

According to Jerald Greenberg and Robert Baron (1997), transformational leaders do more than "articulate a vision"; they "provide a plan for attaining their vision" that makes sense to their followers (p. 510). They are also careful to build relationships with management and employees who feel a special kind of relationship with the transformational leader (Daft & Marcic, 2009). As J. A. Conger (1991) notes, because of this relationship, the transformational leader can "make an appealing dream seem like tomorrow's reality" (p. 44). In brief, the transformational leader has undeniable *charisma* (Bass & Riggio, 2006; Greenberg, 2003). Research supports that these leaders are able to improve performance at all levels of their organizations (Lowe et al., 1996). Unfortunately, not all charismatic leaders are ethical, as indicated in this chapter's Ethics Dilemma story. Williams (2007) describes *unethical charismatics* as leaders who "control and manipulate followers, do what is best for themselves instead of their organizations, want to hear only positive feedback, share only information that is beneficial to themselves, and have moral standards that put their interests before everyone else's" (p. 475).

To determine whether you are a transformational leader with charisma, complete the following Awareness Check.

AP Photo/FRANK FRANKLIN II

Transformational leaders such as Rudolph W. Giuliani inspire followers to exceptional performance, enthusiasm, and loyalty.

AWARENESS CHECK

Charisma Quotient

Directions: Select an answer for each question. You can also fill out this questionnaire online using your Premium Website for *Communicating for Results*.

Answers

1. I worry most about (a) my current competitors or (b) my future competitors. _____

2. I'm most at ease thinking in (a) generalities or (b) specifics. _____

3. I tend to focus on (a) our missed opportunities or (b) opportunities we've seized. _____

4. I prefer to (a) promote traditions that made us great or (b) create new traditions. _____

5. I like to communicate an idea via (a) a written report or (b) a one-page chart. _____

6. I tend to ask (a) "How can we do this better?" or (b) "Why are we doing this?" _____

7. I believe (a) there's always a way to minimize risk or (b) some risks are too high. _____

8. When I disagree with my boss, I typically (a) coax him nicely to alter his view or (b) bluntly tell him, "You're wrong." _____

9. I tend to sway people by using (a) emotion or (b) logic. _____

10. I think this quiz is (a) ridiculous or (b) fascinating. _____

Interpretation:

Charisma leaders answer as follows: 1 (b); 2 (a); 3 (a); 4 (b); 5 (b); 6 (b); 7 (a); 8 (b); 9 (a); 10 (b). If you answered four or fewer questions as listed, you probably don't have much charisma. Seven or more? You ooze it!

Sellers, P. (1996). What exactly is charisma? *Fortune, 133*(1), 68–75.

Leader Responsibilities

Regardless of whether the team is small or large or meeting virtually or face to face, if you are the designated leader, you should be ready to assume certain responsibilities for maximum team success.

Virtual Meetings One of the latest innovations in small-group management is the concept of virtual teams. As discussed previously in the text, a **virtual team** is composed of members in diverse locations, each with a specific expertise, who rarely meet face to face. Business is conducted electronically usually either through the Internet, web conferencing, or tele/videoconferencing. This poses a challenge for leaders: What strategies work best when managing virtual teams? The following suggestions are a good place to begin (Gibson & Cohen, 2003; Robey et al., 2000; VirtualConnection.biz, 2003):

- *Select team members carefully.* Look for good communicators who are self-motivated, self-reliant, creative, adaptable, and expert in needed areas.

- *Avoid micro-management.* Once you have picked a good team, let them function while still providing structure, clear goals, ground rules, and performance criteria.

- *Provide detailed training.* Regular team training plus trust-building exercises and training in information and communication technologies is necessary. In his book, *The Five Dysfunctions of a Team*, Patrick Lencioni (2002) says, "Trust lies at the heart of a functioning, cohesive team. Without it, teamwork is all but impossible" (p. 195). Trust is even more important in virtual teams.

- *Encourage regular and extensive communication.* An initial team-building session (face to face if possible) could include sharing a personal fact, pet peeves, hobbies, and photos. Team building creates morale and trust. Plan regular feedback sessions in which information and resources are shared and hold face-to-face meetings at least once a year if possible.

ETHICAL DILEMMA

Transformational leaders have a charming, almost hypnotic, way about them called charisma. The Greek's defined *charisma* as "gift from God." However, there are two types of charismatic leaders: ethical and unethical. Unethical charismatic leaders are interested in the benefit of self over all others. This was certainly true of Enron's former chief financial officer, Andrew Fastow (Williams, 2007, p. 475).

When Fastow became Enron's CFO, he was essentially an unknown, yet, "suffering delusions of grandeur after just a little time on the job, Fastow ordered Enron's PR people to lobby *CFO* magazine to make him its CFO of the year" (Deutschman, 2005, para. 15). One banker described him this way: "He was so mean in business but so personally delightful" (McLean & Elkind, 2003, p. 139). While Fastow and his team were "creating the financial structures that would allow Enron to hit its profit targets" (p. 141), he was also stealing money directly from Enron. In 2002, his fraudulent deals came to light in court, and Fastow was forced to return $24 million and was sentenced to serve 10 years in federal prison (Deutschman, 2005, para.15).

Robert Hare, professor emeritus at Columbia, refers to corporate charismatic leaders as *corporate psychopaths* because they "ruthlessly seek their own selfish interests" (Deutschman, 2005, para. 6). In a personality scale he devised, he says these people score high on Factor 1, which includes eight traits: "glibness and superficial charm; grandiose sense of self-worth; pathological lying; conning and manipulativeness; lack of remorse or guilt; shallow affect [emotional displays to cover coldness]; callousness and lack of empathy; and the failure to accept responsibility for one's own actions" (para. 12). According to many people who knew him, these traits describe Fastow quite well.

Questions: Why do you think unethical charismatic leaders are able to fool so many people for so long? Would it be as easy to fool a team of 5 to 15 people? Think about the traits of a corporate psychopath listed by Dr. Hare. What verbal and nonverbal communication behaviors do you think team members should be able to detect to identify an unethical charismatic?

Face-to-Face Meetings When more formal face-to-face meetings are needed, leaders are responsible for including the following (adapted from Guffey, 2010, pp. 321–327):

- *Inform everyone involved when and where all meetings are to take place.* Distribute an agenda whenever possible.

- *Select a place for the meeting that will be conducive to effective discussion.* Pay attention to the surroundings—make them as pleasant as possible. Comfortable chairs that can be arranged in a circle are desirable. Serve refreshments if possible.

- *Check the facilities a few minutes before the meeting to see that everything needed is in place.* It can be disconcerting to discover that the media equipment is missing, that there are too few chairs, or that the room has another meeting scheduled at the same time as yours.

- *Welcome people as they come in.* Handshakes, smiles, and friendly greetings go a long way toward creating a favorable climate.

- *Start and end meetings on time.* People have busy schedules and are more likely to attend meetings they know will start and end on time.

- *Preview and stick to the agenda.* Even if the participants already have access to this information, your time will be well spent if you take a few moments to remind them of the points to be discussed. Work to keep the discussion on track.

- *Make sure the secretary/recorder is present.* If not, appoint someone to keep the minutes.

- *Encourage discussion.* It is your responsibility to encourage reticent members of the team to give their points of view and to tactfully block those who try to monopolize or disrupt the discussion.

- *Ask questions skillfully.* Don't get off on side conversations. Know the various types of questions—open-ended, hypothetical open, direct, third-person, and closed—and the kind of responses each type encourages. Using a variety of questions can help ensure an intelligent, productive discussion. (See Chapter 7 for types of questions.)

- *Listen carefully to all comments, even when you don't personally agree with the speaker.* Make sure your nonverbal communication shows interest and respect. Team members may look to see how you are responding to various speakers and take their behavior cues from you.

- *Summarize.* Summarize the main points and decisions as the discussion progresses and provide an overall summary at the conclusion.

- *See to other necessary task and maintenance functions.* These functions may be performed by members of the group, but it is the responsibility of the leader to make sure that the group accomplishes its task.

- *Thank the participants and the audience (if any).* It takes little time for you to express appreciation to the participants and the audience, but it will end the meeting on a positive note.

- *Make sure that all people in the organization who need results of the meeting are properly informed as soon as possible.*

By following these suggestions, you can greatly improve your team's chances of success.

Teamwork

COMMUNICATION SITUATION

A project team is meeting to discuss the most effective way to present its recommendations for implementing a flextime policy on a trial basis. Members of the team are Jason Brown (team leader), Erika Filene, Victoria Lawrence, Bill Williams, and Jensen Chen. They are sitting around a rectangular table with Jason at the head. What are the leadership behaviors depicted in this scenario? Is Jason the only leader, or do other team members contribute leadership to the group? You can use your Premium Website for *Communicating for Results* to answer this question online after you've watched a video clip of this Communication Situation, further critique the interaction among the team members, and, if requested, e-mail your responses to your instructor.

Jason: So we've decided to recommend trying flextime for a 2-month period and with a number of procedures to make sure that people's new schedules don't interfere with productivity. There's a lot of information to communicate to employees, so how can we do that best?

Cengage Learning

Victoria: I think it would be good to use PowerPoint to highlight the key aspects of the new procedures. People always seem to remember better if they see something.

Bill: Oh, come on. PowerPoint is so overused. Everyone is tired of it by now. Can't we do something more creative?

Victoria: Well, I like it. It's a good teaching tool.

Bill: I didn't know we were teaching. I thought our job was to report recommendations.

Victoria: So what do you suggest, Bill? *[She nervously pulls on her bracelet as she speaks.]*

Bill: I don't have a suggestion. I'm just against PowerPoint. *[He doesn't look up as he speaks.]*

Jason: Okay, let's not bicker among ourselves. *[He pauses, gazes directly at Bill, then continues.]* Lots of people like PowerPoint, lots don't. Instead of arguing about its value, let's ask what it is we want to communicate to the employees here. Maybe talking about our goal first will help us decide on the best means of achieving it.

Erika: Good idea. I'd like for us to focus first on getting everyone excited about the benefits of flextime. If they understand those, they'll be motivated to learn the procedures, even if there are a lot of them.

Jensen: Erika is right. That's a good way to start. Maybe we could create a handout or PowerPoint slide—either would work—to summarize the benefits of flextime that we've identified in our research.

Jason: Good, okay, now we're cooking. Victoria, will you make notes on the ideas as we discuss them?

[Victoria opens a notebook and begins writing notes. Noticing that Bill is typing into his personal digital assistant (PDA), Jason looks directly at Bill.]

Jason: Bill, are you with us on how we lead off in our presentation?

Bill: Sure, fine with me. *[He puts the PDA aside but keeps his eyes on it.]*

Erika: So maybe then we should say that the only way flextime can work is if we make sure that everyone agrees on procedures so that no division is ever missing more than one person during key production hours.

Jensen: Very good. That would add to people's motivation to learn and follow the procedures we've found are effective in other companies like ours. I think it would be great if Erika could present that topic because she did most of the research on it. *[He smiles at Erika, and she pantomimes tipping her hat to him.]*

Jason: *[He looks at Erika with a raised brow, and she nods.]* Good. Okay, Erika's in charge of that. What's next?

Victoria: Then it's time to spell out the procedures and—.

Bill: You can't just spell them out. You have to explain each one—give people a rationale for them or they won't follow them. *[Victoria glares at Bill, then looks across the table at Erika, who shrugs as if to say, "I don't know what's bothering Bill today."]*

Jason: Bill, why don't you lead off then and tell us the first procedure we should mention and the rationale we should provide for it. *[Bill looks up from his PDA, which he's been using again.]*

Bill: *[Shrugs and speaks harshly.]* Just spell out the rules, that's all.

Victoria: Would it be too much trouble for you to cut off your gadget and join us in this meeting, Bill?

Bill: Would it be too much trouble for you to quit hassling me?

Jason: *[He turns his chair to face Bill squarely.]* Look, I don't know what's eating you, but you are really being a jerk. If you've got a problem with this meeting or someone here, put it on the table. Otherwise, be a team player.

CHAPTER 10
REVIEW

Andersen Ross/Digital Vision/Getty Images

Key Terms

active listening (263)

authoritarian leadership
  style (272)

big five personality factors (264)

charismatic leader (278)

democratic leadership style (273)

dysfunctional behaviors (267)

function theory (271)

laissez-faire leader (273)

leadership (271)

leadership styles (271)

maintenance roles (266)

open-mindedness (264)

situational contingency
  theory (274)

situational leadership theory (277)

task roles (266)

three-dimension theory (271)

trait theory (269)

transformational leaders (278)

virtual team (279)

Summary

To operate effectively, teams need to do more than just follow the basic problem-solving procedure. Effective group process requires other ingredients. First, it requires committed members, who are willing to devote time and energy to the team, support the decision of the team, and perform needed task and maintenance roles, as well as, avoid nonfunctional behaviors. As participants in a team, you and the other members have a definite effect on its productivity. When members are active listeners and open-minded, are well prepared, view conflict as productive, and are willing to support the leader in any way necessary, the team has a very good chance of producing good decisions and ideas. However, if the members fail to actively listen to one another, are set on their own opinions, fail to prepare or research their ideas prior to the meeting, view conflict as a win-lose situation, and expect the leader to make all the decisions, the team is certain to be nonproductive. Even an excellent, skilled leader would be unable to motivate such members to become a productive team. Effective team members also are able to communicate with teammates of different personality types.

Second, effective teams require leaders who can perform necessary task and maintenance functions, who are adept and flexible at using the democratic, autocratic, and laissez-faire styles of leadership, and who can handle conflicts productively. As the leader of a team, you will directly affect their productivity. "The real test of leadership lies not in the personality or behavior of the leaders, but in the performance of the groups they lead" (Bass & Stogdill, 1990, p. 39).

In your future, you will most likely serve as a team member in some situations and as the team leader in others. This chapter has given you the necessary guidelines to help you perform both roles successfully and productively. Remember, the more you practice these skills, the more effectively you will be able to use them.

Communicating for Results Online

Before continuing to the next chapter, check your understanding of Chapter 10 at the Premium Website for *Communicating for Results*. Your Premium Website gives you quick and easy access to the electronic resources that accompany this text. These resources include:

- **Study tools** that will help you assess your learning and prepare for exams (student companion workbook, digital glossary, key term flash cards, and review quizzes).

- **Activities and assignments** that will help you hone your knowledge, analyze professional communication situations, build your public speaking skills throughout the course, and learn to work effectively in teams (Awareness Checks, Checkpoints, and Collaborative Learning Activities).

- **Media resources** that will help you explore communication concepts online (web links), develop your speech outlines (Speech Builder Express 3.0), watch and critique videos of professional communication situations and sample speeches

(Interactive Video Activities), upload your speech videos for peer reviewing and critique other students' speeches (Speech Studio online speech review tool), and download chapter review so you can study when and where you'd like (Audio Study Tools).

This chapter's key terms, Collaborative Learning Activities, and Checkpoint activities are also featured on the following pages, and you can find this chapter's Awareness Check activities in the body of the chapter. For more information or to access this book's online resources, visit www.cengage.com/login.

Collaborative Learning Activities

1. Ask five to seven people to form a circle in the middle of the room with one or two persons to sit behind and slightly to the right or left of each of the members in the inner circle. Assign each person in the inner circle a task or maintenance role—place a folded card with the name of the role on both sides of the card so the role is visible

to all. The inner circle will discuss; the outer circle will evaluate the discussants' success. The discussion should be over a current problem of concern to the group such as government stimulus package, hiring practices, going green, or tobacco-free businesses and college campuses. The inner group discusses for 5 to 10 minutes with each person performing their assigned role as needed. When the time is up, the outer circle will evaluate how well the inner circle played their roles and comment on which roles seemed to help the group discussion the most. If time allows, have a new set of people form the inner and outer groups and continue the discussion and evaluation process. If different roles are performed, make sure that new place cards indicate the roles.

2. Read the group discussion in the Communication Situation for this chapter, "Teamwork," and then watch to it on the Premium Website for *Communication for Results*. In small groups discuss the effectiveness of the appointed leader (what type leader was he?) and what task, maintenance, and dysfunctional roles were performed by the group members. What changes would you recommend to improve the success of this team? Why?

Checkpoints

Checkpoint 10.1 Considering Your Leadership Style
Fill out the leadership questionnaires in the Awareness Checks in this chapter. Write a brief summary of your leadership tendencies based on the questionnaire results. What seems to be your predominant leadership style? What are your strengths as a leader? What are your weaknesses as a leader?

Checkpoint 10.2 Practicing Task and Maintenance Functions

Checkpoint 10.3 Handling Nonfunctional Behaviors

Checkpoint 10.4 Leadership Traits

Checkpoint 10.5 Assessing Leadership Style

Checkpoint 10.6 The Weakest Link

Checkpoint 10.7 Evaluate Public Leaders

Checkpoint 10.8 Participation and Small Group Leadership Websites

11 Informative Presentations

Christopher Robbins/Getty Images

Case Study: Harry Markopolos: Why Didn't Anyone Listen?

When you hear the name Bernie Madoff, what comes to mind? For many people the name Madoff is synonymous with the phrase Ponzi scheme. Through smooth talking and deception, Madoff managed to steal more than $50 billion of investors' money. Could he have been stopped sooner? Harry Markopolos, an investment veteran, thinks so. Unfortunately for all involved, he was unable to convince the Securities and Exchange Commission (SEC) to take sufficient action. This Ponzi scheme continued unchecked from the time it was discovered by Markopolos in 1999 until Madoff's confession in 2008 ("The Man Who Knew," 2009).

Let's take a look at the role Markopolos played in this situation. In 1999, while working for a rival firm, Markopolos tried to recreate and duplicate Madoff's investment practices but found it was impossible. He took the information to several colleagues and asked for their expert advice; he ran mathematical models. Finally, Markopolos was ready to present his findings, which he did in 2000, 2001, 2005, 2007, and 2008 (American Program Bureau, 2009). The first two times, the SEC ignored him outright, and when they did finally take notice, the investigation led nowhere. In fact, in 2007, Madoff was cleared of charges, a verdict largely due to the lackluster investigation of the SEC. Despite this, "the investigation evidently convinced investigators that Madoff had 'misled' SEC examiners during the 2005 inspection" and additional investigations were considered (Kiel, 2008).

"The World's Largest Hedge Fund" grew as Markopolos' research continued through the years, and by 2005, he had prepared 29 glaring red flags for the SEC to look into. These ranged from the simple, "[W]hy would the world's largest hedge fund manager be so secretive that he didn't even want his investors to know he was managing their money?" to the complex, "It is mathematically impossible for a strategy using index call options and index put options to have such a low correlation in the market where its returns are supposedly being generated from" (Markopolos, 2005). Even with points ranging from common sense to hard data, the SEC failed to listen for almost a decade. Why? Was Markopolos' argument invalid? Could his lack of credibility have been a problem because he didn't sign his name on the first two versions for fear of retribution? No, he claims, the SEC was nonfunctional in its understanding of modern finance (C-SPAN Video, 2009).

A closer look at Markopolos' memo reveals a few distinct problems in his communication style. If, as Markopolos asserts before Congress in his 2009 testimony on reforming the SEC, "the SEC's staff lacks the financial expertise and is incapable of understanding the complex financial instruments being traded in the 21st century" (C-SPAN Video, 2009), he certainly didn't tailor his memo to the level of knowledge of his audience. The pages of his memo reflected well-documented knowledge of the financial industry but failed to clearly lay out the 29 red flags in a way that the SEC's untrained staff could understand. Red flag number one, for example, is buried halfway through a paragraph. For an audience unfamiliar with the topic, Markopolos needed a succinct outline of the 29 red flags, written in plain-English, and instead provided a detailed, technical essay.

Would Madoff have been caught in 1999 if Markopolos' report had communicated more effectively with the SEC, or would the SEC's apparent ineptness have stood in the way regardless? The SEC ignored Markopolos' report multiple times, succinct or not, even when Markopolos "gift wrapped and delivered the largest Ponzi scheme in history" to the SEC (C-SPAN Video, 2009). Perhaps Markopolos' shy demeanor, his stated fear of retribution from Madoff played into the situation as well(C-SPAN Video, 2009). Less than a year after the SEC's investigation clearing Madoff of fraud, Madoff surprised everyone by turning himself in and admitting to fraud. Was his action due to looming government investigations, knowledge of the information gathered by Markopolos, or a bad economy that made continuing the Ponzi scheme impossible? The reason is still unknown. Despite these setbacks, Madoff was eventually brought to justice and was sentenced to 150 years in prison. But not before unbelievable damage was done to hundreds of thousands of lives, from unassuming retirees to famous Hollywood actors to everyday citizens. Apparently, having knowledge of a fraud isn't enough if you can't get those in power to believe you.

Mark Wilson/Getty Images

As you read this chapter, see if you can (a) analyze Markopolos' use of an informative memo as appropriate in light of what happened; and (b) suggest what Markopolos could have done differently once he realized the lack of knowledge on the part his audience (the SEC).

On a short flight from Washington, D.C., to Yale, where he was to give an important economics speech, President John Kennedy decided to make some last-minute changes. When Air Force One arrived at the airport, sheets of paper, some splattered with coffee, lay everywhere. The president's speechwriter was concerned about how little time they had left before the scheduled speech. The president said confidently, "You'll make it!"

They set up a typewriter under the bleachers where the president was to speak, and as the president gave the speech, they handed him the finished pages one at a time. Fortunately, all went well (ter Horst & Albertazzie, 1980). Don't you wish you could be that optimistic about public speaking? Unfortunately, people who are just beginning their careers tend to prepare themselves for every area of business *except* one: giving an oral presentation. For some reason, they don't think they will ever have to do that. If you are one of these people, we suggest you select Google or a search engine like Search, Vivisimo, or AltaVista and run a keyword search on "public speaking." You will be amazed at the number of articles dealing with oral communication skills written by people in your business or profession. Most of us expect only executives in large businesses—such as Intel, General Motors, and Boeing—and professionals—such as lawyers, educators, and presidents—to give oral presentations. But even small organizations need employees who are skilled in oral presentations—for example, high school coaches who must sell the school board on purchasing new equipment and motivate their team; dentists and dental technicians who must deal with patients and supply companies; and salespeople who must present their products and ideas to customers. Even assembly-line workers at General Motors participate in decision-making teams and formally present team ideas to management.

When you first begin working in a firm or organization, most of your oral presentations will be done in-house unless you are in sales. As an employee, you will be expected to present informational reports, proposals, and recommendations to supervisors. As a supervisor, you will be expected to give instructions, to brief employees on various policy decisions or procedures, and even to inspire or motivate employees. Both employees and supervisors are expected to give informal briefings and present reports to their colleagues within the company. Whether your presentations are formal or informal, they will require prior research, careful planning, and proper organization, and they must relate to the needs of your listeners.

The higher you climb up the organizational ladder, the more often you will need to speak either within the organization or to the public through your company's speakers' bureau. A **speakers' bureau** is made up of ordinary employees who have expertise in some aspect of the company and have the ability to share it with the public. Why limit your flexibility as a communicator and maybe even your chances for advancement by failing to learn to make good, relaxed oral presentations?

Informative Presentations: Overview

The place to begin when planning an informative presentation is to know the differences between information and persuasion, the different types of information presentations, what makes a high-quality informative presentation, and the basic outline format to use.

Informative Versus Persuasive Presentations

Presentations can be meant to inform, to persuade, or to entertain. Because entertainment is rarely the purpose of speeches in a business setting, we will discuss only informative and persuasive presentations in this book. Because informative presentations are the most common type of speech found in the business setting, we cover them first in this group of speaking chapters. Persuasive presentations are covered last in Chapter 14. Chapters 12 and 13 cover research, organization, supporting materials, effective visual aids, and delivery—all topics used by both informative and persuasive presenters. Let's begin by discussing the major differences between informative and persuasive speeches. Differences between informative and persuasive written messages are covered in Appendix: Written Communication located at the end of this text.

If your intent is to make the listeners aware of a subject or to present some new ideas or facts, then the presentation is an informative one. **Informative presentations** promote understanding of an idea or body of related facts. Here are some sample topics:

- Nonverbal differences between Japanese and Americans.
- How stress affects employee productivity.
- How to write an effective memo.
- Sales techniques that work.
- The advantages of using blogs for in-house and as a marketing tool.

If your purpose is to get your listeners to change their beliefs, then your presentation is a persuasive one. **Persuasive presentations** influence behaviors or opinions. Here are some sample topics:

- Volunteer work is everyone's responsibility.
- Mandatory drug testing benefits all.
- Stop using sexist language at work.
- Employee Internet use should be restricted.
- Exercise to improve your creativity.

Although persuasive presentations must inform, as well as, persuade, the two types require different approaches. As a speaker, be sure to decide whether your presentation will be informative or persuasive before you begin preparing.

Types of Informative Presentations

Many types of informative presentations are used in business situations. Although the names for various informative presentations differ from company to company, two types that occur most often in the business environment are oral briefings and oral reports.

An **oral briefing** is designed to present a summary of facts in a short period of time (usually 15 minutes or less). A briefing may be given to an individual (such as an employee, supervisor, or client) or to a small group (or, on rare occasions, an entire department).

"Will your presentation have a bloopers part at the end?"

Joel Gordon Photography

Employees, such as this police officer, who can give effective presentations are highly valued by business and professional organizations.

Many briefings are informal, as when an employee or supervisor informally presents information to colleagues at a weekly communications meeting. Other briefings are more formal, such as a briefing on the status of a particular project given to an entire department. Longer presentations require visuals (see Chapter 13).

An **oral report** is designed to present complete details and so is longer than a briefing and usually more formal. A report may include the feasibility of producing a new item, how to use a new company product, or examine a problem and provide recommendations. Often decision-making teams are required to prepare both written and oral reports on a problem and their recommendations for solving it. Suggestions for written informative and persuasive reports are covered in the appendix: "Written Communication."

Characteristics of High-Quality Informative Presentations

In one survey, 450 managers reported that they prefer business communications to be brief, clear, and direct (Bromage, 1970). Eighteen organizations that used oral briefings were asked to list reasons for poor briefings. Their lists include confusing organization, poor delivery, too much technical jargon, too long, and lack of examples or comparisons (Hollingsworth, 1968).

According to the director of a communication consulting firm, business speaking should be "plain, straightforward, and objective" (Wilcox, 1987, p. 11). In addition, information must be communicated ethically and responsibly. According to Lehman and DuFrene (2008, pp. 82–84), informative communicators should do the following:

- Present information in a truthful, honest, and fair manner.
- Avoid embellishment or exaggeration of facts.
- Express ideas clearly and understandably.
- Present objective facts to support views.
- Use tact to preserve the "receiver's self-worth."
- Design visuals so that they don't distort facts or relationships (see Chapter 13).

Effective informative presentations also aid audience understanding. There are four main tools that informative speakers and writers can use to aid understanding that are discussed in detail in Appendix: Written Communication. Briefly, these tools include:

- **Definition**—a definite, explicit, and clear statement of what a thing is followed by use of comparison or contrast, two or one examples, the root meaning of the word, a synonym, or a list of essential features.
- **Description**—a vivid and detailed view of the topic using figures of speech such as a simile or a metaphor.

- **Explanation**—a statement about the relationship between certain items that often answers the questions how, what, and why.

- **Narration**—an illustration or story about things, people, or events told with enthusiasm and vividness.

The specific tools you use will depend on your audience and your speech topic. For example, how much does your audience know about your topic? Is your subject matter easily understood, or does it involve complicated terms, concepts, or processes? Will the main ideas in your presentation be easy for your audience to believe intuitively, or will listeners tend to be skeptical and therefore require special handling (Rowan, 1995)?

Basic Outline for Informative Presentations

The basic organization of an oral briefing and an oral report (whether informative or persuasive) is the same: an **introduction**, a **body**, and a **conclusion**. When preparing a presentation, the body is usually planned first, then the conclusion, and finally the introduction.

Basic Outline for Informative Presentations

Introduction

Capture attention, show benefit to audience, state your qualifications, preview purpose and main points

Body

I. Main Point

    A.

    B.   Supporting materials: explanations, examples, statistics, quotes, visuals, (discussed in Chapters 12 and 13)

    C.

II. Main Point

    A.

    B.   Supporting materials

    C.

III. Main Point

    A.

    B.   Supporting materials

    C.

Conclusion

Summarize purpose and main points, and give closing thoughts

FIGURE 11.1 Basic Outline Format.

> ## Preparation Steps for Informative Presentations
>
> 1. Carefully analyze your potential listeners.
> 2. Determine the general topic.
> 3. Write down your exact purpose in one sentence.
> 4. Plan the body of the presentation.
> 5. Prepare the conclusion and introduction.
> 6. Practice using your notes and visual aids.

Informative Presentations: Preparation Steps

Although there are many different ways to prepare an informative presentation, these six steps will ensure a high-quality presentation.

Step 1: Carefully Analyze Your Potential Listeners

Once the topic has been assigned, all preparation must be guided by the characteristics of your specific listeners. If you want them to listen carefully to your report and understand your ideas, you must be able to relate your presentation to their interests and needs—their frames of reference.

When Speaking Outside the Organization   When making a presentation to a group outside your organization, gather the following information about your listeners from the person who gave you the assignment, the group leader, or a group member:

- Specific type of group.
- Goal or purpose of the group.
- Size of the group.
- Characteristics of the members:

  Ages.

  Occupations.

  Economic status.

  Beliefs and values.

  Interests.
- What knowledge they have about:

  The topic.

  The organization you represent.

When Speaking Within the Organization   When making a presentation to a person or group within your organization, gather the following information about your listeners:

- How many people will be present?
- Are they coming by choice? If so, what do they hope to get out of the presentation?

- Who are they?

  Names, if possible.

  Positions and ranks (Who are the key decision makers?).

  Departments and responsibilities.

- What do they know about your topic?

- Do they know you?

- What is their attitude toward you and your department?

Another way to analyze how receptive an audience will be is to identify them as one of four basic types: (a) friendly, (b) neutral, (c) uninterested, or (d) hostile (Elsea, 1985). Although you should be careful not to stereotype your audience, it is easier to organize your speech, select supporting materials, and plan your delivery when you can place your audience into a general category. Table 11.1 on page 294 outlines strategies for dealing successfully with each audience type. The success of any speech depends on how well the speaker relates the topic to the frames of reference of the audience members. Effective speakers spend a great deal of time analyzing their audiences.

Step 2: Identify the General Topic

Unless you are asked to speak to a group outside the organization and are told to choose any topic you want, the general topic is usually predetermined. Your supervisor may ask for a briefing on a certain project or idea, an engineer may request a technical report on a specific topic, or you may wish to present a new idea to your colleagues or demonstrate a product for a new customer. In all of these cases, the general topic would be obvious. See Figure 11.1 for some sample informative topics.

Step 3: Write Your Exact Purpose in One Sentence

Once your general topic is clear and you have carefully analyzed the potential listeners, you are ready to focus the topic for this specific audience's needs and interests. An **exact purpose** should be written in one sentence describing what the audience will learn. It should begin with "After hearing my presentation, the audience will. . . ." This step is often more difficult than it sounds. Suppose your company has just taken a bold step and implemented a company blog for internal and external communication. Although there are a few younger employees that are familiar with blogs, most of the staff and management view blogging as something only college students do. Each department has been asked to develop its own uses for the company blog and to help develop blogging policies for the company. You have been asked to bring the employees in your department up to speed on the new blog. You have been allotted 15 to 20 minutes for your presentation.

Which of the following statements would best express your exact purpose?
Exact purpose: After hearing my presentation, the audience will . . .

- Understand the company and department benefits from having a blog.

- Appreciate the importance of developing and following specific blogging policies.

- Appreciate the time requirements of each employee to ensure effective blogging.

- Understand possible ethical issues with blogging.

- Realize the do's and don'ts of a good blog response.

TABLE 11.1

Strategies for Dealing Successfully with Four Types of Audiences			
Strategies			
Audience Types	**Organization**	**Delivery**	**Supporting Material**
Friendly audience (predisposed to like you and your topic)	Any pattern; try something new; ask for audience participation	Warm, friendly, open; lots of eye contact, smiles, gestures, and vocal variety	Humor, examples, personal experiences
Neutral audience (consider themselves calm and rational; have minds already made up, but think they are objective)	Present both sides of issue; pro-con or problem-solution patterns; save time for audience questions*	Controlled, even, nothing showy; confident, small gestures*	Facts, statistics, expert opinion, comparison and contrast; avoid humor, personal stories, flashy visuals, and too much color*
Uninterested audience (short attention span; present against their will)	Brief—no more than three points; avoid topical and pro-con patterns that seem long to audience	Dynamic and entertaining, move around, large gestures	Humor, cartoons, colorful visuals, powerful quotations, startling statistics
Do not: Darken the room, stand motionless behind the podium, pass out handouts, use boring visual aids, or expect audience to participate			
Hostile audience (looking for chances to take charge or ridicule speaker; emotional)	Noncontroversial pattern such as topical, chronological, or geographical	Calm and controlled, speak slowly and evenly	Objective data and expert opinion; avoid anecdotes and jokes
Avoid: Question-answer period if possible; otherwise, use a moderator or accept only written questions			

*Also suggested for an audience of mixed audience types.

Source: Compiled from Janet G. Elsea, 1985, "Strategies for Effective Presentations," *Personnel Journal 64* (September), pp. 31–33.

- Feel confident communicating with customers through the blog.
- Know whom to contact when problems arise while using the blog.
- Begin the process of planning the department's blog section and what blogrolls (links to other available and related blogs) the department wishes to use.

If this is your first presentation, you are probably thinking, "There is no way I can cover all the necessary information about the new company blog in 15 to 20 minutes!" However, remember that your presentation will be given to a specific group of listeners, and other presentations will follow. Organize your topic specifically for them.

Suppose that a careful analysis of the listeners in this situation reveals that only five of them have ever used a blog before. Management is as lost as everyone else, and you are sensing some hostility. Although the majority of your potential listeners do not know anything about blogs, they are eager to learn. You finally decide that trying to include specific hands-on training in 20 minutes would only cause confusion. Therefore, you decide to state your exact purpose as follows:

"Biotech" or GMO foods	Ethics in business—what went wrong?	NAFTA's effect on American labor
ADA (Americans with Disabilities Act)	Endangered species—can we save them?	Nursing home costs skyrocket
Advertising and deception	Farmers of the future	Office environments—improving them
Airline safety suggestions	Flexible office hours and traffic problems	Online sales continue to grow
America's role in Iraq	Global warming and business implications	Outsourcing
Anthrax threat—how great?	Globalization and American jobs	Peace coalitions
Bottled water—improving water quality	Healthcare costs	Podcasting—business benefits?
Business blogs—are they safe?	Healthcare for everyone?	Preventing terrorism
Cancer and cell phone usage	Herbal remedies and regulation	Safety in the workplace
Child care and employee recruiting	Hiring older employees	Sexual harrassment—still a problem?
College degrees—are they for everyone?	History of the Internet	Social Security—how safe is it?
Company internships—advantages?	Hospital infections—why the increase?	Spam—how to handle it
Computer hackers—cost of apprehending	Hurricare Katrina	Stock market and retirement
Computer software—new trends	Immigrants and refugees in the workplace	Stress and American workers
Computer viruses—how to stop them	Internet addiction and the workplace	Telecommuting—pros and cans
Cord blood banks	Job seeking on the Internet	Veterans—why can't they find jobs?
Credit cards and the teen market	Land trusts—keeping them safe	Volunteerism—on the increase?
Diversity in the workplace	Library funding decreases—how serious?	Web pages—building good ones
Downsizing—did it really help?	Medical treatments—new vs. old	Working in teams
Dressing professionally on a budget	Mars exploration	World population—declining or myth?

FIGURE 11.2 Sample topics for informative presentations.

After hearing my presentation, the audience will appreciate the important benefits the new blog can provide for customers, employees, and company sales and know who to contact for private instructions or to answer problems. Q-n-A session to follow.

If your listeners were fairly knowledgeable about blogging, you may have decided to jump right into blogging policies and ethics issues or the do's and don'ts of a good blog response. (See Chapter 6 for specifics on the communication aspects of blogs and blogging.)

Step 4: Plan the Body of the Presentation

In planning the body of your presentation, you have four tasks:

1. Decide on your main points.
2. Select the best method for organizing those main points.
3. Expand your main ideas into an outline or storyboards.
4. Add verbal and visual supporting materials.

IT REALLY WORKS!

Speaking Within the Organization

How does one motivate a dying company and pull it back from the edge? Anne Mulcahy was faced with this very challenge when she accepted the position of president and CEO of Xerox in 2001. Bankruptcy for the company seemed certain: Xerox was $17.1 billion in debt; its stock was down to $4.43 a share; it had suffered seven straight quarters of losses; and it was reeling from an accounting scandal that was under investigation by the SEC (Morris, 2003). Many experts didn't think Mulcahy had a chance. She had only a B.A. in English; her experience was in sales, not finance; she was not a board member; and she was the first female CEO in the company's history. But Mulcahy had worked her way up through the company, had successfully managed the desktop division of the company, and was "straightforward, hard-working, disciplined" and "fiercely loyal to Xerox" (para. 6). She knew she had to figure out a way to let employees know she meant business, and she needed to do it quickly. She decided to focus on two important communication skills: listening and speaking.

Beginning in August 2001, Mulcahy spent 90 days traveling, sometimes to three cities a day, meeting with employees and customers. She listened to their ideas about what the company needed to do to succeed, and she promised "to fly anywhere, anytime to help salespeople close tough deals" (Moore, 2001, para. 8). After listening to and analyzing her audience, she also gave many informative and motivational presentations. When she spoke, she used three points as her guide: (a) "Focus on the things that make the company great," (b) "Be brutal about what does not work," and (c) "Be transparent in your communications" (Caminiti, 2005, p. 15). Although Mulcahy may not have expected speaking and listening skills to be so crucial to company success, they have played a large role in her efforts to start the company on the road to recovery.

On July 1, 2009, Mulcahy stepped down as CEO plans to remain as Chair of the Board. The new CEO is Ursula Burns who has become the first Black female CEO of a Fortune 500 company. Will Burns continue to use speaking as a communication tool? According to Xerox.com, Calendar of News and Speaking Events, Burns immediately had speeches scheduled in Georgia and New York for October 5 and 6 and New Jersey on November 3. Xerox appears to be in good hands.

What do you think?
- What effect did Mulcahy's willingness to visit and listen to employees have on her credibility as a speaker?
- What other advantages do you think these visits provided her as a speaker?

NOTE

You can use Speech Builder Express to create your exact purpose. Speech Builder Express is an online speech organization and outlining program that will help you prepare your speeches for this course. You can also use it to create your main points, introduction and conclusion, source list, and more. Access Speech Builder Express through your online resources for this book.

Let's look at each in more detail.

Decide on Your Main Points The first task in planning the body of your presentation is to decide on your main points. Begin by brainstorming a list of possible main points or key ideas that relate to your exact purpose. Then select those that would most benefit your audience. Most speakers cover three main points in their presentations. If you include more than five, you may lose listeners. Research on memory suggests that five bits of information is about all the average person can remember with accuracy at one time (Broadbent, 1975). Therefore, organize your information into five or fewer main points. The number of main points you select should depend on (a) the number of points needed to adequately develop your topic, (b) the time limit, and (c) the knowledge and interests of your audience.

Select the Best Method for Organizing Your Main Points The second task in planning the body of your presentation is to organize your main points. Main points can be organized in a variety of ways. The organization patterns that seem to be most relevant to business and professional situations are topical, spatial, chronological, and causal.

Topical Pattern This is used to divide a topic when no spatial, chronological, or causal relationship exists among the main points. Topical organization is probably the easiest and, therefore, the most popular pattern. It is the most effective if the points are arranged from most to least important, known to unknown, or familiar to unfamiliar.

The director of research and development presented guidelines to her research team, using the following **topical pattern**:

Purpose: After hearing my presentation, the research team will appreciate the guidelines needed for a successful research project.

Main Points:

I.   Obtain top management support.

II. Define research objectives carefully and fully.

III. Be realistic when preparing the budget.

IV. Be prepared to be flexible.

Spatial (or Geographical) Pattern   This pattern organizes main points according to their spatial location, such as front to rear, north to south, bottom to top, or left to right. The layout of a manufacturing plant could be described by its left, center, and right wings; the layout of a park could be explained by proceeding from entrance to exit.

A sales manager gave an informative briefing at a sales meeting using the following **spatial pattern**:

Purpose: After hearing my briefing, the audience will be aware of the company sales increases in the United States.

Main Points:

I.   New England sales have increased 10%.

II. Midwestern sales have increased 5%.

III. West Coast sales have increased 30%.

Chronological (or Time) Pattern   This pattern is used to present events in the order of their occurrence or steps in the order in which they should be followed. For example, the steps to follow in evacuating an office building during a fire could be presented from first to last step; the history of nuclear power could be presented in chronological order from the date when it was discovered to the present.

A building contractor presented a report to area realtors, using the following **chronological pattern**:

Purpose: After hearing my report, area realtors will be familiar with the procedures followed by building contractors in locating land for building.

Main Points:

I.   First, the blueprints for the development are drawn.

II. Second, possible sites are selected.

III. Third, cost and marketing surveys are conducted for each site.

IV. Finally, land is purchased and cleared.

Causal Pattern   When your main points have a cause-effect relationship, you can use the **causal pattern** of organization. In this type of organization, you have only two main points: One is the cause and the other is the effect. You can use a cause-effect order and discuss the problem or condition first and follow with its result or effect.

Organization Patterns

Directions: To check your knowledge of the four organization patterns (typically used in informative briefings and reports), read the main points in the following mini-outlines and identify whether the organization is (a) topical, (b) chronological, (c) spatial or geographic, or (d) causal. Compare your answers to those at the back of this book. You can also take this quiz and view the answers online via your Premium Website for *Communicating for Results*.

_____ 1. The effects of poverty, drugs, and divorce on juvenile crime:

    I. The effect of poverty on juvenile crime

    II. The effect of drugs on juvenile crime

    III. The effect of divorce on juvenile crime

_____ 2. Locating the best theme parks:

    I. Parks in California

    II. Parks in Texas

    III. Parks in Florida

_____ 3. Cigarettes and our health:

    I. Cigarette smoke releases toxic substances into the air.

    II. Toxic substances from cigarettes are linked to several chronic health problems.

_____ 4. Fashions through the ages:

    I. Fashion in the 70s was ugly.

    II. Fashion in the 80s was childish.

    III. Fashion in the 90s was retro.

_____ 5. Tips on becoming a collector:

    I. Where to look for collectibles

    II. How to determine the value of a collectible item

    III. How to bargain with a collector

_____ 6. Eating disorders blamed on society:

    I. Eating disorders

    II. Social preoccupation with appearance responsible for disorders

Or you can use an effect-cause order and present the result first and then discuss the problem or condition that caused it.

A supervisor presented a report on the new company policy limiting e-mail use with the following cause-effect pattern:

Purpose: After hearing my presentation, employees will realize why the company has decided to restrict employee use of e-mail and non-company blogs.

Main Points:

I. Many employees use e-mail and blogs for social and personal business.

II. The company needs to put restrictions on when and how employees use e-mail and blogs.

Expand Your Main Ideas into an Outline or Storyboards The third task in planning the body of your presentation is to turn your main ideas into an outline or several storyboards. Unless you are giving a manuscript presentation, do not write out the speech word for word. It takes twice as long to organize your thoughts this way. It is much faster and easier to work with a simple sentence or keyword outline.

If you plan on using transparencies or computer slides with your presentation, presentation software such as PowerPoint is a good way to work on your outline and visuals at the same time. The AutoContent Wizard in PowerPoint allows you to adjust a basic outline to fit your speech. Each section of the outline becomes a slide. Hundreds of adjustments (including background designs, color, fonts, pictures, and more) can be made at this point. Seeing your speech outline on screen makes organization problems easier to identify and correct. (For more details, see "Creating Visual Aids with Microsoft PowerPoint" via your Premium Website for *Communicating for Results*. Also, for the helpful speech template discussed in Chapter 13, look under the book resources at your Premium Website.)

If you really dislike making outlines, try using storyboards instead. Storyboards don't require the structure or use of symbols of regular outlines, and they provide space to sketch visual aids (thus stimulating right-brain thinking and creativity). Let's look in more detail at both outlines and storyboards.

Outlines Making an outline prior to researching for and planning your speech is a step that experienced speakers never omit because they know how valuable the outline is as a planning tool. An outline tells you at a glance how the main points are organized. When you see your presentation in outline form, it's easy to see the big picture and to know what changes are needed. For guidelines on how to write an effective outline, see the Appendix: Written Communication, which will cover recommended numbering system, reason for indenting, using two supporting items per level, parallel wording, and when to capitalize. The appendix also includes a sample presentation outline similar to the one in Figure 11.3.

Storyboards **Storyboards** are informal planning tools that do not require use of formal outlining rules. They can be used in place of an outline or as the rough-draft stage prior to completing a more formal outline. Take a sheet of paper and divide it into four to nine squares; each square is a storyboard. When you first begin planning a speech, think of each square as a PowerPoint slide and visually plot out your speech. The first square could include your title and a list of your probable main points. The second square could include your first main point, supporting reasons (e.g., a list or pie chart), and a brief sketch of a possible visual aid. As you continue to refine your speech, transfer each storyboard to a separate piece of paper, making sure that each contains at least four parts: a title or thesis statement, supporting statements with sources, a visual aid, and a transition (see Figure 11.4 on page 301).

Normally, you use separate storyboards for the introduction, the conclusion, and each of your main points. Using the storyboard format has the following advantages (Holcombe & Stein, 1996):

- It does not require the structure or use of symbols of regular outlines; bullets or dashes work just as well.
- It is an excellent way to tell if the supporting points and information are adequate.
- It allows for a rough sketch of visuals.

Informative Outline Format

Topic or Title:
Exact Purpose:

INTRODUCTION
- ☐ Attention getter:
- ☐ Audience motivation:
- ☐ Qualifications:
- ☐ Thesis statement:

BODY with SUPPORTS
- **I. Main point #1**:
  - A. Subpoint or supporting material
    - 1. Supporting material
    - 2. Supporting material
  - B. Subpoint or supporting material

  [Transition]

- **II. Main point #2**:
  - A. Supporting material
  - B. Supporting material

  [Transition]

- **III. Main point #3**:
  - A. Subpoint or supporting material
  - B. Subpoint or supporting material
    - 1. Supporting material
    - 2. Supporting material

CONCLUSION
- ☐ Summary:
- ☐ Closing thought:

References:
(Books, magazines, newspapers, Web sites, etc.)

FIGURE 11.3 Informative outline format.

- It encourages you to develop transitions.
- It makes it easy to tell if your arguments flow smoothly.
- It makes it easy for others to read and evaluate your ideas, which is especially important if you are giving a team presentation.

Once storyboards for each main point have been completed to your satisfaction and checked by a friend, colleague, or supervisor, you are ready to add supporting materials and prepare the visual aids and notes for use during the speech.

Add Needed Verbal and Visual Supporting Materials The final task in developing the body of your presentation includes adding your supporting materials. **Supporting materials** are any type of verbal or visual information used to clarify, prove, or

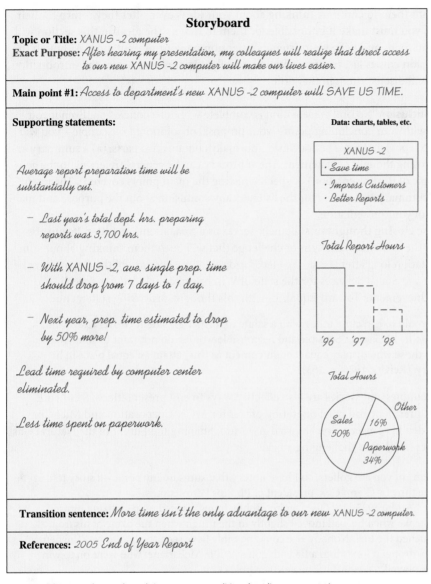

Storyboard

Topic or Title: *XANUS -2 computer*
Exact Purpose: *After hearing my presentation, my colleagues will realize that direct access to our new XANUS -2 computer will make our lives easier.*

Main point #1: *Access to department's new XANUS -2 computer will SAVE US TIME.*

Supporting statements:

Data: charts, tables, etc.

Average report preparation time will be substantially cut.

— *Last year's total dept. hrs. preparing reports was 3,700 hrs.*

— *With XANUS -2, ave. single prep. time should drop from 7 days to 1 day.*

— *Next year, prep. time estimated to drop by 50% more!*

Lead time required by computer center eliminated.

Less time spent on paperwork.

XANUS -2
· *Save time*
· *Impress Customers*
· *Better Reports*

Total Report Hours

'96 '97 '98

Total Hours

Other
Sales 50% 16%
Paperwork 34%

Transition sentence: *More time isn't the only advantage to our new XANUS -2 computer.*

References: *2005 End of Year Report*

FIGURE 11.4 Sample storyboard (compare to traditional outline on p. 300).

add interest to the main points of your presentation. Verbal supporting materials include explanations, comparisons, illustrations, examples, statistics, and expert opinions. Look for supporting materials in printed materials, computer databases, Internet, interviews, and personal experiences. We discuss verbal supporting materials in Chapter 12 and effective visual aids in Chapter 13. Check for accuracy in your research and supporting materials, and make sure that you have not unintentionally plagiarized any of your information.

Step 5: Prepare the Conclusion and Introduction

Many good presentations have failed because of dull introductions and less than memorable conclusions. Just because people show up at your presentation does not mean they plan to listen—unless you make it impossible for them not to. And if you want them to continue thinking about your ideas even after they return to their offices, you must make it impossible for them to forget. The ideas in this section will help you focus and keep your listeners' attention on your presentation. Although the conclusion comes last in a presentation, ideally it is prepared before the introduction, so we will discuss them in that order.

The Conclusion No oral presentation is complete without a conclusion. Even if you began with your concluding point—your proposal or solution, for example—you will need to repeat it again. The conclusion normally contains two parts: (a) a summary and (b) a closing thought or statement. The **summary** can be general (referring to the general topic of the presentation) or specific (listing the main points covered). The intent of the summary is to clarify for the listeners any confusion about the purpose and main points of your presentation.

The **closing thought** or statement serves as a final attention-getter. Its purpose is to give the audience a thought or challenge that will keep them thinking about your presentation long after it is completed. Linda Reivity, secretary of the Department of Health and Social Services for the state of Wisconsin, concluded her speech "Women's Achievements Toward Equality" with this thought-provoking statement:

> I would like to close today with a salute to former President Grover Cleveland, who in 1905 said, "Sensible and responsible women do not want to vote." May all those who display equal enlightenment as [his] attain an equal place in history. (Reivity, 1985, p. 153)

Examples and stories are also effective ways to end presentations. Stephen E. Ewing, president and chief operating officer for MCN Corporation and MichCon, concluded his presentation "Marble and Mud: Shaping the Future of the Natural Gas Industry" with this challenging story:

> Many of you are golfers, so I have a story that sums up my point—a story told at one time by Glenn Cox, president of Phillips Petroleum.
> At the 1925 U.S. Open, golfer Bobby Jones insisted on penalizing himself a stroke when his ball moved slightly in the rough when the blade of his iron touched the turf. Nobody else could possibly have seen the ball move. The penalty dropped Jones into a tie with golfer Willie McFarlane, who went on to win the playoff.
> Tom Kite did the same thing 53 years later in 1978. The self-imposed penalty caused him to lose the Hall of Fame Classic at Pinehurst by one stroke.
> Reporters asked both men why they took the penalties. And both said essentially the same thing—"There's only one way to play the game." Ladies and gentlemen, there is only one way to play our game—and that's with a high ethical sense—even in the fiercely competitive businesses we are in. (Ewing, 1991, p. 491)

Any attention-getters that can be effective in your introduction can also be used successfully to conclude your presentation. One method is to refer back to your opening remarks. For example, if you began with a rhetorical question, you can end by answering or reasking the question; if you began with a quote, mention it again or end with another quote. Other effective ways to close are issuing a challenge or appealing for action.

Ending your presentation without a closing thought is like giving a birthday gift in a brown paper bag: Neither the audience nor the person feels that she received anything special. However, a clever conclusion is like wrapping paper and bow; it dresses up the presentation and leaves the audience feeling like they received a nice gift.

The Introduction The introduction of an oral presentation has four objectives:

1. Capture the attention of your listeners.
2. Motivate them to listen by showing your presentation's benefit to them.
3. Convince them that you are qualified to speak on the subject.
4. Give your thesis statement.

Let's look at each objective in more detail.

1. *Capture the attention of your listeners.* As you begin your presentation, listeners' attention may be focused on many other things. One person may be worrying about a car payment that is due. Another may be reviewing a big business deal that fell through that morning. Others may be wishing they were home eating lunch. Your purpose is to direct attention from individual concerns to your presentation. The following are some common techniques for gaining attention, or what Gladwell (2002, p. 25) calls the Stickiness Factor (when a message "makes an impact. You can't get it out of your head. It sticks in your memory"):

- Reveal one or more startling facts.
- Ask a question. The question may be a rhetorical question (a question that causes the audience to think rather than respond) or an actual question (listener response is usually obtained by a show of hands).
- Tell a joke or humorous story relating directly to the topic. Poorly told jokes do not impress listeners. If you are not good at humor, try something else.
- Briefly cite two or three specific incidents or examples that relate to the topic.
- In detail, recount an actual or hypothetical event (often called an illustration).
- Refer to the specific occasion or event for which you are speaking (such as a company's 50th anniversary).
- Quote or paraphrase a well-known publication or expert.

> ## ETHICAL DILEMMA
>
> In December 2000, Sandra Baldwin was elected the first woman president of the U.S. Olympic Committee (USOC)—an important, prestigious 4-year position. Prior to this, she had served as USOC vice president and previously as president of USA Swimming (Baldwin, 2001). It was hoped that Baldwin would be able to restore the image of the USOC and pull "together the disparate governing bodies of the various Olympic sports" (Litsky, 2002) recently "tainted by the Salt Lake City bidding scandal" and uncertain drug testing procedures (Roberts, 2000).
>
> With each of these positions came speaking opportunities, such as the commencement address titled "Keep the Doors Open" that she gave to the Trinity University graduating Class of 2001 in Washington, D.C. In this presentation, Baldwin stated that it was her dream to "have a lasting effect on the emergence of women in leadership roles, not just in my country, but around the world" (Baldwin, 2001, para. 9).
>
> Unfortunately, Baldwin's dream and the hopes of those who elected her were never finalized. In May 2002, Baldwin stepped down as president because of inaccuracies in her official biography. A reporter writing an article for the University of Colorado's alumni magazine discovered that instead of having a B.A. from the University of Colorado and a Ph.D. from Arizona State University, Baldwin actually had both a bachelor's and a master's from Arizona State but no doctorate (she had never completed her dissertation) and no degree from the University of Colorado, although she had taken classes there (Segin, 2002). Why the lies? Baldwin had experience, obvious abilities, and two degrees—more than enough for the position as president of USOC. In a press release, Baldwin said, "I should have changed it a long time ago, but once it was published it got paralyzing. Now I'm going to have to live with it for the rest of my life" (Litsky, 2002).
>
> **Questions:** Do you think stepping down was the right action for Baldwin to take? If she had stayed in the position, would her resume discrepancies have affected her credibility as a speaker? At this point, is there anything she can do to help restore her image?

- Briefly demonstrate the item or skill you will be discussing in your presentation.

American Robert L. Clarke (1988), while speaking in London, used humor in his introduction to capture audience attention and to establish a common ground with his audience:

> I will in my remarks tonight remain ever mindful of the linguistic ocean that separates the United Kingdom and the United States.
>
> Though I hope you will forgive me if you discover I have lost my bearings between the two shores.
>
> The waters are treacherous even for those with much greater experience with them than I have.
>
> Even Winston Churchill—whose mother, as you know, was American—found himself adrift at times.
>
> During a visit to the United States, Churchill was invited to a buffet luncheon at which cold chicken was served.
>
> Returning for more, he asked politely: "May I have some breast?" His hostess replied: "Mr. Churchill, in this country we ask for white meat or dark meat." Churchill apologized profusely.
>
> The following morning, the hostess received a magnificent orchid from her guest of honor.
>
> The accompanying card read: "I would be most obliged if you would pin this on your white meat." (p. 548)

Although humor can be very effective in a presentation (Detz, 2000), **self-disparaging humor** (where the speaker uses himself or herself as the brunt of a joke) can have a negative effect. More specifically, Hackman (1988) found that when either high- or low-status informative speakers used humor that focused on their personal shortcomings, audiences judged the speeches more humorous; however, the audiences also rated the speakers as being less competent, less interesting, and less desirable to associate with. But Gruner (1985) found that humor directed at one's occupation or profession does not harm a speaker's image.

2. *Motivate the audience to listen by showing your presentation's benefit to them.* Capturing the attention of your listeners does not guarantee that they will listen to the remainder of your presentation. To keep their attention, you must convince them that the presentation will help them satisfy personal or job-related needs.

3. *Convince the audience that you are qualified to speak on the subject.* Unless they believe that you know what you are talking about, few people will take the time to listen to your ideas or proposals, let alone be persuaded by them. You can demonstrate your qualifications to speak on the topic by referring to your personal experience, the research you have done on the topic, and the interviews you have conducted with knowledgeable people.

4. *Give your thesis statement.* A **thesis statement** has two parts: a general statement of purpose and a summary of the main points to be covered. The average listener finds it much easier to follow and remember the ideas contained in your presentation when your introduction lists the key points that will be covered.

Many business speakers also suggest that you "start your presentation with your recommendations or conclusions unless you have a compelling reason not to"

(Wiegand, 1985). This method helps you keep the attention of the typically rushed, tired, and stressed-out business audience. It also helps you determine what background material to leave out; include only the points needed to support your conclusions. However, if your conclusion is bad news, sensitive information, or a controversial proposal, it would be better to report the background data and events *before* stating what you hope is the obvious conclusion or recommended action. Your audience is more likely to listen objectively and less likely to interrupt with questions if such conclusions are presented last.

Although we suggest that you include all four objectives of the introduction in any practice presentation you give in a training seminar or classroom, the presentations you give in business and professional situations may not need to include all four. Which objectives you include depends on your listeners. For example, you may not need to capture their attention (objective 1) if your audience is obviously already interested in your specific topic. You may not have to spell out the benefits of your presentation (objective 2) if your listeners are already motivated to listen or if the benefit to them is obvious. You may not have to convince them of your qualifications (objective 3) if your listeners are already aware of the experience, knowledge, or training that qualifies you to speak on your subject. You might omit your thesis statement (objective 4) if you are trying to build suspense or if, as mentioned previously, you know that the audience you are trying to persuade is against your proposal. In this case, you should hold your proposal until the conclusion of the presentation—the backdoor approach. Check your understanding of when to omit introduction objectives by analyzing the following situations:

Example 1

> Imagine that your supervisor has asked you to present an informative report on the uses of a new piece of machinery. Your audience will consist of your supervisor and her assistant. Which objectives should you include in your introduction?

Obviously, your listeners are already interested, so objective 1 could be omitted. They specifically asked you to give this report, so they are definitely motivated to listen; thus, objective 2 could be omitted. Because you work for them, they already know you are qualified to speak on this topic; objective 3 could also be omitted. Your audience is aware of your general purpose but does not know what main points you plan to cover. Therefore, you should get right to the point by presenting your thesis (objective 4): "This new copy machine can save us time and ease our work load by performing four much-needed tasks for us. These four tasks are . . ."

Example 2

> Suppose you were giving the same report to a large group of foremen and supervisors. Most of the foremen have no idea what your report will be about, several of your listeners have no idea who you are, and three of the supervisors feel that this meeting and the new piece of equipment will be a complete waste of time. Which objectives should you include in your introduction?

This time you will need to include all four objectives! Objective 1 is needed to direct the attention of this diverse group to your topic, especially those foremen who are unaware of the nature of your report. Objective 2 is needed to show the listeners how your topic will benefit them. You'll need to take into account the difference in the personal needs of the uninformed foremen and the supervisors who have already decided that the machine is worthless when planning how to motivate the listeners. Objective 3 is needed because many in your audience are unaware of your qualifications. Objective 4 is needed to make the purpose of your presentation clear.

Before we move to the final step of preparing the presentation, we need to make one more observation about the introduction: As long as you include the necessary objectives, their order can vary. If an attention-getter is needed, it should come first. But the order of the other three objectives depends on you, your topic, and your audience.

Step 6: Practice Using Your Speaking Notes and Visual Aids

Don't mistake your outline for speaking notes. The outline is detailed and used for planning and organizing; speaking notes are a brief keyword outline used as a memory aid while speaking (Leech, 1992). It takes practice to use notes and visual aids smoothly and to feel confident while speaking. Feeling confident while speaking is one of the benefits of rehearsing. For the best results, prepare two ways: visualize yourself giving a successful presentation and practice the presentation aloud. The following suggestions will help you as you practice:

- *Prepare speaking notes on note cards* (one or two are usually enough). If you have any quotes, put each one on a separate note card—typed and double-spaced for ease of reading. If you are using transparencies, the frame area is a handy place for notes. If you are using presentation software such as PowerPoint, turn your slides into an outline (see Figure 11.2) and then condense them even further into speaker notes. Use color and underlining to make keywords stand out, and write personal notes (like *eye contact* or *louder*) in the margins. It's also a good idea to make a hard copy of your PowerPoint slides (six to a page works well) just in case of equipment failure. Figure 11.5 on page 308 shows the speaking notes used by one speaker; an outline of another speaker's presentation is shown in Figure 11.6. (For a look at the speaker's PowerPoint slides, look under the resources for Chapter 11 at the Premium Website for *Communicating for Results*.)

- *Practice your presentation.* Tape-record yourself to get feedback on your vocal delivery, or practice in front of a mirror. If possible, practice in a room similar to the one in which you will be speaking. After you begin to feel comfortable with your speech, practice it in front of a friend or family member. Be sure to ask them for specific comments on your presentation. Don't forget to practice making direct eye contact and using gestures.

- *Practice using your visual aids* with all the needed equipment at least once before the actual speech (two or three times would be better). Videotape yourself if possible or ask a friend to observe one of your final practices.

Informative Presentations: Delivery Methods

Often the success of your presentation depends on the delivery method you select: speaking from memory, from outlined notes, from visuals, from written manuscript, or impromptu. Each of these methods is briefly discussed.

Speaking from Memory

Business and professional speakers seldom select this method of delivery. First, **speaking from memory** takes a great deal of time to memorize a manuscript word for word, and few people have this luxury. Second, speaking from memory makes it difficult to react to listener feedback. A question from a listener can make the speaker forget the next sentence. Even if the listeners make no verbal comments, they make plenty of nonverbal ones. How can a speaker, who sees from facial expressions that a certain idea is not understood, correct the problem when speaking from memory? Any deviation from the practiced speech could cause the speaker to lose concentration and forget the memorized material.

Speaking Extemporaneously (With or Without Notes)

This is the preferred method of delivery for most business speakers. An **extemporaneous speaking** is not memorized or even written out word for word. Instead, the speaker lists in outline fashion on note cards the main ideas to be covered and the verbal and visual supporting materials. Each time the presentation is given, it will be a little different. Speaking from outlined notes allows the speaker to sound conversational, to maintain good eye contact with the listeners, and to alter the speech if listener feedback indicates confusion. The preparation steps discussed in this chapter are the ones used for the extemporaneous method.

Speaking from Visual Aids

Now that so many business speakers use PowerPoint slides during their presentations, another form of extemporaneous speaking exists. Like the extemporaneous presentation, the visual aid speaking method is not memorized or written out word for word. But instead of using note cards, speakers use their PowerPoint slides as a memory device or refer to printed copies of their slides (nine per page works well). If your main points appear at the click of the mouse, it's a good idea to build your own bullets (see the PowerPoint Speaker's Guide located on the Premium Website for *Communicating for Results* for specific bullet instructions). Building your own bullets (which remain stationary with the title) allows you to recall exactly how many points you planned for each slide. In contrast, PowerPoint bullets, which fly in with each point, make it difficult to remember how many points a slide has—especially if you are a bit nervous.

Speaking from a Manuscript

Speaking from a manuscript is much more difficult for most people than speaking from outlined notes. The speaker must read a prepared presentation word for word but make it sound conversational and personal by using good vocal variety and maintaining eye contact with the audience. Unless the speaker deviates from the manuscript occasionally, he or she cannot respond to listener feedback any more than in a memorized presentation.

Nevertheless, for the experienced speaker, there are certain advantages to a manuscript presentation. For example, when the speaker is given a very strict time limit, speaking from manuscript helps to ensure that the presentation will not be too long. For people who speak to audiences outside the company, speaking from the manuscript has the advantage of allowing upper management to read and okay the

Mark Wilson/Getty Images

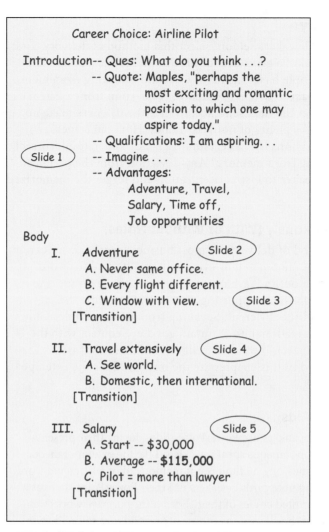

FIGURE 11.5 Sample speaking notes—first note card.

presentation before it is given. This method also protects the speaker from saying something unintentionally and from blatant misinterpretation. Top-level managers and executives, state governors, and the president of the United States often use manuscripts for protection.

If you must use a manuscript sometime in the future, be sure to practice reading it until your pitch, rate, volume, and emphasis make you sound authoritative yet conversational and you are able to glance up and make eye contact with your listeners often enough to look natural.

Impromptu Speaking

Impromptu speaking—speaking without prior preparation and without notes or manuscript—is obviously a hazardous way to give a major presentation. Yet, every time your manager, a client, a newspaper reporter, or a job interviewer asks you a question, your response is an impromptu presentation that must sound intelligent, authoritative, and confident! A hesitant, apologetic, or stumbling answer does not project the professional image you want. When asked to speak impromptu, try the following (Stone & Bachner, 1994):

Sample Informative Presentation

Title: "Bacterial Meningitis" by Emily Wilson

Exact Purpose: After listening to my presentation, the audience will become aware of the danger surrounding meningitis by understanding what it is and how it can hurt us.

INTRODUCTION
- **Attention-getter:** How many of you have heard or been affected by meningitis? How many of you know some-one that has experienced the effects of meningitis? [Visual #1]
- **Qualifications:** I personally have not been affected by meningitis but I do have a friend who has suffered from this silent killer. She has recovered from her experience but still has minor neurological problems.
- **Motivation:** According to the National Meningitis Association there are annually an estimated 3,000 cases of bacterial meningitis in the U.S. and out of those 3,000 cases, about 330 people will die. Teens are more likely to die than younger or older people—so it really relates to us.
- **Thesis:** Today we are going to look at what bacterial meningitis is, how you get it, and what happens when you are infected. These three main points will help you to understand the significant danger of meningitis. [Visual #2]

BODY

I.   What is Bacterial Meningitis?

  A.   Bacterial Meningitis is a serious and dangerous infection of the meninges.

   1.   The infection travels up the spinal cord into the brain.

   2.   Once in the brain, Bacterial Meningitis causes swelling in the normal meninges made up of the Dura mater, the Arachnoid, and the Pia mater. [Visual #3]

  B.   According to the article *Bacterial Meningitis: Disease/Disorder Overview* from the Health and Wellness Resource Center, there are two leading strands of Bacterial Meningitis. [Ref. #1]

   1.   Meningococcal

   2.   Pneumococcal

  Transition: Next, let's look at how we contract a Meningitis infection such as the Meningococcal strand.

II.   How do we get Bacterial Meningitis or where does it strike?

  A.   Bacterial Meningitis is actually found in the body. [Visual #4]

   1.   The bacteria are in everyone's body.

   2.   Bacterial Meningitis is only triggered when your body experiences a drastic change.

  B.   Bacterial Meningitis can be spread unless you are careful.

   1.   Bacterial Meningitis is spread buy coughing, kissing, sharing food. [Ref. #2]

   2.   It is spread through ear, throat, and sinus infections.

   3.   Blood infected by Bacterial Meningitis spreads to the brain.

  Transition: Now that we understand how Bacterial Meningitis is contracted, let's look at what happens when we are infected.

FIGURE 11.6a Sample informative presentation.

- Appear confident (even if you must pretend).
- Decide on your conclusion first so that everything you say can lead up to the conclusion in an organized manner.
- Begin with a general statement or background information to give you time to think of one, two, or three supporting reasons for your conclusion.
- Introduce your supporting reasons with the word *because* until you can stay organized without it. For example:

Q: Do you think speech training should be required for promotion of area managers?

III. What happens when we get it? [Visual #5]

    A. Death or severe brain damage occurs to many people.

        1. Bacterial Meningitis causes swelling in the meninges.

        2. Swelling causes the brain to put extreme pressure against the skull.

    B. Amputations are common.

        1. Amy Purdy was a college student when she contracted Bacterial Meningitis and had to have both of her legs amputated at the knee.

            a. This tragedy struck her overnight.

            b. Within 24 hours she went from being a healthy college student with two perfectly good legs, to an ICU resident with two amputated legs and massive internal damage.

        2. Amy surprised everyone. She not only survived, she continued her love of skiing as you can see in this picture.

    C. Neurological damage may last a lifetime.

        1. Most all survivors have neurological damage.

        2. According to the National Meningitis Association, 20% of cases usually suffer from extreme damage of the kidneys, brain, and liver.

        3. Less serious neurological damage result in such things as loss of hearing and slow response abilities.

CONCLUSION

- Although you may think to yourself that this harmful infection will not happen to you, no one is impervious to this quick, silent killer.

- It is important to remember that it is a serious bacterial infection that can be caught from someone coughing on you and could potentially kill you within the next 24 hours.

- Now that you are aware of Bacterial Meningitis, I hope that you will be able to use this new knowledge in your future.

REFERENCES

1. *Bacterial meningitis: Disease/ disorder overview*. (2008, November). Retrieved from the Health and Wellness Resource Center database.

2. Centers for Disease Control. (2009, August 6). *Meningitis: Transmission*. Retrieved from "http://www.cdc.gov/meningitis/about/transmission.html" http://www.cdc.gov/meningitis/about/transmission.html.

FIGURE 11.6b *(Continued.)*

A: *Because* the average area manager is called on to make at least four formal presentations to the public a year, and *because* they make weekly informal presentations to their employees, I see speech training as a necessary requirement for promotion.

- Answer the question directly and honestly. The exception is those rare instances when you are asked a question you don't wish to answer or for which you don't have an answer (and you feel it would be unacceptable to say, "I don't know"). In those cases it may be justifiable to change the topic to one you do want to answer. Politicians are very good at changing subjects with such comments as these:

  "That's an important question—almost as important as. . . ."

  "Great question! That gives me an opportunity to talk about. . . ."

"Could I come back to that question? I've been wanting to reply to the remark this gentleman made previously. He said. . . ."

"I think we need to look at the problem from a different angle. . . ."

Although there are times when speaking from memory, speaking from a manuscript, and impromptu speaking are appropriate, remember that most successful business speakers do not memorize, read word for word, or speak without prior preparation. *The preferred method of delivery for most business speakers is speaking extemporaneously usually from brief notes or PowerPoint slides.*

Informative Presentations

Now that you've explored different types of informative presentations and how best to prepare and deliver them, use your Premium Website for *Communicating for Results* to watch video clips of several sample informative presentations, including Emily Wilson's presentation on "Bacterial Meningitis" and her PowerPoint slides (see her outline in Figure 11.6) and Elizabeth Lopez's speech on "The Three C's of Down Syndrome" (see her photo below). Other informative speeches include "Chinese Fortune Telling" by Chung-Yang Man and "Retail Theft" by Mark Stephenson (see his speech outline in the Appendix, Figure A.11 and his informative report in Figure A.12).

You can also use your Premium Website to critique each speech and, if requested, e-mail your responses to your instructor.

Cengage Learning

CHAPTER 11
REVIEW

Christopher Robbins/Getty Images

Key Terms

body (291)

causal pattern (297)

chronological pattern (297)

closing thought (302)

conclusion (291)

definition (290)

description (290)

exact purpose (293)

explanation (291)

extemporaneous speaking (307)

friendly audience (294)

hostile audience (294)

impromptu speaking (308)

informative presentations (287)

introduction (291)

narration (291)

neutral audience (294)

oral briefing (289)

oral report (290)

persuasive presentations (289)

self-disparaging humor (304)

spatial pattern (297)

speakers' bureau (288)

speaking from a manuscript (307)

speaking from memory (307)

storyboards (299)

summary (302)

supporting materials (302)

thesis statement (304)

topical pattern (297)

uninterested audience (294)

Summary

In this chapter, we discussed basic information that applies to any formal or informal informative presentation that you may give within an organization or to the public. Effective speakers start by determining the topic and then carefully analyzing the audience. If your presentation does not fit the frames of reference of your audience, you are much less likely to communicate with them successfully.

Once you have determined your listeners' frames of reference, you should determine your topic and write your exact purpose in one simple sentence. When your topic is narrowed, use an outline or story-

boards to plan the body, and then the conclusion and introduction of your presentation. This chapter covered four effective ways to organize the basic parts of an informative presentation: topical, spatial, chronological, and causal. Of course, how you organize your presentation will depend on your listeners' needs, interests, and knowledge; the situation; the time limit; and your own speaking style.

Finally, before the presentation, practice the presentation until you feel comfortable with it. *The best delivery is enthusiastic, conversational, and extemporaneous.*

Communicating for Results Online

Before continuing to the next chapter, check your understanding of Chapter 11 at the Premium Website for *Communicating for Results*. Your Premium Website gives you quick and easy access to the electronic resources that accompany this text. These resources include:

- **Study tools** that will help you assess your learning and prepare for exams (student companion workbook, digital glossary, key term flash cards, and review quizzes).

- **Activities and assignments** that will help you hone your knowledge, analyze professional communication situations, build your public speaking skills throughout the course, and learn to work effectively in teams (Awareness Checks, Checkpoints, and Collaborative Learning Activities).

- **Media resources** that will help you explore communication concepts online (web links), develop your speech outlines (Speech Builder Express 3.0), watch and critique videos of professional communication situations and sample speeches (Interactive Video Activities), upload your speech videos for peer reviewing and critique other students' speeches (Speech Studio online speech review tool), and download chapter review so you can study when and where you'd like (Audio Study Tools).

This chapter's key terms, Collaborative Learning Activities, and Checkpoint activities are also featured on the following pages, and you can find this chapter's Awareness Check activities in the body of the chapter. For more information or to access this book's online resources, visit www.cengage.com/login.

Collaborative Learning Activities

1. In small groups of five to seven, create a series of questions that speakers would likely need to know about their audience to adequately prepare an effective speech including what they know and think about the speaker and the speaker's topic. When the survey is completed, each group should select a speech topic; each member should interview 5 to 10 colleagues using the survey and taking notes. Compare notes and discuss the general level of knowledge on your topic. Finally, using your audience analysis, suggest at least two ways to get those interviewed interested in the topic.

2. In groups of three to five, select four quality topics for informative speeches. Select the topic that the group thinks would make the best speech and create several possible main points that might be included. To show your knowledge of the informative organizational patterns and to show that most topics can be organized into all four patterns, make four different outlines from the same general topic but organize the main points into the topical, spatial, chronological, and causal patterns. When finished, decide which pattern would make the most interesting presentation. Why would it be more interesting? Compare your outlines with those from other groups.

3. In small groups, take the most interesting speech outline from activity 2 and have half of the group prepare an introduction for the speech, and half of the group prepare a conclusion for the speech. Make sure that you include all the steps that are usually found in an effective introduction and conclusion. Ask for volunteers to present both the introduction and conclusion to the entire group who will suggest two strengths and at least one weakness. How could the weakness be changed into a strength?

Checkpoints

Checkpoint 11.1 Preparing and Practicing an Informative Presentation
Prepare a 5-minute informative presentation on a topic you deal with regularly. Videotape yourself if possible. How do you sound? Did you notice any nonverbal problems? Why not volunteer to give this presentation to a real audience? The more you practice, the more professional you become.

Checkpoint 11.2 Using a Speakers' Bureau

Checkpoint 11.3 Analyzing a Presentation

Checkpoint 11.4 Delivery Methods

Checkpoint 11.6 Informative Presentation Websites

12

Researching, Supporting, and Delivering Your Ideas

As you read Chapter 12,

Discuss pointers for researching your topic by using printed materials, commercial databases, the Internet, blogs, and personal interviews without running into any plagiarism problems.

Identify with do's and don'ts the following supporting materials used in quality presentations: Explanations, comparisons, illustrations, examples, statistics, and expert opinion.

Describe how to improve your delivery by using effective visual, vocal, and verbal elements including special stylistic language devices.

Tonis Valing/Shutterstock

Case Study: CNN's Ethical Breach

The credibility of a network's news stories, just like the credibility of a speaker's supporting materials, depends on objective, detailed, and ethical research. In all-news networks like Cable News Network (CNN) that "thrive on controversy, breaking news stories, and stories that go on for days, or even weeks" (McPhail, 2006, p. 142), objective research is especially important. In 1998, CNN reported a story that turned out to have serious research weaknesses and that made an equally serious dent in their credibility.

CNN is a 24-hour U.S.-based cable news station owned by Time Warner. It is largely credited with being the first news station to move to the 24-hour format so widely used today. Between the 1980s and early 2000s, CNN had gone from a small national station to an international one with such force that "in terms of foreign affairs, if it is not on CNN, it does not exist" (McPhail, 2006, p. 157).

A CNN broadcast on June 7 and a *Time* magazine story on June 15, both written by CNN reporters (Oliver et al., 1998), dealt with a shocking story they claimed occurred in Vietnam during Operation Tailwind. It was reported that the U.S. government had "hunted down and killed U.S. defectors and that as part of this operation, the nerve gas sarin was used" (McPhail, 2006, p. 154). Media throughout the world immediately picked up the story. William Cohen, U.S. Defense Secretary at the time, ordered an immediate investigation that eventually concluded "that the military could find 'absolutely no evidence' for either of the allegations" (Thompson, 1998). Despite protests that the story was a hoax, the following week CNN repeated the story, insisting it was true (Reed & Kincaid, 1999). When other journalists and hundreds of military veterans joined the outcry, *Newsweek* printed an article refuting the story (Thomas & Vistica, 1998)—CNN hired an independent media lawyer, Floyd Abrams, to investigate the facts of the story. Adams concluded his 55-page report with the following statement:

> A decision was made by CNN to broadcast accusations of the gravest sort without sufficient justification and in the face of substantial persuasive information to the contrary. CNN should retract the broadcast and apologize to the public and, in particular, the participants in Operation Tailwind. (Abrams, 2000, para. 5)

As a result, the network retracted its story and fired the story's two producers and executive producer Pamela Hill. Peter Arnett, whose name was a byline on the story, was dismissed for other reasons the following year (McPhail, 2006, p. 154). Later dismissals included the CNN president and over 400 CNN staffers (McLaughlin, 2001).

During the retraction, CNN News Group chairman, president, and CEO Tom Johnson noted that "CNN's system of journalistic checks and balances, which has served CNN exceptionally well in the past, failed in this case" ("CNN Retracts Tailwind Coverage," 1998). One reason that the checks and balances failed may be explained by an observation made by the independent investigator (Abrams, 2000, para. 9):

> The CNN journalists involved in this project believed in every word they wrote. If anything, the serious flaws in the broadcast that we identify in this report may stem from the depths of those beliefs and the degree to which the journalists discounted contrary information they received precisely because they were so firmly persuaded that what they were broadcasting was true.

Based on research from the Pew Research Center's Biennial News Consumption Survey (Kohut, 2008), CNN's believability rating which was 42% in 1998 dropped to 28% in 2006 and rose to 30% in 2008. With the exception of 2006, CNN has maintained its standing as the major news organization with the highest credibility rating.

David McNew/Getty Images

As you read this chapter, see if you can determine (a) how trained and experienced reporters could let their own biases cause them to disregard research that disproved their story; (b) what procedures CNN could implement to ensure the credibility and accuracy of future stories; and (c) what lessons public speakers can take from this story. For more details, go to CNN.com and in the cnn.com search box, type in "Operation Tailwind."

H ave you ever walked out of a meeting and heard people making comments like "Wasn't that an interesting talk?" "What a voice!" "That was the first financial report I really understood!" If so, their comments indicate a speaker who researched, supported, and delivered his or her ideas effectively. Research is necessary to make sure your ideas are supported by accurate and up-to-date facts, data, and examples without any bias or plagiarism unlike that found in the CNN opening scenario. Effective support materials keep listeners interested and help them remember the information in your presentation and remain convinced by your arguments even after hearing opposing views. And, of course, a dynamic and enthusiastic delivery not only adds interest and clarity to your words, but it also increases your credibility with your listeners. This chapter will offer helpful ideas on researching, supporting, and delivering your presentations.

Researching Your Topic

In researching their topics, inexperienced speakers often make one of two mistakes: (a) they do too little research because they plan to rely primarily on their personal knowledge and experience or (b) they use only the Internet to do their research (Hamilton, 2009, p. 104). Even if you have a great deal of personal experience with your topic, you need to present additional sources as well. Using information from other respected sources shows that you are an objective and informed speaker, and it adds to your credibility.

Although the Internet can be a wonderful research tool, and many people limit their research to Google or Yahoo!, it is important also to use information obtained from printed materials, electronic databases, and personal interviews.

Printed Materials

If you are relatively unfamiliar with your topic, it's a good idea to begin your search for information by obtaining one or two current books on the topic. Reading them should give you a good overview. Two other excellent sources for up-to-date information are book stores that offer popular books and textbooks on your topic (not only is the information current, but additional valuable sources will also be listed in the footnotes and references) and phone books (where you can find the numbers for local agencies, such as the American Cancer Society, to call and request printed information). Don't overlook the following library sources:

- *Brochures and pamphlets.* Many libraries have a Vertical File Index that lists available pamphlets. Also check with local and national organizations for pamphlets on your topic.

- *Books.* Most city and college libraries have an online catalog for locating books in their collections. To save time, check the Library of Congress Subject Headings for terms under which your topic is likely to be indexed. Also, Amazon.com is an excellent online site to search for books by author, title, or topic. eBooks.com allows you to purchase and download many books. Your college may also have an electronic database for online books through eBooks or netLibrary.

- *Magazines/Journals.* It may be easier to use one of the library's many electronic databases to search for magazines and refereed journal articles—articles selected for their quality by a panel of reviewers. However, don't overlook the reference sections of libraries that contain valuable magazine indexes such as the Business Periodicals Index, Cumulative Index to Nursing and Allied Health, and the Index to Journals in Communication Studies.

- *Newspapers.* Although newspaper accounts may not tell the complete story, they are more current than magazines and books and contain personal details and

David Paul Morris/Getty Images

This speaker is searching a blog to find a story from an authoritative source to use in her presentation.

quotes that can serve as good supporting materials for your speeches. Check your library for local and national newspapers, or use electronic databases that include complete newspaper articles, such as EBSCOhost, *LexisNexis*, and *ProQuest*.

- *Specialized dictionaries and encyclopedias.* If you are new to your topic, begin your research with a specialized dictionary, such as the *Dictionary of American History*, or an encyclopedia, such as the *Encyclopedia of Science and Technology* or the *Physician's Desk Reference*. These reference books contain overviews of basic information in various fields—a good place to find background information. If you find information in Wikipedia.org ("a free encyclopedia that anyone can edit"), be sure to verify all information in at least one other reliable source.

- *Other library resources.* Libraries also contain quotation books such as *Bartlett's Familiar Quotations* and the *Speaker's and Toastmaster's Handbook*; yearbooks like the *Book of lists*, the *Facts on File Yearbook*, and the *Statistical Abstract of the United States*. Also, check with your librarian for government documents, special collections, films, videotapes, and special databases that are relevant to your topic.

Licensed Electronic Databases

Libraries are constantly purchasing new and expanded **electronic databases** that include books, magazine and journal articles, government documents, and more, so if you don't find what you need today, it may well be available soon. Keep asking. Many larger colleges and universities already offer well over 100 different databases for student use. Although search engines such as AltaVista, Yahoo!, or Google can produce many magazine sources, commercial databases such as *EBSCOHost, ProQuest, Opposing Viewpoints Resource Center, Communication and Mass Media Complete,* and LexisNexis Academic give you the option of avoiding "general interest" magazines and limiting your search to scholarly (peer reviewed) journals.

Databases also make available back issues at no charge, whereas most search engines provide only the current issue for free and require you to become a member or pay for back issues.

The Internet

Most people don't realize how recent a creation the Internet is: It has only been in common use since 1992. Yet, the growth of websites is staggering according to web server surveys: 19,000 in 1995, 5 million in 2000, 47 million in February 2004, 92.5 million in August 2006, and 230.4 million in October 2009 ("August," 2006; "February," 2004; "October," 2009; Saunders, 2000).

Although the Internet offers seemingly unlimited access to information, you must keep three facts in mind:

1. *Not all information on the web is authoritative.* Some of it is outdated, fallacious, biased, and basically worthless. You must carefully evaluate what you find. (See the section on page 320 on "Validate Internet Sources.")

2. Unless you know where to look, *it is possible to spend hours on the Internet without finding the information you need.* Surfing the web and researching with the web are not the same. (See the section on page 321 on "Searching More Than One Website.")

3. *Many valuable sources are not available on the web* (or are not available for free). This material is often referred to as the "invisible web" because it cannot be accessed by search engines because search engines cannot type a login or password. Google does have agreements with some academic libraries—thus its new area called *Google Scholar*—but this still only scratches the surface of available materials. It is only through licensed databases found though your college library that this "invisible" information can be found. Therefore, quality research still requires a trip to the library.

Before Going Online Considering the preceding three facts, and to save time and the frustration of an inadequate search, do your homework before going online. First, *prepare a rough-draft outline* of the main points and supporting information you think you might use in your speech. A look at this rough draft should tell you what information sources you already have or know from personal experience and what information (such as facts, statistics, quotes, or examples) are still needed.

Second, when you visit the *library looking for print materials and electronic databases, make a list of keywords and phrases ahead of time* to use when searching the Internet. The information you want may be on the Internet, but if you search using the wrong keywords, you may never find it—or at least, only find part of it. For example, some important documents on positive imagery and speaking can be found only under the keyword *visualization*; other documents appear when the keyword *mental imaging* is used. To narrow a search of "positive imagery" to speaking situations, would you use the keyword *speech, presentation,* or *public speaking*? Consulting print materials on the subject first will help you draw up a list of potential keywords.

Third, *search one or more electronic databases* (such as *InfoTrac College Edition, EBSCOHost,* or *ProQuest*) available through most college libraries and many organizations. You know this information is reliable and can use it to verify the credibility of other sources you find on the Internet.

Now you are ready to go online to look for specific information to supplement your print and electronic database research.

Searching with Boolean Operators   Whether you are using an electronic database or a search engine, **keyword searches,** which look for websites that contain a specific word or phrase, will be more effective if you link your search terms with **Boolean operators** (see Table 12.1). Although the number of hits a search produces is important, the quality of hits is most important. Usually, if the first two pages of hits don't contain what you want, you used the wrong term or search engine. If your search produces too many or too few hits (located websites), try the following suggestions:

TABLE 12.1

Basic Boolean Operators and Their Uses		
Boolean Operator	**Most Databases and Search Engines**	**Google**
• OR (Searches documents with either word & both words = maximum number of hits.)	• *motorcycle* or *racing* • OR = all caps or lowercase	• *motorcycle* OR *racing* • Searches documents with either word but not both words • *motorcycle racing*
• AND (Searches only documents containing both words.)	• *motorcycle* AND *racing* • AND = all caps or lowercase	• *motorcycle racing* • Google default puts AND between all words unless quotes used.
• + [plus sign] (Searches documents with either word but not both words.)	• *motorcycle + racing* • Add space before but not after + sign.	• *"Star Wars Episode +1"* • Google omits words like *in, the, when, how,* and numbers unless a + sign (with space before but not after) is used to force inclusion of these words.)
• "[phrase]" (Searches for content inside quotes as a single word or exact phrase.)	*"motorcycle racing"* • If no quotes, searches each word separately.	• *"motorcycle racing"* skills • If no quotes, puts AND between words.
• NOT or – [minus sign] (Search excludes documents using word or phrase following –, NOT, AND NOT.)	• *motorcycle* NOT *"dirt bike"* • *motorcycle* and not *"dirt bike" motorcycle* – *"dirt bike"* (Use all caps or lowercase.)	• *motorcycle* – *"dirt bike"* • *motorcycle* NOT *"dirt bike"* • NOT must be in all caps. • Add space before the minus but not after.
• * [asterisk] (Searches for truncated endings of the search term.)	• *Listen** • Searches listen, listening, listens, listeners, etc.	• *listen + listeners + listening* • Google does not truncate but will find synonyms if a tilde (~) is placed immediately in front of term: *~food* will find food, recipes, cooking, nutrition, etc.

* For more information on Google searches, go to Google.com/help or Google to find *Googling to the Max* by UC Berkeley.

Too many hits

- *Avoid the Boolean operator OR.* For example, in September 2009 a search for *motorcycle* OR *racing* resulted in 251,000,000 hits on Google!

- *Use phrases* (enclose titles, common phrases, procedures, or names in quotation marks). For example, *motorcycle racing* in Google returned 19, 400,000 hits, but *"motorcycle racing"* found fewer: 4,200,000 hits.

- *Specify additional words using + or AND.* For example, *"motorcycle racing"* +*women* returned 367,000 hits on Google, while *"motorcycle racing* women" found only 33,000 hits.

- Exclude words or phrases using – or NOT. For example, "motorcycle racing" NOT "dirt bike" returned 62,800 hits on Google; "motorcycle racing – dirt bike" found only 312,000 hits.

Too few hits

- Check that spelling and keywords are correct.

- Use the **wildcard** (*) to search for all forms of the word. For example, legisl* will search for legislature, legislation, legislator, and so forth. This type of truncation will not work on Google, but you can search for synonyms by inserting a tilde (~) before search words.

- Use fewer search words.

- Connect search words with OR.

- Use alternate keywords. For example, try automobile instead of car.

- Change full name to initials or initials to full name.

- Don't use -*s*, -*ing*, or -*ed* on search words.

Validate Internet Sources The Internet is a blend of many kinds of sites: educational (identified by web addresses ending in .edu or .cc), commercial (.com), governmental (.gov), organizational (.org), military (.mil), and personal. Therefore, you can't assume that all the information you find on the Internet is authoritative or of the quality you need to support your speeches. Internet searches are likely to include outdated, inaccurate, and biased information along with the valuable. It's up to you to evaluate the credibility of your information by asking the following questions (Drake, 2005):

- *Is the author of the information a qualified expert in the field?* Along with the author's name should be an explanation of his or her occupation, position, education, experience, and organizational affiliations. If no author is given, is the website clearly attributed to a reliable source such as a university or agency?

- *Is the information objective?* Are conclusions based on facts? Are sources cited? Are opinions and personal bias clearly stated? Is the purpose of the website clear—to inform, persuade, or sell? Is the author affiliated with an organization or group that might indicate a bias? For example, an article supporting animal testing of cosmetics on the website beautysupply.com might be biased if the sponsoring site sells animal-tested cosmetics.

- *Is the information accurate?* Generally, avoid websites with grammatical and typographical errors because such errors suggest that content may be faulty as well. Can you verify the facts and conclusions in this website with print or electronic database sources you have read?

Revisiting the Case Study

CNN reporters let bias creep into their research. How can speakers avoid similar problems when researching for supporting materials?

David McNew/Getty Images

- *Is the information current?* When was it written? Has it been updated? Some websites include the date of the last revision. NOTE: Netscape allows you to check the date—go to the File menu, select Document Info, and select Last Modified. Are the sources used by the author up-to-date? If no date is given, the information may be outdated.

As a speaker, you will be expected to use information that is current, accurate, objective, and attributed to a qualified expert. Always verify the credibility of documents obtained on the Internet by comparing them to similar information from other sources.

Searching More Than One Website Check your local college or university to see if they have completed some initial legwork for you by creating a gateway of links to valuable websites, often called subject guides. Many search engines (such as Yahoo! and Google) also provide subject guides—see their Web Site Directory.

Another way to find quality websites is to search with multiple search engines. As mentioned previously, in April 2009, there were 231.5 million websites on the Internet. Obviously, no single search engine can access all available sites. In 2000, Saunders reported that search engines covered less than 16% of the billions of pages of information available on the web; it can only be worse now. When selecting search engines, the following guidelines are recommended (Barker, 2006; Berkman, 2000):

- *For broad or complex subjects*, pick a search engine that uses a **hierarchical index**—a subject directory organized into categories. This way you are more likely to find relevant items. The most popular hierarchical search engine is Yahoo!

- *For specific subjects*, use either a standard search engine, an alternative search engine, or a vertical search engine. With a **standard search engine,** more of the web is searched. This is because computer "robots" search the web, index the pages found, and determine the relevance of the pages by mathematical calculation. Popular standard search engines include AltaVista, Excite, and HotBot. **Alternative search engines** have different ways of sorting or ranking the pages located in the search: AskJeeves, which lets you search by sentences, Google, which ranks hits by how many links to other pages each has, and Ask, which identifies the most authoritative sites on the Web. **Vertical search engines** search less of the Web, but a more specific part of the web (Mossberg, 2005). For example, Indeed searches job openings from thousands of websites and Ziggs searches for professional people (with specific characteristics, and who live in specific locations).

- *To search as many sites as possible*, use a **metasearch engine**—a search engine that searches other search engines. Popular metasearch engines include Dogpile, Surfwax, and Search, which searches 1,000 search engines at a time. Keep in mind that only 10 to 15% of each website is actually searched by metasearch engines; each time you use an engine, different hits will appear; and they focus on "smaller or free search engines and miscellaneous free directories" and are "highly commercial" (Barker, 2006).

Remember—quality searches require the use of multiple search engines.

Blogs and Twitter

Blogs, or weblogs, are personal journals posted on the Internet—blogs don't claim to contain facts but are intended to contain a variety of opinions on various diverse issues. As mentioned in Chapter 6, although the United States has more citizens online than any other country—164.3 million by February 2009—Japan actually has more bloggers (McPhail, 2006; Radwanick, 2009). Twitter.com, a relatively new technology created in 2006, is growing rapidly. Between February and April of 2009, Twitter "quadrupled its audience" to 17 million visitors in the United States (Lipsman, 2009). Most online magazines like forbes.com contain blogs on their own site or on Facebook, MySpace, or Twitter. If you are unclear on current public views, blog research could bring you up to date. Blogs and Twitter comments (called Tweets) could be used by speakers in various ways: an attention-getting narrative in an introduction, supporting examples during the speech, or as clarification of pro and con arguments in a persuasive speech. However, be especially carefully how this information is used—it is opinion not fact. Presenting opinions from one of these sites as though they are fact will hurt your credibility. Before using blogs or tweets in a speech, look for the bloggers frame of reference, goal or purpose, date of the blog, as well as, the credibility of the site (i.e., does the site have restrictions such as real names required?).

Personal Interviews

If your personal knowledge and your library and Internet searches do not provide exactly the type of information you need, you may want to conduct some personal interviews. For interview specifics, see Chapter 7. After you decide on likely candidates, you should plan your questions and conduct the interview following these steps:

1. *Introduction.* Be relaxed and friendly, and make good eye contact. Thank the interviewee for his or her time, and establish rapport by talking about your assignment, the weather (if it's unusual), or the reason you especially wanted to speak with him or her. State why you are there (unless already mentioned), how long you expect the interview to take, exactly what information you are looking for (if there are several areas, list them), and how the responses will be used.

2. *Body.* Here you ask the questions, which you have already planned. Write out your questions and bring them with you. Most interviewees will be more open and relaxed if you do not record the interview. Just listen carefully and take an occasional note to record an important fact, figure, or idea. Use mainly open-ended questions; they will elicit more information. Use probing questions like "Tell me more" or "What happened next?" to keep the interviewee talking. To make sure you haven't missed valuable information, end your questioning with "Is there anything else you think I should know?"

3. *Conclusion.* Use this step to verify information and give closure to the interview. Begin with a brief summary of the main areas you covered in the interview (this allows both you and the interviewee to see if anything important was omitted). If you are planning to quote the interviewee directly, now is the time to review the quote for accuracy and ask for permission to use it in your speech. End by thanking the interviewee, shaking hands, and making a timely exit. As soon as you can, send the interviewee a thank-you note expressing the value of the information to you and your presentation.

Use the results of the interview carefully. Expand your notes as soon as you get back so that you won't forget or misrepresent the interviewee's information. In deciding what, if anything, to use in your speech, be sure to keep all matters confidential that you agreed not to reveal.

Now it's time to select specific pieces of the information you found during your research and use them to support the main points of your presentation.

Geri Engberg Photography

There are many ways to obtain information for a speech. This student is conducting a personal interview.

Avoiding Plagiarism

In addition to researching thoroughly and avoiding bias, you must be careful not to plagiarize. Recall that **plagiarism** is using the ideas of someone else (whether paraphrased or word for word) without giving credit. If you read an article (or hear an ad or TV program) and then use information from it in your speech *without citing the source—even if you only paraphrase the content—you are plagiarizing.* As our ethic's story about ex–school board chairman Keith Cook indicates, using information and parts of speeches from the Internet without giving credit is also plagiarism.

As you are researching for supporting materials on the Internet, you will find many sites willing to sell both canned and custom speeches for classroom or seminar use. Don't be tempted to buy a speech from one of these sites or from a friend; you will be on dangerous ethical ground. If your professor or seminar instructor has questions about your speech, there are several sites that can be used to check it for plagiarism. Turnitin.com is an example of a site that checks both Internet and

ETHICAL DILEMMA

When Keith Cook, a school board chairman from Orange County, North Carolina, found a speech on a web page that listed no author, he thought it would be all right to use a large part of it in his commencement address. The speech used the movie *Titanic* to draw some interesting life lessons that were just perfect for graduating high school seniors. A reporter attending the ceremonies recognized the speech as one given by Donna Shalal[&|udota|&] when she was U.S. secretary of Health and Human Services, and he e-mailed Cook the Internet address ("School board chairman resigns amid plagiarism scandal," 2004). When asked where he got the speech, Cook first replied, "I wrote it" (Norton, 2004, para. 6). Later, he admitted to finding it on the Internet, but because it had no author he thought using it would constitute fair use. It was an "honest mistake," he said (para. 10). Many teachers, students, and community members demanded his resignation, saying that his plagiarism and denial of it set a bad example (Winn, 2004). The high school valedictorian "told a reporter that any student would have been suspended for doing what Cook did" (para. 23). The scandal even reached *Good Morning America, USA Today,* and *Time* magazine (Norton, 2004, para. 14; Winn, 2004, para. 8). Although Cook remained on the board, he resigned as chair. The board thought that this action would take care of the problem. When school board elections were held just 2 months after the controversy, however, Cook was not reelected.

Questions: What do you think? Should Cook have resigned from the board? What effect would his actions have on high school students and possible plagiarism in their assignments?

print sources for plagiarism. There are many reasons to avoid using someone else's speech (Hamilton, 2009, p. 17): It's unethical; the consequences of plagiarism can be severe and long-lasting; you won't learn the successful speech skills needed for business success; it's very difficult to deliver a speech you didn't write—especially if you are nervous; and you will be wasting money when the skills necessary to write a quality speech are available for your use in Chapters 11–14.

Verbal Supporting Materials

The key to understanding what is meant by supporting materials is the verb *support*. One of its dictionary definitions is "to hold up or serve as a foundation or prop for." Therefore, **supporting materials** are informative materials that serve as a foundation for our ideas. Supporting materials have three purposes:

- *Clarify.* If your listeners do not understand your ideas, your presentation will fail. The effective speaker uses visual supports (such as charts, graphs, and pictures) and verbal supports (such as illustrations, comparisons, and explanations) to clarify ideas.

- *Prove.* Often, statements must be proven or substantiated before they are accepted. The effective speaker uses verbal supports (such as statistics, quotes from experts, and illustrations) as evidence for ideas and statements.

- *Add interest.* Because every person has a different frame of reference, not everyone will view a particular support as interesting. An effective speaker uses a variety of supports for each idea or assertion.

The verbal supporting materials most often used by business and professional speakers can be divided into six categories: explanations, comparisons (including figurative and literal comparisons), illustrations (including hypothetical and factual illustrations), examples, statistics, and expert opinions.

Explanations

In an **explanation,** the speaker describes the relationship between certain items, defines a term or word, or gives instructions on how to do something or how to get somewhere. For example, a speaker might describe the relationship between the sales and purchasing departments, give the official company definition of compensation time, or describe how to operate a new piece of machinery. Beginning speakers tend to overuse explanations. If the only support you use is explanation, your presentation will not only lack proof but will most likely lack interest as well. As often as possible, replace or reinforce the explanation you planned to use with some other type of support.

In a speech titled "I Know It When I See It: Moral Judgments and Business Ethics" George Ellard (2007), co-head of the white-collar and corporate compliance section of Baach Robinson & Lewis Law Firm, used the following explanation and definition of business ethics:

> It is an honor to speak with you tonight about business ethics. It is also a very difficult task because the notion "business ethics" rests on the distinction between right and wrong.

REMEMBER

Explanations . . .

- Should be specific but brief.
- Should be used only for clarification, not for proof.
- Are generally used too often by beginning speakers. As often as possible, replace or reinforce the explanation you plan to use with some other type of support.

Most civilizations before the modern epoch accepted the existence of right and wrong, but by the time people reach college age in our society many, if not most, have absorbed the belief dominant in our culture that moral judgments are simply personal preferences (p. 193).

Comparisons

Speakers use **comparisons** to show the similarities or differences between something the listeners know and something they do not know. Suppose, for example, you are speaking to a group of supervisors about an often used but ineffective way of motivating workers—the "dangling carrot" approach. To clarify your point, you could compare this method of motivating workers to a parent motivating a teenager to clean up his room by promising the use of the family car.

There are two types of comparisons: literal and figurative. A **literal comparison** shows similarities or differences between two or more items from the same class or category. The following are examples of literal comparisons: two styles of management, sales of three competing companies, two advertising campaigns, and monthly travel expenses of five top salespersons. Although comparisons are not used as absolute proof, a literal comparison can offer solid evidence for your point if the items being compared are almost identical. For example, Elaine L. Chao (2007), U.S. Secretary of Labor, in a speech titled "Remarks" at the Asian American Government Executives Network, used the following literal comparison:

> And Asian Pacific Americans need to be aware of the cultural differences that may impact the way in which they practice leadership in society. Let me give you an example. This goes back to classroom days.... In traditional Asian American communities, children are discouraged from speaking unless they have something to say. But in American culture, expressing one's opinion is encouraged and rewarded. And this makes sense in this society.... Leaders advance and defend the interests of their organization and their colleagues. So executives need to be articulate, both in written and in oral presentations.... You can see these trends in little children.... But most Asians are taught that it is rude to speak out of turn or to interrupt others. It is proper to defer to others. America, however, is a place where everybody speaks their mind.... I had to overcome my cultural reticence about speaking up (pp. 10–13).

A **figurative comparison** shows similarities or differences between two or more items from different classes or categories. A speaker who compares a salesperson's competitive drive to the drive of a hungry bear is using a figurative comparison. Figurative comparisons are never used for proof, but they do add interest and clarify ideas.

Mike Ruettgers (2003), EMC's Corporation executive chairman of the board, in a speech delivered at Bentley College, Center for Business Ethics, clarified the problem of business ethics by using a figurative comparison:

> There is an old parable about the "boiled frog." Now I don't know why anyone would want to boil a frog, but the story goes that if you put a frog in a pot of boiling water, he'll try to

REMEMBER

Comparisons . . .

- Should relate something unfamiliar to something familiar to the audience. Plan your comparisons to fit the average frame of reference of your audience.
- Are an effective and easy way to add interest to your presentation.
- Are used mainly to clarify ideas. The figurative comparison is used only for clarification and never for proof; the literal comparison can be used in persuasion as a weak proof.

jump out. But place him in room-temperature water and gradually turn up the temperature, and he stays in and eventually is boiled. It seems to me that ethical confrontations are similar. When facing an obvious breach of ethics, you jump out to safety. But when the line between right and wrong is not so obvious, you can get boiled. (p. 151)

Illustrations

An **illustration** is a narrative or story told in vivid detail to paint a picture for the listener. A speaker who recommends that the company provide more conference rooms might present an illustration about a buyer who, when an important client arrives, has no conference room available. A good speaker would give such a vivid picture of the event that the listeners would feel the embarrassment and anger of the buyer trying to negotiate an important purchase in the middle of ringing telephones and competing conversations. Illustrations can be used in the introduction, body, or conclusion of a speech to gain attention and involve the audience personally.

Illustrations can be factual or hypothetical. A **factual illustration** is a detailed narrative about someone, something, or some event that actually happened. In discussing how important encouragement is to each of us, Robert L. Veninga (2006) used the following factual illustration in a commencement address for graduate students at the University of Sioux Falls:

> The importance of encouragement cannot be overemphasized. Recently I had a mid-career student in one of my classes. She took notes religiously, which any professor will tell you is the mark of a highly educated person! Then she would frequently stay after class to discuss class content.
>
> One day, however, I saw sadness written all over her face. I asked her what was wrong. "Just before coming to class my supervisor handed me my performance review," she said. "Would you read it?" I read it and was quite impressed with all her accomplishments. And frankly I was puzzled as to why the student was upset until the student asked me to reread the appraisal. Upon rereading it I understood: There was not a word of thanks. There were no statements of appreciation. It was just a listing of facts related to her job. The student looked at me and said plaintively: "All I wanted was a simple thank you." (pp. 544–545)

A **hypothetical illustration** is a detailed narrative about someone who could exist or some event that could or probably will happen. In other words, the hypothetical illustration is made up by the speaker to fit a particular situation. To be effective, the hypothetical illustration must be possible or likely. Hypothetical illustrations usually begin with a phrase such as "What would you do if...," "Suppose for a moment...," "Imagine...," or "Put yourself in this situation...." During the Civil War, Abraham Lincoln used a hypothetical illustration combined with a figurative comparison to silence critics of his war policy:

> Gentlemen, I want you to suppose a case for a moment. Suppose that all the property you were worth was in gold, and you had put it in the hands of Blondin, the famous

---

REMEMBER

Illustrations . . .

- Should be detailed and vivid, painting a picture for your audience.
- Should relate clearly to the point you are supporting.
- If factual, are used both to clarify and to add proof; the more illustrations you use, the stronger the proof.
- Are used by speakers in introductions to get the attention and personal involvement of the audience.
- If hypothetical, are used only for clarification.

rope-walker, to carry across the Niagara Falls on a tightrope. Would you shake the rope while he was passing over it, or keep shouting to him, "Blondin, stoop a little more! Go a little faster!" No, I am sure you would not. You would hold your breath as well as your tongue, and keep your hands off until he was safely over. Now the government is in the same situation. It is carrying an immense weight across a stormy ocean. Untold treasures are in its hands. It is doing the best it can. Don't badger it! Just keep still, and it will get you safely over. (Ross, 1980, pp. 181–182)

Examples

Examples are brief references to specific items or events that are used for both proof and clarification. Examples can be presented either as lists of items with no detail or as a series of items described with a few brief facts. To be effective, examples are usually presented in groups of two or more. Several examples usually clarify and prove more effectively than a single one. Examples are often included immediately after a factual illustration to add additional proof to the illustration. Time limits usually do not allow for enough detailed illustrations to prove an idea completely. By following the illustration with a series of examples, you are saying to your audience, "And I could include even more facts if I only had the time."

The Chair of Deloitte LLP made a case for the importance of business students being trained for leadership with the following list of statistical examples followed by an explanation of their meaning:

> As an accountant, I've always believed that numbers tell a story. Here are some that have my full attention:

- Currently, age 62 is the median age for retirement in the U.S.
- This year, an estimated 10,000 Baby Boomers will turn 62—every day.
- And in the next 10 years, 43 percent of the population in the U.S. will become eligible to retire.

> That's what's happening at the end of the U.S. talent pipeline—and there appear to be similar trends in Europe, Russia, and Japan. As for what's taking place at the beginning of the talent pipeline, the numbers are equally sobering. Research conducted by Deloitte indicates that in the U.S. there will be fewer young people to replace retiring workers every year for the next 30 years.
>
> With numbers like that, our newest employees probably will be called on to lead earlier in their careers than any previous generation entering the workforce. So we have an urgent need for business students to be fully prepared to become business leaders—sooner rather than later (p. 353).

In a speech to the City Club of Cleveland, Dr. Randolph D. Smoak, Jr. (2001), president of the American Medical Association, used examples to add impact to his statement that many working Americans can't afford insurance:

> The uninsured are all around us— average working Americans like the man who hands you your cleaning when you

---

REMEMBER

Examples . . .

- Are brief references to specific items or events.
- May contain no detail (such as a list of items) or may include a few brief facts.
- Are used for both clarification and proof.
- Are more effective when used in groups of two or more.
- Are often included immediately after a factual illustration to add additional proof to the illustration.

pick it up—the woman behind the cash register at your local diner— and Nancy, who works in the barbershop where I get my hair cut! (p. 443)

In a speech titled "How Women and Minorities Are Reshaping Corporate America," Linda Winikow (1991), vice president of Orange and Rockland Utilities, Inc., used these two longer examples to illustrate how simply being a woman creates barriers to advancement:

> When I first became involved in politics, back in the early 1970s, men found it difficult to swallow that I could be a member of the Zoning Board of Appeals and be pregnant simultaneously!
>
> And when I was a New York state senator, I was stopped by the State Police on the New York State Thruway because they thought my car—with its Senate license plate—must be stolen, since a woman was in it! (p. 243)

Statistics

Statistics are numbers used to show relationships between items. Used correctly, statistics can clarify and add proof to your ideas; used incorrectly, they can confuse and bore your listeners. Statistics can work for you if you follow these important rules.

Relate Statistics to Your Listeners' Frames of Reference This is the most important rule in using statistics. Compare the statistics to something familiar to your listeners so that they will be meaningful. Instead of telling his Indiana University audience that tobacco kills close to 500,000 Americans each year, Lonnie Bristow (1994), chair of the board of trustees of the American Medical Association, made the statistic more meaningful in the following way:

> I ask you to check your watches. Because in this hour, by the time I'm done speaking, 50 Americans will die from smoke-related diseases. By the time you sit down to breakfast in the morning, 600 more will have joined them; 8,400 by the end of the week—every week, every month, every year—until it kills nearly half a million Americans, year in, year out.
>
> That's more than all the other preventable causes of death combined. Alcohol, illegal drugs, AIDS, suicide, car accidents, fires, guns—all are killers. But tobacco kills more than all of them put together. (p. 333)

Eliminate Statistics That Are Not Absolutely Necessary Listeners generally do not pay attention when long lists of statistics are read. If you still want to use several statistics, use a chart or graph to simplify them and make them much easier to understand.

Round Off Statistics to an Easy Number Your listeners will remember a number better if you say, "The amount approaches 25,000" or "approximately 25,000" rather than "The amount is 24,923.002." The following example used in a speech by Mary Sue Coleman (2006) includes statistics that were rounded off:

> Most recently, Hurricane Katrina dealt a blow to the libraries of the Gulf

Statistics . . .

- Are figures used to show relationships between items.
- Are made more meaningful when directly related to the listeners' interests and knowledge.
- Should be used sparingly.
- Are easier to understand and remember when displayed as a line graph, bar graph, or circle graph.
- Should be rounded off.
- Are more credible when cited with the source and the source's qualifications.
- Are used for both clarification and proof.

Coast. At Tulane University, the main library sat in nine feet of water—water that soaked the valuable Government Documents collection: more than 750,000 items…one of the largest holdings of government materials in Louisiana…90 percent of it now lost. (p. 265)

Demonstrate the Credibility of Your Statistics Show credibility by citing the source, the expertise of the source, and the size of the population from which the statistics were compiled. Consider this statistic: "Four out of five managers recommend using employee appraisals." How many managers had to be interviewed to make that statement? Only five! The statements of only five managers out of the thousands that exist are not adequate support for an assertion. However, suppose a survey of 5,000 middle managers from companies of various sizes was conducted by the Independent Business Polling Corporation and that four out of five of the 4,000 managers who replied to the survey (that is, 3,200 managers) recommended the use of employee appraisals. This statistic would be strong support for our claim.

Expert Opinions

Expert opinion refers to the ideas of an expert in the field, either paraphrased or quoted directly by the speaker. Expert opinion is best when kept brief. Supporting your ideas with expert opinion is an excellent way to add both clarification and proof to your presentation. To use expert opinion to prove an idea, be sure to (a) state the name of the expert, (b) briefly describe his or her qualifications unless you are sure the listeners are already familiar with them, and (c) briefly cite where and when the expert reported this information—for example, in a personal interview conducted last Wednesday or in the last issue of the *Harvard Business Review*. When paraphrasing—putting the expert's ideas into your own words—make sure that you don't misrepresent the expert's ideas. Here is a sample of how to introduce a paraphrase:

> In her 2006 book *You're Wearing That?*, Deborah Tannen, university professor and well-known authority on communication, makes the point that…[put information in your own words].

Here is an example of how to introduce a direct quote:

> In response to a question about whether mothers or daughters are more likely to sabotage communication, Dr. Tannen, a well-known authority on communication and author of the popular book *You're Wearing That?*, answered, "[insert quote]."

When using direct quotes, not only should the content be interesting, but as you read the quote, make sure your delivery is lively and convincing.

If your audience is unfamiliar with your experts, you will need to introduce them thoroughly, as Jenny Clanton (1989) did in her speech titled "Plutonium 238: NASA's Fuel of Choice." In her attempt to inform the audience of the danger of Plutonium 238, she included the credentials of the expert she paraphrased:

> Last July, *Common Cause* magazine contacted Dr. Gofman at Berkeley and asked him to place Plutonium 238 in perspective. Before I share Dr. Gofman's assessment, please understand he's no poster-carrying "anti-nuke." Dr. Gofman was co-discoverer of Uranium 233, and he isolated the isotope first used in nuclear bombs. Dr. Gofman told Karl Grossman, author of the article "Red-tape and Radioactivity," that Plutonium 238 is 300 times more radioactive than Plutonium 239, which is the isotope used in atomic bombs. (p. 375)

REMEMBER

Expert Opinions . . .

- May be paraphrased or quoted directly.
- Should be kept brief to keep listener interest.
- May be used for both clarification and proof.
- Should be quoted as though the expert were actually speaking—not read in a dull or monotone voice.
- Should usually include the name and qualifications of the expert and when and where the information was reported.
- Should, in many cases, be followed by an explanation. Don't assume that the listener understood either the content of the quote or your reason for citing it.

If your expert is well known to your audience, it is not necessary to cite the expert's qualifications. For example, speaking to the YWCA Women of Distinction Annual Dinner in Nebraska, Janice Thayer (2001), president of the Excel Corporation, used the following quote, which needed no detailed introduction:

> Barbara Bush must have been heartened when, in his acceptance speech her son said, "I believe in grace, because I have seen it....In peace, because I have felt it....In forgiveness, because I have needed it." (p. 408)

Whether you are paraphrasing or using a direct quote, make sure your audience understands what the expert is saying and your reason for using his or her idea. If you feel there is any chance of confusion, follow the paraphrase or quote with such comments as "In this quote, _____ is making the same argument I made previously"; or "What is _____ saying? He or she is telling us..."; or "I cited _____ because...."

The six types of verbal supporting materials often overlap. For example, you may quote an expert who is explaining an idea by comparing statistics. The effective speaker uses a variety of supports to keep the listeners interested. Don't forget that some supports are used only to clarify, and others are used both for clarification and for proof, as summarized in Table 12.2.

Improving Delivery

Effective speakers must do more than research and prepare well-supported and well-organized ideas—they must present their ideas in a believable manner. "To be successful in the information age," warns Robert V. Smith (2004), "professionals must be dramatic, interesting, and intellectually adventuresome communicators" (p. ix). "As Lee Iacocca (Iacocca & Novak, 1986) said in his autobiography, "You can have brilliant ideas, but if you can't get them across, your brains won't get you anywhere" (p. 16). Your delivery isn't more important than what you say, but without good delivery, your audience may never hear what you have to say. Your words, your tone of voice, and your gestures, eye contact, and appearance must reinforce each other

TABLE 12.2

Verbal Supports	
Used Only for Clarification	**Used for Both Clarification and Proof**
• Explanations	• Literal comparisons (but this is very weak proof)
• Figurative comparisons	• Factual illustrations
• Hypothetical illustrations	• Examples
• Statistics	• Expert opinions

Supporting Materials

To check how well you can identify types of support, take the following quiz. Compare your answers to those at the back of this book. You can also take this quiz online and view the answers via your Premium Website for *Communicating for Results.*

Directions: Identify each of the following types of supporting material by selecting one of the following: (a) explanation, (b) comparison, (c) illustration, (d) examples, (e) statistics, or (f) expert opinion.

_____ 1. Speaking about self-confidence, Eleanor Roosevelt said, "No one can make you feel inferior without your consent."

_____ 2. Abraham Lincoln gives us a dramatic view of the power of attitude:

He was defeated for office in 1832.

His sweetheart died in 1835.

He suffered a nervous breakdown in 1836.

He was defeated for office in 1838 and 1843.

He was elected to Congress in 1846.

He was defeated for office in 1848, 1854, 1856, and 1858.

He was elected president of the United States in 1860.

_____ 3. "Grunting" is a popular technique used to collect earthworms. A stake is driven into the ground and vibrated. The vibrations drive the worms to the surface.

_____ 4. If you had a credit card debt of $2,500 and paid only the minimum payments, it would take approximately 12 1/2 years to pay off that balance.

_____ 5. Imagine that it's a Wednesday morning and your alarm has just gone off. You reach over and after several tries finally get that awful noise to quit. You pull the cover from your head, force your eyes open, yawn, and roll over. You're thinking, "Should I get up and go to work, or should I sleep in a bit longer? After all, the weather is bad today, and I do have a cold...."

_____ 6. Trying to decorate your home without the help of a design consultant works about as well as trying to diet by eating Big Macs.

for your presentation to be most effective. Let's begin the discussion of delivery by looking at it from the visual, vocal, and verbal angles.

Delivery and Nonverbal Behavior

As a speaker, you should appear relaxed, enthusiastic, and natural. You should not become a different person when you give an oral presentation; you should not step into a speaker's disguise. Simply be yourself, presenting your ideas in a natural yet enthusiastic manner. Much of this manner depends on your nonverbal behavior.

To appear natural and relaxed, you need to look directly at your listeners and smile occasionally. Don't look over the heads of or between listeners, or they may decide that you are nervous and lack authority. If you want your listeners to have confidence in what you are saying, you must appear confident! Dressing up for the presentation is one way to feel more confident and a good way to indicate nonverbally that what you have to say is important.

Gestures and a certain amount of movement not only help you appear natural but also add enthusiasm and authority to your presentation. Neither your gestures nor your movements should distract the audience's attention from what you are saying, but too little movement can cause your audience to lose interest. Used correctly, gestures add excitement and reinforce main ideas. Ideally, you will get so involved in your topic that the gestures will come naturally. Stepping forward, backward, or to the side is also an effective way to show enthusiasm, to emphasize a point, or to progress from one idea to another. For the best effect, try to move at either the beginning or the end of a sentence or an idea.

Delivery and Voice

The best speaking voice is one that sounds conversational, natural, and enthusiastic. People are more likely to listen closely to your presentation and to understand your ideas more clearly if you speak much as you do in ordinary conversation. For example, most people automatically use excellent vocal variety when speaking with a friend. Vocal variety, the key to a conversational voice, is achieved by varying volume, pitch, emphasis, and rate in a natural manner.

Volume, the loudness and softness of your voice, is important in several ways to your success as a speaker. First, you must be loud enough to be heard easily from all parts of the room. Second, you also need to vary the volume of your voice to make the presentation interesting. Third, you should increase and decrease volume to emphasize words or phrases.

Pitch, the highness and lowness of vocal tones, is also important to vocal variety. Too little variety in pitch can make your voice a dull monotone (like a piano repeating only one note), whereas extreme changes in pitch can make you sound unnatural and insincere. Effective speakers use step changes in pitch (changes between high, medium, and low pitches) and pitch inflection (gradually rising or falling pitch) to add interest and enthusiasm to their voices and to communicate subtle or implied meanings.

Emphasis, stressing a word with your voice to give it significance, is another important ingredient of vocal variety. In emphasizing a word, two things happen: Your pitch goes up (usually followed by a downward slide) and your volume increases. For a demonstration of this point, say the following question five times, each time emphasizing a different word as shown. Listen to your pitch and volume as you speak. You should be able to give five different meanings to the question.

> *Why* did you fire him?
>
> Why *did* you fire him?
>
> Why did *you* fire him?
>
> Why did you *fire* him?
>
> Why did you fire *him*?

Rate, how fast or how slowly you speak, is especially important in maintaining listener attention. Constantly speaking at the same rate can lull your listeners to sleep. An effective speaker usually speaks faster to show excitement, to build suspense, or for emphasis. A slower speaking rate can also be used for emphasis to show the importance of an idea; combined with low pitch, a slow rate can indicate inappropriate or boring ideas. Be sure to pause after important phrases or ideas to let the listeners absorb them.

Delivery and Language

Listeners expect speakers to use a more informal language style than that of written reports. For example, in oral communication you should use short, simple sentences. In fact, it isn't always necessary to use complete sentences. It is fine to use personal pronouns such as *I*, *we*, *you*, *us*, and contractions such as *I've* or *won't*—forms often avoided in formal written English.

One of the most serious mistakes a speaker can make is to try to impress listeners by using long or extremely technical words or jargon. Do not assume that upper management, employees in other departments, or the public will understand the technical terms and jargon used in your department; they probably won't. The best language is vivid (paints a picture for the listener), specific (gives details), and simple (easy to understand). Your listeners need to understand you the first time.

Here is a sample of the type of language to avoid. The following government memo so upset President Franklin Roosevelt when he read it that he immediately rewrote it and sent it back to the author:

"Could you give a talk to **4,000** angry people in the auditorium in two minutes?"

© 2003 Ted Goff. Reprinted by permission. www.tedgoff.com

IT REALLY WORKS!

Delivery Improvement

Growing up, Bob Love could barely speak without stuttering. It was not until after an injury ended his basketball career at age 45 that Love finally learned to let his voice be heard. Most of the following information comes from an interview published by the American Speech-Language-Hearing Association (Moore, 2004).

Bob Love scored 12,263 points for the Chicago Bulls during his career and is the third-highest scorer in Bulls history—behind only Michael Jordan and Scottie Pippen. He was voted NBA All-Star three times, and for eight seasons averaged 23.0 points per game ("Bob Love," 2006). However, for most of his life, Love got by with being silent. Drafted by the Cincinnati Royals in 1965, he soon realized that, despite his talent, people judged him more on his speaking ability than on his playing ability. He was traded twice for that very reason, and even when he hit his career peak for the Chicago Bulls, he was rarely ever interviewed by reporters and never received any product endorsements. Although he dreamed of being a professional speaker, his stutter was such a problem that upon leaving the Seattle Supersonics from a back injury, the only job he could get was "washing dishes and busing tables for $4.45 an hour" at Nordstrom's (Moore, 2004, p. 8).

This is where a little hard work and likely some luck paid off for Love. Because of his excellent work, Nordstrom wanted to promote him, but first he had to get rid of his debilitating stutter. The CEO of Nordstrom took personal interest in Bob and offered to pay for a speech therapist. The therapist, Susan Hamilton, worked with Love's rate, continuous formation, and breathing patterns, and with hard work and encouragement, his life was completely changed. Now, in addition to serving as the director of Community Affairs for his beloved Chicago Bulls, Love moonlights as a motivational speaker, giving over 300 presentations per year ("Bulls in the Community: Outreach," 2006; "Bob Love," 2006). His dream of becoming a professional speaker achieved, Love's story is now an inspiration to youth and adults.

What do you think?
- Do you think that people really judged Love more by his stutter than by his playing or was he being overly sensitive?
- Based on Love's personal experience with stuttering, what kinds of supporting materials could he successfully use in his motivational presentations?

> Such preparations shall be made as will completely obscure all Federal buildings and non-Federal buildings occupied by the Federal Government during an air raid for any period of time from visibility by reason of internal or external illumination. Such obscuration may be obtained either by blackout construction or by termination of the illumination. (O'Hayre, 1966, p. 39)

Here is President Roosevelt's rewritten version:

> Tell them that in buildings where they have to keep the work going, to put something over the windows; and, in buildings where they can let the work stop for a while, turn out the lights. (O'Hayre, 1966, p. 39)

Alexander Haig, who combined the language of diplomacy with the language of a previous job as general, confused people with such phrases as "careful caution, caveat my response, epistemologically wise, nuanced departures, definitizing an answer, and saddle myself with a statistical fence" (Rackleff, 1988, p. 312).

Putting your ideas into simple, easy-to-understand language that fits the frames of reference of your listeners and is vivid and specific is important for both informative and persuasive speaking. However, persuasive language is generally more straightforward and forceful than informative language. For example, which is the more persuasive language in the examples below—A or B?

Example 1

A.   Although three arguments are frequently presented in favor of legalizing drugs, none of them holds up under careful scrutiny. In fact, as you will see, all three are based on faulty reasoning. The first fallacious argument is…

B.   Let's look at three arguments in favor of drug legalization. The first argument is…

Example 2

A.   When legislation on sobriety checkpoints comes up for a vote in your county, think about what I've said in making your decision.

B.   When legislation on sobriety checkpoints comes up for a vote in your county, vote "Yes." It's time we made our roads safe again.

Example 3

A.   There are three points that I'd like to cover today about the Electoral College.

B.   There are three points I'd like to cover today that will demonstrate how hopelessly out of date and ineffective the Electoral College really is.

In addition to the actual and implied meanings that words carry, words or sets of words can have a texture or "feel"—what persuasion expert Charles Larson (2010) calls the "thematic dimension" of language. The "most important aspect [of words] is their ability to set a mood, a feeling, or a tone or theme for the persuasion" (p. 152). If your listeners are in the correct frame of mind for a particular topic, you will have a better chance of communicating your ideas to them. Therefore, using **stylistic language devices** (see the box on page 335) to establish a mood or feeling at various times during a speech (especially a persuasive speech) is important to the success of your message. Stylistic devices are also used to emphasize and make phrases memorable. They gain their entertaining and persuasive power by "departing from everyday language usage" (Cooper & Nothstine, 1992, p. 168). They

Stylistic Devices

Alliteration—Repetition of consonants (usually the first or last letter in a series of words).

Antithesis—Two parallel but contrasting ideas contained in one sentence.

Assonance—Repetition of vowel sounds.

Hyperbole—Statement containing deliberate exaggeration.

Metaphor—Implied comparison between two items without using *like* or *as.*

Onomatopoeia—Words that sound like their meaning.

Parallelism—Similarly phrased ideas presented in rapid succession.

Personification—Human characteristics or feelings assigned to animals or things.

Repetition—Word or series of words repeated in successive clauses or sentences.

Simile—Direct comparison between two items using the words *like* or *as.*

do this in two basic ways: Most stylistic devices leave word meanings unchanged but rearrange sentences in unusual ways; a few stylistic devices change "the main or ordinary meaning of a word" but maintain normal sentence structure (p. 168).

Speakers also need to be aware that certain words may cause listeners to have either positive or negative reactions. Try to make words work for you, not against you. For example, see the "sweet and sour" words listed in the box on page 336. Chapter 14 presents a detailed discussion of persuasive speaking.

Maintaining a Confident Delivery

Feeling nervous prior to a new communication situation is perfectly normal. We all experience a butterflies-in-the-stomach feeling at times. Your friends do, your boss does, top-level managers do, and so do the vice president and the chief executive officer of your organization. Because speaker anxiety is so prevalent, we included it as an obstacle to communication in Chapter 6. Reread the section "Communicator Anxiety" in that chapter and review whether your anxiety is more situational or trait. Then follow the guidelines for how to manage your type of anxiety.

Don't overlook the importance of practice—stand up, speak out loud, and use your visuals (if you use notes, make sure they are key words only). Practice allows you to check the length and make corrections on any content or transitions that don't seem to flow smoothly. Don't try to memorize the presentation. In fact, each time you practice, it should sound a bit different. Think how much more confident you feel when you have really studied for an exam than when you just skimmed the material. The same is true with speaking—people who practice several times, feel much more confident and in control when giving the actual speech. It is especially helpful to videotape your speech (even practicing in front of a mirror is good) and to give the speech in front of friends or family. Recent research found that students who practiced their speeches in front of others actually received higher grades than students who practiced without an audience (Smith & Frymier, 2006). Also, practicing before larger audiences resulted in higher evaluations than practicing before smaller audiences.

Remember, it doesn't matter how nervous you are inside—just don't admit it to your listeners. Never apologize. If your nervousness causes you to leave out a crucial

Words: Sweet and Sour

Whether you're trying to win an argument, close a sale, or just be personable on paper, the words you use can help or hinder your cause. Research has uncovered the words to which most people react favorably—and unfavorably. Here they are:

Most People Like These Words

advantage	ease	integrity	responsible
appreciate	economy	justice	satisfactory
benefit	effective	kind	service
capable	efficient	loyalty	success
confidence	energy	please	superior
conscientious	enthusiasm	popularity	useful
cooperation	genuine	practical	valuable
courtesy	helpful	prestige	vigor
dependable	honesty	progress	you
desirable	honor	reliable	yours

Most People Dislike These Words

abuse	decline	ignorant	squander
alibi	discredit	imitation	superficial
allege	dispute	implicate	tardy
apology	exaggerate	impossible	timid
beware	extravagance	misfortune	unfair
blame	failure	negligent	unfortunate
cheap	fault	opinionated	unsuccessful
commonplace	fear	prejudiced	waste
complaint	fraud	retrench	worry
crisis	hardship	rude	wrong

From: Ted Pollock, "A Personal File of Stimulating Ideas and Problem Solvers," in *Supervision*, Vol. 46, No. 2 (February, 1984), p. 25. Reprinted by permission. Copyright by the National Research Bureau, Inc., 424 North Third Street, Burlington, IA 52601.

idea, summarize what you have covered so far and insert the idea by saying, "Another topic that needs to be considered is.…" After all, the listeners don't have a script of your presentation, so how will they know you left something out or changed the order of topics? If you do make an obvious error, don't call attention to it. All speakers make a few minor errors—listeners expect it. To look confident, don't toy with pencils, paper clips, or other small items (especially in your pockets) that will distract the listener and make you look nervous and unprofessional. If you want your listeners to have confidence in what you are saying, you must *appear* confident (even if you feel nervous inside). So, practice, practice, practice!

CHAPTER 12 REVIEW

Tonis Valing/Shutterstock

Key Terms

alliteration (335)

alternative search engine (321)

antithesis (335)

assonance (335)

blogs (321)

Boolean operators (319)

comparisons (325)

electronic databases (317)

emphasis (332)

examples (327)

expert opinion (329)

explanation (323)

factual illustration (326)

figurative comparison (325)

hierarchical index (321)

hyperbole (335)

hypothetical illustration (326)

illustration (326)

keyword search (320)

literal comparison (325)

metaphor (335)

metasearch engine (321)

onomatopoeia (335)

parallelism (335)

personification (335)

pitch (332)

plagiarism (323)

rate (332)

repetition (335)

simile (335)

standard search engine (321)

statistics (328)

stylistic language devices (334)

supporting material (324)

vertical search engine (321)

volume (332)

wildcard (320)

Summary

Effective speakers carefully research their topic for current information that can serve as supporting materials for their ideas. They begin their research with print sources, then move to databases if available, then search the Internet for additional specific information, and, if necessary, conduct personal interviews. Then they select pieces of information from their research to be supporting materials that add clarity, proof, or interest to their speeches. Verbal supporting materials include explanations, comparisons, illustrations, examples, statistics, and expert opinions. Effective speakers also realize that they must develop effective delivery to create the greatest impact.

Communicating for Results Online

Before continuing to the next chapter, check your understanding of Chapter 12 at the Premium Website for *Communicating for Results*. Your Premium Website gives you quick and easy access to the electronic resources that accompany this text. These resources include:

- **Study tools** that will help you assess your learning and prepare for exams (student companion workbook, digital glossary, key term flash cards, and review quizzes).

- **Activities and assignments** that will help you hone your knowledge, analyze professional communication situations, build your public speaking skills throughout the course, and learn to work effectively in teams (Awareness Checks, Checkpoints, and Collaborative Learning Activities).

- **Media resources** that will help you explore communication concepts online (web links), develop your speech outlines (Speech Builder Express 3.0), watch and critique videos of professional communication situations and sample speeches (Interactive Video Activities), upload your speech videos for peer reviewing and critique other students' speeches (Speech Studio online speech review tool), and download chapter review so you can study when and where you'd like (Audio Study Tools).

This chapter's key terms, Collaborative Learning Activities, and Checkpoint activities are also featured on the following pages, and you can find this chapter's Awareness Check activities in the body of the chapter. For more information or to access this book's online resources, visit www.cengage.com/login.

Collaborative Learning Activities

1. In small groups, go to EBSCOHost and click on the Military and Government Collection, and look for a Speech that the group likes from a recent *Vital Speeches* magazine. Each group member should read the speech looking for examples of each type of supporting material. Select three of the best and discuss what made them so effective. Select at least one support that you don't think was effective and discuss what the speaker could have done to make it more effective.

2. In small groups, select a topic that the group thinks would make a good speech. Once selected, discuss which types of research would be needed to find quality information for your topic. Have each group member research using two of the types of research. Share your research results and discuss which method of research uncovered the best information and why. Based on your research, decide on three to five main points for your speech. Be prepared to share this list of main points along with at least one research fact with other groups or the class.

Checkpoints

Checkpoint 12.1 Checking Your Voice for Variety and Tone
To get an idea of how your voice sounds to others, leave a detailed message on your answering machine or voice mail system. Do this regularly until your vocal variety and tone project the warmth or enthusiasm or authority you desire (Decker & Denney, 1993).

Checkpoint 12.2 Identifying Types of Verbal Supporting Materials

Checkpoint 12.3 Controlling Nervousness

Checkpoint 12.4 Researching a Speech Topic

Checkpoint 12.5 Practicing your Presentation

Checkpoint 12.6 Source Credibility

Checkpoint 12.7 Familiarizing Yourself with Different Sources

Checkpoint 12.8 Links about Research

Professional Visual Aids

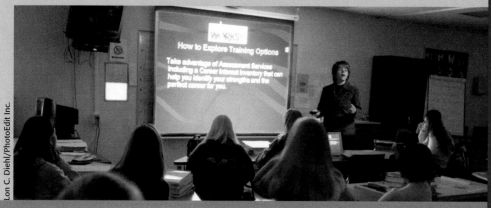

Lon C. Diehl/PhotoEdit Inc.

As you read Chapter 13,

Discuss the benefits of using visual aids in a presentation and list several types of effect visuals.

Identify important guidelines for selecting visual aids including what mistakes to avoid, how many visuals to use, and appropriate size and typeface.

List and briefly **discuss** suggestions for designing visuals including tips for text visuals, graphic visuals, general design principles, and color.

Pinpoint major guidelines for effective use of PowerPoint.

Case Study: PowerPoint Poisoning?

Computer-generated visuals can either aid presentations or they can be so irritating that they work against your best efforts. Over 30 million PowerPoint presentations are made daily—a conservative estimate by Microsoft (Goldstein, 2003). Which leads to Sandberg's (2006) estimate that "bad PowerPoint presentations cost companies $252 million a day in wasted time" (B1). With all these "bad" presentations, the phrases "Death by PowerPoint" and "**PowerPoint Poisoning**" coined by Scott Adams in his Dilbert comic take on real meaning.

Is PowerPoint really all that bad? The military and many businesses think so. For example, the Pentagon is waging war on PowerPoint, which they label as a "growing electronic menace" (Jaffe, 2000, p. A1). Apparently, many military presentations are too long (100 slides or more), too confusing, too wordy, and cluttered with showy effects (e.g., fancy backdrops, distracting slide transitions, spinning pie charts, and "booming tanks"). A former chairman of the Joint Chiefs of Staff, General Hugh Shelton, attempted to solve the problem by placing restrictions on the use of PowerPoint in military presentations. The business world is experiencing similar problems. One meeting facilitator for a software company became so disgusted that he told attendees "they had to leave their PowerPoint at the door" (Maney, 1999, p. 3B).

The real problem may be that "the art of creating a PowerPoint brief frequently has become a substitute for real planning, thoughtful discussion, and cogent analysis" (Wooldridge, 2004, p. 85). As a captain in the U.S. Air Force, Cliff Atkinson (2005) saw PowerPoint abuse first hand. He feels that one of the main problems is that presenters view PowerPoint slides as another piece of paper (Straczynski, 2006) and overload it with information. Tad Simons, past editor-in-chief of *Presentations Magazine*, agrees

AP Photo/Paul Sakuma

As you read this chapter, see if you can (a) suggest what the military and businesses might do to improve the quality of PowerPoint presentations without banning or restricting their use; (b) discover specific tips and guidelines for preparing PowerPoint slides; and (c) determine what lessons public speakers can take from this story. For more details, run a Google or database search for PowerPoint articles.

that the problem lies with the presenter not the software (Bajaj, 2004):

> I think PowerPoint is a fine program that gets horribly misused millions of times every day. Where we went wrong, I think, is in assuming that just because PowerPoint resides on everyone's computer, everyone can and ought to create their own presentation slides. That's the reason there are so many awful PowerPoint presentations in the world—because people without a lick of design sense are out there creating their own slides, inflicting their ineptness on unsuspecting audiences everywhere (para. 13).

In his article, "Bullets May Be Dangerous, but Don't Blame PowerPoint," Simons (2004) indicates that many presenters make two very serious mistakes:

1. *They have forgotten the purpose for using visuals,* which is to aid listener understanding. If your listeners can't grasp the content of a visual in approximately 6 seconds, you are forcing them out of a listening mode and into a reading mode. Audiences can't do both at the same time; so if your audience is reading, they aren't listening to you! Therefore, when you design a PowerPoint presentation, limit the words in the title (use a subtitle if more is needed) and limit the words per line and the number of lines. In addition, nothing on a slide should be random—not the colors, fonts or font sizes, design, images, animation, sounds, or even the number of slides. What to use on the slides depends on your audience, so begin by analyzing them.

2. *Their delivery of the visuals is ineffective.* Many speakers make the mistake of giving PowerPoint presentations in a dark room where the audience can barely see the speaker. Effective presenters need to be in some light (even from a simple can-light in the ceiling) so that they can use eye contact, facial expressions, and gestures to add interest and clarity to their presentations. Speakers also make the mistake of reading from their slides—a sure way to put the audience to sleep. PowerPoint slides should "aid" and reinforce what you are saying. If everything we need to know is on your slides, we don't need you.

Benefits and Types of Visual Aids

Have you ever tried to give instructions verbally on how to get somewhere and finally, frustrated, said, "Here, let me draw you a map"? Such a situation demonstrates the value of visual supporting material. It is easier for people to understand when they can see *and* hear instructions at the same time. A **visual aid,** therefore, is anything presented in a form that listeners can see to supplement the information they hear.

Benefits of Using Visuals

Are visuals worth the time and effort required to prepare them? Absolutely—if in your preparation you have properly designed them (Clark & Mayer, 2008). Claudia Kotchka, vice president for design innovation and strategy for Procter & Gamble, says that when a product is designed and packaged in an interesting, creative manner, people are willing to pay as much as 400 percent more to get it (Reingold, 2005). Therefore, when well-designed, interesting visual aids accompany written or oral messages, they improve listener memory, speed comprehension and add interest, and add to speaker credibility.

Visual Aids Improve Listener Memory Research on listening indicates that a few days after a presentation, most listeners will remember only about 10 to 25% of your presentation (Wolff et al., 1983). And because of frame of reference differences, part of the 25% they do retain may be inaccurate. Better organization, more interesting examples, and more dynamic delivery will not necessarily improve these statistics, *but visual aids can definitely improve what the audience remembers.* Richard Mayer in his book, *Multimedia Learning* (2009), relates two principles to the importance of visual aids. One he calls the **coherence principle** that means that people learn better when words and pictures are used together; the other he calls the **contiguity principle** that says that people learn better when the pictures are placed next to the words they illustrate.

Summarizing research in instructional media, Figure 13.1 shows that verbal and visual information together are more effective than either verbal or visual information alone (Zayas-Baya, 1977–78). Research by the University of Minnesota and the 3M Corporation found that a persuasive presentation that used visual aids (especially color visuals) improved the audience's immediate recall 8.5% and improved delayed recall 10.1% (Vogel et al., 1986, 1990). Hamilton (1999) found that audience recall of an informative presentation was 18% better when visuals were used. High-quality color visuals produced the greatest increase in recall, whereas poor-quality color visuals were the least effective—ranking lower than either high-quality or low-quality black-and-white visuals.

Although research statistics presented in this section differ somewhat, the message is the same: *Speakers should no longer consider visual aids as optional but as absolute necessities!*

Visual Aids Speed Comprehension The old saying "A picture is worth a thousand words" is often true. For example, a single graphic visual could help an audience understand complex, technical information more quickly than either a long verbal explanation or a table loaded with statistics.

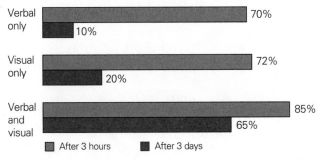

FIGURE 13.1 Audience recall is greater when speakers use visual aids.

A look at right-brain/left-brain theory indicates why visuals speed listener comprehension. Whereas the left hemisphere seems to specialize in step-by-step, analytic processing of information, and pays close attention to details, the right hemisphere seems to specialize in simultaneous processing of information as a whole and pays little attention to details (Bryden & Ley, 1983; Russell, 1979). If you include no visuals or only statistic-heavy tables, you are asking the left side of the brain to do all the work. After a while, you run the risk of audience mistakes in reasoning, information overload, and boredom. In computer terminology, the system shuts down.

On the other hand, in only one glance the right brain can understand complex ideas presented in picture or graphic form (Thompson & Paivio, 1994). In fact, our memory of pictures is almost perfect (Haber, 1970; Nickerson, 1980)—especially when the pictures are vivid (Hishitani, 1991)—and picture memory also is long lasting (Babrick et al., 1975). Picture memory may be more ingrained because pictures and vivid words are coded in both hemispheres (dual coding), making them easier to store and retrieve (Perecman, 1983). Therefore, if you want to increase understanding, add interest, and save time, speak to both sides of your audience's brains.

As an example, look at the data in Table 13.1. Can you quickly tell which advertising medium is now the number one business expenditure? Now look at the same data presented using Microsoft Graph (see Figure 13.2 on page 343). At a glance you can tell that newspapers were the highest expenditure in 1990 and in 1998. However, in 2002 direct mail was the number one advertising expenditure. Therefore, when you need to include complicated data in your presentation, remember that comprehension will be more complete and faster if you present the data in visual form. Keep in mind that because we remember pictures so well, a picture or piece of clipart (if it relates closely to the concept or idea) can serve as an *anchor* and help your audience recall the main points and concepts in your presentation well after the presentation has ended (Alesandrini, 1982). Therefore, select pictures and clipart with care.

In addition, because listeners can comprehend faster when you use visual aids, you can present information in less time. The study by the University of Minnesota and the 3M Corporation found that the use of visuals could reduce the length of the average business meeting by 28% (Antonoff, 1990).

TABLE 13.1

Data Can Often Be Difficult to Grasp			
Advertising Expenditures in Millions of Dollars*			
Medium	**1990**	**1998**	**2002**
Broadcast TV	$26,616	$39,173	$41,830
Direct Mail	23,370	39,620	45,860
Magazines	6,806	10,518	10,990
Newspapers	32,281	44,292	44,380
Radio	8,726	15,073	18,940
Yellow Pages	8,926	11,990	13,720
Total	106,725	160,666	175,720

*For example, $26,616 = $26,616,000,000.

Source: U.S. Bureau of the Census, 2003, *Statistical Abstract of the United States*, Washington, D.C.: GPO, p. 794.

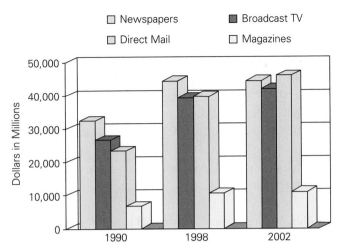

FIGURE 13.2 Data presented in graphic form is easier to understand. (Source: *U.S. Bureau of the Census, 2003,* Statistical Abstract of the United States, Washington, D.C.: GPO, p. 794.)

Visual Aids Add to Speaker Credibility If you are in a situation in which you have fairly low credibility (such as being new to a company, younger than most others in the same position, or unknown to audience members), visuals can be important. One researcher found that low-credibility speakers who use visual aids can overcome an audience's initial doubts about them (as non-authoritative and even untrustworthy) and elicit the same level of audience retention as high-credibility speakers (Seiler, 1971). The study conducted by the University of Minnesota and the 3M Corporation also found that an "average" presenter who uses visuals can be as effective as an "expert" presenter who uses no visuals (Vogel et al., 1986, 1990).

Types of Visual Aids

Now that we know the benefits of using visual aids, let's take a quick look at the most popular types of visuals aids and some tips for using each effectively. Most of the information in later sections of this chapter (such as fonts, point sizes, and design principles) gives advice on designing professional computer slides for electronic and multimedia presentations. The final section of this chapter offers specific tips for using Microsoft PowerPoint for making dynamic visuals.

Audiovisual Aids If used with care, **audiovisual aids** can add definite interest to your presentation. For example, if a DVD player is available, you could show a brief segment of a team-building exercise, such as a rafting trip down the Colorado River. To point out something of special interest, you could set the DVD in slow motion, pause it, or replay a segment. Audiotapes, CDs, and MP3 players can also enhance your presentation. For example, a presentation on types of jazz would be much more informative if the audience could hear brief cuts from well-known jazz selections. Video clips, podcasts, and music clips are readily available on the Internet for use in your presentations. Some of the most popular sites for these items are YouTube, Hulu.com, Google video, and Dailymotion.com. Use your Premium Website for *Communicating for Results* to access the "PowerPoint Speaker's Guide: Advanced Suggestions" for an explanation of how to insert audio and video clips into your

PowerPoint presentations. If you decide to add video or sound to your presentation, follow these tips:

- Make sure the video or audio tape is cued to the right location. Normally the sound should be turned off when showing a videotape, so you can talk during the tape as you would with other visuals.

- Make sure you include a copy of the actual audio or video file in the folder with your PowerPoint presentation. Test it out on a different computer to make sure all is working.

- Keep the audio or video clips short: 15–30 seconds is plenty; if there is sound, test it ahead of time for correct volume.

Electronic and Multimedia Aids   The most popular visual aid in businesses today is the computer-generated presentation. Affordable computer hardware and software make it possible to produce professional sophisticated **electronic and multimedia aids** with color, animation, sound, photos, and video clips. One of the most popular software programs for visual aids is Microsoft's PowerPoint. (In fact, many of the visuals in this chapter were produced with PowerPoint.) To help you create professional visuals, the "PowerPoint Speaker's Guide," with basic and advanced tips, is available to you via your Premium Website for *Communicating for Results.* When using computer-generated visuals, follow these tips:

- *Remember that the main point of using visuals is to aid listener comprehension.* Using too many slides, too much text, too many colors, typefaces, or sounds only distracts from your message. Everything must work together to *simplify meaning* and *direct audience attention.* See "Tips for Designing Text Visuals" (pp. 353–356); "Tips for Designing Graphic Visuals" (pp. 357–359); and the "General Design Principles" for both text and graphic visuals (pp. 359–362).

- *Use sounds sparingly, if at all.* The first time we hear a sound (e.g., applause) it's unique; each additional time we hear it, it's a distraction.

- *Select images carefully and choose the best format for them.* For clip art many people use graphics interchange format (GIF) as their image file format, but GIF uses a much larger file than JPEG or PNG. To change text or pictures into a different image format, open Accessories, Paint, and paste the information/image, adjust it if needed, and Save As a JPEG or PNG.

- *Make sure that the audience can see you when the lights are turned off.* Select a room with appropriate lighting over the speaker stand. If the listeners are likely to take notes, a room with soft lights on a dimmer switch can light both the audience and the speaker. New data projectors are so bright that overhead lights can remain on.

- *Make sure the visuals can be seen by all.* For a small group (probably not more than eight), your computer visuals can be viewed directly on the computer screen. For larger groups, you will need to project the images onto a larger screen using an all-contained video or data projector.

- *Try using a cordless mouse or remote* such as Logitech's Cordless Presenter so you can advance slides and control volume from anywhere in the room.

- *Look at your computer screen and your audience* but do not turn away from the audience to look at the projection screen behind you unless you need to point to something—then, use a laser pointer.

- *Speak in a conversational manner and don't read from your visuals.* According to the **personalization principle** (Mayer, 2009), audiences learn better when speakers use a conversational style instead of a formal one.

- *Before clicking to the next slide, give the oral transition to the next idea*—then change slides (Zelazny, 2000). This keeps the audience from reading the slide before you are ready.

- *Come prepared with a backup plan in case of equipment failure.* For example, bring a copy of your PowerPoint slides to use as notes, three or four transparencies of the most important slides, a second copy of your disk or CD on a USB flash or thumb drive, or e-mail your PowerPoint to yourself so it can be accessed through the Internet.

Flip Charts and Posters There are some definite benefits in using **flipcharts** and **posters**—they tend to set an informal mood, are simple to prepare, and can add a feeling of spontaneity to your presentation if you write on them as you speak. On the other hand, flip charts and posters are awkward to transport and store and can be used only with small groups (fewer than 30 people). If you decide to use them, follow these tips:

- When using flipcharts, leave a blank page between each page you plan to write on or use water-based markers—permanent markers tend to bleed through newsprint. Flip charts normally include only one idea per page as shown in Photo 13.2. When you have finished one idea, simply flip the page to the next idea. The final page should include all your key ideas to refresh the listeners' memory during your summary.

- When several key ideas are included on a poster, *cover each idea with a strip of paper* that can easily be removed as you reach that idea in your talk or give a brief overview of all the items on the poster and then go back and discuss each one in detail. When finished with a poster, cover it with a blank poster or reverse the poster to its blank side.

Posters and flip charts can also be used to *call attention to single words or phrases* (i.e., technical words, new or seldom-used words, or foreign words or phrases) like the poster in Figure 13.3.

Markerboards and Chalkboards Markerboards are usually preferred to **chalkboards** because the glossy white of the markerboard is more attractive and there is no messy chalk residue. Also, small markerboards can be placed on an easel and moved closer to the audience for a more personal feel. However, both markerboards and chalkboards have several drawbacks, which include making speakers look less prepared and less professional than other types of visuals and requiring the speaker's back to be toward the audience while writing on the board. A markerboard is somewhat better because you can stand beside it and still look at the audience occasionally. When using marker and chalkboards, follow these tips:

> **Revisiting the Case Study**
>
> What's wrong with using booming tanks in a military Power-Point presentation? Should the military ban their use?
>
> AP Photo/Paul Sakuma

Effective flip charts should include only one idea per page.

Anne Dowie/Cengage Learning

FIGURE 13.3 Poster.

- *Practice is vital.* Unless you practice ahead, your information may be either too small to see or so large that you run out of space; or you'll need to erase your sketch or repeat it several times to get the proportions correct; or you might forget the spelling of a key word.

- *Learning to speak and draw at the same time requires work.* You will need a great deal of practice to do this well.

- *Make sure that your letters are large enough to be read easily*—generally, a capital should be 3 inches high and basic text at least 1 1/2 inches high. Make sure that colors are bold and avoid pastels.

ETHICAL DILEMMA

In September 2005, Jyllands-Posten, a newspaper in Denmark, posted 12 cartoons and caricatures of Islam's holiest man, the Prophet Mohammed, some of which portrayed him as a terrorist (Eltahawy, 2006; "Muslim cartoon row timeline," 2006). Most controversial was the fact that he was depicted at all—Islam prohibits the portraiture of Mohammed in any visual medium (Eltahawy, 2006). Although the cartoons were originally published in Denmark, they were soon distributed all over the world, and as a result, the newspaper received threats and condemnation from 11 countries (Eltahawy, 2006).

These cartoons generated enormous anger among the Muslim community until February 2006, sparking riots in numerous countries, political tension, and even deaths. Ultimately in a situation like this, the issue becomes not just one involving religious sensibilities but a deeper debate on freedom of expression that has yet to be firmly resolved ("Mohammed cartoon conflict gets even hotter," 2006).

QUESTIONS: What do you think? Given Islam's restrictions regarding portraiture and Muslim religious sensibilities, was it ethical for the Danish newspaper to publish the cartoons? Given the West's belief in freedom of the press, was it ethical for other newspapers to censor the cartoons? What ethical responsibility do speakers have in selecting visuals for use in their presentations?

Objects, Models, and Handouts Objects can be effective visual aids as long as they are large enough to be seen yet small enough to display easily. To keep from distracting audience members, wait until your presentation is completed before passing objects around the audience for a closer view.

If an object is too small, too large, or too dangerous to be used as a visual aid, you might use a **model** instead. For example, a model car, a model office layout, or a model of an atom would all be effective visual aids.

Handouts can be both a help (they limit the audience's need to take notes) and a distraction (the audience may read the handout instead of listening to you). So unless you need the audience to do something with the material while you are speaking (like answer a survey or a checklist), it's better to give handouts at the conclusion of your speech.

Selecting Your Visual Aids

Now that you realize the benefits and drawbacks of some of the most popular types of visual aids, you are ready to discover how much fun it is to create visuals.

Avoid Major Mistakes

Using visual aids, especially computer presentations like PowerPoint can be so much fun that some speakers forget that for effective communication, "less is more" as was indicated in our chapter case study. Surveys of people who view PowerPoint presentations on a regular basis (more than half observed 100 presentations per year) identified the major things that annoy them the most (Cypert, 2007; Paradi, 2005):

- Speakers who read off the slides (62%).
- Text too small to read (47%).
- Text color too difficult to read (43%).
- Complete sentences used instead of phases (39%).
- Too much movement in text and graphics (25%).
- Charts too complex to decipher (22%).

These annoyances (or poisons) are responsible for the dislike that many people have toward PowerPoint presentations. Figure 13.5 offers several antidotes for "PowerPoint Poisoning" (idea adapted from McKenzie, 2000). Use this figure as a guide as you read the remainder of this chapter which gives specific advice on designing professional, poison-free electronic and multimedia presentations.

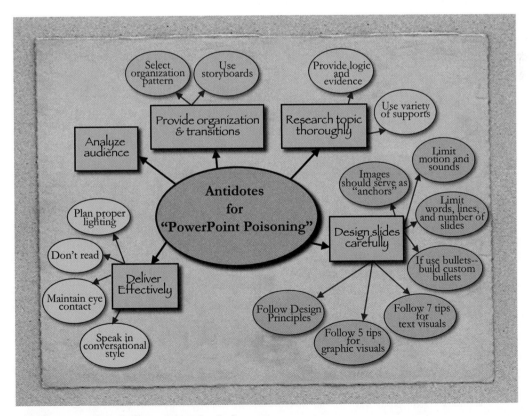

FIGURE 13.4 Antidotes for "PowerPoint Poisoning."

Student and Faculty Text Visuals

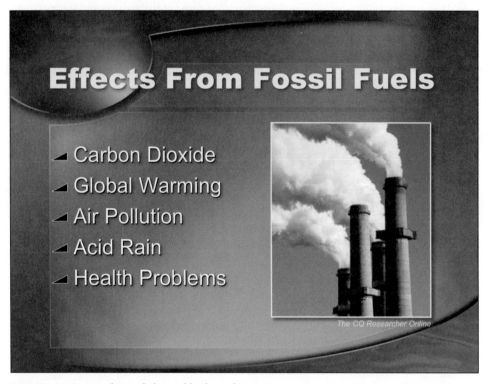

VISUAL 1 Design template and photo add color and interest.

VISUAL 2 Colorful poster and scrolls are used to introduce main points as an alternative to bullets.

VISUAL 3 Note the use of a subtitle and use of arrows to locate sections of a Greek theater.

VISUAL 4 The words "Truth" or "Myth" produced in PowerPoint Word Art fly in to accentuate the answer.

VISUAL 5 Colorful photo used as opening slide.

VISUAL 6 The pictograph and 3D filled line graph draw the eye to important health statistics.

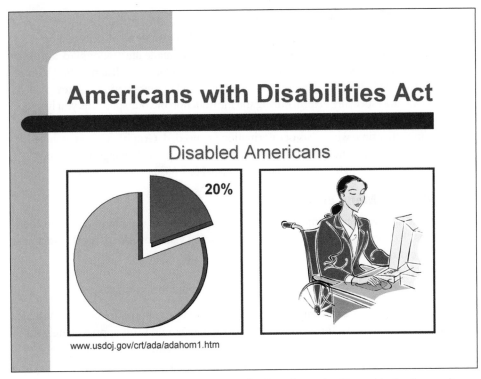

VISUAL 7 An exploded pie chart and clip art with coordinating colors make this graphic visually appealing.

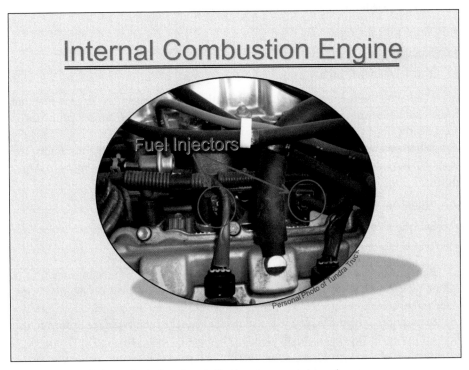

VISUAL 8 Personal photo of a truck engine clarified by reference circles and arrows.

Choose Text or Graphic Visuals

Visuals can be either text visuals or graphic visuals. **Text visuals** are mainly text or printed words with one or two pieces of **clip art**—ready-made illustrations—drawings or photos; the art creates interest and serves as a memory aid for your listeners (see Visuals 1–4 on pages 348–349). The majority of visual aids used in presentations are text visuals. *Text visuals* are especially helpful during the introduction of your speech as you list your main points, during the conclusion of your speech as you summarize the main points, and at any other time when lists of information are needed. **Graphic visuals** include organizational charts and flowcharts, diagrams and schematic drawings, maps, and graphs, with just enough words to clarify the visual (see Visuals 5–8 on pages 350–351).

Decide How Many Visuals to Use

Creating visuals is so enjoyable that some speakers use too many visuals in their speeches. To keep your audience from experiencing visual overload, try this formula when deciding how many visuals to use:

$$\frac{\text{length of speech}}{2} + 1 = \text{maximum number of visuals}$$

For example, for a 6-minute speech, you would want approximately four visuals (6 divided by 2, plus 1); for a 10-minute speech, you would want approximately six visuals (10 divided by 2, plus 1). This formula is only a guide. Fewer visuals could certainly be used, but more visuals should be used with caution.

Using Appropriate Type Size and Typeface

One of the most common mistakes that speakers (even experienced speakers) make in preparing visuals is using text that is too small for easy audience viewing. To make sure your *posters, flip charts, chalkboards, and markerboards* are easy for your audience to read, the following guidelines are suggested:

- Titles 3 inches high.
- Subtitles 2 to 2 1/2 inches high.
- Text 1 1/2 inches high.

When you use these recommended sizes, the text may seem too large at first, but these guidelines will ensure that even the people in the back row can see your message clearly.

When you use electronic computer visuals (such as *PowerPoint*), your audience will have no problems if you use these suggested minimum sizes measured in **points**:

- Title = 30–36 points.
- Subtitle = 24 points.
- Text = 18 points (24 points if no subtitle).

Remember, you can always use larger point sizes—in fact, we recommend it—but no type should be smaller than the sizes suggested here. Obviously, regular print sizes will not work!

In addition to type size, you will also need to select which **typeface** or **font** to use. For our purposes, typefaces are divided into two basic types: sans serif and serif. A **sans serif typeface** (a geometric-looking, simple typeface) is recommended for titles or emphasis. Sans serif typefaces include Futura, Impact, Tahoma, Verdana, Helvetica, and Arial. A **serif typeface** (a typeface with small lines, or finishing strokes, that extend from letter stems) is especially good for text and small labels on charts. Serif typefaces include Times New Roman, Century, Garamond, and Bookman Old Style.

Typefaces can affect the readability of your visuals and will either harmonize with or distract from the overall tone or style of your speech. Imagine your audience's confusion if you were giving a serious business presentation but your visuals used Poster Bodoni, a playful typeface. Here are some suggested typefaces for visuals along with the connotations or tone they project to audiences (compiled from Riggs & Grieshaber, 2009; Williams, 2004, 2008):

- Helvetica (urban)
- Times New Roman (official)
- Arial (professional)
- Century (friendly)
- Garamond (sophisticated)
- Palatino (upbeat)
- Optima (elegant)
- Bodoni (trendy)
- Futura (modern)
- **Poster Bodoni (playful)**

Generally, use no more than two different typefaces per visual, and use the same typefaces for all visuals in a particular presentation. Sometimes the best way to ensure that your visuals are sending the message you desire is to see them projected on a screen. Once they are enlarged, the tone is more obvious.

Designing Your Visual Aids

In addition to having the appropriate fonts and type sizes, as mentioned previously, quality text visuals improve recall if they have one or two pictures or pieces of clip art to *anchor* the audience to the fact or idea you are presenting (Alesandrini, 1982; Paivio, 1986; Thompson & Paivio, 1994). To be effective, the anchor must clearly illustrate or relate to the text content. These visual anchors help the audience remember the related ideas. For example, in a presentation about the four steps realtors follow in selling homes, you could show four steps leading up to the front door of a home with a "For Sale" sign on its door. Later, when the audience tries to remember the main points of your talk, they will picture the "four steps" leading to the home for sale (visual anchors), which will help them remember that you presented four points and even what they were.

Tips for Designing Text Visuals

Quality text visuals also follow specific design tips or guidelines, as discussed by Holcombe and Stein (1996) in *Presentations for Decision Makers*. These guidelines are summarized in Figure 13.6. Before reading further, look at Figure 13.6 to see how many of the tips listed in the visual are not followed in this figure. Then continue reading and see if you were correct. Remember, if visuals require effort to read, the audience is forced into a reading mode rather than a listening mode. They can't pay attention to what you are saying while they are reading your visual. Therefore, a good visual should make sense in 6 seconds or less. Or as Peoples (1996) advises, a good visual aid is "like a billboard on an interstate highway that people can read going by at 65 mph" (p. 249).

Keep the following tips in mind when designing your text visuals:

- *Use no more than four to six lines of text.* Not counting the title and subtitle(s), when a visual contains more than six lines of text, it takes too long for your audience to grasp. Of course, if the text is a list containing single words, seven or eight lines might be fine. In general, if you need more than six lines of text, you probably should split the information into two visuals or simplify your text.

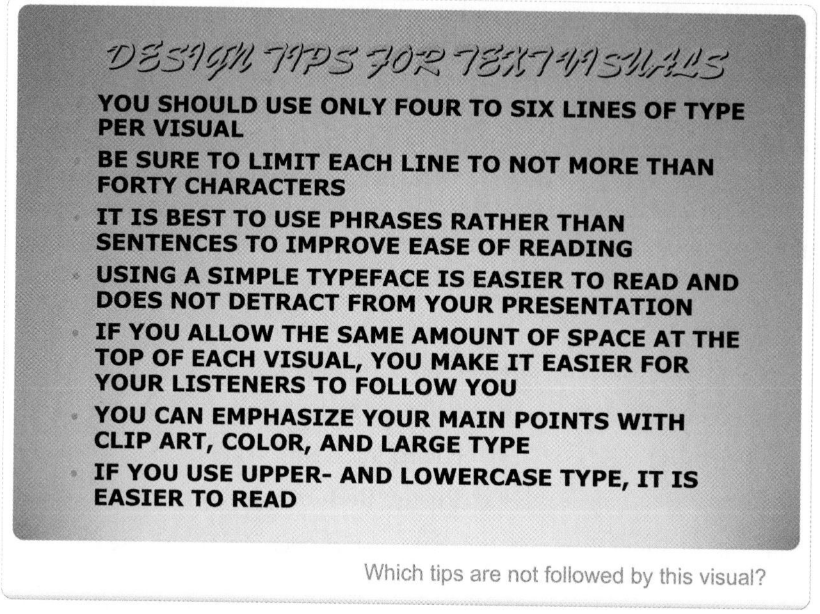

DESIGN TIPS FOR TEXT VISUALS

YOU SHOULD USE ONLY FOUR TO SIX LINES OF TYPE PER VISUAL

BE SURE TO LIMIT EACH LINE TO NOT MORE THAN FORTY CHARACTERS

IT IS BEST TO USE PHRASES RATHER THAN SENTENCES TO IMPROVE EASE OF READING

- USING A SIMPLE TYPEFACE IS EASIER TO READ AND DOES NOT DETRACT FROM YOUR PRESENTATION
- IF YOU ALLOW THE SAME AMOUNT OF SPACE AT THE TOP OF EACH VISUAL, YOU MAKE IT EASIER FOR YOUR LISTENERS TO FOLLOW YOU
- YOU CAN EMPHASIZE YOUR MAIN POINTS WITH CLIP ART, COLOR, AND LARGE TYPE
- IF YOU USE UPPER- AND LOWERCASE TYPE, IT IS EASIER TO READ

Which tips are not followed by this visual?

FIGURE 13.5 How many of these design tips are not followed by this visual?

- *Limit each line to 40 characters.* If your text contains more than 40 characters per line (counting letters *and* spaces), you aren't leaving enough white space (space that contains no text or graphics). White space is essential for fast comprehension and prevents your visual from looking cluttered.

- *Use phrases rather than sentences.* Eliminate unnecessary words so listeners can grasp the content of your visual in 6 seconds or less. Figure 13.6 shows how sentences slow down comprehension. The same information using phrases is displayed in Figure 13.7. Which visual would you rather have an instructor use in a lecture?

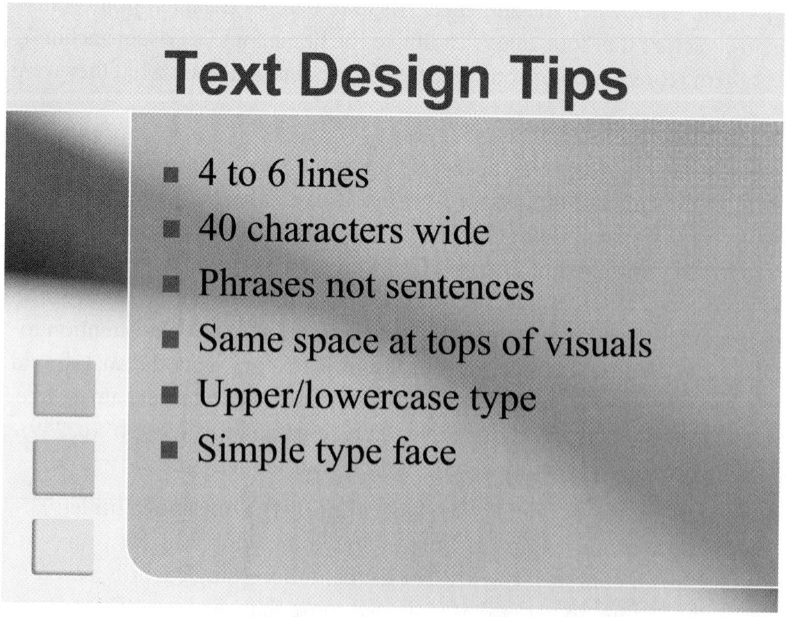

Text Design Tips

- 4 to 6 lines
- 40 characters wide
- Phrases not sentences
- Same space at tops of visuals
- Upper/lowercase type
- Simple type face

FIGURE 13.6 Which visual takes less time to read: this one or Figure 13.5?

FIGURE 13.7 Word recognition experiment.
(Source: Adapted from F. K. Baskette, J. K. Sissors, and B. S. Brooks; 1992, *The Art of Editing*, 5th ed., New York: Macmillan, p. 267.)

- *Use upper- and lowercase type.* Although speakers often put their titles and text into all capital letters because they think it will look larger and therefore be easier to read, research has shown that text in all caps is more difficult to read and to comprehend (Adams et al., 2001). To illustrate why this is true, try a brief experiment using Figure 13.8. The word official has been divided into two lines. Hold your hand over the top line and ask at least four people to read the bottom line. Now hold your hand over the bottom line and ask four other people to read the top line. Which line were more people able to read correctly? The reason that the top line is easier to read is that word recognition comes mainly from the upper half of lowercase letters. However, when the word official is put in all capitals (OFFICIAL), it can look like a shapeless box that cannot be instantly recognized, especially from far away (adapted from Baskette et al., 1992). Therefore, use all caps only for special emphasis.

- *Use a simple typeface.* Script and fancy typefaces are difficult to read. The typefaces suggested previously in this chapter have stood the test of time and are known to work for visual aids. Feel free to experiment, but don't get carried away.

- *Allow the same space at the top of each visual.* Many speakers incorrectly center the content on each of their visuals from top to bottom. This means that some visual aids have only a few lines in the middle of the page, while others utilize the entire page. As a result, each time you project a transparency or slide onto the screen or hold up a poster, the audience has to locate the title—this takes

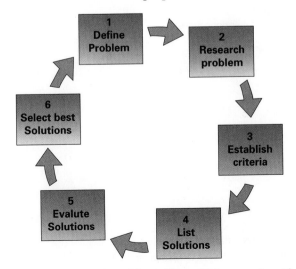

FIGURE 13.8 Flowchart of the problem-solving process from Chapter 9.

valuable time. Your visuals will look more professional if the text begins at the same place on each visual.

- *Use images, larger type, boldface, and color for emphasis.* Clip art, photos, and freehand drawings add emphasis and anchor the content of your visual for your audience. Large-size type, boldface, and color are excellent ways to direct the eye to areas you wish to emphasize. The largest and boldest type will usually be noticed first unless you have also used color. If you want to direct your audience's attention to a portion of a complicated diagram, color is the way to do it. Even on a color visual, a bright, contrasting color will draw your audience's attention.

Types of Graphic Visuals

A search of Google using the image icon produces many graphics and pictures. The most common types of graphic visuals are charts, diagrams and schematics, maps, and graphs.

Organization charts and **flowcharts** are used constantly by business and professional presenters. Figure 13.9 is a flowchart of the problem-solving process from Chapter 9 of this text. Useful flowchart symbols can be found in Word or PowerPoint in AutoShapes/Flowchart.

Diagrams and **schematic drawings** also make effective graphic visuals. You don't need an artist to draw the diagrams or schematics needed in most presentations—you can do them yourself. Use the Drawing toolbar in Word and PowerPoint to access the Diagram Gallery, which includes sample diagrams, or go to Insert/Diagram. If more complicated diagrams are needed, such as the cutaway diagram in Figure 13.10, check for images in Google or ask for assistance from the graphic arts department or from an engineer or draftsperson where you work.

Maps are another type of graphic visual. A presentation on the graying of the United States might include a map of the United States to show which states have more people over the age of 65 (Figure 13.11). Again, click on Images in Google for an amazing number of maps on all sorts of topics. If the map you need isn't there, look in the reference section of your library or in a current magazine on your topic. Scan the map and insert it into your visuals (for Word or PowerPoint use Insert/Picture/From Scanner or Camera). Don't forget to include the source for any images you use.

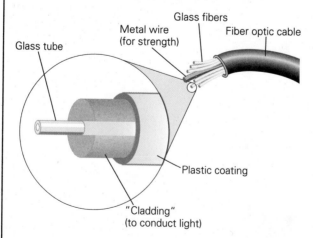

FIGURE 13.9 Cutaway diagram showing construction of a fiber optic cable. (Source: June J. Parsons and Dan Oja, 1995, *New Perspectives on Computer Concepts,* copyright 1995 by Course Technology, Inc., p. 175.)

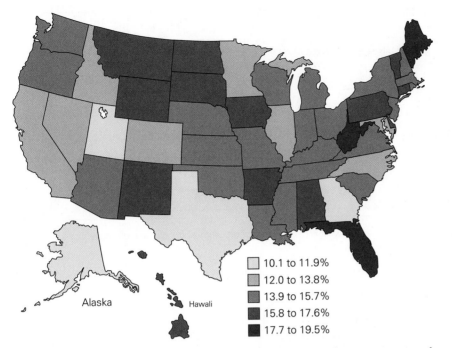

10.1 to 11.9%
12.0 to 13.8%
13.9 to 15.7%
15.8 to 17.6%
17.7 to 19.5%

Alaska   Hawali

FIGURE 13.10 Map of the United States showing the percent of the population over 65 years of age. Source: U.S. Census Bureau, Census 2000 Summary File 1, Matrices P1 and P30.)

Graphs have traditionally been used in industry to display complicated data in simplified, visual form. *Line graphs* show changes in relationships over time; *bar graphs* compare countable data at a specific moment in time; *pie charts* and *stacked bar graphs* show part of the whole or percentages; and *pictographs* replace bars with graphic symbols or icons. Presentation software such as PowerPoint, as well as word processing programs such as Word, provide excellent chart capabilities. In Word go to Insert/Picture/Chart; in PowerPoint go to Insert/Chart/Chart Type or Chart Options. For sample graphs see the following section. (For more specifics, see the "PowerPoint Speaker's Guide" via your Premium Website for *Communicating for Results.*)

Tips for Designing Graphic Visuals

Color, small clip art illustrations, and background images (if used sparingly) can add eye-catching appeal. To be successful, graphic aids should follow the design tips discussed by Holcombe and Stein (1996) in *Presentations for Decision Makers* (illustrated in Figures 13.11 through 13.14):

- *Limit data to what is absolutely necessary.* Figure 13.11 illustrates the importance of using only the data needed to support your verbal points. Because the speech deals with sales, the line graphs for earnings and dividends (as well as the distracting grid lines) are not necessary and actually obscure the seriousness of the sales decline. It is always a good idea, however, to have additional materials ready in case of audience questions. For example, the earnings and dividends line graphs would make excellent overlays, which, if used to answer a question, would certainly be impressive.

- *Combine data when possible.* Figure 13.12 illustrates the principle of grouping data. Grouping seven small categories of costs under the general heading of

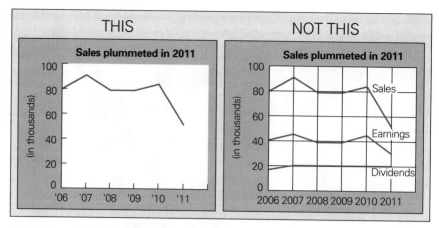

FIGURE 13.11 Limit data to what is needed to support your verbal point and eliminate distracting grid lines.

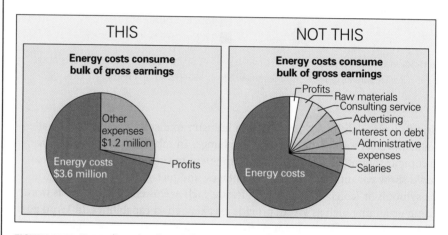

FIGURE 13.12 Group distracting data under a general heading.

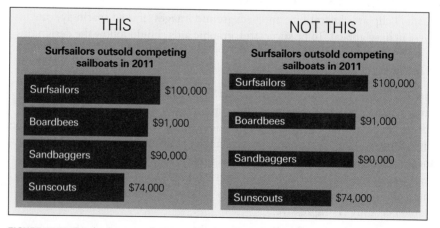

FIGURE 13.13 For viewing ease, the space between bars should be eliminated or be narrower than the bars.

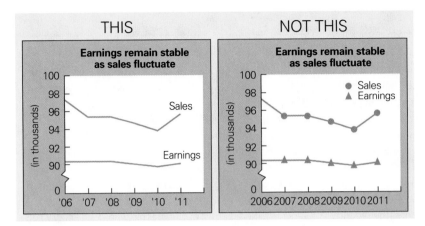

FIGURE 13.14 For viewing ease, eliminate data points.

"Other Expenses" greatly reduced the amount of time needed to get the point of the pie chart. You could follow this visual with a second one that lists the content of "Other Expenses."

- *Make bars wider than the spaces between them.* When the white space between the bars in a bar graph is wider than the bars, as in the right-hand example in Figure 13.13, the white space visually pushes the bars apart, making them seem unrelated (Williams, 2004). For easier audience viewing, make the bars wider than the spaces between them, regardless of whether the bars are horizontal or vertical.

- *Keep background lines and data points to a minimum.* In most cases, grid lines (like those used in Figure 13.11) and data points (like those in Figure 13.14) should be eliminated. They are distracting, take too much time to interpret, and are not necessary for understanding. If you know that your audience expects grid lines and data points, then use them, but include only essential data points and make the grid lines lighter than the data lines.

- *Always use titles.* Whether your graphic visual is a chart, graph, map, or picture, always use a title or heading to reinforce your point. For example, a hand-drawing of a skier in the correct position to begin water skiing might seem obvious to you as the speaker, but without a title or heading, the exact purpose of the visual wouldn't be immediately clear to your audience.

General Design Principles

Before we conclude this chapter on visual supporting material, let's look at four **general design principles** that apply to all visuals, whether text or graphic. A summary of these design principles discussed by Williams (2008, p. 13) follows:

Contrast The idea behind **contrast** is to avoid elements on the page that are merely *similar.* If the elements (i.e., type, color, size, line thickness, shape, space, etc.) are not the *same,* then make them *very different.* Contrast is often the most important visual attraction on a page.

Repetition Repeat visual elements of the design throughout the piece. You can repeat colors, shapes, textures, spatial relationships, line thicknesses, fonts, sizes,

IT REALLY WORKS!

Design Power

Is there power in design? According to Claudia Kotchka, Procter & Gamble's vice president for design innovation and strategy, when customers are presented with the same product packaged in two different styles—one plain and one lively—they are not only more likely to purchase the product with the interesting packaging, but they also will be willing to pay a premium of up to 400% more for it (Reingold, 2005). She illustrates this by comparing a tin of Altoids (not a P&G product) with a hypothetical P&G version designed to save money. The Altoids packaging features the product name, printed in a nostalgic typeface, on a tin that smells of peppermint, looks homemade, and sits inside a liner paper that crinkles. In contrast, the P&G mints are little beige ovals that don't have a peppermint aroma and are packaged in an inexpensive white plastic container with no liner and a less attractive typeface. According to Kotchka, the pleasure gained from using the product is absent, and the product might as well be called "Proctoids" (para. 3)

Kotchka is working to convince designers to "listen with their eyes" (para. 12) so they can develop products that will not only satisfy but also "infuse delight into customers' lives"

(para. 4). One such project is the Mr. Clean Magic Reach cleaning brush. This product was designed with "little details" that make a big difference, such as a connecting lever that makes an "audible 'click'" when assembled correctly, blue cleaning pads (customers consider blue a "clean" color), and a silver handle that gives the whole package a slightly magical feel (paras. 13–14).

Kotchka's attempt to "build design into P&G" has produced many new, creative products (para. 8), but she laments, "There are still a lot of people who don't know what [design] is" (para. 15). However, her decision to embed "top designers in brand teams to help rethink not just the superficials—graphics, packaging, product design—but, more importantly, how consumers *experience* products" (Kalins, 2006) seems to be producing results.

What do you think?
- What specific content in this chapter supports Kotchka's design approach at P&G?
- What specific lessons, if any, can speakers using visuals aids take from P&G's experience with design?

graph concepts, and so on. **Repetition** helps develop the organization and strengthens the unity.

Alignment **Alignment** is important because every element should have some visual connection with another element on the page; nothing should be placed on the page arbitrarily. This creates a clean, sophisticated, fresh look.

Proximity Items relating to each other should be grouped close together. When several items are in close **proximity** to each other, they become one visual unit rather than several separate units. This helps organize information, reduces clutter, and gives the reader a clear structure.

Analyzing Figure 13.15 using design principles Let's illustrate how these four design principles can really improve the quality of a visual aid. Look at Figure 13.15.

First, what's right about this visual aid? The speaker has chosen Century as the typeface (a typeface that gives a caring, friendly impression), which seems appropriate for the topic. The type is large enough for easy audience viewing (the title is 36 points, the subtitle is 30 points, and the main ideas are 26 points), and only necessary words have been used on the visual. Also, an underline separates the title from the subtitle and main points, which helps the audience grasp the organization of the visual. This visual, then, has several good elements.

What's wrong? Notice that the visual is in all caps, making it difficult to read. It's also bland; nothing attracts the eye. Basically, this visual aid doesn't follow Williams's design principles:

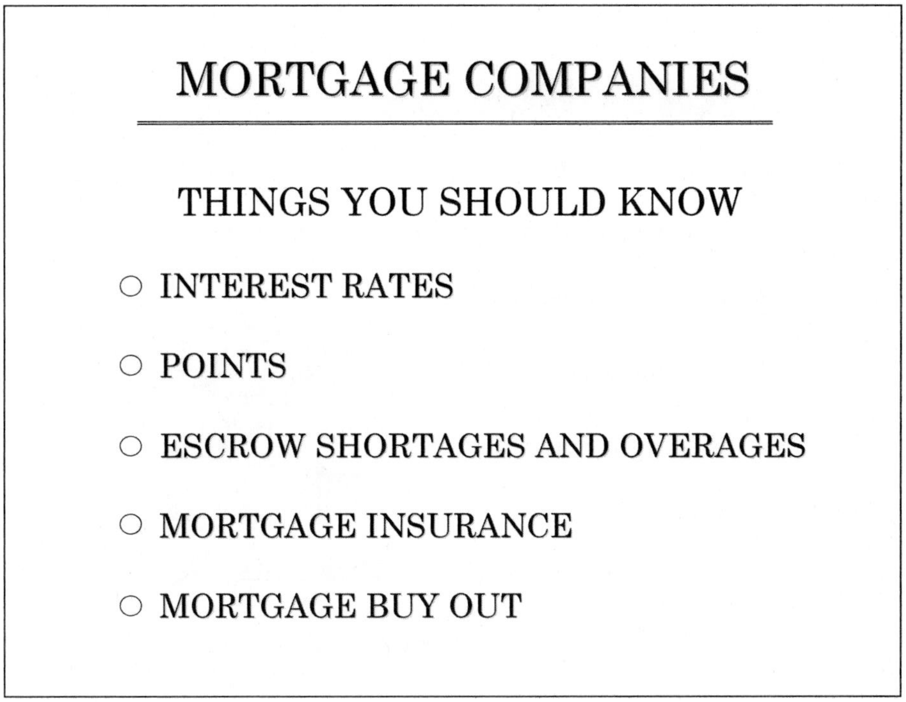

MORTGAGE COMPANIES

THINGS YOU SHOULD KNOW

○ INTEREST RATES

○ POINTS

○ ESCROW SHORTAGES AND OVERAGES

○ MORTGAGE INSURANCE

○ MORTGAGE BUY OUT

FIGURE 13.15 How would you improve this visual?

1. Even with the title in boldface, there isn't enough contrast. The type sizes of the main points and the titles are too similar for contrast.

2. There isn't enough repetition throughout the visual aid. The bullets (circles in front of the main points) do repeat, but they are too bland to be noticed. The bold of the title needs to be repeated somewhere—maybe the bullets could be filled in, the underline could be made wider or bolder, or clip art could repeat the color of the title or bullets.

3. The main points on the page are in alignment, but they don't line up with any of the other elements. If the main points were centered (normally, not a good idea), they would align with the title and underline, which are already centered. Williams says that "every item should have a visual connection with something else on the page" (2008, p. 27). Right now, the title, subtitle, nor the underline does.

4. There is too much space between the title and the underline, the underline and subtitle, and between each of the main points. It almost looks like there are eight separate items on the page. Closer *proximity* among items is needed so they become a visual unit.

Redesigning Figure 13.15 using design principles How can we redesign the mortgage visual to incorporate the four design principles, as well as, the specific design rules for text visuals? Figure 13.16 shows one approach:

1. Change the type from all capitals to upper- and lowercase letters.

2. Revise the title—the main points are about mortgages, not mortgage companies.

3. Add more contrast: The type size of the title is larger (54 points); the subtitle, now 32 points, was changed to Garamond italic; and the type size of the list is

FIGURE 13.16 One approach to redesigning the visual in Figure 13.15.

smaller (28 points). The bullets are now filled in and have a shadow. The color background also adds contrast and interest.

4. Add clip art to provide contrast, color, and interest, as well as, to serve as a visual memory anchor for the audience. To add room for a visual, the main points were rearranged from longest to shortest.

5. Establish repetition by adding a line at the bottom of the visual that is equal in width and parallel to the title underline. The bullets, title, and clip art all add color repetition.

6. Improve the alignment. The title, underline, and bullets line up on the left, whereas the title underline, clip art, and bottom line all align on the right.

7. Improve proximity by grouping main points closer together to appear as a visual unit. The underline and the subtitle are also closer to the title.

Tips for Using Color

It's easy to go overboard when selecting colors for your visuals. When color is poorly used, it can be as great a distraction as too many words or a cluttered graph. When used to highlight, organize, or add interest, color is a definite advantage. A study conducted by the University of Minnesota and the 3M Corporation found that color transparencies were more persuasive and produced better recall than black-and-white transparencies (Vogel et al., 1986, 1990). In addition, Hamilton (1999) found that quality color transparencies produced better recall than poor-quality color or black-and-white transparencies (regardless of quality), and poor-quality color was the least effective. If you want to spend the time to produce quality visuals, color can significantly increase what audience members recall of your presentation. If your preparation time is limited, you would be advised to use black-and-white visuals.

Quality Color Visuals   If used correctly, color is very powerful. For example, color visuals are more persuasive (Vogel et al., 1990) and produce better recall than black-and-white visuals (Hamilton, 1999; Vogel et al., 1990). Color advertisements are 80% more likely to be read, 55 to 78% more likely to be remembered, and 50 to 80% more likely to produce a sale than noncolor ads (Johnson, 1995).

A quality color visual has the same four requirements as a quality black-and-white visual: (a) It follows the design tips for text and graphic visuals on pages 353–356 and 357–359; (b) it follows the four general design principles on pages 359–362; (c) it includes a picture, piece of clip art, or graphic to capture audience interest and attention; and (d) it uses a type size that is large enough to be easily read. In addition, quality color visuals follow specific color principles (Conway, 1988; Johnson, 1995; Marcus, 1982; Pastoor, 1990):

- To show organization, use different hues for unrelated items; use a single hue with different saturation levels for related items. **Hue** is the actual color—each color on the color wheel is a different hue. **Saturation** is the amount of color used in the selected hue (fully saturated colors are vivid; low-saturated colors show more gray and appear paler). Use the fully saturated hues to highlight the most important information.

- For figures (including graphs and charts), use full saturation for all hues. It is easier to see lines and bars if they are in a fully saturated color.

- For backgrounds and texts, select hues low in saturation.

- Use color to indicate distance. Warm colors (such as orange and red) are more active and "jump forward" from a neutral background such as gray. Cool colors (such as green and blue) are more passive and restful. Dark colors appear farther away, while light colors appear nearer.

- Use well-defined boundaries around figures and letters. When light colors (such as pastels) are used for figures, bullets, or letters on a clear or light background, they are difficult to see unless they have a darker outline or shadow, often called a "black zone."

- Use high contrast between figure and background. Dark backgrounds require light letters, bullets, and figures. For example, blue letters on a dark blue or black background are almost impossible to read; white or yellow letters on a dark background are easy to read. In general, the lighter the background, the darker the letters, bullets, and figures need to be for viewing ease. Contrast also can be created by varying the saturation of color selected (such as a fully saturated figure on a partially saturated background). The contrast between lightness and darkness is the most important factor of visibility.

- Avoid colors that tend to look the same at a distance. For example, red and brown often cause confusion when seen from a distance. Other problem combinations include red and orange, orange and yellow, and yellow and green. On the other hand, most basic colors (including red, yellow, blue, green, purple, and pink) are easy to distinguish when not used in the above combinations.

- Avoid placing opposites on the color wheel immediately next to each other. Color opposites (such as blue and orange or red and green) appear to vibrate when placed side-by-side. Therefore, select colors for bar graphs or pie charts with care. Also, be careful with red and green because many people have red-green color blindness.

AWARENESS CHECK

Effective Visual Aids

How aware are you of the tips and guidelines for preparing quality visual aids? To check your knowledge, take the following quiz and check your answers against those in the back of this book. You can also take this quiz online and view the answers via your Premium Website for *Communicating for Results.*

Directions: Identify each question below as T (True) or F (False):

_____ 1. The best visuals are centered on the page.

_____ 2. Using three or more typefaces per visual is recommended for adding contrast and interest.

_____ 3. A sans serif typeface is recommended for titles or emphasis.

_____ 4. When giving a PowerPoint presentation, to move backward to a previous slide, press the number of the desired slide and then press the backspace key.

_____ 5. Saturation is the amount of color used in a selected shade.

_____ 6. For easy audience viewing of a computer slide, titles should be no smaller than 30 points in size.

_____ 7. One way to enhance readability of a computer visual is to use capital letters.

_____ 8. On a poster or flip chart, titles should be approximately 3 inches high.

_____ 9. When used effectively, color visuals are more persuasive and easier to remember.

_____ 10. Using the visual aid formula, a speaker giving a 30-minute speech could easily expect to use 60 slides.

Final Thoughts on Color To be sure that your color choices are effective, project them onto a screen and check the combinations to make sure your visuals are easy to read. Too many colors are also confusing—more than four colors usually makes visuals look cluttered and slows down comprehension. Also, be aware that the colors you see on your computer monitor may not be the exact colors that the audience sees projected on the screen—video projectors and color printers vary in the set of color chips they use and even the way they are adjusted.

Finally, whatever colors you select, use the same ones for all the visuals in a presentation. For example, use the same color background for each visual and the same fonts and colors for each title. *Consistency projects professionalism.*

Using Microsoft Powerpoint

Now that you know how to design an effective visual aid, it's time to familiarize yourself with one of the major presentation software packages: Microsoft PowerPoint. Whether you wish to begin simply by preparing a few computer slides, or wish to go "all out" with an electronic (multimedia) presentation, the following pointers should prove helpful. Although this section is designed for PC users, PowerPoint works basically the same on a Macintosh.

One of the easiest ways to prepare a PowerPoint presentation is to use one of the templates that comes with PowerPoint, or the AutoContent Wizard (which guides you step-by-step through the process) or the *Communicating for Results* **Speech Template** (see step 1 for how to access this template). Even when you use a template, always alter it to follow the design, text, and graphic principles covered in this chapter and to make your presentation unique. *The following steps will help you get ready to create a basic PowerPoint presentation* by customizing a template and show you how to conduct a technological rehearsal once the presentation is completed:

1. *Open the Speech Template* (or AutoContent Wizard). Download a copy of the Speech Template at your Premium Website for *Communicating for Results* (see Figures 13.17a and 13.17b) and paste the template into your PowerPoint data file. Each time you open PowerPoint and click on "Open an existing presentation," the template will appear.

2. *Type in your outline.* The Speech Template will open to Outline view.

3. *View your outline in slide form* by clicking on the Slide Sorter View button (bottom left of screen). *Note*: Any changes you make to individual slides will update the outline; also, any changes you make to the outline will update your slides.

4. *Get ready to customize* the Speech Template—don't skip these steps!

   - From the menu choose View and click on Ruler and Guides if they are not already visible. Drag the vertical guide (dashed line) to where you want your left margin to be. *Note*: The guides will not print but are a great help with alignment. Titles and text are left-aligned in the Speech Template. To change alignment, click on the text; when a text box appears, click on the edge of the highlighted box and use the up, down, left, or right arrow keys to move the text box.

   - Click the Draw button in the Drawing toolbar, choose Snap, and turn off "snap to grid."

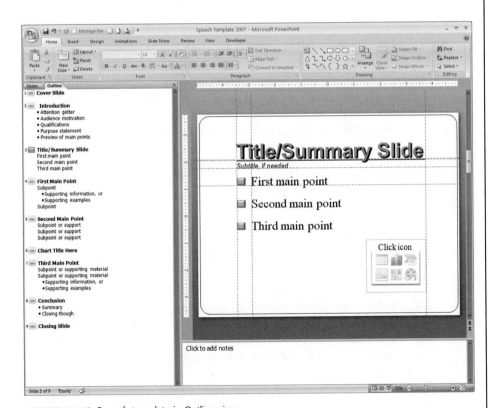

FIGURE 13.17A Speech template in Outline view.

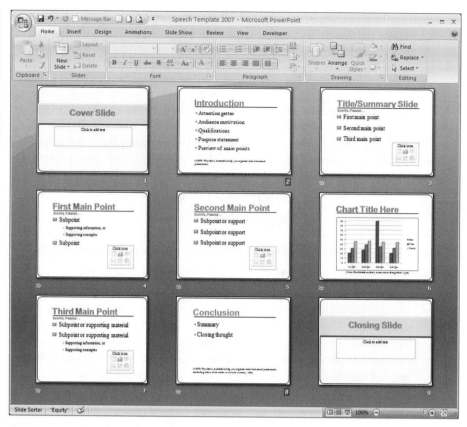

FIGURE 13.17B Speech template in Slide Sorter view.

5. *Begin customizing* titles, text, bullets, clip art, color, sound, movement, and so forth. (See the "PowerPoint Speaker's Guides for Customizing Your Electronic Presentation", accessible via your Premium Website for *Communicating for Results*.) *Note*: If you are worried about being nervous during your presentation, definitely build your own **custom bullets.** Exact instructions given under *Advanced Suggestions* in the Speaker's Guide mentioned previously. Regular PowerPoint bullets fly in with each point, making it hard to remember whether there is another point on the slide or not. However, if you build your own bullets that remain stationary with the title, you will know exactly how many points are located on each slide. This is a real confidence booster—there is no need to memorize your outline!

6. *Conduct a technological rehearsal.*

    *   Test your presentation by trying your disk, CD, or USB flash or thumb drive on a different computer. Note: PowerPoint 2003 and 2007 have a feature under File/Package for CD that lets you to save your entire presentation to a CD. It includes a new Viewer that allows your presentation (created in PowerPoint 2000 or later) to run on any computer operating Windows 98 Second Edition or later even when PowerPoint is not installed on the computer. The Viewer is available free on Microsoft's website.

    *   Use Ctrl + F7 if necessary so you can see the slides on your laptop screen at the same time the audience sees them on the wall screen. Once PowerPoint

has loaded, open your slides to a full-screen presentation by clicking F5. Better yet, save your presentation as a PowerPoint show (.pps)—go to File/ Save As, select PowerPoint Show, and click Save. Now a simple double-click on your presentation icon will immediately show a full-screen view of your opening slide without any indication that PowerPoint is running—much more professional!

- Make sure there is adequate lighting so the audience can see your facial expressions as well as the screen.

- Use remote control if possible—it frees you from the keyboard and gives you speaker control.

- To move back and forth between slides, press the number of the slide and then the Enter key. For example, if you are on slide 6 when someone asks a question about slide 3, simply press 3 and Enter to switch to slide 3.

- Print a paper copy of your slides by selecting Handouts (four to six slides per page) and Frame slides. Number your slides for easy reference in case you need to move back and forth between slides.

- For important presentations, have a backup form of the slides (transparencies or handouts) in case of equipment or power failure.

Student Informative Presentation with PowerPoint

COMMUNICATION SITUATION

Now that you've explored different types of visual aids, use your Premium Website for *Communicating for Results* to watch a video clip of a sample informative presentation that includes examples of PowerPoint slides. "Retail Theft" by Mark Stephenson is one of these speeches (see Mark's outline in Figure A.11). You can also use your Premium Website to critique this speech and, if requested, e-mail your responses to your instructor.

CHAPTER 13

R E V I E W

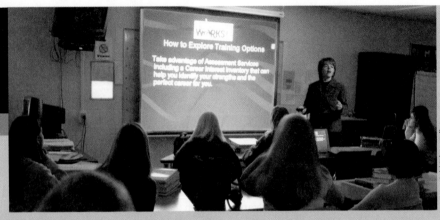

Lon C. Diehl/PhotoEdit Inc.

Key Terms

alignment (360)

audiovisual aids (343)

chalkboards (345)

clip art (352)

coherence principle (341)

contiguity principle (341)

contrast (359)

custom bullets (366)

diagrams (356)

electronic and multimedia aids (344)

flip charts (345)

flowcharts (356)

font (352)

general design principles (359)

graphic visuals (352)

graphs (357)

handouts (346)

hue (363)

maps (356)

markerboards (345)

models (346)

objects (346)

organization charts (356)

personalization principle (345)

points (352)

posters (345)

PowerPoint poisoning (339)

proximity (360)

repetition (360)

sans serif typeface (352)

saturation (363)

schematic drawings (356)

serif typeface (352)

speech template (364)

text visuals (352)

typeface (352)

visual aids (340)

Summary

To improve your presentations and avoid PowerPoint poisoning, use several visual aids to support your ideas—text visuals, graphic visuals, or both. *Visual aids are not optional.* Effective speakers know that audience attention and retention are enhanced when visuals are included. The number of visuals should be about half the number of minutes in the presentation. The type size for all visuals must be large enough to be read by everyone in the room, and the typeface should convey the appropriate tone. The best visuals follow the specific tips for text visuals and graphic visuals (i.e., charts, diagrams, maps, and graphs), as well as, the four general design principles. The tips for text visuals are (a) four to six lines of text per visual,

(b) no more than 40 characters in a line, (c) phrases rather than sentences, (d) upper- and lowercase type, (e) simple typefaces, (f) equal space at the top of each visual, and (g) clip art, large type, boldface, and color for emphasis. The four general design principles are contrast, repetition, alignment, and proximity. Guidelines for color visuals include using the same colors throughout a presentation, the same hues for related items, low-saturation hues for backgrounds, and high contrast between figure and background.

PowerPoint slides are an effective way to add visual aids to your presentation, but for the best effect, you must be sure to alter them to follow the design principles you have learned.

Communicating for Results Online

Before continuing to the next chapter, check your understanding of Chapter 13 at the Premium Website for *Communicating for Results.* Your Premium Website gives you quick and easy access to the electronic resources that accompany this text. These resources include:

- **Study tools** that will help you assess your learning and prepare for exams (student companion workbook, digital glossary, key term flash cards, and review quizzes).

- **Activities and assignments** that will help you hone your knowledge, analyze professional communication situations, build your public speaking skills throughout the course, and learn to work effectively in teams (Awareness Checks, Checkpoints, and Collaborative Learning Activities).

- **Media resources** that will help you explore communication concepts online (web links), develop your speech outlines (Speech Builder Express 3.0), watch and critique videos of professional communication situations and sample speeches (Interactive Video Activities), upload your speech videos for peer reviewing and critique other students' speeches (Speech Studio online speech review tool), and download chapter review so you can study when and where you'd like (Audio Study Tools).

This chapter's key terms, Collaborative Learning Activities, and Checkpoint activities are also featured on the following pages, and you can find this chapter's Awareness Check activity in the body of the chapter. For more information or to access this book's online resources, visit www.cengage.com/login.

Collaborative Learning Activities

1. In small groups, select either Sample Visual 7 or 8 from the Student and Faculty Visual Aids—these are the visuals that need revision and complete the following:

    a. To practice the design rules covered in this chapter, each group member should revise the chosen visual aid and print off their slide to share with group members.

    b. As a group, select the best two versions and make suggestions to make them even better. When these two slides are revised a second time, make a list of why the two slides are effective and how they follow the guidelines given in this chapter.

    c. Using a document camera or a portable USB thumb drive, share your slides with other groups. As a class, select the best slide from all groups.

2. Each student should prepare one or two quality PowerPoint slides they plan to use in their next speech. Print a copy of each visual to share with others. In small groups, critique the slides from each group member covering at least three items that make the slide successful and three suggestions for how to make it even better. If time allows, select the best slide from all slides and share it with the best slide from other groups.

3. Select a manuscript of a recent speech printed in the *Vital Speeches of the Day.* If your library does not carry this magazine, look for it in EBSCO-Host, Military and Government database. In small groups of three to five, discuss what visual aids the speaker could have used with their presentation and sketch out brief storyboards of each visual including suggestions for color, fonts, motion, and sound. In a computer lab or on personal computers, prepare at least three of the visual aids using PowerPoint and following the design guidelines in this chapter. Be prepared to share your results with other group members.

Checkpoints

Checkpoint 13.1 Redesigning Visuals

Practice the design rules covered in this chapter by redesigning one or more of the visual aids in the chapter. Visuals 1 to 8 on pages 348–351, as well as, Figure 13.16 would be especially interesting to redesign.

Persuasive Presentations: Individual or Team

Vince Bucci/Getty Images

Case Study: Dysfunctional Persuasion

When Janet Cooke was interviewed and hired by the *Washington Post*, "every interviewer was impressed" (Green, 1981, para. 4). In fact, after Cooke had received and lost the prestigious Pulitzer Prize, they recalled: "So impressed had the staff been with her and her writing that the usual check of references was done in a cursory manner" (para. 10). The following story was adapted from Kidwell (2004) and Green (1981).

In her first 8 months at the newspaper, Cooke had impressed everyone with her writing and had written "52 byline articles" (Kidwell, 2004, p. 178). However, what she really wanted was to land a front-page story and eventually the Pulitzer Prize (the *Post* had received a Pulitzer for its stories on Watergate). Cooke had heard about an 8-year-old boy who was addicted to heroin, and an editor encouraged her to seek out the child and write his story. After searching for several months with no luck, she decided to just invent a story about a child, his mother, and the mother's boyfriend, who she said injected Jimmy with heroin while she watched. The story began this way:

> Jimmy is 8 years old and a third-generation heroin addict, a
> precocious little boy with sandy hair, velvety brown eyes, and needle
> marks freckling the baby-smooth skin of his thin brown arms. (p. 178).

Cooke's story made the front page on a Sunday morning and immediately "the *Washington Post*'s telephone switchboard lit up like a space launch control room" (Green, 1981, para. 86) with people outraged by the article and concerned for the

As you read Chapter 14,

- **Explain** the meaning of *persuasion*, and the different types of persuasive presentations.
- Briefly **describe** each of the four factors/ theories necessary to make your presentations persuasive, and **pinpoint** at least two practical tips each factor/theory provides the persuasive speaker, including the four methods of citing evidence in a presentation.
- **List** the steps for preparing a persuasive speech, and **describe** each of the following persuasive organizational patterns: claim, causal, problem- solution, criteria satisfaction, compara- tive advantages, and motivated sequence.
- **Identify** three characteristics found in successful team presentations, and **suggest** several tips for handling Q & A.

© Travel Division Images/Alamy

As you read this chapter, see if you can determine (a) whether the *Washington Post* experienced the "instant ethos" or "click-whir" response discussed in this chapter; (b) if this response could be what caused the editors to be so easily persuaded by Cooke; and (c) how we can protect ourselves from this type of dysfunctional persuasion.

child's whereabouts. By Monday, a city-wide search had begun by the police, the schools, and social services. A $10,000 reward was offered for information leading to Jimmy. According to Green (para. 92), "It would be difficult to overestimate Washington's compassion for 'Jimmy' or its anger when the *Post* refused to reveal his identity or address." Yet, after 17 days of intense searching, no child was found. At this point, the police and mayor had serious doubts about the accuracy of Cooke's story. Feeling under attack, the staff went into a "protect the source and back the reporter" mode (para. 150). At one point, a worried editor spoke with Cooke and still remembers his satisfaction at her "gripping account of her visit to 'Jimmy's home'" (para. 152).

Cooke's story was nominated for the Pulitzer Prize by the *Post* leadership, and early the next year it was announced that she had won. The Associated Press and various papers immediately began researching the story behind Cooke's win. A comparison of her Pulitzer biography with her resume showed some discrepancies—she had added an additional six writing awards and fluency in two additional languages to the Pulitzer biography (Kidwell, 2004, p. 179). A further search found that some of her original resume had also been falsified—she had attended Vassar one year, but hadn't graduated from there magna cum laude as stated in her biography. When confronted with the discrepancies by several *Post* editors, Cooke admitted to the resume padding but insisted that her story about Jimmy was true. Finally, only days after receiving the Pulitzer, she admitted to fabricating the story and resigned from the *Washington Post.* Cooke was obviously a good writer, well-liked, highly motivated to achieve, and apparently persuasive enough in her interview and about her feature story that her editors didn't really question her credibility until the story had gone to print (Green, 1981).

Speaking of the incident, the executive editor of the *Post* had this to say (Maraniss, 1981):

> The credibility of a newspaper is its most precious asset, and it depends almost entirely on the integrity of its reporters. When that integrity is questioned and found wanting, the wounds are grievous, and there is nothing to do but come clean with our readers, apologize to the Advisory Board of the Pulitzer Prizes, and begin immediately on the uphill task of regaining our credibility. This we are doing." (para. 4)

For more details, go to WashingtonPost.com. You can easily access this link through your Premium Website for *Communicating for Results.*

A 20-year study of MBA graduates from Stanford University has concluded that no skill is more important to business success than good communication—especially the desire and ability to persuade (Harrell & Harrell, 1984). As we cautioned previously, to overlook the importance of speaking skills is to limit your flexibility as a communicator and perhaps even your chances for advancement.

Persuasive Presentations: Definitions and Types

Although persuasion is one of the most often used business communication skills, it may very well be one of the *least effectively used.* To learn to use persuasion, speakers need to know what persuasion is and understand the many types of persuasion.

Persuasion Defined

Many people either believe that persuasion is simply offering information, or they confuse it with coercion. Some business speakers take a middle-of-the-road approach by covering several possible alternatives but fail to argue for any particular view. They apparently believe that their listeners will do the "right" thing. But simply giving a list of options does not mean your audience will select the one you want them to select. Other business speakers view persuasion as coercion. They think that the only way to get people to do what they want is by force or trickery.

Neither of these methods is effective, and neither is truly persuasion. "Persuasion is communication intended to influence choice" (Brembeck & Howell, 1976, p. 19; see also Williams & Cooper, 2002, pp. 4–5). To *coerce* is to eliminate or exclude options. To *inform* is to increase the number of options (the more you know, the more choices you have). To **persuade** is to limit the options that are perceived as acceptable (Brembeck & Howell, 1976).

There is no force or trickery in persuasion. The receivers of the persuasive message must weigh the logic and evidence and make their own decision. Once that decision has been made, they alone are responsible for it, although the sender helped influence the decision.

Types of Persuasive Presentations

There are two basic types of persuasive presentations: the presentation to convince and the presentation to actuate. The two speeches differ in the degree of audience reaction sought: The presentation to convince seeks intellectual agreement from listeners, whereas the presentation to actuate asks listeners for both intellectual agreement and action of some type.

In a **presentation to convince,** you want your audience to agree with your way of thinking. You aren't asking them to do anything other than agree with you. This approach is especially good when your audience initially disagrees with your position and you realize that moving them to action is unlikely—getting agreement is a more realistic goal.

In a **presentation to actuate,** you want your audience to go one step past agreement to take a particular action. First you must *convince* them of the merits of your ideas; then you want to *actuate* them—move them to action. Most speakers try to persuade the audience to do something they haven't been doing (like join a work team). However, in a presentation to actuate you can also urge the audience to (a) *continue* doing something, such as continue eating balanced meals; (b) *stop* doing something, such as stop waiting until the last minute to prepare reports; or (c) *never start* doing something, such as smoking cigarettes (Fotheringham, 1966). Depending on your topic and your audience, you may want to include more than one action request. For example, in a speech on alcohol you might urge audience members who drink to use a designated driver, those drinkers who have used designated drivers to continue to do so, and those who don't drink to never start.

The type of persuasive presentation you pick may depend on the topic. For example, if your topic is the cultural bias of standardized interview screening tests, your

"That was one wild sales presentation, wasn't it? Ready to buy?"

persuasive presentation will convince rather than actuate. This topic lends itself to *believing* rather than *doing*. On the other hand, topics like the need for volunteers in local schools or the health problems resulting from recycled cabin air in commercial airliners lend themselves to listener action. For the first topic, you might urge your listeners to spend at least 1 hour a week as a volunteer at a local school; for the second topic, you might recommend that your audience write to commercial airlines, state and national government officials, and the Federal Aviation Administration urging that cabin air be continually replaced with fresh air, not recycled.

Persuasion in Business

Persuasion in business includes both written and oral messages. See Appendix: Written Communication for a discussion persuasive written communication and persuasive outlines for oral presentations. Persuasive oral presentations in the business world go be several names (Aubuchon, 1997; Burch, 1996). Some companies label the persuasive presentation a "pitch," others a "proposal," and still others a "presentation." Because the differences are subtle, we will simply use the term *persuasive presentation.*

Many persuasive presentations are informal and are given within the organization by supervisors to their employees or by employees to their supervisors. Supervisors' topics might include convincing employees of the need for a new reorganization plan or urging compliance with a company regulation. Employees' topics might include advocating a new piece of machinery, a policy change, or postponement of a deadline.

Other persuasive presentations are given to an individual or group from outside the organization. Such presentations are more formal. For example, the engineers from one company might plan a formal presentation about a new product for visiting engineers from another company. International business meetings definitely require one or more formal presentations. For these meetings, visual aids are prepared in the language of the guest country. Many companies also give persuasive presentations to the general public in an attempt to create a good public image or to change a negative one. An electric company, for example, might decide to have company representatives deliver persuasive presentations to various clubs and organizations in an attempt to change public opinion about the need for a rate hike. And, of course, salespeople give sales presentations to convince customers to buy their products.

Persuasive Presentations: Theory

There are many theories about persuasion such as the inoculation theory to be discussed on page 380, and the elaboration likelihood model summarized in Table 14.1 and in more detail in the Remember Box on page 376. In addition, persuaders have found that persuasion in business (and in other environments as well) depends on four main factors:

1. Logos: the *evidence and logic* of the message.
2. Ethos: the *credibility* of the persuader.
3. Pathos: the *psychological needs* of the listeners.
4. Opinions: those *held by key people* in the audience.

TABLE 14.1

Persuasion Theories	
Information-Integration Theory	
Basic approach	The way people accumulate and organize information (about a situation, event, person, or object) can result in attitude change (Littlejohn & Foss, 2008, pp. 75–76). Attitudes are affected by the valence and weight of information received. **Valence** refers to whether the information supports (+ valence) or refutes (– valence) previous beliefs; **weight** refers to how much credibility is assigned to the information.
Respected theorist	Martin Fishbein (Fishbein & Ajzen, 1975). A person's intention to change behavior is determined by their attitude toward the behavior *times* the strength (weight) of that attitude *plus* beliefs about what others think they should do *times* the strength of these other opinions.
Consistency Theories	
Basic approach	Because people prefer consistency and balance and feel threatened by inconsistency, attitude change can occur when information creates inconsistency (Littlejohn & Foss, 2008, pp. 78–80).
Respected theorist	Leon Festinger (1957), theory of cognitive dissonance. Dissonance (inconsistency) creates stress and tension in people, which causes them to (a) seek to reduce the dissonance and (b) to avoid other dissonance-creating situations.
Respected theorist	Milton Rokeach (1969, 1973), theory of attitudes, beliefs, values. **Attitudes** are feelings of like or dislike; **beliefs** are the reasons we hold the attitudes we do; and **values** are deep-seated principles that direct behaviors. Persuasion may occur when the speaker shows how certain behaviors are consistent with audience values or when a particular value is shown to be less (or more) important now than in the past.
Elaboration Likelihood Theory	
Basic approach	Elaboration likelihood involves the probability that listeners will evaluate arguments critically (Littlejohn & Foss, 2008, pp. 73–75).
Respected theorists	Richard Petty and John Cacioppo (1986a). When evaluating arguments, people either use the **central route** (elaborate carefully and critically) or the **peripheral route** (decide quickly using little critical thinking). For motivated and able people, elaboration leads to attitudes that are resistant to change.
Social Judgment Theory	
Basic approach	People use internal **anchors** (past experience) as reference points when making judgments about messages (Littlejohn & Foss, 2008, pp. 71–73). Anchors are more likely to influence the judgments of those who are *ego involved* with the topic.
Respected theorist	Muzafer Sherif (Sherif & Hovland, 1961; Sherif et al., 1965). A person's ego involvement determines messages that are acceptable (**latitude of acceptance**), totally unacceptable (**latitude of rejection**), or merely tolerable (**latitude of noncommitment**). The larger a person's latitude of rejection, the more difficult it is to persuade that person. Attitude change results when people perceive that an argument fits within their latitude of acceptance. When an argument falls in their latitude of rejection, a **boomerang effect** may occur, and the original attitude may be strengthened rather than changed.

When Using the Elaboration Likelihood Theory of Persuasion...

When listening to your persuasive arguments, the elaboration likelihood (ELM) theory of persuasion indicates which of two routes for processing arguments audience members will likely use (Petty & Cacioppo, 1986b):

- The *central route*—used if audience members are motivated (involved and interested in your topic) and have the ability to process information. If so, they are likely to use critical thinking and consider your arguments and evidence carefully and ask plenty of questions.

- The *peripheral route*—used if audience members are not motivated (have less involvement or interest in the topic) or are unable to process information. In this case, they are more likely to take a shortcut to decision making and use less critical thinking and evaluation of arguments and instead, focus on senses and cues that aren't directly related to the topic (such as a speaker's credibility or attractiveness).

So what does the ELM model of persuasion suggest to speakers? First, if audience analysis indicates the central route will be used:

- Focus on well-supported logic and evidence.
- Present both sides of the issue (still showing how your position is the better one).

Second, if audience analysis indicates likely use of the peripheral route:

- Focus on catchy visuals, narratives, personal experiences.
- Use immediacy behaviors.
- Organize with rhymes or acronyms.

Each of these factors will be considered in detail so you will be able to utilize the research in improving your persuasive ability.

Evidence and Logic of the Message

Americans like to think of themselves as logical people who make logical decisions. They expect speakers to use logic and evidence in their presentations. And, of course, when the listeners are persuaded, they attribute the persuasion to the superior logic and evidence used by the speaker.

Evidence is defined as factual statements and opinions originating, not from the speaker, but from another source (McCroskey, 1969). Evidence forms the basis for the logical arguments a speaker develops. (See Chapter 12 for supporting materials that can serve as evidence.) **Logic,** from the Greek *logos,* or reason, is "the study of orderly thinking, the sequence and connection of thoughts and ideas as they relate to one another" (Bell, 1990, p. 262). In other words, logic connects the various pieces of evidence in a meaningful and persuasive argument.

Despite its merits, of the four factors leading to persuasion, evidence is the most confusing. Researchers have begun to realize that evidence and logic may not be nearly as effective as previously thought and that certain uses of evidence may even be harmful to persuasion. The following research findings suggest some of the many factors influencing the effect of evidence in presentations (for a summary, see Reynolds & Reynolds, 2002):

- Listeners have difficulty in identifying evidence and intellectual appeals, in distinguishing between logical and illogical messages, and between high-quality evidence and low-quality evidence (Bettinghaus & Cody, 1997). Apparently, even though listeners think logic and evidence are important, they can't necessarily identify them in speeches.

- In order for evidence to produce persuasion, listeners must be aware and accept that the evidence exists (Reynolds & Reynolds, 2002). Therefore, speakers and advertisers who make it obvious that evidence is being presented are more persuasive (O'Keefe, 1998; Pfau & Louden, 1994).

- Low-ability listeners who are not personally involved with the topic will tend to be persuaded when a large amount of evidence is presented—even if the evidence is poor quality (Petty & Cacioppo, 1996).

- Logical-sounding phrases (e.g., "therefore," "as a result," "it is only logical that," and "it is possible to conclude") may cause listeners to judge a presentation as more logical than a presentation without such words (Bettinghaus & Cody, 1997). This finding explains how unethical speakers who use logical-sounding words are sometimes able to fool their listeners.

- Evidence and arguments that are novel or "new" to an audience are more persuasive (Morley, 1987; Morley & Walker, 1987).

- Use of evidence increases the perceived credibility of a low-credibility speaker, thereby increasing persuasiveness (McCroskey, 1970; Olson & Cal, 1984). In a more recent meta-analysis, O'Keefe (1998) found consistent confirmation that citing evidence in a speech improved the credibility of most speakers.

- There is "a significant persuasive advantage for messages providing information source citations" (O'Keefe, 1998, p. 67). When evidence is used, however, mentioning the source of the evidence without explaining who the expert is does not make the presentation more persuasive. In fact, unless the listener is informed about the source's qualifications, citing the source of the evidence may actually make the presentation *less* persuasive (Bostrom & Tucker, 1969; Ostermeier, 1967).

- When giving a source, it is more effective to cite the source and his or her qualifications *after* the evidence is presented. Cite the source *before* the evidence only if you know the listeners consider the source a highly credible one (Cohen, 1964; Reynolds & Burgoon, 1983).

- "Self-reference" speakers (who support their assertions by citing firsthand experiences) are rated higher in trustworthiness and are more persuasive than speakers who refer only to high-prestige sources (Ginossar & Trope, 1980; Koballa, 1989; Reinard, 1988). Personal examples and experiences may be more persuasive than statistical or numerical data (Kazoleas, 1993), especially for listeners who disagree with the speaker (Slater & Rouner, 1996), and they may have a longer-lasting persuasive effect (Ostermeier, 1967; Papageogis, 1963). Statistical evidence may be more persuasive for audience members who already support the speaker (Slater & Rouner, 1996). In most cases, speakers should include both narrative and statistical evidence (Allen et al., 2000).

Figure 14.1 summarizes research findings on the persuasiveness of the following methods of using evidence:

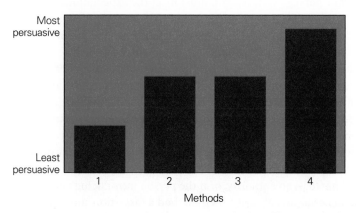

FIGURE 14.1 Persuasiveness of evidence presented in four different methods.

- *Method 1: Assertion plus evidence plus source.* "We need to paint our workroom walls orange [assertion]. Productivity normally increases by 20 percent when walls are painted orange [evidence] according to Kenneth Johnson [source]."

- *Method 2: Assertion plus evidence.* "We need to paint our workroom walls orange [assertion]. Productivity normally increases by 20 percent when walls are painted orange [evidence]." (Here the evidence is not linked to a source or documented in any way.)

- *Method 3: Assertion plus evidence plus source plus qualifications of source.* "We need to paint our workroom walls orange [assertion]. Productivity normally increases by 20 percent when walls are painted orange [evidence], according to Kenneth Johnson [source], the research director for Business Color, Inc. [qualifications of source]."

- *Method 4: Assertion plus firsthand experience.* "We need to paint our workroom walls orange [assertion]. Twice I have been in departments that painted their work areas orange, and both times productivity increased approximately 20 percent [firsthand experience]."

Notice that method 1 is the least persuasive of all four methods. Persuasiveness in this method is increased if the audience already knows the source and the source's qualifications, or views the speaker as highly credible. As discussed previously, citing a source without giving the qualifications of the source may be less persuasive than presenting evidence with no source at all. As Figure 14.1 shows, the most persuasive type of evidence is often firsthand experience. Let's discuss when to use each method.

For Persuasive Presentations Outside the Organization   When speaking outside the organization—at conventions, to educators, to customers, or to the general public—the best methods of using evidence are *method 3* (assertion plus evidence plus source plus qualifications of source) and *method 4* (assertion plus firsthand experience).

There are several reasons for using method 3. First, because these listeners do not know you personally, you enhance your credibility by citing sources that these listeners consider prestigious. Also, these listeners will expect knowledgeable speakers to include documented evidence in their presentations. To appear credible (and to improve your persuasiveness), you must meet the expectations of your listeners.

A second reason for using method 3 when speaking to the general public is that documented evidence may counteract opposing arguments that the listeners hear from other speakers. Communications researcher James McCroskey (1970) found that audiences were less affected by the opposing view (**counterpersuasion**) of a second speaker if the first speaker's message contained documented evidence. Although undocumented evidence can be persuasive, once the listeners begin to think about the arguments and realize that no sources were cited, they may begin to doubt the speaker. Later, when they are exposed to opposing views, they may doubt the original speaker's viewpoint even more.

If you are already known as an authority, or if the person introducing you presents you to the audience as an authority, then method 4 (assertion supported by firsthand experience) can be effective. You can also combine methods 3 and 4.

For Persuasive Presentations Within the Organization When speaking inside the organization to people who know you well, *method 1* (assertion plus evidence plus source) and *method 4* (assertion plus firsthand experience) are good methods for presenting evidence. Method 1 is often used for several reasons. First, in the business world, time is precious to everyone, particularly to management. As a result, individuals rarely have more than 20 to 30 minutes to present their ideas and answer questions. If the topic is very important, they might have as much as an hour. Because of such pressure, management and other listeners tend to view extensive documentation as a waste of time. If they need further verification of a point, they ask for it.

Second, extensive documentation is unnecessary for presentations within the organization because those listening to the presentation are usually already somewhat familiar with the topic being discussed. Even if the presentation concerns a new concept or product, they will normally have enough general knowledge in the field to determine whether the speaker's figures or evidence are reasonable.

Third, the presenter is usually an acquaintance of the listener, so his or her credibility and expertise are already known. If the speaker is relatively unknown or of lower rank than most of the listeners, his or her boss will attend the meeting to add credibility and to answer any problematic questions. Even when a team of speakers from one company travels to another company to present a proposal to people they have never met, each team judges the credibility and expertise of the other by the titles and ranks of the members. This is one reason why titles and positions are so important in business negotiation.

Instead of taking the time to cite the sources during their presentations, business speakers usually include an abbreviated version of the source on the computer visual or transparency they show their audience. For example, at the bottom of a visual demonstrating the results of a business survey, they might simply print, "Dun & Bradstreet, 2004."

Method 4 (assertion plus firsthand evidence) is also a common method of presenting evidence in a persuasive presentation. Would you rather hear about a new way to conduct employee appraisals from a manager who quotes from a book on the subject or from a manager who has firsthand knowledge of how the method works? Suppose that during the last company appraisal, this manager had appraised one-half of the employees using the old method and the other half using the new method. This manager could tell you firsthand whether the theory in the book worked well enough to adopt.

Method 4 should be used only if you have considerable firsthand experience and are an authority on the topic (or at least know more than most of the listeners). Otherwise, method 1 would be the best. However, speakers using method 4 should come prepared with more than just personal experience. They should have made an objective and complete search for relevant evidence (both for and against their idea) before preparing for the talk. They must be sure that their experiences are not exceptions to the rule and that the proposals they are recommending are the best ones for the company. If someone asks for additional evidence, they must be prepared to present it.

Presenting One or Both Sides of the Argument Before we conclude this section on evidence, there is one more question we need to discuss: Should business speakers present only the arguments that support their proposal, or should they introduce and then refute opposing arguments—counterarguments? Following are some recommendations (Allen, 1991, 1998; Hovland et al., 1967; Kamins & Marks, 1987).

Present only your side of the argument when

- *The listeners already agree with your proposal and have a well-developed belief system* (in other words, they are not new to the opinion). Presenting negative arguments that they had not thought of (even if you refute them well) may create some doubt in the listeners' minds and sabotage your attempt at persuasion (boomerang effect). These listeners are more interested in a "pep rally" type presentation.
- *The listeners know nothing about your topic* (too many arguments would cause confusion).
- *You want the listeners to take an immediate action*, such as donating money at the door as they leave.
- *There is little chance that the listeners will hear the other side* from another speaker or the news media.

Present both sides of the argument when

- *The listeners are fairly knowledgeable on your topic.*
- *The listeners already disagree with your proposal.*
- *There is a good chance that the listeners will hear the other side* from another speaker or the news media.
- *The listeners agree but are fairly new to the opinion and have undeveloped belief systems.*

Knowledgeable listeners, especially when they disagree with the speaker, are suspicious of speakers who present only one side of the topic. Presenting both sides also serves to "inoculate" the listeners against later opposing arguments.

Inoculation Theory   According to William McGuire's (1985) **inoculation theory,** inoculating a listener against opposing ideas is similar to inoculating a person against a disease. The person who has never heard any negative arguments on a certain topic will be susceptible to them, just as the person who has lived in a germ-free environment is susceptible to catching a disease. We can create immunity by giving a shot containing a weakened form of the disease, or in the case of a presentation, by motivating receivers to the vulnerability of their beliefs and presenting a brief look at opposing arguments along with their refutation (facts and logic disproving the arguments). Then, when the listener hears opposing arguments, he or she can say, "Oh, yes, I knew that. However, it's not important because research shows that. ... " Presenting both sides also seems to make listeners more resistant even to additional new arguments that the speaker did not cover (Papageogis & McGuire, 1961; Pfau, 1997; Szabo & Pfau, 2002). Apparently, inoculating listeners gives them the immunity needed to continue building their own counterarguments. Whalen (1996) also suggests that "inoculation" can be used with clients or customers who fear opposing views from other people in the organization— you would be supplying them with rebuttal arguments.

To summarize, when speaking (formally or informally) to business audiences *within* the organization, you should normally *present both sides*. Regardless of whether your listeners agree or disagree with you, they will normally be well informed and aware of opposing arguments. However, presenting both sides does not mean that you

Types of Fallacious Reasoning

- Ad hominem—attacking the person rather than the argument.

- Ad populum—arguing that because *everyone* knows an idea is right, it can't be wrong.

- Ad ignoratam—arguing that because no one can prove that a particular belief is false, it must be true.

- Begging the question—asserting that something is because it is.

- Hasty generalization—basing a general conclusion on too few examples or on isolated examples.

- Post hoc—claiming a causal relationship simply because one event followed another event.

- Slippery slope—asserting that taking a particular step automatically will lead to a second undesirable step.

give your opposition equal time. When you are presenting the other side, mention one or more objections to your plan (such as high cost) and then (a) show how each objection is based on inaccurate information or faulty reasoning, or (b) if an objection is accurate, show how it is minor compared to the many advantages of your proposal. After all, every view has some disadvantages. *The key is to show that any disadvantage to your plan or position is minor* but to do so without using **fallacious reasoning** of the kinds listed in the box "Types of Fallacious Reasoning" (Damer, 2000; Walton, 1998).

Credibility of the Speaker

The second factor of persuasion is the **ethos** or **credibility** of the speaker. A credible person is someone whom others view as believable—someone in whom they can place their confidence. In general, research has found that the greater your credibility, the more persuasive you are (O'Keefe, 1990). The importance of speaker credibility for persuasion is illustrated by a study of the decision-making practices of 137 executives and purchasing directors from 70 metal-working companies. The study found that when these executives and directors made decisions on awarding contracts, they were more than twice as likely to base their decisions on the credibility of the suppliers than on any other factor. They felt that finding someone with whom they could work well—someone who was honest and dependable—was even more important than finding a good price (Wilcox, 1987).

Researchers have discovered that a speaker's credibility depends on such factors as the audience's involvement with the topic, the mode of the message, and the audience's similarity to the speaker. Note the following research findings (see O'Keefe, 1990 for summary):

- Listeners who have *very low involvement* with the topic tend to be more persuaded by the expertise of the speaker than by the quality of arguments or evidence. However, listeners who are very *involved* with the topic are more persuaded by quality arguments than by the credibility of the speaker (Petty & Cacioppo, 1996). One explanation for this finding is that involved listeners are more likely to pay attention to and evaluate the speaker's arguments, whereas listeners who are not involved with the topic are less interested in evaluating arguments and more likely to be influenced by their impressions of the speaker (Eagly & Chaiken, 1993; Petty & Cacioppo, 1996).

- When a persuasive message uses an *audio or video mode*, the level of listener persuasion is likely to be determined by the credibility of the speaker; however, when the message is in the *print mode*, the level of listener persuasion is more likely to be determined by the data and quality of evidence (Booth-Butterfield & Gutowski, 1993). This may be because print allows time for careful analysis of data, whereas audio and video do not—listeners must base their evaluation of a speaker's evidence on speaker credibility factors such as sincerity and trustworthiness (Chaiken & Eagly, 1983).

- When a persuasive message is sent by *e-mail or the Internet*, receivers are more persuaded by the perceived credibility of the sender than the presence of any evidence. In fact, when a persuasive message is presented with emotional appeal and fits in with our values, a type of "instant ethos" occurs, which causes us to trust the message even when the author is unknown (Cialdini, 1993; Gurak, 1997).

- Perceived similarity between audience members and the speaker may enhance persuasion by increasing the perceived trustworthiness or competence of the speaker (O'Keefe, 1990, pp. 148–151). Audience members may perceive attitudinal similarities between themselves and the speaker. Attitudinal similarities (even when these similarities don't relate specifically to the topic of the speech) result in increased audience liking for the speaker and a higher rating of *trustworthiness* (Berscheid, 1985; McCroskey & Teven, 1999). Speakers tend to be judged as more *competent*, however, only when perceived similarities are relevant to the topic (O'Keefe, 1990). One way lawyers create attitudinal similarities with witnesses (thereby persuading them to express their views more openly and more convincingly) is by asking questions using the same sensory language previously used by the witness—visual, auditory, or kinesthetic (Swanson, 1981). For example, effective lawyers might ask the *visual witness*, "What did you see?" [I saw this brown Ford coming around the corner…]; the *auditory witness*, "What did you hear?" [I was listening to my Walkman, when I heard the screech of brakes…]; and the *kinesthetic witness*, "What did you feel?" [I had this feeling that something was about to happen, and when it did…] (adapted from Swanson, p. 211).

A speaker's credibility seems to be the result of five basic elements: trustworthiness, competency, dynamism, objectivity, and organizational rank.

Trustworthiness Most listeners determine the credibility of various speakers by observing all five elements and averaging them together. When speakers appear untrustworthy, however, their credibility is questioned regardless of their other qualities (Smith, 1973, p. 309). Therefore, **trustworthiness** (i.e., honesty, fairness, integrity) is the most important of the five elements.

Several factors seem to affect whether listeners perceive speakers as untrustworthy. For example, speakers who avoid eye contact, shift their eyes rapidly from side to side, or always look over the listeners' heads appear to be self-conscious or have something to hide. These speakers may be judged untrustworthy. Speakers with

poor articulation, breathy or nasal voices, or who speak either in a monotone or too rapidly are also perceived as less trustworthy (Addington, 1971).
In addition to having an effective delivery style, speakers can improve their
perceived trustworthiness by presenting both sides of an argument and by
appearing friendly and likeable (Chaiken, 1986). Hosman (2002) also found
that using active instead of passive sentence structure improves the speaker's
believability, although the study dealt with print advertisements.

Financial guru Suze Orman is known
for her personable and dynamic
speaking style.

Competency Another major factor of credibility is **competency.** Listeners
are more likely to judge a speaker credible if they perceive the speaker as
competent (i.e., knowledgeable, experienced, expert) on the topic. However,
speakers who use "nonfluencies" while speaking are often judged as low on
competence. *Nonfluencies* include inaccurate articulation, vocalized pauses
(like "uh," or "and uh"), and unnecessary repetition of words (McCroskey &
Young, 1981). In addition to avoiding nonfluencies, you can appear competent by citing personal experiences that relate to the topic, by citing sources
the listeners feel are prestigious, by speaking confidently, by using high-
quality visual aids, and wearing more traditional, higher status clothing (Behling &
Williams, 1991).

Dynamism Dynamism is another element of credibility. A dynamic speaker is
forceful, enthusiastic, and uses good vocal variety (discussed in Chapter 12). Speakers who avoid direct eye contact, are soft-spoken, use very little vocal emphasis, and
appear hesitant give the impression that they are uncertain about what they are saying (incompetent) or that they are trying to deceive the listeners (untrustworthy). As
a result, the listeners are less likely to be persuaded.

At the same time, the dynamic speaker must also remain conversational.
Researchers found that as speakers move from low to moderate levels of dynamism,
they are perceived as more credible (moderately dynamic speakers are still considered conversational). However, as speakers move from moderate to exaggerated
dynamism, they are perceived as less conversational, less trustworthy, and less credible (Pearce & Conklin, 1971). Speakers with more than moderately dynamic deliveries are perceived as unnatural and phony.

Objectivity The fourth element of speaker credibility is **objectivity.** An objective
speaker is one who is open-minded, impartial, and appears to view evidence and
arguments in an unbiased manner (Smith, 1973; Whitehead, 1968). Speakers usually
seem objective when they discuss all viewpoints of the proposal (of course, they must
conclude by showing why their arguments are best).

Organizational Rank In business, the formal position or **organizational rank** of the
speaker within the organization is another element of credibility—although perhaps
less important than the others. More people would be impressed by a presentation
given by the company's president or assistant vice president than by someone of
lower rank. Therefore, "all other things being equal, the higher the organizational
status of the speaker, the higher his credibility and the greater the effect upon the
audience" (Howell & Bormann, 1979, p. 79).

If the listeners don't know you and are unaware of your credibility, or if you
have low credibility, review the suggestions in the box "To Improve Speaker
Credibility."

Credibility, Fraud, and the Internet As mentioned previously, when a persuasive message is presented with emotional appeal and fits in with our values, a type of "instant ethos" occurs. In *Persuasion and Privacy in Cyberspace* (1997), Gurak notes that this instant ethos causes us to trust the message even when the author is unknown. Similarly, Priester and Petty (1995) found that victims of fraud (especially Internet fraud) give little attention to the substance of the message once they perceive the sender to be honest. Investigations of Internet fraud indicate that criminals use the same credibility-based techniques in Internet scams as they do in telephone and door-to-door scams (Rusch, 1999). In his book *Influence: The Psychology of Persuasion*, Cialdini (1993) discusses several of these persuasive techniques, which he says produce irresistible "click-whir" responses in most of us:

- *Reciprocation*: If you give me something, I feel obligated to reciprocate.

- *Commitment and consistency*: Once I have purchased or committed myself to something, I tend to defend that decision consistently (even if the decision was a poor one).

- *Social proof*: If other people are doing it or believe it, I am more likely to want to do it or believe it.

- *Likeability*: If I like you (usually because we are alike in one or more ways), I am more likely be influenced by you.

- *Authority*: I tend to be influenced by people I perceive to have authority.

- *Scarcity*: When I perceive an item to be scarce, I value it more.

You may also recognize some of these techniques from messages and ads you have received in the mail and over the Internet.

Psychological Needs of the Listeners

To be successful at persuasive speaking, you need more than credibility and logically organized evidence based on reliable sources; you also must adapt your arguments to the **pathos** or **psychological needs** of your listeners (Harris, 1993). In fact, your audience may choose not to believe your evidence no matter how good it is. For example, have you ever had a disagreement with someone when you knew your

To Improve Speaker Credibility...

- *Have a highly credible expert on the topic (or someone of higher rank) introduce you* and establish you as a competent and trustworthy speaker.

- *Support your assertions with up-to-date, carefully documented evidence and sources* considered credible to your listeners.

- *Identify your views* with those of a respected person or institution.

- *Present both sides of an issue* to show your willingness to be fair and honest.

- *Present your ideas in a smooth, forceful, and self-assured manner*, while maintaining good eye contact.

- *Establish a common ground with your listeners* by identifying beliefs, organizations, or problems you share.

- *Recognize* (in content and delivery) the formal status and knowledge of your listeners.

AWARENESS CHECK

Identifying Basic Needs

To check your knowledge of Maslow's Basic Needs, take the following quiz and compare your answers to those at the back of this book. You can also take this quiz online and view the answers at your Premium Website for Communicating for Results.

Directions: Read the following persuasive statements and identify which of the following basic needs each statement is appealing to (**A**) Physiological, (**B**) Safety, (**C**) Social, (**D**) Esteem, or (**E**) Self-actualization.

_____   1. Exercise regularly for a sexier, slimmer you.

_____   2. It may seem like graduation is a long way off, but anything worth having is worth waiting and working for.

_____   3. Unless we take a leadership role in this international crisis, the United States will be viewed as ineffective and weak.

_____   4. Let your children know how you feel about them. Send them off to school each day with a nourishing, hot breakfast.

_____   5. Don't study just to pass this class or seminar; study so you can uncap your business potential.

_____   6. Aren't you tired of being a prisoner in your own home each holiday because of the drunks out on the road? Wouldn't you like to take a car trip this year without worrying about possible consequences to your family?

arguments and evidence were correct, but the person would only say, "I don't care. I don't believe it"? As persuasive speakers, we need to remember that *it isn't evidence unless the audience thinks it's evidence.*

If you can get your audience to relate personally to your evidence—to decide that your topic is important to them and their specific needs—they are more likely to consider your evidence persuasive. The importance of relating to personal needs is illustrated by the following example:

> An excellent vice president had decided to retire early, much to the disbelief of his coworkers. All kinds of inducements (such as a substantial salary increase, more office help, and a new car) were offered to convince him to stay with the company. When inducements didn't work, his colleagues pointed out how much he was needed. Nothing was successful. On his last day with the company, he was having lunch in the executive dining room with the president and two other executives. The president began to discuss a completely new and risky project that the company was contemplating. Almost in jest, the president suggested that the vice president stay and head the new project. He accepted! None of the other appeals had related to his personal need for achievement. The challenge presented by the new project was something he could not resist.

Hierarchy of Needs   Discovering your listeners' basic needs and motives is an essential part of audience analysis. As far back as 1954, psychologist Abraham Maslow believed that all people have the same basic categories of needs or drives, which are shown in Figure 14.2. Think of the **hierarchy of needs** as the rungs of a ladder. Although people may be motivated by several levels at one time, generally a lower rung must be satisfied before the next rung becomes important. As each

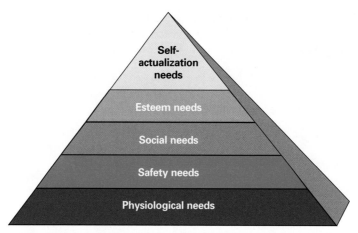

FIGURE 14.2 Maslow's hierarchy of needs.

goal is fulfilled, it is replaced with another. Let's look at each of these basic needs (Maslow, 1954), as well as, our feelings when each need is not fulfilled (Lefton et al., 1980):

- *Physiological needs*: Food, shelter, clothing, air, water, sleep, and sexual attraction. If unfulfilled, we may experience pain, physical discomfort, or illness.

- *Safety needs*: A job and financial security; law and order; protection from injury, poor health, or harm; and freedom from fear. If unfulfilled, we may experience tension, anxiety, fear, or panic.

- *Social needs*: Love, companionship, friendship, and a feeling of belonging to one or more groups. If unfulfilled, we may experience loneliness, boredom, low self-image, or feelings of being unloved or unlovable.

- *Esteem needs*: Pride, recognition from others, status and prestige, and self-recognition. If unfulfilled, we may experience loss of confidence, low self-image, or self-doubt.

- *Self-actualization needs*: Becoming the best person one can—developing to one's fullest capabilities and achieving worthwhile goals. If unfulfilled, we may experience feelings of futility, alienation, or bitterness.

When using emotional appeal, keep in mind that listeners appear to be "more motivated by the thought of losing something than by the thought of gaining something" (Dillard & Pfau, 2002, p. 520). Therefore, when messages are framed to stress potential losses that may occur if certain action is not taken, persuasion is enhanced. Loss framing is especially effective in situations involving risk and uncertainty (De Dreu & McCusker, 1997; Tversky & Kahneman, 1981).

Actively relating to an audience in funny and surprising ways creates good will and audience participation, which helps to make the presentation more interesting and enjoyable for the audience.

Audience Involvement According to Josh Gordon, author of *Presentations That Change Minds* (2006), one of the best and most persuasive ways to relate to audience needs is by getting the audience involved: "Audience involvement means your audience is actively comparing what you are sharing with what they already know, evaluating it, raising concerns, and participating in a dialogue" (p. 4). If you can get your audience actively involved in your presentation, your chance of persuading them is greater. Several successful ways to encourage audience involvement are suggested by Gordon (pp. 4–12):

- *Relevancy*: look at the topic from your audience's viewpoint; what are their problems and what do they want to know. Get them excited and involved right from the start. Show the relevancy of your topic to their needs.

- *Fun and activities*: audiences generally expect most meetings and speeches to be dull and boring. Get them involved by doing something fun and unexpected like completing famous quotations or identifying lines from songs where the activity leads into a key point of the speech (Smith, 2004).

- *Commonality and emotion*: share something you have in common with the audience and do it with emotion. Don't be afraid to show your passion for the topic as you relate it to something that you and the audience both have—same problem, children, pet peeve, or desire to make the world a healthier place.

- *Graphics and Charts*: don't just use charts and graphs to show facts; use them as involvement starters by showing "relationships or contrast between features, competitors, or issues" (Gordon, 2006, p. 9). Ask them if the slide is what they expected or if it agrees with their experience and watch the interest and involvement grow.

These are only a few of the way to get audience involvement; what other ways do you think would work? The key is to get to know your audience ahead of time and approach your topic from their viewpoint. Once they are involved in your topic, they will be more attentive, enjoy your presentation more, and likely be more persuaded.

Opinions of Key Listeners

In almost every group, there is a key person (or persons) whom others look to for advice. To persuade the group, you must first persuade these key people, or **opinion leaders**.

- Opinion leaders tend to have slightly more formal education and a higher

ETHICAL DILEMMA

When Patricia Dunn stepped in as chairwoman of the Hewlett Packard (HP) Board of Directors, taking over from Carly Fiorina, few people expected her to resign a mere 18 months later. On September 22, 2006, Engadget reported the event, citing the "corporate spying scandal that has plagued the company for weeks" (Farivar, 2006) as the reason for her abrupt departure. It started when Dunn learned of a press leak in the board and brought in an outside investigator to look into the matter and expose the leak. Whether she knew it or not, Dunn had just authorized identity theft.

Using the illegal method of pretexting, investigators had obtained the phone records of "more than a dozen people, including current and former board members, nine journalists, two employees and an unspecified number of other people" (Fried, 2006). Although companies legally monitor employee phones and e-mail at work, pretexting, which uses the last four digits of social security numbers to obtain phone records outside the company, is illegal. Dunn maintains that she did not know what techniques the outside investigators were using until June of 2006 and even then she was told the methods were legal. She has cited personal conflict with Tom Perkins—another member of the board—as a reason for the scope of the legal trouble (Kaplan, 2006), and maintains her innocence even after indictment. Dunn has been charged with conspiracy, fraud, and identity theft and has pled not guilty to all the charges in front of the Santa Clara County Superior Court (Pimentel, 2005). The investigation (ongoing at the time this text was published) questions whether Dunn intentionally avoided knowledge of the details so that she could later avoid blame (Kaplan, 2006).

QUESTIONS: What do you think? As CEO, Dunn needed to locate a high-level information leak at HP—the company's competitiveness seemed to depend on it. Were her actions unethical? If you had been a stockholder, would your answer to this question be the same?

IT REALLY WORKS!

Employee Motivation

What is it about J. M. Smucker—the company known for its jams and jellies—that earned it the prestigious honor of Number 1 best company to work for in 2004 (Boorstin, 2004) and Number 8 best company in 2006 (Geoff, 2006)? It may be in part because of its positive motivational philosophy: "Listen with your full attention, look for the good in others, have a sense of humor, and say thank you for a job well done" (Boorstin, para. 2). The company celebrates and motivates its employees with special gifts, food, and holiday events (Williams, 2007, p. 15). "They're always willing to sit down and listen to you," says Bob Jones, a line worker with the company for over 44 years (Wagner, 2002, para. 5). Due in part to this "culture and management style as straightforward and likable as strawberry jam" (Boorstin, para. 2), Tim and Richard Smucker—known as "the boys" (Boorstin, para. 2)—have earned a place of respect for the Smucker's corporation.

Not only does their quiet, unassuming manner influence employees, but it also influences the small community of Orrville, Ohio—their headquarters for 107 years. On their website, Tim and Richard stress that Smucker's will "maintain an environment that encourages personal responsibil-ity within the Company and the community" ("Join our company," n.d., para. 2). It's not surprising that Smucker's is involved with Orrville's schools, the library (which is "progressive," says the director), and many local businesses (Wagner, 2002, para. 7). "This is the best place I've ever lived," says an employee of a metal products manufacturer in Orrville. The teamwork that exists within the company "has shaped the relationship the company has with Orrville and the town's working-class residents" (Wagner, p. 6).

What do you think?

- How do you think the nonassuming method of influence used by Smucker's, with their company of less than 3,000 employees, would have to change if the company grew in size to 100,000 or more employees?
- Based on the organizational models discussed in Chapter 2, which type of organization best describes Smucker's?
- When trying to persuade employees or community members to accept an unexpected change in procedure, which persuasive factor would work the best: evidence and logic, credibility, psychological needs, or key listener opinions? Why do you feel this way?

social status than the people to whom they give advice. Therefore, they serve as models to the others in their group.

- Opinion leaders are usually more knowledgeable than others in those areas about which people seek their opinions.
- Opinion leaders are more likely to converse with others.

If you are speaking within the organization, it should be fairly easy to discover who the key people are and what their opinions are likely to be. Direct your arguments toward these people.

Persuasive Presentations: Preparation Steps

If you follow the steps described here, you will be able to prepare successful persuasive presentations.

Step 1: Analyze Your Expected Listeners and Their Needs

In general, you should obtain the same information about your listeners as you would when preparing an informative presentation. In addition, you need to identify the opinion leaders. Plan your presentation for these key people.

To be persuasive, you must show how your proposal will help fulfill one or more of your listeners' needs. Previously, we compared Maslow's hierarchy of needs

Preparation Steps for Persuasive Presentations

1. Analyze your expected listeners and their needs.

2. Write your exact purpose as a position statement.

3. Determine your initial credibility and plan to increase it if necessary.

4. Research your topic and choose the best method for presenting evidence to this audience.

5. Decide how to organize your presentation for the best effect.

6. Prepare an outline or storyboards to check verbal and visual supports, introduction, and conclusion.

7. Review your presentation to ensure it is ethical.

8. Practice your presentation using your visual aids.

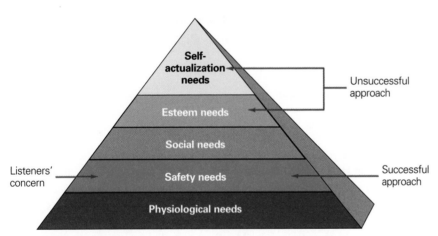

FIGURE 14.3 Relating listeners' needs to a successful persuasive approach.

to a ladder with rungs. Begin with the lowest needs that relate to your topic, and relate your proposal to those needs (see Figure 14.3). For example, if your listeners were concerned with job security and were worried about having enough money to pay their bills, appealing to their desire for self-actualization or their sense of pride would probably be an ineffective way to motivate them to work harder. You would likely have more success if you explained how increased productivity would not only help secure their jobs in the department but would also get them raises at their next evaluation. *The relationship between listener needs and persuasion is very strong. Don't underestimate it.*

Step 2: Write Your Exact Purpose as a Position Statement

Although you probably had your topic in mind before analyzing your listeners and their needs (see Figure 14.4 for sample topics), you will need to adapt it to them specifically. Begin by determining exactly what reaction you hope to elicit from your listeners. Are you hoping to reinforce a current belief or inspire agreement (a presentation to convince) or to request some specific action (a presentation

Air pollution—role of business	Importance of funding space exploration
Avoiding terrorism in the workplace	Making the workplace accessible to the disabled
Business role in helping the homeless	Managing diversity
Business role in health care	Managing employee stress
Cell phones and car accidents	Mandatory drug testing
Company fitness programs	Need for work unions
Company responsibility for child care	Preparing employees for downsizing
Discrimination in the workplace	Raising the minimum wage
Effect of casual dress on job performance	Hybrid automobiles and the environment
Embryonic versus adult stem cell use	Restaurants use organic fruits & vegetables
Employee responsibility for volunteer work	Role of industry in global warming
Empowerment: company blogs	Salary cap for top-level executives
Ethical behavior in the workplace	Sexual harassment in the workplace
401K retirement plans—are they safe	Smoking in the workplace
Hiring the disabled	Using Twitter to advertise
How to solve [select a topic]	Video piracy—penalties too stiff
HPV vaccine—required or optional	Why [select a product] software is best

FIGURE 14.4 Sample topics for persuasive presentations.

to actuate)? Now write your exact purpose in the form of a position statement—a simple sentence that states exactly how you feel about the issue you have chosen. A sample position statement for a presentation to actuate might be "Everyone should take an active role in seeing that cigarette advertising is banned from all sports events." Note that persuasive position statements are different from informative purpose statements. You can use Speech Builder Express to help you create your position statement. Select "Thesis Statement" from the left-hand menu and follow the instructions. For short reminders from this chapter about position statements, click on the "Tutor" button.

Step 3: Determine Your Initial Credibility and Plan to Increase It If Necessary

If your listeners have met you previously, or have heard about you, or have heard about your department or company, you already have some credibility with them. If this initial credibility is positive, it will add to your persuasiveness; if it is negative, you will need to supplement your initial credibility in one or more of the ways suggested previously in this chapter.

One study has shown that 25 to 75% of the customers of small businesses younger than 10 years old come from referrals (Stephenson, 1984). Obviously, for such businesses, employee credibility and company credibility are important to sales, both at the time of presentation and after. A salesperson can continue bolstering personal and company credibility even after a sale:

A telephone call to find out how it's going is worth it; a follow-up session to check on progress; advertising to reassure customers that the purchase was a good one; follow-up mailing of thank you [notes]; feedback questions; newsletters to users; free information on related ideas/products/ services; are all statements of "We care." (Stephenson, 1984, p. 31)

In a popular book, *You've Got to Be Believed to Be Heard*, Decker and Denney (1993) advise the speaker that it is essential "to be liked, believed, and trusted. It's a matter of making emotional contact" (p. 9). Once you've made emotional contact with your audience (as do Carly Fiorina, Katie Couric, and Barack Obama), once they trust and like you, then—and only then—will they really hear you.

Step 4: Research Your Topic and Choose the Best Method for Presenting Evidence to This Audience

Review the methods for presenting evidence discussed previously in this chapter. Suggestions for effective research are covered in Chapter 12. Don't forget to use a variety of supporting materials (also described in Chapter 12) to clarify and add interest, as well as, to support your arguments.

Step 5: Decide How to Organize Your Presentation for the Best Effect

To organize the main points in the body of their presentation, persuasive speakers select from five main patterns: claim pattern (inductive and deductive), causal pattern, problem–solution pattern (problem–solution–benefits or problem–solution–action), comparative advantages pattern, and criteria satisfaction pattern (see Figure 14.5).

Nam Y Huh/AP Image

President Barack Obama makes emotional contact with listeners when he speaks.

PERSUASIVE PATTERNS

I. Claim #1
II. Claim #2
III. Claim #3

Claim Pattern

I. Cause		I. Cause
II. Effect	*(or)*	II. Effect
III. Solution		III. Action

Causal Pattern

I. Problem		I. Problem
II. Solution	*(or)*	II. Solution
III. Benefits		III. Action

Problem–Solution Pattern

I. Any plan must meet the following necessary criteria:
II. Solution X does (or does not) meet the criteria.

Criteria Satisfaction Pattern

I. Plan X is ineffective.
II. Plan Y is superior.
(or)
I. Plan X is average.
II. Plan Y is far better.

Comparative Advantages Pattern

FIGURE 14.5 Organizational patterns for persuasive presentations.

Claim Pattern In the **claim pattern**—so called because the speaker "claims" certain propositions or benefits—the problem is reviewed in the introduction step and the reasons for believing a particular fact, for holding a particular value, or for advocating a particular plan are presented in the body of the presentation. Although the claim pattern is similar to the topical arrangement used in informative presentations, the language is definitely persuasive. The claim pattern often orders the points according to inductive or deductive reasoning. **Inductive reasoning** involves presenting the specific evidence first, then building up to the general conclusion; **deductive reasoning** involves presenting the position or general conclusion first, then providing the supporting evidence. For example, a speech advocating prison reform before a potentially hostile audience might use the following inductive claim pattern (Bidinotto, 1994):

I.   Prison spending costs society over $20 billion each year. *[**claim 1**: specific evidence]*

II. Much of this expense goes to provide recreational equipment and services that even many taxpayers can't afford. *[**claim 2**: specific evidence]*

III. In addition, civil lawsuits filed by inmates are clogging federal and state courts. *[**claim 3**: specific evidence]*

IV. It's time to end the resort status of U.S. prisons. *[**claim 4**: general conclusion]*

Causal Pattern The **causal pattern** in persuasive presentations uses cause-effect reasoning that is followed by either a solution or an action step (see Figure 14.5). Because you are using cause-effect reasoning to prove your point, it's important that the cause-effect relationship you are presenting is real and not just a coincidence. The causal organization pattern was used by Jeff Davidson in his speech titled "Overworked Americans or Overwhelmed Americans? You Cannot Handle Everything" (Davidson, 1993):

I.   The overwhelmed, pressured feeling that Americans have is caused by the complexity of our society. *[**cause**]*
   A.   Population growth
   B.   Expanding volume of knowledge
   C.   Mass media and electronic growth
   D.   Paper trail culture
   E.   Overabundance of choices

II. As complexity increases, these pressured feelings will turn into feelings of overwork and total exhaustion. *[**effect**]*

III. It's not too late to take control of your life. *[**action**]*
   A.   Make choices in what to ignore.
   B.   Avoid engaging in low-level decisions.
   C.   Learn to enjoy yourself.

Problem–Solution Pattern The **problem-solution pattern** can take a variety of forms. The two most popular forms are the problem–solution–benefits and the problem–solution–action patterns. Both patterns begin with a detailed discussion of the problem, its seriousness, and its effect on the audience. Next, a solution (or solutions) is presented to solve or improve the problem. Finally, additional benefits that result from your solution are described, or a particular course of action is recommended to the audience. Nevin S. Scrimshaw (1991) used a *problem-solution–benefit* pattern in his speech titled "The Consequences of Hidden Hunger":

I.	The magnitude and consequences of hidden hunger still devastate a large proportion of the world's population.	[*problem*]
II.	Hunger can be abolished as a public health problem in the world if we are willing to take the required actions.	[*solution*]
III.	Conquering hunger will release human potential for creating better societies.	[*benefits*]

A seminar participant's speech on drunk drivers used a *problem–solution–action* pattern of organization:

I.   The high number of auto/alcohol-related accidents indicates a serious problem.   [*problem*]

   A.   Nationally, 2 of 5 involved in auto-alcohol accidents.

   B.   Nationally, 17,000 killed in auto-alcohol accidents.

   C.   In our state, 1,800 killed in auto-alcohol accidents.

II. There are several workable solutions to the DWI problem.   [*solutions*]

   A.   Year-round sobriety checkpoints

   B.   Legal blood-alcohol level lowered from 0.1 to 0.08

   C.   Stronger penalties for drunk driving

III. Action must be taken now.   [*action*]

   A.   "Lights-on-for-life" promotion

   B.   Letter to state legislators.

Comparative Advantages Pattern The **comparative advantages pattern** of organization is normally used when your audience already agrees with you on the problem but may not agree on the solution. Only a brief mention of the problem is needed during the speech introduction. The comparative advantages pattern concentrates on the advantages of one course of action over another. Usually, you will want to show that one course of action is greatly inferior to your more desirable plan for a number of reasons. Or it is possible that the current plan is okay, but it just doesn't have the advantages of your plan. In his speech on "Aid to Russia," Lawrence M. Lesser (1993) used the comparative advantages pattern:

I.   The current method of giving aid to Russia in the form of cash grants, loans, and credit guarantees isn't working.   [*current plan ineffective*]

   A.   Russia is in default on $600 million of interest payments on $4.2 billion of U.S. agricultural credit guarantees used to purchase U.S. grain.

   B.   Russia has failed to pay $200 million in debts it owes to 57 U.S. companies.

   C.   Russia has defaulted on payments on the $4.5 billion it borrowed from international lenders, forcing the U.S. to pay $180 million in loan loss claims.

II.   Bartering, a concept Russia is very familiar with, is a much better way of providing aid to Russia.   [*new plan superior*]

Criteria Satisfaction Pattern   Whether you are dealing with products, services, or ideas, the **criteria satisfaction pattern** is a successful tool that works well even when audience members oppose your position. First, you establish criteria (guidelines or rules) that should be followed when evaluating possible plans or solutions ("We all want our managers to be knowledgeable and fair"). Second, you show how your plan meets or exceeds the established criteria (e.g., "Not only is Manager X knowledgeable and fair, but she is also a dynamic speaker"). Of course, it's important to carefully consider your audience's values and needs when selecting and explaining why your criteria are important. If you can get your audience to agree with your criteria, the chances are good that they will also agree with your plan. Using the criteria satisfaction pattern, Farah Walters, president and chief executive officer of University Hospitals of Cleveland and a member of the National Health Care Reform Task Force, gave a speech called "If It's Broke, Fix It: The Significance of Health Care Reform in America" (Walters, 1993):

I.   Any health care plan should be measured against six fundamental principles: [*necessary criteria*]

   A.   Provide security for all Americans.

   B.   Provide choice of physician.

   C.   Provide continuity of care.

   D.   Be affordable to the individual, to business, and to the country.

   E.   Be comprehensive in terms of coverage.

   F.   Be user-friendly for consumers and providers.

II.   The health care plan designed by the National Health Care Reform Task Force meets all six of these fundamental principles.   [*plan meets criteria*]

In addition to the five primary organization patterns just discussed, persuasive presentations may use the motivated sequence, which is more than just a pattern of organization for your main points—it includes the introduction and conclusion as well.

The Motivated Sequence The **motivated sequence** was developed by communications professor Alan Monroe more than 50 years ago. It is similar to the problem–solution–action pattern and is especially effective with speeches to actuate an audience to support a particular policy. The motivated sequence involves five steps: attention, need, satisfaction, visualization, and action (Gronbeck et al., 1994). Let's take a brief look at each step.

- *Attention step*: First, grab your listeners' attention (using any of the methods described in Chapter 11) so that they want to continue listening.

- *Need step*: Next, direct the audience's attention to a specific problem that needs to be solved. Describe the problem using credible, logical, and psychological appeals (discussed previously in this chapter), and show how the problem relates specifically to your listeners.

- *Satisfaction step*: In this step, you satisfy the need by presenting a solution to the problem. The following basic framework is suggested: "(a) Briefly state what you propose to do, (b) explain it clearly, (c) show how it remedies the problem, (d) demonstrate its workability, and (e) answer objections" (Gronbeck et al., 1994, p. 209). In demonstrating the workability and feasibility of the solution, as well as, answering possible audience objections, be sure to use supporting materials that will support your statements (see Chapter 12).

- *Visualization step*: After you have presented the solution to your problem, vividly picture the future for your audience, using either positive, negative, or contrast methods. In the positive method, you picture the improved future that the audience can expect when your solution is implemented. In the negative method, you picture the undesirable conditions that will continue to exist or will develop if your solution is not adopted. The contrast method uses both the positive and negative methods, beginning with the negative and ending with the positive. The purpose of this step is to "intensify audience desire or willingness to act—to motivate your listeners to believe, to feel, or to act in a certain way" (Gronbeck et al., 1994, p. 211).

- *Action step*: Conclude your speech by challenging your audience to take a particular action—you want a personal commitment from them. Say exactly what you want them to do and how they can do it.

Step 6: Prepare an Outline or Storyboards to Check Your Verbal and Visual Supports, Introduction, and Conclusion

Review Chapter 12 for suggestions on supporting materials and Chapter 13 for guidelines about preparing professional visual aids of all types. Reread the sections in Chapter 11 on outlines, storyboards, introductions, and conclusions. Be sure to check out the suggestions for effective persuasive outlines for oral presentations included in Appendix: Written Communication. See Figure 14.6 for the persuasive outline format or the storyboard format.

Remember that persuasive conclusions must be persuasive. In addition to summarizing your position and ending in a memorable way, you should issue a

---

Persuasive Outline Format

Topic or Title:
Position Statement:

INTRODUCTION
- Attention-getter:
- Audience motivation:
- Credibility:
- Thesis statement:
- Background of problem or clarification of terms (optional):

BODY
(Use with any of the organizational patterns covered in this chapter; below are two of the most common—claim and problem/solution/action)

  I. Claim I or Problem:
    A. Subpoint or supporting material
      1. Supporting material
      2. Supporting material
    B. Subpoint or supporting material

    [Transition]

  II. Claim II or Solution:
    A. Subpoint or supporting material
    B. Subpoint or supporting material
      1. Supporting material
      2. Supporting material
    C. Subpoint or supporting material

    [Transition]

  III. Claim III or Action:
    A. Subpoint or supporting material
    B. Subpoint or supporting material

CONCLUSION
- Summary of argument, position, or recommendations
- Visualization of future (optional)
- Challenge or appeal for action
- Closing thought

References:
(Books, magazines, newspapers, Web sites, etc.)

FIGURE 14.6 Persuasive outline format.

challenge or appeal for action. It's also a good idea to add one last persuasive push by vividly picturing the future for your audience. The visualization step of the motivated sequence listed previously explains how to use the positive, negative, or contrast methods in visualizing the future.

You can use Speech Builder Express to help you create your introduction and conclusion. Select "Introduction" and "Conclusion" from the left-hand menu and follow the instructions. For short reminders from this chapter about introductions and conclusions, click on the "Tutor" button.

Step 7: Review Your Presentation to Ensure It Is Ethical

Ethical problems are more likely to occur in persuasive rather than informative situations. Speakers may be led into unethical behavior when they are deciding which emotional and logical appeals to use and how to establish speaker credibility. In

Chapter 1 we defined *ethics* as "the moral principles that guide our judgments about the good and bad, right and wrong, of communication" (Shockley-Zalabak, 2009). It is not always easy to see the rightness and wrongness of communication. Does the end ever justify the means? How about the following:

- A passenger who talks a hijacker into giving up his gun by telling the hijacker lies.

- A union leader who gets union members to vote a certain way by making up statistics.

- An advertising promoter who doubles previous sales by making false promises about a certain product.

- A student who invents the evidence used in his speech because he has no time for research due to a family illness.

- Parents who greatly exaggerate a problem to convince their child not to participate in a highly dangerous activity.

What if any of the listeners in the preceding examples found out they had been lied to? Should the possibility of getting caught determine a speaker's ethical standards? Although we can't deny that ethics may depend at times on the situation, *real persuasion does not involve manipulation, trickery, coercion, or force.* In persuasion, the individual's right to decide cannot be prevented. According to Joseph DeVito (2008, p. 112), *communicators are ethical "to the extent* that they facilitate a person's freedom of choice by presenting the person with accurate information." On the other hand, DeVito says that: "*Communicators are unethical to the extent that they* interfere with people's freedom of choice by preventing them from securing information relevant to the choices they will make." With this definition, speakers who lie or twist evidence, or use extreme emotional or fear–threat appeals, would be considered unethical regardless of the rightness or goodness of their purpose.

Because speakers have a great deal of *influence* on their audiences, they also have a great deal of *responsibility* to their audiences.

Step 8: Practice Your Presentation to Gain Confidence

Work for a dynamic yet conversational delivery. While you practice, videotape your presentation. Practice makes it easier to manage any situational anxiety that may stifle your forcefulness. As you know, a dynamic yet relaxed delivery improves your credibility and persuasiveness. You can see video clips of sample persuasive speech on your Premium Website for *Communicating for Results*. See the end of this chapter for more information about these sample speeches.

Team Presentations

In some organizations, team presentations of two or more people are more common than individual presentations. The team presentations given by IBM, for example, are well known in the industry. Team presentations are more common in larger organizations where the budgets are large and the stakes are high—for example, a manufacturing team bidding on a building contract, or a cable TV company asking for a city franchise. Team presentations can also be successful with only two or three speakers and a limited budget—for example, a team of insurance salespeople explaining a policy to a client or two partners attempting to get a bank loan to start a small business.

Team presentations have the obvious advantages of shared responsibility, more expertise during the presentation and the question–answer period, and an impressive appearance. But team presentations are difficult to coordinate, time consuming, and fairly expensive.

Effective Team Presentations

Successful team presentations have three characteristics (Leech, 2004):

- Well-organized, well-supported, smooth-flowing content.
- Creative, professional, and well-used visual aids.
- Smooth, polished, and dynamic team performance.

Content Team presentations can be either informative or persuasive and should follow the basic steps discussed in Chapters 11 and previously in this chapter. In the initial organization stage, you might benefit by having members write their ideas on sticky notes—one idea per note ("Rules for Team Presentations," 2004). Use the wall or tabletop to organize the notes, moving them around until a basic outline is formed.

Later, each presenter can prepare storyboards of their part of the presentation—again, tape each person's storyboards to the wall for ease of viewing by other members. While you read them, imagine that you are an audience member. Is each presentation completely clear? Are the main points obvious? Would you doubt any of the main points? What additional information or visual aids would ease those doubts? Does each member's presentation flow smoothly into the next? Finding and correcting problems early in the planning process is very important. Otherwise, you may be forced to make last-minute changes requiring new visuals. Then, instead of a relaxed dry run of the entire presentation, you'll have a tense, frantic session.

Visual Aids Visual aids should be consistent in appearance throughout the presentation. If one member has professional-looking computer visuals and another has handwritten transparencies, the overall impact is diminished. We suggest that all the team's final visuals be prepared by one group member or by the graphic arts department in your organization. If individuals are responsible for their own visual aids, decide early on such things as font style, size, and color for titles and text; background color or template; and style of graphics. Review Chapter 13 for specific suggestions on preparing effective visual aids.

Team members should practice using their visual aids in front of at least one other team member who can offer suggestions if needed. Awkward handling of visuals can ruin the effect of a well-organized presentation.

You can estimate the length of the team presentation by the number of visuals you plan to use. Most people spend 1 to 2 minutes per visual. Twenty visual aids at 2 minutes per visual would make at least a 40-minute presentation. Stay within the time prearranged with your audience.

Performance A polished and dynamic team performance requires practice, revision, and more practice. Each member should practice alone or with a partner, and then the team should have one or more dry runs of the entire presentation. Videotape the practice sessions if possible.

One team member needs to be the coordinator/leader—preferably a member with past team experience, speaking experience, and leadership abilities. Marjorie Brody (2003) recommends that a team leader should be a "subject matter expert." An effective team leader also must be objective in critiquing and directing the presenters. During the actual presentation, the coordinator presents the introduction and conclusion, introduces members, provides transitions if members fail to do so, and directs the question-and-answer session.

If you decide to have a question-and-answer session, plan ahead how you will handle it. Anticipate possible questions and determine who has the most expertise to answer specific topic areas. In addition, the leader should:

- Mention in the introduction that there will be a brief question-and-answer period at the end of the presentation and ask audience members to jot down questions during the presentation. Then, at the end of the presentation, either ask for questions by a show of hands or collect the questions from the audience. This allows you to answer several good questions and ignore undesirable ones.

- Rephrase any confusing or negative questions in a clear and positive manner.

- If a question appears irrelevant or will take too long to answer, thank the audience member for the question and offer to speak personally with him or her after the session.

- Before directing the question to a group member, repeat the question to make sure that everyone heard it.

- End the session on time with (a) a final summary of the presentation that refocuses audience attention back to the main ideas or proposals presented by the group and (b) a pleasing, memorable closure.

Adapting Team Presentations to the Media

Mass media, especially television and teleconferencing, are now used by businesses and organizations of all sizes to advertise products, project company image, answer criticisms, educate employees on company policy and procedures, and train employees in job skills. As your career advances, you will probably be asked to tape a team presentation for closed-circuit viewing or even to participate in a local talk show or news interview. You will feel much more relaxed and confident as an interviewee and will be prepared to do what you can to help the process work more smoothly if you also are aware of the following tips (Blythin & Samovar, 1985):

- Avoid white clothing. Even a white shirt or blouse, white trim on clothes, or a white handkerchief in your suit pocket can give the camera technicians problems.

- Stripes, polka dots, or patterns tend to bleed together. Solid colors are best.

- Avoid warm or hot colors such as red, pink, or orange. Cool colors (blues and greens) are preferred.

- Avoid clothing with sharp color contrast or clothing made of shiny material. A slight contrast is desirable, however.

- Both women and men look slimmer in clothing fitted at the waist.

- Avoid shiny jewelry (e.g., rings, necklaces, tie clasps, and so on).

- Men generally do not need makeup. If you have a heavy beard or a shiny fore-head, the producer may want you to apply some powder. Women should wear regular makeup (e.g., eyeliner is suggested).

- Studio lights are hot, so you may wish to wear lightweight fabrics. If the lights are so bright that you are squinting, tell the floor manager so they can be adjusted.

Adapting your team presentation to the media is not difficult once the team members have become familiar with the technical equipment and environment used.

We hope we have not only convinced you that speaking skills are necessary for successful business and professional people, but also have included enough specific information in this chapter to enable you to prepare an effective persuasive presentation. Speaking skill is not learned overnight, it takes practice. Rather than trying to avoid assignments, *volunteer* for them if you are serious about improving your speaking skills. With careful planning and practice, you can become a successful speaker.

Sample Persuasive Presentation

Title: "Untreated Depression in America" by Sean Stewart
Position Statement: Untreated depression in the United States has reache epidemic proportions and should no longer be tolerated.

INTRODUCTION
- **Attention-getter:**
  --For Dr. Leon Rosenberg, the quality of life was something that he never took for granted.
  --With a stellar career as a genetics professor at Princeton University, Rosenberg's career continued to reach new heights. [Ref. 1]
  --Unfortunately, so did his mood disorder. As the Baltimore Sun of September 1, 2003, asserts, Rosenberg had suffered from a mood disorder for more than 30 years but had declined treatment for fear that his career could be adversely affected. [Ref. 2]
- **Audience motivation:** According to ABCNews.com of June 17, 2003, some 33 million or more Americans suffer from the debilitating condition of depression. But even more shocking is that over 78 percent receive insufficient care, which means there are some 25 million of us who are victims of the growing epidemic of untreated depression.
- **Thesis:** We will look at the problem surrounding this disease, determine why it persists, and suggest some possible solutions that are desperately needed.

BODY
I. **Untreated depression is a rampant problem in today's society.**
   A. Depression affects people in their prime working years. [Ref. 3] (NMHA website)
      1. Untreated depression accounts for more than 200 million workdays lost yearly.
      2. According to the AMA, 97 percent of those reporting depression said the disease affected their work, home life, and relationships. [Ref. 4]
      3. These untreated affects cost the United States economy $148 billion annually. [Ref. 5]
   B. Depression is a leading cause of suicide.
      1. The elderly have the highest suicide rate—largely due to untreated depression. [Ref. 6]
      2. Untreated depression is the leading cause of suicide and the third leading cause of death for 15- to 24-year-olds; the sixth leading cause of death for 5- to 14-year-olds. [Ref. 3]
      3. 12-year-old Timothy O'Clair was treated for depression, but 6 weeks later hanged himself in his closet shocking everyone from his parents to his doctors. *Transition*: Now that we see how serious untreated depression is, let's look at the causes. [Ref. 7]

II. **Untreated depression persists for two reasons.**
   A. Reason one is the social stigma surrounding depression.
      1. Many people still view depression as a weakness and fear the reactions of others. [Ref. 8]
      2. Even famed *60 Minutes* journalist Mike Wallace never sought treatment. In the book *On the Edge of Darkness*, Wallace states:

FIGURE 14.7a Sample persuasive speech outline.

"I was ashamed. For years depression meant the crazy house. For years I never sought treatment, and as I look back on it, my depression seems like damned foolishness, which is one of the reasons why I speak of it now." [Ref. 9]

3. According to Dr. John Zajecka of St. Luke's Medical Center in Chicago, many people would rather live with the disorder than face the stigma of treatment. [Ref. 10]

B. Reason two is the lack of insurance coverage.
   1. Most insurance companies cover mental illness differently than physical illness.
   2. Stricter limits are placed on mental health care than for physical ailments such as cancer and diabetes. [Ref. 11]

Transition: Although limited health-care coverage and social stigma have prevented millions from seeking treatment of depression, there are things we can and must do.

III. There are several solutions to untreated depression.
   A. First, we must educate those lacking knowledge of depression.
      1. Read books like *Darkness Visible* or *On the Edge of Darkness* [Refs. 12 & 9]
      2. Look for behaviors like persistent sadness, anxiousness, empty moods, difficulty concentrating, lack of sleeping, limited health, or a waning sex drive [Refs. 3 & 13]
   B. Second, we must encourage and help those suffering from depression.
      1. Speak about the nature of depression and offer to take them to the doctor.
      2. If you are depressed, make an appointment with a doctor and go to the website for college students (www.Ulifeline.org) which offers help 24/7. [Ref. 14]
   C. Finally, we must do our part to enact health care legislation like Timothy's Law in the state of New York.

CONCLUSION
- While Dr. Rosenberg finally received treatment for this mental disorder, there are over 25 million of us who are victims of this disease.
- By looking at the problem, its causes, and enacting some solutions, hopefully one day we can finally end the depressing consequences of our neglect.

REFERENCES:
1. Bor, J. (2003, September 1). Hopkins professor wrote to inspire others. *Baltimore Sun*, 11A.
2. *ABCNews.com*. (2003, June 17).
3. *National Mental Health Association website*. (2003). Accessed at http://www.nmha.org.
4. Glass, R. (2003, June 18). Awareness about depression. *Journal of the American Medical Association*, 289(23), 3169-3170.
5. Depression Fact Sheet. (2003, July 17). Accessed at http://www.med.umich.edu/opm/newspage/2003/depressionfact.htm
6. *Washington Post*. (2003, November 25).
7. *Post Standard* of Syracuse, New York. (2003, August 14).
8. University of Nebraska's Department of Obstetrics and Gynecology website. (2004, January 6). Accessed at http://www.unmc.edu/olson.
9. Cronkite, K. (1994). *On the Edge of Darkness*. New York: Delta.
10. Zajecka, J. (2003, September 2). St. Luke's Medical Center in Chicago. Depression white paper.
11. *New York Times*. (2003, September 1).
12. Styron, W. (1990). *Darkness Visible: A memoir of madness*. New York: Random House
13. Hasemyer, D. (2003, September 28). Depression lurks on road through midlife. *San Diego Union-Tribune*, 5.
14. *ULifeLine.org*. (2004). Accessed at http://www.ulifeline.org/main/Home.html.

FIGURE 14.7b Persuasive speech outline (continued).

Student Persuasive Presentation

Now that you've explored different types of persuasive presentations and how best to prepare and deliver them, go to your Premium Website for *Communicating for Results* to watch a video clip of a sample persuasive presentation given by a student. This speech, "Untreated Depression in America," was given by Sean Stewart at the Texas Intercollegiate Forensics Convention in February 2004 (see

his outline in Figure 14.7). You can also use your Premium Website to critique this speech online and, if requested, e-mail your response to your instructor.

Additionally, you can use your Premium Website to watch and critique several other persuasive speeches including "No More Sugar!" by Hans Erian, "Counterfeit Drugs" by Lindsay Wakefield, "Reduce Your Alcohol Intake" by Susan Cramer, and "Endometriosis: Possible Cause Will Surprise You" by Rebecca DeCamp (see her speech outline in the Appendix, Figure A.13 and as a persuasive report in Figure A.14).

CHAPTER 14
REVIEW

Vince Bucci/Getty Images

Key Terms

anchors (375)

attitudes (375)

beliefs (375)

boomerang effect (375)

causal pattern (392)

central route (375)

claim pattern (392)

comparative advantages pattern (393)

competency (383)

counter persuasion (378)

consistency theories (375)

credibility (381)

criteria satisfaction pattern (394)

deductive reasoning (392)

dynamism (383)

elaboration likelihood theory (375)

ethos (381)

evidence (376)

fallacious reasoning (381)

hierarchy of needs (385)

inductive reasoning (392)

information-integration theory (375)

inoculation theory (380)

latitude of acceptance (375)

latitude of noncommitment (375)

latitude of rejection (375)

logic (376)

logos (376)

motivated sequence (395)

objectivity (383)

opinion leader (387)

organizational rank (383)

pathos (384)

peripheral route (375)

persuade (373)

presentation to actuate (373)

presentation to convince (373)

problem-solution pattern (393)

psychological needs (384)

social judgment theory (375)

trustworthiness (382)

valence (375)

values (375)

weight (375)

Summary

Persuasive presentations are formal or informal presentations designed to influence the audience's choices. Successful persuasion depends on the evidence and logic of the message, the credibility of the persuader, the psychological needs of the listeners, and the opinions held by key audience members.

Preparing a persuasive presentation begins with analyzing your listeners and their needs, writing your purpose, and planning ways to increase your credibility, if necessary. Following that, you must research your topic and decide on the best method of presenting the evidence, decide how to organize your presentation, plan the verbal and visual supports, ensure that your presentation is ethical, and practice the presentation.

Persuasive presentations are sometimes given as a team; such presentations are effective if the team presents well-organized, well-supported content, uses visual aids that are consistent in appearance and unify the overall presentation, and practices its performance. If your team presentation must be adapted to the media, you and your team members will need to become familiar with the media equipment and environment to be used and, as always, practice the presentation.

Communicating for Results Online

Check your understanding of Chapter 14 at the Premium Website for *Communicating for Results*. Your Premium Website gives you quick and easy access to the electronic resources that accompany this text. These resources include:

- **Study tools** that will help you assess your learning and prepare for exams (student companion workbook, digital glossary, key term flash cards, and review quizzes).

- **Activities and assignments** that will help you hone your knowledge, analyze professional communication situations, build your public speaking skills throughout the course, and learn to work effectively in teams (Awareness Checks, Checkpoints, and Collaborative Learning Activities).

- **Media resources** that will help you explore communication concepts online (web links), develop your speech outlines (Speech Builder Express 3.0), watch and critique videos of professional communication situations and sample speeches (Interactive Video Activities), upload your speech videos for peer reviewing and critique other students' speeches (Speech Studio online speech review tool), and download chapter review so you can study when and where you'd like (Audio Study Tools).

This chapter's key terms, Collaborative Learning Activities, and Checkpoint activities are also featured on the following pages, and you can find this chapter's Awareness Check activity in the body of the chapter. For more information or to access this book's online resources, visit www.cengage.com/login.

Collaborative Learning Activities

1. In groups of four to seven, pick a good topic for a persuasive presentation. Determine the following: (a) a well-worded position statement; (b) the type of organization that would work best with your topic and why; (c) at least two specific ways to create audience involvement with your topic—be creative. Be prepared to share your results with other groups.

2. In small groups, discuss the use of logos and ethos in presenting a persuasive presentation. Identify two key pointers for each factor that you think would be the most help for persuasive speakers and why. Be sure to discuss the different ways to cite evidence in a speech. Why is one way more persuasive than the others?

3. Take a look at the section on persuasive messages in Appendix: Written Communication In small groups of three to five, compare the advice on persuasion from the appendix with the information on persuasion in this chapter. What are the main differences? What are the similarities? Thinks of examples from past job experiences to

404 COMMUNICATING FOR RESULTS: A GUIDE FOR BUSINESS AND THE PROFESSIONS

add to your discussion. Be prepared to share your conclusions with other groups.

Checkpoints

Checkpoint 14.1 Preparing and Practicing a Persuasive Presentation
Prepare a 10-minute persuasive presentation on a topic you deal with regularly. Videotape yourself if possible. How do you sound? Did you notice any nonverbal problems? Why not volunteer to give this presentation to a real audience? The more you practice, the more professional you become.

Checkpoint 14.2 Determining What Persuades Businesspeople

Checkpoint 14.3 Fitting Presentation Method to Audience Type

Checkpoint 14.4 Can Somebody Call the Doctor?

Checkpoint 14.5 There Is No "I" in Team

Checkpoint 14.6 Team Persuasion: Organizational Policy?

Checkpoint 14.7 Persuasive Presentations (Individual and Team) Links

Written Communication

As you read this Appendix,

Determine the four functions of effective written communication, and **list** specifics on writing successful e-mail messages and letters.

Discuss guidelines for writing effective resumes including the conventional, scannable, e-mail, and web resumes.

Pinpoint guidelines for writing to inform –especially informative outlines and informative reports.

Summarize guidelines for writing to persuade –especially persuasive outlines and persuasive reports.

Effective communicators need to know more than just how to communicate orally; they must also know how to use written communication. Sometimes your first contact with people is through written messages such as e-mail or a letter of application. Therefore, the first impression you make on a person is often written as well. How impressive are your written messages? If you aren't sure or already know that your writing needs some improvement, the specific written skills covered by this appendix should help. We will cover e-mail messages, letters, resumes, writing to inform, and writing to persuade. By polishing each of these skills, you will improve your business and professional communication by enriching both the clarity of your writing and the impression you make with it.

Before we look at specifics on each type of written communication, let's refer to some general information that relates to most all written messages.

Effective Written Communication

The best written communication performs at least four important functions: it adapts to the audience, makes a good first impression, is effectively organized, and looks professional with proper formatting and typeface.

Adapts to the Audience

The key to all communication whether spoken or written is to know your audience. Therefore, effective written communication adapts to the audience. For example, your language and specific references should differ when writing to a college friend, a business professional, or a retired adult. This means that you will have to do enough research to discover their needs, preferences, and expectations. Once you have a clear picture of your readers, imagine them sitting across from you while you write. When you imagine that you are talking to an actual person as you write, your tone will sound more natural and friendly.

Consider how your audience is likely to react while reading your message: how would *you* react if you received this same e-mail or letter? Remember that because there are no facial expressions or gestures to accompany a written message, an accurate interpretation is more difficult to make. It's a good idea to read your message out loud and think of possible misinterpretations especially if you are angry or disappointed as you write the message. When possible, adapt to your audience by giving them the benefit of the doubt and a way to save face—you never know what impact you may have.

In an online class, I received an assignment that was so well written and witty, so far above anything a freshman would turn in that I was certain that the student had either plagiarized or had a more experienced student write the assignment for her. I thought about giving the student a failing grade, but at the last moment I decided to give her the benefit of the doubt and assigned her an "A" and wrote the following: "Your poem analysis is so far above the normal freshman writing that I am amazed. If you actually wrote this analysis, I want you to know that you have a special writing talent that I hope you nurture because it is outstanding." She replied: "I just wanted to say thank you for the comments you left about my poem analysis. I have always loved writing. My father and one of my brothers are very gifted writers, combining subtle wit with clever insight. I especially needed that shot of confidence right now, while I'm struggling with my thesis in my Comp class. Maybe your uplifting comments will help me to tap into the writer that exists in me and apply that talent to my writing class."

Makes a Good First Impression

Once you are writing to a specific audience, it is easier to make a good first impression. Just like an effective personal interview or oral presentation grabs attention and motivates the listener to pay attention, it is important to make a good first impression in written communication if you hope to grab the reader's interest. Why is reader interest important? Because "writing that isn't interesting usually isn't read" (Newsom & Haynes, 2008). Also, writing that creates a negative first impression is unlikely to get the response you were seeking whether from a colleague, client, or job interviewer. There are several ways to make a good first impression:

- *Focus on the receiver's interests and needs.* A cover letter that accompanies a resume should focus on how you can meet the needs of the organization; an e-mail addressed to team members should also focus on team benefits. Limit your use of *I* and *we* and use more of *you, your,* and *our.*

- *Keep your tone friendly yet professional.* Generally this means keeping your words and sentences relatively short in length, using correct grammar, and avoiding spelling and punctuation errors. If you have to include some bad news, try to include something pleasant in the same sentence (Lehman & Dufrene, 2008). Which would you rather read:

  1. Your overall grade on the exam was satisfactory.

  2. Your overall grade on the exam was satisfactory; however, your written analysis on the case study was excellent.

- *Get to the point quickly making key ideas obvious.* Using bullets and boldface will highlight key ideas and present an organized and professional appearance to an e-mail message, a memo, or a letter.

- *Proofread* at least twice after completing the message to check for sentence structure, misspellings, and typos. As the cartoon on this page so effectively illustrates, errors occur to the best of us but do not make a good impression.

Is Effectively Organized: Proper Clarity and Length

The basic information on organization that we covered in the speaking chapters applies to written communication as well. Effective written communication contains a *greeting* that grabs the reader's attention and makes the purpose of the message clear; a *body* that presents the main points in an organized manner and clarifies and supports them with materials such as statistics and examples; and a *closing* that summarizes your purpose and main points and ends with a final thought or reference to any needed action.

Ineffective writers often leave off the introduction and conclusion and concentrate on the body, which makes the content more difficult to understand. It is the introduction and conclusion that add clarity and give the reader direction, which allows for fast reading and better memory of your content. Content that takes too long to read or understand is often ignored and certainly not read all the way to the

© 2009 Ted Goff

© 2009 Ted Goff. Reprinted by permission. www.tedgoff.com

"And now, it's time for me to present this year's Typo Awerd."

end. If people are asking you the same questions that you answered in your written message, it's pretty clear that they didn't read all that you wrote. Check your writing style. Did you include the introduction and conclusion? Did you use bullets to speed up reading of the content?

In addition to lack of organization and clarity, length is a problem in written communication. Ideally, an e-mail or memo should include only one major idea or purpose—you might be able to include two or possibly three different ideas or purposes if you separate each with boldfaced titles and use good transitions between them. More than three, it's best to send multiple e-mail or messages. You can include more ideas in a letter but still need to segment each idea with a clear title and easy-to-read paragraphs or bullets. If your communication is sent in two or more messages, be sure to label each as Part 1or Part 2.

Looks Professional: Proper Formatting and Typeface

Much of the advice for effective formatting and typeface choices you have already read about in Chapter 13, *Professional Visual Aids*. For example, in Chapter 13 we discussed the differences between a *serif* typeface which has small lines that extend from letter stems used to move the eyes along when reading text and a *sans serif* typeface which is a geometric-looking, simple typeface that is easy to read and great for titles. Either works for written messages but normally no more than two typefaces should be used in a single message—perhaps a serif such as Times New Roman or Century for your text and a sans serif such as Arial or Verdana for titles. Another suggestion from Chapter 13 is to avoid using all capitals in your writing unless a single word or short phrase is needed for emphasis. Words in all capitals are more difficult to read than words in upper and lower case because the instant recognition we gain from letter extensions such as the *l* and *f* and the dot over the *i* are missing (Adams et al., 2001). In addition, in e-mail, words in all capitals looks like you are shouting and may offend the reader. In Chapter 13 we also discussed the importance of not overloading a page with too much text and of leaving empty space called *white space* around the document. White space keeps the document from looking cluttered and speeds reading comprehension. Besides setting your margins to allow for at least 1 inch, using ragged right margins instead of justified margins allows for more white space. All these suggestions apply to all types of written messages as well as PowerPoint slides. One additional point deals with the size of type to use in your written messages. This will be discussed later in the section on writing resumes, but in general the best advice is to use 11-point or 12-point type for your text. Any smaller is too difficult to read especially if the print quality is poor; any larger looks like you didn't have enough to say and wanted to fill more space. Titles can use a larger size such as 14-point or even a 16-point type.

Writing Successful E-mail Messages

Although instant messaging (IM) and text messaging have their place, e-mail is the preferred method of communication in the business setting when face-to-face isn't possible and there's no time to mail a written letter or memo. Although personal friends may overlook misspelled words, use of lower case in place of capitals, and shorthand abbreviations used in text messages and chat rooms, your business associates won't.

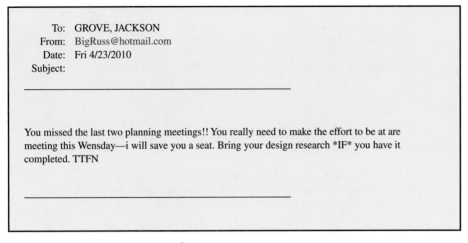

To: GROVE, JACKSON
From: BigRuss@hotmail.com
Date: Fri 4/23/2010
Subject:

You missed the last two planning meetings!! You really need to make the effort to be at are meeting this Wensday—i will save you a seat. Bring your design research *IF* you have it completed. TTFN

Figure A.1 Inappropriate e-mail.

How would you feel if you received the e-mail message in Figure A.1? It isn't professional and certainly doesn't send a good impression, does it? Here are just a few things that are wrong with this email:

- It has no subject line to indicate key information.
- It was sent from a personal e-mail address with a non-professional handle.
- It has no greeting or closing.
- It is too brief to include all necessary information, such as where the meeting will be held and the time of the meeting.
- It has a misspelled word, an incorrect word, and a lower-case "i."
- It has a negative and accusatory tone that will likely make the recipient angry.
- It includes shorthand more appropriate to a text message.

The worst part of this email may be the tone that is used. According to Raymond Friedman and Steven Currall (2003), because messages sent by e-mail have no vocal or nonverbal cues to meaning, and because people tend to read them more than once, even messages that aren't intended as critical "can be easily misinterpreted as being more aggressive than intended" (p. 1342). If you have ever received an e-mail that made you instantly angry, you have experienced this phenomenon. Therefore, it is important to read your e-mail from the receiver's viewpoint and edit it carefully listening for tone and possible interpretation. Be ready to apologize if the reaction you receive is negative—even if you don't think it is your fault. Take a look at Figure A.2 for a more professional approach than our original e-mail in Figure A.1.

Writing a Successful Letter

Although letters are more formal than e-mail, they still have tone and carry an impression. Let's look at three types of letters you are the most likely to send: the letter of application that accompanies your resume, the thank-you letter sent after an interview, and the follow-up letter used if you do not receive an invitation for an interview.

> To: GROVE, JACKSON
> From: Russell J. Hampton (Russell.Hampton@YardConstruction.com)
> Date: Fri 4/23/2010
> Subject: Important planning meeting on Wednesday, May 5 at 1:00 p.m.
>
> ―――――――――――――――――――――――――
>
> Dear Jackson,
>
> Please arrange your schedule to attend our next **Strategic Planning Meeting** on **Wednesday, May 5 at 1:00 p.m.** in Building B, Room 29.
>
> I know that you have been extremely busy working on the Yarley project and hope it is wrapping up as you and your customers anticipated. Your design expertise has undoubtedly made this an outstanding landscape. I am looking forward to the tour this Friday.
>
> It is your design expertise that is so needed in the Strategic Planning Meeting on May 5th. We concentrated on other issues in the previous meetings because you were unable to attend and have them almost completed. However, to stay on budget, our next meeting should be our last meeting and we need your input. Two weeks remain before the meeting, so please call me or drop by the office if I can help you in any way.
>
> Hope to hear from you soon,
> Russ
>
> Russell J. Hampton
> Chair, Strategic Planning
> Yard Construction Services
> E-Mail: Russell.hampton@yardconstruction.com
> Phone: (817) 515-9934
> Cell: (972) 229-7227

Figure A.2 Appropriate e-mail.

The Letter of Application or Cover Letter

The *letter of application*—sometimes called a cover letter—should give just enough information about you and your capabilities to interest the employer in talking with you personally (Kennedy, 2009; Lurie & Welz, 2006; Yate, 2008c). Each letter should relate specifically to the company and person to whom you are writing (see Figure A.3). Therefore, if you haven't already done so, find out as much as you can about each firm and individual you plan to ask for an interview. Try to talk with someone who has been working with the firm; ask for literature, such as the annual report, that explains the firm and its policies; check the company's website or blog (look on Google for both); or read about the organization at the following sites: CareerBuilder.com, FastCompany. com, Monster.com, QuintCareers.com, Wetfeet.com, or Jobster.com. (You can access links to these sites through your Premium Website for *Communicating for Results*.)

You can also check your college or city libraries for the following databases:

- Business and Company Resource Center by the Gale Group (type in company name or browse; also includes links to articles about the company).

- Associations Unlimited by the Gale Group (contains information on nonprofit organizations).

- EBSCOHost (click on Company Profiles, then type company name or browse; includes complete company reports in PDF format).

1355 Edna Street
Napa, CA 94558

September 20, 2010

Mr. John F. Schmitz, Owner
Schmitz Furniture & Carpet
705 North Locust Street
Dulsura. CA 94661

Dear Mr. Schmitz:

Since I have received the honor of being named top salesperson for the past three years by my employer, Fabric Imports, I believe that I could make a valuable contribution to Schmitz Furniture & Carpet. Your advertisement in today's *Los Angeles Times* indicated that you were looking for a carpet salesperson. My experience and communication skills qualify me for this position.

Last year at Fabric Imports, I added ten new accounts because of my ability to sell to walk-in customers. I enjoy the close working relationship with key accounts. In addition, my knowledge of Spanish and personal computers can reach out to a variety of customers thereby increasing your sales.

I would like to personally meet with you to discuss more thoroughly my qualifications for this position. Although mornings work best for me, another time can be arranged to meet your schedule. For your convenience, I have enclosed a copy of my resume. You may contact me at my home or cell phone as referenced on my resume or you may leave a message at (415) 666-4332.

Thank you for your consideration. I look forward to hearing from you soon.

Sincerely,

Joel C. Reyes

Joel C. Reyes

Enc: Resume

Figure A.3 Sample letter of application.

If the company doesn't have a website and is too small to appear in any of the preceding sources, call the company receptionist or the sales, marketing, public relations, or human resources departments for information. Once you have discovered as much about the company as possible, you are ready to complete your letter of application. Keep in mind that your letter is the first indication the reader has of both your communication skills and your writing style so be sure to have someone proofread it for errors and for readability. The following guidelines are suggested when writing a letter of application:

- *Address it to a specific person by name.* Include the job title in the inside address. If you address your letter to the "Personnel Manager," "Manager," or a similarly vague title without a name, the letter may never reach the right person; or if it does, the letter may not be answered. If you address the letter to a specific person, he or she has a responsibility to answer it. Also, that person may be impressed that you cared enough to find out his or her name.

- Include the following:
  - A brief greeting including how you heard about the opening.
  - The position for which you are applying.
  - Your basic qualifications for the position and any accomplishments or career highlights that might interest the employer enough to contact you.
  - Any other information you feel is pertinent to the specific job without repeating information found in your resume; justify any holes in the resume if necessary. If you have additional information/resumes on your personal website, be sure to mention it. Be enthusiastic; sell yourself.
- *End with a paragraph requesting an interview*, including your phone number and when you can be reached.
- *Be sure that you include the date, a return address, and an inside address (e-mail letters do not need to include addresses), closing, and a signature.* Sign the letter in dark blue or black ink.

The Thank-You Letter

After every interview whether actual or informational, you will want to send a *thank you letter* or card. A survey of 150 interviewers found that almost 90% of them "consider a written thank you influential in evaluating candidates" (Lublin, 2008, B1). Although an e-mail thank you may be effective, a hand-written card or letter shows more professionalism and indicates that you are really interested in the position (see Figure A.4). For effective thank-you messages, consider the following suggestions (adapted from Guffey, 2010 and Lehman & DuFrene, 2008):

- Keep the tone of your thank-you message formal yet friendly—avoid sounding chummy.
- Your message should be fairly short but include enough details so the interviewer will recall your specific interview.
- Begin by thanking the interviewer for the interview—mention the specific job and the date of the interview.
- If something out-of-the-ordinary occurred during the interview, be sure to mention it to help the interviewer recall your specific interview. Otherwise, remind the interviewer of one or two key issues or problem areas discussed and how your skills, communication abilities, and experience could help solve those problems. If the interviewer is having difficulty deciding between you and one or two other candidates, your letter reinforcing your strengths may be just the persuasive nudge needed to get you another interview or a job offer.
- Be sure to mention your interest and enthusiasm for the position.
- If the interviewer asked for any additional information or you thought of something that you forgot to mention during the interview, be sure to cover it now or include an enclosure.
- End with something similar to "I am looking forward to hearing from you soon."

1355 Edna Street
Napa, CA 94558

October 15, 2010

Mr. John F. Schmitz, Owner
Schmitz Furniture & Carpet
705 North Locust Street
Dulsura. CA 94661

Dear Mr. Schmitz:

Thank you for the delightful interview on Friday, October 8 for the position of carpet salesperson. If you recall, you had just received a shipment of allergy-free carpet made from bamboo and we looked through it together. It was my first time to feel and smell this new carpet and I can't wait to sell it to people like my sister who has put off buying new carpet because of her allergies. In fact, I called her as soon as I got home and she may have already come by the showroom to see it.

You mentioned that you were hoping to double your sales this year. With my experience as top salesperson for the past three years and my communication skills in handling a wide variety of customers, I think I am just the person to help you achieve your goal. In addition, you have many Hispanic customers who do not speak English and I am fluent in Spanish.

You will find me a diligent and enthusiastic employee and I look forward to working with you and your outstanding staff. For your convenience, an updated copy of my resume is enclosed. Please contact me at my home or cell phone as referenced on my resume or you may leave a message at (415) 666-4332.

Thank you for your consideration. I hope to hear from you soon.

Sincerely,

Joel C. Reyes

Joel C. Reyes

Enc: Resume

Figure A.4 Sample thank you letter.

The Follow-up Letter

If a few weeks have passed since your interview and you have not heard from the interviewer even after sending a thank-you note and after calling to the office to restate your interest, it most likely means that you were not selected for the position. Whether you received an official rejection notice or not, don't overlook the importance of a follow-up letter that stresses your continued interest in working for the company (See Figured A.5). You never know—the person hired may not work out or may take another job or additional jobs may become available. If the job seemed to be a perfect fit for you or you are especially interested in the particular company, a follow-up letter is a must. Here are some suggestions for effective follow-up letters:

- Express your disappointment at not receiving the position but thank the person for interviewing you and for notifying you promptly (if they did).

Mr. John F. Schmitz, Owner   October 25, 2010
Schmitz Furniture & Carpet
705 North Locust Street
Dulsura. CA 94661

Dear Mr. Schmitz:

Thank you for interviewing me for the position of carpet salesperson. I'm very disappointed that someone
else was hired for the position because I think my sales experience and communication skills are a good fit for
your company and goals of doubled growth. Even though I wasn't hired, I appreciate your letting me know so
quickly. Please keep my resume in your active file and let me know if you have another opening. Your showroom and product lines are excellent and I look forward to the possibility of working with you in the future. I
will call you later in the year to see if any new job openings are available.

Sincerely,

Joel C. Reyes

Joel C. Reyes
1355 Edna Street,
Napa, CA 94558
(415) 555-5760

Figure A.5 Sample follow-up letter.

- If you suspect that you did not get the position because of lack of experience or skill and are taking steps to correct the problem (such as working with a mentor or enrolling in a course), be sure to mention it. You may want to include a revised resume as well.

- If, in your reading, you come across an article that relates to a problem area discussed during the interview that you think will interest the interviewer, include a two-sentence review and the link to access the article. If the article isn't too long, make a copy and include it with your letter. Sharing information is a good way to make your name stand out and it shows your professionalism.

- End by expressing your interest in working for the person or company and ask that your resume remain in the active file. You might suggest that you will call in a couple of months to touch base and see if any new job openings are available.

Writing an Effective Resume

The basic types of resumes were discussed in Chapter 8—the conventional paper resume, the scannable resume, the e-mail resume, and the web resume. Although the scannable and e-mail resumes are used less often, in today's high tech world, you never know when one will be required. Because a quality resume can give you an advantage over others applying for the same position, it is good to have several different types prepared and ready to use at a moment's notice. Let's look at some specifics on how to write effective resumes.

The Conventional Paper Resume

Conventional resumes are the most fun to prepare because you can design in a professional wow factor. They are formatted to hand to the interviewer or to send through the mail—but are not meant to be scanned by computers or stored electronically. Use the information you gathered during your information-seeking interviews to help you decide whether to use a short, one-page resume or a longer, more detailed, two-page resume. There are many excellent resume books and Internet articles available (see for example, Kennedy, 2009; Whitcomb, 2006; Yate, 2008a). Sample conventional resumes are shown in Figures A.6 and A.7.

Joel C. Reyes
1355 Edna Street, Napa, CA 94558
Home phone: (415) 555-5760
Office: (415) 555-5745

OBJECTIVE Sales, Leading to Sales Supervision

AREAS OF
KNOWLEDGE

Personal selling	Team problem-solving
Correspondence	Customer relations
Fluent in Spanish	Time Management
Stock handling	Microsoft Office 2010
Data entry, 55wpm	Presentation skills
Complaint handling	Office Procedures

WORK EXPERIENCE

July 2007 to
Present

Salesperson, Fabric Imports, Napa, California
<u>Responsible</u> for sales, Spanish-speaking accounts, and customer relations.
<u>Achievements</u> include being top salesperson for last three years and adding ten new accounts.

Jan. 2005 to
June. 2007

Assistant to Dean of Instruction and Student Services
Richland College, Dallas, Texas
<u>Responsible</u> for maintaining calendar of student activities, coordinating on-campus student organizations, and meeting with student leaders to discuss goals, activities, budgets, and scholarships.
<u>Achievements</u> include developing a new procedure for handling student complaints.

Feb. 2004 to
Dec. 2004

Fountain clerk (part-time), Jack–in-the-Box, Dallas, Texas
<u>Achievements</u> include creating a best-selling shake flavor.

EDUCATION Associate of Arts Degree, 2007, Richland College, Dallas, Texas. Major in business with emphasis in sales and communication.

High School Diploma, 2004 Willard High School, Dallas, Texas.

EXTRACURRICULAR
ACTIVITIES
Student Government Representative
Young Salespeople of America
Phi Beta Kappa

REFERENCES Available upon request.

FIGURE A.6 Sample one-page conventional paper resume.

Basic Organization

Regardless of the length, conventional resumes usually follow the chronological, the functional, or the combination style. *Chronological resumes*—the resume style used most often by interviewees (Guffey, 2007, 2010; Yate, 2008a)—"emphasizes what you did, when you did it, and for whom you did it" (Brett, 1990, pp. 25–26). Work experience is highlighted and presented in reverse chronological order; dates are prominent. Include responsibilities and achievements for each position—in other words, don't just tell what you did, but also how well you did it. Don't forget awards and commendations. The sample resumes in this appendix follow the chronological style.

The *functional resume* emphasizes skills rather than work experience; it highlights accomplishments, with dates playing a less prominent role. The functional resume is normally for experienced job seekers who have a variety of experiences and wish to highlight specific skills. It is also recommended if you are changing careers, have been unemployed for a long period of time, or are near retirement (Enelow & Kursmark, 2006; Guffey, 2007, 2010; Yate, 2008a). Employers, however, generally prefer the chronological style.

There is a third type of resume—the *combination or hybrid resume*—that includes both chronological and functional aspects. According to Martin Yate (2008a), upward-moving, experienced professionals often prefer the combination resume. After the introductory information or summary, the combination resume begins with a functional look at achievements, skills, and personal abilities; follows with a chronological work history listing companies, positions, and accomplishments; and ends with education and any final items.

Information to Include

Experts recommend that both chronological and functional paper resumes include the following basic information:

- Name, address, and home and work telephone numbers.
- Objective or position desired.
- Education and (for recent graduates) educational highlights, including a brief list of job-related courses you have completed. If you have a college degree or a special certification or license, there is normally no need to list high schools attended.
- Areas of knowledge or professional highlights.
- Job experience, including job accomplishments and responsibilities. Usually, your jobs should be listed in reverse chronological order beginning with the most recent one. If you have little or no job experience, list your volunteer experience. The interpersonal and supervisory skills that the volunteer develops are as valuable as those developed in a paid position.

Other information of interest can be added if it shows character and is job related:

- Veteran
- Professional organizations
- Publications or patents
- Job-related hobbies, activities, or interests
- Accreditations or licenses
- Scholarships, awards, or honors
- Language ability (including knowledge of computer languages and programs)

RESUME

Joel C. Reyes
1355 Edna Street
Napa, CA 94558
Home phone: (415) 555-5760
Cell: (415) 229-5745

OBJECTIVE	Sales, Leading to Sales Supervision

AREAS OF KNOWLEDGE

Personal selling	Microsoft Office 2010
Customer relations	Team problem-solving
Office Procedures	Stock handling
Correspondence	Complaint handling
Presentation skills	Time management
Data entry, 55wpm	Fluent in Spanish

EXPERIENCE

July 2007 to Present

Fabric Imports, Napa, California
Position: Salesperson
Responsibilities:
• Personally sell to customers, including key accounts
• In charge of all Spanish-speaking customer accounts
• Handle customer complaints and adjust satisfactorily
• Assist in ordering stock and in promoting warehouse sales
Achievements:
• Top salesperson for the company for the last three years
• Added ten key accounts last year

Jan. 2005 to July 2007

Richland College, Dallas, Texas
Position: Assistant
Responsibilities:
• Provided assistance to the Dean of Instruction and Student Services
• Maintained calendar of student programs
• Coordinated on-campus student organizations and met with the student leaders to discuss goals, activities, budgets, and scholarships
Achievements:
• Developed new procedure for handling student complaints

FIGURE A.7 Sample two-page conventional paper resume.

The phrase "References available upon request" is often included in a resume, but some experts believe this statement is not necessary. Whether included or not, you should take a list of references with you to the interview. Normally, family members should not be used as references. Select people who know you well and can comment on either your communication and people skills or your work abilities and experiences, or both. Usually, three to five impressive references will work. Ask ahead of time if they are willing to serve as references, and include contact information for each interviewer.

Joel C. Reyes
Resume, Page 2

Feb. 2004 to Dec. 2004	Jack-In-the-Box, Dallas, Texas **Position:** Fountain Clerk (part-time) **Responsibilities:** • Took orders from drive-through window. • Prepared fountain items such as carbonated drinks and ice-cream orders. **Achievements:** • Created best selling new shake flavor
EDUCATIONAL HIGHLIGHTS	**Business** Salesmanship Advertising Principals Retailing Principles Motivation Seminar **Office Administration** Word-Processing Skills on Microsoft Word Shorthand Speed Building Office Management Administrative Procedures Business Correspondence in Spanish **Additional Courses** Business and Professional Communication Business Communication Counseling Spanish I-IV
EDUCATION	Richland College, Dallas, Texas, May 2007 Associate of Arts Degree in business with emphasis in sales and communication.
LANGUAGES	Speak and write fluent Spanish and am familiar with the Spanish dialects used in Southern California and Texas.
REFERENCES	Available upon request.

FIGURE A.7 (*Continued*)

Information to Avoid

Regardless of the style in which your resume is organized, it should use personal data in a way that indicates an awareness of current laws. Both federal and state legislation make it unlawful to discriminate in employment hiring on the basis of race, color, religion, sex, national origin, and, in most cases, age and physical disabilities. Even so, some companies prefer that personal data be included in the resume. It is not unlawful for you to include such data if you wish or if you feel it would be to your advantage. However, if you include personal data and other non-job-related information, there is no guarantee that this information will not be used against you in some way. For similar reasons, it is also advisable to omit specific salary preferences. If an application form asks you to state a desired salary, you can write "negotiable." Unless the information is pertinent in some way to the job, you are advised to omit the following kinds of information:

- Hobbies, activities, or interests that do not relate to the job. (Exception: hobbies, activities, and interests that reveal your creativity, leadership, character, and volunteerism usually should be included).

- Past, present, or desired salary.

- Personal data, such as race, gender, age, date of birth, city and state of birth, marital status, health, height, weight, number and ages of children, type of military discharge, or spouse's name.

When Preparing a Conventional Paper Resume:

- *Put the most important information first.* The reader may only read the top half of the page. Don't start with education unless it is outstanding. If both education and experience are weak, begin with areas of knowledge or accomplishments.

- *Include the basic information* under "Information to Include."

- *Make sure all information is job related.*

- *Make it neat.* No misspelled words.

- *Make it easy to read.* Use wide margins to make the resume appealing to the eye. Use phrases instead of complete sentences when possible. The reader should be able to skim the page to get basic information.

- *Keep it brief.* Usually one to two pages in length.

- *Print on heavy bond paper.* Make sure the print is letter quality.

The Scannable Resume

A *scannable resume* is a conventional paper resume that has been altered into a "computer-friendly" format that can be scanned into an electronic file, which can then be stored, searched, and downloaded (Whitcomb, 2006; Weddle, 2005, 2009b). The scannable resume serves two purposes: It provides a professional showcase of your abilities in paper form, and because of its formatting, it can be stored in a database and retrieved as needed. Employers, employment agencies, and search firms use scannable resumes to reduce their paper load and quickly locate qualified candidates in their database, although many prefer resumes directly downloaded onto their website. The scannable resume provides an acceptable compromise between a conventional paper resume and the e-mail or American standard code for information interchange (ASCII) resume. It is more professional looking than the latter, but it doesn't have to be sent as an attachment, which some employers and agencies reject because of possible virus infection.

Because scannable resumes are read by an optical character recognition (OCR) scanner, they must be plainer than conventional resumes. This means you should avoid colored or patterned paper; type sizes smaller than 12 point (scanners have problems reading small print); and fancy fonts or formatting, such as underlining, italics, or boxes (although boldface type works well).

When writing a scannable resume, think in keywords. *Keywords* (also called *tags*) are used by employers to describe a specific job. If your resume does not include the latest industry keywords (or their synonyms), it will not be selected during a computer search. Once your resume has been searched for keywords and identified as appropriate for a job vacancy, it is downloaded and printed out to be read by the

Joel C. Reyes
1355 Edna Street
Napa, CA 94558

(415) 555-5760 (Res.)   (415) 229-5745 (Cell)

KEY WORD SUMMARY

Sales and sales supervision. Four years in fabric import sales. Customer relations. Customer complaints. Team problem-solving. Files & records. Correspondence. Microsoft Office 2010. Data entry, 55 wpm. Fluent in Spanish. A.A., Business-2007.

EXPERIENCE

Fabric Imports   **Napa, California**
• Salesperson   7/07-Present
• Awarded top salesperson for the last three years.
• Strengthened customer relations with Spanish speaking accounts.
• Generated 10 new key accounts during last year.
• Ordered stock, promoted warehouse sales, and handled customer complaints.

Richland College   **Dallas, Texas**
• Assistant   1/05-7/07
• Assistant to Dean of Instruction and Student Services.
• Maintained calendar of student activities.
• Coordinated on-campus student organizations.
• Met with student leaders to discuss goals, activities, budgets, and scholarships.
• Developed less complicated procedure for handling student complaints.

Jack-in-the-Box   **Dallas, Texas**
Fountain Clerk (part-time)   02/04-12/04
• Took orders from drive-through window.
• Prepared fountain items such as carbonated drinks and ice-cream orders.
• Cleaned counters and tables.
• Created best-selling new shake flavor.

EDUCATION

Richland College   **Dallas, Texas**
Associate of Arts Degree in Business   May 2007

PROFESSIONAL AFFILIATIONS

Napa Sales Club. Chamber of Commerce. Phi Beta Kappa.

FIGURE A.8 Sample scannable resume.

person who will do the interviewing. Therefore, a scannable resume must appeal both to the computer and to the human reader as well.

A scannable resume usually begins with a *Keyword Summary*, as shown in Figure A.8, which lists multiple keywords or phrases that describe you, your skills, and your interpersonal traits. Or if you prefer to use longer phrases to highlight your abilities, knowledge, or skills, begin your resume with a *Summary of Qualifications* (but still include keywords). Read more about the qualifications summary and sample keywords in Chapter 8. In both kinds of summaries, each word/phrase should begin with a capital and end with a period. For help in developing your keyword summary, check your paper resume for descriptive nouns, look carefully at the terms used in the job description, consult one of the excellent resume books by such authors as Karsh and Pike (2009), Kennedy (2007), and especially consult *2500 Keywords to Get you Hired* (Block & Betrus, 2002). Use the terms that best describe you while including the jargon used by the industry (Lehman & DuFrene, 2008). Scannable resumes generally include four headings: *Keyword Summary, Experience, Education,* and *Professional Affiliations and Awards.* As with the conventional resume, references aren't included; in the scannable resume, the Keyword Summary usually replaces the Objective. Although the chronological pattern is also effective for scannable resumes, simply telling what you can do isn't enough. You need to show the end result or benefit of your actions. For example, taking "customer complaints" as a keyword, you might state that you "handled customer complaints." However, saying that you "developed a faster procedure for handling customer complaints" not only shows what you can do, but it also indicates how well you can do it.

When Preparing a Scannable Resume:

- *Include basic information*: Name (address/phone/e-mail), Keyword Summary, Education, Experience, and Professional Affiliations and Awards.
- *Use boldface* (for titles and subtitles) but avoid boxes, lines, italics, underlining, shading, or graphics; they don't scan well. Bullets must be dark and filled in.
- *Use white paper (20 to 60 lb.) and black ink.* Send only original copies from a laser or ink-jet printer.
- *Use simple fonts*, like Times New Roman or Arial in 12 to 14 point. A scanner can read 14-point type more easily, but a one-page resume will become two pages.
- *Print on only one side of the paper.* If you use two pages, do not staple them. Use a paper clip instead. Be sure to put your name and page number at the top left side of the second page.
- *Place dates on the right side of the resume* so they will still be readable when compressed. Write dates as May 2010 or 5/10.
- *Avoid columns.* The scanner will read each column as a separate page.
- *Send the resume in a large envelope without folding it* (folds make print impossible to scan legibly).

The E-Mail Resume

The ASCII resume—also called an e-resume—is a plan text, "bare bones" resume designed to be pasted into an e-mail message and read by any computer in the world that is connected to the Internet. Because ASCII resumes must be readable by any type of computer and any e-mail or word processing program, they must be even plainer and use less formatting than scannable resumes. Even boldface should be avoided; fonts should be nonproportional fonts, such as Courier or Courier New (although this is changing). All text should be left-aligned, and any indenting must be done with the space bar, not the tab key.

Fortunately, there are a few ways to make the plain text resume more readable. You can emphasize your name and the main heads using *all caps* or set off the main heads between two *lines of dashes* and use all caps for your name and the secondary heads (such as the companies for which you have worked). Highlight your accomplishments with a *plus sign* (+) or *asterisk* (*) instead of bullets. And you can double-space to separate sections. See Figure A.9 and Figure 8.1 in Chapter 8 for two variations on preparing your ASCII plain text resume. Which one do you think is easier to read?

You will notice that the main headings for scannable and ASCII resumes are the same: *Keyword Summary, Experience, Education, and Professional Affiliations/Awards.* Of course, these are only guides. You may wish to change the wording or the order of these headings, or you may even wish to add or delete at times. If you feel that adding an objective is necessary, you might try setting off the heading "Keyword Summary" with dashes but replace the heading title with your objective(s) instead (see Figure A.9 for an example).

The e-mail resume does not take the place of a paper resume. You will want to take a hard copy with you to interviews. It does, however, eliminate the need to send multiple resumes through the mail and speeds the job search.

A large number of employers post openings on free sites (such as Indeed.com, Simplyhired.com, or Jobster.com), their own websites, or on employment websites like Monster.com or Careerbuilder.com. Employers search for resumes and applicants on employment websites, Google, and Zoominfo.com, (Dikel & Roehm, 2008; Weddle, 2009b). Job sites can be used for more than just posting your resume or looking for job openings. They are also an excellent source of information, such as interviewing advice, facts about specific companies or jobs, an up-to-date list of average salaries, cost of living across the country, and names of people you may want to call for additional information (Bolles, 2009). You can even get ideas by looking at other people's resumes.

Most employers now have their own websites where they post job openings. To see if a company you are interested in has a website, do a Google search, or go to Monster.com, Weddle.com, or JobHuntersBible.com for a listing of company sites. (You can find links to these sites through your Premium Website for *Communicating for Results.*) Some companies include an Internet address in their newspaper ads and instruct applicants to e-mail their resumes. Virtual job fairs allow you to check who's hiring in your area and to post your resume for jobs that are of interest.

When Preparing an ASCII Plain Text Resume:*

- *Before beginning, turn off any AutoFormat or AutoFormat as You Type* features (i.e., lines, dashes, or "smart quotes"). ASCII reads only keyboard characters.
- *Begin with name and Keyword Summary* and limit them to a total of 15 lines (including any double-spaced lines). The reader may only look at the information visible on the first screen and may not take time to scroll down your resume.
- *Include the basic information* used in scannable resumes.
- *Use only nonproportional fonts,* such as Courier New or Courier, and avoid boldface, italics, underlining, bullets, boxes, special characters or symbols, pictures, or graphics. In place of bullets, use a plus sign (+) or an asterisk (*). Add a space after the plus sign/asterisk before beginning your text.
- *Use the space bar to indent*—ASCII does not read tabs.
- *Left-align all text* (even your name), *and limit lines to 60 characters.* Many e-mail readers accept only 60 characters without wrapping lines. For the proper line length, set your margins so your text is approximately 4 3/4 inches—for 10-point Courier New, set margins at 1.89 inches.

* Adapted from Isaacs, 2000; "Resume Makeover II," 2000; Weddle, 2005; Yate, 2008a.

```
Joel C. Reyes
1355 Edna Street
Napa, CA 94558
415)555-5760/JCR805@online.com


KEY WORD SUMMARY

Sales and sales supervision. Four years in fabric
import sales. Customer relations. Complaint
handling. Team problem-solving. Files & records.
Correspondence. Microsoft Office 2010. Data entry,
55 wpm. Fluent in Spanish. AA in Business-2007.


EXPERIENCE

Fabric Imports — Napa, California
Salesperson, 7/07 to Present
+ Awarded top salesperson for the last three years.
+ Strengthened customer relations with Spanish-
  speaking accounts.
+ Generated 10 new key accounts during last year.
+ Ordered stock, promoted warehouse sales, and
  handled customer complaints.

Richland College, Dallas, Texas
Assistant, 1/05-7/07
+ Assisted the Dean of Instruction and Student
  Services.
+ Maintained calendar of student activities.
+ Coordinated on-campus student organizations.
+ Met with student leaders to discuss goals,
  activities, budgets, and scholarships.
+ Developed less complicated procedure for
  handling student complaints.

Jack-in-the-Box, Dallas, Texas
Fountain Clerk (part-time), 2/04-12/04
+ Took orders from drive-through window.
+ Prepared fountain items such as carbonated
  drinks and ice-cream orders.
+ Cleaned counters and tables.
+ Created best-selling new shake flavor.


EDUCATION

Richland College, Dallas, Texas
Associate of Arts Degree in Business, May 2007


PROFESSIONAL AFFILIATIONS

Napa Sales Club.
Chamber of Commerce.
Phi Beta Kappa.
```

```
Joel C. Reyes
1355 Edna Street
Napa, CA 94558
415)555-5760/JCR805@online.com

------------------------------------------------
Sales, Leading to Sales supervision
------------------------------------------------
Personal selling. Four years in fabric import sales.
Customer relations. Complaint handling. Data entry,
55wpm. Team problem-solving. Files & records.
Correspondence. Microsoft Office 2010. Presentation
skills. Fluent in Spanish. AA in Business-2007.


------------------------------------------------
Experience
------------------------------------------------
FABRIC IMPORTS — Napa, California
Salesperson, 7/07 to Present
* Awarded top salesperson for the last three years.
* Strengthened customer relations with Spanish-
  speaking accounts.
* Generated 10 new key accounts during last year.
* Ordered stock, promoted warehouse sales, and
  handled customer complaints.

RICHLAND COLLEGE, Dallas, Texas
Assistant, 1/05-7/07
* Assisted the Dean of Instruction and Student
  Services.
* Maintained calendar of student activities.
* Coordinated on-campus student organizations.
* Met with student leaders to discuss goals,
  activities, budgets, and scholarships.
* Developed less complicated procedure for
  handling student complaints.

JACK-IN-THE-BOX, Dallas, Texas
Fountain Clerk (part-time), 2/04-12/04
* Took orders from drive-through window.
* Prepared fountain items such as carbonated
  drinks and ice-cream orders.
* Cleaned counters and tables.
* Created best-selling new shake flavor.

------------------------------------------------
Education
------------------------------------------------
RICHLAND COLLEGE, Dallas, Texas
Associate of Arts Degree in Business, May 2007

------------------------------------------------
Professional Affiliations
------------------------------------------------
Napa Sales Club.
Chamber of Commerce.
Phi Beta Kappa.
```

FIGURE A.9 Comparison of two e-mail plain text resumes.

- *End each line with a space followed by a hard return.* Do not let lines automatically wrap to the next line, or your paragraphs will look as ragged as many e-mail messages you have probably received.
- *Emphasize your name and main headings with all caps, or set off main heads with lines of dashes* (and save caps for subheads). Overuse of caps will dilute effectiveness. Limit lines made with dashes to 4 1/2 inches (for 10-point Courier New).
- *Save the resume in plain text format.* Select Save As and click on Plain Text or Text Only (.txt).
- *Test the formatting by pasting the resume into an e-mail message and sending it to yourself.* Fix any formatting problems before sending it to potential employers.

The Web Resume or e-Portfolio

The *Web (HTML) resume* or electronic portfolio (Lehman & DuFrene, 2008) is a resume posted to your personal website. It is especially useful for applicants in creative or high-tech fields. A Web resume includes your ASCII resume (as well as links to your professional resume and even to a multimedia resume) posted to your personal website. The suggestions illustrated in Figure A.10 are adapted from Lehman and DuFrene (2008) and Guffey (2007, 2010):

- Include your name, e-mail address, and objective or goal near the top (address and telephone number should probably be omitted for security purposes).
- Include a link to your ASCII resume.
- Include a link to a more professionally formatted resume.

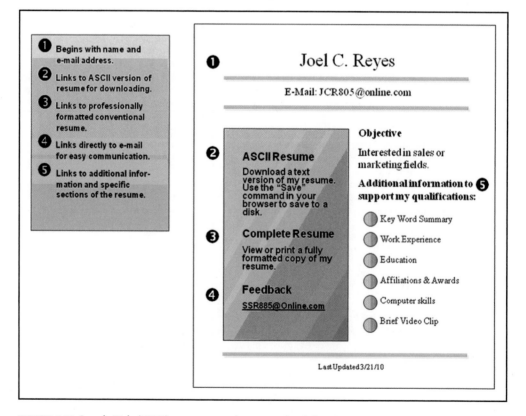

FIGURE A.10 Sample Web (HTML) resume posted to personal website.

- Design an attractive set of links to specific areas of your resume and to additional information that showcases your qualifications and abilities (include work samples, past projects, and even a brief video clip introducing yourself or a PowerPoint presentation).

- Keep all information job related (avoid personal photos or statements that indicate your gender, age, ethnic background, marital status, or religion).

Your e-portfolio can easily be burned onto a CD or DVD and mailed to prospective employers (Guffey, 2010). The newest resume is called a bioblog or biographical blog. If you are a blog user, be sure to read *Bioblogs: Resumes for the 21st Century* (Smith, 2006).

E-mail and interviewing aren't the only places that written communication plays an important role in the workplace. Informative oral presentations and reports are regular occurrences in the workplace and require careful thought and preparation. A survey of employers conducted by the National Association of Colleges and Employers (NACE) reported that the skills/qualities most sought after by employers are oral and written communication skills; however, communication skills were also reported as the "number one skill that is most lacking in new college graduate hires" (Job Outlook 2009, p. 24). Improving your oral and written communication skills can definitely improve your employability.

Writing to Inform

Informative presentations or reports promote understanding of an idea or a body of related facts through a well organized presentation of data. There is no persuasion involved—the reader or audience member is expected to reach their own interpretation and possible application of the data. Recall the general pointers for effective writing given at the beginning of this appendix—adapt to the audience, impress with your opening words, organize for clarity and brevity, and create a professional look with proper formatting and typeface choices. These pointers apply to informative messages whether used to organize a report or an oral presentation.

In messages to inform there are four suggested tools that aid understanding:

- *Use a definition if your audience is unfamiliar with your topic or if the topic is complicated.* According to the *New World Dictionary*, a definition is "a statement of what a thing is; being definite, explicit, and clear; absence of fuzziness." Defining the word *entrepreneur* as "to undertake or to set out on a new mission or venture" (Platt, 2004, p. 541) is an example of a definition. To ensure clarity, follow each definition with one of the following: a comparison or contrast, one or two examples, the etymology or root meaning of the word, a synonym, or a list of essential features needed if the definition is to be complete and correct.

- *Use a description to paint a vivid, detailed picture of the topic if clarity and maintaining audience attention are especially important.* Effective descriptions use concrete words and figures of speech such as similes, metaphors, and onomatopoeia. *Similes* compare items using the word *like* or *as*—"your eyes work like a camera"; *metaphors* are implied comparisons and do not use *like* or *as*—"the pupil of the eye is the camera aperture"; and onomatopoeias sound like their meanings, such as *buzz, bark, swish, ring*—"the hiss of the snake was worse than its slither."

- *Use explanations when your subject matter is complex, may be difficult to comprehend, or requires the clarification of some process.* As discussed in Chapter 12, an explanation is a statement about the relationship between certain items and often answers the questions how, what, and why. Good explanations are enhanced by quality visual aids, use of clear connecting words (like *because* or *for example*), and comparison of old knowledge with new (Rowan, 1995). With complex topics, it's best to start with the "big picture" and then show how the parts or processes work and interrelate. When speaking on a topic that listeners may find difficult to believe, it is best to first discuss the "lay" theory or belief and why it seems plausible, then discuss why it is inaccurate, and then present the more acceptable concept or theory (Rowan, 1991).

- *Use a narration to improve understanding and grab audience interest*—also called illustrations or storytelling (Ballard, 2003). A *narration* is a story about real or imagined things, people, or events told with detail and enthusiasm. Narrations are even used in business to enliven "speeches, sales pitches, training sessions, and other presentations on otherwise dry or technical topics" (Quinones, 1999). In fact, Quinones reports that executives pay as much as $4,000 for an "executive storytelling" seminar (p. 4). According to Fisher (1987), an outstanding narration or story should have two important qualities: (a) *Probability*—the story is easy to follow and makes sense, and (b) *Fidelity*—the story rings true to the audience.

Informative Outlines

Whether used with a written report or an oral presentation, informative outlines are important. Don't make the mistake of thinking that you can just "wing" oral presentations because they are spoken. An informative presentation given without a carefully written outline is unlikely to impress the audience. When used correctly, an outline can be an effective planning tool. An outline tells you at a glance how the main points are organized. When you see your presentation in outline form, it's easy to see the big picture and to know what changes are needed. To be effective, outlines need to follow a few basic guidelines:

- *Use standard numbering.* Roman numerals, capital letters, and Arabic numerals are recommended. The levels most typically used in outlines are:

  I. First main point

     A. Subpoint or supporting material

        1. Supporting material

- *Indent for faster comprehension.* When each main point and level is indented (instead of all left-aligned), you can spot your main and supporting points quickly.

- *Include at least two supporting items per level*, when possible. In other words, if you have an "A," you need a "B"; if you have a "1," you need at least a "2." However, don't force an unnatural division just to have two parts.

- *Use parallel wording for each level.* If the item in "A" is a sentence, then "B" should also be a sentence (or both could be phrases). The items need to have similar structure, and sentences should be in the same voice (either active or passive). For example, in a speech on the common cold, the following main points are not parallel:

  I. Many remedies have been tried.

  II. Modern therapy is best.

  III. Curing the cold with vitamin C

The first two points are sentences (I is passive voice and II is active voice) and the third one is a sentence fragment. To make them parallel, you could use the following noun phrases: Ancient remedies, Modern therapy, and Vitamin C cure.

- *Capitalize the first word in each level.* It only takes a glance to know where a new level begins when the first word in each level is capitalized.

- *If your outline is intended for an oral presentation, it should also include the following: transitions between main points, sources, and a list of your references.*

For a sample informative outline, check out Figure A.11. How well does this sample outline follow the guidelines for effective outlines?

Sample Informative Presentation

Title: "Retail Theft" by Mark Stephenson
Exact Purpose: After listening to my presentation, the audience will know the three types of retail theft and how to recognize (and hopefully deter) each type.

INTRODUCTION
- **Attention-getter:** Who has stolen from a store? A candy bar? A shirt? *[Slide1]* A CD you thought you couldn't live without? The fact is, theft in retail is abundant. It remains the common string that affects all merchants from malls to flea markets.
- **Qualifications:** As a retail store manager, I've seen countless attempts at theft and I've partnered with my company's Retail Loss Department to minimize theft.
- **Audience motivation:** According to the University of Florida's National RetailSecurity survey, U.S. retailers lost over $10 billion due to shoplifting last year.*[Slide2]* What this study really shows is that theft prevention produces a morestable economy so people like you and I won't have to face inflated prices and will want to purchase that CD or candy bar. *[slide3]*
- **Thesis:** Retail theft is caused by three main types of individuals: professionals, amateurs, and employees. By recognizing and understanding the various methodsused to conceal merchandise, stores can more aptly deter retail theft.

BODY
I. The first type of retail theft is caused by professional shoplifters. *[Slide 4]*
  A. Organized Retail Crime (ORC) groups have stolen millions of merchandise.
    1. These groups travel to cities and work in groups—one group scouts the store, another enters and prepares the merchandise (by removing sensors or moving merchandise toward the entrance), a final group enters and conceals the goods.
  B. Methods of concealment used by professionals are the most advanced. *[Slide 5]*
    1. Bags lined with foil to defeat security systems are popular and easily obtained.
    2. Hidden pockets and expandable waistbands have also been successfully used.
  C. ORC groups seldom go further than 20 feet from the entrance. *[Slide 6]*
    1. They prefer to remove merchandise from the front area (tables, etc.)
    2. The closer to the front, the quicker the escape.

Transition: Professionals aren't the only shoplifters.

II. The second type of retail theft is caused by amateurs.
  A. Usually, amateur shoplifters are younger than the professionals. *[Slide 7]*
    1. They tend to steal for the thrill rather than lack of funds.
    2. They usually steal in groups of two or more—if opportunity arises.
  B. Methods of concealment are more basic and spontaneous. *[Slide 8]*
    1. The back of the store is preferred to the front—more concealment.
    2. Fitting rooms are especially useful because of their privacy.
    3. Amateurs prefer to steal small items that fit into a pocket or purse.

Transition: In additional to professionals and amateurs, there is a third type of shoplifter.

FIGURE A.11a Informative outline for oral presentation.

III. Employees compose the final group of shoplifters *[Slide 9]*
   A. Internal theft contributes to 78% of retail theft.
   B. Methods of concealment are carefully planned. *[Slide 10]*
      1. Employees have more opportunity to remove security devises.
      2. Employees may put merchandise in the trash before taking it out.
      3. Now a personal story about an employee and her "disposable" cup . . .

   Transition: Now that we've discussed types of shoplifting, let's focus on prevention.

IV. Knowing the "alert signals" of each type shoplifter increases prevention.
   A. Recognizing alert signals for professions is very difficult. *[Slide 11]*
      1. Professionals avoid employees, wear sunglasses, and talk on cell phones.
      2. They also seem uninterested in merchandise sizes or styles.
      3. They communicate by leaving pennies or toothpicks on the floor.
   B. Spotting alert signals used by amateurs is easier. *[Slide 12]*
      1. Amateurs seem nervous and look at employees more than merchandise.
      2. They form tight groups to limit visibility by employees and others.
   C. Recognizing alert signals for internal theft is very important. *[Slide 13]*
      1. Look for employees who frequent the restroom (especially before leaving work), who bring large bags or purses to work; and who have friends who visit often.
      2. Use tools such as Microsoft's Smarter Retailing Initiative program.

CONCLUSION

- Theft is a plague that hurts businesses, individuals, and the economy. The National Retail Federation is working with law enforcement to crack down on retail theft.[Slide 14]
- The Retail Loss Prevention Ltd. estimates a total of 60,000 cases will be handled successfully in 2006. May be you should re-think stealing that CD . . .

REFERENCES:

1. Herbst, M. (2006, March 12). Hello, we're keeping an eye on you. *Fort Worth Star-Telegram*, G7 (Sunday Life).

2. *Microsoft technology helps Trax tackle inventory shrinkage problems*. (2004, August 25). Accessed at http://www.microsoft.com/industry/retail/LossPrevention.mspx. .

3. Organized Retail Crime, A Growing Trend. (2005). *Retail Industry.com*. Accessed at http://retailindustry.about.com/b/a/203293.htm.

4. About RLP: Background. (2006). *Retail Loss Prevention Ltd*. Accessed at http://www.lossprevention.co.uk/background.html.

FIGURE A.11b *(Continued)*

Informative Reports

Informative reports play an important role in the business communication of both supervisors and employees. Employees' informative reports are the only way supervisors can stay up to date on all the information they need to make sound decisions. Employees also use informal and formal reports to communicate ideas and proposals horizontally to fellow workers and to present information or demonstrate product use to clients. Supervisors use reports to communicate company policies and operational procedures downward to employees. In addition to the suggestions for quality written messages given at the first of this appendix, and the suggested ways to add clarity to informative messages included in this section, effective informative reports whether informal or formal generally include these items:

- *Present a brief, clearly worded statement of purpose.* The best statements take a reader-centered approach to get the reader involved from the beginning.

- *Follow a deductive approach* and make the purpose and perhaps even the results of the report clear from the beginning. The rest of the report would then include facts, examples, and data to support and expand the purpose and results presented at the beginning of the report.

- *Organize the supporting information and subtopics into brief, clearly divided paragraphs.* Each paragraph should include data and information with sources cited and illustrated with quality visual aids (see Chapter 13 for suggestions for preparing effective visual aids).

- *Use concrete, vivid words and a variety of supporting materials to keep reader interest.* Take a reader-centered approach as you try to answer the questions that a reader might have and use a variety of supporting materials to keep interest and clarify including definitions, descriptions, explanations, and narratives discussed previously. See Chapter 12 for types of supports that add proof and interest to reports and presentations.

- Additional items: In *formal reports*, you may wish to add a title page (including title, names of participants and date), table of contents (including headings with page numbers and a list of tables and figures), and even an abstract or synopsis (placed at the beginning which briefly includes the problem, the process followed, and the conclusions and recommendations that were reached).

For a sample informative report, check out Figure A.12 on the following pages. How clearly does this informal report follow the suggested guidelines and how well does it communicate?

Writing to Persuade

Although information may be used more often in the workplace than persuasion, persuasive oral presentations and reports run a close second. Convincing employees or management to take a particular course of action or presenting how a particular product will meet the needs of a client require carefully prepared arguments. *Persuasive presentations and reports* take a definite position and present arguments to convince the audience to either agree with the position or to take a particular action. Presenting information on both sides of an issue and then asking the audience or reader to make up their own minds is not persuasion. Although persuasive messages definitely need to include information, the overall intent is to change opinions and encourage action without trickery or manipulation. Don't forget to use the general pointers for effective writing given at the beginning of this appendix—adapt to the audience, impress with your opening words, organize for clarity and brevity, and create a professional look with proper formatting and typeface choices. In addition, effective persuasive messages do the following:

- *Use an inductive pattern of organization.* If you begin your persuasive message with a specific request or recommendation as is done in informative messages, the audience is likely to be more resistant to your position. Therefore, persuasive messages are usually more successful when you convince the audience that a serious problem exists before suggesting any solution or recommendations. Such approach is called *inductive* because it presents arguments building up to a conclusion or

Sample Informative Report

January 10, 2010.
Retail Theft Report for Toys Ahoy.
Prepared by Mark Stephenson

Introduction

Retail theft and shoplifting are a serious problem for businesses of all sizes. This is especially true for new businesses because they are unaware of what to expect. Because of my experience in retail and management, a new children's store named Toys Ahoy has asked me to prepare a report discussing the main types of retail theft for which they should prepare prior to opening their first store this coming summer. My research on this topic found that the three main types of retail theft have not changed since my presentation to the city council on the topic four years ago. The three types of retail theft to be discussed in this report include: Professional shoplifters, Amateur shoplifters, and Employees.

Background

The most recent retail loss statistics were presented in July 2009 by the University of Florida's National Retail Security survey at the National Retail Federation Loss Prevention Conference in Los Angeles. According to NRSS retail theft accounted for approximately $36 billion in losses in 2008 (Hollinger, 2009). Also, the 21st Annual Retail Theft Survey prepared by Hayes International ("Shoplifters and Dishonest Employees," 2009) found that 22 major retailers with over 19,000 stores lost $6 billion in 2008. Over 904,000 thieves were apprehended and $182 million recovered. Retail theft remains a serious problem that retailers need to recognize and, deter.

Findings

Finding One: Retail theft is conducted by three different types of individuals: the professional, the amateur, and the employee:

- *The first type of retail theft is caused by professional shoplifters.*
    1. Organized Retail Crime (ORC) groups have stolen millions of merchandise.
    2. These groups travel to cities and work in groups—one group scouts the store, another enters and prepares the merchandise (by removing sensors or moving merchandise toward the entrance), a final group enters and conceals the goods.
- *The second type of retail theft is caused by amateurs.*
    1. Usually, amateur shoplifters are younger than the professionals.
    2. They tend to steal for the thrill rather than lack of funds.
    3. They usually steal in groups of two or more—if opportunity arises.
- *Employees compose the final group of shoplifters*
    1. Internal theft contributes to 78% of retail theft.
    2. Employees tend to steal seven times more per theft than other types of shoplifters—$969 per employee versus $135 per non-employee ("Shoplifters and Dishonest Employees," 2009).

Finding Two: Each type of thief tends to use different *methods of concealment:*

- *Methods of concealment used by professionals are the most advanced.*
    1. Bags lined with foil to defeat security systems are popular and easily obtained.
    2. Hidden pockets and expandable waistbands have also been successfully used.
    3. ORC groups seldom go further than 20 feet from the entrance.
        a. They prefer to remove merchandise from the front area (tables, etc.)
        b. The closer to the front, the quicker the escape.

FIGURE A.12a Sample informative report.

position; the *deductive* approach more often used in informative messages begins with the conclusion or position and follows with arguments to support it.

- *Clearly spell out one or more problems that need to be addressed.* Why should your target audience change their beliefs or actions unless there is a compelling reason to do so? It is up to you to show that a situation exists that is serious enough to require a change by presenting quality evidence and citing impressive sources. See Chapter 12 for effective ways to cite information from authorities.

- *For the amateur, methods of concealment are more basic and spontaneous.*
    1. The back of the store is preferred to the front—more concealment.
    2. Fitting rooms are especially useful because of their privacy.
- *Employees carefully plan their methods of concealment.*
    1. Employees have more opportunity to remove security devises.
    2. Employees may put merchandise in the trash before taking it out.
    3. One employee even put jewelry items in her "disposable drinking cup."

Finding Three: Each type of thief can be spotted using different "signals."

- *Recognizing alert signals for professions is very difficult.*
    1. Professionals avoid employees, wear sunglasses, and talk on cell phones.
    2. They also seem uninterested in merchandise sizes or styles.
    3. They communicate by leaving pennies or toothpicks on the floor.
- *Spotting alert signals used by amateurs is easier.*
    1. Amateurs seem nervous and look at employees more than merchandise.
    2. They form tight groups to limit visibility by employees and others.
- *Recognizing alert signals for internal theft is very important.*
    1. Look for employees who frequent the restroom (especially before leaving work), who bring large bags or purses to work; and who have friends who visit often.
    2. Use tools such as Microsoft's Smarter Retailing Initiative program

Summary

Theft is a plague that hurts businesses, individuals, and the economy. The National Retail Federation is working with law enforcement to crack down on retail theft ("2009 Organized retail crime survey," 2009). Law enforcement is important, but well-trained employees—employees who know the findings presented above—are a better bet for lowering retail theft. Well-trained employees realize that there are three different types of individuals who commit retail theft, that each type of thief uses different methods of concealment, and that each can be spotted using different "signals."

Works Cited

1. About Us: Statistics. (2009). *Retail Loss Prevention Ltd.* Accessed at "http://www.lossprevention.co.uk/stats.aspx" http://www.lossprevention.co.uk/stats.aspx.
2. Herbst, M. (2006, March 12). Hello, we're keeping an eye on you. *Fort Worth Star-Telegram,* G7 (Sunday Life).
3. Hollinger, R. (2009, July). 2008 National Retail Security Survey: Preliminary Results. Presented at the 2009 NRF Loss Prevention conference & Expo in Los Angeles. Retrieved from "http://www.nrf.com/Attachments.asp?id=25036&rid=984555" http://www.nrf.com/Attachments.asp?id=25036&rid=984555.
4. *Microsoft technology helps Trax tackle inventory shrinkage problems.* (2004, August 25). Accessed at http://www.microsoft.com/industry/retail/LossPrevention.mspx. .
5. 2009 Organized Retail Crime survey. (2009). *National Retail Federation.* Accessed at "http://www.nrf.com/modules.php?name=Documents&op=showlivedoc&sp_id=3137" http://www.nrf.com/modules.php?name=Documents&op=showlivedoc&sp_id=3137.
6. Shoplifters and dishonest employees are apprehended in record numbers by US retailers. (2009). Hayes International. Retrieved from "http://www.hayesinternational.com/ts_rtl_thft.html" http://www.hayesinternational.com/ts_rtl_thft.html.

FIGURE A.12b (*Continued*)

- *Clearly spell out recommended beliefs or actions needed to solve the problems presented.* Don't assume that an audience will arrive at the same conclusion as you after hearing the problem. They may be unsure which solution would be best or arrive at a completely different conclusion if left on their own. Therefore, messages are more persuasive when they clearly specify recommended beliefs and actions that will help solve the problems presented.

- *Show incentives and additional benefits if recommendations followed.* Any type of audience from a client reading your proposal to people listening to an oral presentation is more likely to be persuaded if you give them a personal incentive or show that your recommendations not only will solve the problem, but will also provide additional benefits. These benefits may occur immediately or slowly over time; they may be personal, relate to the organization, or benefit society as a whole. For additional approaches to organizing persuasive messages, see Chapter 14.

- *Support all recommendations with carefully researched and ethical evidence,* relate it to the psychological needs of the audience, and demonstrate your credibility. Effective persuasive messages contain logos (logic and reasoning), pathos (emotional appeal), and ethos (ethical appeal)—all three are needed for persuasion. *First,* instead of asserting that problems exist, prove that they do by presenting evidence such as examples, statistics, quotations, and comparisons connected by logic that is clear and persuasive. *Second,* show how the problem and the evidence relate directly to the audience's needs—evidence will be persuasive to the extent that the audience feels personally involved or emotional about it. Audience analysis is a must in order to know the needs of your audience and how to relate your position or product to them and their needs. *Third,* demonstrate your credibility as a writer or speaker toward the specific topic. In other words, how can we know that you are trustworthy, knowledgeable, and fair? People with little knowledge or involvement with the topic are especially persuaded by your expertise—your experience with the topic; people with knowledge and experience want to know that you have expertise but are especially persuaded by the evidence you present (Eagly & Chaiken, 1993). All audience members want to know that you are trustworthy. Presenting both sides of the argument while showing why one side is the better position reveals to an audience that you are trustworthy and knowledgeable and have a complete grasp of the topic (Chaiken, 1986). Using active instead of passive sentence structure is another way to add to your trustworthiness (Hosman, 2002). For more specifics on logos, pathos, and ethos, see Chapter 14.

Persuasive Outlines

Effective persuasive outlines follow the guidelines presented previously for informative outlines but follow an inductive overall pattern. The conclusion of a persuasive message is important because it is your last chance to persuade. Therefore, careful, prior planning of your conclusion is a must. All persuasive outlines include an introduction and conclusion and many include these major headings: (1) Problem, Solution, Benefits or (2) Problem, Solution, Action.

Persuasive outlines expand the conclusion beyond the summary and the closing thought used in informative outlines to include a visualization of the future and a call for belief or action. Let's look at each of these:

- *Visualize the future for the audience.* At this point in trying to persuade your audience, there may be a few or many people who are still undecided. Visualizing the future for your audience may be what finally makes them decide to support your position. Therefore, using evidence and available authorities to predict the future will show what is likely to happen if your recommendations are not adopted—here is the time to paint a vivid picture showing how bad things may get for your audience. Contrast this dire prediction with how good things will likely become for the audience if your recommendations are adopted—again painting a vivid picture of the future. If the predictions are unlikely to affect the people in your audience, appeal to their sense of fair play and desire to help others by building a strong economy and country.

- *Call for belief or action.* Many persuasive messages end in a general summary assuming that the audience will make the right decision. People are much more likely to make a decision requiring a change of belief or action when they are directly asked to do so. Not only should you ask for a change of belief or action, but you should also show how this can be done easily and quickly if possible. If you have made the change yourself, be sure to mention it. If you can do it, so can they.

For a sample persuasive outline, check out Figure A.13. How does this sample outline differ from the informative outline presented in Figure A.11? How persuasive do you think the oral presentation represented by this outline would be for the typical audience?

Persuasive Reports

Persuasive reports are often referred to as analytical reports because they do more than just present data and information on a problem; they also analyze the problem and offer suggested solutions in the form of recommendations. Although reports differ in specific topics included, effective persuasive reports include a form of the following:

- *A problem section clearly defining the problem.* Not only should the problem be clearly stated and demonstrated through prior research and quality sources, but you will also want to conclude this section with a statement of purpose giving the goal of your report and its scope or boundaries. This is especially difficult when there are multiple problems closely related—you will want to limit your report to a manageable size.

- *A method section describing how the information was collected.* When researching for information, include only credible Internet sites such as government or organization sites, electronic databases such as Lexis-Nexis or ABI/Inform, first-hand surveys you plan to conduct by mail, telephone, or personal interviews, and other collection methods.

- *A results section describing the data and information collected with explanatory charts and graphs to simplify data.*

- *A conclusions and recommendations section listing and explaining all recommendations.*

- *A reference section listing the sources used in APA or MLA style.*

- *Additional items*: If your report is formal, you may want to add a title page (including title, names of participants and date), table of contents (including headings with page numbers and a list of tables and figures), and even an abstract or synopsis (placed at the beginning which briefly includes the problem, the process followed, and the conclusions and recommendations that were reached).

For a sample persuasive report, check out Figure A.14, which shows the first part of most pages. To read the entire report, go to your Premium Website for *Communicating for Results.*

Sample Persuasive Presentation

Title: "Endometriosis" by Rebecca DeCamp
Position Statement: Endometriosis is a dominant cause of pain in women and immediate industry and individual action is needed.

INTRODUCTION
- **Attention-getter:**
  --At the age of 26, Laurie Calcaterra was ready to start a family but after a few years of trying, she was unable to conceive.
  --Laurie started having pelvic pain that the doctors couldn't figure out. She started missing work around her periods since she couldn't walkFinally, one day, she was in so much pain her husband rushed her to the emergency room.
  --After an ultrasound, the doctors discovered that she had a large cyst on her right ovary. Taken directly to surgery, they found that Laurie has late stages of endometriosis.
- **Audience Motivation:** Nearly 5.5 million women in the United States are affected by endometriosis according to *The Contra Costa Times of Walnut Creek California* on February 20th, 2009. That is twice the amount of patients with Alzheimer's and seven times as many as those with Parkinson's.
- **Thesis:** To help us understand the affects of endometriosis, let's look at what endometriosis is, then the new cause and finally what the government, industry and even we can do to solve this problem.

BODY
I. **Endometriosis is a crippling disease with three ineffective real cures.**
   A. The definition of endometriosis in the July 21, 2009 *Irish Times* is a condition in which cells from the lining of the womb travel to other parts of the body, and often adhere to the ovaries, fallopian tubes and abdominal cavity.
      1. These patches respond to the hormones of the menstrual cycle and each month they thicken, build up with blood and then break down.
      2. But, unlike the lining of the womb, they have nowhere to go and can cause damage, like inflammation, internal scarring and adhesions.
      3. The most common symptoms include increasing levels of pain before and during periods, unusually long and heavy periods, painful urination, inability to have sex, and in most cases; infertility.
   B. To some, these symptoms can sound like normal period pain or "cramps." Let me assure you that women with endometriosis are in pain well beyond the normal limits.
      1. During their periods, women with endometriosis usually don't move around much. The increasing levels of pain manifest into days that they are unable to walk.
      2. If it isn't the pain that has these women stay home, then it is the heavy bleeding that keeps them close to a bathroom. In many cases they change a tampon or pad every thirty minutes as opposed to every 4 to 6 hours.
      3. Endometriosis can cause pain depending on where the adhesions are located. There may be only a little on a sensitive internal organ that can cause severe pain, but there can also be internal scarring that attaches the organs together sometimes causing the uterus to completely flip over.
   C. So, how do we cure such terrible affects of this disease? Certainly there must be some good medical research going on to prevent a disease of this magnitude. But there isn't a cure. Women with endometriosis are given only three options.
      1. First includes taking continuous birth control which prevents a period at all, causes many side effects, and doesn't help when a couple is trying to conceive.
      2. For later stages of endometriosis, there is a shot doctors can administer that is called Lupron, which shuts down estrogen production and causes your body to go into early menopause. Lupron has a whole other set of side effects, like early osteoporosis.
      3. And the third option is having a hysterectomy, which is the complete removal of a woman's uterus and ovaries. Surprisingly, after a hysterectomy, some women still suffer from the pain of adhesions not removed in the abdominal cavity.

   Transition: Now that we've seen what endometriosis is, how it affects women and what cures are available, I want to talk about a new dominant cause that has recently emerged.

II. **Surprisingly, dioxins and feminine hygiene products appear to contribute to endometriosis.**

FIGURE A.13a Sample persuasive outline for an oral presentation.

A. According to the *EPA*, on September 22nd, 2009, dioxins are an accidental byproduct of a multitude of industrial processes in which chlorine is present —such as chemical and plastics manufacturing, pesticide and herbicide production and pulp and paper bleaching.

B. This may seem like something that wouldn't affect anyone that doesn't live directly by a plant that produces these products, but there is something that women use once a month that is.

    1. According to the *US Food and Drug Administration* on January 27, 2009, tampons and sanitary pads made of rayon or bleached cotton contains low levels of dioxins.

    2. These levels are tested in parts per trillion, so the risk was originally thought of as low. The *National Institutes of Health* has been researching health risks to women, including counts of endometriosis from the presence of dioxins.

    3. They found that dioxins build up in the body over time in a process of bioaccumulation and it concentrates in fatty tissues. If the National Institutes of Health know about this, why are these dioxins still allowed in our most sensitive products you may be wondering?

C. Companies haven't changed because of the money being made on these products.

    1. *Proctor & Gamble* reported that the *Tampax* brand is one of their half-billion dollar brands in their 2008 yearend report.

    2. "Let's do the math" says the November 10, 2008 *The Gazette from Montreal*, "If a woman used four tampons and four pads per day, five days a month for about 35 years, that adds up to 16,800 tampons and pads…" Now, for a woman with endometriosis, changing every half hour for even 12 hours results in 24 tampons and pads for five days for 35 years…this adds up to 50,400 tampons and pads.

    3. Companies like *Kimberly-Clark*, producer of Kotex, who report in their annual financials that they net 8.3 billion, *Playtex Products Inc*, and *McNeil-Personal Products Company* who produce O.B. tampons also report in the millions.

    4. You see why the big companies are not willing to change—we really are talking about millions and billions of dollars these companies are making on feminine products.

    Transition: Now that we have talked about what Dioxins are, where they come from, and why big companies aren't doing anything to change from what they are currently producing, I want to talk about solutions on a government, industry and personal level.

III. **Solutions require immediate action on the part of our government, the companies that make tampons, and from each of us.**

A. As stated in our very own Constitution, our government is here to "establish justice, insure domestic tranquility, provide for the common defense, promote the general welfare, and secure the blessings of liberty to ourselves and our posterity."

B. The research is out there, it is just not being enforced.

    1. There is legislation, introduced in Congress back in January 2003 about health risks to women from tampons.

    2. But rules don't make one bit of difference if they are not enforced. The USFDA was put in place to make sure those ingredients, purposefully in a product or not, are safe for use.

C. *The National Center for Toxicological Research* has a goal to "Strengthen and improve scientific and human capital management and expand training and outreach to retain and train scientific experts critical to address FDA's scientific needs." as reported on their website last updated on July 10th, 2009.

    1. If the legislation and government enforcement was effective, the companies would have to follow suit.

        a. Go to any of the companies' websites that I mentioned before and you will see on all of them a section about Toxic Shock Syndrome, a disease that is related to the absorbency of a tampon and the length of time you leave a tampon inside your body, but not anywhere will you see anything about dioxins.

        b. These companies should have an organic option and start putting information on their web pages about the dangers of dioxins.

    2. As for the rest of us, our action should be in education.

        a. As a whole, women's periods are still a "hush-hush" subject. We all should be talking about it. Not just mother to daughter, but single father to daughter as well.

FIGURE A.13b Sample persuasive outline for an oral presentation (continued).

b. There are some alternative products out there. Neither are these organic products advertised nor are they readily available, but we can all start asking for them at our local grocery stores. Products like Seventh Generation and Natracare are two producers of organic non-chlorine bleached tampons. They are usually found in upscale supermarkets like Whole Foods and Market Street and are more expensive than their dioxin-caring counterparts.But if we all start asking for them, those big companies may find that they have to change to the new market trends and accommodate us.

c. The more we talk about it in public the more women and young girls will know about the seriousness of not talking and not knowing. We could have a huge impact.

CONCLUSION

- Today, we have discussed what endometriosis is, the new dominant cause, dioxins, and what solutions there are.
- Women are creatures of habit, the products that your mother first bought you; you will buy your growing daughter when the time comes.
- I believe that the only way to change our current path is thru research and education. Laurie Calcaterra, my sister; is currently on her first round of Lupron. Every day is a new experience for her. Between the mood swings, bone pain and night sweats, she is learning how to make her way thru this ordeal. Let's all be a part of the solution so that cases like Laurie become a thing of the past.

REFERENCES

1. Beaudin, M. (2008, November 10). Time of the month revisited; 'Women look at the DivaCup like it fell from outer space,' but reusable feminine hygiene products earn good reviews – and converts – among a group of local women. *The Gazette (Montreal)*. Retrieved from http://thegazette.canwest.com.
2. DeVito, M.J., & Schecter, A. (2009, January 27). Exposure assessment to dioxins from the use of tampons and diapers. *Environmental Health Perspectives, 1*(1), 23-28. Retrieved from http://www.endometriosisassn.org.
3. *The Irish Times*. (2009, July 21). East meets west for treatment of endometriosis.
4. Proctor & Gamble yearend financial report (unaudited). (2008, December 22). Retrieved from http://www.pg.com/investors/annualreport2008/financials.
5. *U.S. EPA*. (2009, September 22). Risk characterization of dioxin and related compounds—Draft Dioxin Reassessment. Washington D.C., Bureau of National Affairs. Retrieved from http://www.endometriosisassn.org.
6. *U.S. Food and Drug Administration Report*. (2009, January 17). Tampons, asbestos, dioxin & toxic shock syndrome. Retrieved from http://www.endometriosisassn.org.
7. Yadegaran, J. (2009, February 20). Endometriosis a painful, puzzling reproductive disease. *Contra Costa Times* (Walnut Creek, California).Retrieved from http://www.contracostatimes.com.

FIGURE A.13c Sample persuasive outline for an oral presentation (continued).

The Crippling Effect of Endometriosis:
What Industry and Individuals Can Do To Minimize It
Prepared by Rebecca DeCamp
February, 2010

INTRODUCTION

At the age of 26, Laurie Calcaterra was ready to start a family but, after a few years of trying, she was unable to conceive. Laurie started having pelvic pain that the doctors couldn't figure out. The pain was severe and caused her to miss work on the days surrounding her periods. Finally, one day, she was in so much pain her husband rushed her to the emergency room. After an ultrasound, the doctors discovered that she had a large cyst on her right ovary. Taken directly to surgery, they found that Laurie had severe endometriosis. The chances are that you know someone with endometriosis because nearly 5.5 million women in the United States experience its painful effects according to *The Contra Costa Times of Walnut Creek California* (February 20, 2009). This is twice the number of patients with Alzheimer's and seven times as many as those with Parkinson's.

PROBLEM

No one wants to experience or stand by while others experience the excruciating pain involved with endo-metriosis. I certainly don't—Laurie is my sister and watching her painful struggle led me to begin researching this problem and to begin searching for a cure. As this report will show, there appears to be no effective cure for endometriosis, but one of the causes of endometriosis is someth[...]
part of government, industry and individuals. To help us understand[...]
will include:

• A clear definition of endometriosis.
• A look at current ineffective cures for endometriosis.
• A new, startling cause of endometriosis.
• Why involved industries are not taking corrective action.
• Recommendations that may save young women from endomet[...]

FACTS & RESULTS

The following facts and results are based on current research [...]
report) and validated through discussions with Laurie's do[...]
endometriosis.

Endometriosis Defined

According to the July 21, 2009 *Irish Times*, endometriosis is a cond[...]
womb travel to other parts of the body, and often adhere to the ova[...]

1. These patches respond to the hormones of the menstrual cycle a[...]
   blood and then break down.
2. Unlike the lining of the womb, these cells have nowhere to go a[...]
   internal scarring and adhesions.
3. The most common symptoms include increasing levels of pain [...]
   and heavy periods, painful urination, inability to have intercours[...]

If you are thinking that these symptoms sound like normal period p[...]
me assure you that women with endometriosis are in pain well bey[...]

1. During their periods, women with endometriosis usually don't r[...]
   pain manifest into days that they are unable to walk.
2. If it isn't the pain that has these women stay home, then it is [...]
   to a bathroom. In many cases they change a tampon or pad ev[...]
   to 6 hours.
3. Endometriosis can cause differing amounts of pain dependi[...]
   There may be only a little on a sensitive internal organ that [...]
   be internal scarring that attaches the organs together somet[...]
   flip over.

Ineffective Cures for Endometriosis

What is the cure for his disease? Certainly one thinks there must be some good medical research going on to prevent a disease of this magnitude. Currently, there is no cure. Women with endometriosis are given only three options.

1. One ineffective cure to endometriosis includes taking continuous birth control which prevents a period at all, causes many side effects, and doesn't help when a couple is trying to conceive.
2. For later stages of endometriosis, there is a shot doctors can administer that is called Lupron, which shuts down estrogen production and causes your body to go into early menopause. Lupron has its own set of side effects, like early osteoporosis and growth of facial hair.
3. The third ineffective option is having a hysterectomy, which is the complete removal of a woman's uterus and ovaries. Surprisingly, after a hysterectomy, some women still suffer from the pain of adhesions not removed from the abdominal cavity.

A Startling Cause of Endometriosis

Surprisingly, dioxins in feminine hygiene products appear to contribute to endometriosis. According to the *EPA*, on September 22, 2009, dioxins are an accidental byproduct of a multitude of industrial processes in which chlorine is present—such as chemical and plastics manufacturing, pesticide and herbicide production and pulp and paper bleaching. This may seem like something that wouldn't affect anyone that doesn't live directly by an industrial plant that produces these products, but feminine hygiene products, tampons and sanitary pads, are created using these processes, and are used by women once a month.

1. According to the *US Food and Drug Administration* on January 27, 2009, tampons and sanitary pads made from rayon or bleached cotton contain low levels of dioxins.
2. These levels of dioxins are tested in parts per trillion, so the risk was originally thought to be low. The *National Institutes of Health* has been researching health risks to women, including counts of endometriosis from the presence of dioxins.
3. Researchers found that dioxins build up in the body over time in a process of bioaccumulation and are concentrated in fatty tissues. If the National Institutes of Health know about this, why are these dioxins still allowed in our most sensitive feminine hygiene product[...]

Why Involved Industries Are Not Taking Corrective Ac[...]

It appears that companies that produce and sell tampons an[...]
because of the money being made on these products.

1. *Proctor & Gamble* reported that the *Tampax* brand is o[...]
   yearend report.
2. "Let's do the math" says the November 10, 2008 *The* [...]
   tampons and four pads per day, five days a month for a[...]
   pads…" Now, for a woman with endometriosis, changing [...]
   tampons and pads for five days for 35 years…this adds [...]
3. Companies like *Kimberly-Clark*, producer of Kotex, w[...]
   billion, *Playtex Products Inc*, and *McNeil-Personal Pr*[...]
   report in the millions.

CONCLUSIONS AND RE[...]

Millions of women experience the crippling pain of endom[...]
a cause of endometriosis that could be eradicated if the co[...]
pads would remove all traces of dioxins from these produc[...]
that make sanitary products, our government, and the Ame[...]

Action needed by Industry

Companies are not unaware of the effects of dioxins; they [...]
nies' websites (mentioned above) and you will see on all o[...]
disease that is related to the absorbency of a tampon and th[...]
body. However, nowhere will you see anything about the d[...]
sanitary pad industry to take responsibility for their role in[...]
about the dangers of dioxins, and offer organic non-chlori[...]

Action Needed by Government

If the sanitary product industry refuses to do what is right, the federal government must step in. As stated in our very own Constitution, our government is here to "establish justice, insure domestic tranquility, provide for the common defense, promote the general welfare, and secure the blessings of liberty to ourselves and our posterity."

1. In January 2003, Congress introduced legislation about health risks to women from Toxic Shock Syndrome. This legislation does not include information on dioxins. This legislation needs revision.
2. Rules, or legislation, don't make one bit of difference if they are not enforced. The USFDA was put in place to make sure those ingredients, purposefully in a product or not, are safe for use.
3. *The National Center for Toxicological Research* has a goal to "Strengthen and improve scientific and human capital management and expand training and outreach to retain and train scientific experts critical to address FDA's scientific needs." as reported on their website last updated on July 10th, 2009.

Action Needed from American Public

We can't just stand by and hope that industry and the government take the appropriate action. Now that we are informed of the problem, cause, and possible solution, we need to inform others.

1. As a whole, women's periods are still a "hush-hush" subject. We all should be talking about it. Not just mother to daughter, but single father to daughter, and in the larger public arena as well.
2. There are some alternative products out there. Although these organic products are not advertised or readily available, they will be if we start asking for them at our local grocery stores. Products like Seventh Generation and Natracare are two producers of organic non-chlorine bleached tampons. They are usually found in upscale supermarkets like Whole Foods and Market Street and are more expensive than the products that contain dioxins. But if we all start asking for them, industry may find that they have to change to the new market trends and accommodate us.
3. The more we talk about it in public the more women and young girls will know about the seriousness of dioxins and endometriosis. We, the American public, could make a huge impact.

SUMMARY

• This report has included what endometriosis is, ineffective cures, a new, startling cause—dioxins, why industry is not removing these dioxins from tampons and sanitary pads, and needed actions.
• Women are creatures of habit, the products that your mother first bought you, you will buy your growing daughter when the time comes.
• I believe that the only way to change our current path is through research and education. Laurie Calcaterra, my sister, is currently on her first round of Lupron. Every day is a new experience for her. Between the mood swings, bone pain and night sweats, she is learning how to make her way through this ordeal. Let's all be a part of the solution so that cases like Laurie become a thing of the past.

REFERENCES

1. Beaudin, M. (2008, November 10). Time of the month revisited; 'Women look at the DivaCup like it fell from outer space,' but reusable feminine hygiene products earn good reviews – and converts – among a group of local women. *The Gazette (Montreal)*. Retrieved from "http://thegazette.canwest.com"http://thegazette.canwest.com.
2. DeVito, M.J., & Schecter, A. (2009, January 27). Exposure assessment to dioxins from the use of tampons and diapers. *Environmental Health Perspectives*, 1(1), 23-28. Retrieved from "http://www.endometriosisassn.org"http://www.endometriosisassn.org.
3. *The Irish Times*. (2009, July 21). East meets west for treatment of endometriosis.
4. Proctor & Gamble yearend financial report (unaudited). (2008, December 22). Retrieved from "http://www.pg.com/investors/annualreport2008/financials" http://www.pg.com/investors/annualreport2008/financials.
5. *U.S. EPA*. (2009, September 22). Risk characterization of dioxin and related compounds—Draft Dioxin Reassessment. Washington D.C., Bureau of National Affairs. Retrieved from "http://www.endometriosisassn.org"http://www.endometriosisassn.org.
6. *U.S. Food and Drug Administration Report*. (2009, January 17). Tampons, asbestos, dioxin & toxic shock syndrome. Retrieved from "http://www.endometriosisassn.org"http://www.endometriosisassn.org.
7. Yadegaran, J. (2009, February 20). Endometriosis a painful, puzzling reproductive disease. *Contra Costa Times* (Walnut Creek, California). Retrieved from "http://www.contracostatimes.com"http://www.contra-costatimes.com.

3

FIGURE A.14 Sample persuasive report.

Putting Your Knowledge to Work: Collaborative Learning Activities

1. In small groups have each group member bring three or four e-mail messages received either at home or at work. At least one of these e-mail messages should be one that caused the member to get angry or be confused. As a group, read through all the e-mail samples and select one that was the worst written and one that was the best written. Make a list of what made each e-mail effective or ineffective. Last, take the worst written e-mail and have each group member rewrite it into an acceptable format. Select the best of all those written and discuss what makes it the best. Be prepared to share your examples with other groups.

2. Divide into small groups of four or six members. Each member should prepare a conventional, paper resume and print off enough copies for each person in the group. As a group, look at each resume and do the following:

   a. Select the two that look the most impressive. Why are they more impressive than the other resumes? Be specific and list at least four reasons.

   b. Which resume does the best job with the experience section—look for ease of reading, use of bullets, and achievements.

   c. Which resume does the best job with the education section—why was it best? Be specific.

   d. Look at the areas of knowledge, educational highlights, and keyword summary sections when used. Select the best in each category and discuss why it was outstanding.

   e. Select the best overall resume and be prepared to share it with the class or other groups saying why it was best.

3. In teams, select a problem on campus or in the community; Research the problem and prepare a persuasive report with recommendations. Prepare a formal copy of the report to turn in to your professor. Also, plan to give a 5- to 7-minute team presentation using PowerPoint slides that describes your problem, process, results, and recommendations. Make sure that all team members play a role in research and preparation of both the report and the presentation.

Answers to Awareness Check Quizzes

Chapter 1

Communicator Quiz (page 20)
Results:
If you have 7 or more A answers, you are an outstanding communicator.
If you have 7 or more A + B answers, you are an average communicator.
If you have 7 or more C answers, you need immediate improvement. Begin by rereading Chapter 1.

Chapter 2

Organization Models (page 58)
1. B (human relations); 2. D (systems/contingency); 3. E (transformational); 4. A (traditional); 5. B (human relations); 6. C (human resources); 7. D (systems/contingency); 8. A (traditional); 9. E (transformational); 10. C (human resources)

Chapter 3

Styles Survey—Short Form (page 69)
Answers will vary.

Communicator Styles (page 76)
1. A (closed); 2 B (blind); 3. D (open); 4. C (hidden); 5. B and D (blind and open); 6. C (hidden); 7. B (blind); 8 D (open); 9. C (hidden); 10. A (closed)

Chapter 4

Gender Barriers (page 109)
1. *Men.* Despite the folklore that women talk more, research shows that in the classroom and the workplace, men talk more than women (Mulac, 2006). In one experiment, male and female subjects were asked to orally describe pictures. The women's average description was approximately 3 minutes, while the average time for men was 13 minutes. Deborah Tannen (1994) reports a study of seven university faculty meetings that concluded that men "spoke more often and, without exception, spoke longer. . . . The longest contribution by a woman was still shorter than the shortest contribution by a man" (pp. 278–280).

2. *Women.* Women generally tend to be more proficient than men at nonverbal decoding (Wagner et al., 1993). In a meta-analysis of 61 relevant studies, J. A. Hall (1979; 1984) found that women were more accurate decoders than men. Women's success at decoding may be due to the high priority they tend to place on relationship development.

3. *Same.* Past research was inconclusive, but leaned toward women using more tag questions (Mulac, 2006) either in a non-assertive, hedging style, or to exhibit politeness. Palomares (2008) found that use of tentativeness depends on the topic of discussion—men are more tentative when the topic is feminine; women are more tentative when the topic is masculine; when the topic is gender-neutral, both men and women are equally tentative. Calnan and Davidson (1998) found that powerful people of either gender use tags more often than powerless people, and they use them to confirm, support, or soften their verbal comments. Because of the importance of teams in today's work environment, tag questions would seem to be valuable tools (McCowen, 1989)—they leave "open the door for others to respond and express their opinions" (Wood, 2009, p. 130).

4. *Men.* According to Julia Wood, communication rules taught during child play differ for men and women. Females are encouraged to develop interpersonal connections with others whereas males are encouraged to develop "independence and status" (Wood, 2009, p. 238). As a result, women tend to use talk cooperatively—"and regard communication as a primary way to establish and maintain relationships with others"—whereas men tend to use talk competitively—"and regard communication" as an arena for proving oneself and negotiating prestige" (p. 128–130).

5. *Women.* Women work much harder than men to maintain a discussion: They initiate more topics than men (Fishman, 1978), and show attention and interest by using listening responses such as "Tell me more" or "How was your day?" (Wood, 2009, p. 129). Men, on the other hand, are less likely to be responsive and may even "kill" topics by failing to respond or by giving only minimal response cues, such as, "yeah" or "um" or "uh-huh" (Guerrero et al., 2006; Maltz & Borker, 1982). Such minimal

response cues signal lack of involvement to women. Julia Wood (2009) attributes these gender differences to the cultural rules each is taught while young: Women are taught the importance of empathy and support; men generally are not.

6. *Men.* Researchers found that men are more likely to interrupt others (Borisoff & Merrill, 1992; Mulac et al., 1988) and are especially likely to interrupt women (Borisoff & Merrill, 1992). Judy Pearson and colleagues paired men and women and found that men interrupting women accounted for 96% of all interruptions (Pearson et al., 1991). On the other hand, after reviewing the current research on interrupting behavior, Deborah James and Sandra Clarke (as cited in Tannen, 1994) found the results inconclusive.

7. *Men.* Although both genders certainly ask questions, Deborah Tannen notes that men tend to be more aware that asking a question is a public statement of lack of knowledge and that they may be judged less capable by those in power—reputation and even career may be affected. As a result, men are less likely to ask questions (Tannen, 1994). The problem is illustrated by an intern who received a low grade from her supervising physician:

   It took her by surprise because she knew that she was one of the best interns in her group. She asked her supervisor for an explanation, and he replied that she didn't know as much as the others. She knew from her day-to-day dealings with her peers that she was one of the most knowledgeable, not the least. So she asked what evidence had led him to his conclusion. And he told her, "You ask more questions." (Tannen, 1994, p. 26)

8. *Women.* Although 69% of adults consider men and women to be equally good leaders (pewresearch.org, 2008)—women are seen as slightly more supportive and better listeners. In a 2006 study by Coprnicus and *Brandweek* magazine ("Discovery of the Month," 2006), 57% of the people surveyed considered women to be better listeners). Both male and female subordinates report higher morale and job satisfaction when supervised by a woman (Rozema & Gray, 1989).

Listening Skills (page 110)

If you answered "yes" or "sometimes" on less than three questions, you perceive yourself to be a good listener. If you answered "yes" or "sometimes" on three to six questions, you are an average listener. If you answered "yes" or "sometimes" on seven or more questions, you need immediate improvement of your listening skills.

Chapter 5

Nonverbal Symbols Across Cultures (page 143)

Situation 1. Africans enjoy parties and usually are happy to reciprocate with parties that include both food and drink. Although your guests may have been surprised by your American-style (drinks only) party, it is doubtful that this was more than a slight influence in this situation. The best answer is probably Answer *b* When they get to know you better, you will probably be invited to their homes. Be patient.

Situation 2. Although the English managers may be upset that an outsider has been sent to solve one of their problems, eye blinking is not the way the English show unhappiness. Actually, the British use prolonged eye contact and eye blinking as a way to show that they are paying attention (answer *c*). Absence of eye contact and eye blinking might be a nonverbal sign that you were not getting through to the managers. Because private offices are rare in England, the noises Americans make to show they are listening would intrude on nearby conversations almost as much as loud talking. Both are considered examples of extremely poor manners and low class!

Chapter 6

Giving Instructions (page 158)

Situation: Project F. Answers will vary.

Facts Versus Inferences (page 163)

1. T   That's what the story says.
2. ?   Story does not say whether he did or not.
3. F   Story says he did produce something new.
4. ?   Story does not say whether or not Harris had authority to spend.
5. ?   Story does not say whether other than the three mentioned had such authority.
6. T   That's what the story says.
7. ?   Not all executives are necessarily men.
8. ?   Story suggests this but does not specify it.
9. ?   If Harris is one of the three given authority to spend $50,000, this would be true, but the story does not specify whether he is one of those three.

10.   T   That's what the story says.

11.   ?   Story does not specify whether Phillips gave such authority to his best men.

Meanings of Terms (page 165)
Answers will vary.

Chapter 7

Types of Questions (page 195)
1. B (hypothetical open); 2. E (loaded); 3. D (closed); 4. A (open); 5. H (verbal probe); 6. F (leading); 7. H (verbal probe); 8. B (hypothetical open); 9. C (direct/ specific); 10. C (direct/specific); 11. G (third-person); 12. D (closed)

Chapter 8

Lawful and Unlawful Questions (page 224)

1. *Unlawful.* Unless absolutely necessary to obtain information for a preemployment investigation, this question is unlawful. How can the maiden name of a man's wife in any way relate to his job qualifications?

2. *Lawful.* This information is necessary to ensure that the applicant has a legal work permit that allows permanent stay in the United States. It is unlawful, however, to ask if a person is a naturalized citizen of the United States or to ask when the person acquired citizenship.

3. *Unlawful.* Arrest does not necessarily mean conviction. An applicant could have been arrested simply because he or she happened to be driving the same type of car as a reported robbery getaway car. Should this be on the applicant's record? Unfortunately, some employers might feel that the applicant is suspect, regardless of the reason for the arrest, and refuse employment. It is lawful to ask if the applicant has been convicted of a felony, but this can be used for employment rejection only depending on the number of convictions, the nature and time of the convictions, and if the conviction is job-related (e.g., if the position requires the employee to be bonded).

4. *Questionable.* There is probably nothing wrong with asking this question, but if challenged the burden of proof would be on the employer to show that the question was job-related.

5. *Unlawful.* The Age Discrimination in Employment Act prohibits discrimination against persons between the ages of 40 and 60, and in most cases, to 70 years of age. Because of child protection laws in most states, it is legal (even required) to ask if the applicant is 21 or older. The exact age, however, should not be asked.

6. *Unlawful.* Both documents contain information that is unlawful to obtain. Even if the employer owned a liquor store and could not legally hire anyone under the age of 21, the employer could not ask for proof of age in the preemployment interview. Once the applicant has been hired, it is legal to obtain proof of age.

7. *Lawful.* This information would be job-related if the job requires the applicant to type. The employer may ask the applicant to take a standardized typing test if all applicants are given the same test.

8. *Unlawful.* This question is unlawful unless the job requires certain physical skills for successful performance of duties. It would be better to ask, "Do you have any physical or health problems that may affect your job performance?"

9. *Questionable.* The employer must be able to prove that the question is job related.

10. *Lawful.* The response would tell of the applicant's skill and abilities.

11. *Lawful.* This is necessary to determine an applicant's qualifications. The employer should request the applicant to sign a release form so that the schools in question may legally release this information.

12. *Unlawful.* Even men could be discriminated against by this question. Some employers consider a young man who is married to be more stable and therefore a better employee than a young man who is single.

13. *Unlawful.* Questions referring to pregnancy, marital status, number or names of children, care of children when sick, and other similar questions are illegal because they are mainly used to discriminate against women and are not job related. An employer who is worried that a woman may take off too much time to tend sick children merely needs to ask for the woman's attendance record for the past year.

14. *Lawful.* As long as the information is job related, it is lawful. However, to ask how the applicant acquired the ability to speak, read, or write a foreign language is unlawful. If a definite competency level is required, all applicants can be given a language test.

15. *Lawful.* The response would tell of the applicant's job-related skills and knowledge.

16. *Unlawful.* Type of discharge is not job related; neither is the branch of the military in which the applicant served. It is lawful to ask, "Are you a veteran?"

17. *Unlawful.* This could reveal personal information used to discriminate against the applicant.

18. *Unlawful.* A photograph could easily be used to discriminate against the applicant on the basis of race, sex, age, or national origin. Sometimes, a job applicant will send a photograph even when not requested. Normally it is advisable not to send a photograph because employers aware of federal regulations will separate it from the application and destroy it anyway. Once an applicant has been hired, the company can request a photograph or have the employee photographed.

19. *Unlawful.* This question could be used to discriminate against an applicant because of his or her religion. However, if the applicant has voluntarily stated religious preferences, the interviewer may ask, "Do you expect to have your religious holidays off?"

20. *Lawful.* This question is job related if the job requires the operation of machines.

21. *Questionable.* Asking for names of clubs, lodges, or organizations that relate to sex, race, or religion is unlawful. It is also unlawful to ask if the applicant is or was a member of a fraternity or sorority. However, it is lawful to inquire about any unions or trade or professional organizations that are job related.

22. *Unlawful.* This is not job related and tends to discriminate against the poor, young, and minority groups. For the same reasons, it is also unlawful to ask if an applicant owns a car (unless it's a job requirement) or has an established credit record.

23. *Unlawful.* Such personal data are used to discriminate against applicants for the same reasons listed in answer 18. Personal data have rarely proven to be job related. Applicants are not advised to include such data in their resumes or personal data sheets.

24. *Unlawful.* The Immigration Reform and Control Act (IRCA) prohibits discrimination based on national origin. Areas given special consideration by EEOC and IRCA include discrimination against a person who is foreign looking, who speaks with an accent, who fails to meet company height and weight requirements, and who speaks a language other than English in personal conversations and on breaks.

25. *Questionable.* Although not actually unlawful, it would be hard for the employer to prove that the applicant's answer was not used in a discriminatory manner. The safest policy would be to omit questions such as this one, or ask, "What types of people do you least like working with?"

Chapter 9

Use of Criteria (page 250)
1. A (want); 2. D (operational); 3. D (operational); 4. C (task); B (want); 5. C (task); A (must); 6. D (operational); A (must)

Chapter 10

Answers will vary to all Awareness Checks in the chapter.

Chapter 11

Organization Patterns (page 298)
1. a (topical); 2. c (geographic); 3. d (causal); 4. b (chronological); 5. a (topical); 6. d (causal)

Chapter 12

Supporting Materials (page 332)
1. f (expert opinion); 2. d (examples); 3. a (explanation); 4. e (statistics); 5. c (hypothetical illustration); 6. b (figurative comparison)

Chapter 13

Effective Visual Aids (page 365)
1. F (false); 2. F (false); 3. T (true); 4. F (false); 5. F (false); 6. T (true); 7. F (false); 8. T (true); 9. T (true); 10. F (false)

Chapter 14

Identifying Basic Needs (page 388)
1. a (physiological need of sexual attraction); 2. d (esteem need of sense of achievement);
3. d (esteem need of status and prestige); 4. c (social need to give and receive love); 5. e (self-actualization need of being the best person possible); 6. b (safety need of protection from injury)

References

1988–2002 award recipients' contacts and profiles (2003, August 15). Retrieved from http://baldrige.nist.gov/Contacts_ Profiles.htm

A million little lies. (2006, January 8). *The Smoking Gun.com.* Retrieved from http://www.thesmokinggun.com/archive/0104061jamesfrey1.html

A powerful story. (2005, October 26). *Oprah.com.* Retrieved from http://www.oprah.com/tows/slide/200510/20051026/slide_20051026_350_101.jhtml

A true tale of a case interview gone bad. (n.d.). *Quintessential Carreers.com.* Retrieved November 11, 2009, at http://www.quintcareers.com/bad_case_interview.html

About eBay. (2009). *eBay.com.* Retrieved from http://news.ebay.com/about.cfm

About NEADS. (2009). *National Education for Assistance Dog Services, Inc.* Retrieved from http://www.neads.org/ about_us/index.shtml

About Technorati. (2006). *Technorati.com.* Retrieved from http://www.technorati.com/about

Abrams, F. (2000). Report on CNN Broadcast. *CNN.com.* Retrieved from http://www.cnn.com/US/9807/02/tailwind.findings/index.html

Adams, J. M., Faux, D. D., & Rieber, L. J. (2001). *Printing technology* (5th ed.). Albany, NY: Delmar.

Addington, D. W. (1971). The effects of vocal variations on ratings of source credibility. *Speech Monographs, 38,* 242–247.

Adler, N. J., & Gundersen, A. (2008). *International dimensions of organizational behavior* (5th ed.). Cincinnati, OH: South-Western.

AFA Online. (2002, July). Parents hammer A&F over children's thong underwear. *AFA Journal.* Retrieved from http://www.afa.net/journal/july/2002/noi.asp

Aggarwal, P., Castleberry, S. B., Ridnour, R., & Shepherd, C. D. (2005). Salesperson empathy and listening: Impact on relationship outcomes. *Journal of Marketing Theory and Practice,* Summer, 16–31.

Aguilar, F. J. (1994). *Managing corporate ethics.* New York: Oxford University Press.

Albrecht, T., & Hall, B. (1991). Facilitating talk about new ideas. *Communication Monographs, 58,* 273–288.

Alesandrini, K. L. (1982). Image eliciting strategies and meaningful learning. *Journal of Mental Imagery, 6,* 125–140.

Allen, J. G. (2009). *Instant interviews: 101 ways to get the best job of your life.* New York: Wiley.

Allen, M. (1991, Fall). Meta-analysis comparing the persuasiveness of one-sided and two-sided messages. *Western Journal of Speech Communication, 55,* 390–404.

Allen, M. (1998). Comparing the persuasive effectiveness of one- and two-sided messages. In M. Allen & R. W. Preiss (Eds.), *Persuasion: Advances through meta-analysis* (pp. 87–98). Cresskill, NJ: Hampton Press.

Allen, M., Bruflat, R., Fucilla, R., Kramer, M., McKellips, S., Ryan, D. J., & Spiegelhoff, M. (2000). Testing the persuasiveness of evidence: Combining narrative and statistical forms. *Communication Research Reports, 17,* 331–336.

Allen, M., Hunter, J., & Donohue, W. (1989). Meta-analysis of self-report on the effectiveness of public speaking anxiety treatment techniques. *Communication Education, 38,* 54–76.

Alvey, R. J. (2005, December). Creating an effective crisis communication team. *Tactics, 12,* 12–13.

Amason, A. C. (1996). Distinguishing the effects of functional and dysfunctional conflict on strategic decision making: Resolving a paradox for top management teams. *Academy of Management Journal, 39,* 124–148.

Amason, A. C., Thompson, K. R., Hochwarter, W. A., & Harrison, A. W. (1995). Conflict: An important dimension in successful management teams. *Organizational Dynamics, 24*(2), 20–35.

Ambady, N., Halahan, M., & Conner, B. (1999). Accuracy of judgments of sexual orientation from thin slices of behavior. *Journal of Personality and Social Psychology, 77,* 538–547.

AMD.com. (2009). History of AMD: 1969–73. Retrieved from http://www.adm.com/en-US/news/Facts/Pages/default.aspx

American Hearing Research Foundation. (2006). Noise induced hearing loss. Retrieved from http://www.american-hearing.org/name/noise_induced.html

American Program Bureau. (2009). Harry Markopolos: Madoff Whistleblower. Retrieved from http://www.apbspeakers.com/speaker/harry-markopolos

Andersen, P. A. (1999). *Nonverbal communication: Forms and functions.* Mountain View, CA: Mayfield.

Andersen, P. A., & Wang, H. (2009). Beyond language: Nonverbal communication across cultures. In L. A. Samovar, R. E. Porter, & E. R. McDaniel (Eds.), *Intercultural communication: A reader* (12th ed., pp. 264–281). Boston: Wadsworth.

Andrews, A. H., & Baird, J. E., Jr. (1999). *Communication for business and the professions* (7th ed.). Dubuque, IA: Brown & Benchmark.

Antonoff, M. (1990, July 27). Presentations that persuade. *Personal Computing, 14,* 62–68.

Applicant Interview. (1998). HRdirect sample. *HRdirect.com.* Retrieved from http://www.hrdirect.com/GRAPHICS/ProductPage-Extras/A291_ApplcntIntrvw.pdf

Archer, D., & Akert, R. M. (1977). Words and everything else: Verbal and nonverbal cues in social interpretation. *Journal of Personality and Social Psychology, 35,* 443–449.

Argyle, M. (1973). The syntaxes of bodily communication. *International Journal of Psycholinguistics, 2,* 78.

Argyle, M., & Ingham, R. (1972). Gaze, mutual gaze and proximity. *Semiotica, 6,* 32–49.

Arkowitz, H., Westra, H. A., Miller, W. R., & Rollnick, S. (Eds.) (2008). *Motivational interviewing in the treatment of psychological problems.* New York: Guilford Press.

Armstrong, D., & Burton, T. M. (2009, June 18). Medtronic paid the surgeon accused of falsifying study nearly $800,000. *Wall Street Journal,* p. B1.

Atkinson, C. (2005). *Beyond bullet points.* Redmond, WA: Microsoft Press.

Aubuchon, N. (1997). *The anatomy of persuasion: How to persuade others to act on your ideas, accept your proposals, buy your products or services, hire you, promote you.* New York: AMACOM.

Augstums, I. M., & Halkias, M. (2006, August 30). E-mail: You're fired. *The Dallas Morning News,* pp. 1D, 4D.

August 2006 Web Server Survey. (2006, August 1). *Netcraft.com.* Accessed August 12, 2006, at http://news.netcraft.com/archives/ 2006/08/01/august_2006_web_server/html.

Axtell, R. E. (1998). *Gestures: The do's and taboos of body language around the world.* New York: Wiley.

Axtell, R. E. (2007). *Gestures: The do's and taboos of body language around the world* (3rd ed.). New York: Wiley.

Ayres, J., & Hopf, T. S. (1995). An assessment of the role of communication apprehension in communicating with the terminally ill. *Communication Research Reports, 12*(2), 227–234.

Ayres, J., Hopf, T. S., & Ayres, D. M. (1994). An examination of whether imaging ability enhances the effectiveness of an interview designed to reduce speech anxiety. *Communication Education, 43*(3), 252–258.

Ayres, J., Hopf, T. S., & Ayres, D. M. (1997). Visualization and performance visualization: Applications, evidence, and speculation. In J. A. Daley, J. C. McCroskey, J. Ayres, T. Hopf, & D. M. Ayres (Eds.), *Avoiding communication: Shyness, reticence, and communication apprehension* (2nd ed., pp. 401–422). Cresskill, NJ: Hampton.

Babrick, H. P., Babrick, P. O., & Wittlinger, R. P. (1975). Fifty years of memory for names and faces: A cross-sectional approach. *Journal of Experimental Psychology, 104,* 54–75.

Bachman, G. (2000). Brainstorming deluxe. *Training & Development, 54*(1), 15–17.

Bajaj, G. (2004, March 26). An interview with Tad Simons. *Presentations.com.* Retrieved from http://www.indezine.com/products/powerpoint/personality/tadsimons.html

Baldwin, S. (2001, Summer). Keep the doors open. *Trinity Magazine Online.* Retrieved from http://www.trinitydc.edu/ news_events/mags/summer01/doorsopen.htm

Ballard, B. (2003, June). Six ways to grab your audience right from the start. *Harvard Management Communication Letter, 3–5.*

Baltes, B. B., Dickson, M. W., Sherman, M. P., Bayer, C. C., & LaGanke, J. S. (2002). Computer-mediated communication and group decision making: A meta-analysis. *Organizational Behavior and Human Decision Processes, 87*(1), 156–179.

Barge, J. K. (1994). *Leadership: Communication skills for organizations and groups.* New York: St. Martin's.

Barker, J. (2006). Meta-search engines. *UC Berkeley.* Retrieved from http://www.lib.berkeley.edu/TeachingLib/Guides/Internet/MetaSearch.html

Barnard, C. I. (1938). *The functions of the executive.* Cambridge: Harvard University Press.

Barnlund, D. C. (1989). *Communicative styles of Japanese and Americans: Images and realities.* Belmont, CA: Wadsworth.

Barrionuevo, A. (2006, May 26). Two Enron chiefs are convicted in fraud and conspiracy trial. *The New York Times.* Retrieved from http://www.nytimes.com/2006/05/26/business/businessspecial3/26enron.html

Bartoo, H., & Sias, P. M. (2004, Winter). When enough is too much: Communication apprehension and employee information experiences. *Communication Quarterly, 52,* 15–27.

Baskette, F. K., Sissors, J. Z., & Brooks, B. S. (1992). *The art of editing* (5th ed.). New York: Macmillan.

Bass, B. (1995). Concepts of leadership: The beginnings. In J. T. Wren (Ed.), *The Leaders' companion* (pp. 49–52). New York: Free Press.

Bass, B. M. (1985). *Leadership and performance beyond expectations.* New York: Free Press.

Bass, B. M., & Riggio, R. E. (2006). *Transformational leadership* (2nd ed.). Mahwah, NJ: Lawrence Erlbaum.

Bass, B. M., & Stogdill, R. M. (1990). *Bass and Stogdill's handbook of leadership: Theory, research, and managerial applications* (3rd ed.). New York: Free Press.

Beamer, L., & Abraham, K. (2002). *Let's roll.* Wheaton, IL: Tyndale House.

Beatty, M. J. (1988). Situational and predispositional correlates of public speaking anxiety. *Communication Education, 37*(1), 28–39.

Beatty, M. J., Balfantz, G. L., & Kuwabara, A. Y. (1989). Traitlike qualities of selected variables assumed to be transient causes of performance state anxiety. *Communication Education, 38*(3), 277–289.

Beatty, M. J., McCroskey, J. C., & Heisel, A. D. (1998). Communication apprehension as temperamental expression: A communibiological paradigm. *Communication Monographs, 65,* 197–219.

Beebe, S. A., & Masterson, J. T. (2006). *Communicating in small groups: Principles and practices* (8th ed.). Boston: Pearson Education.

Behling, D. U., & Williams, E. A. (1991). Influence of dress on perceptions of intelligence and expectations of scholastic achievement. *Clothing and Textiles Research Journal, 9*(4), 1–7.

Behnke, R. R., & Sawyer, C. R. (1999). Milestones of anticipatory public speaking anxiety. *Communication Education, 48*(1), 49, 165–172, 187–195.

Belcher, J. (2006, August). The business of blogging: A review. *eMarketer.com.* Retrieved from http://www.emarketer.com/Reports/All/Blogs_aug06.aspx

Bell, A. (1991, January-February). What price ethics? *Entrepreneurial Woman,* 68.

Bell, A. H. (1989). *The complete manager's guide to interviewing: How to hire the best.* Homewood, IL: Dow Jones-Irwin.

Bell, D. (2002). The Eden alternative. Retrieved from http://www.pbs.org/thoushalthonor/eden/index.html

Bell, K. (1990). *Developing arguments: Strategies for reaching audiences.* Belmont, CA: Wadsworth.

Bellezza, F. S. (1982). Updating memory using mnemonic devices. *Cognitive Psychology, 14,* 301–327.

Benne, K. D., & Sheats, P. (1948). Functional roles and group members. *Journal of Social Issues, 4,* 41–49.

Benson, P. L., Korabenick, S. A., & Lerner, R. M. (1975). Pretty please: The effects of physical attractiveness, race, and sex on receiving help. *Journal of Experimental Social Psychology, 18,* 409–415.

Berg, D. M. (1967). A descriptive analysis of the distribution and duration of themes described by task-oriented small groups. *Speech Monographs, 34,* 172–175.

Bergen, G. L., & Haney, W. V. (1966). *Organizational relations and management action: Cases and issues.* New York: McGraw-Hill.

Bergeron. J., & Laroche, M. (2009). The effects of perceived salesperson listening effectiveness in the financial industry. *Journal of Financial Services marketing, 14*(1), 6–25.

Berkman, R. (2000, January 21). Searching for the right search engine. *Chronicle of Higher Education,* p. B6.

Berlo, D. K. (1960). *The process of communication.* New York: Holt, Rinehart & Winston.

Berry, L. L., & Bendapudi, N. (2003). Clueing in customers. *Harvard Business Review, 81*(2), 100–106.

Berscheid, E. (1985). Interpersonal attraction. In G. Lindzey & and E. Aronson (Eds.), *The handbook of social psychology* (3rd ed., Vol. 2, pp. 413–484). New York: Random House.

Bettinghaus, E. P., & Cody, M. J. (1997). *Persuasive communication* (5th ed.). New York: Holt, Rinehart & Winston.

Bidinotto, R. J. (1994, November). Must our prisons be resorts? *Reader's Digest, 145,* 65–71.

Bigger liars out there [Online message board comment]. (2006, January 25). *Oprah.com.* Retrieved from http://boards.oprah.com/WebX?13@@.f0e3cc6!DYNID=1ABZLJJHGM1ENLARAZ2SFEQ

Binkley, C. (2008, April 17). Business casual: All business, never casual. *The Wall Street Journal,* pp. D1, D8.

Bippus, A. M., & Daly, J. A. (1999). What do people think causes stage fright? Naive attributions about the reasons for public speaking anxiety. *Communication Education, 48*(1), 63–72.

Birdwhistell, R. L. (1970). *Kinesics and context: Essays on body motion communication.* Philadelphia: University of Pennsylvania Press.

Bishop, T. (2003, October 30). Microsoft fires worker over weblog. *Seattle Post-Intelligencer.* Retrieved from http:// seattlepi.nwsource.com/business/146115_blogger30.html

Blake, R. R., & Mouton, J. S. (1964). *Managerial grid.* Houston: Gulf.

Blake, R. R., & Mouton, J. S. (1985). *The managerial grid III: The key to leadership excellence.* Houston: Gulf.

Blakeman, M., et al. (1971). *Job-seeking skills reference manual* (3rd ed.). Minneapolis: Minnesota Rehabilitation Center.

Blanchard, K. H., & Johnson, S. (1982). *The one minute manager.* New York: William Morrow.

Blau, P. M. (1974). *On the nature of organizations.* New York: Wiley.

Block, J. A., & Betrus, M. (2002). *2500 Keywords to get you hired.* Boston: McGraw-Hill.

Blythin, E., & Samovar, L. A. (1985). *Communicating effectively on television.* Belmont, CA: Wadsworth.

Bob Love. (2006). *SportsStarsUSA.com.* Retrieved from http://www.sportsstarsusa com/basketball/love_bob.html

Bochner, A. P. (1984). The functions of human communicating in interpersonal bonding. In C. C. Arnold and J. W. Bowers (Eds.), *Handbook of rhetorical and communication theory* (pp. 554–621). Boston: Allyn & Bacon.

Boland, R., & Hoffman, R. (1983). Humor in a machine shop. In L. Pondy, P. Frost, G. Morgan, and T. Dandridge (Eds.), *Organizational symbolism* (pp. 187–198). Greenwich, CT: JAI Press.

Bolles, R. (2009). *What color is your parachute? 2009: A practical manual for job-hunters and career-changers.* Berkeley: Ten Speech Press.

Boor, M., Wartman, S. A., & Reuben, D. B. (1983). Relationship of physical appearances and professional demeanor to interview evaluations and rankings of medical residency applicants. *Journal of Psychology, 113,* 64.

Boorstin, J. (2004, January 12). 1 J. M. Smucker. *Fortune, 149,* 58–59. Available from Business Source Premier Database.

Booth-Butterfield, M., & Booth-Butterfield, S. (1992). *Communication apprehension and avoidance in the classroom.* Edina, MN: Burgess.

Booth-Butterfield, M., & Booth-Butterfield, S. (1994). Communication anxiety and signing effectiveness: Testing an interference model among deaf communicators. *Journal of Applied Communication Research, 22,* 273–286.

Booth-Butterfield, S., & Gutowski, C. (1993, Winter). Message modality and source credibility can interact to affect argument processing. *Communication Quarterly, 41,* 77–89.

Bordwin, M. (1998). The courts get you coming and going. *Management Review, 87*(10), 51–53.

Borenstein, S. (2006, July 11). Experts: NASA's shuttle program is back. *Associated Press News Release.* Retrieved from http://news.yahoo.com/s/ap/20060711/ap_on_sc/space_shuttle&printer=1

Borisoff, D., & Merrill, L. (1992). *The Power to communicate: Gender differences as barriers* (2nd ed.). Prospect Heights, IL: Waveland.

Bormann, E. G., Howell, W. S., Nichols, R. G., & Shapiro, G. L. (1969). *Interpersonal communication in the modern organization.* Englewood Cliffs, NJ: Prentice-Hall.

Bostrom, R. N. (1988). *Communicating in public: Speaking and listening.* Edina, MN: Burgess.

Bostrom, R. N., & Tucker, R. K. (1969, March). Evidence, personality, and attitude change. *Speech Monographs, 36,* 22–27.

Bourhis, J., & Allen, M. (1992). Meta-analysis of the relationship between communication apprehension and cognitive performance. *Communication Education, 41*(1), 68–76.

Bovee, C. L., & Thill, J. V. (2004). *Business communication today* (8th ed.). Upper Saddle River, NJ: Prentice-Hall.

Bowen, W. (1981, March 9). How to regain our competitive edge. *Fortune,* 74–90.

Boyd, J. (1999). Wrong questions can turn job interview into lawsuit. *Business Journal, 14*(11), 29–30.

Boyle, R. C. (1999). A manager's guide to effective listening. *Manage, 51*(1), 6–7.

Bradford, D. L., & Cohen, A. R. (1984). *Managing for excellence: The guide to developing high performance in contemporary organizations.* New York: Wiley.

Breen, B. (2000, February). New rules for landing a job. *Readers Digest, 156,* 86–90.

Brembeck, W. L., & Howell, W. S. (1976). *Persuasion: A means of social control* (2nd ed.). Englewood Cliffs, NJ: Prentice-Hall.

Brett, P. (1990). *Writing for results: A resume workbook.* Belmont, CA: Wadsworth.

Brilhart, J. K. (1978). *Effective group discussion* (3rd ed.). Dubuque, IA: Brown.

Brinkley, D. (2006). *The great deluge: Hurricane Katrina, New Orleans, and the Mississippi Gulf Coast.* New York: HarperCollins.

Bristow, L. R. (1994, March 15). Protecting youth from the tobacco industry. *Vital Speeches, 60,* 333.

Broadbent, D. E. (1975). The magic number seven after 15 years. In A. Kennedy & A. Wilkes (Eds.), *Studies in long-term memory* (pp. 3–18). London: Wiley.

Brockner, J. (1992). The escalation of commitment to a failing course of action: Toward theoretical progress. *Academy of Management Review, 17,* 39–61.

Brody, M. (1994, June). Listen up! Do you hear what people are saying? *American Salesman, 39,* 14.

Brody, M. (2003). Team presentations: A winning combination. *3M Meeting Network.* Retrieved from http:// www.3m.com/meetingnetwork/articles_advice/ marjorie/ 03-summer.html

Bromage, M. C. (1970). Defensive writing. *California Management Review, 13,* 45–50.

Brown, M. (2005, August 29). First responders urged not to respond to hurricane impact areas. FEMA. Press Release.

Brownell, J. (2003, November). *The skills of listening-centered communication.* Paper presented at the National Communication Association convention, Miami, Florida.

Brownell, J. (2006). *Listening: Attitudes, principles, and skills* (3rd ed.). Boston: Allyn and Bacon.

Bruce, S. D. (1988). Exit interview: Potent managerial tool. *Chemical Engineering, 95,* 105–108.

Bryden, M. P., & Ley, R. G. (1983). Right hemispheric involvement in imagery and affect. In E. Perecman (Ed.), *Cognitive processing in the right hemisphere* (pp. 116–117). New York: Academic Press.

Buckingham, M., & Coffman, C. (1999). *First, break all the rules: What the world's greatest managers do differently.* New York: Simon & Schuster.

Buckley, R. (1999, October). When you have to put it to them. *Across the Board,* 44–48.

Buller, D. B., & Aune, K. (1988). The effects of vocalics and nonverbal sensitivity on compliance: A speech accommodation theory explanation. *Human Communication Research, 14,* 301–332.

Bulls in the Community: Outreach. (2006). *Bulls.com.* Retrieved from http://www.nba.com/bulls/community/outreach.html

Burch, G. (1996). *The art and science of business persuasion: Mastering the power of getting what you want.* Secaucus, NJ: Birch Lane Press.

Burgoon, J. K. (1983). Nonverbal violations of expectations. In J. M. Wiemann & R. P. Harrison (Eds.), *Nonverbal interaction* (pp. 11–77). Beverly Hills: Sage.

Burgoon, J. K. (1993). Interpersonal expectations, expectancy violations, and emotional communication. *Journal of Language and Social Psychology, 12,* 30–48.

Burgoon, J. K., Birk, T., & Pfau, M. (1990). Nonverbal behaviors, persuasion, and credibility. *Human Communication Research, 17,* 140–169.

Burgoon, J. K., Buller, D. B., & Woodall, W. G. (1996). *Nonverbal communication: The unspoken dialogue.* New York: McGraw-Hill.

Burgoon, J. K., & Hoobler, G. D. (2002). Nonverbal signals. In M. L. Knapp and J. A. Daly (Eds.), *Handbook of interpersonal communication* (3rd ed., pp. 240–299). Thousand Oaks, CA: Sage.

Burgoon, J. K., & Le Poire, B. A. (1993). Effects of communication expectancies, actual communication, and expectancy disconfirmation on evaluations of communicators and their communication behavior. *Human Communication Research, 20,* 75–107.

Burke, L. A., & Wise, J. M. (2003, May-June). The effective care, handling, and pruning of the office grapevine. *Business Horizons, 46,* 73–74.

Burnett, J. R., & Motowidlo, S. J. (1998). Relations between different sources of information in the structured selection interview. *Personnel Psychology, 51*(4), 963–1083.

Burns, J. M. (1978). *Leadership.* New York: Harper & Row.

Burtt, T. (2006). Baseball strength training. Retrieved from http://www.beabetterhitter.com/text/conditioning/strengthtraining/baseball-stregthtraining.htm

Business casual can be confusing. (2006, July 11). *The Wall Street Journal,* p. B5.

Caldwell, D., & O'Reilly, C. (1982). Task perceptions and job satisfaction. *Journal of Applied Psychology, 67,* 361–369.

Callarman, W. G., & McCartney, W. W. (1995, March). Identifying and overcoming listening problems. *Supervisory Management, 30,* 38–42.

Calmes, J., & Story, L. (2009, March 18). Outcry builds in Washington for recovery of A.I.G. bonuses. *The New York Times.com.* Retrieved from http://www.nytimes.com/2009/03/18/business/18bailout.html

Calnan, A. C. T., & Davidson, M. J. (1998). The impact of gender and its interaction with role and status on the use of tag questions in meetings. *Women in Management Review, 13,* 19–36.

Cameron, K. S. (1994). Investigating organizational downsizing—fundamental issues. *Human Resources Management, 33*(2), 183–188.

Caminiti, S. (2005, January/February). The people company (pp. 12–6). *NYSE.*

Canines for combat veterans. (2009). *National Education for Assistance Dog Services, Inc.* Retrieved from http://www.neads.org/services_new/military_dog.shtml

Canseco, J. (2005). *Juiced: Wild times, rampant 'roids, smash hits, and how baseball got big.* New York Regan Books.

Caputo, J. S., Hazel, H. C., & McMahon, C. (2000). *Interpersonal communication: Competency through critical thinking.* Boston: Allyn & Bacon.

Carroll, D. (2009). United Airlines Song Background (detailed version). *Dave Carroll Music.com.* Retrieved from http://www.davecarrollmusic.com/story/united-breaks-guitars/

Carr-Ruffino, N. (1985). *The promotable woman: Becoming a successful manager* (Rev. ed.). Belmont, CA: Wadsworth.

Carr-Ruffino, N. (1997). *The promotable woman* (3rd ed.). Franklin Lakes, NJ: Career Press.

Carson, C. L., & Cupach, W. R. (2000). Facing corrections in the workplace: The influence of perceived face threat on the consequences of managerial reproaches. *Journal of Applied Communication Research, 28,* 215–234.

Carter-Jackson, S. (n.d.). Online friendships and collaborations. *Wired Woman.* Retrieved from http://www.wiredwoman.com/technoculture/friendships.html

Carzo, R., Jr., & Yanouzas, J. N. (1969). Effects of flat and tall organization structures. *Administrative Science Quarterly, 14,* 178–191.

Cascio, W. F. (1998). *Applied psychology in human resources management* (5th ed.). Upper Saddle River, NJ: Prentice-Hall.

Case, J. (1995, June). The open-book revolution. *Inc.com.* Retrieved from http://www.inc.com/magazine/19950601/2296.html

Cashdan, E. (1998). Smiles, speech, and body posture: How women and men display sociometric status and power. *Journal of Nonverbal Behavior, 22,* 209–228.

Caudron, S. (1998). They hear it through the grapevine. *Workforce, 77*(11), 25–27.

Cavanagh, G., Moberg, D., & Velasquez, M. (1990). The ethics of organizational politics. In S. Corman., S. Banks, C. Bantz, & M. Mayer (Eds.), *Foundations of organizational communication: A reader* (pp. 243–254). New York: Longman.

CBCNews.com. (2006, February 17). RadioShack CEO apologizes for resume errors. Retrieved from http://www.cbc.ca/story/business/national/2006/02/16/radio-060216.html

Ceniza-Levine, C. (2009, February 4). Ask-A-Recruiter: Telephone interview tips. *The Glass Hammer.com.* Retrieved from http://www.theglasshammer.com/news/2009/02/04/ask-a-recruiter-telephone-interview-tips

Chaiken, S. (1986). Physical appearance and social influence. In C. P. Herman, M. P. Zanna, & E. T. Higgins (Eds.), *Physical appearance, stigma, and social behavior: The Ontario Symposium* (Vol. 3, pp. 143–177). Hillsdale, NJ: Erlbaum.

Chaiken, S., & Eagly, A. (1983). Communication modality as a determinant of persuasion: The role of communicator salience. *Journal of Personality and Social Psychology, 45,* 241–256.

Chao, E. L. (2007). Remarks. *Department of Labor.* Retrieved from www.dol.gov/_sec/media/speeches/20070712_agen.htm

Chaplin, W. F., Phillips, J. B., Brown, J. D., Clanton, N. R., & Stein, J. L. (2000). Handshaking, gender personality, and first impressions. *Journal of Personality and Social Psychology, 79,* 110–117.

Chell, E., & Tracey, P. (2005). Relationship building in small firms: The development of a model. *Human Relations, 58*(5), 577–616.

Chen, G., Liu, C., & Tjosvold, D. (2005). Conflict management for effective top management teams and innovation in China. *Journal of Management Studies, 42*(2), 277–300.

Chesbrough, H. W., & Teece, D. J. (1996). When is virtual virtuous? Organizing for innovation. *Harvard Business Review, 74*(1), 65–73.

Chicago Tribune. (2006, June 9). Baseball's next scandal, Editorial. Retrieved from LexisNexis Academic.

Choi, S. H. (1991). Communicative socialization processes: Korea and Canada. In B. B. Schieffelin & E. Ochs (Eds.), *Language socialization across cultures* (pp. 213–250). Cambridge: Cambridge University Press.

Cialdini, R. B. (1993). *Influence: The psychology of persuasion.* New York: Quill.

Clampitt, P., & Downs, C. (1983, November). *Communication and productivity.* Paper presented at a meeting of the Speech Communication Association, Washington, DC.

Clanton, J. (1989, April 1). Plutonium 238: NASA's fuel of choice. *Vital Speeches, 55,* 375.

Clark, R. C., & Mayer, R. E. (2008). *e-learning and the science of instruction: Proven guidelines for consumers and designers of multimedia learning* (2nd ed.). San Francisco: Pfeiffer/Wiley.

Clarke, R. L. (1988, July 1). Hard times and great expectations: The condition of the national banking system. *Vital Speeches, 54,* 548.

Cleveland, J. N., Murphy, K. R., & Williams, R. E. (1989). Multiple uses of performance appraisal: Prevalence and correlates. *Journal of Applied Psychology, 74,* 130–135.

Cliff, S. (1998). Knowledge management: The well-connected business. *Harvard Business Review, 76*(4), 17–21.

CNN retracts Tailwind coverage. (1998, July 2). *CNN.com.* Retrieved from http://www.cnn.com/US/9807/02/tailwind.johnson

Cohen, A. (2008, January 25). Going, going, gone: Meg Whitman leaves eBay [Web log posting]. *The New York Times,* Retrieved from http://theboard.blogs.nytimes.com/2008/01/25/going-going-gone-meg-whitman-leaves-ebay

Cohen, A. R. (1964). *Attitude change and social interaction.* New York: Basic.

Cohen, R. (1991). *Negotiating across cultures: Communication obstacles in international diplomacy.* Washington, DC: U.S. Institute of Peace.

Coleman, M. S. (2006, February 15). Google, the Khmer Rouge and the public good. *Vital Speeches, 72,* 263–269.

Columbia Accident Investigation Board. (2003, August). *Report* (Vol.1). Washington, DC: Government Printing Office.

Colvin, G. (2009). The world's most admired companies 2009. *Fortune, 159*(5), 75–78.

Comer, L. B., & Drollinger, T. (1999, Winter). Active empathetic listening and selling success: A conceptual framework. *Journal of Personal Selling and Sales Management, 19,* 15–29.

Conditt, C. M. (2000). Culture and biology in human communication: Toward a multi-casual model. *Communication Education, 49*(1), 7–24.

Conger, J. A. (1991). Inspiring others: The language of leadership. *Academy of Management Executive, 5,* 31–45.

Conrad, C. (1990). *Strategic organizational communication.* New York: Holt, Rinehart & Winston.

Conrad, C. (1994). *Strategic organizational communication: Toward the twenty-first century* (3rd ed.). New York: Harcourt Brace.

Conrad, C. (2003). Setting the stage. *Management Communication Quarterly, 17,* 15–19.

Conrad, C., & Poole, M. S. (2002). *Strategic organizational communication: Into the twenty-first century* (5th ed.). Fort Worth: Harcourt Brace.

Conrad, C., & Poole, M. S. (2005). *Strategic organizational communication* (6th ed.). Belmont, CA: Wadsworth.

Conway, J. A. (1988). The interaction of color code type and information type on the perception and interpretation or visual displays. *Dissertation Abstracts International, 48,* 2123–2124.

Cook, M. (1970). Experiments on orientation and proxemics. *Human Relations, 23,* 61–76.

Cooper, K. (1987). *Body business.* New York: AMACOM.

Cooper, L. O. (1997). Listening competency in the workplace: A model for training. *Business Communication Quarterly, 60*(4), 75–84.

Cooper, M. D., & Nothstine, W. L. (1992). *Power persuasion: Moving an ancient art into the media age.* Greenwood, IN: Educational Video Group.

Corporate Recruiters Survey: 2009 General Data Report. (2009). *2009 Graduate Management Admission Council.* Retrieved from http://www.gmac.com/NR/rdonlyres/06C3E039-7335-4814-AD1D-16-F501AB70E9/0/2009CRS_GeneralDataReport.pdf

Coughlan, R. (2003, May). Demystifying business ethics. *Successful Meetings, 52,* 33.

Covey, S. M. R. (2006) *The speed of trust: The one thing that changes everything.* New York: Free Press.

Covey, S. R. (1990). *The seven habits of effective people: Powerful lessons in personal change.* New York: Fireside.

Covey, S. R. (2005). *The 8th Habit: From Effectiveness to Greatness.* New York: Free Press.

Cowan, N. (2001). The magical number 4 in short-term memory: A reconsideration of mental storage capacity. *Behavioral and Brain Sciences, 24,* 87–14.

Cozby, P. (1973). Self-disclosure: A literature review. *Psychological Bulletin, 79,* 73–91.

Cravens, D. W., & Piercy, N. F. (2003). *Strategic marketing* (7th ed.). New York: McGraw-Hill.

Credo. (2009). Credo for Communication Ethics. The National Communication Association (Natcom.org). Retrieved from http://www.natcom.org/index.asp?bid=514

C-Span Video. (2009, February 4). House Financial Services Hearing on Madoff Investigation. Retrieved from http://www.c-span.org/Watch/watch.aspx?MediaId=HP-A-15082

CultureChangeNow.com. (n.d.). Topic: Welcome to our neighborhood. Retrieved from http://www.culturechangenow. com/askpact.html

Customer service commitment. (2009). *Southwest.com.* Retrieved from http://www.southwest.com/about_swa/customer_service_commitment/customer_service_commitment.html

Cyphert, D. (2007, April). Presentation technology in the age of electronic eloquence: From visual aid to visual rhetoric. *Communication Education, 56*(2), 168–192.

Daft, R. L. (2007). *Organization theory and design* (9th ed.). Mason, OH: South-Western.

Daft, R. L. (2008). *Management* (8th ed.). Mason, OH: Thomson South-Western.

Daft, R. L., & Lengel, R. H. (1986, May). Organizational information requirements, media richness and structural design. *Managerial Science, 32,* 554–572.

Daft, R. L., & Marcic, D. (2006). *Understanding management* (5th ed.). Mason, OH: Thomson South-Western.

Daft, R. L., & Marcic, D. (2009). *Understanding management* (6th ed.). Mason, OH: South-Western Cengage Learning.

Daly, J. A., & Friedrich, G. W. (1981). The development of communication apprehension: A retrospective analysis of contributory correlates. *Communication Quarterly, 29,* 243–255.

Daly, J. A., Vangelisti, A. L., & Weber, D. J. (1995). Speech anxiety affects how people prepare speeches: A protocol analysis of the preparation process of speakers. *Communication Monographs, 62,* 383–397.

Damer, T. E. (2000). *Attacking faulty reasoning: A practical guide to fallacy free arguments* (4th ed.). Belmont, CA: Wadsworth.

Damhorst, M., & Fiore, A. M. (2000). Women's job interview dress: How the personnel interviewers see it. In M. L. Damhorst, K. A. Miller, & S. O. Michelman (Eds.), *The meaning of dress* (pp. 92–97). New York: Fairchild.

Damhorst, M., & Reed, J. A. P. (1986). Clothing, color value and facial expression: Effect on evaluations of female job applicants. *Social Behavior and Personality, 14*(1), 89–98.

Damp, D. V. (2005). *The book of U.S. government jobs* (9th rev. ed.). Ashland, OH: Brookhaven Press LLC.

Dartnell Corporation. (1995). *1995 cost of a business letter* [Dartnell study]. Chicago: Author.

Davenport, T. H., & Pearlson, K. (1998). Two cheers for the virtual office. *Sloan Management Review, 39*(4), 51–65.

Davidson, C. (2009, June 26). Your asked for it: Introducing the mini Starbucks card!! *MyStarbucksIdea.com.* Retrieved from http://blogs.starbucks.com/blogs/customer/default.aspx

Davidson, J. (1993, May 15). Overworked Americans or overwhelmed Americans? You cannot handle everything. *Vital Speeches, 59,* 470–473.

Davis, D. C., & Scaffidi, N. M. (2007, May). Leading virtual teams. Conference Papers—International Communication Association Annual Meeting.

Davis, K. (1972). *Human behavior at work.* New York: McGraw-Hill.

Deal, T. E., & Kennedy, A. A. (1999). *The new corporate cultures: Revitalizing the workplace after downsizing, mergers, and reengineering.* Reading, MA: Perseus Books.

Decker, B., & Denney, J. (1993). *You've got to be believed to be heard.* New York: St. Martin's.

De Dreu, C. K., & McCusker, C. (1997). Gain-loss frames and cooperation in two-person social dilemmas: A transformational analysis. *Journal of Personality and Social Psychology, 72,* 1093–1106.

Deetz, S. (1995). *Transforming communication, transforming business: Building responsive and responsible workplaces.* Cresskill, NJ: Hampton.

Deetz, S. (2001). Conceptual foundations. In F. M. Jablin & L. L. Putnam (Eds.), *The new handbook of organizational communication: Advances in theory, research, and methods* (pp. 3–46). Thousand Oaks, CA: Sage.

de Janasz, S. C., Dowd, K. O., & Schneider, B. Z. (2002). *Interpersonal skills in organizations.* Boston: McGraw-Hill.

Delbecq, A. L., Van de Ven, A. H., & Gustafson, D. H. (1986). *Group techniques for program planning: A guide to nominal group and delphi process.* Westport, CT: Green Briar.

Dennis, A. R., Aronson, J. E., Heninger, W. G., & Walker II, E. D. (1999). Structuring time and task in electronic brainstorming. *MIS Quarterly, 23*(1), 95–108.

Dennis, A. R., & Valacich, J. S. (1993). Computer brainstorms: More heads are better than one. *Journal of Applied Psychology, 78,* 531–537.

Dentzer, S. (2002, February 27). A nursing home alternative. Retrieved from http://pbs.org/newshour/bb/health/jan-june02/eden_2-27.html

DeSantis, J. (2009, March 25). Resignation letter. *New York Times,* p. A29. Retrieved from http://www.nytimes.com/2009/03/25/opinion/25desantis.html

Detz, J. (2000). *It's not what you say, it's how you say it.* New York: St. Martin's Griffin.

Deutschman, A. (1991, November 4). Dealing with sexual harassment. *Fortune,* 145–148.

Deutschman, A. (2004, December 2004). The fabric of creativity. *FastCompany.* Retrieved from http://pf.fastcompany.com/magazine/89/open_gore.html

Deutschman, A. (2005, July). Is your boss a psychopath? *Fast Company, 96,* 44. Retrieved from http://www.fastcompany.com/magazine/96/open_boss.html

DeVito, J. A. (2008). *Interpersonal messages: Communication and relationship skills.* Boston: Allyn & Bacon.

Dewey, J. (1910). *How we think.* Boston: Heath.

Did he con his readers? (2006). *Oprah.com.* Retrieved from http://www.oprah.com/tows/slide/200601/20060126/slide_20060126_350_107.jhtml

Did Medtronic promote dangerous off-label use? (2008, September 4). Did Medtronic promote dangerous off-label use of Infuse Bone Graft? *NewsInferno.com.* Retrieved from http://www.newsinferno.com/archives/3760

Diehl, L. A. (1996). Raising expectations: Institutional responsibility and the issue of sexual harassment. *Initiatives, 57,* 1–10.

Dikel, M., & Roehm, F. (2008). *Guide to Internet job searching 2008–09.* New York: McGraw-Hill.

Dillard, J. P., & Pfau, M. (2002). *The persuasion handbook: Developments in theory and practice.* Thousand Oaks, CA: Sage.

Di Mare, L., & Waldron, V. R. (2006). Researching gendered communication in Japan and the United States: Current limitations and alternative approaches. In K. Dindia and D. J. Canary, *Sex differences and similarities in communication* (pp. 195–215). Mahweh, NJ: Erlbaum.

Dimmick, S. (1995). *Successful communication through NLP.* Hampshire, UK: Gower.

Dindia, K. (1994). The intrapersonal-interpersonal dialectical process of self-disclosure. In S. W. Duck (Ed.), *Dynamics of relationships* (Vol. 4, pp. 27–57). Thousand Oaks, CA: Sage.

Discovery of the Month. (2006, November). Women in Marketing: Succeeding. . . . Naturally! *The Copernicus MZine.* Retrieved from http://www.copernicusmarketing.com/about/mzine/monthlyeds/nov06.shtml

Douglas, J., Jr. (2005, January 22). 'Hook 'em Horns' sign has different meanings in other cultures. *Fort Worth Star-Telegram.* Available from Gale Database.

Downs, A.. (1967). *Inside bureaucracy.* Boston: Little, Brown and Company.

Drake, A. (2005). *Evaluating information found on the World Wide Web* [handout]. Tarrant County College Library Workshop, Fort Worth, Texas.

Drake, J. D. (1998). *The panel interview.* Melville, NY: DBM Publishing.

Drucker, D. (2000, April 4). Virtual teams light up GE. *Internetweek, 808,* 1–2.

Duff, D. C., Levine, T. R., Beatty, M. J., Woolbright, J., & Park, H. S. (2007). Testing public anxiety treatments against a credible placebo control. *Communication Education, 56*(1), 72–88.

Duncan, R. (2006, February 2). The Blog Herald blog count February 2006: 2000 million blogs in existence. *The Blob Herald.com.* Retrieved from http://www.blogherald.com/2006/02/ 02/the-blog-herald-blog-count-february-2006-200-million-blogs-in-existence/

Dunworth, J. (1980, January 1). Six barriers to basics: Education depends on you. *Vital Speeches, 46,* 190.

du Pre, A. (2000). *Communicating about health: Current issues and perspectives.* Mountain View, CA: Mayfield.

Dwyer, K. K. (2000). The multidimensional model: Teaching students to self-manage high communication apprehension by self-selecting treatments. *Communication Education, 49,* 72–81.

Eagly, A. H., & Chaiken, S. (1993). *The psychology of attitudes.* Fort Worth: Harcourt Brace Jovanovich.

EdenAlt.com. (2006, March). *Newsletter: Stories from Eden Alternative registered homes, 5*(2). Retrieved from http://www. edenalt.com/pdf/MarchApril2006Master.pdf

Edinger, J. A., & Patterson, M. L. (1983). Nonverbal involvement and social control. *Psychological Bulletin, 93,* 30–56.

Edmunds, H. (2000). *The focus group research handbook.* New York: McGraw-Hill.

EEOC. (2004, September 2). Discriminatory practices. *U.S. Equal Employment Opportunity Commission.* Retrieved from http:// www.eeoc.gov/abouteeo/overview_practices.html

Einhorn, L. J. (1981). An inner view of the job interview: An investigation of successful communication behaviors. *Communication Education, 80,* 216–228.

Eisenberg, C. (2009, April 29). Chesapeake Energy accused of giving CEO 'personal' bailout. Muckety News. Retrieved from http://news.muckety.com/2009/04/29/chesapeake-energy-accused-of-giving-ceo-mcclendon-personal-bailout/14991

Eisenberg, E. M., Goodall, H. L., Jr., & Trethewey, A. (2010). *Organizational communication: Balancing creativity and constraint* (6th ed.). New York: Bedford/St. Martin's.

Eisenberg, E. M., Monge, P., & Miller, K. (1983). Involvement in communication networks as a predictor of organizational commitment. *Human Communication Research, 10,* 179–201.

Ekman, P. (1992). Are there basic emotions? *Psychological Review, 99*(3), 550–554.

Ekman, P. (1994). Strong evidence for universals in facial expressions: A reply to Russell's mistaken critique. *Psychological Bulletin, 115,* 268–287.

Ekman, P. (2003). *Emotions revealed: Recognizing faces and feelings to improve communication and emotional life.* New York: Times Books.

Ekman, P., & Friesen, W. V. (1969). The repertoire of nonverbal behavior: Categories, origins, usage, and coding. *Semiotica, 1,* 49–98.

Ekman, P., Friesen, W. V., O'Sullivan, M., Chan, A., Heider, K., & Diacoyanni-Tarlatzis, I. (1987). Universals and cultural differences in the judgments of facial expressions of emotion. *Journal of Personality and Social Psychology, 53*(4), 712–717.

Elashmawi, F., & Harris, R. (1998). *Multicultural management* 2000. Houston, TX: Gulf Publishing.

Ellard, G. (2007). I know it when I see it: Moral judgments and business ethics. *Vital Speeches.*

Ellis, A. (2004). *Rational emotive behavior therapy: It works for me—it can work for you.* Amherst, New York: Prometheus Books.

Ellison, S. (2004, July 12). Colgate CEO: Grooming his replacement. *Wall Street Journal,* p. B1.

Elsea, J. G. (1985, September). Strategies for effective presentations. *Personnel Journal, 64,* 31–33.

Eltahawy, M. (2006, January 28). A mountain out of a molehill over Danish cartoons. *Muslim Wakeup! Inc.* Retrieved from http://www.muslimwakeup.com/main/archives/2006/01/a_mountain_out.php

Enelow, W. S., & Kursmark, L. M. (2006). *Expert resumes for baby boomers.* Indianapolis: JIST Works.

Erickson, F. (1979). Talking down: Some cultural sources of miscommunication in interracial interviews. In A. Wolfgang (Ed.), *Nonverbal behavior: Applications and cultural implications* (pp. 99–126). New York: Academic.

Ethics training a low priority. (2004, January 29). *USA Today,* p. 1B.

Evangelista, B. (2009, June 1). Assessing Napster-10 years later. *San Francisco Chronicle,* p. A1. Retrieved from http://www.sfgate.com/cgi-bin/article.cgi?f=/c/a/2009/06/01/MNI917R8PB.DTL.

Ewing, S. E. (1991, June 1). Marble and mud: Shaping the future of the natural gas industry. *Vital Speeches, 57,* 491.

Exline, R., & Eldridge, C. (1967, April). *Effects of two patterns of a speaker's visual behavior upon the perception of the authenticity of his verbal message.* Paper presented to the Eastern Psychological Association Convention, Boston.

FAQ's. (2009). *National Education for Assistance Dog Services, Inc.* Retrieved from http://www.neads.org/services_new/ faqs.shtml

Farivar, C. (2006, September 22). HP chairwoman Patricia Dunn resigns, effective immediately. *Engadget.com.* Retrieved from http://www.engadget.com/2006/09/22/hp-chairwoman-patricia-dunn-resigns-effective-immediately/

Fast, J. (1991). *Subtext: Making body language work in the work place.* New York: Viking.

Fayol, H. (1949). *General and industrial management.* London: Pitman & Sons.

February 2004 Web Server Survey. (2004). Retrieved February 3, 2004 from http://news.netcraft.com/archives/web_server_survey.html

Feeley, T. H., Hwang, J., & Barnett, G. A. (2008). Predicting employee turnover from friendship networks. *Journal of applied Communication Research, 36*(1), 56–73.

Fernandez-Araoz, C., Groysberg, B., & Nohria, N. (2009). The definitive guide to recruiting in good times and bad. *Harvard Business Review, 87*(5), 74–84.

Ferraro, G. P. (1998). *The cultural dimension of international business* (3rd ed.). Englewood Cliffs, NJ: Prentice-Hall.

Festinger, L. (1957). *A theory of cognitive dissonance.* Stanford: Stanford University Press.

Fiedler, F. E. (1967). *A theory of leadership effectiveness.* New York: McGraw-Hill.

Fiedler, F. E. (1978). Contingency model and the leadership process. In L. Berkowitz (Ed.), *Advances in experimental social psychology* (Vol. 11, pp. 60–112). New York: Academic Press.

Fiedler, F. E. (1993). The leadership situation and the black box in contingency theories. In M. M. Chemers & R. Ayman (Eds.), *Leadership theory and research: Perspectives and directions* (pp. 1–28). San Diego: Academic Press.

Fiedler, F. E. (1996). Research on leadership selection and training: One view of the future. *Administrative Science Quarterly, 41,* 241–250.

Fiedler, F. E., & Chemers, M. M. (1974). *Leadership and effective management.* Glenview, IL: Scott Foresman.

Fiedler, F. E., Chemers, M., & Mahar, L. (1976). *Improving leadership effectiveness.* New York: Wiley.

Fill, C. (1995). *Marketing communications: Frameworks, theories, and applications.* Upper Saddle River, NJ: Prentice Hall.

Finder, A. (2006, June 11). When a risque online persona undermines a chance for a job. *The New York Times,* p. A1.

Finkelman, D., & Goland, T. (1990). The case of the complaining customer. *Harvard Business Review, 68*(3), 9–21.

Fishback, B. W., & Krewson, C. (1981, February 16). Design team simplifies interiors to aid patient recuperation. *Hospitals, 55,* 151–156.

Fishbein, M., & Ajzen, I. (1975). *Belief, attitude, intention, and behavior.* Reading, MA: Addison-Wesley.

Fisher, A. (1998). Don't blow your new job. *Fortune, 137*(12), 159–162.

Fisher, A. B. (1992, September 21). When will women get to the top? *Fortune,* 44–56.

Fisher, W. R. (1987). *Human communication as narration: Towards a philosophy of reason, value, and action.* Columbia: University of South Carolina Press.

Fishman, P. M. (1978). Interaction: The work women do. *Social Problems, 25,* 15–21.

Floyd, K., & Parks, M. (1995). Manifesting closeness in the interactions of peers: A look at siblings and friends. *Communication Reports, 8,* 69–76.

Ford, C. H. (1982). *Think smart, move fast: Decision making/problem solving for super executives.* New York: AMACOM.

Forsythe, S. (1990). Effect of applicant's clothing on interviewer's decision to hire. *Journal of Applied Social Psychology, 20,* 1579–1595.

Fotheringham, W. C. (1966). *Perspectives on persuasion.* Boston: Allyn & Bacon.

Frank, M. S., & Gilovich, T. (1988). The dark side of self- and social perception: Black uniforms and aggression in professional sports. *Journal of Personality and Social Psychology, 54,* 74–85.

Frankel, R. M. (1995). Emotion and the physician-patient relationship. *Motivation and Emotion, 19,* 163–173.

Frantz, C., & Jin, K. (1995). The structure of group conflict in a collaborative work group during information systems development. *Journal of Applied Communication Research, 23,* 108–122.

Fraser, B. (1999). Rules of the road for navigating the information superhighway. *Human Rights, 26*(1), 17–21.

Freed, L. (2000, April 18). Videoconferencing software—You've bought a camera for videoconferencing. Now which software should you use to manage your videoconferences? *PC Magazine,* 165.

Freiberg, K. L., & Freiberg, J. A. (1996). *NUTS! Southwest Airlines' crazy recipe for business and personal success.* Austin: Bard Press.

Fremouw, W. J., & Scott, M. D. (1979). Cognitive restructuring: An alternative method for the treatment of communication apprehension. *Communication Education, 28,* 129–133.

Fried, I. (2006, September 28). Dunn grilled by Congress. *ZDNET News.com.* Retrieved from http://news.zdnet.net/ 2100-9595_22-6120625-2.html?tag=st.next

Friedman, R. A., Tidd, S. T., Currall, S. C., & Tsai, J. C. (2000). What goes around comes around: The impact of personal conflict style on work conflict and stress. *The International Journal of conflict Management, 11*(1), 32–55.

Friedman, R. A., & Currall, S. C. (2003). Conflict escalation: Dispute exacerbating elements of e-mail communication. *Human Relations, 56*(11), 1325–1347.

Friedman, T. L. (2005). *The world is flat: A brief history of the twenty-first century.* New York: Farrar, Straus and Giroux.

Frierson, J. G. (1987, December). National origin discrimination: The next wave of lawsuits. *Personnel Journal, 66,* 97–108.

Fry, R. W. (2006). *101 great answers to the toughest interview questions* (5th ed.). Clifton Park, NY: Thomson Delmar Learning.

Fulk, J., & Collins-Jarvis, L. (2001). Wired meetings: Technological mediation of organizational gatherings. In F. M. Jablin & L. L. Putnam (Eds.), *The new handbook of organizational communication: Advances in theory, research, and methods* (pp. 624–663). Thousand Oaks, CA: Sage.

Fusaro, P. C., & Miller, R. M. (2002). *What went wrong at Enron: Everyone's guide to the largest bankruptcy in U.S. history.* Hoboken, NJ: John Wiley & Sons.

Galanes, G. J., & Adams, K. (2010). *Effective group discussion* (13th ed.). Boston: McGraw-Hill.

Galbraith, J. R. (1967). Influencing the decision to produce. *Industrial Management Review, 9,* 97–107.

Gallupe, R. B., Cooper, W. H., Grise, M., & Bastianutti, L. M. (1994). Blocking electronic brainstorms. *Journal of Applied Psychology, 79,* 77–86.

Gallupe, R. B., Dennis, A. R., Cooper, W. H., Valacich, J. S., Bastianutti, L. M., & Nunamaker, J. F. (1992). Electronic brainstorming and group size. *Academy of Management Journal, 35,* 350–369.

Geddes, D. (1992). Sex roles in management: The impact of varying power of speech style on union members' perception of satisfaction and effectiveness. *Journal of Psychology Interdisciplinary and Applied, 126,* 589–608.

Geoff, C. (2006, January 23). The 100 best companies to work for 2006. *Fortune, 153*(1), 70–74.

Gibson, C. B., & Cohen, S. G. (2003). *Virtual teams that work: Creating conditions for virtual team effectiveness.* San Francisco: Jossey-Bass.

Gilbert, S. (1976). Empirical and theoretical extension of self-disclosure. In G. Miller (Ed.), *Explorations in interpersonal communication* (pp. 197–215). Newbury Park, CA: Sage.

Ginossar, Z., & Trope, Y. (1980). The effects of base rates and individuating information on judgements about another person. *Journal of Experimental Social Psychology, 16,* 228–242.

Gioia, D. (1992, May). Pinto fires and personal ethics: A script analysis of missed opportunities. *Journal of Business Ethics, 11*(5–6), 379–389.

Gittell, J. H. (2003). *The Southwest Airlines way: Using the power of relationships to achieve high performance.* New York: McGraw-Hill.

Gladwell, M. (2002). *The tipping point: How little things can make a big difference.* New York: Little, Brown & Co.

Gladwell, M. (2005). *Blink: The power of thinking without thinking.* New York: Little, Brown and Company.

Glanz, J., & Schwartz, J. (2003, September 26). Dogged engineer's effort to assess shuttle damage. *New York Times,* p. A1.

Glatthorn, A. A., & Adams, H. R. (1983). *Listening your way to management success.* Glenview, IL: Scott Foresman.

Goby, J. & Lewis, H. (2000). The key role of listening in business: A study of the Singapore insurance industry. *Business Communication, 63*(2), 290–298.

Golden, N. (1986). *Dress right for business.* New York: Gregg Division, McGraw-Hill.

Goldhaber, G. M. (1993). *Organizational communication* (6th ed.). Dubuque, IA: Brown & Benchmark.

Goldstein, M. (2003). It's alive! The audience, that is, but some presenters don't seem to know it. *Successful Meetings, 52*(2), 20.

Gonzalez, J. L. (2006, January). Textbook review for *Communicating for Results* 8th edition. Belmont, CA: Wadsworth. Reviewer from Delta College, University Center, Michigan.

Gordon, J. (2006). *Presentations that change minds: Strategies to persuade, convince, and get results.* New York: McGraw-Hill.

Gordon, N. J., & Fleisher, W. L. (2001). *Effective interviewing and interrogation techniques.* New York: Academic.

Gorham, J. (1988). The relationship between verbal teacher immediacy behaviors and student learning. *Communication Education, 37,* 40–53.

Goss, B. (1982). Listening as information processing. *Communication Quarterly, 30,* 306.

Graceful Competitor. (2008, September 1). Nastia Liukin: Graceful Competitor. *US Weekly, 707,* 48–49.

Green, B. (1981, April 19). *The players: It wasn't a game. Washington Post,* p. A12. Available from LexisNexis Academic Database.

Green-Hernandez, C., Quinn, A. A., Denman-Vitale, S., Falkenstern, S. K., & Judge-Ellis, T. (2004). Making nursing care culturally competent. *Holistic Nursing Practice, 18,* 215–218.

Greenberg, J. (2003). *Organizational behavior: The state of the science* (2nd ed.). Mahwah, NJ: Erlbaum.

Greenberg, J., & Baron, R. A. (1995). *Behavior in organizations* (5th ed.). Englewood Cliffs, NJ: Prentice-Hall.

Greenberg, J., & Baron, R. A. (1997). *Behavior in organizations: Understanding and managing the human side of work* (6th ed.). Upper Saddle River, NJ: Prentice-Hall.

Greenberg, J., & Baron, R. A. (2007). *Behavior in organizations: Understanding and managing the human side of work* (9th ed.). Upper Saddle River, NJ: Prentice-Hall.

Greenleaf, C. T. (1998). *Attention to detail: A gentleman's guide to professional appearance and conduct.* New York: Mass Market Press.

Gronbeck, B. E., McKerrow, R. E., Ehninger, D., & Monroe, A. H. (1994). *Principles and types of speech communication* (12th ed.). New York: HarperCollins.

Groves, R. M., Biemer, P. P., Lyberg, L. E., Massey, J. T., Nicholls II, W. L., & Waksberg, J. (2001). *Telephone survey methodology.* Hoboken, NJ: Wiley.

Gruner, C. R. (1985). Advice to the beginning speaker on using humor: What the research tells us. *Communication Education, 34,* 142–147.

Guerrero, L., Jones, S., & Boburka, R. (2006). Sex differences in emotional communication. In K. Dindia & D. J. Canary (Eds.), *Sex differences and similarities in communication* (pp. 242–261). Mahweh, NJ: Erlbaum.

Guffey, M. E. (2007). *Essentials of business communication* (7th ed.). Mason, OH: South-Western.

Guffey, M. E. (2010). *Essentials of business communication* (8th ed.). Mason, OH: South-Western.

Gurak, L. J. (1997). *Persuasion and privacy in cyberspace: The online protests over Lotus Marketplace and the Clipper Chip.* New Haven: Yale University Press.

Gutek, A. (1985). *Sex and the workplace.* San Francisco: Jossey-Bass.

Haber, R. N. (1970). How we remember what we see. *Scientific American, 222*(10), 104–112.

Hachmann, R. (2008, March 27). Chrysler listens, Starbucks wants ideas. *Web Jungle.com.* Retrieved from http://www.web-jungle.com/2008/03/27/chrysler-listens-starbucks-wants-ideas

Hackman, M. Z. (1988, Winter). Reactions to the use of self-disparaging humor by informative public speakers. *The Southern Speech Communication Journal, 53,* 175–183.

Hackman, M. Z., & Johnson, C. (2000). *Readership: A communication perspective.* Prospect Heights, IL: Waveland.

Haddock, S. M. (1996). Beware! Your e-mail could haunt you later. In P. R. Timm & J. A. Stead (Eds.), *Communication skills for business and professions* (pp. 148–149). Upper Saddle River, NJ: Prentice-Hall.

Hall, B. J. (2002). *Among cultures: The challenge of communication.* Fort Worth: Harcourt.

Hall, E. T. (1969). *The hidden dimension.* Garden City, NY: Anchor.

Hall, E. T. (1973). *The silent language.* Garden City, NY: Anchor.

Hall, E. T. (1976). *Beyond culture.* Garden City, NY: Doubleday.

Hall, E. T. (1983). Proxemics. In A. M. Katz & V. T. Katz (Eds.), *Foundations of nonverbal communication: Readings, exercises, and commentary* (pp. 5–27). Carbondale: Southern Illinois University Press.

Hall, E. T., & Hall, M. R. (1990). *Understanding cultural differences: Germans, French and Americans.* Yarmouth, ME: Intercultural Press.

Hall, E. T., & Whyte, W. F. (1960, Spring). Intercultural communication: A guide to men in action. *Human Organization, 19,* 5–12.

Hall, J. A. (1975). Communication revisited. In M. S. Worthman, Jr., & F. Luthans (Eds.), *Emerging concepts in management* (2nd ed., pp. 135–148). New York: Macmillan.

Hall, J. A. (1979). Gender, gender roles, and nonverbal communication skills. In R. Rosenthal (Ed.), *Skill in nonverbal communication: Individual differences.* Cambridge, MA: Oelgeschlager, Gunn & Hain.

Hall, J. A. (1984). *Nonverbal sex differences: Communication accuracy and expressive style.* Baltimore: Johns Hopkins University Press.

Halloween at the airlines. (2009, October 30). *Nuts about Southwest blog.* Post retrieved from http://www.blogsouthwest.com/news/halloween-airlines

Hallowell, E. M. (1999, January-February). The human moment at work. *Harvard Business Review, 77,* 64.

Hamilton, C. (1999). *The effect of quality and color visual aids on immediate recall, attitude toward speaker, and attitude toward speech* (Unpublished dissertation). University of North Texas, Denton.

Hamilton, C. (2009). *Essentials of public speaking* (4th ed.). Boston: Wadsworth/Cengage Learning.

Hamilton, C. R. (2005, November 1). Medical ethics and performance-enhancing drugs. *American Medial Association*. Retrieved from www.ama-assn.org/ama/pub/category/15633.html

Hamilton, D. (2000, March). Prepare and practice. *Officepro*, 14.

Hamm, S. (2007). *Bangalore tiger: How Indian tech upstart wipro is rewriting the rules of global competition*. New York: McGraw-Hill.

Hammer, M., & Champy, C. (1993). *Reengineering the corporation: A manifesto for business revolution*. New York: Harper Business.

Haney, W. V. (1973). *Communication and organizational behavior: Text and cases* (3rd ed.). Homewood, IL: Irwin.

Haney, W. V. (1986). *Communication and organizational behavior: Text and cases* (5th ed.). Homewood, IL: Irwin.

Hansen, K. (2006). *New twists and turns mark a decade of Internet job-hunting: A Quintessential Careers annual report 2006. Quintessential Careers*. Retrieved from http://www.quintcareers.com/printable/Internet_job-search_report.html

Hansson, T. (1999, Spring). Etiquette for globetrotters. *Writers block*. Retrieved from http://www.writersblock.ca/spring1999/essay.htm

Harcourt, J., Richerson, V., & Waitterk, M. J. (1991). A national study of middle managers' assessment of organization communication quality. *Journal of Business Communication, 28*, 348–365.

Harper, R. G., Wiens, A. N., & Matarozzo, J. D. (1978). *Nonverbal communication: The state of the art*. New York: Wiley.

Harrell, T. W., & Harrell, M. S. (1984). *Stanford MBA careers: A 20-year longitudinal study* (Research Paper No. 723). Stanford: Stanford University, Graduate School of Business.

Harris, T. E. (1993). *Applied organizational communication: Perspectives, principles, and pragmatics*. Hillsdale, NJ: Erlbaum.

Heath, D. (1991). *Fulfilling lives: Paths to maturity and success*. San Francisco: Jossey-Bass.

Hechinger, J. (2008, September 18). College applicants, beware: Your Facebook page is showing. *Wall Street Journal*, p. D6.

Heerden, I., & Bryan, M. (2006). *The storm*. New York: Viking.

Heider, F. (1958). The psychology of interpersonal relations. New York: Wiley.

Heller, R. (1998). *Communicate clearly*. New York: DK Publishing.

Hempel, J. (2009, March 11). How Facebook is taking over our lives. *Fortune*. Retrieved from http://money.cnn.com/2009/02/16/technology/hempel_facebook.fortune/index.htm

Hentz, M. C. (2009). Phone interview etiquette can propel you to the next step in the hiring process. *Quintessential Careers*. Retrieved from http://www.quintcareers.com/phone_interview_etiquette.html

Hersey, P., & Blanchard, K. H. (1996). *Management of organizational behavior* (7th ed.). Englewood Cliffs, NJ: Prentice-Hall.

Hersey, P., Blanchard, K. H., & Johnson, D. E. (2007). *Management of organizational behavior* (9th ed.). Upper Saddle River, NJ: Prentice-Hall.

Hewitt, H. (2005). *Blog: Understanding the information reformation that's changing your world*. Nashville: Nelson Business.

Hirokawa, R. Y., Erbert, L., & Hurst, A. (1996). Communication and group decision-making effectiveness. In R. Y. Hirokawa & M. S. Poole (Eds.), *Communication and group decision making* (2nd ed., pp. 269–300). Thousand Oaks, CA: Sage.

Hirokawa, R. Y., & Pace, R. (1983). A descriptive investigation of the possible communication-based reasons for effective and ineffective group decision making. *Communication Monographs, 50*, 269–370.

Hirokawa, R. Y., & Rost, K. (1992). Effective group decision making in organizations. *Management Communication Quarterly, 5*, 267–388.

Hishitani, S. 1991. Vividness of image and retrieval time. *Perception and Motor Skills, 73*, 115–123.

Hitt, M. A., Ireland, R. D., & Hoskisson, R. E. (1999). *Strategic management: Competitiveness and globalization* (3rd. ed.). Cincinnati: South-Western.

Hoevemeyer, V. A. (2005). *High-impact interview questions: 701 Behavior-based questions to find the right person for every job*. New York: AMACOM.

Hof, R. D., Gross, N., & Sager, I. (1994, March 7). A computer maker's power move. *Business Week*, 48.

Hofstede, G. (2001). *Culture's consequences: Comparing values, behaviors, institutions, and organizations across nations* (2nd ed.). Thousand Oaks, CA: Sage.

Hofstede, G., & Hofstede, G. J. (2005). *Cultures and organizations: Software of the mind* (2nd ed.), pp. 78-79. New York: McGraw-Hill.

Hogan, G. W., & Goodson, J. R. (1990). The key to expatriate success. *Training and Development Journal, 44*, 50–52.

Holcombe, M. W., & Stein, J. K. (1996). *Presentations for decision makers* (3rd ed.). New York: Wiley.

Hollingshead, A. B., & McGrath, J. E. (1995). Computer-assisted groups: A critical review of the empirical research. In R. A. Guzzo, E. Salas, & Associates (Eds.), *Team effectiveness and decision-making in organizations* (pp. 46–48). San Francisco: Jossey-Bass.

Hollingsworth, J. E. (1968, August). Oral briefings. *Management Review, 57*, 2–10.

Holm, J. H. (1981). *Business and professional communication*. Boston: American Press.

Holt, K. (1996). Brainstorming—from classics to electronics. *Journal of Engineering Design, 7*(1), 77–84.

Horne, J. (2006). *Breach of faith: Hurricane Katrina and the near death of a great American city*. New York: Random House.

Horton, T. R. (1983). Using your managerial ear. *Management Review, 72*, 2–3.

Hosman, L. H. (2002). Language and persuasion. In J. P. Dillard & M. Pfau (Eds.), *The persuasion handbook: Developments in theory and practice* (pp. 233–258). Thousand Oaks, CA: Sage.

House, R. (1971). A path–goal theory of leader behavior. *Administrative Science Quarterly, 16*, 321–339.

House, R., & Mitchell, T. (1974). Path–goal theory of leadership. *Journal of Contemporary Business, 3*, 81–98.

House, R. J., & Aditya, R. M. (1997). The social scientific study of leadership: *Quo Vadis? Journal of Management, 23*, 409-473.

Houston, J. (1997). *The possible human: A course in enhancing your physical, mental, and creative abilities* (reprint ed.). Los Angeles: Tarcher.

Hovland, C. I., Lumsdaine, A. A., & Sheffield, F. D. (1967). The effects of presenting "one-side" vs. "both sides" in changing opinions on a controversial subject. In R. L. Rosnow & E. J. Robinson (Eds.), *Experiments in persuasion* (pp. 201–225). New York: Academic.

How to blog safely. (2005, May 31). How to blog safely (about work or anything else). *Electronic Frontier Foundation Whitepaper*s. Retrieved from http://www.eff.orgwp/blog-safely

How to conduct a lawful employment interview. (1978). Des Moines, IA: Batten, Batten, Hudson and Swab.

Howell, W. S., & Bormann, E. G. (1971). *Presentational speaking for business and professions*. New York: Harper & Row.

Howell, W. S., & Bormann, E. G. (1979). *Presentational speaking for business and the professions*. New York: Harper & Row.

Hsu, C. (2004, Fall). Sources of differences in communication apprehension between Chinese in Taiwan and Americans. *Communication Quarterly, 52*, 370–390.

Hubbell, A. P., & Chory-Assad, R. M. (2005). Motivating factors: Perceptions of justice and their relationship with managerial and organizational trust. *Communication Studies, 56*(1), 47–70.

Hudson, A. (2006, January 20). Brown takes blame for Katrina missteps. *Washington Times*, A10.

Hylmö, A., & Buzzanell, P. M. (2002). Telecommuting as viewed through cultural lenses: An empirical investigation of the discourses of utopia, identity, and mystery. *Communication Monographs, 69*(4), 329–356.

Hymowitz, C. (1988, November 4). Spread the word: Gossip is good. *Wall Street Journal*, p. B1.

Hymowitz, C. (2000, February 8). Racing onto the web, one manager's secret is simple: Listening. *Wall Street Journal*, p. B1.

IABC News Centre. (2006, May 22). Less than half of companies encourage discussion of ethical issues at the workplace. Retrieved from http://news.iabc.com/index.php?s=press_releases&item=97

Iacocca, L., & Novak, W. (1986). *Iacocca: An autobiography* (Rev. ed.). New York: Bantam.

Ilkka, R. J. (1995). Applicant appearance and selection decision making: Revitalizing employment interview education. *Business Communication Quarterly, 58*(3), 11–18.

Ingram, T. N., LaForge, R. W., Avila, R. A., Schwepker, Jr., C. H., & Williams, M. R. (2004). *Sales management: Analysis and decision making* (5th ed.). Mason, OH: South-Western.

Ingram, T. N., Schwepker, C. H., & Hutson, D. (1992, August). Why salespeople fail. *Industrial Marketing Management, 21*, 225–230.

Ingram, T. N, LaForge, R. W., Avila, R. A., Schwepker Jr., C. H., & Williams, M. R. (2008). *Professional selling: A trust-based approach* (4th ed.). Mason, OH: South-Western.

Internet Activities. (2009, January 6). Pew Internet and American Life Project Tracking surveys (March 2000–December 2008). *Pew Internet. org.* Retrieved from http://www.pewinternet.org/Trend-Data/Online-Activities-Total.aspx

Isaacs, K. (2000). How to convert your resume to ASCII format. Retrieved from http://content.monster.com/resume/resources/asciiresume

Ishaya, T., & Macaulay, L. (1999). The role of trust in virtual teams. *Electronic Journal of Organizational Virtualness, 1*(1), 140–157.

Issac, A. R., & Marks, D. F. (1994, November). Individual differences in mental imagery experience: Developmental changes and specialization. *British Journal of Psychology, 85,* 479–497.

Ivancevich, J. M., & Matteson, M. T. (1996). *Organizational behavior and management* (4th ed.). Chicago: Irwin.

Ivancevich, J. M., & Matteson, M. T. (2002). *Organizational behavior and management* (6th ed.). Chicago: McGraw- Hill/Irwin.

Jablin, F. M. (1985). Task/work relationships: A life-span perspective. In M. Knapp & G. Miller (Eds.), *Handbook of interpersonal communication* (pp. 615–654). Newbury Park, CA: Sage.

Jablin, F. M., Putnam, L. L., Roberts, K. H., & Porter, L. W. (Eds.). (1987). *Handbook of organizational communication: An interdisciplinary perspective.* Newbury Park, CA: Sage.

Jablin, F. M., & Tengler, C. D. (1982, Winter). Facing discrimination in on-campus interviews. *Journal of College Placement,* 57–61.

Jackson, C. V. (2009, July 9). Passenger uses YouTube to get United's attention. *ChicagoSun-Times.com.* Retrieved from http://www.suntimes.com/technology/1658990,CST-NWS-united09.article

Jackson, S. E. (1983). Participation in decision making as a strategy for reducing job-related strain. *Journal of Applied Psychology, 68,* 3–19.

Jaffe, G. (2000, April 26). What's your point, lieutenant? Just cut to the pie charts—The Pentagon declares war on electronic slide shows that make briefings a pain. *Wall Street Journal,* p. A1.

James, D. L. (1989, November). The art of the deal (Japan-style). *Business Month, 134*(5), 93.

Janis, I. L. (1971, November). Groupthink. *Psychology Today, 5,* 43–46, 74–76.

Janis, I. L. (1982). *Groupthink: A psychological study of foreign policy decisions and fiascoes* (2nd ed.). Boston: Houghton Mifflin.

Janis, I. L. (1989). *Crucial decisions: Leadership in policymaking and crisis management.* New York: Free Press.

Janus, T., Kaiser, S. B., & Gray, G. (2000). Negotiations at work: The casual business wear trend. In M. L. Damhorst, K. A. Miller, & S. O. Michelman (Eds.), *The meaning of dress* (pp. 264–269). New York: Fairchild.

Jarboe, S. (1996). Procedures for enhancing group decision making. In R. Y. Hirokawa & M. S. Poole (Eds.), *Communication and group decision making* (2nd ed., pp. 345–383). Thousand Oaks, CA: Sage.

Jarvis, J. (2008, March 20). Starbucks listens—at last. *BuzzMachine.com.* Retrieved from http://www.buzzmachine.com/2008/03/20/starbucks-listens-at-last

Job Outlook 2009. (2008, November). How employers view candidates. *National Association of Colleges and Employees.* Retrieved from http://www.naceweb.org

Johnson, D. D. (1995). Color adaptation for color deficient learners. *Visual Arts Research, 21*(2), 26–41.

Johnson, D. W., (2002). Being open with and to other people. In J. Stewart (Ed.), *Bridges not walls,* pp. 232–236. Boston: McGraw-Hill.

Johnson, D. W., & Johnson, F. P. (2002). *Joining together: Group theory and group skills* (8th ed.). Boston: Allyn & Bacon.

Johnson, K. (1992). *Busting bureaucracy.* New York: Irwin.

Johnston, L. M., & Gao, H. (2009). Resolving conflict in the Chinese and U.S. realms for global business entities. *China media Research, 5*(2), 104–117.

Join our company: Career opportunities (n.d.). *Smuckers.com.* Retrieved from http://www.smuckers.com/fc/hr/default.asp?

Jones, G. R. (2007a). *Business ethics and the legal environment of business.* New York: McGraw-Hill.

Jones, G. R. (2007b). *Introduction to business: How companies create value for people.* New York: McGraw-Hill.

Jones, J. M. (2009, May 14). Americans more likely to say moral values "getting better:" Still overwhelmingly believe values are getting worse.

Gallup.com. Retrieved from http://www.gallup.com/poll/118387/Americans-Likely-Say-Moral-Values-Getting-Better.aspx

Jones, S. (2003). A uniform look for Sears clerks. *Crain's Detroit Business, 26*(24), 1–2.

Jourard, S. M. (1968). *Disclosing man to himself.* Princeton, NJ: Van Nostrand.

Journalists speak out. (2006). *Oprah.com.* Retrieved from http://www.oprah.com/tows/slide/200601/20060126/slide_20060126_350_202.jhtml

Kacmar, K. M., Kelery, J. E., & Ferris, G. P. (1992, August 16–31). Differential effectiveness of applicant IM tactics on employment interview decisions. *Journal of Applied Social Psychology,* 1250–1272.

Kagan, D., Meserve, J., Malveaux, S., & Gupta, S. (2006, February 10). Former FEMA director Michael Brown testifies before Senate Homeland Security committee. CNN Live Event, February 10, 2006. Available from Newspaper Source Database.

Kahn, R. L. (1984). Productive behavior through the life course: An essay on the quality of life. *Human Resource Management, 23*(1), 14.

Kalins, D. (2006, May 23). Going home with the customers. *Newsweek.* Retrieved from http://www.msnbc.msn. com/id/7856259/site/newsweek

Kamins, M. A., & Marks, L. J. (1987). Advertising puffery: The impact of using two-sided claims on product attitude and purchase intention. *Journal of Advertising, 16,* 6–15.

Kanter, D., & Mirvis, P. (1990). *The cynical American: Living and working in an age of discontent and disillusionment.* San Francisco: Jossey-Bass.

Kanter, R. M. (1983). *The change masters.* New York: Simon & Schuster.

Kaplan, D. A. (2006, September 18). Suspicions and spies in Silicon Valley. *Newsweek, 148*(12), 40–47.

Karlin, B. E., & Zeiss, R. A. (2006). Environmental and therapeutic issues in psychiatric hospital design: Toward best practices. *Psychiatric Services, 57*(10), 1376–1378.

Karsh, B., & Pike, C. (2009). *How to say it on your resume: A top recruiting director's guide to writing the perfect resume for every job.* New York: Penguin Group (Prentice Hall Press).

Katz, D., & Kahn, R. L. (1966). *The social psychology of organizations.* New York: Wiley.

Kazoleas, D. C. (1993, Winter). A comparison of the persuasive effectiveness of qualitative versus quantitative evidence: A test of explanatory hypotheses. *Communication Quarterly, 41,* 40–50.

Kellett, J. B., Humphrey, R. H., & Sleeth, R. G. (2006). Empathy and the emergence of task and relations leaders. *Leadership Quarterly, 17*(2), 146–162.

Kelley, L. (1989). Implementing a skills training program for reticent communicators. *Communication Education, 38,* 85–101.

Kelly, L., & Keaten, J. A. (2000). Treating communication anxiety: Implications of the communibiological paradigm. *Communication Education, 49,* 45–57.

Keltner, V., & Holsey, M. (1982). *The success image: A guide for the better dressed business woman.* Houston: Gulf.

Kendon, A. (1994). Do gestures communicate? A review. *Research on Language and Social Interaction, 27,* 175–200.

Kennedy, J. L. (2007). *Resumes for dummies* (5th ed.). Foster City, CA: IDG Books.

Kennedy, J. L. (2009). *Cover letters for dummies* (3rd ed.). Indianapolis: Wiley.

Kepner, C. H., & Tregoe, B. B. (1981). *The new rational manager: A systematic approach to problem solving and decision making.* New York: McGraw-Hill.

Ketcham, H. (1968). *Color planning for business and industry.* New York: Harper & Brothers.

Keyton, J. (1999). *Group communication: Process and analysis.* Mountain View, CA: Mayfield.

Keyton, J., Harmon, N. A., & Frey, L. R. (1996, November). *Grouphate: Implication for teaching group communication.* Paper presented at the Speech Communication Association Convention, San Diego.

Kidwell, R. E., Jr. (2004, May). "Small" lies, big trouble: The unfortunate consequences of résumé padding, from Janet Cooke to George O'Leary. *Journal of Business Ethics, 51,* 175–184.

Kiel, P. (2008, December 18). The world's largest hedge fund is a fraud. *ProPublica.com.* Retrieved from http://www.propublica.org/article/the-worlds-largest-hedge-fund-is-a-fraud-1219.

Kiewra, K. A. (1985). Investigating note-taking and review: A depth of processing alternative. *Educational Psychologist, 20,* 23–32.

Kiewra, K. A., DuBois, N. F., Christian, D., McShane, A., Meyerhoffer, M., & Roskelley, D. (1991, June). Note-taking functions and techniques. *Journal of Educational Psychology, 83,* 240–245.

Killian, R. (1968). *Managing by design . . . for executive effectiveness.* New York: American Management Association.

Killion, A. (2004, March/April). Animal assisted therapy: One family's experience. *The Autism/Asperger's Digest Magazine.* Retrieved from http://home.comcast.net/~akillio1/ AMK_Files/Autism_Aspergers_Digest_2004.htm

Kilmann, R., & Thomas, K. W. (1975). Interpersonal conflict-handling behavior as a reflection of Jungian personality dimensions. *Psychological Reports, 37,* 971–980.

Kimble, G. A. (1989). Psychology from the standpoint of a generalist. *American Psychologist, 44*(3), 491–499.

Kinnick, K. N., & Parton, S. R. (2005). Workplace communication: What the Apprentice teaches about communication skills. *Business Communication Quarterly, 68*(4), 429–456.

Kirk, D. (1988, August). *Gender differences in the perception of sexual harassment.* Paper presented at the Academy of Management National Meeting, Anaheim, CA.

Kirkpatrick, S. A., & Locke, E. A. (1991). Leadership: Do traits matter? *Academy of Management Executive, 5,* 48–60.

Kirkwood, W. G., & Ralston, S. M. (1999). Inviting meaningful applicant performances in employment interviews. *Journal of Business Communication, 36*(1), 55–76.

Klyukanov, I. E. (2005). *Principles of intercultural communication.* Boston: Allyn & Bacon.

Knapp, M. L., & Hall, J. A. (1997). *Nonverbal communication in human interaction* (4th ed.). Fort Worth: Harcourt Brace.

Knapp, M. L., & Hall, J. A. (2002). *Nonverbal communication in human interaction* (5th ed.). Belmont, CA: Wadsworth.

Koballa, T. R., Jr. (1989) Persuading teachers to reexamine the innovative elementary science programs of yesterday: The effect of anecdotal versus data-summary communications. *Journal of Research in Science Teaching, 23,* 437–449.

Koehler, J. W., Anatol, K. W., & Applbaum, R. L. (1976). *Organizational communication: Behavioral perspectives.* New York: Holt, Rinehart & Winston.

Kohut, A. (2008, August 17 news release). Audience Segments in a changing News Environment. The Pew Research Center for the People & the Press. Retrieved from http://people-press.org/reports/pdf/444.pdf

Koneya, M., & Barbour, A. (1976). *Louder than words: Nonverbal communication.* Columbus, OH: Merrill.

Konrad, M., & Gutek, B. A. (1986). Impact of work experiences on attitudes toward sexual harassment. *Administrative Science Quarterly, 31,* 422–438.

Korda, M. (1991). *Power: How to get it, how to use it* (Reprint ed.). New York: Ballantine.

Kosslyn, S. M., Pascula-Leone, A., Felician, O., Camposano, S., Keenan, J. P., Thompson, W. L., Ganis, G., . . . Alpert, N. M. (1999). The role of area 17 in visual imagery: Convergent evidence from PET and rTMS. *Science, 284,* 167–170.

Kosslyn, S. M., & Rosenberg, R. S. (2006). *Psychology in context* (3rd ed.). Boston: Allyn & Bacon.

Kostner, J. (2001). *Bionic teamwork: How to build collaborative virtual teams at hyperspeed.* Chicago: Dearborn Trade Publishers.

Kouzes, J. M., & Posner, B. Z. (2002). *The leadership challenge* (3rd ed.). San Francisco: Jossey-Bass.

Kowinski, W. (1975, March 7). Shedding new light. *New Times, 4,* 46.

Kramer, M. W., Kuo, C. L., & Dailey, J. C. (1997). The impact of brainstorming techniques on subsequent group processes: Beyond generating ideas. *Small Group Research, 28,* 218–242.

Krames, J. A. (2003). *What the best CEO's know: 7 exceptional leaders and their lessons for transforming any business.* New York: McGraw-Hill.

Krannich, R., & Krannich, C. (2006). *Resume, application and letter tips for people with hot and not-so-hot backgrounds: 150 tops for landing the perfect job.* Atascadero, CA: Impact Publishers.

Kreitner, R. (2007). *Management* (10th ed.). Boston: Houghton Mifflin.

Kreps, G. L. (1990). *Organizational communication* (3rd ed.). New York: Longman.

Kulhavy, R. W., & Schwartz, N. H. (1980, Fall). Tone of communication and climate perceptions. *Journal of Business Communications, 18,* 23.

Kunda, G., & Van Maanen, J. (1999). Changing scripts at work: Managers and professionals. *Annals of the American Academy of Political and Social Science, 561,* 64–80.

LaBarre, P. (1994). The other network. *Industry Week, 243*(17), 33–36.

Lamb, C. W., Hair, J. F., & McDaniel, C. (2004). *Marketing.* Mason, OH: South-Western.

Lamb, C. W., Hair, J. F., & McDaniel, C. (2006). *Essentials of Marketing* (5th ed.). Mason, OH: Thomson South-Western.

Lancaster, H. (1999, August 31). Herb Kelleher has one main strategy: Treat employees well. *Wall Street Journal,* p. B1.

Lander, M. S., Lander, S., & Cagwin, D. (2008). A comparative study of ethical values of business student: American vs. Middle Eastern cultures. *Journal of College Teaching & Learning, 5*(8), 27–43.

Landy, H. (2006, February 14). RadioShack CEO's resume in question. *Star-Telegram.com.* Retrieved from http://www.dfw. com/mld/dfw/13867927.htm?template=contentModules/printstory.jsp

Larson, C. E., & LaFasto, F. M. J. (1989). *Teamwork: What must go right/what can go wrong.* Newbury Park, CA: Sage.

Larson, C. U. (2010). *Persuasion: Reception and responsibility* (12th ed.). Belmont, CA: Wadsworth, Cengage Learning.

Lashinsky, A. (2003, September 1). Meg and the machine. *Fortune,* 68–78.

Lawlor, M. (1998). Dynamic executive centers bolster corporate revenue. *Signal, 52*(9), 89–94.

Lee, F. (1993). Being polite and keeping MUM: How bad news is communicated in organizational hierarchies. *Journal of Applied Social Psychology, 23,* 1124–1149.

Lee, R. A. (1996). Miranda's revenge: Police interrogation as a confidence game. *Law & Society Review, 30*(2), 259–288.

Leech, T. (2004). *How to prepare, stage, and deliver winning presentations* (3rd ed.). New York: AMACOM.

Lefton, R. E., Buzzotta, V. R., Sherberg, M., & Karraker, D. L. (1980). *Effective motivation through performance appraisal: Dimensional appraisal strategies.* Cambridge: Ballinger.

Lehman, C. M., & DuFrene, D. D. (2008). *Business communication* (15th ed.). Mason, OH: South-Western.

Lencioni, P. (2002). *The five dysfunctions of a team: A leadership fable.* San Francisco: Jossey-Bass.

Lenhart, A., & Fox, S. (2006, July 19). *Bloggers: A portrait of the internet's new storytellers.* Washington, DC: Pew Internet & American Life project.

Lerner, M. A. (1983, May 16). A dead stick at 23,000 feet. *Newsweek,* 40.

Lesser, L. M. (1993, August 15). Aid to Russia: Barter transactions. *Vital Speeches, 59,* 651–653.

Levine, L. R., Bluni, T. D., & Hochman, S. H. (1998). Attire and charitable behavior. *Psychological Reports, 83,* 15–18.

Lewicki, R. J., McAllister, D. J., & Bies, R. J. (1998). Trust and distrust: New relationships and realities. *Academy of management Review, 23,* 438–458.

Likert, R. (1961). *New patterns of management.* New York: McGraw-Hill.

Likert, R. (1967). *The human organization: Its management and value.* New York: McGraw-Hill.

Lipsman, A. (2009, May 12). Twitter.com quadruples to 17 million U.S. visitors in last two months. *ComScore.com.* Retrieved from http://blog.comscore.com/2009/05/twitter_traffic_quadruples.html

Listen up. (2001, July-August). *Flight Safety Australia,* 36–37.

Litsky, F. (2002, May 25). U.S. Olympic chief quits over her lies on college degrees. *The New York Times,* p. A1.

Littlejohn, S. W., & Foss, K. A. (2008). *Theories of human communication* (9th ed.). Belmont, CA: Wadsworth.

Loehr, J. (1989, March). Seeing is believing. *World Tennis, 36,* 16ff.

Lombardo, J. P., & Wood, R. D. (1979). Satisfaction with interpersonal relations as a function of level of self-disclosure. *Journal of Psychology, 102,* 21–26.

Lowe, K. B., Kroech, K. G., & Sivasubramaniam, N. (1996). Effectiveness correlates of transformational and transactional leadership: A meta-analytic review of the MLQ literature. *Leadership Quarterly, 7*(3), 385–425.

Lublin, J. S. (2008, February 5). Notes to interviewers should go beyond a simple thank you. *Wall Street Journal,* p. B.1.

Luft, J. (1969). *Of human interaction.* Palo Alto, CA: National Press Books.

Luntz, F. I. (2007). *Words that work: It's not what you say, it's what people hear.* New York: Hyperion Books.

Lurie, R., & Welz, S. (2006). *Killer cover letters and resumes: Wetfeet insider guide.* San Francisco: Wetfeet, Inc.

Lutz, B. (2009, July 13).Webchat: Bob Lutz on reaching customers in his new role. *GM Fastlane.com.* Retrieved from http://fastlane.gmblogs.com/archives/2009/07

Mack, D., & Rainey, D. (1990). Female applicant's grooming and personnel selection. *Journal of Social Behavior and Personality, 5,* 399–407.

McKenzie, M.L. (2005). "Managers look to the social network to seek information." *Information Research, 10*(2) paper 216. Retrieved from http://InformationR.net/ir/10-2/paper216.html

Maher, K. (2004, October, 5). Job seekers and recruiters pay more attention to blogs. *CareerJournal.com.* Retrieved from http://www.careerjournal.com/jobhunting/usingnet/20041005-maher.html?jobhunting-whatsnew

Malandro, L. A., Barker, L., & Barker, D. A. (1989). *Communication* (2nd ed.). New York: Random House.

Maltz, D. N., & Borker, R. A. (1982). A cultural approach to male-female miscommunication. In J. J. Gumperz (Ed.), *Language and social identity.* Cambridge: Cambridge University Press.

Maltz, M. (1960). *Psycho-cybernetics.* Englewood Cliffs, NJ: Prentice-Hall.

Maney, K. (1999, May 12). Armed with PowerPoint, speakers make pests of themselves. *USA Today,* p. 3B.

Manz, C. C., & Sims, H. P. (2001). *The new superleadership.* San Francisco: Berrett-Koehler.

Maraniss, D. A. (1981, April 16). Post reporter's Pulitzer Prize is withdrawn; Pulitzer board withdraws Post reporter's Prize. *Washington Post.* Available from LexisNexis Academic Database.

March, J., & Sevon, G. (1982). Gossip, information, and decision making. In L. Sproull & P. Larkey (Eds.), *Advances in information processing in organizations* (Vol. I). Greenwich, CT: JAI Press.

Marcus, A. (1982). Color: A tool for computer graphics communication. In D. Greenberg, A. Marcus, A. Schmidt, & V. Garter (Eds.), *The computer image: Application of computer graphics.* Reading, MA: Addison-Wesley.

Markopolos, H. (2005, November 7). The world's largest hedge fund is a fraud. Retrieved from http://online.wsj.com/documents/Madoff_SECdocs_20081217.pdf

Marks, D. F. (1999). Consciousness, mental imagery and action. *British Journal of Psychology, 90,* 567–585.

Marx, E. (2001). *Breaking through culture shock: What you need to succeed in international business.* London: Nicholas Brealey Publishing.

Maslow, A. (1954). *Motivation and personality.* New York: Harper & Brothers.

Mastropieri, M. A., & Scruggs, T. E. (1998). Enhancing school success with mnemonic strategies. *Intervention in School & Clinic, 33,* 201–208.

Mattioli, D. (2009, July 20). Leaks grow in world of blogs: Companies search for new ways to stop disclosures of sensitive information. *The Wall Street Journal,* p. B4.

Maxwell, J. C. (2006). *The 360-degree leader: Developing your influence from anywhere in the organization.* Nashville: Nelson Impact.

Mayer, R. E. (2009). *Multimedia learning* (2nd ed.). New York: Cambridge University Press.

Mayo, E. (1933). *The human problems of an industrial civilization.* New York: MacMillan.

Mayo, E. (1945). *The social problems of an industrial civilization.* Boston: Graduate School of Business Administration, Harvard University.

Maysonave, S. (1999). *Casual power: How to power up your nonverbal communication and dress down for success.* Austin: Bright Books.

McAllister, H. A. (1980). Self-disclosure and liking: Effects for senders and receivers. *Journal of Personality, 48,* 409–418.

McCaskey, M. B. (1979). The hidden messages managers send. *Harvard Business Review, 57,* 148.

McCowen, C. (1989, September). Teaching teamwork. *Management Today,* 107–111.

McCroskey, J. C. (1969, April). A summary of experimental research on the effect of evidence in persuasive communication. *Quarterly Journal of Speech, 55,* 169–176.

McCroskey, J. C. (1970, August). The effects of evidence as an inhibitor of counter-persuasion. *Speech Monographs, 37,* 188–194.

McCroskey, J. C. (1972). The implementation of a large-scale program of systematic desensitization for communication apprehension. *Speech Teacher, 21,* 255–264.

McCroskey, J. C., & Beatty, M. J. (1998). Communication apprehension. In J. C. McCroskey, J. A.. Daly, M. M. Martin, & M. J. Beatty (Eds.), *Communication and personality: Trait perspectives* (pp. 215–231). Cresskill, NJ: Hampton Press, Inc.

McCroskey, J. C., & Beatty, M. J. (2000). The communibiological perspective: Implication for communication in instruction. *Communication Education, 49,* 1–6.

McCroskey, J. C., Fayer, J. M., & Richmond, V. P. (1985). Don't speak to me in English: Communication apprehension in Puerto Rico. *Communication Quarterly, 33*(3), 185–192.

McCroskey, J. C., & Teven, J. (1999). Goodwill: A reexamination of the construct and its measurement. *Communication Monographs, 66,* 90–103.

McCroskey, J. C., & Young, T. J. (1981). Ethos and credibility: The construct and its measurement after three decades. *Central States Speech Journal, 32,* 24–34.

McGarvey, R. (1990, January–February). Rehearsing for success: Tap the power of the mind through visualization. *Executive Female,* 35.

McGovern, T., & Ideus, H. (1978, Spring). The impact of nonverbal behavior on the employment interview. *Journal of College Placement, 38,* 51–53.

McGregor, D. (1960). *The human side of enterprise.* New York: McGraw-Hill.

McGuire, W. J. (1985). Attitudes and attitude change. In G. Lindzey & E. Aronson (Eds.), *The handbook of social psychology* (3rd ed., Vol. 2, pp. 233–346). New York: Random House.

McGwire mum on steroids in hearing. (2005, March 17). *CNN.com.* Retrieved from http://www.cnn.com/2005/ALLPOLITICS/03/17/steroids.baseball.

McKenzie, J. (2000, September). Scoring power points. *The Educational Technology Journal.* Retrieved from http://fno.org/sept00/powerpoints.html.

McKnight, D. H., Cummings, L. L., & Chervany, N. L. (2006). Initial trust formation in new organizational relationships. In R. M. Dramer, *Organizational trust: A reader* (pp. 111–139). New York: Oxford University Press.

McLaughlin, B. (2001, June). Hard times at CNN. *World and I, 16*(6), 62. Available from Opposing Viewpoints Resource Database.

McLean, B., & Elkind, P. (2003). *The smartest guys in the room.* New York: Portfolio/Penguin Group.

McPhail, T. L. (2006). *Global communication: Theories, stakeholders, and trends.* Malden, MA: Blackwell Publishing.

Mears, B., Isidore, C., & Crawford, K. (2005, May 31). Andersen conviction overturned. *CNNMoney.com.* Retrieved from http://money.cnn.com/2005/05/31/news/midcaps/scandal_andersen_scotus/index.htm

Medtronic.com. (2008, August 3). What is Infuse Bone Graft and how does it compare to the natural protein in my body that helps bones to grow? *Medtronic.com.* Retrieved from http://www.medtronic.com/your-health/lumbar-degenerative-disc-disease/surgery/questions-and-answers/index.htm

Meer, J. (1985, September). The light touch. *Psychology Today, 19,* 60–67.

Mehrabian, A. (1969). Significance of posture and position in the communication of attitude and status relationships. *Psychological Bulletin, 71,* 359–372.

Mehrabian, A. (1980). *Public places and private spaces.* New York: Basic.

Merskin, D. (2004). Reviving Lolita? *American Behavioral Scientist 48*(1), 119–121.

Merx, K. (2003). Dress blues. *Crain's Detroit Business, 19*(35), 1c.

Meyerson, D., Weick, R. E., & Kramer, R. M. (1996). Swift trust and temporary groups. In R. M. Kramer &T. R. Tyler (Eds.), *Trust in organizations: Frontiers of theory and research,* pp. 261–287. Thousand Oaks, CA: Sage.

Michelsen, M. W., Jr. (1993). How to make a good first impression. *American Salesman, 38*(5), 16–19.

Miell, D. E., & Duck, S. W. (1986). Strategies in developing friendship. In V. J. Derlega & B. A. Winstead (Eds.), *Friendship and social interaction* (pp. 129–143). New York: Springer.

Miles, R. (1965). Keeping informed—Human relations or human resources? *Harvard Business Review, 43*(4), 148–163.

Miles, R. (1975). *Theories of management.* New York: McGraw- Hill.

Miller, G. A. (1994). The magical number seven: Some limits on our capacity for processing information. *Psychology Review, 101,* 343–352.

Minter, R. L. (1972, June). Human rights laws and pre-employment inquiries. *Personnel Journal,* 431–433.

Mohammed cartoon conflict gets even hotter. (2006, February 2). *DW-World.de, Deutsche Welle.* Retrieved from http://www.dw-world.de/dw/article/0,2144,1889584,00.html

Molloy, J. T. (1988). *New dress for success.* New York: Warner.

Monk, R. (1994). *The employment of corporate non-verbal status communicators in Western organizations* (Unpublished doctoral dissertation). The Fielding Institute, Santa Barbara, CA.

Montgomery, B. M. (1984). Behavioral characteristics predicting self and peer perception of open communication. *Communication Quarterly, 32,* 233–240.

Moore, J. R., Eckrich, D. S., & Carlson, L. T. (1986). A hierarchy of industrial selling competencies. *Journal of Marketing Education, 8*(1), 79–99.

Moore, M. (2004, May 11). Bob Love Speaks His Dream. *ASHA Leader,* pp. 8, 14.

Moore, P. (2001, August 1). Anne Mulcahy: She's here to fix the Xerox. *BusinessWeek.Com.* Retrieved from http://www.businessweek.com/magazine/content/01_32/b3744090.htm?chan=mz

Morgenstern, J. (2005, May 29). The fifty-nine-story crisis. *The New Yorker,* 45–53. Retrieved from http://www.duke.edu/~hpgavin/ce131/citicorp1.htm

Morley, D. D. (1987, June). Subjective message constructs: A theory of persuasion. *Communication Monographs, 54,* 183–203.

Morley, D. D., & Walker, K. B. (1987). The role of importance, novelty, and plausibility in producing belief change. *Communication Monographs, 54,* 436–442.

Morris, B. (2003, June 23). The accidental CEO. *Fortune.* Retrieved from http://money.cnn.com/magazines/fortune/fortune_archive/2003/06/23/344603/index.htm

Morris, D. (1994). *Body talk: The meaning of human gestures.* New York: Crown.

Morris, M. H., Davis, D. L., & Allen. J. W. (1994). Fostering corporate entrepreneurship: Cross-cultural comparisons of the importance of Individualism and Collectivism. *Journal of International Business Studies, 25*(1), 65–89.

Moskowitz, M. (1985, Winter). Lessons from the best companies to work for. *California Management Review, 27,* 43.

Mossberg, W. S. (2005, April 6). Product reviews: Vertical search sites promising. *Tucson Citizen.* Retrieved from http://www.tucsoncitizen.com/news/business/040605d1_vertical

Motley, M. T. (1993). Facial affect and verbal context in conversation: Facial expression as interjection. *Human Communication Research, 20,* 3–40.

Motley, M. T. (1995). *Overcoming your fear of public speaking: A proven method.* New York: McGraw-Hill.

Mottet, T. P., Parker-Raley, J., Beebe, S. A., & Cunningham, C. (2007). Instructors who resist "college lite": The neutralizing effect of instructor immediacy on students' course-Workload Violations and perceptions of instructor credibility and affective learning. *Communication Education, 65*(2), 145–167.

Muchinsky, P. M. (1999). *Psychology applied to work* (6th ed.). Belmont, CA: Wadsworth.

Mudrack, P. E., & Farrell, G. M. (1995). An examination of functional role behavior and its consequences for individuals in group settings. *Small Group Research, 26,* 542–571.

Mulac, A. (2006). The gender-linked language effect: Do language differences really make a difference? In K. Dindia & D. Canary (Eds.), *Sex differences and similarities in communication* (pp. 219–239). Mahwah, NJ: Erlbaum.

Mulac, A., Wiemann, J. M., Widenmann, S. J., & Gibson, T. W. (1988). Male/female language differences and effects in same-sex and mixed-sex dyads: The gender-linked language effect. *Communication Monographs, 55,* 315–335.

Mullen, B., Futrell, D., Stairs, D., Tice, D. M., Baumeister, R. F., Dawson, K. E., Riordan, C. A., Radloff, C. E., Goethals, G. R., Kennedy, J. G., & Rosenfeld, P. (1986). Newscasters' facial expressions and voting behavior of viewers: Can a smile elect a President? *Journal of Personality and Social Psychology, 51,* 291–295.

Munter, M. (1993, May-June). Cross-cultural communications. *Business Horizons, 36,* 76.

Murray, M. (2009). Corporate recruiters survey: 2009 general data report. *Graduate Management Admission Council.* Retrieved from http://www.gmac.com/NR/rdonlyres/06C3E039-7335-4814-AD1D-16-F501AB70E9/0/2009CRS_GeneralDataReport.pdf

Murtha, R. (2005). Workplace conflicts challenge businesses. *Fairfield County Business Journal, 44*(20), 42.

Muslim cartoon row timeline. (2006, February 19). *BBC News.* Retrieved from http://news.bbc.co.uk/go/pr/fr/-/2/hi/ middle_east/4688602.stm

Mutzabaugh, B. (2009, July 9). Disgruntled United flier gets hit song on Web with revenge video. *Today in the Sky* [Web log posting]. Retrieved from http://www.usatoday.com/travel/flights/item.aspx?type=blog&ak=68493997.blog

Nadler, R. (2008). Text messaging craze. *CollegeOutlook.net.* Retrieved from http://www.collegeoutlook.net/co_ca_on_campus_c.cfm

Naisbitt, J., & Aburdene, P. (1985). *Re-inventing the corporation.* New York: Warner.

Nasaw, D. (2003, June 12). Instant messages are popping up all over. *The Wall Street Journal,* p. B4.

National Association of Colleges and Employers. (2008). NACE research: Job outlook 2009. Retrieved from www. naceweb.org

Navarro, J., & Karlins, M. (2008). *What every "body" is saying: An ex-FBI agent's guide to speed-reading people.* New York: Harper Collins.

NCAOnline.org. (n.d.). *The Eden alternative: A life worth living.* Retrieved from http://www. ncaonline.org/ncpad/eden.shtml

Needleman, S. E. (2009a, June 1). More ways to ace a phone interview. *The Wall Street Journal* Online. Retrieved from http://online.wsj.com/article/SB124389975664774435.html

Needleman, S. E. (2009b, June 2). The new trouble on the line. *The Wall Street Journal,* p. B7. Retrieved from http://online.wsj.com/article/SB124439348922474789.html

New suit against Medtronic. (2009, January 15). New suit against Medtronic for off-label use of Infuse. *Medical Device Daily, 13*(9), 6.

Newsom, D., & Haynes, J. (2008). *Public relations writing: Form & style* (8th ed.). Belmont, CA; Thomson Wadsworth.Newstrom, J. W., & Davis, K. (1996). *Organizational behavior: Human behavior at work* (10th ed.). New York: McGraw-Hill.

Nichols, M. (1996). *The lost art of listening: How learning to listen can improve relationships.* New York: Guilford Press.

Nickerson, R. S. (1980). Short-term memory for complex meaningful visual configurations: Demonstration of capacity. *Canadian Journal of Psychology, 19,* 155–160.

Nierenberg, G. I., & Calero, H. H. (1973). *How to read a person like a book.* New York: Pocket.

Nishimura, S. (2009, August 9). A whole lot of resumes, but not very much luck. *Star-Telegram,* 1D & 3D.

Northouse, P. G. (1997). *Leadership: Theory and practice.* Thousand Oaks, CA: Sage.

Norton, C. (2004, June 14). Board opts not to censure member. *Herald Sun.Com.* Retrieved from http://www.heraldsun. com/orange/10-490970.html

Oat, J. S. (1989). *The organizational culture perspective.* Chicago: Dorsey.

O'Brian, B. (1992, October 26). Southwest Airlines is a rare air carrier: It still makes money. *Wall Street Journal,* p. A1.

Occupational Safety and Health Administration. (2008, April 4). Computer workstations. Retrieved from http://www.osha.gov/SLTC/etools/computerworkstations/index.html

October 2009 Web Server Survey. (2009). Retrieved October 28, 2009, from http://news.netcraft.com/archives/web_server_survey.html

O'Hayre, J. (1966). *Gobbledygook has gotta go.* U.S. Department of the Interior, Bureau of Land Management. Washington, DC: U.S. Government Printing Office.

O'Keefe, D. J. (1990). *Persuasion: Theory and research.* Newbury Park, CA: Sage.

O'Keefe, D. J. (1998). Justification explicitness and persuasive effects: A meta-analytic review of the effects of varying support articulation in persuasive messages. *Argumentation and Advocacy, 35,* 61–75.

Oliver, A., Arnett, P., Kasarda, A., & Smith, J. (1998, June 15). Did the U.S. drop nerve gas? A CNN investigation charges that the U.S. used gas in 1970 to save troops sent into Laos to kill defectors. *Time Australia, 24,* 33–35. Available from the Business Source Premier Database.

Olson, J. M., & Cal, A. V. (1984). Source credibility, attitudes, and the recall of past behaviors. *European Journal of Social Psychology, 14,* 203–210.

O'Reilly, B. (1994, October 17). 360-degree feedback can change your life. *Fortune*, 93–100.

O'Reilly, C. A. (1980). Individuals and information overload in organizations: Is more necessarily better? *Academy of Management Journal, 23*, 684–696.

Orlitzky, M., & Hirokawa, R. (2001, June). To err is human, to correct for it, is divine: A meta-analysis of research testing the functional theory of group decision-making effectiveness. *Small Group research, 32*, 313–341.

Osborn, A. F. (1993). *Applied imagination* (3rd ed.). Buffalo, NY: Creative Education Foundation.

Ostermeier, T. H. (1967, June). Effects of type and frequency of reference upon perceived source credibility and attitude change. *Speech Monographs, 34*, 137–144.

Ouchi, W. G. (1981). *Theory Z: How American business can meet the Japanese challenge*. Reading, MA: Addison-Wesley.

Our Stores: The Best Service. (2009). *Container Store.com*. Retrieved from http://www.containerstore.com/learn/index.jhtml#stores

Overman, S. (2004). Mentors without borders. *HR Magazine, 49*, 83–85.

Paivio, A. (1986). *Mental representations: A dual coding approach*. New York: Oxford University Press.

Palan, E. (2008, May 29). 7 people fired for blogging. *MentalFloss.com*. Retrieved from http://www.mentalfloss.com/archives/15329

Palmeri, C. (2006, October 25). Southwest: The street's love fades. *BusinessWeek.com*. Retrieved from http://www.business-week.com/investor/content/oct2006/pi20061025_660770.htm?chan=top+news_top+news+index_businessweek+exclusives

Palomares, N. A. (2008) *Women are sort of more tentative than men, aren't they? How men and women use tentative language differently, similarly, and counterstereotypically as a function of gender salience.* Paper presented at the annual meeting of the International Communication Association in May in Montreal, Quebec. Retrieved from from http://www.allacademic.com/meta/p231545_index.html

Papageogis, D. (1963). Bartlett effect and the persistence of induced opinion. *Journal of Abnormal and Social Psychology, 67*, 61–67.

Papageogis, D., & McGuire, W. (1961). The generality of immunity to persuasion produced by pre-exposure to weakened counterarguments. *Journal of Abnormal and Social Psychology, 62*, 475–481.

Paradi, D. (2005). What annoys audiences about PowerPoint presentations? *ThinkOutsideTheSlide.com*. Retrieved from http://www.think-outsidetheslide.com/pptresults2005.htm

Paradi, D. (2009, October 20). Results of the fourth annoying PowerPoint survey. Dave Paradi's PowerPoint Blog. Retrieved from http://pptideas.blogspot.com/2009_10_01_archive.html

Park Place Lexus. (2005). *Malcolm Baldrige National Quality Award*. Retrieved from http://baldrige.nist.gov/PDF_files/ Park_Place_Lexus_ Profile.pdf

Pastoor. S. (1990). Legibility and subjective preference for color combinations in text. *Human Factors, 32*(2), 157–171.

Pearce, W. B., & Conklin, F. (1971). Nonverbal vocalic communication and perceptions of a speaker. *Speech Monographs, 38*, 241.

Pearce, W. B., & Sharp, S. M. (1973). Self-disclosing communication. *Journal of Communication, 23*, 409–425.

Pearson, J., Turner, L. H., & Todd-Mancillas, W. (1991). *Gender and communication* (2nd ed.). Dubuque, IA: Wm. C. Brown.

Penley, L. E., Alexander, E. R., Jernigan, I. E., & Henwood, C. I. (1991). Communication abilities of managers: The relationship to performance. *Journal of Management, 17*, 57–76.

Peoples, D. A. (1996). *Presentations plus: David People's proven techniques* (Rev. ed.). New York: Wiley.

Perecman, E. (Ed.). (1983). *Cognitive processing in the right hemisphere*. New York: Academic.

Perez, J. (2005, February 16). Three minutes: Fired Google blogger. *PC World*. Retrieved from http://www.pcworld.com/article/119715/three_minutes_fired_google_blogger.html

Perkins, N. L. (1991, March). What you need to know about the Americans with Disabilities Act. *Supervisory Management*, 4–5.

Perkins, N. L. (1992). *Americans with Disabilities Act*. New York: Wiley.

Perry, K. (1994). Increasing patient satisfaction: Simple ways to increase the effectiveness of interpersonal communication in the OPSA/PACU. *Journal of Post Anesthesia Nursing, 9*, 153–156.

Peters, T. J., & Waterman, R. H. (1982). *In search of excellence*. New York: Random House.

Petit, C. W. (1999, October 11). NASA's costly deviation: Metric-English slip doomed Mars craft. *U.S. News & World Report*, 63.

Petras, K., & Petras, R. (1995). *The only job hunting guide you'll ever need: The most comprehensive guide for job hunters and career switchers*. New York: Simon & Schuster.

Petronio, S. (1991). Communication boundary management: A theoretical model of managing disclosure of private information between marital couples. *Communication Theory, 1*, 311–335.

Petty, R. E., & Cacioppo, J. T. (1986a). *Communication and persuasion: Central and peripheral routes to attitude change*. New York: Springer-Verlag.

Petty, R. E., & Cacioppo, J. T. (1986b). The elaboration likelihood model of persuasion. In L. Berkowitz (Ed.), *Advances in experimental social psychology* (Vol. 19, pp. 123–205). San Diego: Academic.

Petty, R. E., & Cacioppo, J. T. (1996). *Attitudes and persuasion: Classic and contemporary approaches*. Boulder: Westview Press.

Petzinger, T., Jr. (1999, December 31). The WSJ millennium (a special report: industry and economics—so long, supply and demand): There's a new economy out there—and it looks nothing like the old one. *Wall Street Journal*, p. R31.

Pew Research.org. (2008, August 25). Men or women: Who's the better leader? Retrieved from http://pewresearch.org/pubs/932/men-or-women-whos-the-better-leader

Pfau, M. (1997). Inoculation model of resistance to influence. In G. A. Barnett & G. J. Boster (Eds.), *Progress in communication sciences: Advances in persuasion* (Vol. 13, pp. 133–171). Norwood, NJ: Ablex.

Pfau, M., & Louden, A. (1994). Effectiveness of adwatch formats in deflecting political attack ads. *Communication Research, 21*, 325–341.

Pfeffer, J., & Veiga, J. F. (1999). Putting people first for organizational success. *Academy of Management, 13*(2), 37–48.

Phillips, G. M. (1991). *Communication incompetencies: A theory of training oral performance behavior*. Carbondale: Southern Illinois University Press.

Philpott, J. S. (1983). *The relative contribution to meaning of verbal and nonverbal channels of communication: A metaanalysis* (Unpublished master's thesis). University of Nebraska.

Pimentel, B. (2005, November 16). Dunn pleads not guilty in HP spy probe. *San Francisco Chronicle*, p. D1. Retrieved from http://sfgate.com/cgi-bin/article.cgi?f=/c/a/2006/11/16/HP.TMP

Pinel, J. P. J. (2006). *Biopsychology* (6th ed.). Boston: Allyn & Bacon.

Pinsonneault, A., & Barki, H. (1999). Electronic brainstorming: The illusion of productivity. *Information Systems Research, 10*(2), 110–133.

Pitts, L., Jr. (1999, January 20). Rumors yield sour fruit on electronic grapevine. *Fort Worth Star-Telegram*, p. 13.

Planty, E., & Machaver, W. (1977). Upward communications: A project in executive development. In R. C. Huseman, C. M. Logue, & D. L. Freshley (Eds.), *Readings in interpersonal and organizational communication* (3rd ed.). Boston: Holbrook Press.

Platt, L. (2004, June 15). Accepting risk—daring greatness: An entrepreneurial credo. *Vital Speeches, 70*(17), 541–543.

Pletcher, B. (2000, January 10). Plan of reaction: Finding calm from stress lies just a deep breath away. *Fort Worth Star-Telegram*, p. 11.

Pollock, T. (1984, February). A personal file of stimulating ideas and problem solvers. *Supervision, 46*, 25.

Poole, M. S. (1991). Procedures for managing meetings: Social and technological innovation. In R. A. Swanson & B. O. Knapp (Eds.), *Innovative meeting management* (pp. 53–109). Austin: 3M Meeting Management Institute.

Poole, M. S., Putnam, L. L., & Seibold, D. R. (1997). Organizational communication in the 21st century. *Management Communication Quarterly, 11*(1), 127–139.

Poole, M. S., & Roth, J. (1989). Decision development in small groups IV: A typology of decision paths. *Human Communication Research, 15*, 323–356.

Porter, K. (2003). *The mental athlete: Inner training for peak performance in all sports*. Champaign, IL: Human Kinetics.

Porter, K., & Foster, J. (1986). *The mental athlete: Inner training for peak performance in all sports*. New York: Ballantine Books.

Powell, G. N. (1986). Effects of sex role identity and sex on definitions of sexual harassment. *Sex Roles, 14*, 9–19.

Powell, J. T. (1983). Listen attentively to solve employee problems. *Personnel Journal, 62*, 580–582.

Powers, V. (2004, November). Finding workers who fit. *Business2.0.com*. Retrieved from http://www.dynamicexperiencesgroup.com/Articles/Business2.0%20article.pdf

President and Commerce Secretary announce recipients of nation's highest honor in quality and performance excellence. (2003, November 25). Retrieved from http://www.nist.gov/ public_affairs/releases/2003baldrigewinners.htm

Press release, "First Responders Urged Not to Respond to Hurricane Impact Areas," FEMA, August 29, 2005.

Preston, P. (2005, January–February). Teams as the key to organizational communication. *Journal of Healthcare Management, 50,* 16–18.

Priester, J. R., & Petty, R. E. (1995). Source attributions and persuasion: Perceived honesty as a determinant of message scrutiny. *Personality and Social Psychology Bulletin, 21*(6), 637.

PRNewswire.com. (2006, May 18). Seventy percent of U.S. employers fail to grasp legal training requirements: ELT Survey Results. Retrieved from http://www.prnewswire.com/ cgi-bin/stories.pl?ACCT=104&STORY=/www/story/05-18-2006/0004364539&EDATE

Pulizzi, J., & Barrett, N. (2009). *Get content get customers: Turn prospects into buyers with content marketing.* New York: McGraw-Hill.

Punyanunt-Carter, N. M. (2006). An analysis of college students' self-disclosure behaviors on the Internet. *College Student Journal, 40*(2), 329–331.

Purdy, M. (2003, April). *Listening and community.* Paper presented at the Eastern Communication Association Convention, Washington, DC.

Quackenbush, R. L. (1987). Sex roles and social perception. *Human Relations, 40,* 659–670.

Quinones, E. (1999, August 1). Companies learn the value of storytelling. *New York Times,* p. 4.

Rackleff, R. B. (1988, March 1). The art of speech writing. *Vital Speeches, 54,* 312.

Radwanick, S. (2009, April 16). U.S. Hispanic Internet audience growth outpaces total U.S. online population by 50 percent. *ComScore.com.* Retrieved from http://www.comscore.com/Press_Events/Press_Releases/2009/4/U.S._Hispanic_Internet_Audience_Growth

Rahim, M., & Magner, N. (1995). Confirmatory factor analysis of the styles of handling interpersonal conflict: First-order factor model and its invariance across groups. *Journal of Applied Psychology, 80,* 122–132.

Rain, J. S., Lane, I. M., & Steiner, D. D. (1991). A current look at the job satisfaction/life satisfaction relationship: Review and future considerations. *Human Relations, 44*(3), 287–307.

Ralston, S. M., & Kirkwood, W. G. (1999). The trouble with applicant impression management. *Journal of Business and Technical Communication, 13*(2), 190–208.

Ramsey, R. P., & Sohi, R. S. (1997). Listening to your customers: The impact of perceived salesperson listening behavior on relationship outcomes. *Journal of the Academy of Marketing Science, 25*(2), 127–137.

Rao, A., Schmidt, S., & Murray, L. (1995). Upward impression management: Goals, influence strategies, and consequences. *Human Relations, 48*(2), 147.

Ray, G. B. (1986). Vocally cued personality proto-types: An implicit personality theory approach. *Communication Monographs, 53,* 266–276.

Reardon, K. K. (2000). *The secret handshake: Mastering the politics of the business inner circle.* New York: Random House.

Redding, W. C. (1964). The organizational communicator. In W. C. Redding & G. A. Sandborn (Eds.), *Business and industrial communication: A source book* (pp. 29–58). New York: Harper & Row.

Reed, I., & Kincaid, C. (1999, September 1). Costly Tailwind bedevils CNN. *Accuracy In Media.* Retrieved from http://www.aim.org/media_monitor/3231_0_2_0

Reeves, E. G. (2009). *Can I wear my nose ring to the interview?* New York: Workman Publishing.

Reinard, J. C. (1988, Fall). The empirical study of evidence: The status after fifty years of research. *Human Communication Research, 15,* 3–59.

Reingold, J. (2005, June). The interpreter. *FastCompany, 95,* 59–61. Retrieved from http://www.fastcompany.com/magazine/95/open_design-kotchka.html

Reigning in office rumors. (2004, November). *Inc., 26,* 60.

Reisner, R. (1993, June). How different cultures learn. *Meeting News, 17,* 31.

Reivity, L. (1985, December 15). Women's achievements toward equality. *Vital Speeches, 52,* 153.

Remland, M. S. (1981). Developing leadership skills in nonverbal communication: A situational perspective. *Journal of Business Communication, 3,* 17–29.

Remland, M. S. (2000). *Nonverbal communication in everyday life.* Boston: Houghton Mifflin.

Resume makeover II. (2000). *Monster Career Center.* Retrieved from http://content.monster.com/resume/samples/resumes/bennett_new

Reynolds, R., & Burgoon, M. (1983). Belief processing, reasoning and evidence. *Communication Yearbook, 7,* 83–104.

Reynolds, R. A., & Reynolds, J. L. (2002). Evidence. In J. P. Dillard & M. Pfau (Eds.), *The persuasion handbook: Developments in theory and practice* (pp. 427–444). Thousand Oaks, CA: Sage.

RIAA.com. (2006). Frequently asked questions—Napster and Digital Music. Retrieved from http://www.riaa.com/ news/filings/napster_faq.asp#shut

Rice, R. E., & Gattiker, U. E. (2001). New media and organizational structuring. In F. M. Jablin and L. L. Putnam (Eds.), *The new handbook of organizational communication: Advances in theory, research, and methods,* (pp. 544–584). Thousand Oaks, CA: Sage.

Richmond, V. P., & McCroskey, J. C. (1998). *Communication: Apprehension, avoidance, and effectiveness* (5th ed.). Scottsdale, AZ: Gorsuch Scarisbrick.

Richmond, V. P., & McCroskey, J. C. (2003). *Nonverbal behavior in interpersonal relations* (5th ed.). Boston: Allyn & Bacon.

Ricks, D. A. (2006). *Blunders in international business* (4th ed.). Maiden, MA: Blackwell Publishing.

Riger, S. (1991, May). Gender dilemmas in sexual harassment policies and procedures. *American Psychologist, 46,* 498.

Riggs, T., & Grieshaber, J. (2009). *Typeface: Classic typography for contemporary design.* New York: Princeton Architectural Press.

Robbins, S. P. (2003). *Organizational behavior* (10th ed.). Upper Saddle River, NJ: Prentice-Hall.

Roberts, S. (2000, December 4). U.S.O.C. elects woman as head for first time. *The New York Times,* p. D2.

Robertson, A. K. (1994). *Listen for success: A guide to effective listening.* Burr Ridge, IL: Irwin.

Robey, D., Minkhoo, H., & Power, C. (2000, February). Situated learning in cross-functional virtual teams. *Technical Communication, 47,* 51–66.

Robinett, B. (1982). The value of a good ear. *Personnel Administrator, 27,* 10.

Robinson, J. (2009, June 11). What leaders must do next. *The Gallup Management Journal.* Retrieved from http://gmj.gallup.com/content/120791/Leaders-Next.aspx?version=print

Roch, S. G., & Ayman, R. (2005). Group decision making and perceived decision success: The role of communication medium. *Group Dynamics: Theory, Research, and Practice, 9*(1), 15–31.

Rockwood, K. (2009, November). Windows into the soul. *Fast Company, 140,* 56–58.

Roethlisberger, F. J., & Dickson, W. J. (1939). *Management and the worker.* Cambridge: Harvard University Press.

Rogers, E. M., & Agarwala-Rogers, R. (1976). *Communication in organizations.* New York: Free Press.

Rogers, P. (2006, June 16). Selig takes battle on drugs to fans. *Chicago Tribune.* Available from LexisNexis Academic Database.

Rokeach, M. (1969). *Beliefs, attitudes, and values: A theory of organization and change.* San Francisco: Jossey-Bass.

Rokeach, M. (1973). *The nature of human values.* New York: Free Press.

Rosaluk, W. J. (1983). *Throw away your resume and get that job!* Englewood Cliffs, NJ: Prentice-Hall.

Rosenfeld, L. B. (1979). Self-disclosure avoidance: Why I am afraid to tell you who I am. *Communication Monographs, 46,* 72–73.

Rosenfeld, P. (1997). Impression management, fairness and the employment interview. *Journal of Business Ethics, 16*(8), 801–808.

Ross, J. A. (1997). Does friendship improve job performance? *Harvard Business Review, 75,* 8–9.

Ross, L. D. (1977). The intuitive psychologist and his short-comings: Distortions in the attribution process. In L. Berkowitz (Ed.), *Advances in experimental social psychology,* Vol. 10 (pp. 173–220). New York: Academic.

Ross, R. S. (1980). *Speech communication* (5th ed.). Englewood Cliffs, NJ: Prentice-Hall.

Roter, D. L., Stewart, M., Putnam, S. M., Lipkin, M., Jr., Stiles, W., & Inui, T. S. (1997). Communication patterns of primary care physicians. *Journal of the American Medical Association, 277*, 350–357.

Rothfeder, J., Bartimo, L., & Therrien, L. (1990, July 2). How software is making food sales a piece of cake. *Business Week*, 54–55.

Rowan, K. E. (1991). When simple language fails: Presenting difficult science to the public. *Journal of Technical Writing and Communication, 21*, 369–382.

Rowan, K. E. (1995, July). A new pedagogy for explanatory public speaking: Why arrangement should not substitute for invention. *Communication Education, 44*, 236–250.

Rowe, P. M. (1989). Unfavorable information and interview decisions. In R. W. Eder & G. R. Ferris (Eds.), *The employment interview: Theory, research, and practice* (pp. 77–89). Newbury Park, CA: Sage.

Roy, M. C., & Gauvin, S. (1996). Electronic group brainstorming. *Small Group Research, 27*, 215–249.

Rozema, H. J., & Gray, J. W. (1989, July). How wide is your communication gender gap? *Personnel Journal, 66*, 98–105.

Ruettgers, M. (2003). Responsibility lies in leadership: The integrity of management and the management of integrity. *Vital Speeches, 70*(5), 150–155.

Rules for team presentations. (2004). *Epson Presenters Online*. Retrieved from http://www.presentersonline.com/basics/delivery/rulesforteam.shtml

Rusch, J. J. (1999). The *"social engineering" of Internet fraud*. INET'99 Proceedings. Retrieved from http://www.isoc.org/ inet99/ proceedings/3g/3g_2.htm

Russell, P. (1979). *The brain book*. New York: Dutton.

Ryfe, D. M. (1999). Franklin Roosevelt and the fireside chats. *Journal of Communication, 49*(4), 80–103.

Saad, L. (2008, November 24). Nurses shine, bankers slump in ethics ratings. *Gallup Poll.com*. Retrieved from http://www.gallup.com/poll/112264/Nurses-Shine-While-Bankers-Slump-Ethics-Ratings.aspx

Salopek, J. J. (1999). Is anyone listening? *Training & Development, 53*(9), 58–59.

Salter, C. (2002, February). (Not) the same old story. *Fast Company, 55*, 78–86. Retrieved from http://pf.fastcompany. com/magazine/55/new-wisdon.html

Samovar, L. A., & Porter, R. E. (2004). *Communication between cultures* (5th ed.). Belmont, CA: Wadsworth.

Samovar, L. A., Porter, R. R., & McDaniel, E. R. (2010). *Communication between cultures* (7th ed.). Boston: Wadsworth/Cengage Learning.

Sandberg, J. (2003, February 12). Workplace email can turn radioactive in clumsy hands. *Wall Street Journal*, p. B1.

Sandberg, J. (2006, November 14). Tips for PowerPoint: Go easy on the text; please, spare us. *The Wall Street Journal*, p. B1.

Sandler, B. (1996, June 27). Letter to the editor. *Wall Street Journal*, p. A19.

Sashkin, M., & Morris, W. C. (1984). *Organizational behavior: Concepts and experiences*. Reston, VA: Reston.

Saunders, F. (2000, June). Web wonders. *Discover, 21*(6), 31–32.

Sayles, L. R. (1993). *The working leader*. New York: Free Press.

Schab, F. R., & Crowder, R. G. (1989) Accuracy of temporal coding: Auditory-visual comparisons. *Memory and Cognition, 17*, 384–397.

Schnake, M. R., Dumler, M. P., Chochran. D. S., & Barnett, T. R. (1990). Effects of differences in superior and subordinate perceptions on superiors' communication practices. *Journal of Business Communication, 27*, 37–50.

Schneider, A. E., Donaghy, W. C., & Newman, P. J. (1975). *Organizational communication*. New York: McGraw-Hill.

Schnurman, M. (2006, February 22). Pay attention to the power of the blog. *Star-Telegram.com*. Available from LexisNexis Academic Database.

School Board Chairman resigns amid plagiarism scandal. (2004, June 7). *NBC17.com*. Retrieved from http://www. nbc17.com/3392052/detail.html

Schramm, W. (1955). *The process and effects of mass communication*. Urbana: University of Illinois Press.

Schumer, A. A. (1988, July 1). Employee involvement: The quality circle process. *Vital Speeches, 54*, 563–566.

Schwartz, H., & Davis, S. (1981). Matching corporate culture and business strategy. *Organizational Dynamics, 10* (Summer), 30–48.

Scrimshaw, N. S. (1991, December 15). The consequences of hidden hunger: The effect on individuals and societies. *Vital Speeches, 58*, 138–144.

Segal, U. A. (1982). The cyclical nature of decision making: An exploratory empirical investigation. *Small Group Behavior, 13*, 333–348.

Segin, J. L. (2002, June 16). Lies can have a (long) life of their own. *The New York Times*, p. BU4.

Segrin, C. (1993). The effects of nonverbal behavior on outcomes of compliance gaining attempts. *Communication Studies, 44*, 169–187.

Seiler, W. J. (1971, Winter). The conjunctive influence of source credibility and the use of visual materials on communication effectiveness. *Southern Speech Communication Journal, 37*, 174–185.

Sellers, P. (1996). What exactly is charisma? *Fortune, 133*(1), 68–75.

Sewell, C., & Brown, P. B. (1998). *Customers for life: How to turn that one-time buyer into a lifetime customer*. New York: Pocket Books.

Shannon, C., & Weaver, W. (1949). *The mathematical theory of communication*. Urbana: University of Illinois Press.

Shea, S. C. (1998). *Psychiatric interviewing: The art of understanding* (2nd ed.). Philadelphia: Saunders.

Sherif, M., & Hovland, C. I. (1961). *Social judgment*. New Haven: Yale University Press.

Sherif, M., Sherif, C., & Nebergall, R. (1965). *Attitude and attitude change: The social judgment-involvement approach*. Philadelphia: Saunders.

Sherman, S. (1996, March 18). Secrets of HP's "muddled team." *Fortune*, 116–120.

Sherman. (2009).

Shockley-Zalabak, P. (2009). *Fundamentals of organizational communication* (7th ed.). Boston: Allyn & Bacon.

Showband of the Southwest. (2002, October 7–14). *University of Texas. edu*. Retrieved from http://www.utexas.edu/features/archive/2002/band.html

Sias, P. M., & Cahill, D. J. (1998). From coworkers to friends: The development of peer friendships in the workplace. *Western Journal of Communication, 62*(3), 273–299.

Sias, P., Krone, K. J., & Jablin, F. M. (2002). An ecological systems perspective on workplace relationships. In M. Knapp & J. A. Daly (Ed.), *Handbook of interpersonal communication* (3rd ed., pp.615–642). Newbury Park, CA: Sage.

Sifry, D. (2007, April 5). State of the Live Web, April 2007. *Technorati.com*. Retrieved from http://www.sifry.com/alerts/archives/000493.html. ipsman and Twitter.

Simon, A. M. (1991, September). Effective listening: Barriers to listening in a diverse business environment. *The Bulletin, 54*, 73–74.

Simons, T. L., & Peterson, R. S. (2000). Task conflict and relationship conflict in top management teams: The pivotal role of intragroup trust. *Journal of Applied Psychology, 85*, 102–111.

Simmons, D. B. (1985). The nature of the organizational grapevine. *Supervisory Management, 30*(11), 39–42.

Simonson, I., & Staw, B. M. (1992). Deescalation strategies: A comparison of techniques for reducing commitment to losing courses of action. *Journal of Applied Psychology, 77*, 419–426.

Sims, H. P., & Dean, J. W., Jr. (1985, January). Beyond quality circles: Self-managing teams. *Personnel*, 31.

Singel, R. (2007, July 19). Nearly ten percent of companies have fired bloggers, survey claims. *Wired.com*. Retrieved from http://www.wired.com/threatlevel/2007/07/nearly-ten-perc

Skooglund, C. (2003). Ethics at IT. Retrieved from http://www.ti.com/corp/docs/company/citizen/ethics/employ.shtml

Slater, M. D., & Rouner, D. (1996). Value-affirmative and value-protective processing of alcohol education messages that include statistical evidence or anecdotes. *Communication Research, 23*, 210–235.

Smeltzer, L. R., & Kedia, B. L. (1985, July–August). Knowing the ropes: Organizational requirements for quality circles. *Business Horizons, 28*, 32–34.

Smith. C. (2000). The ethical workplace. *Association Management, 52*, 70–73.

Smith, M. H. (2006). *Bioblogs: Resumes for the 21st century*. New York: HarperCollins.

Smith, P. B., & Bond, M. H. (1994). *Social psychology across cultures: Analysis and perspective*. Boston: Allyn & Bacon.

Smith, R. G. (1973). Source credibility context effects. *Speech Monographs, 40*, 303–309.

Smith, R. V. (2004). *The elements of great speechmaking: Adding drama & intrigue*. Lanham, MD: University Press of America.

Smith, T. E., & Frymier, A. B. (2006, February). Get "real": Does practicing speeches before an audience improve performance? *Communication Quarterly, 54*, 111–126.

Smoak, R. S., Jr. (2001, May 1). Health care coverage: For all Americans. *Vital Speeches 67*, 443.

Solomon, D., & Williams, A. (1997). Perceptions of social-sexual communication at work: The effects of message, situation, and observer characteristics on judgments of sexual harassment. *Journal of Applied Communication Research, 25*, 196–216.

Sommer, R. (1967). *Personal space: The behavioral basis of design*. Englewood Cliffs, NJ: Prentice-Hall.

Sommerhoff, E. W. (1998). Quality videoconferencing: Not light years away. *Facilities Design and Management, 17*(2), 50–56.

Sorenson, S. (1981, May). *Grouphate*. Paper presented to the International Communication Association Annual Convention, Minneapolis.

Southwest.com/Careers (2009). Retrieved from http://www.southwest.com/careers/?int=FOOTSITE_CAREER

Spencer, E. E. (1994). Transforming relationships through ordinary talk. In S. W. Duck (Ed.), *Dynamics of relationships* (Understanding Relationship Processes Series, Vol. 4, pp. 58–86). Thousand Oaks, CA: Sage.

Sproull, L., & Keisler, S. (1992). *Connections: New ways of working in the networked organization*. Cambridge: MIT Press.

SSM Health Care—leading the way. (2003, April 29). Retrieved from http://www.nist.gov/public_affairs/releases/ ssmhealth.htm

State of the Blogosphere 2008. (2008, September 22). *Technorati.com*. Retrieved from http://technorati.com/blogging/state-of-the-blogoshpre

Steele, F. (1975). *The open organization: The impact of secrecy and disclosure on people and organizations*. Reading, MA: Addison-Wesley.

Stefani, L. A., Samovar, L. A., & Hellweg, S. A. (1997). Culture and its impact on negotiation. In L.A. Samovar & R. E. Porter (Eds.), *Intercultural communication: A reader* (8th ed.), 307–317. Belmont, CA: Wadworth.

Steil, L. K., Barker, L. L., & Watson, K. W. (1983). *Effective listening: Key to your success*. Reading, MA: Addison-Wesley.

Steil, L. K., Summerfield, J., & deMare, G. (1984). *Listening—it can change your life: A handbook for scientists and engineers*. New York: Wiley.

Steiner, J. L. (2004, March). Successful Edenization through education: suggestions for encouraging LTC staff to embrace the change of the Eden Alternative. *Nursing Homes, 53*(3), 46, 48–49.

Steinfield, C. W. (1990). Computer-mediated communications in the organization: Using electronic mail at Xerox. In B. D. Sypher (Ed.), *Case studies in organizational communication* (pp. 289–292). New York: Guilford.

Stengel, J. R., Dixon, A. L., & Allen, C. T. (2003). Listening begins at home. *Harvard Business Review, 81*(11), 106–117.

Stepanek, M. (1999, December 13). Using the Net for brainstorming. *Business Week*, 55–57.

Stephan, K. M., Fink, G. R., Passingham, R. E., Silbersweig, D., Ceballos-Baumann, A. O., Frith, C. D., & Frackowiak, R. S. J. (1995, January). Functional anatomy of the mental representation of upper extremity movements in healthy subjects. *Journal of Neurophysiology, 73*, 373–385.

Stephenson, H. B. (1984, Summer). The most critical problem for the fledgling small business: Getting sales. *American Journal of Small Business, 9*, 27.

Stettner, M. (1998, November 19). How to use curiosity to listen effectively. *Investor's Business Daily*, p. A1.

Stevens, C. K., & Kristof, A. L. (1995). Making the right impression: A field study of applicant impression management during job interviews. *Journal of Applied Psychology, 80*, 587–606.

Stewart, C. J., & Cash, Jr., W. B. (2008). *Interviewing: Principles and practices* (12th ed.). Boston: McGraw-Hill.

Stewart, J. (1973). Clear interpersonal communication. In J. Stewart (Ed.), *Bridges not walls: A book about interpersonal communication* (pp. 116–130). New York: Random House.

Stewart, J., & Logan, C. (1999). Empathic and dialogic listening. In J. Stewart (Ed.), *Bridges not walls: A book about interpersonal communication* (7th ed.) (pp. 217–237). Boston: McGraw-Hill College.

Still, D. J. (2006). *High impact hiring: How to interview and select outstanding employees* (3rd ed.). Dana Point, NY: Management Development Systems LLC.

Stogdill, R. M. (1948). Personal factors associated with leadership: A survey of the literature. *Journal of Psychology, 25*, 35–71.

Stolberg, S. G. (2009, January 29). White House unbuttons formal dress code. *The New York Times*. Retrieved from http://www.nytimes.com/2009/01/29/us/politics/29whitehouse.html

Stone, B. (2009a, March 29). Is Facebook growing up too fast? *The New York Times*. Retrieved from http://www.nytimes.com/2009/03/29/technology/internet/29face.html

Stone, B. (2009b, May 26). Facebook. *The New York Times*. Retrieved from http://topics.nytimes.com/top/news/business/companies/facebook_inc/index.html?inline=nyt-org

Stone, B., & Stelter, B. (2009, February 19). Facebook withdraws changes in data use. *The New York Times*. Retrieved from http://www.nytimes.com/2009/02/19/technology/internet/19facebook.html

Stone, J., & Bachner, J. (1994). *Speaking up: A book for every woman who wants to speak effectively*. New York: Carroll & Graf.

Straczynski, S. (2006, November 4). It's not your fault, PowerPoint! *Presentations.com*. Retrieved from http://www.presentations.com/msg/content_display/presentations/e3i1bc82f141111910da929f1eae51a1199

Sullivan, J., & Kameda, N. (1991). Bypassing in managerial communication. *Business Horizons, 34*(1), 71–81.

Swanson, S. L. (1981, Winter). Sensory language in the courtroom. *Trial Diplomacy Journal, 37*–43.

Sykes, C. (2007, October 1). When it's time to say goodby. *Hardware Retailing*. Retrieved from http://www.highbeam.com/doc/1G1-169716537.html

Szabo, E. A., & Pfau, M. (2002). Nuances in inoculation: Theory and applications. In J. P. Dillard & M. Pfau (Eds.), *The persuasion handbook: Developments in theory and practice* (pp. 233–258). Thousand Oaks, CA: Sage.

Tamaki, J. (1991, October 10). Sexual harassment in the workplace. *Los Angeles Times*, p. D2.

Tannen, D. (1994). *Talking from 9 to 5: How women's and men's conversational styles affect who gets heard, who gets credit, and what gets done at work*. New York: Morrow.

Tapscott, D., Tiscoll, D., & Lowy, S. (2000). *Digital capital: Harnessing the power of business webs*. Boston: Harvard Business School Press.

Taylor, F. W. (1911). *Scientific management*. New York: Harper & Row.

Telephone Interview Techniques. (2009). Prepare for phone interview questions: Telephone interview techniques. *Best-Job-Interview.com*. Retrieved from http://www.best-job-interview.com/phone-interview-questions.html

ter Horst, J. F., & Albertazzie, R. (1980). *Flying White House: Story of Air Force One*. Des Plaines, IL: Bantam.

Thayer, J. (2001, April 15). The purpose of life: Where have all the heroes gone? *Vital Speeches, 67*, 408.

The Editors. (2009, February 18). Facebook rules. *The New York Times, Room for Debate*. Retrieved from http://roomfordebate.blogs.nytimes.com/2009/02/18/facebook-rules

The ethical enterprise. (2006). Survey by the American Management Association / Human Resource Institute, pp. vii & 2. Retrieved from http://www.amanet.org/images/HREthicsSurvey06.pdf

The GAAP rap by southwest airlines' rapping flight attendant. (2009, May 20). Video retrieved from http://www.blogsouthwest.com/video/the-gaap-rap-southwest-airlines%E2%80%99-rapping-flight-attendant

The Man Who Knew. (2009, June 14). *CBS, 60 Minutes*. Retrieved from http://www.cbsnews.com/video/watch/?id=5088137n

The Oxford English Dictionary. (1989). (Vol. II, Rev. ed.). Oxford: Clarendon.

There's No Containing Our Growth. (n.d.) *Container Store.com*. Retrieved from http://www.containerstore.com/learn/index.jhtml#growth

The Waterline. (2006, April 12). Navy designates next-generation Zumwalt destroyer. Retrieved from http://www.dcmilitary.com/dcmilitary_archives/stories/041206/40719-1.shtml

The world's 50 most innovative companies. (2009, March). *Fast Company, 133*, 52–97.

Thomas, D. C. (2008). *Cross-cultural management*. Thousand Oaks, CA: Sage.

Thomas, E., & Vistica, G. L. (1998, June 22). What's the truth about Tailwind? *Newsweek, 131,* 32.

Thomas, J. (1999). So you hear what I hear? *Women in Business, 51*(1), 1–14.

Thomas, K. W. (1992a). Conflict and conflict management: Reflections and update. *Journal of Organizational Behavior, 13,* 265–274.

Thomas, K. W. (1992b). Conflict and negotiation processes in organizations. In M. D. Dunnette & L. M. Hough (Eds.), *Handbook of industrial and organizational psychology* (2nd ed.) (Vol. 3, pp. 651–718). Palo Alto, CA: Consulting Psychologists Press.

Thomas, W. H. (1999). *Learning from Hannah: Secrets for a life worth living.* Acton, MA: Vanderwyk & Burnham.

Thomas, W. H. (2004). *What are old people for? How elders will save the world.* Acton, MA: Vanderwyk & Burnham.

Thompson, L. A., Driscoll D., & Markson, L. (1998). Memory for visual-spoken language in children adults. *Journal of Nonverbal Behavior, 22,* 167–187.

Thompson, M. (1998, August 3). "Absolutely no evidence": A U.S. investigation dismisses a CNN-Time report on the use of sarin in Indochina. *Time, 152*(5), 54.

Thompson, V. A., & Paivio, A. (1994). Memory for pictures and sounds: Independence of auditory and visual codes. *Canadian Journal of Experimental Psychology, 48*(3), 380–395.

Thorne, B., Kramarae, C., & Henley, N. (Eds.). (1983). *Language, gender and society.* Cambridge, MA: Newbury House.

Thourlby, W. (1990). You are what you wear: Business and casual style in a "clicks and mortar" world (Expanded ed.). New York: Forbes/Wittenburg & Brown.

Tice, L. (1980). *Investment in excellence* [cassette series]. Seattle: The Pacific Institute.

Tichy, N., & Sherman, S. (1994). *Control your destiny or someone else will.* New York: HarperCollins.

Timm, P. R. (1986). *Managerial communication: A finger on the pulse* (2nd ed.). Englewood Cliffs, NJ: Prentice-Hall.

Ting-Toomey, S. (1988). Intercultural conflict styles: A face negotiation theory. In Y. Kim & W. Gudykunst (Eds.), *Theories in intercultural communication* (pp. 213–235). Newbury Park, CA: Sage.

Ting-Toomey, S. (2000). Managing intercultural conflicts effectively. In L. A. Samovar & R. E. Porter (Eds.), *Intercultural communication: A reader* (9th ed., pp. 388–400). Belmont, CA: Wadsworth.

Ting-Toomey, S., Gao, G., Trubisky, P., Yang, Z., Kim, H. S., Lin, S., & Nishids, T. (1991). Culture, face maintenance, and styles of handling interpersonal conflict: A study in five cultures. *International Journal of Conflict Management, 2,* 275–296.

Townsend, A. M., deMaire, S. M., & Hendrickson, A. R. (1998). Virtual teams: Technology and the workplace of the future. *Academy of Management Executive, 12*(3), 17–30.

Treviño, L. K., & Nelson, K. A. (2004). *Managing business ethics* (3rd ed.). Hoboken, NJ: John Wiley & Sons.

Triandis, H. C. (1995). *Individualism and collectivism.* Boulder: Westview.

Triandis, H. C., & Albert, R. D. (1987). Cross-cultural perspectives. In F. M. Jablin, L. L. Putnam, K. H. Roberts, & L. W. Porter (Eds.), *Handbook of organizational communication* (pp. 280–281). Newbury Park, CA: Sage.

Trottman, M. (2001, September 21). Southwest Airlines considers cutbacks, halts delivery of planes from Boeing. *Wall Street Journal,* p. A4.

Tse, T. M. (2009, October 16). Bank of America CEO to get no salary for 2009. *Washington Post.com.* Retrieved from http://www.washingtonpost.com/wp-dyn/content/article/2009/10/15/AR2009101503929.html

Tubbs, S. L. (2009). *A systems approach to small group interaction* (10th ed.). Boston: McGraw-Hill.

Turner, D. (2007). Conceptualizing oral documents. *Information Research, 12*(4). Retrieved from http://InformationR.net/ir/12-4/colis/colis32.html

Turner, M. E., & Pratkanis, A. R. (1998). Twenty-five years of groupthink theory and research: Lessons from the evaluation of a theory. *Organizational Behavior and Human Decision Processes, 73,* 105–115.

Tversky A., & Kahneman, D. (1981). The framing of decisions and the psychology of choice. *Science, 211,* 453–458.

UnityFirst.com. (2003, November). $1.8 million awarded to 1,100 dental professionals. Retrieved from http://www.unityfirst.com/pressreleasecolgate.htm

U.S. Department of Labor. (2009). Women in the labor force in 2008. *United States Department of Labor: Women's Bureau.* Retrieved from http://www.dol.gov/wb/factsheets/Qf-laborforce-08.htm

U.S. Equal Employment Opportunity Commission. (2003, July). *EEOC litigation settlements, July 2003.* Retrieved from http://www.eeoc.gov/litigation/settlements/settlement07-03.html

U.S. Equal Employment Opportunity Commission. (2006, June 1). Wal-Mart to pay $315,000 to settle two EEOC suits for sexual harassment at store in central Florida [Press Release]. Retrieved from http://www.eeoc.gov/press/6-01-06.html

U.S. Equal Employment Opportunity Commission. (2009, March 11). Sexual harassment. Retrieved from http://www.eeoc.gov/types/sexual_harassment.html

Vaas, L. (1999, May 31). Brainstorming: Before opening the floodgates to new KM technologies, IT managers should make sure users are ready, willing and able to share what they know. *PC Week, 16,* 65.

Valacich, J. S., Dennis, A. R., & Connolly, T. (1994). Idea generation in computer-based groups: A new ending to an old story. *Organizational Behavior and Human Decision Processes, 57,* 448–467.

Van Gundy, A. B. (1984, June). Brainstorming: Variations on a theme. *Quality Circles Journal, 7,* 14–17.

Van Gundy, A. B. (1987). *Managing group creativity: A modular approach to problem solving.* New York: American Management Association.

Van Gundy, A. B. (1994). *Brain boosters for business advantage: Ticklers, grab bags, blue skies, and other bionic ideas.* San Diego: Pfeiffer.

Varner, I., & Beamer, L. (1995). *Intercultural communication in the global workplace.* Chicago: Irwin.

Veninga, R. L. (2006, July 1). Star throwing 101. *Vital Speeches, 72,* 544–545.

Verschoor, C. C. (2003, May). New evidence of benefits from effective ethics systems. *Strategic Finance, 84,* 20, 22.

Veruki, P. (1999). *The 250 job interview questions you'll most likely be asked . . . and the answers that will get you hired!* Holbrook, MA: Adams Media.

Vicers, M. (1997, April 14). Video interviews cut recruiting costs for many firms. *International Herald Tribune,* p. 15.

Video-conferencing: A strategic business tool in an information age. (1995). *Chain store age executive with shopping center age, 71*(3), B8–B10.

VirtualConnection.biz. (2003). Tip of the month: Virtual Connection. Retrieved from http://www.virtualconnection.biz/pages/TipOfMonth.html

Vogel, D. R., Dickson, G. W., & Lehman, J. A. (1986). *Persuasion and the role of visual presentation support: The UM/3M study* [3M Study] (pp. 1–20). St. Paul: 3M Corporation.

Vogel, D. R., Dickson, G. W., & Lehman, J. A. (1990, July 27). Persuasion and the role of visual presentation support: The UM/3M study. In M. Antonoff, Presentions that persuade. *Personal Computing,* 14.

Volokh, E. (2000). Freedom of speech, cyberspace, harassment law, and the Clinton administration. *Law and Contemporary Problems, 63*(1–2), 299–335.

von Bertalanfy, L. (1968). *General systems theory.* New York: Braziller.

Vroom, V., & Jago, A. G. (1988). *The new leadership: Managing participation in organizations.* Englewood Cliffs, NJ: Prentice-Hall.

Vroom, V., & Yetton, P. (1973). *Leadership and decision making.* Pittsburgh: University of Pittsburgh Press.

Wagner, H. L., Buck, R., & Winterbotham, M. (1993). Communication of specific emotions: Gender differences in sending accuracy and communication measures. *Journal of Nonverbal Behavior, 17,* 29–53.

Wagner, J. A., & Hollenbeck, J. R. (2010). *Organizational behavior: Securing competitive advantage.* New York: Routledge.

Wagner, V. A. (2002, February 17). Preserving jams, jellies, and tradition. *AmericanProfile.com.* Retrieved from http://www.americanprofile.com/issues/20020217/20020217mid_1855.asp

Wallack, T. (2005, January 24). Blogs: Beware if your blog is related to work. *San Francisco chronicle.* Retrieved from http://www.sfgate.com/cgi-bin/article.cgi?f=/c/a/2005/01/24/BUGCEAT1I01.DTL

Wall Street Journal's Workplace Ethics Quiz. (1999, October 21). *The Wall Street Journal,* p. B1.

Walters, F. M. (1993, September 1). If it's broke, fix it: The significance of health care reform in America. *Vital Speeches, 59,* 687–691.

Walters, L. (1993). *Secrets of successful speakers.* New York: McGraw-Hill.

Walton, D. (1998). *Ad hominem arguments.* Tuscaloosa: University of Alabama Press.

Walton, E. (1961). How effective is the grapevine? *Personnel, 28,* 46.

Wardell, C. (1998). The art of managing virtual teams: Eight lessons. *Harvard Management Update, 3*(11), 4–6.

Waterman, R., Waterman, J., & Collard, B. (1994). Toward a more career-resilient workforce. *Harvard Business Review, 72*(4), 87–95.

Watson, K. W., & Smeltzer, L. R. (1982, June). Perceptions of nonverbal communication during the selection interview. *ABCA Bulletin,* 30–34.

Watts, F. N. (1983, June). Strategies of clinical listening. *British Journal of Medical Psychology, 56,* 115.

Weaver II, R. L. (1984). *Understanding business communication.* Englewood Cliffs, NJ: Prentice-Hall.

Weaver, G. R., Trevino, L. K., & Cochran, P. L. (1999). Corporate ethics practice in the mid 1990s: An empirical study of the Fortune 1000. *Journal of Business Ethics 18*(3), 283–294.

Weber, H. R. (2006, May 26). Home Depot CEO blocks debate over his own pay. *Fort-Worth Star-Telegram,* p. 2C.

Weber, J. (1993). Institutionalizing ethics into business organizations: A model and research agenda. *Business Ethics Quarterly, 3,* 419–436.

Weber, M. (1947). *The theory of social and economic organization.* New York: Oxford University Press.

Weddle, P. D. (2005). *Weddle's wiznotes: Writing a great resume.* Stamford, CT: Weddle.

Weddle, P. D. (2006a). Networking online as your mother taught you. *Weddle's Newsletter: October 3 Edition.* Retrieved from http://www.weddles.com/seekernews/issue.cfm? Newsletter=183

Weddle, P. D. (2006b). *Weddle's 2006/7 guide to employment web sites.* Stamford, CT: Weddle.

Weddle, P. D. (2008, March 27). Weddle's Annual Source of Employment Survey. *Weddle's Recruiters Newsletter.* Retreived from http://www.weddles.com/recruiternews/issue.cfm?Newsletter=226

Weddle, P. (2009a). *Work strong: Your person career fitness system.* Stamford, CT: Weddle.

Weedle, P. (2009b). *Weedle's guide to employment-related web sites 2009/10: For recruiters and job seekers.* Stamford, CT: Weedle.

Weinstein, B. (1993). *Resumes don't get jobs: The realities and myths of job hunting.* New York: McGraw-Hill.

Weitz, B., Castleberry, S., & Tanner, J. (2008). *Selling: Building partnerships* (7th ed.). McGraw-Hill/Irwin.

Welch, J. F. (2001). *Jack: Straight from the gut.* New York: Warner Books.

Whalen, D. J. (1996). *I see what you mean: Persuasive communication.* Beverly Hills, CA: Sage.

Wheeless, L. R., & Grotz, J. (1977). The measurement of trust and its relationship to self-disclosure. *Human Communication Research, 3,* 250–257.

Whitcomb, S. B. (2006). *Resume magic: Trade secrets of a professional resume writer* (3rd ed.). Indianapolis: JIST Works.

White, R., & Lippitt, R. (1968). Leader behavior and member reaction in three "social climates." In D. Cartwright & A. Zandor (Eds.), *Group dynamics* (3rd ed., pp. 318–335). New York: Harper & Row.

Whitehead, J. R. (1968). Factors of source credibility. *Quarterly Journal of Speech, 54,* 61–63.

Wiegand, R. (1985, July–August). It doesn't need to be dull to be good: How to improve staff presentations. *Business Horizons, 28,* 36.

Wiemann, J. M., & Knapp, M. L. (1975). Turn-taking in conversations. *Journal of Communication, 25,* 75–92.

Wilcox, R. P. (1987). *Communication at work: Writing and speaking* (3rd ed.). Boston: Houghton Mifflin.

Wilkins, B. M., & Andersen, P. A. (1991). Gender similarities and differences in management communication: A meta-analysis. *Management Communication Quarterly, 5,* 6–35.

Williams, C., (2003). *Management* (2nd ed.). Mason, OH: South-Western.

Williams, C., (2007). *Management* (4th ed.). Mason, OH: South-Western.

Williams, C. C. (2005). Trust diffusion: The effect of interpersonal trust on structure, function, and organizational transparency. *Business & Society, 44*(3), 357–368.

Williams, M. R., & Cooper, M. D. (2002). *Power persuasion: Moving an ancient art into the media age* (3rd ed.). Greenwood, IN: Alistair Press.

Williams, R. (2004). *The non-designer's design book: Design and typographic principles for the visual novice* (2nd ed.). Berkeley: Peachpit.

Williams, R. (2008). *The non-designer's design book: Design and typographic principles for the visual novice* (3rd ed.). Berkeley: Peachpit.

Wilson, B. (2009, July 9). United Airlines sees power of viral PR up close and personal. *Things with Wings: The Commercial Aviation blog.* Retrieved from http://www.aviationweek.com/aw/blogs/commercial_aviation/ThingsWithWings/index.jsp?plckController=Blog&plckScript=blogScript&plckElementId=blogDest&plckBlogPage=BlogViewPost&plckPostId=Blog%3a7a78f54e-b3dd-4fa6-ae6e-dff2ffd7-bdbbPost%3aa4e8ba09-2f49-4152-a158-04dc14892ace&plckCommentSortOrder=TimeStampAscending

Wilson, D. O. (1992). Diagonal communication links with organizations. *Journal of Business Communication, 29*(2), 129–143.

Wilson, G. L. (1991, September). Preparing students for responding to illegal selection interview questions. *The Bulletin of the Association for Business Communication,* 47–48.

Wilson, J. (1993). *The moral sense.* New York: Free Press.

Wimbush, J. C., & Shephard, J. M. (1994). Toward an understanding of ethical climate: Its relationship to ethical behavior and supervisory influence. *Journal of Business Ethics, 13,* 637–647.

Winikow, L. (1991, February 1). How women and minorities are reshaping corporate America. *Vital Speeches, 57,* 243.

Winn, P. (2004, June 8). School board chairman gives up top post. *The Chapel Hill News.* Retrieved from http://www.chapelhillnews.com/front/story/1317148p-7439 660c.html

Wise, R., Chollet, F., Hadar, U., Friston, L., Hoffner, E., & Frackowiak, R. (1991). Distribution of cortical neural networks involved in word comprehension and word retrieval. *Brain, 114,* 1803–1817.

Wolff, F. I., Marsnik, N. C., Tracey, W. S., & Nichols, R. G. (1983). *Perceptive listening.* New York: Holt, Rinehart & Winston.

Wood, J. T. (1984). Consensus and its alternatives: A comparative analysis of voting, negotiation and compromise as methods of group decision-making. In G. M. Phillips and J. T. Wood (Eds.), *Emergent issues in human decision making.* Carbondale: Southern Illinois University Press.

Wood, J. T. (2009). *Gendered lives* (8th ed.). Boston: Wadsworth/Cengage Learning.

Wood, J. T. (2010). *Interpersonal communication: Everyday encounters* (6th ed.). Boston: Wadsworth/Cengage Learning.

Wood, J. T., Phillips, G. M., Pedersen, D. J., & Young, K. S. (2000). *Group discussion: A practical guide to participation and leadership* (3rd ed.). Prospect Heights, IL: Waveland.

Woodward, J. (1965). *Industrial organization: Theory and practice.* London: Oxford University Press.

Wooldridge, E. T, III. (2004, December). Order a PowerPoint stand-down. *Proceedings of the United States Naval Institute, 130,* 85.

Workers are surveyed on communication. (2004, December 26). *Arizona Republic,* p. D6.

Worldwide facts. (2009). *UPS.com.* Retrieved May 26, 2009 from http://www.ups.com/content/us/en/about/facts/worldwide.html

Worthy, W., Gary, A., & Kahn, G. M. (1969). Self-disclosure as an exchange process. *Journal of Personality and Social Psychology, 13,* 59–63.

Wright, J. (2006). *Blog marketing.* New York: McGraw-Hill.

Wright, P. H. (1982).Men's friendships, women's friendships, and the alleged inferiority of the latter. *Sex Roles, 8,* 1–20.

Wright, P. H. (2006). Toward an expanded orientation to the comparative study of women's and men's same-sex friendship. In K. Dindia & D. J. Canary (Eds.), *Sex differences and similarities in communication* (pp. 37–57). Mahwah, NJ: Erlbaum.

Wrobbel, E. D. (1991, November). *A conversation analytic look at the yes/no question.* Paper presented at the annual meeting of the Speech Communication Association, Atlanta.

Yager, J. (1997). *Friendships: The power of friendship and how it shapes our lives.* Stamford, CT: Hannacroix Creek Books.

Yang, J. L. (2009, January 23). Get your dream job. *Money/CNN.com.* Retrieved from http://money.cnn.com/galleries/2009/fortune/0901/gallery.bestcompanies_hiring.fortune/4.html

Yate, M. (2008a). *Knock 'em dead resumes* (8th ed.). Avon, MA: Adams Media.

Yate, M. (2008b). *Knock 'em dead 2009: The ultimate job search guide.* Avon, MA: Adams Media.

Yate, M. (2008c). *Knock 'em dead cover letters* (8th ed.). Avon, MA: Adams Media.

Young, D. J. (2006). *Foundations of business communication.* New York: McGraw-Hill/Irwin.

Yrle, A. C., & Galle, W. P. (1993). Using interpersonal skills to manage more effectively. *Supervisory Management, 38*(4), 4.

Zagacki, K. S., Edwards, R., & Honeycutt, J. M. (1992, Winter). The role of mental imagery and emotion in imagined interaction. *Communication Quarterly, 40,* 56–68.

Zayas-Baya, E. P. (1977–78). Instructional media in the total language picture. *International Journal of Instructional Media, 5,* 145–150.

Zelazny, G. (2000). *Say it with presentations: How to design and deliver successful business presentations.* New York: McGraw-Hill.

Zhang, Y., Butler, J., & Pryor, B. (1996). Comparison of apprehension about communication in China and the United States. *Perceptual and Motor Skills, 82,* 1168–1170.

Zillmann, D. (1994). Cognition-excitation interdependencies in the escalation of anger and angry aggression. In M. Potegal & J. F. Knutson (Eds.), *The dynamics of aggression: Biological and social processes in dyads and groups.* Hillsdale, NJ: Lawrence Erlbaum.

Zima, J. P. (1983). *Interviewing: Key to effective management.* Chicago: Science Research Associates.

Zumwalt, E. R., Jr. (1976). *On watch,* 187–189. *The Waterline.* (2006, April 12). Navy designates next-generation Zumwalt destroyer. Retrieved from http://www.dcmilitary.com/dcmilitary_archives/stories/041206/40719-1.shtml

Zumwalt, E. R., Jr. (2006). USN, historic record. *Naval Historical Center Home Page.* Retrieved from http://www. history.navy.mil/photos/pers-us/uspers-xz/e-zumwt.htm

Zunin, L., & Zunin, N. (1994). *Contact: The first four minutes* (Rev. ed.). New York: Ballantine.

Credits

This page constitutes an extension of the copyright page. We have made every effort to trace the ownership of all copyrighted material and to secure permission from copyright holders. In the event of any question arising as to the use of any material, we will be pleased to make the necessary corrections in future printings. Thanks are due to the following authors, publishers, and agents for permission to use the material indicated.

Author Index

Subject Index